Unive

Subjec

http

Tracing Education Policy

The last thirty years have seen unprecedented change in education. A field that used to be a backwater in terms of government policy has now become a central – and high-profile – priority in many countries around the world.

This book brings together key articles that trace the development of British education policy since 1975 and provides a valuable route map to developments within education policy during this period. It includes twenty-six seminal articles from the journal *Oxford Review of Education*, written by many of the leading authors in the field, and covering issues and topics with a wide significance beyond Britain.

In one, easy-to-access place, this authoritative reference book provides a collection of articles that have made an important impact on policy studies and cover a broad range of significant policy issues, including:

- equality in education
- school effectiveness
- special educational needs
- school choice
- fourteen to nineteen education
- the structure of the educational system

The book has been compiled by the current and previous editors of the journal to show the development of the field, and their specially written Introduction contextualises the selection and introduces students to the main issues and current thinking in the field.

This volume is from the *Education Heritage* series. For details of other books in the series, please go to www.routledge.com/education

David Phillips is Professor of Comparative Education and Fellow by Special Election of St Edmund Hall at Oxford University, UK. **Geoffrey Walford** is Professor of Education Policy and a Fellow of Green College at the University of Oxford, UK.

Education heritage series

Other titles in the series:

From Adult Education to the Learning Society
21 years from the *International Journal of Lifelong Education*
Peter Jarvis

A Feminist Critique of Education
Edited by Christine Skelton and Becky Francis

Overcoming Disabling Barriers
18 years of *Disability & Society*
Edited by Len Barton

Tracing Education Policy
Selections from the *Oxford Review of Education*
Edited by David Phillips and Geoffrey Walford

Making Curriculum Strange
Essays from the *Journal of Curriculum Studies*
Edited by Ian Westbury and Geoff Milburn

Tracing Education Policy

Selections from the *Oxford Review of Education*

Edited by
David Phillips and Geoffrey Walford

Routledge
Taylor & Francis Group

LONDON AND NEW YORK

First published 2006
by Routledge
2 Park Square, Milton Park, Abingdon, Oxon OX14 4RN

Simultaneously published in the USA and Canada
by Routledge
270 Madison Ave, New York, NY 10016

*Routledge is an imprint of the Taylor & Francis Group, an informa
business*

© 2006 David Phillips and Geoffrey Walford

Typeset in Sabon by Wearset Ltd, Boldon, Tyne and Wear
Printed and bound in Great Britain by TJI Digital, Padstow,
Cornwall

British Library Cataloguing in Publication Data
A catalogue record for this book is available from the British Library

Library of Congress Cataloging in Publication Data
A catalog record for this book has been requested

ISBN10: 0–415–39861–4

ISBN13: 978-0-415-39861-9

Contents

Introduction   1

PART I
**1975–1979 Labour Government, The Great Debate and
the Callaghan years**   9

1 The concept of equality in education   11
   MARY WARNOCK

2 Sociology and the equality debate   20
   A.H. HALSEY

3 Equality and education: fact and fiction   39
   H.J. EYSENCK

4 The impossibility of a core curriculum   50
   ALAN HARRIS

5 The impossibility of a core curriculum: a reply to
   Alan Harris   62
   JOHN WHITE

6 Authority, bureaucracy and the education debate   68
   A.H. HALSEY

7 Power and participation   90
   VERNON BOGDANOR

8 The seventy thousand hours that Rutter left out   105
   ANTHONY HEATH AND PETER CLIFFORD

PART II
1979–1986 Conservative Government, Margaret Thatcher and slow change 127

9 The educational consequences of Mr Norman Tebbit 129
STUART MACLURE

10 Reconciling the irreconcilable: declining secondary schools rolls and the organisation of the system 150
W. F. DENNISON

11 Educational attainment in secondary schools 163
JOHN MARKS AND CAROLINE COX

12 Problems in comparing examination attainment in selective and comprehensive secondary schools 194
KEN FOGELMAN

13 Selection does make a difference 207
PETER CLIFFORD AND ANTHONY HEATH

14 The expansion of special education 223
SALLY TOMLINSON

PART III
1987–1997 Conservative Government, the Education Reform Act and after 235

15 Evolution or revolution: dilemmas in the post ERA management of special educational needs by local authorities 237
CATHERINE CLARK, ALAN DYSON AND ALAN MILLWARD

16 Equality fifteen years on 255
MARY WARNOCK

17 'British schools for British citizens'? 266
BARRY TROYNA AND RICHARD HATCHER

18 Specialisation and selection in secondary education 282
TONY EDWARDS AND GEOFF WHITTY

19 Choice and diversity in education: a defence   296
    JAMES TOOLEY

20 Through the revolution and out the other side   313
    STUART MACLURE

21 14–19 Education: legacy, opportunities and challenges   338
    MICHAEL YOUNG AND KEN SPOURS

PART IV
1997–2005 Labour Government, change and continuity   357

22 From City Technology Colleges to sponsored
    grant-maintained schools   359
    GEOFFREY WALFORD

23 Faith-based schools and state funding: a partial argument   376
    HARRY JUDGE

24 School admissions and 'selection' in comprehensive schools:
    policy and practice   391
    ANNE WEST, AUDREY HIND AND HAZEL PENNELL

25 Labour government policy   416
    RICHARD PRING

26 Reinventing 'inclusion': New Labour and the cultural politics
    of special education   433
    DERRICK ARMSTRONG

    Index   452

Introduction

The first issue of the *Oxford Review of Education* appeared in March 1975. The initiative for the new journal came from the Department of Educational Studies of the University of Oxford, and the two general editors and one editorial board member were from that Department, but the remaining thirteen editorial board members were from various departments and colleges throughout the University. This was, and remains, an important feature of the journal. As the first chair of the editorial board, Alan Bullock, then Master of St. Catherine's College, wrote in his forward to the first issue:

> Education has come to play so large and important a part in society – or at least in our thinking and talking about it – that many people who have never thought of themselves as educationalists are drawn or driven into taking an active interest in it. Most educationalists welcome this: the problem is *how* to invoke the others – from philosophers to medical scientists – whom everyone would like to see taking part in the discussion of educational issues. The *Oxford Review of Education* is an attempt to provide a forum for such an enlarged discussion.

While the editorial board was restricted to Oxford, this was 'for purely practical reasons', and the intention from the start was to 'make the *Review* international in scope both in the subjects it treats and in the writers invited to contribute'. The word 'invited' is important: the journal was not originally a refereed journal in the sense that it is now. Given the strength of the editorial board, however, one might argue that scrutiny was much greater at this point than for most current journals where just two or three referees judge the articles. This freedom to invite contributions meant that special issues on particular themes could be a particular regular feature of the journal, and this remains true today. Now, of course, the *Review* is a fully peer-reviewed publication, usually counted among the top four UK-based education journals.

The *Review*'s first editors were W.D. (Bill) Halls and Kevin

Marjoribanks. Bill Halls continued as joint editor until 1984, but Kevin Marjoribanks resigned after the publication of the first issue in order to take up a chair in Australia. He was succeeded by the philosopher John Wilson. Over the next nine years Halls and Wilson together gradually established the journal as a serious forum for the discussion of educational issues. The editorial board fixed a routine of two meetings a year which were attended by most board members and which provided stimulus in particular for the commissioning of special issues. In 1984 David Phillips succeeded Bill Halls and worked as co-editor with John Wilson until Wilson resigned. Phillips then continued as sole editor, resigning after twenty years in the editor's chair and being succeeded by Geoffrey Walford in 2004.

The *Review* has been fortunate to have a succession of committed chairs of the editorial board. Alan Bullock steered it through its early years and was succeeded by A.H. Halsey. He was followed by Harry Judge and the historian Janet Howarth. The present chair is the sociologist Anthony Heath.

The first issue contained the following statement of objectives for the journal:

> The object of the *Oxford Review of Education* is to advance the study of education. It especially wishes to promote the elaboration and evaluation of a body of speculative and empirical theory, the development of which might improve practice and help to establish education more firmly as a legitimate field of academic enquiry. The journal publishes papers on the theory and practice of education from scholars throughout the world in a variety of disciplines: philosophy, political science, economics, history, anthropology, sociology, psychology and medicine. The editorial board seeks to provide a common forum and, on occasion a focal point of controversy for the discussion of research findings, of historical and contemporary issues and of the functioning of educational systems. Articles are also published relating to the introduction of new statistical and methodological approaches, or to matters of educational policy, administration and planning.

Such a wide remit makes the selection of chapters for an edited book such as this a difficult prospect. It would be possible, for example, to trace developments in psychology or the history of education. Similarly, over the years, there have been many debates on the philosophy of education or on research methodology conducted within the pages of the journal. But the emphasis on multidisciplinarity and on the desire to use 'speculative and empirical theory' to improve practice has led us to focus here on educational policy. The journal has had a consistent interest in educational policy and has published a great many articles that report on policy developments and which often seek to influence future policy. These articles draw on a range of academic disciplines and both reflect and have helped to shape the nature of education policy in the UK. Even here, we have had to be extremely selective and we have chosen articles that deal with just a limited range of issues.

In making our selection we have divided the whole time period from 1975 to 2005 into four:

- 1975–1979 Labour Government, the Great Debate and the Callaghan years;
- 1979–1986 Conservative Government, Margaret Thatcher and slow change;
- 1987–1997 Conservative Government, the Education Reform Act and after;
- 1997–2005 Labour Government, change and continuity.

Part I: 1975–1979 Labour Government, the Great Debate and the Callaghan years

When the first issue of the *Oxford Review of Education* appeared in 1975 the United Kingdom was some months into a new Labour government. Edward Heath had lost the 1974 election, called after protracted problems with the trades unions. Throughout Heath's premiership Margaret Thatcher had been Secretary of State for Education: the only woman in his cabinet, she was not moved to any other post during the four years he was in power.

It had not been widely expected that the Labour Party would win the 1974 election. Heath's confrontation with the unions was expected to strike a popular chord. In fact, Harold Wilson found himself Prime Minister for a third period. He stayed in office only until April 1976, when he suddenly resigned, making the way clear for James Callaghan to succeed him. Callaghan was a politician of the old school: the only Prime Minister ever to have held all three great offices of state (Foreign Secretary, Chancellor of the Exchequer, and Home Secretary), his roots were in the original conception of the Labour movement and he was keen to complete the radical changes in the structure of secondary education begun with Anthony Crosland's Circular 10/64. 'Equality of Opportunity' was still the catchphrase for change. And questions of equality provided the rationale for the *Review*'s first collection of papers.

The first issue had a stunning cast of contributors writing on different aspects of 'Equality and Education'. The list included: Mary Warnock, A.H. Halsey, James S. Coleman, Jerome S. Bruner, H.J. Eysenck, Arthur R. Jensen and Mary Jean Bowman. It is clear from the original contributions that the first editors did not shun controversy! (In 1991 the Review revisited the topic, as we shall see, and seven of the original contributors wrote again on the subject, some fifteen years on.) It is thus appropriate that the first three chapters in this book are selected from this first issue.

Together, they provide something of a background to educational policy-making in the 1970s.

In Chapter 1, Mary Warnock applies a philosophical framework to the concept of equality and focuses on two areas where difficulties arise. First, she examines the claim that everyone has an equal right to education, interpreted, as it often is, to mean everyone has an equal right to an equal opportunity for education. Second, she examines the contention that there should be equality between the participants in the educational process itself – that teacher and student should, in some sense, have equal rights. In Chapter 2, A.H. Halsey provides a discussion of the sociological interpretation of the equality debate. In addition to providing a first glimpse of some data from the Oxford Social Mobility Survey showing how few from the working class were entering university, he examines three possible obstacles to equality and egalitarianism: occupational hierarchies, the importance of schooling, and genetic distributions. This third aspect is taken up in the third chapter by H.J. Eysenck who argues that equality of endowment is a myth, 'a fiction dreamed up for ideological and political reasons'. Moreover, he sees it as a myth that is dangerous if it dictates educational policies that go counter to biological reality. A version of equality of opportunity is seen as a more realistic ideal to follow.

The key educational event of 1976 was undoubtedly Prime Minister James Callaghan's Ruskin College speech, given in Oxford but in an independent trades-union sponsored college rather than in a college of the University. What exactly the Prime Minister meant by what he said is still debated, but the thrust was that education should prepare children for work as well as be an avenue for personal development. What was important was that this was the first significant speech on education ever to be given by a British Prime Minister. Education had become a major issue – the details were less important. However, one of the key ideas to come from this speech was that of a core curriculum for schools – in particular, one that would include more vocational and work-related elements. Chapters 4 and 5 of this book present an exchange of views on this matter between Alan Harris and John White. In spite of the title of Harris's paper, he is really arguing against a core curriculum because of its arbitrariness and unsatisfactoriness. He claims that ideological and political pressure will lead to diversity of possible curricula and that it is impossible to agree on a sensible basis for a core curriculum. John White takes him to task.

In Chapter 6, A.H. Halsey tackles face-on the Prime Minister's Great Debate, which followed from his Ruskin College speech and was orchestrated by the Secretary of State, Shirley Williams. The article is based on a BBC Radio 3 talk given a little while after Callaghan's speech. It is thus unusual in style, but it puts forward an argued view where he applies his previous discussions of authority and bureaucracy to the educational situation.

Volume 5, Issue 2, was a special issue on 'Policy issues for the eighties and after', guest edited by Stuart Maclure. Chapter 7, by Vernon Bogdanor, again responds in part to the Great Debate and considers the desirable balance between the various participants involved in education. The fundamental problem is seen as that of encouraging consensus and continuity through stronger central frameworks, while giving to individuals and to educational institutions the freedom to develop their contribution to social objectives in the way they think best.

The final chapter in this section discusses one of major research reports of the 1970s – *Fifteen Thousand Hours* (by Michael Rutter *et al.*), which launched the school effectiveness movement in Britain. Anthony Heath and Peter Clifford are critical of many aspects of the analysis presented in the book, in particular the possibility that correlation does not indicate causality and that it may be good pupils who are producing good schools rather than the reverse. They wish to emphasise 'the seventy thousand hours that Rutter missed out' in his analysis. Given the crucial role of school effectiveness research in current policy, the argument is still important and one that warrants greater consideration. A response from Rutter was published in the *Oxford Review of Education* issue 6 (3) and a further reply in issue 7 (1).

Part II: 1979–1986 Conservative Government, Margaret Thatcher and slow change

The year 1979 saw the start of a long period of Conservative rule, and Volume 7 marks the second of our four divisions in the development of the *Oxford Review of Education*. The first few years of Margaret Thatcher's government saw few new educational policies from the Department of Education and Science. Embracing the message of the Ruskin College speech, and believing that the Department was likely to inhibit change, many of the education-related policies of these first years were directed through the Department for Employment and the Manpower Services Commission. In Chapter 9, Stuart Maclure examines 'the educational consequences of Mr Norman Tebbit' who was, at that point, Secretary of State for Employment. He shows the ways in which the Manpower Services Commission had rapidly expanded and begun to influence schooling as well as education and training for those outside schools. At the higher education level, the main decision made at this time (which turned out to be overturned by events) was that there should be no expansion of provision. The proportion of young people in higher education was actually predicted to fall for a few years while the 'hump' in eighteen year olds was 'tunnelled through' until it again declined.

At school level, the decline in student numbers was already apparent. In Chapter 10 W.F. Dennison examines one of the central concerns of the 1980s and 1990s – declining secondary school rolls and the organisation of the system. As Dennison argues, the decline in school rolls was so sharp that it automatically led to many schools having a considerable number of spare places. Competition between schools for pupils was an automatic result as parents searched for what they saw as the most desirable schools.

Volume 10, issue 1, was again a special issue, this time on Comprehensive and Selective Schooling. It is a response to the publication of three pieces of research that came to differing conclusions on the effectiveness of the two systems. The debate about whether a selective system of secondary education produced better overall examination results than one based on common schooling in comprehensive schools had raged throughout the 1970s as the selective systems of local education authorities had gradually become comprehensive. The issue came to prominence again because some of those on the political right saw the possibility of urging a Conservative government to reintroduce selection, albeit in new forms. The first of the chapters reprinted here is by former Black Paper contributors John Marks and Caroline Cox who had produced one of the three research reports. They discuss their own work which claimed that selective schooling produced better overall results and the public reception of their research. They then draw comparisons between their work and that of others. This chapter is followed by a short response and discussion by Ken Fogelman who examines the problems of such comparative work, and a further chapter by Peter Clifford and Anthony Heath that discusses the different assumptions made by the researchers and calls for more research into the nature of school effectiveness.

In Chapter 14 Sally Tomlinson examines the expansion of special education at a time when youth unemployment was high and it was predicted that a large group would be either partially or permanently unemployed. She concludes that the concept of special needs has become an ideological rationalisation which obfuscates the educational, political and economic needs actually served by the expansion.

Part III: 1987–1997 Conservative Government, the Education Reform Act and after

While 1986 marked the announcement of greater diversity of schools with the City Technology Colleges, it was the 1988 Education Reform Act that dramatically changed much of schooling in England and Wales. The Act legislated for a National Curriculum with associated testing at seven, eleven and fourteen; local management of schools; grant-maintained schools; the abolition of the Inner London Education Authority and many other important changes. The *Oxford Review of Education* was not slow to include articles that commented on these various policy developments and presented research that showed their effects. Catherine Clark *et al.* focus on the management of special educational needs by local authorities. They follow the effects of increasing special education provision in mainstream schools, and present examples where more collaborative approaches between schools and local authorities have been successful.

Issue 17(2) was the 50th issue of the journal and was marked by a series of papers that returned to the subject of the very first issue – Equality and Education. Many of the contributors to the original issue agreed to write again for this anniversary issue, including Mary Warnock, James S. Colman, H.J. Eysenck, Arthur R. Jensen, Mary Jean Bowman and Kevin Marjoribanks. We have chosen Mary Warnock's article on 'Equality fifteen years on' to represent this special issue.

Chapter 17 takes up another aspect of equality by examining the National Curriculum and its effects on anti-racist education. Barry Troyna and Richard Hatcher argue that the centralist impulses of the National Curriculum are anathema to the development and legitimation of anti-racist education.

The next two chapters were first published in a special issue on 'Choice, diversity and equity in secondary schooling'. The first, by Tony Edwards and Geoff Whitty, considers the effects of specialisation and selection on secondary education. While the 1992 White Paper on Choice and Diversity identified specialisation rather than selection as its main direction for secondary schooling, later publications emphasised selection as well. It is argued that in the English system of secondary schooling, both the causal relationships between choice and diversity and the likelihood of specialisation without selection are highly questionable. This is followed by a chapter by James Tooley who argues that, while the then current policies on choice and equity did not satisfy equity, three simple reforms could make the system equitable. Choice is examined from first principles, and the peculiar powers it has for the promotion of human good are identified. An argument for a broader understanding of choice in a more authentic market in education is offered, and objections to this are countered.

Chapters 20 and 21 are again taken from a special issue – this time titled 'Through the revolution and out the other side', which examined the effects of the Education Reform Act up to the fall of the Conservative government in 1997. Stuart Maclure, who edited the issue, gives an overview of the whole period. The account discusses the changes as they affected the school curriculum, the role of local authorities, the management of the system, and the role of market forces. Michael Young and Ken Spours deal with 14–19 education over the same period. They analyse the changes since the 1980s and consider the tensions in the legacy. Both of these chapters also look forward and speculate about how the new Labour government will change or develop these policies.

Part IV: 1997–2005 Labour Government, change and continuity

The year 1997 saw the return of a new Labour government to power, and one that had, it had told the electorate on may occasions, 'education, education, education' as its first three priorities. The chapter by Geoffrey Walford examines two different policy initiatives for secondary schools –

City Technology Colleges and sponsored grant-maintained schools. Both were originally ideas of the Conservative government to encourage the supply-side of schooling and bring new providers into the market. The second was continued and eventually added to by the Labour government, thus marking the continuities in policy between the two parties in power. The encouragement of new providers to enter schooling was an important part of Labour's first and second term in office. The chapter by Harry Judge comes from a special issue devoted to 'The State, Schools and Religion'. In it he examines provision by faith-based groups and argues that any extension of state support for faith-based schools is likely to lead to an unwelcome fragmentation of society and a diversion of resources away from schools committed to developing a common culture, whilst respecting a diversity of cultural identities.

The next chapter, by Anne West *et al.*, gives further new data on admissions and selection in comprehensive schools. The authors show that, in spite of some attempts by the Labour government to reform school admissions, there was still considerable selection taking place.

The final two chapters are from a special issue published in early 2005 on 'Education and the Labour Government: An Evaluation of Two Terms'. The first, by Richard Pring, assesses Labour policy and practice on 14–19 education and training. Pring examines five aspects of policy: reform of qualifications, participation and retention, work-based learning, institutional provision, and equality of esteem, and he finds the overall results wanting. He assesses the government's initiatives as rather half-hearted and even contradictory, and he has doubts about the government's ability to manage the massive interrelated system that has emerged. Finally, Derrick Armstrong gives his evaluation of Labour's policy on special education and inclusion. He argues that Labour policy on inclusive education has shifted responsibility for meeting special needs on to teachers in ordinary classrooms and failed to engage with the issue of the cultural politics of special education and inclusion. The result has been massive contradictions in policy with little evidence of real change in the system.

Over the first thirty years or so of its existence the *Oxford Review of Education* has progressed from being a forum for the discussion of education largely among a group of Oxford-based scholars in a range of disciplines germane to, but essentially outside of, educational studies, to being an international journal to which educationists from around the world are keen to contribute. Its strengths lie not only in the breadth of its coverage and in its tradition of identifying key themes for the commissioning of special issues but also in the dynamic contribution its active editorial board makes in steering its future. We hope that this present selection of articles will give something of a flavour of the *Review*'s coverage of policy issues in education and that the quality of the contributions included here will be reflected in future papers accepted for publication.

Part I

1975–1979 Labour Government, the Great Debate and the Callaghan years

1 The concept of equality in education

Mary Warnock

Source: 'The concept of equality in education', *Oxford Review of Education*, 1(1): 3–8, 1975

Historically it has always been a matter of extreme difficulty to separate the two notions of equality and justice, nor is it probably very profitable to try to do it. We may take them as twin, related concepts. Both of them together entail the notion of behaviour *according to a rule*. If it is just to give a piece of cake to each person, then the rule lays down that the cake shall be divided between those persons present.

Let us look a little more in detail at this somewhat hackneyed example. If a number of people are hungry, and there is a cake available, over which, as a whole, no one has any special rights, then it is just to give everyone a piece of it. So the rule will be that everyone shall have a piece of cake and it will be, so far, under this rule that everyone will have an *equal right*; everyone counts for one, and none for more than one.

But the rule may be more explicit than this. It may specify that everyone present has to have a piece of cake of the same size, or it may devise some way of proportioning the size of the piece to the person, either matching size for size, or inventing a measure of greater hunger or greater need. So there could be a rule which laid down that men had twice as much as women and women twice as much as children. Any principle capable of being expressed could be the principle of division; and under such a principle equality and justice would demand that *everyone* should be treated as having a right, *according to the rule*. None should forgo his right, such as it is. Equality in this case simply ensures that *each* gets what the rule allows. Now it is clear that, in the example given, some may think that the rule should be changed, perhaps in such a way that what the men, women and children get is the same amount each. So the rule itself may be criticized as unjust, and the claim made that in some deeper sense everyone has a right to an equal amount. And this presupposes an argument to the effect that the discrimination envisaged in accordance with age or sex, although such differences do indeed exist, is not a fair basis for the division of rights. But that this argument is possible does not in the least change the fact that under the original rule everyone had an equal right, though not a right to a bit of cake equal to his neighbour's.

These are familiar points, and have been explored in detail by Richard Wollheim (*Proceedings of the Aristotelian Society*, 1955/6). I mention them simply to bring out the obvious difference between 'everyone has an equal right to education' and 'everyone has a right to equal education'. According to the first proposition *what* education each has a right to may be laid down by some rule or criterion so far unspecified. But the second proposition suggests that everyone has a right to the *same* education, and is itself therefore a specifying rule. It is the second proposition, not the first, which is generally known as the principle of Egalitarianism. Isaiah Berlin, in the same volume of the Aristotelian Society Proceedings, suggested that a pure egalitarian would have as his ideal that everyone one should be the same as everyone else. For if there were no differentiating characteristics between one person and another there could be found no specifying rule to proportion different lots of the cake, or whatever was in question, to one person rather than another. For from this pure point of view any difference *may* be taken as a ground for different and unequal allocation. Therefore ideally differences should be eliminated. But perhaps this is a somewhat misleading way of putting it. What is true is that sometimes different treatment of different people is regarded as intrinsically unfair, and where it is so regarded then egalitarianism looks like a demand for absolute uniformity between people, as well as between the way they are treated. So egalitarianism itself tends to get a bad name. For the natural human vices of envy and spite very often enter into an argument which starts as an argument about natural justice. Coherently to claim one's 'rights' where there is no law laying down the rights, and where one is in fact saying that there *should* be such a law, is a difficult thing to do; and such claims are often vitiated by the intrusion of resentment and envy. But in any case, it is doubtful whether anyone could hold to a 'pure' egalitarian view, in Berlin's version of it. Such an ideal looks more like what one would ascribe to one's enemies rather than ever admit to oneself.

I want now to consider, in the light of these opening remarks, two separate, though connected, areas in which the question of equality arises in education, and in which it poses problems. First, I want to look at the general claim that everyone has an equal right to education, interpreted, as it often is, to mean everyone has an equal right *to an equal opportunity for education*. The moment one starts to examine this interpretation, difficulties multiply. First of all there is an implicit assumption which I do not wish seriously to dispute that the situation is in *some* sense like the familiar cake situation, in that education is a good thing, and a thing which is wanted. As people can be hungry, and satisfied by a bit of cake, so they can be in need of education, and be satisfied by getting it. Further, it must be supposed that education is an available commodity which can be distributed more fairly or less. But whereas a hungry man will, if given his bit of cake presumably eat it, in the case of education, though we may all need it, we do not all necessarily want it, and may reject what is offered. This is why we have to speak of the benefit to be distributed not, after all, as *education itself*, but as *the opportunity for education, if it should seem desirable*.

But the introduction of the concept of opportunity immediately changes the picture. For we do not really believe that *all* we need distribute is the opportunity to be educated. We also believe that we must compel people to be educated whether they want it or not and so, to some extent, distribute education. When we speak in terms of equal opportunity we speak as though education were an undoubted good, but one which is in short supply. Everyone, we suggest, must have as good a *chance* as everyone else to get some, but this does not entail that everyone will get some, and it certainly does not entail that everyone will get the same. All it means, so far, is that no one may rightfully deprive another of his chance to be educated. But at the same time we probably want to say, as well, that everyone ought *actually to get* some education as of right, and that no one may rightfully deprive another of his actual education, not merely his chance. And in this sense we stop speaking as though education were something for which we have to compete against each other and speak instead as if it were a commodity which was not scarce, like fresh air.

The position seems to be this. We hold that everyone should have an equal right to two different things; to a certain amount of education, and the chance or opportunity to get more than this if they want it. The split between these two goods to be distributed arises partly because, in the nature of the case, education, being something primarily for children, cannot be thought of exactly as cake is thought of, namely as actually desired. Instead it has to be thought of as needed. So, as we saw, there is a split, not envisaged in the simple cake example, between what people want and what they need; and that is why we have to say that someone has a duty to provide education, and everyone has a right to receive *it*, not just the opportunity for it. To give a child the opportunity to go to school may be good, but it may not be enough. He might not actually choose to go. His parents might say that certainly he was free to go to school, but since he did not wish to, they did not wish to press him. But on the other hand it is generally held that there must be a limit to compulsory education; and after this limit is reached, all that a child has a right to, or anyone has a duty to provide, is a *chance* for more. So one question which obviously has to be answered is the question at what point has a child had enough *education* as of right? Or in other words, at what point does his right become a right to equal *opportunity* to be educated?

A satisfactory way to answer this would be to say that everyone has an equal right to as much education as may enable him to have more if he wants it; and when he has been educated so far, he thereafter has a right to equality of *opportunity* for more. Whether he actually gets more will depend upon his inclinations, upon the amount of the commodity available, and the kind of competition involved in getting it. Of course if the commodity is not scarce then equality of opportunity simply means that everyone can have as much as he likes, and the right to have it means that no one can rightfully prevent him. But if the commodity is scarce, then all he may have, as of right, is the right to enter the competition.

But this answer, though formally satisfactory, cannot in practice be very informative. For although we have succeeded in separating two different rights which are equally held, namely the right to education up to a certain point, and the right to opportunity for more, the actual nature of the goods to be distributed has not been seriously mentioned. What is it that every child should have, such that when he has got it, he should then have the opportunity for more? Are we saying that every one should have a *taste* of cake, so that if they then develop a liking for it, they should have the opportunity for more? Somewhere in this description there is lurking an assumption about what is the minimum quantity of the stuff that will count as a 'taste'. Now in the case of some useful skills, such as swimming, or indeed reading and writing, it is sensible to argue that everyone ought to have at least the bare minimum amount of skill (to enable them, for instance, to keep afloat if they fall into the river) even if it takes more time and resources to teach some people than to teach others. But then whether they go on and get really expert is up to them. But perhaps nowadays it would be hard to find anyone to argue that it was only to such a bare educational minimum that everyone had a right, although they may be agreed to have a right to this among other things. People have a more grandiose notion of education; and the moment we start saying that education should be the development of an ability to think independently, or to appreciate one's cultural heritage, then the notion of a *bare minimum* becomes impossible to apply. Moreover the objection that for some people it is going to be far more difficult than for others to reach a comparable minimum standard in cultural-heritage-appreciation or independent thought takes on a new dimension. Does the equal right to be educated to a reasonable standard, when this kind of thing counts as education, entail that the naturally disadvantaged should have more education than those to whom it may come more easily? Where there is some fairly definite goal such as the ability to swim enough to prevent oneself drowning in a river, then it makes sense to argue that one must press on with the inept until they reach the goal, even though it takes a comparatively long time and much patience. But where the goal has become vague and elusive, no such simple argument will apply. Notoriously political theorists concerned with education have to try to devise further arguments to justify this particular policy or that, in their distribution of resources. All I hope to have suggested is that no appeal to equality will on its own help one to make good decisions in this field, since one might almost say that the concept of equality is precisely what introduced the difficulties in the first place. For in the simple cake example, one either had to be a total egalitarian (upholding the right of each to an equal amount of cake) and follow this as the distributive rule, or one had to devise another rule which would proportion that to which the right was held to the bearer of the right. Similarly, in the case of education, one has to try to devise a rule. And the devising of such a rule is further complicated, in this instance, by the fact that, as we have seen, the stuff to be distributed changes its character. At one stage it appears as education itself, at another as the opportunity for education. Perhaps the difficulties of devising the distributive rule need hardly be further elaborated. I am inclined to think that, in this area, equality, and therefore justice, must form an element of the considerations involved, but that, through lack of clarity, they cannot form the whole of such considerations. A quite different principle may inevitably crop up, a principle concerned with what it is desirable that people should learn, concerned with the needs, that is to say, of society. Educational purists and egalitarians may both deplore this, but I believe that it is so, and, if so, should be acknowledged. Too great a reliance on the confusing principle of equality may conceal the facts of the case.

Let us now turn to the second area within which difficulties arise over the concept of equality. I want briefly to consider the kind of arguments which have become fairly familiar in recent years, not about equality in the distribution of education, but about equality between the different participants in the educational process itself. Egalitarianism in this field amounts to the view that the teacher and his pupil are equal, and that education is a transaction carried on for the ultimate benefit of the pupil (though for the financial benefit of the teacher) in which the rights of the parties to the transaction are the same.

Having thus roughly characterized this kind of egalitarianism, a difficulty immediately arises when we try to go on and discover in more detail what these equal rights are supposed to be equal rights *to*. In practice, there appear to be several different claims, but two seem to be dominant. The first is the claim that pupil and teacher have equal rights to their own *opinions*, and especially their opinions as to what is and what is not valuable. Therefore a teacher has no right to impose his opinions or values upon his pupils. The second is a sub-class of this claim, namely that pupil and teacher have equal rights to decide what is to be taught. The teacher has no more right than has the pupil to lay down the subject-matter of education. This denial obviously arises out of the claim to equality in respect of values, since the teacher might be thought, in selecting and determining subject-matter, to be thereby imposing as of right his own view of what is fit to be taught or valuable to learn, upon his pupil. Now although the first claim is wider and perhaps more serious, I want to confine myself in this essay to the discussion of the second, for various reasons. First there is the consideration of space. Secondly the question of rights to opinion or values becomes variously confused according to whether one is talking about education at school, where some of the participants are children, or at university where they are not (and as some children are younger than others, egalitarianism has accordingly to be adjusted along the line). Moreover a further complication arises out of the identification, in some cases, of teachers with the middle classes and pupils with the working classes, and so this kind of egalitarianism may turn into the claim that working class values should have as much right to be accepted as middle class values. It is not that I do not think such issues are worth discussing. It is rather that to try to sort out the part played by the concept of equality in such arguments would take too long, since not only are there complications in this concept itself, as we have seen, but there are vast difficulties lurking in the notion of 'value' and 'the imposition of values on another'. Into these I shall not at present enter. I want, instead, to take a fairly limited instance of the second of the two claims listed above, that teacher and pupil have an equal right to determine the subject-matter taught. And I want to confine even this instance to university education where both parties to the transaction may be thought to be grown-up.

The view that the teacher determines what is taught, while the pupil takes what is given to him is of course a crude and inadequate account of what may be observed to occur in any university. On the one hand, the teacher may feel as much bound by an existing syllabus as his pupils, and he may feel himself obliged to teach what the syllabus demands. However syllabuses can be changed, though slowly, and it is still true that teachers probably have more power to change them than their pupils, though they may have little power as individuals to do so. But even leaving on one side the question of a fixed syllabus, still the picture of the teacher handing out *the subject* to his pupils who sit passively by and receive it may also seem exaggerated. For in so far as pupils are supposed to think and write, they may be thought to be preparing themselves to change the look of the subject, perhaps to change its boundaries. What remains, however, is the fact that even at a university, the teacher is supposed to know more than his pupil, and that this knowledge creates an *authority*, which, in the particular educational relation between teacher and pupil, is inimical to equality. As teacher, the teacher has rights which his pupil has not, simply in virtue of the fact that he is an expert. It is sometimes argued, indeed, that education entails being taught, that being taught entails the existence of teacher and pupil, and that therefore education *entails* a lack of equality between the parties to it. It is against this notion of the teacher as expert or authority, that the egalitarian claim has grown up. In its extreme form, it is difficult to see clearly what it amounts to. But perhaps it is important to try to make it clearer. In a recent volume called *Counter Course*[1] there is a number of essays which are aimed both to demonstrate the legitimacy of the egalitarian claim within university education and also to suggest ways of exercising the rights of students against their teachers. In a particularly interesting essay on medical education the author, Robert Silman, says this, in passing (his main concern is with the notion of the doctor as a 'sacred object', and with this we are not concerned), "... It would be nice to analyse how it would be possible to overcome the problems raised by the accumulation of medical knowledge or information by an élite group i.e. those who practice and research in medicine. These are critical problems, since knowledge or information is a form of wealth with its own laws of accumulation and distribution. Not only has information a value which can be exchanged against money, it seems to possess a value which can resist economic devaluation. This ought to be the starting-point of a critique of medical education." The problem is that some people are going to know more than other people, and that this will give them not only more money, but more of something else, something which seems to be valuable, and which at present is unequally distributed throughout the world. Expertise, the possession of more information than another man has, is something which should be regarded, according to this view, as *intrinsically* inequitable. This is the pure voice of egalitarianism.

The same kinds of points are made more specifically by Robbie Gray in an essay on History as a university subject. Mr. Gray allows that "a certain degree of technical expertise" is necessary for an historian, if mere dogmatic assertion is not to be substituted for conclusions based on evidence. But he goes on to argue that such expertise or specialization is commonly illegitimate in that "it is used in a manipulative way to exert power over ... students". And he argues that most alternative courses so far proposed in universities "reduplicate the authoritarian approach", in that they use "superior knowledge to dominate". Even political propaganda, he says, "reflects the dominant educational process in society; it is characterized by distance between the 'expert', and an audience that must passively receive instruction". "In the teaching situation", he says, "superior knowledge is taken as conferring the right unilaterally to define the questions asked and the kind of evidence deemed relevant, thus preventing the development of a shared understanding". And he goes on to sketch the kinds of 'alternative relationships' which ought to replace the 'teaching situation'. These he sees as social and collective activity, motivated by a common search for understanding and including a recognition of total equality within the group.

Now it is true that such exploratory groups exist in universities and that the excellent and exciting thing about them, at their best, is precisely the feeling that the argument, whatever it is, can be pursued wherever it leads, that no one is in a position to tell anyone else what conclusion he ought to draw, that anyone can contribute evidence or relevant considerations to the common pool. Such groups may be groups of colleagues, all expert in their field, or groups of graduate-students or mixed groups. But the one thing that is essential to the proper functioning of such a group is that no one should have come to it either to instruct or be instructed. And it seems to me obvious, though perhaps it is not strictly entailed by this, that therefore there must exist some *other* form of educational occasion as well as the kind of groups envisaged. People can, of course, get their instruction out of books. But even so, they need help and advice about the reading of books, and in giving such advice, expertise is essential. There must be someone somewhere who is regarded as knowing better than his pupil, even if it is only a matter of knowing better what to read, and in what order. If such guidance and advice were withdrawn then there could be no progress, not only for the individual but within the subject as a whole. It is essential to learning that the discoveries of others should be capitalized, and used by subsequent workers in the field. The concept of such capitalization entails that there exist authorities, who can be consulted. Where the goal is that knowledge should be increased, it is plain that superior knowledge will, in a sense, dominate. It is plain, also, that pupils often wish to be dominated, that is, to be told things which will help them themselves to become expert. One ought not to regard such a wish to be dominated as a psychological disaster nor as the result of sociological conditioning. To consult an authority is no disgrace, nor is it an unnatural or servile act. Indeed it is inconceivable that one should not do it and do it willingly if only as a means to becoming an authority oneself. In such a situation, the question of *rights* hardly seems to arise. But *if* it arises, then the person who knows has a right to say what he knows to be true, and a right to be heard.

There are, of course, questions within any university about the content of the courses and syllabuses to be taught, and perhaps about the methods of teaching. But, once again, to suppose that these practical questions can be answered by an appeal to the doctrine of equality or justice seems to me to mistake the nature of the questions. There are doubtless principles in accordance with which answers can be attempted. But there is no reason to suppose that these will be principles of equality.

The two areas from which I have derived problems with regard to equality in education are in fact related. For it may be argued that a particular view of the role of teacher vis-à-vis his pupil is an élitist view, which will spill over into élitism with respect to who ought to be educated and how much. In a somewhat immoderate article on the philosophy of R. S. Peters, David Adelstein (op. cit.) attacks Peters for dividing the process of education into two parts, "those who do the thing and those to whom it is done. This inherent division gives rise to the teacher as authority and ultimately to the whole class division of society which is mediated in the educational system". The demand for equal rights as between teacher and taught is another aspect of the demand that everyone should, as of right, have the *same knowledge*, that is, the same education. My somewhat negative contribution to these controversies has been to suggest that while there are genuine difficulties in both these areas, in neither will the concept of equality alone be sufficient to produce solutions. If conceptual analysis has any merit, it is to clarify certain concepts in order to see what they are and what they are not fitted to do. To show that the concept Equality may not be as powerful as has sometimes been supposed is worth doing, if one can thereby open the way for less misleading discussions of possible educational policies.

Note

1 Published by Penguin Books.

2   Sociology and the equality debate

A. H. Halsey

Source: 'Sociology and the equality debate', *Oxford Review of Education*, 1(1): 9–23, 1975.

Though sociologists have contributed heavily to the debate about equality, the problem is much more than a sociological one. In 1651 Hobbes wrote:

> Nature hath made man so equall, in the faculties of body, and mind; as that though bee found one man sometimes manifestly stronger in body, or of quicker mind than another; yet when all is reckoned together, the difference between man, and man, is not so considerable, as that one man can thereupon claim to himselfe any benefit, to which another may not pretend, as well as he.
>
> (Thomas Hobbes, *Leviathan*, London Everyman edition, 1934, p. 63)

Egalitarian claims and anti-egalitarian rebuttals are probably more strident now, and certainly more often couched in sociological terms, than they were in Britain in the seventeenth century. Yet Hobbes' formulation (substituting 'person' for 'man' and a pronoun for both sexes if the English language possessed one) defines the contemporary debate as well as anything written in the intervening three hundred years. We would say now that it contains empirical propositions from both genetics and sociology, the one referring to natural differences and the other (about claiming and pretending) referring to the social psychology of men's perceptions of social rights. But the central assertion is an evaluative one, as it must be. For the debate is fundamentally about the values which ought to be reflected in the actual relations of men and women in society.

Controversy goes on at three relatable but not necessarily related levels. First, there is a clash of priorities between different values presumed to be realisable in society. Second, there is the philosophically and logically difficult intellectual task of clarifying the language of the debate and third, there is the tedious labour of relating theoretical constructions to the changing empirical realities of the social world. The distinctive contribution of sociology must clearly be at the third level. It is well-known, of course, that the political persuasion of the majority of western sociologists has leant towards egalitarian politics by contrast with the typical orientation of biologists and psychologists since Herbert Spencer and social Darwinism. Perhaps there is a sociology of intellectual culture which might partly explain these persistent political differences in terms of the social consciousness induced by work in the different disciplines and the selective effect of their popular representations on the recruitment of personalities to them. At all events, whatever the provenance of ethical discussion, the premises of argument are set by a moral affirmation about the value of equality in relation to other values such as liberty or fraternity sought by people in their dealings with others. In this sense the debate, I suspect, is unresolvable and simple and for that reason all the better phrased in the blunt banality used by R. H. Tawney to dismiss the inegalitarian—"if a man likes that sort of dog then that is the sort of dog a man likes".

Yet to begin with this fundamental simplicity is in no way to detract from the work of those who have contributed to the second level of discussion by seeking greater conceptual clarity as to the meaning of the terms used in the debate.[1] John Rawls' *A Theory of Justice* is a recent and notable case in point. He adopts the device of the 'original position'—an 'if so' story of the rational choices that might be expected from an individual contemplating different societies with known different systems of social relationship and distribution but an unknown position within them for the contemplater—to illuminate the problem of value choice. Brian Barry's *Political Argument* (1965) is another example of a book which educates us to avoid terminological confusion and to use words to the fullest extent of their potential for precise distinction. Yet if we only consider Brian Barry's short book (*The Liberal Theory of Justice*, O.U.P., 1973), or Rawls' long one, it becomes clear that no amount of conceptual clarification, however sophisticated and erudite, solves the problem of what I have referred to as the first level. Thus Barry, through an argument of delicate philosophical dissection, clearly demonstrates how a minimal adjustment to Rawls' social and psychological assumptions opens up the possibility of a crucial shift from liberal to egalitarian forms of society. Nevertheless, the problem at the first level remains. Thus Barry ends with a personal statement of preferences which he does not offer as compelling, only as consonant with his preceding argument. "I feel a strong attachment to liberalism in relation to ideas while believing that in matters of political, social and economic organisation altruistic collaboration is worth giving up a good deal of efficiency for, and fearing that hierarchy is more soundly based in human psychology than I would altogether like".[2]

At the same time, this passage indicates the existence of a third level of argument which sustains the first and second levels by challenges to test concept against relevant fact, typically under conditions where either the pace of social change or the ingenuity of theorists outpaces the capacity of empirical enquiry.

Of course, politicians can be more or less serious even at the first level. Thus, when Mr. Prentice tells us from the D.E.S. that he does not like the private sector of education but that the cost of abolition is too great a financial burden for a Labour government to face for the time being, he is offering an honest if debatable ordering of priorities. But when a previous Secretary of State, the then Sir Edward Boyle, prefaced the first Newsom Report with: "The essential point is that all children should have an equal opportunity of acquiring intelligence, and of developing their talents and abilities to the full", and then goes on to tell us that he favours the retention of direct grant schools, the reader or listener is understandably baffled as to what priorities are being offered. It is only by hearing the first affirmation as amiable rhetoric or the second as assuming the (false) empirical proposition that opportunity to develop intelligence is equal as between children in direct grant and comprehensive schools that the two quotations can be reconciled. In the latter case, given conceptual clarity, empirical enquiry can settle useless debate. This I take to be the distinctive business of the social scientist.

Now that there is widespread disillusionment concerning the possibilities of reaching an egalitarian society through educational reform, much sociological effort is needed to determine what education might contribute to wider participation in the material and cultural abundance potentially available to the members of a rich society. We are, of course, invited on every hand to espouse various utopias among which Ivan Illich's developing outline of a convivial society is a fashionable one.[3] Nevertheless, whether we lean towards Illichian or other nostrums, there is inescapable controversy as to the relation between theory and policy, or what means might appropriately and effectively make our dreams into realities. My own view is basically that the society of equals has to be created by economic and political reform and that the role of education must largely be to maintain such a society once it has been attained.

A good deal may be learned by looking back over the debate on the relation between equality and education and in this connection Harold Silver's *Equal Opportunity in Education* (Methuen, 1974) is an adroit selection from twentieth century writings which gives a fair picture of this element of intellectual and political history.[4] But, as I shall argue, the origins of the mainstream of theory on which policy has been floated are to be found further back in the nineteenth century.

The liberal theory of educational embourgeoisement[5]

Looking back over the history of official policy in Britain, there is an unmistakable thread of egalitarianism. No less striking, however, is the fact of failure to realise egalitarian ends by educational means—a failure to which the virulence of current debate is itself a major witness. The basic reason is that the theory which has formed the foundation of our policy edifice is a false one, consisting of liberal concepts which have not stood the test of historical experience.

This liberal theory came out of the tradition of political economy in which, in Britain at least, the boundaries between economics and sociology were not drawn as sharply as they are now. The classic statement of the theory is to be found in a paper written by Alfred Marshall a hundred years ago and delivered at a converzatione of the Reform Club in Cambridge on 'The Future of the Working Class'.[6] This famous essay is the *locus classicus* of liberal theories about the relation of education to social class.[7] The question, as Marshall put it, was "whether it be true that the resources of the world will not suffice for giving to more than a small proportion of its inhabitants an education in youth and an occupation in after-life, similar to those which we are now wont to consider proper to gentlemen" ... "The question is not whether all men will ultimately be equal—that they will certainly not—but whether progress may not go on steadily if slowly till the official distinction between working men and gentlemen has passed away; till, by occupation at least, every man is a gentleman".

Marshall's high-minded Victorian conception of the stratification system was focused on culture and character. These were the defined class attributes to which policy had to be directed. The theory was that culture and character were functions of education (which determine occupation) and occupational experience. The mediating variable was experience in work. The occupations of gentlemen he saw as directly promoting high culture and refinement of character—qualities which require a careful and long-continued education. He further saw the occupational structure of his day as descending (in terms of its propensity to generate admirable personal qualities) through fine gradations from the high professions through the "intermediate classes" down to "that darker scene which the lot of unskilled labour presents" ... "Vast masses of men who, after long hours of hard and unintellectual toil, are wont to return to their narrow homes with bodies exhausted and minds dull and sluggish...".

Marshall's proposals for liberation from mid-nineteenth century conditions were contained in a sketch of a 'fancied country' from which the brutalising effects of long hours of toil had been excluded and in which no one would have an occupation which tended to make him anything else than a gentleman. This would be assured by technical progress, extensive education and short hours of work.

He argued that such an education, economy and society would be practical; "We know, then, pretty clearly what are the conditions under which our fancied country is to start; and we may formulate them as follows. It is to have a fair share of wealth, and not an abnormally large population. Everyone is to have in youth an education which is thorough while it lasts, and which lasts long. No one is to do in the day so much manual work as will leave him little time or little aptitude for intellectual and artistic enjoyment in the evening. Since there will be nothing tending to render the individual coarse and unrefined, there will be nothing tending to render society coarse and unrefined".

But then, could such a society be maintained? Marshall went on to rebut the objections which were seriously advanced in Victorian England. First, he argued against the fear that a great diminution of the hours of manual labour would lead to economic ruin. This argument was the stock-in-trade of British employers from the middle of the nineteenth century and survived up to the slump years of the 1930s. Thus, when the Bill presenting the Fisher Act of 1918 was before Parliament, we find R. H. Tawney repeating the Marshall argument against a memorandum of the Education Committee of the Federation of British Industries. The proposal was to abolish all exemption from school attendance for children under fourteen. The F.B.I. argued that: "A period of eight hours a week taken out of working hours would impose a burden upon many industries which they would be quite unable to bear except on a basis of very gradual development".

Tawney couched the rebuttal in terms of outraged irony. "To suggest that British industry is suspended over an abyss by a slender thread of juvenile labour, which eight hours of continued education will snap, that after a century of scientific discovery and economic progress it is still upon the bent backs of children of fourteen that our industrial organisation, and national prosperity, and that rare birth of time, the Federation of British Industries itself, repose—is not all this, after all, a little pitiful?"[8] Marshall's version of the argument is more sober but otherwise identical. It is based on technological progress and the high return to skilled labour exploiting technologically advanced forms of capital.

That knowledge is power was already a well-worn cliché, but that man could possess it with reduced toil was revolutionary thought, contrary to the common-sense of all previous experience. None the less, Marshall went so far as to assert that the total work done per head of the population would be greater than it then was. All labour would be skilled and there would be no premium on setting men to tasks that required no skill. Inventions would increase and would be readily applied. His argument at this point reads like the familiar contemporary thesis of official policy throughout the industralised and industrialising world—that investment in man is the cure for all things—but, as was consonant with his elevated view of man and society, he stressed the vigorous exercise of increased faculties and saw the direct outcome as an improvement in the level of civility and sensibility and only indirectly as an increase in material wealth. When Tawney developed this theme in the twentieth century the paramountcy of social over economic values became even more sharply emphasised.

In arguing the possibility of maintaining the new society once it had been attained, Marshall also dealt with the objection that a high standard of education could not be kept up because some parents would neglect their duty to their children. "A class of unskilled labourers might again grow up, competing for hard toil, ready to sacrifice the means of their own culture to increased wages and physical indulgences. This class would marry inprovidently: an increased population would press on the means of subsistence, the difficulty of imparting a high education would increase, and society would retrograde until it arrived at a position similar to that which it now occupies—a position in which man, to a great extent, ignores his duty of anticipating, before he marries, the requirements of the bodily and mental nurture of his children; and thereby compels Nature, with her sorrowful but stern hand, to thin out the young lives before they grow up to misery".

We see here the Malthusian spectre which continued to haunt the Victorians into the 1870s. Marshall pinned his faith on the two forces of self-respect (born of education) and external restraint ("Society would be keenly alive to the peril to itself of such failure, and would punish it as a form of treason against the state"). Thus Marshall concluded, "every single condition would be fulfilled which was requisite for the continued and progressive prosperity of the country which we have pictured. It would grow in wealth—material and mental".

Marshallian theory in hindsight

To look at Britain a century later is to see that the pre-conditions postulated in his 'fancied country' have, if anything, surpassed his youthful expectations. If unskilled labour is the measure of degradation and brutality, its proportion in the total occupied population of Great Britain had fallen from 14.8 per cent in 1931 to 8.5 per cent in 1966.[9] Indeed, the white-collar occupational groups (what he called the intermediate classes) grew by 176 per cent between 1911 and 1966 and now approach 40 per cent of the total. Moreover, within their ranks the growing number of skilled scientific and technical workers has proliferated, reflecting a vast investment in human capital and an increasingly scientific and capital-intensive technology.

Meanwhile, hours of work have been reduced from 54 to 44.5 a week between 1900 and 1968 and there has been a marked increase, especially since the Second War, in paid holidays. By 1972 three-quarters of the manual workers in the United Kingdom were enjoying three weeks paid holiday, compared with 1 per cent in 1951.[10] There have been rising standards of housing, and health. Affluence has accumulated: the gross national product was £1,846m. in 1900 and rose to £36,815m. in 1968. In some respects at least, the material conditions of the ordinary man now are superior to those of the gentleman in Marshall's day.

On the other hand, the redistribution of what in Marshall's day was an almost exclusive concentration of private capital ownership in the hands of the richest 5 per cent of the nation—conditions approximating most closely to a simple Marxist definition of class—has proceeded at no more than a snail's pace. In 1911 it was 86 per cent and by the 1950s 67 per cent[11] and by 1970 55 per cent.[12] Moreover, the small minority of the extremely wealthy is matched by another and larger minority of the poor. At the end of 1971 three million people were receiving supplementary benefit and these, with their dependants, numbered four and a half million, including about a million children under sixteen.[13] Though the middle mass of white-collar and affluent workers enjoys a considerable material prosperity and though the miners in 1973 may have accelerated sharply the trend towards a more even income balance as between the markets for 'uneducated' and 'educated' labour, a steep hierarchy of income, power and advantage remains.

Universal compulsory education to age sixteen has arrived, together with expanded provision at the secondary and further stages. But educational inequality has also remained. Its documentation is a recurrent theme of the sociology of education. To take a recent example—a report of the National Child Development Study[14]—"first there is clearly a strong association between social class and reading and arithmetic attainment at seven years of age. The chances of an unskilled manual worker's child (Social Class V) being a poor reader are six times greater than those of a professional worker's child (Social Class I). If the criterion of poor reading is made more stringent the disparity is much larger. Thus the chances of a Social Class V child being a non-reader are fifteen times greater than those of a Social Class I child ... There appears to be a substantial division between the children from non-manual, or middle-class, homes on the one hand, and those from manual, or working-class, homes on the other. This suggests that whatever the factors are which social class indirectly measures, they are fairly sharply differentiated as between middle-class and working-class homes, at least as far as their effect on attainment or ability is concerned". Similar disparities of educational attainment according to social origin can be shown for the secondary schools.[15] The major burden of recent work is to show that the disparities persist despite educational expansion. Thus, educationally at least, there has been no assimilation of the working-class into the middle-class though studies at various points in the century show a rising trend of aspirations for the education of their children among working-class families.

Marshall stood at the Victorian origin of a century of liberal theories concerning the relations between education, occupation and class. I have traced the subsequent history of this tradition and theory elsewhere[16] and argued that it has failed even in its own terms. Its aim—equality of opportunity in education—has eluded the policy makers. It may be, as James Coleman argues, that, as a pure object of policy, whether defined in input or output terms, the concept is useless in a pure form. Of course, if there were universal provision of all stages of education, the aim would be achieved definitionally: but in fact, selection and differential attainment between sexual, class and social groups have remained an integral feature of passage to further stages of education and of entry to the hierarchy of occupational advantage.

Marshall himself, it may be noted, avoided the meritocracy problem which has faced later versions of the liberal theory,[17] by building in the supply, demand and price argument with respect to different kinds of labour on the assumption of technological advance. This advance has been realised, and in the post-War period, has resulted in more diverse origins among those in the most elevated occupational destinations. But this pattern of recruitment to 'the top' co-exists with a very large measure of self-recruitment among manual workers.[18]

Education in Britain has remained predominantly an avenue for the stable transmission of status from one generation to another, though this has not been incompatible with some inter-generational occupational mobility, not only through the relative expansion of skilled work (because of technical advance) and through the 'replacement' of 'deficient' numbers among the high-born (because of an inverse relation of social class to fertility) but also through successful educational and career competition by a minority of children born in the lower strata. Exactly how much and what kind of mobility through education had been experienced by the 1972 population is not known until the results of the current study at Nuffield College, Oxford, are published in 1975. We can, however, have an anticipatory glimpse of the findings with respect to university graduates.

Of the men born in England and Wales between 1930 and 1949, 6.88 per cent reached a university compared with 2.6 per cent of those born before 1930 (i.e. those who went to school before the 1944 Act). The trends and distribution of university attendance are shown in Table 2.1.

A sample of ten thousand men in England and Wales in 1972 are here classified in two ways—by date of birth and by the occupation of their fathers. We have thus two birth cohorts and a division of social origins into an upper and a lower middle class and an upper and a lower working class. Three assertions can be made on the basis of these statistics. First, the expansion of university places since the War has benefited all classes; second, there remain impressive inequalities of opportunity for university education between classes; and third, inequality is rather less than it was before the post-War expansion.

Table 2.1 Percentage who reached university from origins in various occupational groups

Birth	*Professional administrative and managerial*	*Inspectoral, supervisory and non-manual*	*Skilled manual*	*Semi-skilled, unskilled manual*	*Total*
1910–29	12.3	2.81	1.37	0.64	2.63
1930–49	22.73	7.73	4.14	1.92	6.38

Table 2.2 Indices of university access from origins in various occupational groups

Birth	Upper middle class	Lower middle class	Upper working class	Lower working class
1910–29	5	1	$\frac{1}{2}$	$< \frac{1}{4}$
1930–49	3	1	$\frac{1}{2}$	$< \frac{1}{2}$

A simple measure of the trends in class differences of access to the universities may be had by standardising each of the percentages in the table. This means expressing each percentage of the whole age group who attended universities (i.e. to divide the cell values by the total row percentage). The resulting rough and rounded indices of relative chances of graduating from given social class origins are as shown in Table 2.2.

In this form the statistics show the steepness of the remaining inequality, with the upper middle class children having three times better than average chance and the lower working class having less than half an average chance. Nevertheless, the degree of inequality has lessened with reduction at the top and slight relative improvement at the bottom of the hierarchy of social birth. So much for the progress of educational equality.

Marshall was, in essence, advancing a particular version of the embourgeoisement thesis, i.e. the theory that class is inexorably abated by the assimilation of the working class into the middle class as industrial society advances to ever higher levels of wealth and income. For Marshall this assimilation was assured by technological progress leading to an amelioration of economic circumstances in work and social opportunities and attitudes in non-work for the working classes. Normative assimilation was also crucial to his theory—the spread, that is, of gentlemanly character and culture, partly from occupational experience but reinforced by increased and prolonged education.

However, though Marshall is not specifically mentioned, the theoretical and empirical demolition of the liberal version of the embourgeoisement thesis by Goldthorpe and Lockwood[19] is completely applicable to his essay. As these modern Cambridge authors have argued, "increases in earnings, improvements in working conditions, more enlightened and liberal employment policies and so on, do not in themselves basically alter the class situation of the industrial worker in present-day society. Despite these changes, he remains a man who gains his livelihood through placing his labour at the disposal of an employer in return for wages, usually paid by the piece, hour or day ...". Characteristic differences in the work situations of manual and non-manual employees still widely persist. Hence these writers regard with some scepticism the broad evolutionary perspectives of western industrialism in which "the emergence of a 'middle-class' society is seen as a central process resulting more or less automatically from continuing economic growth". Rising affluence and advances in the technical organisation of industry are not likely in themselves to bring about a radical restructuring of the stratification hierarchy. At best there is a classless inegalitarianism. And the interpretation which Goldthorpe puts on the developments that have occurred is rather one of "normative convergence between certain manual and non-manual groups".

Marshall's version of the embourgeoisement prediction has not been confirmed by events. Not only has there not been a 'one-way' assimilation of the character and culture of working-class life into middle-class life but it has also not taken the direction of universalising the life-style of an ideal late-Victorian Cambridge don. Marshall did not address himself to the complications of a sophisticated theory of social consciousness. He in effect assumed that the gentlemanly culture of his day would be the common culture of a rich society. He was only dimly aware of the high cost in cultural terms of the extreme forms of division of labour that have been necessitated by technologically based economic growth. The occupational experiences of dons and professional people, which he assumed would spread throughout society, are characterised by high degrees of autonomy and discretion as well as by relations of high trust.[20] Perhaps he was appreciating the dangers of developing low discretion and low trust relationships in and between highly specialised occupational groups in his hope for the development of producer co-operatives as a form of industrial organisation. And he certainly was aware of the dilemma which exists as between the values of efficiency on the one hand and humane work-relationships on the other. But, as Goldthorpe and Lockwood have shown, the problem has turned out to be much more complicated. Biblical appeal is not enough to combat the tendencies of instrumentalism to generate low-trust organisations. The gift relation as described by Titmuss in the case of the British organisation of blood supplies[21] does not generalise itself in any automatic way. Yet without it we are unlikely to achieve either equality or high character and culture.

We are at this point suggesting in other words that, quite apart from its intricate relation to liberty, equality also presupposes a social basis in fraternity. Socialism as fellowship[22] is central to the native brand of political thought which runs from William Morris through Tawney to Titmuss. It is this tradition which lends most coherent support to the idea of community schooling[23] as an educational means towards both fraternity and equality.

Determinism and openness in social change

Sociological debate on the possibility of a more egalitarian society is riven by dispute about the character of social change. Goldthorpe and his colleagues are most concerned to argue, both as against the liberal evolutionist determinism and the alternative determinism of the neo-Marxists, that tensions remain in the structure of society along class lines but that the outcomes for social movements are open. There is neither an automatic social levelling nor an inevitable revolution arising out of increasingly manifest alienation. "It is, in our view, likely that a sense of deprivation will tend to increase as improvement in material standards reaches the point at which the old wants are satisfied and aspirations of a new type arise—aspirations that are less closely related to consumption of a private character and less easily fulfilled. To illustrate but one possibility, it may be recalled that among our Luton couples, parents' aspirations for their children appeared already to be running well beyond the latter's actual chances of success within the existing system of educational provision. Thus, in circumstances of this kind, the *potential* support for politics of social change is evident enough but whether this potentiality is realised and, if so, how, will depend upon the degree and the manner in which the awareness of deprivation becomes articulate and directed". Thus, in their perspective of the new working class the 'degrees of freedom' that exist are crucial. Accordingly, they lay great emphasis on the possibilities of polit- ical leadership, "that is, purposive action on the part of elites and organi- sations, aimed at giving a specific and politically relevant meaning to grievances, demands and aspirations, which have hitherto been of a sub- political kind and thus mobilising mass support for a programme or movement".

This last point is of considerable importance when set against the liberal tradition of theory concerning the relationship between class and educa- tional movement. The liberal conceptions underlying official policy have always lacked an adequate theory of learning. Recent work, for example that born of the experience of the British E.P.A.s[24] or the American Com- pensatory Education movements[25], has had the effect of locating the origins of inequality at earlier and earlier stages in the life-cycle. But in the end the criticism of the liberal approach becomes attack on the conception of class held by Marshall and later liberal theorists. In its recent history, enshrined particularly in the analysis of achievement made by Peaker for the Plowden Committee,[26] the concept of class is trivialised to the point where differences of parental attitude are conceived of as separate factors rather than as an integral part of the work and community situation of children. There are, of course, and always have been, variations of ambi- tiousness and levels of aspirations at any given economic or income level. But it is essential to insist that the effect of class on educational experience is not to be thought of as one factor from which parental attitudes and motivations to succeed in education are independent. A theory which explains educational achievement as the outcome of a set of individual attributes has lost the meaning of those structural forces which we know as class. An adequate theory must also attend to those structural inequal- ities of resource allocation which are integral to a class society.

Thus, any attempt to free education from its antecedents and con- sequences in the class system has to include structural forces as well as individual attributes. Both within and outside the formal educational system there are social forces which weight systematically against working-class children in respect of those types of learning which make for educational success and subsequently for advantageous occupational placement. These include the quality of linguistic and other stimulation in family and neighbourhood, the expectations of teachers, the efficiency of co-operation between teachers and parents, and the occupational horizons which can be seen by children at different social vantage points. Above all, it is a matter of resources. At every point, again both inside and outside the schools, the working-class child has a great deal less spent on his opportunities for learning than has his more fortunate middle-class contemporary. The association of social class with educational achievement will not therefore be explained by a theory or eliminated by a policy which falls short of including changes in public support for learning in the family and the neighbourhood, the training of teachers, the production of relevant curricula, the fostering of parental participation, the raising of standards of housing and employment prospects and, above all, the allocation of educational resources. The translation of such a theory into action would require political leadership with the will to go beyond the confines of traditional liberal assumptions.

Obstacles to equality. 1. An ineluctible occupational hierarchy

There are three current types of argument against the viability of egalitarian theory which deserve specific consideration. The first concerns the immutability of occupational hierarchy, postulating a *de facto* necessity for some jobs to be more distasteful, unrewarding and injurious to health than others despite (and possibly because of) the technical advances on which Alfred Marshall pinned so much hope. Given that life-chances in wide measure are determined by the individual's occupation, a hierarchy of social advantage seems to be inescapable and equality as opposed to equality of opportunity therefore unobtainable. But even accepting the postulate, a more egalitarian society is not thereby rendered sociologically impossible. It is not difficult to imagine a wide range of counteracting social policies (apart from the obvious one of progressive taxation, wealth taxes, etc. against which objections are lodged in the name of liberty and economic efficiency). As Brain Barry has argued, "the first line of attack would be to spread the nastiest jobs around by requiring everyone, before entering higher education or entering a profession to do, say, three years of work wherever he or she was directed. (This would also have educational advantages). To supplement this there could be a call-up of, say, a month every year, as with the Swiss and Israeli armed forces but directed towards peaceful occupations. These steps would, of course, constitute a limited interference with occupational choice but one whose justice would, it seems to me, be difficult to deny".[27] And there are other such institutional reforms, both inside and outside education, which can be brought into play without making outrageous assumptions about 'human nature' or the price to be paid in terms of other widely held values in society.

Value choice is again the nub of the issue. Hence, with a view to suggesting that equality and liberty need not come immediately and directly into conflict when a more equal society is sought, we may refer to the set of ideas which are labelled recurrent education and the views of the Swedish economist Gosta Rehn.[28]

The average industrial man spends something like 100,000 hours of his life at work. There is here, therefore, a large arena for the application of both egalitarian and libertarian ideas. Rehn is a post-Keynesian economist who takes it for granted that responsible government on behalf of individual liberty has to go beyond the enforcement of contracts voluntarily entered and the natural tendencies of men to conspire against the rigours of the free market. He takes modern society to be committed to the efficient production of abundance, the maintenance of full employment and the abolition of all unnecessary labour. On these assumptions he advocates arranging deliberately for greater variation and diversity in the life-patterns of education, work, leisure and retirement, in such a way as to transfer decision as far as possible from the bureaucracy to the individual. The underlying conception is of a modified social contract. The individual has a life-long bargain with society to work in exchange for material rewards and social security. In Rehnian society the individual, within a broad framework of agreed rules, would determine the phasing and placing of the exchange, week by week, year by year and over the course of his whole life-time. The sharp divisions of the life-cycle and the established patterns of education, leisure and work, bequeathed by the harsh necessities of preindustrial society and entrenched in the rigid formulae of statutory school leaving ages, weekly hours, annual holidays and compulsory retirement ages would go. Instead, there would be 'flexi-time', study rights at personal discretion, vacation rights not tied to calendar years, sabbaticals and temporary retirements not tied to old age.

In order to effect these new freedoms, which are in any case gradually and patchily appearing in the rich countries, it would be desirable, though not absolutely necessary, to systematise the present piece-meal arrangements for providing income to those who are not in paid employment because they are young and in school or unemployed or pregnant or sick or old and therefore retired. Collectively, it would require decisions on the generalised drawing rights to be allocated to each citizen. Obviously, there would have to be safeguards against improvidence and the absence of 'deferred gratification patterns'. But the general idea is one of institutional movement towards the reduction of bureaucracy and enlargement of personal choice. For example, there would be an age of compulsory schooling but not as high as that currently set in the richer countries. Then everyone would have a basic study credit, which could go to all age groups, not only to children and the unborn, to cover living and tuition costs for X years. The individual could claim his educational rights according to his own career management and would not be pressed to extend his childhood as he characteristically now is. He would thus be encouraged to have low-skill jobs in youth and occupational status could become more a matter of age than class. And the right to further education could be transferred to leisure or to more affluent retirement if the individual so chose.

The point is here that recurrent education may in principle serve to increase both equality and liberty. The possibility of bringing about greater equality between generations is obvious enough. The danger is, however, that it could so easily be trivialised into gestures towards a more generous provision of adult education, classes, sabbaticals, day release, Open University and sandwich courses. It would only be if recurrent education were taken seriously as a citizenship right, like social security or pensions, that the transformation of the established system in an egalitarian direction would be possible and this would require ambitious institutional inventiveness, much more flexible relations between work and education, more optimistic definitions by teachers of educability and curriculum, a vast development of community schooling and more bounteous educational budgets.

Obstacles to egalitarianism. 2. The importance of schooling

The second obstacle to be considered may be turned the Jencks pessimism. We are not here concerned with the relation of educational opportunity and educational attainment to social origin, which has always been close and continues to be so, but with the linkage of education to subsequent life-chances, and therefore the possibilities of education as as instrument for changing social distributions. This issue lies at the centre of the controversy which has been so explosively refuelled by Christopher Jencks' *Inequality*.[29] Jencks has given a much-discussed interpretation of the study by Blau and Duncan[30] that the American occupational structure is open in the sense that a relatively loose relation between social origin and occupational destination is largely to be accounted for by factors which, as far as the individual is concerned, might be regarded as luck, even though some of them have a structural basis. Thus in his formulation, largely derived from the Blau and Duncan findings, Jencks writes, "While occupational status is more closely related to educational attainment than to any other thing we could measure, there are still enormous status differences among people with the same amount of education. This remains true when we compare people who have not only the same amount of schooling, but the same family background and the same test scores. Anyone who thinks that a man's family background, test scores and educational credentials are the only things that determine the kind of work he can do in America is fooling himself. At most, these characteristics explain about half the variation in men's occupational statuses. This leaves at least half the variation to be explained by factors which have nothing to do with family background, test scores or educational attainment".

Some of this unexplained variation is attributable to intra-generational occupational mobility. But Jencks is concerned to stress a different set of causative factors: "Much of the variation is probably due to chance (one steel worker gets laid off and takes a temporary job as a painter, while another keeps his job because his plant happens to be busier). Some is due to choice (a business man decides to give up making underwear and become a clergyman)". And on income equality, Jencks adds: "Income also depends on luck: chance acquaintances who steer you to one line of work rather than another, the range of jobs that happens to be available in a particular community when you are job-hunting, the amount of overtime work in your particular plant, whether bad weather destroys your straw-berry crop ... and a hundred other unpredictable accidents".

Jencks' book starts from reaction to the recently orthodox view that education reform was the best mechanism for breaking the inter-genera-tional curse of poverty. In one sense, then, he has produced an essay in the demolition of popular explanations of economic inequality: "We cannot blame economic inequality primarily on genetic differences in men's capac-ities for abstract reasoning, since there is nearly as much economic inequality among men with equal test scores as among men in general. We cannot blame economic equality primarily on the fact that parents pass along their disadvantages to their children, since there is nearly as much inequality among men whose parents have the same economic status as among men in general. We cannot blame economic inequality on differ-ences between schools, since differences between schools seem to have very little effect on any measurable attribute on those who attend them".

Academic critics have questioned Jencks' statistical analyses,[31] on the whole unsuccessfully. But it must be noted that no less an authority than James Coleman is not entirely satisfied with them. He criticises Jencks essentially for failing to distinguish clearly between two meanings of inequality—inequality of opportunity and inequality of result. He argues, quite correctly, that Jencks' intention is to discuss inequality of result but in fact spends his time on inequality of opportunity. What Jencks demon-strates, of course, is that equalising opportunities through schooling will not change inequality of income between individuals. Schooling explains only about 12 per cent of the variance in income. Coleman complains that the explanation for the inequality of income accruing to jobs is not what would explain who happens to occupy those jobs. The former problem is not directly tackled by Jencks. By demonstrating the absence of a relation between income distribution and distribution of schooling and family characteristics he on the one hand, however negatively, points to the direct truth that the basic trouble with the poor is that they have no money. But on the other hand, by the form of analysis adopted, he is left with a large unexplained variance in income which, in various formulations, he attributes to luck and a capriciously if not arbitrarily distributed competence. James Meade's recent discussion of Jencks underlines the crucial import-ance of resolving the question of how far life-chances are determined by luck as distinct from what Meade calls fortune (i.e. "the basic structural genes, property, education and social contacts"[32]). Jencks stresses the luck hypothesis. Meade is less sure. In so far as Jencks is right, then action against inequality has to be concentrated more on day to day redistribu-tion of unequal income and wealth created by luck. Clearly, such measures are possible. But until the case (or rather cases) is given less controversial empirical grounding, the structural theories, Marxist or non-Marxist, cannot meanwhile be discarded. Certainly there is no reason to suppose that because we cannot identify the causes of a result we should infer that they are random rather than part of some systematic feature of society.

Obstacles to egalitarianism. 3. Genetic distributions

The third obstacle is the alleged structural feature on which Professor Jensen in America and Professor Eysenck in London lay so much stress—the argument that differences in educational attainment are rooted in genetic differences between races and classes. The most notorious recent formulation of this argument was published by Arthur Jensen in the *Harvard Educational Review* ('How much can we boost I.Q. and scholas-tic achievement?') in 1969, of which his *Genetics and Education*[33] is an extended version and of which a popular version was published by Profes-sor Hans Eysenck under the title *Race, Intelligence and Education.*[34]

Much of Professor Jensen's extensive marshalling of the evidence is uncontroversial. Whether you take social classes or racial minority groups in America, there are incontrovertible differences in the average scores. On all this it may be said that the scientific mapping of measured perfor-mances is necessary to informed discussion, but the explanation for test differences and even less the question of the relation between test scores and the distribution of whatever we might mean by intelligence (other than that which is measured by I.Q. tests) remains.

The distributions and correlations of test scores are not at issue. The importance of Jensen is that he advances a theory about causes and also advice about consequences. In both of these realms reasonable men can differ.[35]

On the side of causes or explanations, the question he asks is whether the average difference between American negroes and American whites in I.Q. (a difference of ten to fifteen points) is (i) genetic, or (ii) a combination of genetic and environmental influences, or (iii) environmental. Eysenck cheated by calling the second type of theory hereditarian and the third type environmentalist, whereas obviously the first is hereditarian and the third environmentalist and the second a combination of the two. Jensen is more careful, especially in the preface to his book. He acknowledges that one cannot formally generalise from within-group heritability to between-group heritability but concludes that "a largely genetic explanation of the evidence on racial and social group differences in educational performance is in a stronger position scientifically than those explanations which postulate the absence of any genetic differences in mental traits and ascribe all behavioural variation between groups to cultural differences, social discrimination, and inequalities of opportunity—a view that has long been orthodox in the social sciences and in education".

Jensen thus places himself behind the second type of explanation, excluding the purely hereditarian view and regarding the purely environmentalist theory as dubious almost to the point of impossibility. My own view of the evidence is that the purely environmentalist theory is much less implausible. For one thing, I take seriously the calculations of heritability produced by Christopher Jencks in his *Inequality*. Curiously enough Jensen ignores Jencks' calculations which yield much lower estimates than his own of the variance in I.Q. attributable to genetic factors. And second, I accept the remarks of the distinguished if anonymous reviewer in the *Times Literary Supplement*.

> A few years ago W. F. Bodmer and L. L. Cavalli in ascertaining the evidence on genetic and environmental influences on race-I.Q. differences, came to the not very startling conclusion that current techniques and data could not resolve the question. While not excluding the possibility of a genetic component, it seemed that the I.Q. differences could be explained by environmental factors, many of which we still knew nothing about. There is no reason to believe that the situation has changed since then.[36]

Still more important is the issue of consequences, for these take us from science to politics. Jensen is last, if not first, an American individualist and with Sir Cyril Burt pleads for diversity of opportunity and treatment in a way which reflects his appreciation, perhaps over-appreciation, of the huge variability in genetic make-up which is such an important fact about the human species. No reasonable man could quarrel with that as such. But, like Eysenck, Jensen has the blinkers of a psychologist and vastly overestimates the importance of I.Q. He half-recognises this when he notices that I.Q. differences are relevant to differences in levels of performance in *traditional school structures*. But he assumes, along with many of his environmentalist opponents, that I.Q. is overwhelmingly important in determining the placing of individuals in the economy. In respect of income distribution in America this is certainly not the case. In addition to Jencks' evidence, Professors Bowles and Gintis have shown[37] that I.Q. is of negligible importance by comparison with socio-economic background and years of schooling in determining economic success as measured by a combination of occupational status and income. Jensen made no mention of this article in his book. But if the Bowles-Gintis argument is taken seriously, the Jensen wrangle becomes largely irrelevant to the underlying questions of political and economic justice for American blacks and the American working class. In this sense, the Jensenist controversy is but a storm in the academic tea-cups. As the T.L.S. reviewer summed it up, so will I:

> We do not at present know the answer to the question of how much is the genetic component to the race-I.Q. difference, we do not have the techniques at hand to find the answer and the answer does not seem to matter anyway. Let us then forget this question and move on to more important matters for our present-day society.

These important matters I take to include theories and their application as policies which will liberate education from its recent history as the victim of false argument from both the Left and the Right.

Notes and references

1 James Coleman's contribution to this issue of this journal (p. 27) is an admirable example. He is responsible for shifting the terms of the debate from the older liberal conception of equality of opportunity in the sense of access to equality of outcome in the sense of attainment. The reference is, of course, to average members of social groups and not to individuals.
2 Barry, B. (1973) *The Liberal Theory of Justice* (London, Oxford University Press), p. 168.
3 Illich, Ivan (1971) *Deschooling Society* (London, Calder & Boyars), and (1973) *Tools for Conviviality* (London, Calder & Boyars).
4 In addition to the authors and sources used by Silver I would also strongly commend Basil Bernstein, *Class, Codes and Control*. (London, Routledge & Kegan Paul). Volume I 1970, Volume II 1973 and Volume III forthcoming.
5 In this section I have drawn heavily on my 'Education and Social Class in 1972'. In Jones, K. (ed.) (1973) *The Year Book of Social Policy 1972* (London, Routledge & Kegan Paul).
6 In 1923 Marshall added a manuscript footnote to this paper that "it bears marks of the over-sanguine temperament of youth", but he left it unaltered to be published by Professor A. C. Pigou in *Memorials of Alfred Marshall*. (London, Macmillan, 1925).
7 For the most distinguished descendant of the political economy tradition see James Meade (1964) *Efficiency, Equality* and the *Ownership of Property* (London, George Allen & Unwin), and (1973) *The Inheritance of Inequalities: Some Biological, Demographic, Social and Economic Factors, Proceedings of the British Academy*, Volume 59 (London, Oxford University Press). Meade's work as a modern liberal theorist is not vulnerable to the criticisms offered here against Marshall's essay.
8 Hinden, Rita (ed.) (1964) *The Radical Tradition* (London, George Allen & Unwin), p. 48.
9 Halsey, A. H. (1971) *Trends in British Society since 1900* (London, Macmillan), p. 113, Table 4.1.
10 *Social Trends* (London, H.M.S.O., 1973), p. 78, Table 26.
11 Halsey, A. H. (ed.), *op. cit.*, p. 96, Table 3.19.

12 *Social Trends*, p. 11, Table VIII.
13 *Social Trends*, p. 11. The most thorough recent attempt to measure poverty in Britain is by Professor A. B. Atkinson ((1969) *Poverty in Britain and the Reform of Social Security*, University of Cambridge Press) on the official definition of poverty (i.e. receipt of supplementary benefit). He decided that between 4 per cent and 9 per cent of the total population were poor and the figure is towards the upper end of this range. Most of the poor are single, or married couples without children, and especially old people. At the same time, one-third are children and—a comment on the distribution of effective relations with the productive system—some 20 per cent have earnings as their primary source of income.
14 Davey, Ronald *et al.* (1972) *From Birth to Seven* (London, Longman). This is the second report of the National Child Development Study, which is following a national school of children born in 1958.
15 See, for example, Douglas, J. W. B. (1968) *All Our Future.*
16 See my *Educational Priority: Problems and Policies*, Vol. I, chapter I.
17 Young, Michael *The Rise of the Meritocracy* and Herrnstein, R. J. (1973) *I.Q. in the Meritocracy* (London, Allen Lane).
18 For quantified detail on mobility in relation to the shift in occupational structure, see the forthcoming monograph by J. H. Goldthorpe & C. Llewellyn which forms part of the report on the Nuffield College social mobility enquiry to be published by Oxford University Press.
19 Goldthorpe, J., Lockwood, D., Bechhofer, Frank & Platt, Jennifer (1969) *The Affluent Worker in the Class Structure* (Cambridge University Press).
20 For an elaboration of analysis in these terms, see Fox, Alan (1974) *Beyond Contract: Work, Power and Trust Relations* (London, Faber & Faber).
21 Titmuss, R. M. (1971) *The Gift Relation: from human blood to social policy* (London, George Allen & Unwin).
22 See Terrill, Ross (1973) *R. H. Tawney and his Times: Socialism as Fellowship* (Harvard University Press).
23 See my *Educational Priority*, Vol. I, chapters 9–12, and George and Teresa Smith (1974) Scottish Education Dept., Bulletin. Occasional Paper no. 3.
24 See Halsey; A. H. (ed.) (1972), *op. cit.* (London, H.M.S.O.), and Vols. II, III, IV and V, 1974.
25 Smith; G. & Little, A. (1971) *Strategies of Compensation: a review of educational projects for the disadvantaged in the United States* (Paris, O.E.C.D.).
26 *Children and their Primary Schools* (London, H.M.S.O., 1967).
27 Barry, B., *op. cit.*, p. 164.
28 Rehn, G. (1972) O.E.C.D. paper.
29 Jencks, Christopher (1972) *Inequality: A Reassessment of the Effect of Family and Schooling in America* (New York, Basic Books).
30 Blau, P. & Duncan, O. D. (1968) *The American Occupational Structure* (New York, John Wiley).
31 See *Harvard Educational Review* (Perspectives on Inequality), 1973.
32 Meade, J. E. (1974), p. 28.
33 Jensen, Arthur (1972) *Genetics and Education* (London, Methuen).
34 Eysenck, Hans (1971) *Race, Intelligence and Education* (London, Temple Smith).
35 Which is in no way to condone but on the contrary to condemn those who seek to prevent argument by violence.
36 *The Times Literary Supplement*, August 3rd, 1963, p. 891.
37 Bowles, Samuel & Gintis, Herbert (1972) 'I.Q. in the U.S. Class Structure', *Social Policy*, November/December 1972, January/February 1973.

3   Equality and education: fact and fiction

H. J. Eysenck

Source: 'Equality and education: fact and fiction', *Oxford Review of Education*, 1(1): 51–58, 1975.

In recent years, the discredited notion of *equality of endowment* has gained many adherents, and practical steps have been taken in education particularly to try and adapt reality to this mythology. Equality of endowment (as opposed to equality of opportunity) takes literally the famous statement from the Declaration of Independence that "all men are created equal", and deduces from this erroneous premise a number of equally erroneous consequences. Equality, so conceived, is of course politically impossible, philosophically meaningless, and biologically absurd; Hayek (1960), in his famous classic *The Constitution of Liberty*, has adequately documented the first two statements, and any text on behavioural genetics, such as Dobzhansky's (1973) *Genetic Diversity and Human Equality*, will equally well document the third. As he points out, "equality is confused with identity, and diversity with inequality." (p. 3.) And he goes on to point out that "the easiest way to discredit the idea of equality is to show that people are innately, genetically, and therefore irremediably diverse and unlike. The snare is, of course, that human equality pertains to the rights and to the sacredness of life in every human being, not to bodily or even mental characteristics." (p. 4.) This point was well expressed in the 1952 UNESCO statement on race: "Equality of opportunity and equality in law in no way depend, as ethical principles, upon the assertion that human beings are in fact equal in endowment." Defenders of equality become entangled in this snare when they attempt to minimize or deny human genetic diversity. "They overlook, or fail to understand, that the diversity is an observable fact of nature, while equality is an ethical command." (p. 4.)

It is sometimes said that arguments against the notion of equality of endowment are directed at a man of straw, and that no one actually posits literally equality of the genetic basis of intelligence, or personality. This clearly is not true. In the U.S.A., to take one example, Professor L. J.

Kamin, Chairman of the Psychological Dept. at Princeton University, has explicitly stated his belief that there is no evidence to indicate genetic determination of individual differences in IQ. Students in psychology and sociology have boycotted lecturers who attempt to lecture on the application of genetic principles to human behaviour, and have made it impossible for such lectures to be given. Even more frequent than an explicit disavowal of the importance of genetic diversity is an implicit denial; researchers and theoreticians simply disregard intelligence and any other genetically determined factors in their investigation of educational policies and outcomes. Only two examples will be given. The first is the report of the National Child Development Study (Davie *et al.*, 1972), which purports to trace the causal influences which determined the educational and social development of the large number of children followed up over many years. Neither IQ nor intelligence, neither genetics nor heredity are even mentioned in the Index, and the whole performance of Hamlet goes on without the appearance of the Prince of Denmark!

The second example is Boudon's (1973) book *Education, Opportunity, and Social Inequality*; the author attempts to develop a theoretical model for social mobility and educational equality, but again without any mention of heredity, genetics, and their influence on IQ and social mobility. Boudon even incorporates his prejudices in his very definition of inequality of educational opportunity; he states that "by inequality of educational opportunity, I mean the differences in level of educational attainment according to social background." (p. xi.) Clearly, all consideration of differences in attainment due to genetic differences in ability is ruled out of court by the very definition given! These examples could be multiplied a hundredfold, but this would surely not be necessary; all readers of educational journals and books will be well aware of the fact that it is only the most exceptional paper or book in this field that will take cognizance of genetic factors, or incorporate such factors into the design of an experiment—regardless of the fact that without such an incorporation the whole experiment becomes impossible to interpret. Arguments against the notion of equality of endowment are therefore not directed at a man of straw, but rather at the overwhelming majority of writers in this field, whether they be theoreticians or experimentalists. Their failure to recognize that heredity and environment are but the opposite sides of the same coin, always acting together to determine the observable phenotype, takes their contribution right outside the field of scientific discourse.

It is sometimes stated that attempts to give numerical estimates of the degree of heritability of intelligence, or extroversion, or scholastic achievement, are doomed to failure, and that no such estimate is possible. There are two points to be made regarding this objection. In the first place, for most purposes a precise numerical estimate is not required; no geneticist doubts that heredity contributes a large amount to the final measured phenotype in these fields. No geneticist doubts that heredity and environment interact to produce the observed IQ score, or the observed degree of extraversion. Whether the degree of heritability is 50%, 80% or 90% is not particularly important for most purposes (although it might be in particular circumstances); what is important is the undeniable relevance of genetics to mental ability. Given that this is so, those who explicitly or implicitly deny the role of genetics in this interaction process are doing a disservice to education, and inevitably to the children whose future may be fatally disrupted by unwise and ideologically motivated decisions based on erroneous premises.

In the second place, the objections to a numerical estimate of heritability were reasonable before the growth, in recent years, of biometrical genetical analysis. The new methods introduced by Mather & Jinks (1970) among others, for constructing genetic models and testing these experimentally against reality have made them obsolete. It is noteworthy that the critics who maintain the point of view that heritability cannot be assessed quantitatively have in the vast majority of cases expressed this view without apparent knowledge of the actual methods used by geneticists (e.g. Jinks & Fulker, 1970, for an application of these new methods to the analysis of heritability of intelligence, scholastic achievement, and personality,) and in popular papers and journals, rather than in the technical literature. Criticism in science demands full knowledge of that which is being criticized, rather than a mere repetition of ancient shibboleths; it will only be possible to evaluate the criticisms of these new methods when they are expressed in statistical terms, and published in the appropriate journals. Simple statements of denial of the possibility of doing something that has already been done are hardly convincing; something more is surely required when complex scientific arguments are concerned.

Granted that human beings are divergent with respect to mental abilities (Jinks & Fulker, 1970), personality (Eysenck, 1974), and almost every conceivable component of scholastic achievement, it surely behoves us to consider seriously the consequences of this diversity for optimal scholastic success, and even for the achievement of that 'equality of opportunity' that we feel may be within our grasp if only we knew how to set about getting it. The first, and the most obvious deduction to be made from the fact of the existence of biological human diversity is perhaps the simple statement that doing the same to everyone is not likely to afford equal opportunity to everyone. Blake's famous words about the Ox and the Lion come to mind; how can one create equality of opportunity for two such unlike protagonists? Let us take a simple example. In a particular, clearly demarcated learning task, would it be more helpful to give rules before or after practice? Leith & Trown (1970) showed that extroverted children did better when the rules were given after practice; introverted children did better when the rules were given before practice. Other work has shown that extroverted children prefer instruction by teacher to instruction by machine, and do better that way, while introverted children show the opposite effect (Eysenck, 1967). Other studies have shown differences in the reaction of extroverted and introverted children to blame and praise (Thompson & Hunnicutt, 1944).

If we were now to use identical methods on all children, our choice of motivational procedure (praise or blame), of teaching method (person or machine), and of discovery vs. rule setting method would inevitably disadvantage the more extroverted, or the more introverted children, depending on the precise choice made. Clearly there is no equality of opportunity when all children are treated equally; equality of opportunity, if the term is to have any meaning, implies that conditions are optimized for each particular child, given his own particular personality, pattern of ability, and general biological make-up. This is a very difficult aim to achieve, but it may serve to remind us of what it is we have to strive for. Clearly implicit in this aim is the acquisition of sufficient psychological knowledge to make it possible to gear the child's tuition to his or her personality, using this term in its widest sense, i.e. embracing abilities as well as temperament. In the absence of such knowledge (and the current egalitarian climate is making it more and more difficult to mount experiments which will give us information on genetic diversity in the educational setting, and the optimal interaction patterns to be selected) all talk of equality of opportunity is rather idle chatter; we simply don't know how to achieve any such thing.

Even under the best conditions, and assuming much more knowledge than we have now, equality of opportunity, as defined above, does not mean equality of outcome. There are no conceivable conditions of educational methodology which would guarantee that the dullest, most idle and destructive child, motivated only for mischief and violence, would achieve as much scholastically as the brightest, most determined and hardworking child, motivated highly for achievement and intellectual development. There are no conceivable political or social conditions which would remove the biological handicap under which many children labour, and even to suggest such a possibility is little better than a cynical and cruel joke played on the least fortunate of our children. Any attempt to achieve equality of outcome must make use of the methods of Procrustes – cut off the feet of those who are too tall to fit on your bed, and stretch on the rack those who are too small. Even then it is doubtful if mental characteristics respond as readily to such treatment as did the physical characteristics of Procrustes' guests.

It follows clearly from what has been said that many modern educational policies are counter-productive, and do not serve any useful function. The idea of forcing all children to go to school for an additional year after the age of 15 is clearly born of the notion of equality of endowment; if such an additional year is useful for some, it must be useful for all. (In Holland, discussions are going on to make education compulsory until the end of the 18th year; this extends the same principle with a vengeance.)

But children differ, not only in temperament, or in intelligence, but also in motivation for education; are we entitled to force them, against their will, to do what we regard as in their best interests—often incorrectly? This surely is manipulation of the worst kind, a refusal to honour the diversity of human nature, and an imposition of our will, regardless of any suffering that may result, on individuals powerless to resist. (They can, and do, vote with their feet, of course; the increase in truancy and criminality which followed this law has served, as nothing else could have done, to convince teachers of the absurdity of a rule which previously many had in fact championed.)

This whole notion can of course be taken further. If all children can benefit from education up to 16, why not University education? Already Holland has introduced the idea that all children who pass the (rather low level) school leaving certificate are entitled to go to University; when the Universities could not cope with the numbers they introduced a lottery—students were not selected on the basis of their past scholastic achievements, but on a purely chance basis. The next step no doubt will be to admit all adolescents, if need be on the basis of drawing lots, to University, including mental defectives and schizophrenics (why should they be omitted?); after that we will begin to draw lots who shall be the professor to teach these unteachables. Given the basis of equality of endowment, all this might make sense; given the facts as they are, this seems the most certain method of ensuring national suicide that mankind has ever devised.

Certainly this egalitarian procession in the democratic countries, advocated most strongly by Marxists and their militant student followers, contrasts quite markedly with procedures in the Communist countries. Nowhere in the world is the meritocratic principle more in evidence than in the schools of the U.S.S.R., the D.D.R., Poland, Hungary and Czechoslovakia. Here advance is entirely on the basis of scholastic achievement (except for the occasional Commissar's son who gets by on the strength of his family connections). The result has been remarkable; standards are much higher than in the democratic countries, and in the special centres of excellence where specially chosen children are educated in mathematics and the 'hard' sciences achievements are similar to those reserved in the Western countries for Universities. But then of course Marx himself would have nothing to do with egalitarianism, which he considered absurd; his ideal of "from each according to his ability" clearly recognized innate differences in ability. It is these differences in ability that modern Communist states build on. The often expressed Communist sentiment: "We will bury you yet" is likely to come true if they continue to cooperate with nature, while we desperately (and no doubt for the best motives) go on fighting against it.

One particular application of the notion that equality of treatment does not make for equality of opportunity highlights a curious development that has recently taken place. ESN pupils have for many years been given special training, as they are unable to take part in ordinary class work. This is a good and welcome realization of the principle in question; ESN pupils require different types of teaching to normal children in order to achieve whatever they are able to achieve. This type of schooling was a benevolent and sensible recognition of inexorable fact, and it has benefited many thousands of children who would otherwise have been lost in the hurly-burly of ordinary teaching. Now many groups complain that children from certain backgrounds are over-represented in these classes, and demand parity—a kind of quota system in reverse. In other words, they are saying that these children should not be allowed to benefit from this benevolent institution on the grounds of some hypothetical egalitarian notion. Next no doubt will come the demand that all ESN educational facilities should be dismantled, on the grounds that they discriminate. Such objections do not take into account the fact that these facilities discriminate in favour of ESN children; the objectors would presumably prefer failure under conditions of equality to success under conditions of special help. Or possibly they are confused as to what they want, or how what they want can be justified; the arguments presented do not usually enable one to discover the logic presumably underlying them.

At the other end of the ability scale there has also occurred a very counter-productive change, namely the abolition of differential types of schooling, of 'streaming' and other methods of grouping together children of similar ability levels. Again, this has been justified in the name of 'egalitarianism', the hypothesis being presumably that if all children are really equal in innate ability, then they ought to be brought up and taught together, without any selection whatever. But as we have seen, they are not equal in ability, and to treat them as if they were is illogical and likely to be to the detriment of both the abler and the less able children. In my *The Inequality of Man* I have discussed this point at some length, and will not do so here again (Eysenck, 1973); let me only add that teachers who have had experience of these developments have reacted quite strongly against the obvious consequences of boredom for the able and stress for the dull. I have also discussed in that book some of the difficulties which arise in carrying out research in this complex field; most of the published work clearly fails to take these complexities into account.

The search for equality in education is usually discussed in purely verbal terms, thus making any quantitative statements impossible. Yet there is no reason why such quantitative statements should not be made, and I believe that doing so will illuminate the whole discussion as nothing else can do. An example for the work of R. C. Atkinson (1972) of Stanford University may serve to illustrate this approach. The work in question concerns the development of computer-assisted instruction programmes for teaching reading in the primary grades (CAI for short). The programme provides individualized instruction in reading and is used as a supplement to normal classroom teaching. Performance is measured on a standardized reading achievement test, and the child spends from 0 to 30 minutes each day on the computer. It has proved possible to construct a statistical model which predicts the child's future test performance as a function of the time he spends on the CAI system (see discussion in Eysenck, 1973). This enables us to decide on how best to allocate rare resources (time on the computer) in such a way as to obtain the best results. But how are we to decide on what results are 'best'? Normally such decisions are made without proper consideration of the alternatives, on the basis of political or social prejudice, and without knowledge of the actual outcomes involved. In the present case, however, the model enables us to make quite explicit statements about the outcomes of different actions. Let P stand for the performance of the children on the terminal test. We can then state four different objectives which might be chosen as 'most desirable'. These objectives are:

(a) Maximize the mean value of P over the class of children.
(b) Minimize the variance of P over the class of children, i.e. try to equalize their performance as much as possible.
(c) Maximize the number of children who score at grade level at the end of the first year.
(d) Maximize the mean value of P, but satisfy at the same time the constraint that the resulting variance of P is less than or equal to the variance that would have been obtained if no CAI were administered. (In other words, try for maximum performance all round, but without increasing the existing differences between children.)

Objective (a) maximizes the gain for the class as a whole; objective (b) aims to reduce differences among children by making the class as homogeneous as possible; objective (c) is concerned specifically with those children who fall behind grade level; objective (d) attempts to maximize performance but insures that differences among children are not amplified by CAI. Now we can calculate the outcomes which attend these four courses of action. If we follow objective (a) we find that the mean performance of the class is 15% higher than if we had allocated time equally to all children; unfortunately, there is also an increase in variance of 15%—in other words, the difference between the best and worst readers has increased! If we accept objective (b) we find that compared with an equal distribution of time on the computer there is a reduction of overall performance of 15% but there is also a reduction of 12% in variability. Adopting policy (c), we have a reduction in overall performance, compared with equal time allocation, of 9%, and also a reduction in variability of 10%. Objective (d), which attempts to strike a balance between (a) on the one hand, and (b) and (c) on the other, yields an increase in performance over equal time sharing of 8%, and yet reduces variability by 5%. Objective (a) is the most 'meritocratic', objectives (b) and (c) are the most 'mediocratic', while objective (d) attempts to accommodate both the desiderata that there should be maximum improvement, but also a reduction in variability.

It is by translating policies into quantitative estimates of this kind that both adherents and opponents of the doctrine of equality in education can begin to form some idea of the consequences of any particular action they advocate. And when they do so, they may find that both may well agree on a particular programme, rather than fight to the death over ideological niceties. Clearly nothing of this kind can at present be done for most of our educational policies, from the use of the 11+ examination to the retention or not of 'streaming' from comprehensive schooling to the retention of grammar schools. No wonder that our councils are so confused, and that strife abounds. "One's knowledge of science begins when he can measure what he is speaking about, and express it in numbers", said Lord Kelvin, and Kepler pointed out that "as the ear is made to perceive sound and the eye to perceive colour so the mind of man has been found to understand not all sorts of things, but quantities. It perceives any given thing more clearly in proportion as that thing is close to bare quantities as to its origin, but the further a thing recedes from quantities, the more darkness and error inheres in it." No wonder that so much darkness and error inhere in the usual political and ideological arguments about equality; not only are the participants ignorant of the facts of genetic determination of intelligence and personality, but they cannot translate their ideas into quantitative terms, and point to the expected results on their policies. Only advances in educational research can remedy this lack, and it can hardly be said that present day educational research is leading us towards this promised land. Until it does our children will suffer for the ideological sins of their fathers.

In what has been said so far many will read (erroneously) a denial of the role of social factors in causing low measured IQ, and failure to reach high level of scholastic achievement. No geneticist, brought up in the tradition of marking the difference of genotype from phenotype, would dream of underestimating the influence of environment; all theories are phrased in terms of *interaction* between heredity and environment, nature and nurture. Even the estimate that 80% of the total variance in IQ is contributed by genetic causes, 20% by environmental ones still gives to environment half the importance that is given to heredity; this amounts to a very considerable sum. It is possible to assess the changes in IQ which best and worst environments, as we know them, can make to measured IQ (Jensen, 1973), and these are quite substantial. (All demonstrated IQ changes which have been achieved in experimental conditions fall well short of the theoretical extremes.) Adherence to the genetic point of view does not therefore imply in any way a reluctance to improve conditions making for inequality of opportunity at present; such improvements can and should be made, and there is no doubt that they will have a beneficial impact on society. What is asserted here is simply that the interactionist position implies that there are definite *limits* to what can be done along these lines; that biology sets a limit to environmental manipulation which cannot be transgressed; and that attempts to enforce equality of outcome will have the most deleterious effects on our social well being. Communist countries have recognized these verities; why must our militants attempt to be holier than the Pope?

A good demonstration of the limitations of egalitarian policies comes from two types of experiment. We can study the effect on the reduction in variability of IQ of bringing up children under circumstances as identical as human ingenuity can make them (Lawrence, 1931). Taking babies from their mothers and putting them into an orphanage in which they are treated as alike as possible, in closely similar environments with identical food, drink, care, facilities and education, should reduce any differences in IQ between them to vanishing point *if environment were the crucial variable*; in fact nothing of the kind happens—the variability in IQ between children so brought up is reduced by only about 10%, if that! It is unlikely that we could ever succeed in making society as egalitarian, as similar in its environmental effects, as is done in an orphanage; society cannot do much to reduce the differential effect of bright vs. dull parents, for instance. Consequently it is extremely unlikely that even the most egalitarian society would be able to reduce the variability in IQ we observe in our own society to any noticeable extent. And if it were able to do this, then it would also follow that the remaining IQ differences were determined by heredity to an even greater degree than is true today; the elimination of practically all environmental factors would leave IQ phenotype = IQ genotype!

The other study was carried out by Waller (1971) who looked at social mobility within families. He discovered that when two sons of the same parents differed in IQ, it was the brighter one who went up the social scale, the duller one who sank down towards the bottom. His replication of earlier work by Burt and other shows how irrelevant can be the many features of the environment which are so often presented as important in determining IQ; as the differences between the children compared arose within the family, between family causes are irrelevant to the upward and downward social mobility experienced later. This is in good agreement with the genetic evidence which finds little causal role for between family factors. And even the most egalitarian might hesitate to follow Plato and advocate the elimination of the family in order to eliminate within family environmental variance! This study may also give reason to pause to those who argue that social class causes IQ differences, rather than the other way about; here is direct evidence that IQ differences in children coming from the same social class background determine their future social class. The evidence would be conclusive even without this study (Eysenck, 1973), but it does help to illustrate a feature of our modern society which is not always appreciated sufficiently by egalitarians, namely that genetic factors of ability play an important part in raising (or lowering) a person's social status irrespective of his social class at birth.

We may conclude that equality of endowment is a myth, a fiction dreamed up for ideological and political reasons; that this myth is dangerous if we allow it to dictate educational policies which go counter to biological reality; and that equality of opportunity presents us with a much more realistic ideal to follow. We must also conclude that equality of opportunity is not as obvious a concept as it appears at first sight, and that thorough, quantitative studies are required in education before we can even begin to know what we are doing. Choices have to be made at all times, and until these choices are presented to us in a more quantitative manner than is customary at present, they are not likely to be made in a wise and moderate manner. Last, there is nothing in the genetic interaction model which says that environmental sources of inequality should not be reduced or eliminated, in order to achieve greater equality of opportunity (in so far as this does not interfere with liberty; Hayek has pointed out the danger of emphasizing one ideal to the exclusion of other equally or even more important ones!). What the evidence does suggest is that the consequence of such reduction of inequality would be strictly limited, and very much smaller than hoped for by egalitarians. Children will continue to take out of education what they bring into it; the bright will take out a lot, the dull only little. There is not much that educationalists can do about this at the present; the possibility always exists that new methods may change this situation, but until these new methods have been discovered, and proved themselves, it may be suggested that they are more likely to increase than decrease the differential existing at present between bright and dull children with respect to school achievement. Unless we adopt a deliberate policy of handicapping our bright children—a policy whose malevolent cruelty would only be exceeded by its debilitating effects on our national welfare—our best hope is probably to adopt the suggestion by Jensen (1973), namely to capitalize on the existing association-forming abilities of the duller children, rather than to force them to make use of precisely those forms of learning in which they are genetically inferior to the brighter children.

References

Atkinson, R. C. (1972) 'Ingredients for a theory of instruction,' *American Psychologist*, 27, pp. 921–931.

Bourbon, R. (1973) *Education Opportunity, and Social Inequality* (London, Wiley).

Dobzhansky, T. (1973) *Genetic Diversity and Human Equality* (New York, Basic Books).

Davie, R., Butter, N., & Goldstein, H. (1972) *From Birth to Seven* (London, Longman).

Eysenck, H. J. (1974) Genetic factors in personality development. In A. R. Kaplan (ed.) *Human Behavior Genetics* (Springfield, C. C. Thomas).

Eysenck, H. J. (1973) *The Inequality of Man* (London, Temple Smith).

Eysenck, H. J. (1967) *The Biological Basis of Personality* (Springfield, C. C. Thomas).

Hayek, F. A. (1960) *The Constitution of Liberty* (London, Routledge & Kegan Paul).

Jinks, J. L. & Fulker, D. V. (1970) 'A comparison of the biometrical, genetical, MAVA and classical approaches to the analysis of human behavior,' *Psychological Bulletin*, 73, pp. 311–349.

Jensen, A. R. (1973) *Educability and Group Differences* (London, Methuen).

Lawrence, E. M. (1931) 'An investigation into the relation between intelligence and inheritance,' *British Journal of Psychology*, Monog: Supplement, 16, No. 5.

Leith, G. V. M. & Trown, E. S. (1970) 'The influence of personality and task conditions in learning and transfer,' *Programmed Learning*, 7, pp. 181–188.

Mather, K. & Jinks, J. J. (1971) *Biometrical Genetics* (London, Chapman & Hall).

Thompson, G. C. & Hunnicutt, C. U. (1944), 'The effect of repeated praise or blame on the work achievement of "Introverts" and "Extroverts",' *Journal of Educational Psychology*, 25, pp. 257–266.

Waller, J. H. (1971) 'Achievement and social mobility,' *Social Biology*, 18, pp. 252–259.

The impossibility of a core curriculum

Alan Harris

Source: 'The impossibility of a core curriculum', *Oxford Review of Education*, 3(2): 171–180, 1977.

Throughout the country gaggles of educationalists are responding to the Prime Minister by trying to devise 'a core curriculum' which would be acceptable both to the government and to teachers. Perhaps they may even try to take into account the pupils as well. It seems to me unlikely that there could ever be a satisfactory outcome to their endeavours.

The problem is this: even if the general principle of having a core curriculum were thought desirable, questions about how it should be constituted are no less than questions about the whole nature of educational aims and methods – questions to which few clear answers have emerged despite the rise of education as an academic study in universities throughout the world. The likelihood is that any core curriculum actually adopted would be as arbitrary and unsatisfactory as what it replaced.

In this paper I shall expound two reasons for my pessimism. The first is that ideological and political pressures in this country are infinitely more powerful influences than the work of curriculum theorists, and that these influences would favour the development of an *irreconcilable* variety of core curricula. The second is that even if it were possible to eschew ideological or political bias it would still be impossible to agree on a sensible basis for a core curriculum, and this point I shall illustrate by attempting to devise one.

In the first place, questions about the curriculum are inseparable from questions about the educational ideologies of the society in which the curriculum is designed: and the first barrier to the design of a generally acceptable core curriculum is that there is no obvious way of deciding which ideology is 'best'. In practice the outcome would be decided by political pressure. Let me illustrate this problem by adumbrating three educational ideologies which currently have influence in Britain. By 'ideology' I do not mean a coherent set of educational principles: I mean a cluster of attitudes, beliefs and customs which are value-laden and which have practical consequences for the organization and methodology of education. (The terminology I am using is that of the earlier units of the Open University course *Curriculum Design and Development* (E203, Open University Press, 1976), and was devised by Professor Malcolm Skilbeck.)

The first of these 'clusters' I shall refer to as 'classical humanism'. In brief, its emphasis can be summarized thus: "What education ought, centrally, to do is to transmit to pupils what is most valuable in their cultural heritage". Since schools cannot teach *everything*, the curriculum must be a selection from what is available in the way of human knowledge, and classical humanism implies the selection of 'high culture'. It is an ideology which places much weight upon the authority of teachers: 'authority' in the sense of knowing better than parents and pupils what is of value and therefore what should be taught. Teachers will not only know what subjects are important but will also be authorities *in* those subjects: they will (as academics) know their specialized field and will (as pedagogues) know how to pass on their knowledge of this field.

However, not all pupils may be capable of appreciating high culture, so (according to Bantock, for example)[1] there should be a *dual* curriculum, with the ablest pupils following more or less the pattern offered in grammar schools; and the others a curriculum which is academically less demanding, more vocational, more practical, and more tolerant of the values of folk culture and 'low-order' art forms.

A core curriculum for the ablest pupils would presumably begin with an emphasis on rapidly developed literacy and numeracy (conceived as preconditions for effective *reception* of the messages to be transmitted) followed by intensive teaching of selected 'goodies' from the Arts, Sciences, History and Languages. It is difficult to see what could rationally be excluded from the traditional academic curriculum in order to form a 'core'; but certainly vocational training would be peripheral, and so would domestic science, health education, metalwork, home economics, sport, physical education, and so on. This state of affairs (good or bad) struck me forcibly on a recent visit to a prestigious Direct Grant school where I was sounding out the possibility of trying out an experimental course in 'moral education'. Apart from the fact that my proposals were instantly translated into potential examination components ("A-level philosophy? – no, not enough likely Boy candidates") it also struck me how impossible it would be for the Boys ever to be seriously engaged in (say) a study of the culinary arts.

The other area of Bantock's dual curriculum seems to demand a core of practical studies in addition to initial training in language and number skills. A similar sort of authoritarianism must exist: teachers must *know* that boys in a particular area must be prepared for the sort of jobs and life expectations available to them; and girls too, will be trained as efficiently as possible to cope with their likely futures in short-term employment and housewifery. On the periphery will be a smattering of high culture, a critical study of pop-music, of fashion in clothes, of the media, and so on; and, of course, plenty of time spent on emergent subjects such as 'child-care' and 'personal relationships'. Whatever the 'core' consisted of it would be functional: a preparation of pupils for life in society as it exists now.

My second ideology is 'progressivism'. Here the cluster of beliefs and attitudes will include the following:

(a) education should start from the needs and interests of every individual pupil;
(b) the teacher is not so much an authority on specific subjects as one who enables pupils to learn and discover for themselves, who manipulates the school environment so that maximal learning can take place, who refrains from pre-judgements about what *ought* to be learned, for whom the main-aim of education is the promotion of personal autonomy.

Again, this is not a coherent set of educational principles, but a vague con-glomeration of value judgements. In its less dogmatic manifestations it pro-duces curricula such as those found in what used to be called the West Riding primary schools. A typical day might consist of a morning devoted to creative activities of all sorts, with each child having considerable freedom to work from starting points of his own choice. Teachers would take pride in the range and quality of the work produced and talk of goals such as the development of self-expression, of social confidence, of co-operativeness. By contrast the afternoon may well be devoted to highly structured study of mathematics, English language, geography and history. In most cases the ethos of such a school seems to preclude technological pursuits: mysteriously boys taken to see a mechanical excavator will be inspired to take pictures of it, or mime it, rather than find out how it works.

What, in such a school, could become the core curriculum? The emphasis is on creativity, so would the morning's work become the 'core', the *indispensable* area of education? Notice that there is still a stress on lit-eracy and numeracy, though the pedagogic approach will be subtly differ-ent (and, *perhaps*, more effective) with an emphasis on the acquisition of these skills enabling self-expression rather than (as it were) opening the child's mouth wide enough to swallow educational nutrition.

Extreme forms of progressivism exist. There are schools where the whole educational process is conducted through the pupils' pursuit of his own interests. The teacher may still want his pupils to acquire specific skills, but the emphasis will be *modes of enquiry* rather than specific pack-ages of 'fact'. The pupil who finds the remains of a Saxon pot, for example, and who is encouraged to pursue the questions about it which interest him will be helped to acquire skills of historical enquiry, but will, in order to tackle associated problems, need to acquire mathematical skills (for surveying), language skills (for research into local records, books on archaeology, and so on). As well as acquiring the familiar basic skills he will also encounter areas of knowledge which have never been traditional school subjects.

In such a situation it seems absolutely impossible that a core curriculum could be isolated. One could set out a list of achievements which will, hopefully, occur; and even test the pupils accordingly. But the absence of a formal timetable would preclude lessons being set aside for the coverage of specific academic areas.

The last ideology is 'reconstructionism' (currently more influential in the Third World than here; but times are changing). Central is the notion that education should change society for the better: society will be reconstructed along more democratic lines, with everyone playing a full part in creating a proud, self-reliant nation. In Tanzania, for example, the old colonial system of education (derived directly from British schools) has been eliminated in favour of communal education where all pupils learn the skills necessary for Tanzania to become economically and agriculturally self-reliant, where they all participate in local projects such as building a new school, or making agricultural innovations, as well as receiving formal instruction towards literacy and numeracy. The latter are still seen as indispensable, but the emphasis is political: it is only through literacy, for example, that all citizens can take a full role in social reconstruction, or even (as in the case of Brazil) begin to fight against tyrannical oppression.

Such an ideology is obviously likely to have appeal in impoverished countries which have suffered from dictatorial regimes, and where there is considerable inequality. But it has its advocates in Britain too. What is wrong with the nation at present, asserts the Prime Minister, is that it is technologically backward. Society must change to the extent that more prestige will be given to work in industry, and education must give more prominence to preparing pupils to participate in a technological society.

Basically the idea is that the stress in education should be on catering for *social* needs rather than for individual ones, and perhaps it would be far too complacent to suggest that Britain is rich and stable enough to concentrate on the latter. But what would such a policy mean for the core curriculum? Nothing, as far as I can see. Even if one agreed with Mr. Callaghan's diagnosis (I don't personally) it would be nonsense to suggest that the solution is simply to make technology and allied subjects the main part of a 'core curriculum'. For one thing, the 'allied subjects' turn out not only to span the entire curriculum but also areas never traditionally taught in schools. Numerate and literate technologists must be (though it would be impossible to define *how* literate and *how* numerate). But should technologists necessarily be pure scientists? Do they need skills in physics and chemistry? Do they need aesthetic awareness? Could they operate effectively without some knowledge of economics? Or of politics? Should they not also be alert to ecological, geographical and moral issues? Or to put these questions the other way round, could it be justifiable, educationally, to produce technologists with no regard for the quality of human life, no respect for landscape, no concept of the politics or economics of technological innovation, no real understanding of the scientific principles underlying their work? Only, surely, in the most desperate of emergencies.

And anyway, there are many different opinions about what social changes are needed, My own is that we ought to develop a society *less* dependent on technology, and concentrating (for economic survival) on widespread but small-scale ventures involving old-fashioned craftsmanship; a society offering greater job satisfaction and less concerned with material prosperity.

But even if everyone agreed, there wouldn't be a case for a core curriculum consisting of weaving, carpentry, metalwork, baking, brewing and so on. On theoretical grounds the development of crafts needs support from the pure and applied sciences; and craftsmen need awareness of aesthetic, economic and political issues, to name but a few.

Even in utilitarian terms we are left with the need for a broad curriculum where it would be impossible to indicate absolute priorities: unless, that it were morally acceptable to extend Bantock's notion in the direction of Brave New World. If we opted for a society which had Epsilons as well as Alphas we might well be able to devise core curricula for the latter, according to their designated function in society. We would never be able to design a core curriculum for the Alphas.

The first half of this paper has been intended to show that the ideological and political pressures at work in education are unlikely (in our pluralistic society) to lead to any generally acceptable educational policy, or even to a core curriculum which would be the logical outcome of any *particular* ideological view or educational aims. Now, I wish to look at the sort of considerations which arise from *within* educational theory, where we shall find refinements of some of the views previously considered.

We have, for example, Paul Hirst's 'knowledge-based' approach,[2] where the implications for curriculum design are generally taken to be that liberal education should initiate pupils into the various 'forms of thought' which people have found important to contribute to their understanding of the universe. But even on the assumption that all pupils *ought* to have a 'liberal' education (whatever their abilities or interests, and even if the economics of the country could sustain such education), there are no clear inferences about what a core curriculum ought to consist of. All pupils, presumably, should have a fair chance to acquire the skills involved in *all* modes of enquiry: so how could one isolate a 'core'? John White[3] has suggested that every child should continue until at least sixth-form level to study all of Hirst's forms of thought: mathematics, the arts, the human and physical sciences, religion, morality, history and so on. These forms of thought are seen as central to the curriculum, and every pupil should go as far as his ability allows in each of them.

Superficially this looks like the traditional grammar school curriculum (and indeed Hirst has often been accused of simply rationalizing the ideology of 'classical humanism'). Yet few schools actually do give as much importance to the human sciences as to the physical sciences, and very few schools try seriously to teach morality (or even religion) as a mode of thought. Philosophy, too, is rare in schools. So really Hirst is adding to the traditional curriculum by attempting to give a *comprehensive* list of the constituents of the mind (but not, as far as I know, suggesting that these constituents, or forms of thought, should necessarily appear separately on the time-table: nothing follows from the analysis about *ways* of initiating pupils into the various elements).

I feel uneasy about John White's suggestion for the following reasons:

(a) The forms of thought should certainly be represented in the curriculum, but could it not be argued that there are other equally important educational goals? Hirst has very little to say about cognitive aspects of education such as the acquisition of social skills, or the sort of skills involved in craftsmanship, child care, sport, keeping fit, and so on. Is not social competence more important for the average person than advanced mathematical skill? Is not the knowledge of foreign languages more important to some people than a knowledge of physics? Furthermore, when Hirst talks about the arts he seems to mean 'aesthetic modes of thought' rather than creative artistic activity; and many people would place at least as much importance upon such activity as upon the acquisition of cognitive skills. It would be ridiculous if the main educational motive for fostering creativity was simply to give pupils more understanding of aesthetic theory.

(b) Despite White's arguments I cannot really believe that a pupil who has no competence in (say) mathematics should be encouraged to pursue the subject beyond the level of simple computation. Would not most adolescents gain a lot more benefit from activities which gave them more insight into personal relationships?

(c) What about the *fields* of knowledge, such as geography, technology, archaeology, medicine, and so on, which combine two or more of the forms of thought? Are they no more than heuristic devices for stimulating progress in their component 'forms'? Or are such fields *inherently* important and valuable to one's understanding of the world?

(d) I fear that in practice, however illogical this may be, national plans for a forms-of-thought-based core curriculum would lead to excessive compartmentalization of the time-table, and a regressive disregard for other important educational goals. It would be a good side-effect, however, if every school in the country were seen to need teachers competent in the teaching of philosophy and the human sciences.

If one doesn't opt to argue from an analysis of knowledge, then another approach is to argue from human *needs*; though apart from the fact that 'needs' cannot be identified except by reference to 'values' (which takes us back into ideology) all needs-based theories that I have encountered (except the most naive of them) leave curriculum questions almost entirely open.

The most sophisticated attempt at such curriculum theory (in my experience at least) is that of Professor John Merritt[4] where at least the analyses of individual human needs is not arbitrary – and indeed has a compelling logic to it. In brief, he says that all human beings (a) need to function efficiently biologically, (b) need to communicate with others on whom their existence depends, (c) need to acquire knowledge of their environment, and (d) need to resolve conflicts between other needs, which involves presumably (among other things) being able to make moral decisions. Professor Merritt's own suggestions for how this approach can lead to curriculum design are in themselves very interesting, especially as they throw a refreshing emphasis on currently under-valued educational goals such as (to take small examples) teaching people to *breathe* efficiently, to *relax* physically and mentally); but nothing can be deduced from them about educational *priorities*, and without priorities there can be no basis for a core curriculum.

It should be noticed, however, that it would seem distinctly odd for the curriculum to ignore any of the above needs altogether. Some sort of 'health education' is clearly indicated, if only (thinking in educational terms) because some degree of health is a precondition of effective learning. But if it is to be health *education* (as distinct from tips on keeping fit) then this area becomes massive in scope; for among other things it should help towards the pupil's developing his *own* concepts of what constitutes physical and mental health, as well as understanding the medical and psychological sciences and services upon which he can call for help. Even trying to decide what 'minimally' ought to be taught to all pupils in all schools present problems. Should yoga, for example, be universally taught? All these questions, significantly, are raised by Professor Merritt's approach.

With regard to (b) above, 'communication needs' range from 'learning' as a baby to signal needs to one's mother, to understanding the rules, laws and mores which are acknowledged by those with whom one wishes to communicate, quite apart from some knowledge of individual and social psychology. How much of all this (weakly represented in current curricula) should be given priority?

Analysis from *social* needs seems more promising. If a primitive village survives exclusively by fishing, then (given obvious value judgments) children ought to learn how to fish. But the more complex the society, and the more complex its relation with other societies, the more difficult it seems to draw any conclusions about curriculum priorities (and the more dangerous seem the possibilities of political manipulation). Yes, if a country is at war, or in other dire straits, then it may be necessary to abandon gentle educational theorizing and to train everyone to fight (core-curriculum – the basic arts of warfare as currently conceived). But it is not always so easy to judge what counts as the sort of emergency which justifies educational directives of this sort (as the technology question reveals).

Yet it would seem distinctly odd for the curriculum to *ignore* social needs. Doesn't common sense indicate that education should render people employable in tasks necessary to the survival (and development?) of society as we know it? That social needs such as those for law and order, public health or the military defence of the state, must always have some degree of educational priority?

But what follows from all this with regard to the *school* 'core curriculum'? 'Employability' is a need whose implications vary from person to person and place to place: what possible core of knowledge would *always* be apposite? (Unless we are dictatorial, and say, for example, that 'all boys living within three miles of Longbridge will work in car factories'.)

Or take the social need for adequate defence resources. This surely doesn't mean that all schools should train cadets: only that military training should be *available* beyond a certain age. As with all the other areas, when one begins to decide what *school* curriculum is relevant there seems no end to what is relevant: history, economics, international politics, physics, chemistry, geography, physical and mental health, and even knitting socks for the troops. War nowadays is as complex as life itself.

In brief, an analysis of social needs can throw up *contingent* educational needs (i.e. contingent to a particular situation) but it cannot indicate what ought in the long term to be central curricular aims. Nor can more recent doctrines, such as 'cultural analysis' as expounded by Professor Malcolm Skilbeck,[5] which seem to say no more than that educationalists ought to take into account what's going on around them. (But how does one then decide what the educational priorities should be?)

I conclude this paper with some of my own thoughts on educational priorities. I do not think that they solve any of the problems delineated above; but at least they may serve to illustrate more clearly why I have no faith in any conceivable 'core curriculum'.

In brief, I believe that education should, *sub specie aeternitatis*, have the following goals. It should, minimally:

(a) enable one to communicate with others
(b) foster greater understanding of one's own and of other people's needs, wishes and feelings,
(c) foster knowledge and understanding of the society in which one lives and
(d) develop one's capacity for making moral judgments.

But suppose we now try to translate these high-sounding goals into a core curriculum.

(a) Communication involves (in our society) literacy. But how much literacy? A Shakespearian capacity for verbal communication? The ability to comprehend elaborate legal documents? All right then: it should be a central educational aim to promote maximal linguistic skills in every pupil (whatever *that* may mean). Literacy is an elaborate concept, and 'teaching' it involves many value judgements. Currently, for example, it is possible to pass O-level 'comprehension' exercises while at the same time making 'errors' of grammar and punctuation which would have failed candidates ten years ago; and, conversely, modern teachers would think very little of what often passed for 'creative writing' thirty years ago. Likewise, notions of what constitute 'oracy' vary enormously from place to place, and from time to time. (I wonder, even now, how many schools would place the *development of conversational skills* at the top of its hierarchy of goals?) It's far more common to find that only perhaps one period a week, and then in a grossly amateurish way, is devoted to such a goal.

And anyway, it is not only through words that we communicate. How many schools give any real importance to the education of the whole body as an instrument of communication? Quite a few primary schools, perhaps: but in secondary schools it must be comparatively rare.

(b) It seems obvious enough, at a common sense level, that children should be taught to understand themselves and others. So why isn't *psychology*, appropriately taught, a core subject? Shouldn't we teach pupils about their own mental and emotional development, and foster insight into conscious and unconscious psychological needs?

But such insight (even if it demands a serious study of psychology) also needs illumination through all the arts, so these become core subjects as well.

Again, there is no way of setting a minimal limit to the extent that schools should foster such awareness, and therefore no way of prescribing how much 'psychology' should be mandatory.

(c) Who could not agree that people should learn 'to understand the society in which they live'? Surely this must be central to education? And doesn't this involve *sociology*, appropriately taught, as a core subject? (Already it seems, we have two necessary core subjects which seldom actually appear in the school time-table, and we have several other yet to come.) Yet in most schools (especially elitist ones) the nearest equivalent (Social Studies) tends to be a low-prestige area, seldom a serious contender in the examination stakes.

Again, sociology is not by any means the *only* key to social understanding, which must surely need a central place for history, politics (yet another subject rarely taught) and, again, all the arts. And what about archaeology, ecology, economics, foreign languages, applied science, technology, and so on *ad infinitum*? If 'understanding society' is centrally important, then so are all these subjects.

(d) Lastly, does 'education' deserve the name if people leave school without the capacity to think *morally* (with rationality, coherence, and love) about their personal and social responsibilities? Hardly. Yet the central academic study here would be moral philosophy (appropriately taught) and this rarely finds a place outside a handful of sixth forms. As with psychology and sociology, moral philosophy is only one key to a particular goal, this time moral awareness: it must be backed up by other illuminations of moral issues (hence, again, all the arts, especially literature); and, among many other things, hard factual knowledge and genuine understanding concerning the mores of other cultures and sub-cultures). Many people would think that religious education, too, had a necessary (or even fundamental) contribution to make in this area.

Conclusions

(1) Even the most generally agreed educational needs, literacy and numeracy, are difficult to define as part of a core curriculum. Literacy, in particular, is not only acquired in 'literacy lessons' but (and far more importantly) via the use of language in all aspects of school and home life.

If national 'tests' of basic skills were devised and applied at intervals throughout a child's school life, it is more than likely that teaching would become geared to these tests, with the results that brighter pupils would under-achieve and that a good deal of richness and variety in language teaching would be lost. Inevitably, the tests would be narrow in scope in order to be assessable, and would doubtless lead to the production of textbooks, equally narrow in scope, aimed at getting through the test. Individual teachers and schools would feel the need to compete with others in having high average marks for their pupils: and all towards a very dubious end. Such tests would necessarily be abitrary: the notion of 'competence' in the basic skills is highly complex and debatable, and to some extent ideologically defined. Paulo Freire's notion of competence would be very different from that of users of the 'Janet and John' books.

(2) The above may sound suspiciously like the relativism favoured by the more tiresome sort of sociologist, so I shall qualify it.

I do not doubt that it is possible to construct reasonably objective tests of certain skills needed in the comprehension, writing and speaking of 'standard' English, nor even that such tests, properly conducted and interpreted, could be useful to teachers. My argument is simply that they would be tests on a very narrow front, and if sanctified by being given national importance would have bad effects on pedagogy. We have plenty of awful warnings from such tests devised in the past which tend to promote banal, cliche-ridden English.

(3) With regard to number skills, obviously a far greater degree of objectivity is possible because of the logical structure of mathematical

language. However, it is not by any means certain that the consequences of national tests would be pedagogically desirable. They could promote learning rituals which suited some children better than others, and might discourage the sort of curriculum where number skills are successfully acquired during the process, say, of individual or group project work (a process which may be as effective in the long run but which can involve varying *paces* of learning).

Despite the 'objectivity' referred to above, there are various ideological positions which could still have a profound effect upon the realization of mathematics as a core subject. Just as instances:

(a) "Mathematics is the purest form of knowledge, and therefore deserves a privileged place in the curriculum." (I have also heard it claimed that mathematics offers the deepest possible insight into the nature of God.)

(b) "Mathematics of all subjects offers least contribution to our understanding of real life, and is not, therefore, of central importance for most pupils."

(c) "We should encourage academically gifted children to go as far as possible with the subject; but most pupils need only learn mathematical processes relevant to everyday life."

(d) "Our country is backward technologically, and since mathematics is an essential ingredient we ought to place a lot more emphasis on its place in the curriculum for all pupils."

(e) "Every human being should have the opportunity of acquiring as much mathematical skill as possible, since liberal education involves initiation into every possible way of understanding the universe."

(4) In this paper I have avoided questions about the *definition* of a core curriculum. I have not, for example, distinguished between (a) a core curriculum specified in general terms by a central committee but interpreted and administered at the discretion of individual schools and individual teachers, and (b) a core curriculum involving external directives on the educational procedures of all schools. Nor have I distinguished between (a) a core curriculum which formally occupies a defined proportion of the timetable with a defined content, and (b) a more flexible system whereby any methodology and curriculum content may exist provided that pupils of a particular age have acquired particular, measurable skills. Nor have I considered compromises, whereby the Department of Education and Science, the Schools Council, schools and parents could all have a defined role to play in determining a core curriculum.

These are all important questions in themselves; but do not, I believe, have any consequences for the main argument presented in this paper, which is:

(5) That I cannot conceive any theoretical process by which *any* sort of

core curriculum which would be both appropriate and morally justifiable for all pupils could be established. Except in a Brave New World situation, where some social groups are treated as less than human, no core curriculum could, in my opinion, satisfy *all* the ideological demands of a pluralistic society. The outcome would be a core curriculum determined by political pressure and would be largely arbitrary.

(6) If this paper were *merely* a response to current political debates it would be extremely naive. I don't suppose for a moment that Mr. Callaghan (or Shirley Williams for that matter) really believes that a core curriculum would have any specific relevance to our immediate social needs. All he really means is that there should at the present time be greater emphasis on the teaching of technological subjects (just as a few years ago successive governments thought there should be a rapid expansion in teacher training to meet future social needs).

However, in the background of the debate there are hawkish threats to a free-flying educational system that has some virtues as well as many gross faults. I hope, therefore, that all educationalists will take the debates seriously.

References

1 Bantock, G. H. (1977) 'Towards a theory of popular education,' *Times Educational Supplement*, 12 and 19 March.
2 Hirst, Paul H. (1969) 'The logic of the curriculum,' *Journal of Curriculum Studies*, 1, 2.
3 White, John (1969) 'The curriculum mongers: education in reverse,' *New Society*, 6 March.
4 Merritt, John (1974) *What Shall We Teach?* (London, Ward Lock).
5 Skilbeck, Malcolm (1976) *Culture, Ideology and Knowledge*, E203, units 3 and 4 (Open University Press).

5 The impossibility of a core curriculum: a reply to Alan Harris

John White

Source: 'The impossibility of a core curriculum: a reply to Alan Harris', *Oxford Review of Education*, 3 (2): 181–184, 1977.

Harris' title might lead one to think his thesis is that a core curriculum is impossible. But this can't be right, because he presupposes later that a core curriculum may be 'actually adopted' (p. 171). Nearer the mark is his claim that it is likely that 'any core curriculum actually adopted would be as arbitrary and unsatisfactory as what it replaced' (*ibid.*) A 'core curriculum' is to be understood very broadly here as covering any curricula or curricular objectives laid down at national level (I take it) as indispensable for all children. It is not clear whether Harris sees politicians and the Department of Education and Science as necessarily having a hand in determining a core curriculum or whether a core curriculum could in principle be set up, at national level, by a purely professional body. A big issue arises here, of course: that of the schools' accountability to the community for their curricula. But as far as I can see, Harris is not taking sides on this, since it seems, from the reasons he advances, as if he is opposed to core curricula of both a politically determined and a professionally determined sort. ... Or is he really objecting to the former only? There are certain indications that he might be. But let us take the more inclusive alternative. The thesis is, then, that it would be wrong for any body, political or professional, to lay down any curricula or curricular objectives at national level as indispensable for pupils. To do so would be 'arbitrary and unsatisfactory'. Why so? Harris offers two reasons:

> The first is that ideological and political pressures in this country are infinitely more powerful than the work of curriculum theorists and that these would favour the development of an irreconcilable variety of core curricula. The second is that even if it were possible to eschew ideological or political bias it would still be impossible to agree on a sensible basis for a core curriculum ... (p. 171).

Elaborating the first of these arguments, Harris shows how different educational ideologies – 'classical humanism', 'progressivism' and 'reconstructionism' – have different, and mutually exclusive, curricular implications. Let us agree, for the sake of argument, that he is broadly right about this. The problem is: how does this truth support the main conclusion, that any imposition of a core curriculum would be 'arbitrary' and therefore morally wrong? The mere fact of radical disagreement does not show that all those disagreeing are adopting an arbitrary position. Some people believe the earth is round, others that it is flat. Does this imply, on Harris' view, that there can be no reason for adopting one belief rather than the other? In this case we don't give up the ghost as soon as we find a disgreement: we look into the arguments each side puts up and examine them objectively. If objective assessment is possible here, why isn't it in the case of educational ideologies? I see no reason why it shouldn't be. Would it necessarily be arbitrary, for instance, to impose a core curriculum of a 'reconstructionist' sort? What if the alternative ideologies were riddled with bad argument and if the reconstructionist case were as well-founded as the thesis that the earth is round? Harris has to do more than merely present his three alternatives: he has to show that none of them could ever be well-founded. Let me throw him down a gauntlet. I can see holes in 'classical humanism' and in 'progressivism', but I cannot for the life of me see what is wrong in 'reconstructionism'. In Harris's words, "central is the notion that education should change society for the better: society will be reconstructed along more democratic lines, with everyone playing a full part in creating a proud self-reliant nation" (p. 173). On this definition, with possible reservations about the 'self-reliant', count me in as a reconstructionist. I challenge Harris to argue through a case why this view is 'arbitrary and unsatisfactory'.

I guess he might find this rather difficult, since so many of his own curricular judgements, scattered throughout his paper, seem to uphold the importance of social aims. He says, quite rightly, that it's not enough to produce highly specialized technologists: they need to be equipped with an understanding of the social context and significance of their work. In addition, all his preferred goals on p. 176 are connected with the pupil's social relations.

But by this point in the paper we are dealing with Harris's second reason against a core curriculum: "even if it were possible to eschew ideological or political bias it would still be impossible to agree on a sensible basis for a core curriculum" (p. 171). He elaborates this by showing disagreements arising *within* education theory, e.g. between a Hirstian, 'forms of knowledge', approach and his own curricular preferences, just mentioned.

A problem here is that I can't see a difference between this second reason and the first. In both cases the argument is that there are differing theoretical standpoints about aims and curricula, so any particular standpoint must be arbitrary. In both cases these standpoints are within educational theory. Why, then, are Bantock and progressivism discussed as part of the first reason and Hirst and myself as part of the second?

Harris appears to think that only some theories – i.e. those of the first sort – are 'ideological and political'. Others, presumably, are in some sense politically and ideologically neutral. I fail to see how one could make any useful distinction here.

The second reason, then, collapses into the first: people differ about aims and curricula, so any particular proposal must be arbitrary. The fallacy in the 'second' reason is the same as that in the first: the fact that opinions differ does not imply arbitrariness.

Harris says on p. 50 that he will illustrate the force of his second reason by attempting to devise a core curriculum. He does so in his elaboration of the four sub-goals already mentioned. The thought here seems to be that in stating his personal preferences, their difference from others' positions, and hence their arbitrariness, will become apparent.

But does Harris really think his own position is as good as any other? Or does he think there are any considerations in its favour? Perhaps he is uncertain. Although his main thesis should incline him to the former, he *does* produce reasons, and often convincing ones, for a certain sort of education.

Why not, then, see how far the path of reason will take one before concluding that anything goes? Why not, in particular, see just what mileage there is in the proposition, which both Harris and I and many others seem to share, that education should be directed primarily towards social ends? If all us 'social-enders' go around saying, "This, of course, is just my view. I believe it, of course, but I don't expect anyone else to", we may miss a great opportunity. We may isolate ourselves within our own systems of beliefs instead of working together to see how much common ground we can find – or make – between us. We might find, if we do so work together, that there is far more room for agreement than we at first imagined. We might even prove collectively strong enough to act as a new theoretical pressure-group, helping to shift the educational system towards agreed social ends at all levels from national politics through to school staff meetings. Why not? Why must we continue to bedevil ourselves with the thought – strange in supporters of a social end – that individual differences of belief on a topic like this are to be cherished rather than diminished?

But, it may be said, some individual differences in belief may go pretty deep, resting on fundamental gulfs of a metaphysical or other kind. Even here, however, Harris's pessimism would not be warranted. For those who differ so fundamentally might *not* differ when it comes to curriculum objectives. Take someone opposed to all forms of abortion on religious grounds and set him against a supporter of abortion on demand – an apparently irreconcilable gulf here. But both parties could agree that, as far as curricular objectives go, all children should be exposed to all the main arguments for and against abortion. Or take Harris's own opinion that society should evolve away from large-scale technology towards a craft-economy. An opponent may rest his case on fundamentally different beliefs about how men should best live. But both may be unwilling to ram their own views down schoolchildren's throats, preferring them to be equipped with an understanding of both positions and the intellectual tools to make up their own minds between them.

So if believers in social ends did find no common ground in some areas, that would not imply the end of the quest for an agreed core curriculum.

But this is jumping the gun a little. The first task is to see just what common ground there can be. To launch this (who knows?) historic enterprise, let me start by picking up one or two of Harris's various points about social ends and seeing if we two at least can't come to some closer agreement. One very strong claim that he makes is that "an analysis of social needs can throw up *contingent* educational needs (i.e. contingent to a particular situation) but it cannot indicate what ought in the long term to be central curricular aims" (p. 57). If this were true, then a core curriculum on this social foundation would indeed be impossible. But that it is not true, at least in Harris's eyes, is evident from a number of other remarks he makes in his paper. For example, "social understanding ... must surely need a central place for history, politics and all the arts ..." (p. 58). "Does 'education' deserve the name if people leave school without the capacity to think *morally* (with rationality, coherence and love) about their personal and social responsibilities? Hardly" (p. 59). These are only two out of many examples: his belief that technologists should have a broad understanding of social and political problems is another. In none of these cases does an analysis of social needs eventuate in such situation-specific curricula that a core curriculum at national level is automatically ruled out.

Perhaps Harris could agree to all this? If so, that would at least be a start. We could then go on to see how far we saw eye to eye on the relation between 'social' and 'individual' aims. In one passage Harris seems to imply that once a country becomes rich and stable enough, it can switch priorities from the former to the latter (p. 53). This would seem to imply a rather narrow view of 'social' aims, as concerned only with such things as increasing the G.N.P. I doubt from all sorts of other things he says that Harris *does* want to restrict things in this way, but we would clearly need to thrash out together what we meant by 'social' and 'individual' aims and whether we saw these as in any way exclusive. (For me, seeing that society is made up of individuals and individuals are not atomic entities but essentially social creatures, the statement that education must have the aim of improving society already incorporates within itself some aims of an 'individualistic' sort. To spell this out would obviously be a long job. I attempt to do so in a book which I hope will shortly be published, called *The Aims of Education*.)

One thing that seems to bother Harris is that once you begin to look at education from a social point of view, all kinds of subjects come knocking for a place on a core curriculum. He cites archaeology, ecology, economics, foreign languages, applied science, technology, history, politics, the arts, sociology, psychology, philosophy, religious education. I'm not sure of his conclusion from this, but I take it it is that there are just too many, and too many sophisticated, subjects for all schoolchildren to be expected to master. Suppose he is right in this. Does it follow that a core curriculum is impossible? I don't see why. We might indeed conclude, as those splendid fighters for Continuation Schools did before and after the first world war, that there should be at least part-time compulsory education for all up to the age of eighteen, with an emphasis on historical, political, economic, literary and other forms of understanding which are less meaningful to younger children. Core curriculum requirements at the pre-sixteen level could then be determined in the light of this later learning. There is indeed a lot which any pupil should be expected to master overall, but by laying proper foundations at primary school level and by extending compulsory schooling beyond sixteen, much can be done to relieve the burden on the secondary school. Compromises between ideals and actualities may well have to be made all along the line: we might to have to settle for rather lower terminal expectations than we would wish at the end of the compulsory period, leaving a large part of the task to be finished by voluntary organs of education like the media and adult education, and by the practice of industrial democracy. Organizations like these might come to be harnessed, partly by legislation or regulation, partly by pressure-group activity, to the same social ends which I believe should direct the school system. All of this points to the complexity of the task ahead of us; but none of it rules out the possibility or desirability of core curricula.

Alan Harris despairs too soon. To be consistent, he should set his face not only against core curricula but also against any curriculum which a school imposes on its pupils, even schools who decide their curricula wholly autonomously. For if a core curriculum is likely to be 'arbitrary', then so are the broad curricular objectives of any particular school. If these have been thought through at all, they will necessarily rest on *someone's* beliefs about education, whether the head's, the staff's, the governors', or all combined. Since these beliefs are likely not to be shared by other people, on Harris's argument the resulting curricular objectives will probably be as arbitrary as any core curriculum. Perhaps he would be willing to agree. Perhaps he is as opposed to the arbitrary powers of headmasters as to those of a national body. All right. But what, positively, does he suggest we do about school curricula? Do we let children do what they like? He seems, quite rightly, not to be in favour of that. But what policy *is* he in favour of?

Harris is not the first educational subjectivist to have caught himself in this particular lobster pot. But unlike those tedious and too familiar sociologists of knowledge who express no views at all on what pupils should learn, because *any* suggestions, from them or anyone else, would simply be reflections of bourgeois ideology and have no objective validity, Harris at least stands for *something*. What's more, the kind of thing he stands for – a socially orientated education – is something which, when further refined and elaborated, is rationally defensible as an alternative to the present dominant ideologies. Most of these, whether advocating a 'child-centred' education, or 'initiation into intrinsic worthwhileness' or – most dominant of all – an education which opens as many doors as possible to different jobs and/or leisure pursuits, put excessive weight on the good of the individual pupil as something hivable off from the good of the community. In those increasing numbers of us who are dismayed by the egocentric tendencies of those dominant ideologies, Harris's social preferences will strike a sympathetic chord.

One final note. I have attempted to show in this paper that Harris's arguments against a core curriculum will not do. I have not attempted the further, and longer, task of coming to a final judgement on whether we need such a curriculum.

6 Authority, bureaucracy and the education debate

A. H. Halsey

Source: 'Authority, bureaucracy and the education debate', *Oxford Review of Education*, 3(3): 217–233, 1977.

A preliminary note

It so happened that I had agreed in the autumn of 1976 to give three talks on BBC Radio 3 – in their '*Personal View*' series. The first and second were devoted respectively to authority and bureaucracy: for I was using the occasion to put forward a personal view of what seem to me to be fundamental changes in contemporary life. But before I could deliver the third and final talk, on relations between the generations, the Prime Minister opened the 'great education debate' with a speech at Ruskin College, Oxford.

The opportunity was not to be missed and I therefore responded to Mr. Callaghan's invitation in the light of the views I had advanced in the first two talks. The result is sharply different in form from that of the conventional academic article. But when the editors of the *Review* offered publication I decided not to change the format except for minimal concessions to written rather than spoken English.

Authority

Bad news is the staple fare of the mass media. Take virtually any day's content of any paper or radio or television news and you are bombarded with metaphors of menace and violence. Here are some from a single day in 1976:

FRENCH GANGS IN BLOODY EXIT
TRUCE AFTER FORDS NIGHT OF VIOLENCE
MAOIST HIJACK GANG BROKEN
POLICE SHOW MUSCLE IN PAY DISPUTE
ESCAPE TO WEST FOILED BY SPIES
BRITONS CHARGED WITH MURDER

THE POUND'S CRISIS
LABOUR RANK AND FILE TAKE POT-SHOTS AT
GOVERNMENT LEADERS
NO NEED TO PANIC, SAYS CALLAGHAN

and MISERY GO-ROUND, which is a commentary column by Peter Jenkins in which he says that the Government is "staring itself and pending disaster in the eye".

The impact of it all is to raise the Hobbesian spectre of the collapse of civil society into conditions where every man's hand is against every other man's hand and life is nasty, brutish and short. Is this our fate? Or is it a miasma created by a sensationalist press? – a sort of horror comic, offering vicarious excitement to the suburban commuter on his monotonously orderly round? My own view is certainly less alarmist than that of the mass media. Nevertheless, there is a lot in the news under the headlines which invites reflection on Thomas Hobbes's analysis of a conflict-ridden England in the seventeenth century and his solution – the Leviathan, an all-powerful authority.

Authority. The very word has an archaic ring about it nowadays. What a frail thing it is! I write below about a type of authority – the rational–legal in Max Weber's inelegant phrase – which bids to dominate us in the modern world in the form of bureaucracy. What is rational and legal about this type of authority is that it claims to apply general rules to particular cases. Its deeper justification comes, at least in our country, from the fact (or at least the theory) that the general rules are arrived at by democratic legislation. It rests ultimately on the preferences of the major-ity. But, I argue, bureaucrats all too easily and frequently break the chain from popular will to executive decision.

Now there is a second type of authority of which the newspapers fre-quently remind us. This is *charisma* – the personal authority of the inspired leader who is trusted by his followers. His word is the criterion of truth and worth. This type of authority also has its frailties. Those who have it, like Mao Tse Tung, must one day die. Those who aspire to it, like Jim Callaghan or David Steel, must face the ordeal of their Annual Party conferences. And there is a third type of authority to complete the picture. This is tradition. Today's orders are justified on the grounds that we have always done it that way. It is ancestral wisdom. But I hardly need to explain the frailty of traditional authority in our world of rapid social change. In the village where I grew up custom decreed that all adults, within limits well understood, could and should act in *loco parentis*. There was intergenerational authority. A friend of mine aged 50 went to see the Notting Hill carnival last year and was robbed in the street by four adoles-cents who addressed him contemptuously as 'Grandad'. This is the absence of intergenerational authority.

It seems almost, once one's thoughts begin to run on these lines, that the newspapers, the radio and the television are concerned with nothing else than authority, the conditions for its exercise and the causes of its rupture. Car workers rampage through the management canteen at the Ford plant, prisoners rebel against warders in the gaol at Hull. Condemned members of the Irish Republican Army refuse to recognise an Irish court.

There is no doubt that authority is not what it used to be. My friend Paul Cheetham recently sent me a copy of a passport signed by Lord Palmerston in 1851. Here is indeed a document of authority:

> We, Henry John Viscount Palmerston, Baron Temple, a Peer of Ireland, a Member of Her Britannic Majesty's Most Honorable Privy Council, a Member of Parliament, Knight Grand Cross of the Most Honorable Order of the Bath, Her Majesty's Principal Secretary of State for Foreign Affairs, request and require in the Name of Her Majesty all those whom it may concern to allow Mr. Edward Holroyd, his wife Mrs. Holroyd, two daughters and three sons, travelling on the Continent. with a man and a maid servant, to pass freely without let or hindrance, and to afford them every assistance and protection of which they may stand in need. Given at the Foreign Office, London, the 10th day of July 1851.

Notice the symbols of authority here. And, perhaps even more telling, the confident description of social hierarchy from Her Majesty down through the Viscount to Mr. Holroyd and thence to sons and daughters, and finally a man and a maid servant.

Honi soit qui mal y pense, says the heraldry. No matter that, three years before, Marx and Engels in the Communist Manifesto of 1848 had, with no less confidence, announced the impending fall of the capitalist state, the overthrow of imperial authority by the rising revolutionary proletariat.

Recently I read, in the *Daily Mirror*, Geoffrey Goodman's brilliant tabloid history of the twentieth-century rise of *new* authorities – the TUC, and the Parliamentary Labour Party – from Downing Street, Manchester, to Downing Street, London, to become what the journalists now describe as the natural government of the country. But Goodman ended his account with a remark about the Annual Conferences, that they were a much-cherished opportunity for the rank and file to have a bash at their masters on the platform, rather as we know many primitive tribes have annual rituals in which the chief is ceremoniously reviled and insulted by licensed warriors before the assembled people.

On the next day we learned that the paternal, or is it more apt to say avuncular, Jim had disciplined Reg Prentice against rocking the boat with a speech hostile to the proposed Labour policy programme. Meanwhile, news continued to come in from China about bitter struggles for succession to the places emptied by death among the founding gerontocracy of that regime.

I choose these diverse examples partly to emphasise that the problem of authority is ubiquitous in human relationships, extending from the encounter in the street through those small human groups which are sufficiently bound by rules for us to call them institutions, like the family or the youth club or the office, and on up to the great political organisations of party and parliament.

From all these instances, we can discern the three basic forms of authority – rational-legal, charismatic and traditional – combining and contending with one another. And we can further see that social change makes each of them uncertain as sources for stable and peaceable relations between people. The examples emphasise that authority is not a synonym for law. The adults in my village had no legal authority over children: but they had the authority of long-established tradition. Jim Callaghan has no legal control over Reg Prentice's expression of opinion but he too has the sanction of tradition – the fraternal solidarity of the platform – plus, and perhaps more effective, the power of a prime minister to exclude people from his cabinet. Neither law nor prime ministerial prerogative in these cases was absolute. The Notting Hill adolescents were breaking the law and prime ministerial power did not in fact prevent Reg Prentice from giving utterance. When the law against theft had only my friend to deliver it to the adolescents, its authority was insufficient, at least temporarily. Jim might have silenced Reg by sheer force of the other type of authority – charisma.

Certainly Mao exercised enormous charisma in his progress from young revolutionary in Yenan Province to the chairmanship in Peking. But charisma too has no universal writ. It may be routinised, as with Christ's authority in the institution of the papal succession. But that does not silence the notorious Danish film-maker and Mao's charisma, if it does not die with him, at least cannot prevent a power struggle among the survivors.

Charisma is historically like the wind which bloweth where it listeth. Churchill is thought of in this country as having had this type of authority. He gained it at a moment of desperate external threat to a country at war. External threat does, in fact, accelerate the process whereby many are called and few are chosen. Our present economic condition seems to approach a somewhat similar intensity of threatened collapse. But let us be clear that the possibility of new and dramatic leadership, which our infirmity invites, is highly dangerous. Charisma is no necessary friend of democracy – *explicitly* not if it comes from the political extreme Right and *actually* not if it comes from the extreme Left, for all its ideological clothing in rhetoric proclaiming the will of the people.

No, neither the charismatic nor the rational-legal can be our primary source of authority. We must look to tradition. And that must mean democracy – the consensus of free men, free to assemble, to express opinion, to persuade and to elect but, having done so, willing to accept the will of the majority whose rule will be tempered by consideration for the minority among whom they may at any time find themselves. Democracy is not a long tradition. It was a usurper at the end of the eighteenth century, fighting a previous tradition of feudal custom. And it was slow in coming – for example, universal suffrage took from 1832 to 1948 to be legally enacted as 'one adult, one vote'. And it has yet to be fully realised beyond the formalities of the polling booth in those spheres of life, particularly the work place, where it lays claim to be applied.

I am not of course, suggesting that democracy can be applied mechanically to all forms of human association. What I am suggesting is that it must be the ultimate court of appeal for our secular lives. Families cannot be full democracies: they are not bands of brothers and the lesser responsibility of childhood is an inescapable fact: but they can be and can be judged as nurseries of responsible citizenship. Schools and universities cannot be democracies, whatever is said by the National Union of Students. If you are a teacher and I come to learn then your knowledge must have authority over my ignorance: but again the school you run is successful precisely in so far as it brings me to competent citizenship in the trade, profession or subject you teach me: and from that moment I have the right to democratic relations with you.

That is all obvious enough. But we are far from laying the democratic foundation for traditional authority in all the spheres to which our modern evolution points. Let me take two spheres of life where this is conspicuously so – our nation state and our industrial organisation – two areas in which the democratic principle could be more firmly applied.

The starting point in both spheres is that we have come to organise ourselves by extremely specialised division of labour. But in national affairs we have over-reached ourselves. We are tied into a huge apparatus of international markets. We have given over a great deal of our effective authority to international agencies through our membership of the EEC, the development of multi-national companies and our trading relations all over the world. And we occupy a specialist position within this complex through the London money market which we call the City. We are very far from being an autonomous economy and, quite apart from internal dissension, the extent to which our government can control inflation, price levels and standards of life is feeble. To domesticate authority within our shores – and so to give ourselves a chance to run an effective democracy – would probably entail considerable cost to our general standards of living.

I for one would prefer that we paid that material price. In saying this I am assuming democratic justice in the distribution of the burden. But it must be pointed out in defence of this 'little Englandism' that no economist or politician in the current debate who seeks solutions within the international framework holds out any immediate prospect of relieving the misery of a million and a half unemployed. That is one painful and inequitably distributed cost of our persistence with the large and therefore undemocratic system we have.

I said, "quite apart from internal dissension". That brings me to the other sphere which needs greater democratisation and here I would point to the perceptive analyses which have been offered by my colleague, Alan Fox.

Mr. Fox's main attention in his book *Beyond Contract* is focused on the experience of work in the office, the factory and the workshop. Work relations in the past have given low discretion and low trust to subordinates *vis-à-vis* their superiors. This was the triumph of the so-called scientific management which reached its most extreme form in the modern factory assembly line. The low-discretion syndrome, as Mr. Fox describes it, contrasts the rank and file production worker with the professional. The worker on the shop floor has little sense of being an expert; of commitment to a calling; of autonomy on the job; or obligation to produce high-quality work, and he has little or no sense of identification with the organisation in which he works.

Alan Fox has also analysed the low levels of trust which lie behind the struggles between different groups of organised workers. Obviously a better society would organise its work by the opposite principles of high-trust relations, both vertically and horizontally. Professional work at its best requires and involves a high level of trust between people. Rigidly hierarchical forms of industrial authority produce at best the solidarity of the resentful.

Industrial democracy is a vital element in our unfinished programme of creating a society which commands willing and widespread allegiance. I, like Mr. Fox, do not go far with those who announce the arrival of the corporate society as the new Leviathan. Our evolution has strong roots in liberal individualism and little or nothing in those Hegelian or organic conceptions of society which see the individual and his purposes as having meaning only in terms of corporate membership. Indeed, Britain has the strongest shop-steward organisation in the world. Its indiscipline against corporatism is far more impressive than the corporative hierarchy of the TUC, which Paul Johnson and the mass media are quick to portray as the modern demon. What is more important than shop-steward radicalism is that this shop-floor organisation is the most conspicuous form of democracy in contemporary Britain. Nevertheless, the low discretion, low trust principle still dominates work organisation. And we pay a price for it far beyond our lives as producers.

These tendencies could, however, be reversed. Reversal, of course, would carry its considerable price – and not only in terms of cars and television sets (at least in a transitional period). The extension of high trust relations would be at the expense of the expectation of affluence. And I can see little prospect of the bargain being eagerly sought either by those presently in authority (who have vested interest in their present power), or the workers, patients, consumers and citizens (who are conditioned to prefer a bit more of what material benefits they already have). Only those who experience autonomy and relations of trust can fully appreciate their satisfactions.

Yet surely the tradition of democracy is our essential means to a better society. It offers the basis of willing co-operation. It is our main defence against rejection of society by the dissatisfied – and infinitely preferable to social control through the discipline of mass unemployment. I see no other direction in which free Britons can make a society they would uphold as authentic.

Bureaucracy

Hardly a day passes without the newspapers complaining about this ugly polysyllable. *The Times* recently (23.8.76) reported a new book by Gordon Tullock, describing it as a "comprehensive criticism of politicians and civil servants for being more interested in feathering their own nests than serving the public". Professor Tullock argues that civil servants are just like other men and that therefore "they will make most of their decisions in terms of what benefits them, not society as a whole". And, "as a general rule, a bureaucrat will find that his [interests are best served] ... if the the bureaucracy in which he works expands".

A few days later (1.9.76) the papers announced that the two large civil service unions, alarmed by what their leaders described as a "hate campaign against civil servants", have distributed a pamphlet to MPs and other Unions defending the incumbents of public offices against exaggerated rumours of their pay and pensions and against misrepresentation of their conduct towards citizens. The Civil Service Unions had also protested against cuts in public expenditure in general and public service jobs in particular. No one ought to need reminding that forced unemployment is a private tragedy and a public failure, but anyone could be forgiven, after reading or watching the news this past year, for thinking that there has been a sharp reduction in the number of officials, if not from the arrival of the Conservative Government of 1970 then at least since Mr. Healey. And this would be especially marked in the case of local government with its alleged reorganisation for greater economy and efficiency. In fact the opposite is the case.

The Joint Manpower (Watch) Survey – made jointly by central and local government-records that, between March 1975 and March 1976 – a much publicised 'No Growth' period – there was an *increase* in English and Welsh local government staff of over 30,000. On a longer view it is clear that Governments of either colour preside over continuous bureaucratic growth. There were a million and a quarter local government employees in 1960. It was two million when Labour displaced the Tories in 1964. They added over 400,000 before the Conservatives came back in 1970 determined to turn the tide. But the tide flowed on. By 1975 there were 2,875,000 despite the fact that 77,000 were transferred to the NHS and Water Services in 1974 and so did not appear in the 1975 total. No wonder NALGO is the fourth largest union in the country.

Taking a still wider view it can be seen that in the twentieth century the occupational structure has shifted its centre of gravity from basic productive employment to the tertiary sector of services and administration. One measure of the change is that between 1911 and 1966 white collar numbers went up 176 per cent while manual jobs rose only 5 per cent and actually decreased after 1931.

These figures reflect an increasingly organised world in which bureaucracy is the dominant working principle. Though the word 'community' also spatters its pages, the contemporary newspaper habitually looks out, sees organisations everywhere, and tells us in a more or less sensationalist way how people enter them in pursuit of their interests only to lose themselves. Yes, you may say – it is really a roundabout way of telling us that we are drifting towards socialism. I will come to that. But, lest anyone should imagine that all criticism of bureaucracy comes from the political Right, identifying bureaucracy with socialism, it is as well to mention the article by Paul Johnson in *The New Statesman* which constitutes attacks of spectacular verbal violence on the leaders of the TUC. For Paul Johnson this organisational élite are the greatest threat to democracy in modern times and the closed shop the greatest blow against freedom in his life time.

It is, he writes:

> the thesis of the bureaucratic brothers that they represent the people; that what they are doing, in erecting their private empires, in extending their bureaucratic control and grabbing jobs for their boys, in remorselessly driving their juggernaut over the prostrate bodies of individual men and women, that all this is done by, with, for and in the name of the people. Jack Jones, who might well be described as the Louis XIV of the trade union takeover, has seemingly convinced himself that 'Le peuple, c'est moi!' ...[1] But all the available evidence suggests that, at a time when so many members of the Establishment – ministers and MPs, dons and civil servants, experts and publicists – are hurrying to pay their respects to the new totalitarianism, and sell their shares in individual liberty, the ordinary decent people of Britain are strongly opposed to rule by trade union bureaucrats.

I would persuade you that serious resistance to the very real threat to democracy and freedom which comes from bureaucracy, if it is possible at all, is more likely to be inspired by our native political traditions of socialism than by either Conservative or Communist political theory.

In common speech, of course, the word 'bureaucracy' is an established term of abuse. The word 'bureau' referred originally to the cloth covering the desks of French government officials in the eighteenth century. With its suffix added it came to refer to the rule of government, and a host of ocracies have since been added to the vocabulary of politics as commentators have searched desperately to find the ultimate seat of power in modern society. The pejorative use of the term then spread throughout Europe during the nineteenth century, at first to ridicule the high-handed arrogance of officials in absolutist regimes and later more generally as a whip for the backs of unresponsive organisations, tortuous methods of administration, and large-scale enterprises (whether of government, business, church or recreation) in which power was concentrated into the hands of the administrative few.

There is, on the other hand, a technical, social-scientific use of bureaucracy to describe a type of social organisation deliberately devised by men for the rational and efficient pursuit of defined purposes. The classic source for the analysis of bureaucracy in non-evaluative terms is the German sociologist Max Weber who wrote at the turn of the nineteenth and twentieth centuries. No one saw more clearly than he that bureaucracy and large-scale organisation were the fundamental phenomena of modern political, social, and economic life. And Weber's account of bureaucracy, from one point of view, reminds us of its virtues. Bureaucracy, he noted, was distinguished from other forms of human authority and control by its routinised rationality, its capacity to attain a high degree of efficiency, its stability, the stringency of its discipline, and its reliability. It is a matter of national pride for us in Britain that we showed the world how to escape from the corrupt control of administration by the privileged into uncorrupt and dedicated public service recruited on merit in open competition. That was the Northcotte-Trevelyan and Gladstonian reform; and that was the acceptable face of bureaucracy.

It is true that Weber at the same time saw the tragedy of the highly organised world into which industrialisation would take us – a world of disenchantment, robbed of magic and mystery. Even charisma, the gift of grace, would be routinised within it and freedom and individuality could be destroyed by it. Nevertheless, in company with both the Leftists and the Rightists of his age, Weber identified modernity with the spread of bureaucratic administration. "This is true", he wrote,

> of church and state, of armies, political parties, economic enterprises, organisations to promote all kinds of causes, private associations, clubs, and many others. However many forms there may be which do not appear to fit this pattern such as collegial representative bodies, parliamentary committees, soviets, honorary officers, lay judges, and what-not, and however much people may complain about the 'evils of bureaucracy', it would be sheer illusion to think for a moment that continuous administrative work can be carried out in any field except by means of officials working in offices. The whole pattern of everyday life is cut to fit this framework. For bureaucratic administration is,

other things being equal, always from a formal technical point of view, the most rational type. For the needs of mass administration today, it is completely indispensable. The choice is only that between bureaucracy and dilettantism in the field of administration.

Adherents of different ideological traditions than that of Weber's liberalism echoed his celebration of the inevitable march of bureaucracy as well as his ambivalence towards it. Sheldon Wolin, in his *Politics of Vision* (1960), gives us a subtle and scholarly account of the origin of this view in all political camps. Whatever differences there were in diagnosis and prescription, most of the major writers have been agreed on the general formula for developing wealth, welfare and social order – organisation. Thus for the nineteenth-century French conservative De Maistre the organisation of society into a vast hierarchy of authority would reinstitute stability and peace under the command of king and pope assisted by a public-spirited aristocracy. For his compatriot, Auguste Comte, there would be an organised hierarchy of savant-priests. For yet another compatriot, Emile Durkheim, the organisation of society had to be on the basis of professional and producing groups, and for the proponents of managerial élitism in the twentieth century the best organisation of society is one under the control of the professional managers and administrators who alone possess the requisite knowledge for maintaining social equilibrium in the age of successive technological revolutions.

Weber himself remorselessly drove home the inference from the indispensability of bureaucracy that it made no difference whether an economic system was organised on a capitalist or a socialist basis. And he adds:

> though by no means alone, the capitalistic system has undeniably played a major role in the development of bureaucracy. Indeed, without it capitalistic production could not continue and any rational type of socialism would simply have to take it over and increase its importance. Its development, largely under capitalistic auspices, has created an urgent need for stable, strict, intensive and calculable administration. It is this need which gives bureaucracy a crucial role in our society as the central element in any kind of any large-scale administration.

Bureaucracy, I would stress, in theories of the Right and the Left, has been seen as an instrument not only for efficiency but also of social control. There is accordingly an élitism of the Left as well as of the Right. Lenin is perhaps the outstanding example. In Professor Wolin's phrase 'organisation was to mass in Lenin's theory what idea had been to matter in Plato's: that which imparted form to the formless". Lenin was the first to seize the implications of transferring politics to the plane of organisation. He taught that politics had meaning only within an organisational setting. The trick was not to destroy the political but to absorb it into organisation to create a new compound. ... The irony is that his prescription for revolution has also been used to preserve giant capitalism. Democracy has no meaning in such élitist thought except in so far as it is consonant with the imperatives of organisation. Thus Lenin wrote:

> Bureaucracy *versus* democracy is the same thing as centralism *versus* (local) democracy as opposed to the organisational principle of the opportunists of Social Democracy. The latter want to proceed from the bottom upwards ... The former proceed from the top, and advocate the extension of the rights and powers of the centre in respect of the parts ... My idea is 'bureaucratic' in the sense that the Party is built from the top downwards....[2]

No nonsense Lenin. But the historical roots of British socialism were never like that. Let us be clear that democracy came to us from the bottom upwards. The urban working classes of the nineteenth century were uprooted newcomers to the growing provincial industrial towns who responded to their circumstances with extraordinary social inventiveness to give Britain in the first half of the twentieth century its most characteristic popular organisations – the Cooperatives store, the Trade Union and the Labour Party as well as the dance hall, the football club and the Friendly Society. The first and the greatest three of these were experiments in democracy. This urban proletariat created its own local, communal welfare societies. Nothing could have been more democratic than the constitution of the Co-op, nothing more fraternal than the Miners' Lodge. Nowhere could we find more sturdy institutional protection for individuals against becoming a mass to be manipulated.

Then, with political organisation as its instrument, the Labour movement set out to nationalise democracy and welfare; to translate fraternity, equality and liberty from the local community to the national state.

What has been the outcome? In 1973, very near to the end of his life, R. H. S. Crossman gave an account in the form of a review of the Labour movement as he had experienced it. It was in essence a lament for the eclipse of voluntarism by bureaucratic organisation – a disappointment in Westminster and a despair in Whitehall. Let me quote him:

> From the 1920s on, the normal left wing attitude has been opposed to middle-class philanthropy, charity, and everything else connected with do-gooding. Those of us who became socialists grew up with the conviction that we must in this point ally ourselves with the professionals and the trade unions and discourage voluntary effort particularly since it was bound to reduce the number of jobs available to those in need.
>
> I am now convined that the Labour Party's opposition to philanthropy and altruism and its determined belief in economic self-interest

as the driving dynamic of society has done it grievous harm. For ironically enough the Party, the trade unions, and the Co-operative were all a hundred years ago inspired by a profound and passionate altruism – a belief in a new Jerusalem – linked with an urgent sense of duty – a conviction that it was an essential part of socialism to practise what one preached by volunteering to help comrades in distress.[3]

So the movement which had invented the social forms of modern participatory democracy and practised them in Union Branch and Co-op meeting, thereby laying a Tocquevillian foundation for democracy, was ironically fated to develop through its political party the bureaucratic corporate state.

And the supreme irony now is that when my friend and colleague Norman Dennis protests against these emerging tyrannies with the authentic voice of a deeply-rooted English socialism, he is heard with approval by Sir Keith Joseph and dismissed as a nuisance by the Labour establishment. Mr. Dennis has written, for example, a completely convincing demolition of our planning practices[4] from the standpoint of democratic socialism in the English tradition of which I have been speaking.

Planning is, of course, associated with left-wing politics and the illogical 'therefore' is frequently added that criticism of it is comfort to the Right. But the 'hidden hand' is also 'a planner' with the market as its instrument. This form of 'planning', however, is vitiated by unequal distributions of power, wealth and income between citizens; it does not accurately reflect the preferences of citizens in community as opposed to individuals in a market.

Studies of planning do often turn out to be a more or less sophisticated attack on socialism and a plea to 'return to the market'. With Mr. Dennis, however, the criticism is directed to the planner's indifference to egalitarian notions of income and power, and his ignorance of the preferences and values of the community he is appointed to serve.

On what grounds can we accept or reject the theory or principle by which a bureaucracy is guided in its action? Sociologists call these grounds the 'legitimation' of the organisation and its activities. Max Weber pointed out that organisations differ greatly when they come to decide whether what they are doing is 'morally right' and based upon 'the correct and relevant data'. One type of organisation accepts the word of its leader on both these matters. This is Charisma. *Ipse dixit* – the sayings of the leader are the criteria of both truth and worth. A second type of organisation rests its activities upon a piety for what has actually, allegedly or presumably always existed and upon a belief in the every day routine as being the inviolable norm of conduct. This is organised authority based on tradition. Thirdly, there are organisations to which Weber gave the term bureaucratic, which appeal to the rule of general laws applying to all within the jurisdiction of the organisation without regard to differences of race, age, family background or social condition. The legitimacy of such an organisation's authority does not depend upon the actual benefits given to particular persons, but upon the legality of the general rule which has been purposely thought out and enacted. Authority here is based on formal as distinct from substantive justice.

This said, it is immediately apparent how enormously ambitious is the claim, scientific and moral, for a bureaucratic organisation.

The task is relatively easy, and successful bureaucratic routine administrations have emerged, where the same service can (and especially where it must) be provided day after day in an identical way to large numbers of people. This is the case with, for example, gas, water and electricity supplies and transport and postal services. Bureaucratic administration is also appropriate, if more problematic, in the production of houses when, because of chronic shortage, large numbers of identical dwellings must be produced. It may even be appropriate to the demolition of houses where a few formal characteristics – for example, whether the house is at all damp or possibly where a measurable amount of dampness is present – enable an official to distinguish unequivocally between a slum house and a non-slum house. But when we come to the service of more subtle and varied human needs in medicine, social security, or education difficulties multiply and a fourth type of legitimation appears which is increasingly important in the modern world. The activities of an organisation are not 'proved' right and good because they are the command of a charismatic leader, or because of tradition, or because they can be subsumed under some general rule, but because they are so certified by the trained members of the organisation whose special function it is to evaluate the particular issue. This is professional authority. Decisions, characteristically in the form of 'advice', are made by those who have been appointed to a 'sphere of competence' on the basis of qualifications attested by a professional group of peers.

As long as the group of professionals make claims only in the technical sphere; as long as they merely say 'this is the given task, we know the most economical means of accomplishing it', the organisation will show many acceptable bureaucratic characteristics. But it is also possible for professionals to make claims in such a way, or to such an extent, that their legitimation resembles that of the inspired leader. These claims to legitimation typically take the form of a kind of group charisma. Each case is adjudicated not by an appeal to strictly formal conceptions unambiguously established, made public and safely recorded 'in the files', but by informal judgements rendered by the personal incumbent of the professional status in terms of concrete ethical or practical valuations. These valuations may be quite opaque to those outside the profession. The professional, by definition, is absolved from justifying his decision; he does not need to reveal his basis in theory or fact or value.

Thus the legitimacy of professional bureaucratic decisions must be judged in two ways. The first is scientific. Decisions ought to be made in the light of ascertainable knowledge. No one can read Mr. Dennis's account of planning in Sunderland and retain confidence in the profession-alism of planners. (Their numbers, by the way, increased nearly 5 per cent in the 'No Growth' year.) And here, speaking more generally (and with examples from many branches of public policy which I do not have time to rehearse) is R. H. S. Crossman again:

> But I was even more worried, particularly when I became a Minister and was able to see a good deal for myself, by the inexplicable decisions under which I found our social services to be operating, decisions which in themselves were inhuman and stupid. And yet as I knew full well they had been made by intelligent, well-intentioned people. How could it be possible that now we had abolished the amateurism of philanthropy and placed the administration of our welfare state in highly professional hands such decisions could be made?[5]

The second way of judging professional bureaucracies emphasises the capacity of ordinary people to reach rational decisions about matters which directly affect them. But even more it emphasises the moral proposi-tion that the exercise of personal discretion is itself a social and personal good. When such discretion has to be abbreviated, as is unavoidable on countless grounds, the case of those who desire to impose restrictions must be well based in fact and convincing in terms of political, social and moral argument. Otherwise we are all to likely to forget, in a fog of pseudo science, that, as Mr. Dennis likes to say, "the citizen is usually his own best expert".

The outlook, you may conclude, is gloomy – the huge private business we have created, and the public servants we invented to realise justice, freedom and equity will become our tyrannical masters. Even the Ombuds-man will turn out to be another professional bureaucrat.

What, then, is to be done? I can pretend to no easy answer. But if there are answers I am convinced that they lie in our own heritage of democracy and socialism. Our hardwon civil liberties need new defence from a radical overhaul of administrative laws. We have an unfinished programme of economic and social equality. But the fraternity which underpins it all cannot survive the national organisation we have erected. Such a scale only generates Robert Michel's 'Iron Law of Oligarchy'. Weber saw only one escape from bureaucratic tyranny – a return to small scale. Subsequent writers following this line have been dismissed as proposing economic absurdity as did William Morris in *New from Nowhere* or medieval romanticism as did G. K. Chesterton in *The Napoleon of Notting Hill Gate*.

But perhaps there is hope in education to which on Mr. Callaghan's invitation I now turn.

The Prime Minister's seminar

It is not often that a Prime Minister invites us all to a seminar. Why, you may ask, should Mr. Callaghan suddenly depart from the established tradition of Prime Ministerial indifference to education? It is said, and it is true, that he has the advantage over his predecessors of having suffered the educational disadvantage of pre-war elementary schooling and no Oxford. He had had, in other words the schooling experience of the majority. I don't doubt that this helped to produce the first major Prime Ministerial speech on education that I can remember. More cynically, it may be observed that Mr. Callaghan is a canny politican who has sensed that some electoral advantage may be held by the Tories in the direction of parental discontent and therefore wishes, perfectly properly, not to leave the definition of the issues to the so-called *Black Paper* writers. Nevertheless, I like to think that he announced this new and very open university course for us all because the subject is important: (for it is certainly that, and certainly deserved, from the political headmaster himself, a contribution to the 'what about our children' politics which have been going on since before the 1944 Act).

So I welcome the Prime Minister's invitation (for all its avuncular quality and irrespective of any narrow party political motives that may have underlain it). My fear is, however, that the debate, as he phrased it, may be about the wrong things. The emphases of his speech were three-fold: on the need for a common core curriculum, the monitoring of standards and the link between education and industry.

The curriculum problem is not, in my view, a serious one. Of course, legalistically defined, the only prescribed element is the daily act of worship. But actually or anthropologically, what strikes me is the sameness or commonality of what goes on in schools. It is very hard to find any primary or secondary school which does not attend to the basic literacies and numeracies. No doubt the Secretary of State should have powers and procedures to stop those conspicuous lunacies which occasionally appear. But the debate should not be about this standard fare of cognitive instruction. It should be about what you might call the hidden curriculum of values and assumptions and choices which define the relation between adults and children – the connection, if you like, between one generation and the next.

That will be my theme: and I approach it from the standpoint of a Christian socialist. The approach is difficult. Our Christian civilisation is virtually at its end after a millenium of powerful influence over the transmission of values and meanings from adults to children. Difficult, too, because many if not most of those in the democratic socialist tradition do not see themselves as Christians. And most difficult because so many of those who join the debate notice that much of our analysis is Marxist – for example, our understanding of education in terms of power, class interests and exploitations – but fail to notice that Marxist *analysis* does not at all require Communist *prescriptions*.

I will come back to all this in a minute. Briefly, meanwhile, on the other two Callaghan emphases. Monitoring? Yes, of course, why not? If we want to be intelligent about what we get for the £6,000 m we spend each year, then we ought to have a running account. That means systematic, regular testing of attainments in literacy and numeracy. It also means tests of much less easily measured products of schooling – creativity, imagination, satisfaction and involvement – and the definitions of all of these in practical terms are inevitably contentious. No matter; so long as the premises on which the measures are constructed are made explicit, we can argue them publicly, include alternatives, and change them in the light of experience. But monitoring must also mean much more than testing of cognitive learning. It has always seemed strange to me that, in the country which invented political arithmetic, and in an area of public life like education which is so quintessentially political (that is the process of public influence over the social personality of the next generation) we do not have official statistics of who gets what out of the £6,000 m.

For example, we have been committed officially to equality of educational opportunity at least since the passing of the 1902 Education Act. But monitoring our progress towards that ideal has never been laid as a duty on the Department of Education and Science. Instead, it is left to the private labours of individuals (who are then, ironically, often criticised as I have been for wasting public money on frivolous and impertinent enquiry). Or again, if you quite reasonably want to know how much is being spent on the education of children of different social origins or men of different trades and professions with their different incomes you ought to be able to find the answers in the official records. How else can a democracy know if it is measuring up to the ideals of fairness and efficiency by which it claims to live? And how else can the professional administrators and teachers rationally and intelligently do the job they are paid to do? Yet in fact it is private investigation instead of public record-keeping that supplies what incomplete answers there are to these essential questions.

On Callaghan's third point – connecting school to work – I would make one immediate comment. It is an old story: which is not to say it is untrue. Every single generation in the history of Britain as an industrial nation has been told that the schools are failing to provide the skills of workers and and managers and professionals needed by a modernising economy. This was the case when we led the world in the rate of economic growth just as much as it is the case now when we are portrayed as the ailing, clapped-out Western country, the sick man of Europe, the ageing bankrupt, etc. That, of course, is another big story, and I have suggested in my first two talks that the picture could be quite differently presented as one of a country with a deep and lively tradition of democracy and one which is leading the world rather than trailing behind it in pursuing the application of democratic principles beyond the polling booth in the factory and work-place, the home and the school.

Let's leave that, however, and note instead that Callaghan is unknow-ingly right if he means that there is a rather tenuous connection between educational and occupational change in modern Britain. Some of my col-leagues and I at Nuffield College have spent several years of work studying the familial, and educational and occupational history of the British adult population of 1972. From these studies one thing is clear – that both the output of qualified people from the educational system and the intake of professional, managerial and white-collar manpower into the work force have risen year by year throughout the century. But there is no automatic supply/demand relation between the two upward movements. They have proceeded independently of each other and no simple conclusion can be drawn along the lines of praising or blaming the schools for the level of efficiency or national income or unemployment or any other aspect of the economy. Of course, for an individual, job choice and protection against unemployment are improved the longer he stays in school and the more he collects educational certificates. But the wealth of the nation, the range of occupational opportunities and the level of employment for our society as a whole are determined by quite other forces such as the amount of invest-ment, the international market and the collective attitudes towards work and leisure which prevail at any given time. Education alone cannot create either wealth or welfare.

Hence my fears about the terms on which Mr. Callaghan's invitation may be interpreted. So let me now say positively what I think the debate has to be about. In a phrase, it is about the social reproduction of genera-tions. In another phrase, it is about social engineering. By the way, one of the irritating features of the Black Paper ideology put out by Mr. Rhodes Boyson, Professor Cox, the Institute of Economic Affairs and other reac-tionaries is that they say of me and other radicals that we believe in using the schools for social engineering while they want to get back to educa-tion. This is a verbal swindle. It illicitly suggests that we have a choice, which we don't. The reproduction of a generation is *always* social engin-eering. The issue is engineering for what? For me it is to make a reality of democratic values. For them it is social engineering for a society of market liberalism and hierarchy. We should argue these ends and not pretend that the socialists are somehow and sinfully introducing corrupting politics into the purity of learning.

I missed this fundamental element in Mr. Callaghan's speech. It is true that he dismissed the excesses of Black Paperism; and he firmly rejected the often implicit and sometimes explicit claims of the organised teachers to a monopoly over decisions as to what should happen in schools. What he did *not* do was to challenge the conventional wisdom that upbringing is to be equated in practice with the formal relations of pedagogy. To accept conventional wisdom is to allow the education debate to be monopolised by the competing interests of the professionals in their common rooms, union branches and conferences and by the bureaucrats in their offices, County Halls and Elizabeth House. He certainly hinted at what I hope the Taylor Committee will insist – namely, a substantial shift of power from where it at present resides among the organised administrators and teachers to the parents and the local community served by schools. As things are, parental involvement in the school side of their children's upbringing is largely a ritual, largely tokenism, often humiliating, seldom enlightening and generally frustrating. I will say more in a minute about the plight of the modern mother. But the point at the moment is that, despite its qualifications, Callaghan's syllabus for the national debate is fatally restricted to the concerns of the powerfully organised.

This is strange when you consider how much the twentieth century deserves its description as the 'century of the child'. So much of modern politics has been about children. Not only increasing educational expenditure but also infant and maternity services, population policies, family allowances, adoption and fostering, treatment of young offenders and so on. Even the principal objective all over the world of economic growth is essentially justified as 'for the children'. The old are relatively political outcasts. The future is all. "Trailing clouds of glory do they come." We have lived through a revolution, demographic, economic and social, as a result of which the child has become the quality product of industrial society. The recalcitrant Andy Capp who says, "What have my grandchildren done for me that I should care for them?" is at best a pre-Freudian anachronism.

No. We should start by recognising the frustration of the modern parent – whether a West Indian mother in Brixton who is baffled by the apparent failure of the school to teach her boy either good letters or good manners or the anxious suburban father calculating the costs and benefits of buying a place for his boy in the private sector now that the comprehensive school is the only alternative to a subsidised place in the direct grant school. He, or more particularly she, looks out on a world which simultaneously takes away control while psychologically thrusting responsibility on parents for the fate of their children. Most parents have lived through a dramatic shift in the standards expected of them. It is not enough, as it once was, to look after bodily health and physical security. Parents must also accept the burden of responsibility for the mental and moral development of their sons and daughters while all around they see influences from the street, the so-called peer group, the mass media and youth culture which they are less and less able to control. They are increasingly made to feel amateurs in a difficult professional world. The old 'Us and Them' of the working-class mother is now a more generalised division as between the inner life of families of all classes and the external public influences, some of which, like the television, have comprehensively invaded the privacy of the hearth. Such circumstances, together with the appreciation of schooling as an instrument largely beyond family control which determines the future jobs and incomes of their children add up to a situation of intense frustration. That is what the debate has to be about. Who is ultimately responsible?

It is said that the monitoring role of Her Majesty's inspectors has been lost in recent years and, if this is so, it is partly because they have lost confidence as to what schools ought to be doing and therefore the authority to guide those they inspect. They deserve sympathy, for the loss of confidence is not only theirs. We *all* live in confusion as to what is the good life. Rereading Richard Hoggart's account of working-class life before the 1950s, I am struck by the integration of ordinary families in those days with the moral traditions of the old class and Christian society which he so accurately and lovingly described. That moral structure has ebbed away fast under the assault of the classless inequalities and the secular materialism of the post-war world and, in the process, the familial controls over upbringing have steadily attenuated.

A traditional culture weakened by multiple forces of change falters in its transmission to the next generation and the lonely crowd of adolescent age-mates look to each other for guidance. They too, like their parents, are essentially powerless, for all their newly-found access to relative material prosperity. Their powerlessness is reflected in their collective amnesia, their unknowingness of the history of their conditions and even more in their uncertainty as to their future. No wonder that fashionability, hedonism and a desperate individualism serve as substitutes for a securely held morality. Hoggart's working-class family is romantically remote now.

Of course, they were never church or chapel attenders in substantial proportions but, if I may quote him:

> They believe, first, in the purposiveness of life. Life has a meaning, must have a meaning. One does not bother much about defining it, or pursue abstract questions as to its nature or the implications which follow from such a conclusion: 'We're 'ere for a purpose', they say, or, 'There must be some purpose or we wouldn't be 'ere.' And that there is a purpose presupposes that there must be a God. They hold to what G. K. Chesterton called 'the dumb certainties of existence', and Reinhold Niebuhr, 'primary religion'. Equally simply, they hold to what George Orwell called 'those things (like free-will and the existence of the individual) which we know to be so, though all the arguments are against them'.
>
> [Richard Hoggart, *The Uses of Literacy*, p. 95.]

Since Hoggart wrote, I suspect that, not only the eclipse of church and chapel, but also two changes in the typical position of married women – their reduced fertility and their sharply increased rate of paid employment – have been of greater moment in changing the character of the learning process among children than all the expansion and reorganisation of schools which has gone on since the 1944 Act.

In short, a weakening of the bond between parent and child is a fundamental and paradoxical part of the so-called century of the child. From one point of view this may be seen in the growing power of public authorities to over-ride the traditional rights of parents over children, albeit justified in the name of ever-rising standards of child care. Standards belong to experts. From another point of view, the weakening bond is seen in child-avoidance by adults. This was, of course, always the way of the rich down the ages through such bodies as house-slaves, nannies, tutors and (in this context aptly named) public schools. Characteristically now it takes the form, in middle-class districts, of an endless round of parties and play activities which in effect share out the stint of child-minding on an informal rota system, releasing the other mothers. In the working-class, as Brian Jackson keeps reminding us, the child-minding industry has become an essential adjunct of recognised women's employment, punitively contained by a public administration in the vain hope that it will somehow go away. From another point of view the parent and the teacher tacitly conspire to retreat from the harsh realities of their own lack of confidence to leave the children corralled before the television set. And later adolescents are given up to their peer-group activities in segregated territories which they increasingly monopolise, such as the disco, the football terrace, the student union and the pop music festival.

These age-segregated phenomena are surely what the Martian anthropologist would pick out as the significant features of a modern urban upbringing and that is what Callaghan's debate should be about.

But, you may object, this is all strange talk from one who has stridently and tediously over a quarter of a century clamoured for educational expansion, the abolition of private schooling and the development of comprehensives. What has it all to do with my faith in democracy as the principal source of traditional authority? And is it not all these things which have brought us to the mess I have described? Well, certainly this is what the *Black Papers* would have us all believe. But their answer is an impossible plea for return to the class tradition. A better and a practical answer lies in understanding the democratic tradition to which I have pointed in all three of these talks.

In a pure class society it is, or was, material capital which differentiated the classes and education basically served to put a stamp of class culture on fates already decided by class origin. The social reproduction of generations was primarily a transmission of material capital and therefore of its attendant inequality of income and opportunity.

But as our economy slowly developed its technology and gradually complicated its division of labour, that fate of a family's children began to turn more on the successful transmission of cultural rather than material capital. Both still exist, of course, and are partially interchangeable – for example, conspicuously in a private or marketed system of schools. But cultural capital is of increasing importance. It is affirmed and publicly recognised in degrees, certificates and credentials. And it is acquired first and foremost through familial transmission – for example, through knowledge of how to use the public properties of libraries and museums, through elaborated language codes which are indispensable to success at school, through appropriate levels of academic aspiration reinforced in the home, through information about learning or job opportunities.

The result is (just as much in Communist Russia or Capitalist America as in whatever you want to call Britain) that the social reproduction of generations is a reproduction of a hierarchy of cultural capital. This permits considerable mobility for a minority upwards and downwards in the hierarchy but its main feature remains the continuity of familial status between generations.

The remedy for these inequalities lies in wider application of democratic tradition which I have advocated in talking about bureaucracy and authority in the workplace and in local and central administration. We must pursue the democratisation of our cultural institutions and, above all, we must challenge the usurpation of authority by experts (whether they appear as teachers or as administrators) and grant full citizenship to the amateur parents against the professional pedagogues. This is what is meant, for instance, by the community school. Not parent governors as tokens in a ritual but genuine parental and community government of schools.

Families have unequal shares of cultural capital. The remedy is positive discrimination. Not the narrow professionalism of subject-teaching but the immensely more challenging professionalism of support for the family as the fundamentally educative institution and the professionalism which sets out to integrate and orchestrate all the educative influences which are brought to bear on a child inside and outside the school.

The material base for parenthood does not measure up to democratic standards of fairness. It is true that, no thanks to government, babies now tend to be born rather more in the better-off and less in the worse-off houses. Fertility is coming to be positively correlated with family income – a reversal of the previous absurdity. But mothers, and especially working-class mothers, are still at once both the most hard-worked and the least-rewarded members of our working population. They are an essential element of the social division of labour but, unlike nurses, teachers, social workers and the like, are excluded from the paid occupational division of labour. They deserve income commensurate with their service to society and not merely as appurtenances of their husbands. They deserve publicly provided facilities in street child centres and play groups to relieve their isolated labours in raising the under-fives. We should look again at our priorities and redistribute income from outside and, if necessary, inside education to the first educators – the mothers. The family is our best carrier of the basic core curriculum of each new generation. An enlightened social policy should recognize this and define the experts and specialists, the schools and the child services as agents for the support, not the replacement, of family upbringing.

Notes and references

1 Johnson, Paul (1976) *New Statesman*, 3rd September.
2 Lenin, *Selected Works*, vol. II, pp. 447–448, 456.
3 Crossman, R. H. S. (1976) The role of the volunteer in a modern social service. In Halsey, A. H. (ed.) *Traditions of Social Policy*, (Oxford, Basil Blackwell) p. 278.
4 Dennis, N. (1970) *People and Planning* (London, Faber); (1972) *Public Participation and Planners' Blight* (London, Faber).
5 Crossman, R. H. S., *loc. cit.*, p. 268.

7 Power and participation

Vernon Bogdanor

Source: 'Power and participation', *Oxford Review of Education*, 5(2): 157–168, 1979.

The balance of power in education

The Education Act of 1944 created an educational system comprising "a complex web of interdependent relationships among the manifold participants"—central government and local authorities, politicians and officials, teachers and inspectors, schools and parents. If Sir Toby Weaver is correct in arguing that "The mode and degree of participation of the different interests varies with the issues involved",[1] then it makes no sense to argue about the degree of influence of each of the policy-making agents *in vacuo*. The 'efficient secret' of the system, to adapt Bagehot, was that no *one* individual participant should enjoy a monopoly of power in the decision-making process. Power over the distribution of resources, over the organisation and over the content of education was to be diffused amongst the different elements and no one of them was to be given a controlling voice.

Such a structure securing a 'balance' between the different interèsts involved was, for Lord Alexander, "the envy of the world".[2] It offered clear and obvious advantages not only for the administrator concerned with the efficient working of the system but also for the liberal, anxious to avoid the concentration of power and the pluralist, insistent that different interests are properly represented. For parallel to the formal relationships between central and local government, embodied in statute and convention, there grew up a network of professional communities whose role it was to soften the political antagonisms which might otherwise render the system unworkable. The process through which particular interest groups (such as the National Association of Schoolmasters or the National Union of Students), became legitimate and thus eligible for consultation, was admittedly one of the more arcane mysteries of British public administration: but it did ensure that the major interests involved in policy-making were consulted before decisions were taken. If the result of such consultation has become in recent years less the creation of an educational consensus, than a babble of discordant voices, that, perhaps, has less to do with the intrinsic weakness of the process of consultation, than with wider factors serving to undermine the consensus. What could at least be said for the structure of educational policy-making was that, if an incipient consensus *did* exist, the process of consultation would ensure that it was actualised.

A corollary of the representative nature of the system was that decisions took longer to reach than would have been the case in a more centralised structure. Indeed, few policy initiatives in education can be carried out within the lifetime of a single parliament, and it is a misconception of the role of the Secretary of State for Education and Science to imagine that he or she can lay down policy by fiat. Educational institutions have an "organic nature ... which even the omni-competence of Parliament cannot force into conformity with the electoral timetable".[3] But, in exchange for the delays which could prove so frustrating to the reformer, the system at its best gave rise to a process of mutual accommodation which, for that very reason, ensured a greater degree of legitimacy than decisions taken by executive fiat. The diffused structure of decision-making led, it could be argued, to better decisions because it ensured a wide basis of agreement before changes were made.

Obviously different views are possible as to how well this system worked since 1944, although it would not be unduly controversial to claim that it was accorded general approval until the end of the 1960s, and has come under continual and growing criticism since. But before outlining and evaluating these criticisms, it is essential to look at the *presuppositions* behind the structure of educational decision-making to see how they have been eroded.

Within a system of diffused decision-making, accountability is ensured not through confining responsibility for decisions within watertight institutional compartments, but through a system of checks and balances. No doubt each actor within the system would seek to extend his influence through a process of aggrandisement, but he would find himself checked by an opposed interest, and a pattern of constraints would be developed resulting in a balance of power. The precise balance, of course, would differ from issue to issue, but it would in each case be based upon a willingness to compromise in the broader interest of educational advance. "A large consensus on a second best solution is preferred to an assumed optimum obtained under duress".[4] Were any element in the system to seek to use its formal powers to the full, the system could not work. Mutual restraint, as in the Hobbesian universe, is the precondition of success, and the war of all against all would make progress in education impossible.

Central–local relations

There must, therefore, be limits upon the degree of politicisation in the education service if it is to operate successfully. It is clearly impossible for the basic structure of education to be altered every time there is a change of political control at either central or local level. It is undesirable for either the Secretary of State for Education and Science or a local education authority to insist upon its prerogatives in the face of the political opposition of the other. Moreover, given the long time-scale of major educational policies and the need for some degree of continuity, the civil service is bound to have a greater impact upon the process of decision-making in the DES than in many other Whitehall departments. Civil servants, therefore, were "the guardians of consensus" in education. Since the war, the average spell in office of the minister responsible for education has been a little under two years, and this is hardly long enough to make a continuing impact on policy in the face of the continuity of civil service attitudes. In local authorities, the chairmen of education committees frequently enjoy a longer period of tenure, but nevertheless it is remarkable that innovations in education tend to be associated with Chief Education Officers—with Mason of Leicestershire, Clegg of the West Riding, Ralphs of Norfolk or Newsom of Hertfordshire—rather than with their committee chairmen.

In the immediate post-war years, the danger of conflict between central and local government was alleviated by the fact that local authorities themselves were so much less politicised than they have since become. In rural areas, especially, many local authorities were dominated by Independents—there was, it was held, no Labour or Conservative method of running schools, local health services or emptying dustbins. As late as 1970, over one-third—21—out of the 58 county councils in England and Wales outside London were controlled by Independents. Even where local authorities were under party control, the style of government displayed many of the features of the consensus model. The links between the central party organisations and their local counterparts seemed less powerful, and local authorities whose political complexion was different from that of the government of the day did not seek to coordinate policy with the Opposition to inflict 'defeats' upon the Government. Similarly, the government seemed less constrained by its grass-roots supporters to ensure that it in turn was not 'defeated' by local authorities. The style was consensual with the implication that there was a clear path of educational advance which could be discerned by any sensible person of goodwill whether his policies were of the Right or the Left.

This approach of minimising political conflict was greatly helped by the climate of educational expansion after 1944, and the broad satisfaction which it engendered until the end of the 1960s. When there are financial resources for expansion, conflict is likely to be less severe, since each interest can secure a share of what is available. Expansion, moreover, engendered optimism. The inflationist, as Harold Macmillan has recently reminded us, is the optimist, while the deflationist is the pessimist. Accompanying this optimism, there was what must appear in retrospect as an extraordinary confidence in the ameliorative effects of education, a confidence which reached its apogee in Anthony Crosland's (1956) *The Future of Socialism* in which educational reform, rather than public ownership or other economic measures, was seen as the key to the attainment of a socialist society. Education could be seen as a countervailing force to the selfish commercialism which allegedly lay behind the affluent society of the 1950s, and the teacher was, in Jean Floud's words, a "missionary in the slums" and a "*crusader* in the suburb".[6] Faced with so exalted a conception of their role, it would have required, surely, a very querulous teacher or educationalist to question the beneficent legacy of the Education Act of 1944, and the balance of power which resulted from it.

The balance undermined

A number of factors can be isolated as being responsible for current disenchantment with this legacy. The first is the feeling that whatever the benefits of the distribution of power in education from the point of view of pluralist theory, the education system has simply failed to make a sufficient contribution to the achievement of national objectives. The litany of accusations made against the schools for failing to produce a sufficient number of literate, numerate and technically qualified young people, is too familiar to bear repetition, and can perhaps best be summarised in Mr Callaghan's claim in his Ruskin College speech of October 1976, launching the 'Great Debate', that teachers had not satisfied parents and industry that "what you are doing meets their requirements and the needs of their children". Since that speech, the participants in the education system have found themselves on the defensive, unsure of whether they can rely upon public support, and confused about what it is that they are supposed to do.

The uncertainty has been compounded, of course, by the shortage of financial resources. It is generally accepted that the period of expansion in educational expenditure ended (paradoxically enough) when Mrs Thatcher left the DES; and further expansion is unlikely not only for the demographic reasons mentioned by Stuart Maclure, and the need for economy in public spending, but also because education, as compared to, for example, health is not seen as having a priority claim on such limited resources as may be available. Educationalists have become scapegoats rather than crusaders.

Concern for the achievement of national objectives, together with the need for financial retrenchment, has brought into question the central/local division of responsibility in education. If the schools are failing to produce pupils able to cope with the exigencies of technological change, perhaps the fault lies with the failure of central government to establish and monitor national standards of achievement, and the abdication by central government from involvement with curricular issues. If the colleges of further education and the polytechnics are not producing sufficient technicians to cope with the problems of modern industry, perhaps the fault lies with central government for failing to provide machinery to ensure that agreed national objectives can actually be implemented. This is the kind of criticism that has come increasingly to be heard from those anxious as to whether a structure of diffused responsibility is still appropriate for an advanced but stagnating industrial society.

The need to control public expenditure has also served to undermine belief in local autonomy. From the point of view of the Treasury, the independent taxing powers enjoyed by local authorities constitute a loophole in the system of control: and it can be argued that, with resources severely limited, there can be no real scope for local autonomy, and that greater reliance upon central government is needed to ensure that the taxpayer is getting value for money. If it is agreed that there should be a clearer definition of priorities in the education service, then, it may be argued, what agent other than the DES is capable of laying down these priorities? Questions such as these are bound to be raised with increasing insistence unless and until there is a radical change in the economic environment faced by governments.

From this standpoint, then, the very merits of the 1944 Act come to be seen in a very different light. For what from one perspective is a pluralist system of government, controlled by an intricate and informal machinery of checks and balances, can also seem to be a system in which accountability is so blurred that, in the final resort, it becomes difficult to ascribe responsibility for failure to any particular element of it. Where constitutional arrangements establish a clear demarcation of powers and division of responsibilities, the aggrieved citizen knows where to direct his complaint; but where, as in education, the system operates through a complex inter-governmental network, the scope for shuffling off responsibility—or, in less elegant language 'passing the buck'—must be very great.

Current arrangements for financing the activities of local government add enormously, of course, to the blurring of responsibility, for in the post-war period the allocation of functions to local authorities and the pattern of public finance have come to be increasingly divorced from each other. This has meant that although local authorities are in theory given very wide responsibilities in areas such as education, housing and the social services, in practice their powers are circumscribed by dependence upon central government for funds. The key factor in the life of the local authority becomes not its standing with its local electorate, but its relationship to Whitehall, and in particular how much money it can squeeze out of the Cabinet in the annual rate support grant negotiations. For it is upon the degree of success of the local authority as a pressure group upon Whitehall, rather than the quality of its management of resources, that improvement in local services primarily depend. Moreover, the rate support grant negotiations through their very nature serve to weaken the role of local councillors *vis-a-vis* civil servants and local government officers, since two noticeable features of these negotiations are their secrecy and the lack of any involvement of elected members until the very last stage.

The Report of the Layfield Committee on local government finance is commonly regarded as having advocated greater autonomy in place of creeping centralisation. But that is not a wholly accurate interpretation of the Committee's position. For the argument was that *first*, a choice had to be made as to whether a more centralised or a more localised system was desirable; and *then* a structure of finance had to be developed to sustain the chosen allocation of responsibilities; rather than, as at present, the financial structure pre-empting political choices.

Characteristically perhaps, central government has avoided the challenge posed by Layfield. In the Green Paper, *Local Government Finance* (Cmnd. 6813, May 1977), Layfield's proposal of a local income tax to buttress local autonomy was rejected, but the government did not have the courage of its convictions to advocate a wholly centralist solution either. Instead it proposed that a unitary grant, based upon the unit cost of providing local services, might replace the rate support grant. This proposal, although clothed in the rhetoric of 'partnership' would in reality make for greater central control, since the unit allocation on local authority services would be decided by central government using indicators of local authority need. This would intensify the trend towards a common pattern of local authority spending, since authorities which spent more than the unit allocation would be under pressure to economise, while those which spent less would be urged to raise spending to common standards decided nationally. It is not necessary to argue that the trend towards greater centralisation is necessarily mistaken—although a strong case could be made out that it is—but only that if centralisation is desirable, it should come about as the result of a political decision, and not as a by-product of financial constraints. It is in this area above all that a clarification of responsibilities and objectives is most urgent.

Such a clarification would be of considerable benefit to the education service, and especially to local education authorities. Because existing financial arrangements obscure the true location of responsibility, governments have been able to announce education policies without providing the resources needed for their implementation. This has created false expectations amongst voters, and the disillusionment when it comes tends to be directed towards local authorities who bear the odium for failure. The most striking recent example of such a pattern lies in the Education Act of 1976, requiring local authorities to organise their secondary schools along comprehensive lines, but without providing the financial resources to ensure success. It is extremely doubtful whether anything but makeshift schemes could have been undertaken within this constraint. Education, then, can benefit more than other local authority services from the principle enunciated by the Layfield Committee that "whoever is responsible for spending money should also be responsible for raising it so that the amount of expenditure is subject to democratic control".[7]

The participation of interests

The balance created by the 1944 Act can be seen, therefore, to have been a precarious one. It has been threatened not only by external pressures arising from Britain's parlous economic condition and the shortage of resources for the public services, but also by pressures internal to the education system itself. In particular, the move towards greater participation in education has done much to undermine traditional arrangements. For the system of consultation worked best, when only a small number of interests were involved whose rank and file were content to defer to elites, and could, therefore, be relied upon to act 'sensibly'. This process of elite accommodation reached its apogee during the post-war period when, so it was believed, many policy decisions in education were taken over lunch at the National Liberal Club by a troika consisting of Sir William Alexander, Secretary of the Association of Education Committees, Sir Ronald Gould, the General Secretary of the NUT and the Permanent Secretary at the Department of Education. If these three agreed on some item of educational policy, it would, more often than not, be implemented. Such at least was the general belief and, even if it was a caricature, it is at least significant that it was widely held.

The demand for participation has, as Maurice Kogan has reminded us, at least two faces. First, there is the demand for greater control by the *client*—the parent—and, secondly, the demand for greater participation by the professional—the teacher. The first demand gives rise to the risk of schools being dominated by the parochial interests of the consumer, while the second exposes the education service to the risk of the system being undermined by a form of self-interested syndicalism which has little to do with the true aims of the education.[8] Indeed a hostile observer of the activities of the teachers' associations might be tempted to correlate their rise to influence with a marked decline of the professional ethic, so that these associations have become able to subordinate the interests of the education to their own corporate convenience. "Teacher control", it has been said, "has too often meant control by cohorts of teachers more involved in the politics of associations and unions than in the work of the classroom".[9] Indeed self-interested syndicalism may have reached its zenith when two spokesmen for the teachers' associations confessed themselves unable to distinguish between the self-interest of their members, and the needs of education, in their comments made to the Expenditure Committee

Every improvement in teachers' conditions is inevitably an improvement in the education of children in our schools. Equally every improvement in educational conditions within schools improves teachers' conditions. The two things go together like that."
(Mr Max Morris, Ex-President of the National Union of Teachers.)

One tends to look at educational problems from what seems to me to be a very rational point of view, that the interests of teachers in the end are completely consonant with the interests of the education service.
(Mr Terry Casey, General Secretary of the National Association of Schoolmasters.)[10]

It is likely, however, that the growth in the power of the various interest groups has already reached its peak, and their influence is likely to decline sharply in the years to come. The increase in the number of the interest groups has itself served to limit their power, since there is bound to be more difficulty in securing a consensus amongst a multiplicity of groups than amongst a cosily delimited network; and where there is no consensus amongst the different voices, government cannot evade the responsibility of making a judgment as to the relative weight to place upon their different submissions.

Neither is a period of contraction favourable to the aggrandisement of interest group power. When the system is expanding, the interests are only too glad to propose priorities for extra expenditure; but when economies are being made, the response of any group asked to suggest items of expenditure which might be redundant, is likely to be a pained insistence that everything is essential; and that is not very helpful to the policy-maker. Moreover, economic uncertainties often mean that the decision to retrench has to be taken at extremely short notice so that there is no time to consult the interests affected. The consensus of the immediate post-war period may well have presupposed a rather longer time-scale during which policy was formulated; in less leisured times, the system is bound to become more autocratic.

The driving force behind the 'Great Debate' was, unquestionably, a determination to make the education service more publicly accountable by rescuing the DES from the departmentalism which threatened to engulf it. The DES, so it was alleged, had become a ministry which was "*responsive* rather than either controlling or initiating".[11] Influence over the curriculum and over examinations had been wrongly delegated to the Schools Council, which, dominated as it was by the teachers' associations, had been unable to evolve a coherent policy on examinations which could secure general approval. The multiplicity of interests in the education system had so diffused the power of veto that the public interest, as represented by the formal institutions of parliamentary government, found it difficult to gain expression. "It is ironic", the Expenditure Committee commented, "that it should have seemed natural that, in defending its record of consulting interest groups, the DES made no mention of Parliament, the group with the widest range of interests of all. The elected representatives of the people may ask questions of the DES or speak in debates on education but they are never consulted".[12]

The government of education had become a system of pluralism run mad, and it was difficult even for the hardened professional, let alone the informed citizen, to determine where responsibility for particular decisions lay. A corporate system of government had come to be increasingly out of harmony with the system of representative democracy which it was intended to complement.

The history of the relationships between the DES and the other agents of educational policy-making since the beginning of the Great Debate, can be understood very largely in terms of the reassertion of the public interest against the partial interests which had arrogated themselves the right to decide the aims and purposes of the education system. The 1980s will show how the insertion of the public interest into the existing pattern of educational government, modifies current institutional arrangements.

Parent power

The demand for greater participation by the client in the education service has been a further intrusive element in the system. The 1970s have seen the claims of 'parent power', the demand by parents or, perhaps more accurately, of a small and possibly unrepresentative section of parental opinion, for representation within the system. That parents be given a powerful voice on the governing bodies of schools, has been a central objective and it was supported both by the Taylor Committee of Inquiry into the government and management of schools, and by the Labour Government in 1978, and the Conservative Opposition, which both accepted the Committee's proposals. In fact, however, the implementation of these proposals would create governing bodies perhaps more representative of parental opinion, and certainly more powerful, but lacking any genuine accountability. For financial responsibility will remain with the elective institutions of government, and it will be impossible for governing bodies to make sensible decisions on the curriculum or internal organisation of schools, without also being aware of, and accountable for, their financial implications. How, for example, would it be possible for school governors to support the introduction of Nuffield Science without enjoying the power to finance the required expenditure? The post-Taylor governing body will be in a curious position *vis-à-vis* its local education authority, and far from securing a clarification of the role of professional, elected and lay members in the education service, the likelihood is that chains of accountability will become entangled, and responsibility for what

actually occurs in schools will be obscured. The governing bodies themselves are likely to become heavily politicised, and the parental places
might well become prey to control by highly unrepresentative minority
groups with the time and ability to organise on a scale beyond the scope of
many parents. Indeed one objection to the Taylor proposals may be
couched in a similar form to Oscar Wilde's objection to socialism, namely
that it would take up too many evenings!

For it is, in the last resort, questionable whether parents *qua* parents
have interests in the education system separate from their interests as citizens represented by Parliament and by local authorities, or whether the
urge to participate can be so intense as to sustain for long parents who do
not belong to any other organised interest. In any case, it is probably a
misinterpretation to regard parental pressures as being demands for participation, rather than complaints about the quality of education offered by
the schools, coupled with the desire to exercise greater freedom of choice
in education. For participation, as Sir Isaiah Berlin has so trenchantly
reminded us, is not the same as freedom of choice, and only confusion can
follow from equating the two.[13]

Monitoring

If the anxieties of parents *qua* citizens, as opposed to the anxieties of
parents *qua* activists, are to be satisfied, it must be by ensuring that the
quality of education is improved. The Bullock Report on standards of literacy showed how extraordinarily difficult it was even to evaluate, let alone
improve, the performance of the schools. Nevertheless, unless and until
satisfactory indicators of performance are developed, a great deal of educational discussion will resemble argument in a vacuum between ignorant
armies which clash by night. For, as Maurice Peston has argued, "It seems
... absurd that we rely on *ad hoc* studies and are still in 1976 having some
debate as to whether literacy is going up or down when it is simply a
matter of spending some resources to engage in a continuing monitoring
picture".[14]

The DES was, of course, not alone among Whitehall departments in
being more concerned with the quantity of resources put into the service
for which it was responsible, rather than with the quality of the service
itself. Indeed the very sophistication of the PESC machinery for deciding
upon the allocation of resources, tended to concentrate attention upon
'inputs' rather than 'outputs'. So intense was the battle for extra resources,
so exhausting the struggle that, after it was over, the temptation was to
avoid the question of whether the resources which had been so hardly won
were actually being put to good use, or whether governmental programmes were really yielding the results which their protagonists had so
confidently predicted.

The Assessment of Performance Unit (APU) offers only a partial remedy for these ills. For its concern is with the measurement of national changes in the performance of pupils from year to year. It will not test either individual pupils or individual schools, and therefore it cannot monitor the progress of individual pupils, nor can it contribute to the evaluation of different types of school. Yet these were precisely the areas of concern which led to the public pressure for monitoring. It is likely that this pressure will continue and intensify, so that the APU will be forced to expand its remit. Future generations will find it difficult to understand how governments could spend £8 billion pounds a year on education while being so little interested in whether this vast sum was being well spent.

Central/local relations in the 1980s

The DES response to 'The Great Debate' was to insist upon the need for more centralised control in education. In a confidential document, leaked a few days before Mr Callaghan's speech inaugurating the Debate, and known, from the colour of its cover, as the 'Yellow Book', the Prime Minister was urged to make "an authoritative pronouncement on the division of responsibility for what goes on in schools suggesting that the Department should give a firmer lead". Indeed, the combination of the circular 14/77 enquiry into curriculum control, the introduction of APU, the 1976 Education Act and increased control over local authority expenditure, are all serving to concentrate power at the centre.

Moreover in the 1980s such educational expansion as there is, will probably occur in the spheres whose importance for the national economy is only now being fully recognised—day-release and part-time education for school-leavers who lose all contact with education at 16, adult education and retraining—and these developments may require a greater degree of central direction than the education service has hitherto been accustomed to. It may be argued that in these areas of policy there is greater need for specific grants to local authorities, rather than funding through the rate support grant machinery, to ensure that local authorities actually implement new programmes; it may even be argued that local authorities are not the appropriate bodies to initiate programmes of so wide a scope and importance, and that they should therefore be administered directly from the centre. This would, of course, involve a significant weakening in the responsibilities of local authorities in post-school education.

Whether increasing centralisation is seen as something to be welcomed or deplored, it is likely to cause serious problems for the education service. For it could plausibly be argued that the DES is already a prime victim of governmental 'overload', of having so wide a range of diverse responsibilities, that it has become almost impossible for it to plan effectively for the future. If the DES is to take on new responsibilities, the question of the devolution of some of its powers to local authorities is bound to take on new urgency. It will become necessary to scrutinise very carefully the whole range of departmental regulations, and to ask which of them are strictly necessary, and which could with advantage be removed, trusting to the good sense and public spirit of local authorities to ensure that services do not fall below an acceptable standard. Such a course might appear especially reasonable at a time when stronger education authorities have been created as a result of local government reorganisation, authorities well able to discharge some of the regulatory and supervisory tasks hitherto undertaken by the DES. Indeed, one of the central arguments for local government reorganisation was precisely that the newly created authorities would be powerful enough to render much central supervision unnecessary. A clarification and re-assessment of central/local relations is therefore badly needed, and could be of great benefit to the education service, For if educational policy is to become more effective in the 1980s, "the main desideratum" "... in relation not only to long term educational policy but public administration in general, ... is general reform of the machinery of government so that ministers and senior civil servants have more time for systematic thought and discussion on the matters for which they are responsible".[15]

Such a clarification of relationships may, however, prove increasingly difficult to achieve in the face of the politicisation of local authorities. The reorganisation of local government in 1974 gave a tremendous impetus to the growth of party politics in local government, and of the 21 county councils which, before reorganisation, were controlled by Independents, only five have resisted the head-long rush to organisation along party lines. The traditional rural style of local politics—characterised by an authority dominated by Independents with few contested elections—has been overcome by the expansion of the county borough style of local politics, with local elections being fought on party lines, and the authority being organised to reflect party divisions. At the same time, the traditional rural elites, the 'social leaders' whose election to the council was but a reflection of their status in the community, have been replaced by 'public persons' whose status is acquired only through election to the council.[16]

The greater dominance of party politics in local government may have beneficial effects in education, in that a set of aspirations can only be transformed into a policy through the medium of a political party. But there can be little doubt that there will be, as a result, great strains in the relationships between the DES and local education authorities. The links between the central organisation of the political parties and their local offshoots may become closer, so that local authorities may be encouraged to resist the government of the day when that government is of a different political colouring. The recourse of the Labour government to the law in the Tameside case in 1976 was "A sure indication of the break-up of consensus ..."[17] since the 1944 Education Act had presupposed that central and local government could work together in education in comparative harmony. The DES was not given strong formal powers to secure the implementation of its policies, precisely because it was assumed that both central government and local education authorities were managed by men of goodwill whose main concern was to improve the service, and whose reflective judgments remained untainted by the intrusion of party ideology. Such an assumption can hardly be made any longer.

The government's response to signs of increasing divergence between central departments and local authorities, has been to establish formal consultative machinery in an attempt to limit the damage. Yet the new machinery can hardly be said to have improved matters significantly. CLEA (The Council of Local Education Authorities) has not proved itself to be a powerful body, and it has been overshadowed by the Consultative Council on Local Government Finance. Yet the Consultative Council is not a body designed to secure consensus between two different branches of government; its function is rather to secure the acquiescence of local authorities in the distribution of rate support grant. Local authorities do not, in practice, have very much influence over the distribution of grant, which remains a matter for the Cabinet. So, even if the form of the machinery is consultative, the spirit remains centralist.

If, therefore, the greater politicisation of local government is not to lead to an unhealthy polarisation of view in education, it will be necessary for both central government and local authorities to be more aware of each other's problems, and to show a sense of self-restraint in pressing their respective claims. For this purpose, it might well be desirable to secure the establishment of some genuinely inter-locking machinery, such as a Select Committee of the House of Commons on Local Government, on which members of local authorities, as well as MPs, would sit, to discuss common problems; perhaps, governments would be willing to consult such a Committee before introducing legislation which affected the functions and powers of local authorities, so that they could be made aware of the consequences of such legislation upon local government.

The development of the European Community, and the increasingly complex problems of bargaining and negotiation at an inter-governmental level, makes the construction of institutional links between different layers of government a matter of growing importance. For educational progress depends upon central government and local authorities seeing their roles not as independent, but as *inter-dependent* providers of public resources. The success of education policy in the 1980s will depend, to no small degree, upon whether these two arms of government can work together in tact and harmony, rather than engaging in an unseemly squabble over the division of political spoils. But such tact and harmony are perhaps less likely to be displayed in a system which is suffering from the pains of contraction, than in the expanding system of the post-war period.

Conclusions

It is perhaps not too fanciful to see educational policy-making in dialectical terms, as an attempt to resolve conflict between different partial interests so as to secure the greater good of the education service as a whole. Different institutional interests—central and local, professional and lay—legitimately conflict, but, until recently at least, it could have been argued that such conflict played a positive role in the striving for agreement. If one is bound now to register a less confident verdict, it is surely because social and economic developments have led to a confusion of roles, and to a situation in which many of those whose task it is to manage the system no longer know what is expected of them. It may be that such confusion can only be dissipated through a new Education Act clarifying the roles of the various participants in the system for, without new legislation, it is difficult to see how new role patterns compatible with the stability of the education system, can be expected to develop. Governments in peacetime are, however, unwilling to submit themselves to the exercise of self-criticism which such clarification would involve, and it is probable that they will attempt to muddle on within a structure which was developed for a form of society that has now passed away.

One consequence of this muddling through, is that it is proving increasingly difficult to "develop deliberative institutions which can sustain a line of policy over a period of time".[18] Our political institutions, far from encouraging consensus, militate against it; and perhaps the confusion of responsibility in educational policy-making is, in large part, a reflection of the decaying state of our political and constitutional structure. If that is the case, then we will be unable to resume the smooth progress of educational advance until our political system offers less hostages to the rigours of adversary politics; any consideration of the problems likely to be faced by education in the 1980s must conclude that they cannot be solved without reference to issues of political and indeed constitutional organisation.

Such a conclusion itself raises the important question of how, in a pluralist society, there can be a place for the politics of agreement, so that a consensus can be secured on central social objectives broad enough to sustain an attack upon the educational problems of the 1980s. Pluralism and diversity are in themselves strengths and not weaknesses, and the traditional ethos of British education has recognised, in a quite admirable way, the importance of giving to individuals and to educational institutions the freedom to develop their contribution to social objectives in the way they think best. The problem now is to ensure that a tighter framework of central control does not undermine autonomous sources of progress in society, and that the framework itself is such as to make possible the achievement of agreed national aims.[19] That problem is one that faces all democracies, and not just this country; but other democracies have attempted to solve these problems with rather more energy and imagination than this country has latterly shown; and the record of successive governments in recent years does not inspire confidence that they will rise to the level of the challenges that are involved. Our educational malaise is but a symptom and not a cause of more fundamental problems in the British economy and society, and one can only hope that, through a reassertion of national will, we recover the energies which sustained the framers of the Education Acts of 1870, 1902 and 1944.

Notes and references

1 Sir Toby Weaver: Tenth Report from the Expenditure Committee 1975–76: Policy Making in the Department of Education and Science (HC 621), p. 379, paras 2 & 4 (afterwards cited as HC 621).
2 HC 621, p. 267, para. 857.
3 Memorandum by Stuart Maclure, HC 621, p. 30.
4 OECD (1975) *Educational Development Strategy in England and Wales* (Paris), p. 27.
5 Davies, Bryan, MP HC 621, p. 274, para. 901.
6 Eloud, Jean (1962) 'The teacher in the affluent society,' *British Journal of Sociology*, 13, 305.
7 Committee on Local Government Finance (Cmnd. 6453) 1976, Chap. 15, p. 283, para. 2.
8 Kogan, Maurice (1978) *The Politics of Educational Change* (London, Fontana), p. 71.
9 Judge, Harry (1974) *School is Not Yet Dead* (London, Longman), p. 31.
10 HC 621, p. 141, para. 509; p. 223, para. 755.
11 Memorandum by Dr Halsey, HC 621, p. 191, para. 2.
12 HC 621, Report, p. xxxiv, para. 98.
13 Berlin, Sir Isaiah (1969) Two concepts of liberty. In: *Four Essays on Liberty* (Oxford University Press).
14 HC 621, pp. 206–7, para. 708.
15 Memorandum by Lord Robbins, HC 621, p. 184.
16 I discussed this theme in my article: Education, politics and the reform of local government, *Oxford Review of Education*, Vol. 2, No. 1, 1976, where I took what now seems to me an over-optimistic view of the effects of the spread of party politics in local government.
17 Kogan, *op. cit.*, p. 86.
18 Memorandum by Stuart Maclure, HC 621, p. 30.
19 I owe this point to Mr W. L. Weinstein who developed it at a meeting of the All Souls Group in the autumn of 1976.

8 The seventy thousand hours that Rutter left out

Anthony Heath and Peter Clifford

Source: 'The seventy thousand hours that Rutter left out', *Oxford Review of Education*, 6(1):3–19, 1980.

A visitor to a number of Inner London secondary schools will come away with strong impressions. Even in this relatively small geographical area there will be wide differences between schools, not only in the standards of behaviour and level of attainment of the pupils but also in the general appearance of the pupils and the attitudes and work habits of the staff. After some reflection the visitor might argue as follows: good behaviour and high levels of attainment are found mainly in schools which appear to be neat and orderly, so a neat and orderly appearance must be a good thing; if all schools could be given this appearance, our visitor might conclude, there would be a general raising of educational standards.

We can easily imagine the reception our visitor's argument would be given if he were to propound it in the staff room. There would be a heated discussion and the staff would raise some powerful objections which would leave the visitor shaken if not wholly contrite. What Rutter and his colleagues have done in their book *Fifteen Thousand Hours*[1] is to formalise the visitor's arguments and to quantify his observations. In essence their theory is that, all other things being equal, bright and clean, well-ordered schools promote the production of well-behaved pupils with high academic attainment. To test such a theory satisfactorily would require a carefully designed experiment in which the staff at a number of schools actually changed their modes of operation and in which the pupils' behaviour was carefully monitored and compared with that in a 'control group' of schools.

Clearly, there are serious technical problems and ethical reservations which would arise with such an experiment (although they are not perhaps quite as daunting as is usually assumed). Rutter and his colleagues decided to avoid the Scylla of experimentation, however, preferring the equally dangerous waters of the Charybdis of statistical analysis. They quantify the qualitative impressions of the casual visitor and then use statistical techniques to assess the relationship between school characteristics and pupil achievements. But quantification only superficially changes the nature of the evidence. The fact that the appearance of the schools and the behaviour of the pupils have been expressed numerically does not alter the fact that only a few schools have been studied; neither does it alleviate doubts about whether differences in intake from school to school have been taken adequately into account. And the fact that an association has been established statistically does nothing to enable us to determine what is cause and what is effect. Do good pupils produce good schools or good schools produce good pupils? The objections of the staff room remain valid. In the present review therefore our role will be to see that such commonsense reservations are not neglected amid the maelstrom of technical arguments and statistical manipulations. But let us first consider in greater detail the claims which Rutter makes.

"Do a child's experiences at school have any effect; does it matter *which* school he goes to; and which are the features of school that matter?" (p. 1).[2] These are the questions which Rutter and his colleagues start with, and as a result of their investigations they felt able to conclude that "the research findings provide a clear 'yes' in response to the first two questions. Schools do indeed have an important impact on children's development and it does matter which school a child attends" (p. 1). They found that the schools studied differed in their 'success'—in their records at 'O' level and the CSE for example—and that these differences persisted even when allowance was made for the differences in their intake. The schools with the best or worst records were not necessarily those with the brightest or socially most advantaged pupils. The implication is therefore that the character of the schools themselves matters too, and Rutter went on to claim that his results "provide strong indications of what are the particular features of school organisation and functioning which make for success" (p. 1).

These features were not physical ones such as the size of the school or the age of its buildings; neither did it matter whether the school was single-sex or co-educational, a state school or a church school. Rather, they were features which in combination gave the impression that the school was run as a 'tight ship'. More successful schools tended to be ones where home-work was set frequently and there was some check on whether teachers really had set it; where lessons started promptly and ran for their full length; where the school was kept clean and tidy and well painted with attractive pictures and furniture in good repair; where there was a generally accepted set of standards for classroom discipline prevalent throughout the school rather than individual teachers being left to establish their own standards; where decisions were made at senior level rather than in the staff room. These are but a sample of the various features of the school which Rutter picks out, and he emphasises that they "were probably less important in their own right than in the part they played in contributing to a broader school ethos or climate of expectations and modes of behaving" (p. 55). The implication is that teachers, by doing the things listed, could help establish a beneficial climate throughout the school as a whole. The climate, then, was not merely a reflection of the attitudes and expectations which the pupils brought to the school but was, at least to some extent, under the direct control of the teachers themselves.

The 'mix' or balance of pupils in the school also affected success, Rutter claimed. Examination success tended to be better in schools with a substantial nucleus of children of at least average ability, and delinquency rates were higher in those with a heavy preponderance of the least able. Rutter is not merely stating the obvious here; he is saying more than that cleverer pupils get better results. He is arguing that the presence of cleverer pupils improves the performance of the others as well.

> The presence of a relatively high concentration of pupils in the upper ability groups may work to the advantage not only of those pupils themselves, but also of their peers. In a similar way, a largely disadvantaged intake might depress outcomes in some cumulative way, over and above the effects of a disadvantaged background on the individual pupil.
>
> (p. 154)

If Rutter and his colleagues are correct in these claims, their book becomes very important indeed. It purports to tell us not only that schools differ—we know that already—but also that schools with *identical* intakes differ in their success, that the factors which make for success or failure are under the control of the staff or administrators, and that a school's record can thus be changed. In that sense it is a very optimistic book. It purports to tell us what we can do if we are to improve our schools. But there is of course another side to the coin. If we accept Rutter, then we have also to accept that schools which fail to change and achieve better results have defaulted: they have not made the efforts that they could, and therefore should, have done. So if Rutter is wrong he may be laying up trouble for schools and teachers that lag behind. The carrot of improved results which he holds out also gives parents, local authorities and governments a stick with which to beat the less successful school. It will not be possible for schools to hide behind the claim that they had to deal with worse areas, lower ability children, apathetic parents, poor buildings or higher teacher turnover. If Rutter is right, these things are by no means all-important. Those things which are under the direct control of teachers and administrators are important too.

But Rutter may be wrong. True, he does put in various caveats. "Firm conclusions about causation can only come from controlled experimental studies", he warns, but he immediately adds that in a non-experimental study such as his own "the *pattern* of statistical associations can nevertheless provide quite good guidance as to whether a relationship is likely to reflect a causal effect" (p. 180) and the implication is that his study does give this good guidance. In any event, one suspects that the casual reader may not pay quite the attention to the caveats that one would wish. In a book which addresses sensitive social and political issues it is important not only to put the caveats in but also to make them sufficiently prominent so that even the reader who wants to believe the conclusions has to take pause for thought. Rutter hardly does this. Indeed, he ends with the confident conclusions that "the results carry the strong implication that schools can do much to foster good behaviour and attainments, and that even in a disadvantaged area, schools can be a force for the good" (p. 205).

Quite aside from the caveats, however, there are serious problems with Rutter's conclusions. We claim that the guidance his statistical associations give is not nearly as good as he implies. We would go further. There are serious doubts about all Rutter's main conclusions. The environment of home and neighbourhood is almost certainly more important than he thinks, the characteristics of the school as a social institution are almost certainly less important, and these characteristics may be much less under the control of the staff than he thinks.

To defend these counter-claims we must examine closely the nature of Rutter's evidence and the statistical manipulations to which he subjects it. Unfortunately, *Fifteen Thousand Hours* is a highly technical book with a great deal of statistical manipulation which makes it very difficult for the non-statistical reader to check Rutter's conclusions. For example, if he wishes to check the basis for the conclusion that a school's academic or ethnic mix is more important than its social class mix, all he has to go on is that G^2 attributable to academic balance groups is 123.46, attributable to ethnic balance groups is 129.81 and attributable to occupational balance groups is 32.88. Even the statistical reader who understands what G^2 attributable to a parameter means is still at a disadvantage for he cannot check to see whether an alternative statistical technique would have produced the same conclusion. Remarkably few raw data from which we could draw our own conclusions are presented in the book, and we are therefore at the mercy of Rutter's choice of techniques. Unfortunately, we have serious doubts about his choice, but before we go on to this let us first look at the data.

Rutter's data come from twelve schools which serve an area of inner London. All were currently non-selective and none had been selective in the past. However, they varied in other respects. Size varied from 450 to 2000 pupils; there were all-boys, all-girls and coeducational schools; there were voluntarily aided (i.e. Church) schools and maintained schools. Information was then collected on certain characteristics of the pupils when they entered the schools, on a huge range of internal features of the schools, and on four measures of outcome.

The characteristics of the intake were obtained from records routinely collected by the ILEA, the ones most often used being the pupils' verbal reasoning scores at the age of 10 and parental occupation—defined as the occupation of the main family 'breadwinner'. Information on the schools, however, was collected by the research team itself and was based partly on their own observations in the classroom, on interviews with senior staff and a proportion of rank-and-file teachers, and on questionnaires administered to the pupils. This was a highly sophisticated and impressive research effort producing a wealth of information about the schools. For the measures of outcome, however, the research group relied largely on existing records as they had with the characteristics of the intake. The four outcomes measured were attendance, academic attainment, delinquency and behaviour. The schools' own records of attendance and of the pupils' performance in the 'O' level, CSE and CEE examinations were used for the first two, the records of the Metropolitan Police Juvenile Bureaux for the third, while only the fourth was based on direct research by the team. They obtained information from the pupil questionnaires and their own classroom observations on twenty-five items such as the number of times a pupil deliberately missed a lesson, how many times he had not worn uniform, the number of broken windows or broken furniture in the school, the amount of graffiti on the walls, and so on. No attempt was made to obtain scores for individual pupils, comparable to their individual scores for the other three outcomes. Instead they obtained the school's average on each item and placed the twelve schools in rank order for each of the twenty-five items. Finally, an overall behaviour score was obtained by averaging each school's positions on the twenty-five rankings. This distinctly complex procedure means that we have come rather a long way from the original data and that the measure becomes hard to interpret. It is certainly not a measure of 'good' and 'bad' pupil behaviour as the layman would understand these concepts. After all, the amount of broken furniture or graffiti will to some extent reflect the efficiency of the cleaners and maintenance staff and conceivably it might even reflect the quality and age of the furniture itself.[3] It is doubtful if it can simply be blamed on the pupils.

The major data-gathering effort thus went into the collection of information about what went on inside the schools. The research on this front was enormously thorough and produced extremely high quality data. At the end of the day the research team must have had a fascinating picture of the internal life of the schools they studied. They constructed a total of 46 'process' measures of what went on inside the schools, and they must have had the information to compile even more had they wished. In comparison the information about what went on outside the schools is sparse and of poorer quality—official records of cautions and convictions, for example, are notoriously fallible guides to children's delinquent activities.[4]

The first major defect of the book, then, is the unequal effort of the research group on the different fronts. While the attention given to what goes on inside the schools is a valuable corrective to earlier studies which focused on out-of-school factors, they stack the cards in favour of the in-school factors simply by finding out so much more about them With only one measure of family background, but forty-six measures of school processes, it is hardly surprising that some aspects of the school turn out to be important. We shall return to this point shortly. A second defect is that the reader is never really given the benefit of the marvellously detailed picture which the research team must have acquired of the twelve schools. It would have been extremely easy, and perhaps more illuminating, to have produced profiles of each of the twelve schools rather than all the correlation coefficients and log-linear analyses. There are all kinds of questions that spring to mind which these profiles might have answered. What was the 'best' school (as measured by the four outcomes) like? Was it a single-sex Church of England voluntary school, oversubscribed by eager parents, with few black children and with a long history of being run as a tight ship? What was the worst school like? Was it clearly the worst on all four outcomes, lagging some way behind the others? And were there any features specific to this one school (assuming there was such a school in the sample) which gave it particularly intractable problems to deal with? Statistical manipulation can often put up a barrier between the reader and data. It can obscure as well as illuminate. If the sample really did contain a few extreme cases while all the others were much of a muchness, it might have been better to give a literary analysis of the few distinctive schools, tracing the origins of their peculiarities in the fashion of the historian or anthropologist, rather than lose their distinctiveness in an array of scales and correlation coefficients. It is important for the social scientist to learn when statistics are not appropriate as well as to use them correctly when they are. However, we must make do with what Rutter has given us, so what we shall now do is go through some of his major claims and examine in more detail their foundations.

> (I) Our investigation clearly showed that secondary schools varied markedly with respect to their pupils' behaviour, attendance, exam success and delinquency. This had been observed before, but the demonstration that these differences remained *even after taking into account differences in their intake* was new. This suggested that, contrary to many views, secondary schools *do* have an important influence on their pupils' behaviour and attainments.
>
> (p. 205)

This is perhaps the most important claim in the book. Everything else becomes suspect if it turns out that Rutter has not taken differences in intake sufficiently into account. If there are characteristics of the intake which other studies have shown to be important but which Rutter ignores, then we cannot be nearly so sure that secondary schools do have an important influence on their pupils' behaviour and attainments. So how does Rutter control for intake?

Consider examination success. Each child has been given a score based on his number and grades of pass in public examinations. His verbal reasoning score at the age of 10 is also available and Rutter uses this to group the children into seven verbal reasoning (VR) groups. Analysis of variance is then used to find the extent to which the children's examination scores vary according to their VR group and school. It turns out (according to table 5.9) that 27% of the variance is explained by VR group, 6.5% by the schools, and the remaining 66.5% remains unexplained.[5] One way to interpret this, quite properly, is that the school a child attends makes very little difference to his prospects in the public examinations included in the measure, that his verbal reasoning score is much more important, but that factors not included in the model at all are doing most of the work. Rutter, however, chooses, also quite properly, to point out the fact that 6.5% of the variance is explained by the schools means that differences remain in the average attainments of pupils at the twelve schools even when we have controlled for their verbal reasoning scores. This is the result which he prefers to emphasise, and it is not perhaps irrelevant to speculate that a Jencks or Eysenck, faced with identical results, might have emphasised quite different aspects. A Jencks might have emphasised that neither verbal reasoning nor school explained much of the variance—and he might have pointed out that there is almost as much variation in the results of pupils at the same school as there is in the sample as a whole. An Eysenck might have emphasised that verbal reasoning was the best of the known predictors—and he could have pointed out that children in the top quarter of the ability range obtained results that were 500% better than those of children in the bottom quarter.[6] But Rutter emphasises that schools nonetheless make a difference—and he points out that the best school's examination results were 71.2% better than would have been expected given the ability of its children, while the worst had results 55.4% worse—"large differences indeed", he says (p. 86). Large differences, like beauty, are very much in the eye of the beholder. Our other two beholders might have seen them rather differently. All three would in some sense have been correct, but it is essential to recognise that none has a monopoly of the truth.

So far Rutter has controlled only for verbal reasoning, but of course there is an enormous sociological literature showing that family background also affects a child's attainment. As we have already mentioned, Rutter's one measure of family background is parental occupation. He groups occupations into three broad categories—professional, managerial and clerical occupations in one category, skilled manual in a second, and semi-skilled, unskilled and unemployed in the third. It is not really a satisfactory classification. The first category is far too broad, and there is plenty of evidence that children from professional and managerial backgrounds have considerably higher educational attainments on average than those from routine clerical origins.[7] By putting these groups in the same category Rutter is simply throwing information away and is rendering his measure of parental occupation a less powerful one than it might be. In the case of parental occupation the use of broad categories would probably not make a great deal of difference to Rutter's results, but his habit of using broad categorisations where finer ones would be perfectly practicable is rather irritating and there is circumstantial evidence later in the book that it does make a difference.

Thus in the case of verbal reasoning Rutter sometimes divides the children's scores into seven groups, but at other times he uses only three, broader, bands. Now, as we have already noted, table 5.9 shows that verbal reasoning, when divided into seven groups, explained 27% of the variance in academic attainment. But, contrarily, table 9.4 shows that verbal reasoning explained only 14%. It is far from clear from Rutter's presentation what accounts for the discrepancy, but one possibility is certainly that he has used different classifications of verbal reasoning in the two tables.[8] The point is a worrying one of course: a crude categorisation will not do as much explanatory work as a finer one, and will leave more scope for other variables to do some apparent work. Thus if children from higher status homes and with higher verbal reasoning scores are more likely to attend some schools rather than others, and if we use crude measures of parental status and verbal reasoning, then we will almost certainly exaggerate the school 'effects' and erroneously attribute to schools 'effects' which really derive from their pupils' social origins and verbal reasoning abilities.[9]

Even more serious than this, however, is the fact that Rutter fails to control for any other aspects of family background. It is commonplace now that parental interest and encouragement affect a child's attainment and that they have important effects even when we have controlled for parental occupation and IQ. After all, while a child may spend 15,000 hours in school, he will probably spend at least another 70,000 hours out of school, and many of these will be spent with his family. We need to put as much effort into capturing the effects of these hours as we do into capturing the effects of those spent at school.

Failure to capture these out of school influences leaves Rutter extremely vulnerable to counter-attack. The dangers can be illustrated easily enough from a variety of post-war studies but for the sake of convenience let us take the material presented in *Origins and Destinations*.[10] The authors of *Origins and Destinations* present estimates of the effect of a variety of home background variables on academic attainment, but let us make do with a relatively simple example that will almost certainly understate the magnitude of the dangers facing Rutter. As our dependent variable let us take the children's school-leaving age (a variable that correlated very highly with examination success). We find that IQ and father's social class together explain 29.9% of the variance of school-leaving age, but if we then add just one more, relatively crude, measure of family background—namely father's education—we can immediately increase the variance explained to 32.9%.[1]

Father's education is at best a very rough proxy for parental interest and encouragement, and there can be little doubt that a more sensitive measure would have increased the variance explained much further. Neither can there be much doubt that the inclusion of similar measures in Rutter's analysis would have increased the variance which he managed to explain in academic attainment or school attendance. As it stands, he simply has not controlled for all the non-school factors which are well known to affect children's school careers. This is clearly going to be important if these omitted factors are themselves correlated with the school attended (as incidently Rutter found parental occupation to be). It means that the variations in examination results which Rutter attributes to schools might in whole or part be truly a consequence of these omitted factors. And since schools explained only 6.5% of the variance, we may not need very much in the way of unmeasured factors to wipe out their apparent effect.

We can again illustrate the point from the material in *Origins and Destinations*. This material by and large relates to the period before comprehensive re-organisation and so what we can do is look at the effect of school type (i.e. independent, grammar, technical and secondary modern) on school-leaving age. Following a similar procedure to Rutter's we find that, once account has been taken of father's social class and pupil's IQ (but ignoring father's education) school type explains 15.4% of the variance in school-leaving age. However, if we take account of father's education as well, the additional variance explained by school type falls to 13.6%.[12] By leaving out father's education, therefore, we would have exaggerated somewhat the importance of schooling. True, we do not wipe it out—far from it. But then the *Origins and Destinations* material suggested that school type had much more effect to start with than schooling did in Rutter's study. Indeed, it would not be altogether outrageous to draw the inference from this that it mattered a great deal in England and Wales in the 1950s and 1960s whether your child went to a grammar school rather than a secondary modern, but that it mattered relatively little in Inner London in the 1970s which of the available comprehensives he attended.

We cannot strictly compare the two studies because the nature of the samples and the data collected differed considerably, but the basic point must surely be true. If Rutter had been able to control more fully for family background, he would have reduced, although not perhaps eliminated, the size of the school effects which he claimed to find. This further means that many of the specific internal features of the schools which he found to be correlated significantly with outcomes after controlling for characteristics of the intake would lose their place. Setting homework, starting lessons promptly, and so on, might turn out to be correlated significantly with outcomes after all. But alas we have no way of anticipating which would be likely to survive the slaughter.

Another equally puzzling omission is that of all mention of primary schools. At least one-half of Rutter's 15,000 hours are actually spent in these schools rather than in the secondary schools which he studied, so they surely warrant some treatment. To a certain extent the primary school which a child attends tells us something about his family background, if only as a geographical measure, and of course it might have some independent influence of its own on a pupil. It would seem to be a simple variable to include in any prediction of a child's performance at secondary school but one which Rutter might find difficult to live with. Let us suppose, for example, that each secondary school has a more or less exclusive set of feeder primary schools; this would mean that the pupils at a given secondary school are distinctive not only by virtue of their attendance at that secondary school but also by virtue of their attendance at the relevant feeder schools. What could we then conclude about the difference in the success rates of the various secondary schools? In short, we have an insuperable problem of identification. If all the children at a given secondary school have had the prior experience of attending a unique set of primary schools, we cannot possibly decide which of the two is responsible for the children's eventual behaviour. To be sure, the problem will not in practice take on quite this extreme form, but it is one that Rutter should surely have faced up to given his title of *Fifteen Thousand Hours*. Moreover, he could easily have collected information on the primary schools which the children did attend, and it would have been no difficult matter to compare the eventual attainments of such children as attended the *same* primary but *different* secondary schools. In this way some leverage at least might have been brought to bear on the problem.

> (II) These differences in outcome between schools were *not* due to such physical factors as the size of the school, the age of the building or the space available; nor were they due to broad differences in administrative status or organisation. It was entirely possible for schools to obtain good outcomes in spite of initially rather unpromising and unprepossessing school premises, and within the context of somewhat differing administrative arrangements.
>
> (p. 178)

Having controlled, as he thought, for differences in intake, Rutter moved on to consider whether the remaining differences between schools could be explained by their physical or administrative arrangements. And he concluded that, having controlled for intake, no significant differences remained between voluntary-aided and local authority maintained schools; between boys', girls' and mixed schools (except in the case of delinquency); between small, medium and large schools; between schools with old and new buildings; between schools which operated streaming, banding or mixed ability teaching. He concluded that these physical and administrative differences "had thus failed to offer any pointers to account for the outcome variations" (p. 105).

There were a number of other negative findings which Rutter also reports, and it is convenient to treat these here too before we move on to his positive results. Thus he claimed that school differences were not simply a product of neighbourhood differences, nor were they significantly associated with 'parental subscription rates'—the proportion of children at a school whose parents had put that school down as their first choice at the time of transfer from primary to secondary school.

With these negative findings Rutter appears to have cleared the ground and left himself free to move on to those factors which actually are significantly associated with outcome. Having dismissed these physical and administrative factors, he then ignores them in all future analyses. But is he right to do so? Other studies have shown that some at least of these factors are important, and Rutter surely needs to be on firm ground before rejecting them. His main criterion throughout for accepting and rejecting hypotheses is the test of significance, and it is of course highly desirable in such a study with a small sample of schools that tests of significance be calculated. However, it is by no means clear that they should be used as the *sole* criterion. Statistical tests should be our guides, not our masters. Thus if other larger samples have shown, for example, that school size has a significant correlation with outcome, and if Rutter then finds from his own small sample that there is a consistent relationship between these two variables—with big schools having better outcomes than medium, and medium than small schools—but one that falls short of statistical significance, he is hardly entitled to conclude that he has 'no pointers' to the factors that account for school differences, and he is hardly entitled to ignore size in his later analyses.

This is important because Rutter does indeed find some consistent, but non-significant, relationships of the kind that could have been anticipated from other material. Thus voluntary-aided schools were found to have better results, on all four measures of outcome, than did the maintained schools. None of the four individual associations between school status and outcome was significant, but the overall pattern in the results is persuasive. Similarly there is a consistent pattern of association between parental subscription rates and outcomes, although none of the four individual associations is significant. In the other cases (school size, split sites, neighbourhood differences, and so on) the patterns are not so clear, but it would certainly seem unwise to reject the hypothesis that school status and parental subscription rates account for some of the differences between schools, and it would seem highly desirable to control for differences in status and subscription rates when investigating the relationship between outcomes and the internal features of the schools (the process variables). Since Rutter also reports a consistent (but non-significant) relationship between subscription rates and school process score, it is at least plausible that correlations between process and outcome would be reduced (perhaps to a non-significant level) once parental subscription rates were properly controlled for. It is surely quite reasonable to speculate that voluntary-aided schools attract more interested and educationally ambitious parents, hence having higher subscription rates, and that they also tend to run a 'tighter' ship with more emphasis on uniforms, homework, lessons starting on time and the like. If this were so, it might be quite wrong to attribute their success to the 'tight ship' style of management; the quality and motivation of their intake might simply provide them with the conditions under which a tight ship can be run without mutiny—the school's *modus operandi* is supported and reinforced by the parents. But Rutter does not seriously consider alternative accounts of this kind.

As in the case of parental occupation, moreover, Rutter stacks the cards against the physical, administrative and ecological aspects of the schools by his use of broad categories. As before, he sometimes groups his data into categories within which there is likely to be considerable variation, thus throwing away information and making it harder to achieve statistically significant results. For example, there is no need to group parental subscription rates—he could quite well obtain 'parental subscription' scores for each of his twelve schools (as he does with all his process variables) and then correlate these scores with the four outcome measures. This would be very easy for him to do, and it would be interesting to see if the results were any closer to significance if he did so.

By far the most important case where his use of broad categories stacks the cards in favour of his preferred hypothesis is the case of neighbourhood differences. Rutter uses a classification devised by the Centre for Environmental Studies to classify the electoral wards in which his sample were resident. Over one-half turn out to come from a single category described as including "a very large amount of low status inner London combining high proportions of multi-occupancy, privately rented accommodation, single non-pensioners, immigrants and women at work" (p. 148). The next largest proportion of the sample came from a category associated with traditional dockland areas "picked out by their very low levels of skill, their high unemployment and their serious overcrowding". It is hardly surprising that Rutter still finds highly significant school differences within these categories. The categories are far too coarse and it would really be rather remarkable if a category which included one-half of the sample was a good predictor of school outcomes. What is needed is a much finer classifications based on a far smaller area than the ward and making more subtle discriminations. We all know of areas or estates within a ward that are relatively 'rough' or 'respectable', and an afternoon with the local police, probation or social services department would surely enable Rutter to get a picture of much smaller areas than the ones he uses. It is something that he could still easily do—and we strongly suspect that if he were to do it, statistically significant variations would be found which did in part account for the school variations.

> (III) The differences between schools in outcome *were* systematically related to their characteristics as social institutions. Factors as varied as the degree of academic emphasis, teacher actions in lessons, the availability of incentives and rewards, good conditions for pupils, and the extent to which children were able to take responsibility were all significantly associated with outcome differences between schools. All of these factors were open to modification by the staff, rather than fixed by external constraints.
>
> (p. 178)

Rutter goes through a long list of these 'process' factors—other ones which he mentions are the emphasis of homework, the display of children's work on the walls, the proportion of lessons ending early. His method here was to obtain a score for the school on each of the process items and then to correlate the schools' rank-order on a given item with their 'adjusted' ranking on each of the four outcome measures. The 'adjustment' is an attempt to take account of the differences in the schools' intakes, and it is obviously of some importance. Unfortunately, Rutter does not describe at all clearly in *Fifteen Thousand Hours* how he set about adjusting the outcome scores, but he apparently proceeded some-what as follows.[13] First, he calculated what the overall relationships were for the sample as a whole between parental occupation, verbal reasoning and the four outcome measures. This gave him four regression equations (one for each outcome) showing how outcome depends on verbal reasoning and parental occupation. He then used these equations to calculate 'expected' outcome scores for each school—these scores tell him what level of outcome would be expected in each school given the parental occupation and verbal reasoning scores of its intake. He can next compare these 'expected' scores with the actual ones, and the difference between the two gives a measure of the school's success. These differences can finally be ranked, and its position in the rank order of differences gives the school's adjusted score.

The need for adjustment is clear. Since parental occupation and verbal reasoning are known to affect outcomes, and since the schools differ in the number of children entering with given ability and parental occupation, a school's unadjusted rank on an outcome must partly reflect the character-istics of its intake. What Rutter wants to do is to revise this rank order so that it reflects how well the school does after the characteristics of its intake have been taken into account.

One obvious drawback with this procedure which we have already emphasised is that it excludes many other characteristics of the intake that ought properly to have been included. But even aside from this there is a serious statistical defect in Rutter's procedure. By basing his 'adjustment equations' on the sample as a whole he is effectively giving more weight to the bigger schools. The schools vary from 450 to 2000 pupils and this means that the adjustment equations will tend to reflect the relationship between outcome and intake characteristics in the bigger schools. This will not of course matter if there are identical relationships in all twelve schools, but Rutter reports that the relationships are not in fact identical (see p. 88). Now if the relationship differs in big and little schools, then the adjustment equations will be an inappropriate basis for calculating 'expected' outcomes for the smaller ones. Rutter needs to give equal weighting to all twelve schools in his adjustment equations, since he needs his adjustments to be equally good in all twelve cases. He accordingly ought to check and revise his adjustments if necessary; it would be interesting to see whether his revised scores lead to any change in the 'adjusted rank orders' and hence in the correlations between process and adjusted outcome scores which he finds statistically to be significant. Since many of his correlations are only barely significant, they might be quite sensitive to small changes in the adjusted scores. For example, with a sample of 12 schools a correlation of 0.5 is needed to obtain a statistically significant result at the 0.5 level; the correlation between adjusted academic outcome and children's work displayed on the wall is a bare 0.5; a small change in the adjusted rank ordering therefore might easily reduce the correlation below the nominal significance level (although equally it might push it up to something beyond 0.5). At any rate we have to regard these statistics as unstable—with a new method of adjustment we might find that a different set of process items were 'significantly' associated with outcome.

These worries about the method of adjustment and the failure to control for relevant intake, area and school characteristics mean that we have to be extremely cautious in drawing any conclusions whatsoever from the analysis of the 46 process items. Even taking them at face value however, and ignoring these problems, they are rather worrying. The behaviour outcome is the most so, since there is a strong risk of circularity in the correlations. For example, school decorations and care of buildings correlates significantly with behaviour (and has low or negligible correlations with the other outcomes), but the amount of graffiti observed on school walls was itself one of the components of the behaviour scale. Also with some of the process items there is a strong risk that the direction of causation is the opposite of the one Rutter prefers. Thus behaviour correlates significantly and consistently with various measures of teacher actions—the percentage of time spent by the teacher on the topic, amount of disciplinary intervention, and so on. Rutter admits that the association might merely represent the teachers' responses to the behavioural disruption, but, he says, "it certainly does not constitute the whole explanation"

(p. 115). He gives no grounds for this strong assertion, and it is also worth noting that all seven measures of teacher actions correlate significantly with behaviour, but only two correlate significantly with the other three outcome measures.

These worries about circularity and causation do not apply to the other outcome measures to the same extent, although it is worth noting that there are far more significant correlations with the behaviour measure, 23 of the 46, whereas only 15 out of the 46 are significant with academic attainment, 12 with attendance, and eight with delinquency. If we ignore the behavioural measure because of these worries, the results are not nearly so impressive. Rutter does not however rest his case on these individual correlations with individual process items. He rightly recognises that

> in a study where a large number of statistical comparisons are made, some significant associations will arise just by chance. It is necessary, therefore, to take steps to determine as far as possible which *statistically* significant associations are real (in the sense of not arising by chance) and hence educationally significant.
>
> (p. 140)

The answer that he comes up with is that what is actually crucial is the overall school ethos or climate of expectations and modes of behaving rather than individual process items; these might help to establish the ethos but their effect on the pupil is mediated by the ethos. His grounds for asserting this is that when the different statisically significant process items are combined to give an overall process score, this correlates far more highly with the various outcome measures than do any of the individual process items. "The school process measures which correlated with the four types of pupil outcome included a wide variety of factors", Rutter points out.

> Doubtless ... they operated by a variety of different mechanisms. It was striking, however, that their *combined* effect was much more powerful than that of any individual factor considered on its own. For this and other reasons, we have suggested that some kind of overall school 'ethos' might be involved.
>
> (p. 132)

Preece has already entertainingly demonstrated that a completely random allocation of scores to schools, when subjected to the identical statistical procedures as Rutter's, could also produce a more powerful combined effect than that of the individual process items.[14] So we hardly have powerful evidence as yet that an overall school 'ethos' was involved. However, while we are all familiar with the fallacy in the argument that 'all cats are animals; this is an animal; therefore it must be a cat' we must also remember that if we do stumble across an animal in the dark it really might turn out to be a cat. Rutter has stumbled across a powerful combined effect, and it certainly might turn out to be an indication of school ethos. We simply have to inspect it rather more closely first.

The concept of ethos is an attractive one. Our visitor to the Inner London secondary schools would doubtless feel the existence of different climates and modes of behaving. At one extreme he might find a couple of schools which were orderly and happy places with shared standards, high academic expectations and their own distinctive cultural patterns emphasising learning and hard work. At the other extreme he might find some schools which were perhaps equally happy and with an equal consensus on the expected modes of behaving, but where the *content* of the expectations was rather different. The leisure ethic of the working-class adolescent might predominate and might be tolerated by the staff who preferred to work with the pupils rather than against them.

At both these extremes we could reasonably talk of a 'school ethos' but what are we to say about all those schools in the middle (and for some reason the middle always seems to predominate) where it is the *variability* within the school that most impresses the visitor? In some classrooms we find order, the appearance of hard work, and old-fashioned discipline. In others there is a more relaxed and slightly cheeky atmosphere where the pupils keep just the right side of that dividing line between order and disorder. And in a few others the teacher is fighting a losing battle to keep in control. The same variability exists within the playground or staff room. There are no standards shared by all pupils or staff alike. Instead the school is a microcosm of society with its cliques and subcultures, its official rules and their infractions, its tensions and contradictions. Surely, we cannot say *tout court* that there is a 'school ethos' here, and surely Rutter cannot extrapolate from the small group studies that he quotes to the conclusion that "All these studies have shown that any relatively self-contained organization tends to develop its own culture or pattern; this also applies to secondary schools" (p. 184). It would be a matter of great interest and considerable empirical difficulty to establish whether the "well-nigh universal tendency for individuals in common circumstances to form social groups with their own rules, values and standards of behaviour" (p. 184) operates in the same way in a secondary school of 1000 boys and girls with different ethnic, religious and social class backgrounds as it does in the groups of eleven-year-olds in Sherif's 'robber cave' experiments.[15]

Of course, this is not to deny that we could devise some overall measures of school functioning which took into account both the content of the school's standards and the degree of consensus on these standards. The crucial question then becomes whether functioning can be changed by the actions of the staff and whether it would then have a causal effect on outcomes. As Rutter rightly points out, only controlled experimentation can provide a satisfactory answer to these questions. In the absence of experimental studies we could quite reasonably argue that *both* outcome *and* functioning were merely consequences of the kinds of pupils that attended these schools, the kind of parental encouragement that they received, and the kind of adolescent subcultures that developed in the neighbourhood. On this line of argument, some schools have the good fortune to be working with promising material under favourable circumstances; others have much more difficult conditions to contend with and a more mutinous crew which makes it much harder to run a tight ship; the staff get poorer results and doubtless less satisfaction from their work, and to add insult to injury actually get blamed for their troubles. Before we dismiss this line of reasoning, we have to be fairly sure of our ground.

We have already dealt with one defect of Rutter's attempt to demonstrate a causal effect of school processes on outcome—his failure to control for relevant background variables. But he has another important string to his bow. As backing for a causal influence he argues that

> Of course, interactions will take place in both directions, but the much greater correlation between school process and children's behaviour/attainment at the *end* of secondary schooling strongly implies a greater effect of schools on children than of children on schools. We may infer that it is very likely that school processes *do* influence pupil outcome.
>
> (p. 181)

Somewhat surprisingly it is very hard to find where in the book Rutter reports the correlations between school process and outcomes at the *beginning* of secondary schooling from which he could conclude that they had risen by the end. He does give a little evidence on the proportion of children at two schools with behavioural difficulties prior to intake and at 14 years, and this certainly shows a vastly wider gap between the two schools at 14 than at intake (p. 27). But this is not in itself important. What we need are the rank correlations between the relative positions of schools on the relevant measures of behaviour and attainment at the beginning and end of secondary schooling. Even more to the point, Rutter should investigate the *changes* in the ranking over this period and the extent to which they are related to the internal features of the schools. If it could be shown that the schools which had climbed the league table were distinguished by a particular ethos, while those which fell had a different one (or lack of one), we should be more favourably inclined to the view that ethos has a causal effect.

> (IV) Outcomes were also influenced by factors *outside* teachers' immediate control. The academic balance in the intakes to the schools was particularly important in this connection. Examination success tended

to be better in schools with a substantial nucleus of children of at least average intellectual ability, and delinquency rates were higher in those with a heavy preponderance of the least able.

(p. 178)

As Rutter rightly points out, this finding, if sound, has extremely important implications for educational policy. A system which allowed unlimited freedom for parents to choose between schools might well lead to heavy concentrations of able pupils in some schools and of less able in others. We could take the argument further (Rutter does not). We could argue that a system which allowed high IQ children to have assisted places at independent schools thereby reduced the prospects for educational success of those children left behind in the maintained sector. Indeed, since the major independent schools in general recruit disproportionate numbers of high IQ children,[16] it would provide further ammunition for those (such as both the authors of this article) who urge the abolition of the independent sector altogether.

But even although Rutter's conclusions might coincide with one's personal preferences, we must assess his statistical reasoning as carefully as ever. The major caveat about his reasoning is now familiar. If he has failed to control satisfactorily for relevant out-of-school variables such as home background or neighbourhood, he may erroneously attribute to school characteristics effects which are properly those of the unmeasured variables. This is as relevant in the case of 'balance' as it is in that of 'process'. There is also our familiar worry about the use of broad classifications of non-school factors where finer ones would be more desirable. And then there is the curious case, so to speak, of the dog that did not bark—the dog in this case being verbal reasoning. As we mentioned earlier, table 5.9 shows that verbal reasoning *on its own* explains 27% of the variance in examination scores while table 9.4 shows that it has shrunk to only 14% and that verbal reasoning, parental occupation and balance *between them* account for only 25%. This is really very curious. We suggested one possible explanation—perhaps the classification of verbal reasoning had changed—but no doubt many others are possible too.[17] But whatever the explanation, the worry remains: if Rutter had controlled for verbal reasoning in the way that he did in table 5.9, would there have been any work left for balance to do? Perhaps balance will turn out to have no effect at all once we have controlled for verbal reasoning in a way which gives that variable maximum scope. We must wait for Rutter to elucidate the paradox.

As well as these old problems, balance raises a new and particularly interesting one. If, for the sake of argument, we allow that balance does have an effect, then we have to postulate some mechanisms which underly it. Rutter's own suggestion (which seems not at all unreasonable) is that the influence of intellectual mix did *not* operate primarily through its effect on teacher attitudes or behaviour, nor through its effects on overall school functioning. ... The inference to be drawn is that the main mechanism was likely to be of some other kind—probably related to some aspects of the peer group itself.

(p. 200)

The idea is simply that pupils influence each other, an idea that has long been familiar in the study of deviance with theories of 'differential association'. But unfortunately this could have rather serious consequences. The statistical techniques which Rutter, in company with most sociologists, uses assume *independence* whereas peer group pressures clearly require us to assume *dependence*. If we are investigating children's height, for example, we can reasonably assume that it will be independent of the height of other children in the class or neighbourhood; if they have similar heights, therefore, we can reasonably infer that it is because of such things as common nutritional patterns and not because one boy's height directly affects another's. But we cannot so comfortably assume this of delinquency. If boys in a particular school have relatively similar patterns of delinquent activity, it clearly could be because they directly influence each other rather than because they share a common school experience.

Consider the following hypothetical and highly artificial example. We randomly allocate children to a set of identical schools with identical facilities and teaching practices. The pupils themselves, prior to allocation, will almost certainly vary in their characteristics—in their liking for different ball games for example. Now random allocation of these pupils will not mean that all the schools will get the same mix of pupils. Some will—purely as a result of chance—have relatively more footballers, others more cricketers, and so on. If the pupils now tend to interact predominantly with the other children in their own school, the pupils within a given school will tend to become more similar to each other in their sporting preferences. In other words they will become less variable than they were on allocation to the school although the school averages may stay exactly the same. This reduction in variability of course has had nothing to do with the characteristics of the schools as institutions since we have already specified that they are identical.

Why is this important? Well, let us suppose that there is an innocent statistician who has been given no advance warning about the experiment that has taken place and who has come to test the hypothesis that the observed differences in the sporting preferences of the pupils at the different schools are due to some school effect. What our statistician no doubt will do is measure the current variability in the preference of the sample as a whole and use a statistical formula to calculate whether the observed differences between schools could have occurred by chance alone. If his formula assumes independence he is quite likely to 'discover' that the between-school differences are greater than the chance expectation. His formula tells him that the between-school differences are greater than the ones that would have been expected given the overall variability within the pupil sample. What he has forgotten is that that variability has been reduced by pupil interaction and that he should have used a different formula for calculating the expected differences in school averages.

Rutter (and, let us be fair, nearly all sociologists) is in the same position as our innocent statistician. In the greater part of his book which precedes the discussion of balance he uses statistical techniques which assume independence. He thus finds that statistically significant differences remain between schools in their levels of deliquency, attendance, behaviour and attainment even when he has controlled for pupil characteristics. But then right at the end of the book he advances the hypothesis that pupils influence each other, thus casting doubt on the assumption of independence that he has used throughout. To put the matter in a nutshell, if a pupil's ability and attainment is affected by the abilities of those around him, then a formula which wrongly assumes independence will wrongly amplify statistical differences between school outcomes.

We shall not attempt a laborious summary of the points that have been made. In essence our case is that Rutter has not demonstrated satisfactorily that his conclusions follow from the evidence his team had collected. The reader may feel that we have been overly stringent, but one of the functions of an academic community is to subject their colleagues' work to rigorous scrutiny. True, it is always easy to suggest some magic variable X that would have transformed one's colleague's conclusions if he had had the providence to foresee it (or perhaps, more realistically, the inflated budget needed to collect the additional data). But we have also tried to be more constructive and to suggest ways that Rutter could use even now to re-analyse his data. We recognise that he cannot now sensibly hope to make good the gaps in his knowledge of the children's family backgrounds, but surely he could attempt to use a finer classification of neighbourhood differences, of verbal reasoning and parental occupation; he could take some account of the primary schools which the children attended; he could control for parental subscription rates and differences in school status; he could attempt a new method of adjusting the process scores—and he might even manage to think of a formula that assumes dependence rather than independence (we would be glad to see it).

We therefore invite Rutter and his colleagues to re-analyse their data and to sort out the paradoxes that baffled us. In the meantime we cannot believe that *Fifteen Thousand Hours* gives a sufficiently strong basis for teachers or administrators to change their practices. No doubt it is desirable in itself to finish lessons on time, to put pictures on the wall, to organise one's teaching so that time is spent on the topic rather than on giving out equipment, but teachers are not entitled to use Rutter's book as proof that this will improve outcomes. Rutter himself would assuredly not wish teachers to do this. We must remember his caveat that firm conclusions about causation can only be drawn from experimental studies. The acid test therefore is whether, if we bodily swopped the children from the best and the worst schools (as measured on the adjusted outcome scores), the schools would retain their positions in the league table. It will never be done, but it would be interesting to hear what the staff rooms think might happen.

Acknowledgments

We are very grateful to David Hargreaves and John Ridge for the help they have given us in the preparation of this paper.

Notes and references

1 Rutter, M., Maughan, B., Mortimore, P., & Ouston, J., with Smith, A. (1979) *Fifteen Thousand Hours: secondary schools and their effects on children* (London, Open Books).

2 Page references throughout are to Rutter, *op. cit.* The italics used in the quotations are those given in the original text.

3 One complaint often raised in the staff room is that small secondary modern schools turned comprehensive tend to be given very little money for furniture and other resources compared with the larger purpose-built 'show-school' comprehensives.

4 See, for example, Belson, W.A. *The Extent of Stealing by London Boys and Some of its Origins.* No. 39 in the reprint series of The Survey Research Centre, the London School of Economics and Political Science. For a general discussion of the unreliability of the official statistics on criminal behaviour see Box, S. (1971) *Deviance, Reality and Society* (New York, Holt, Rinehart & Winston), Chapter 3.

5 See Rutter, *op. cit.,* Appendix G, p. 239.

6 This is a rough-and-ready estimate derived from inspection of figure 5.6, p. 86.

7 See, for example, Halsey, A.H., Heath, A.F. & Ridge, J.M. (1980) *Origins and Destinations: Family, class and education in modern Britain* (Oxford, Clarendon Press).

8 Another contrast occurs between Tables 5.1 and 9.8. In Table 5.1 VR *band* explains 2.1% of the variance in 5th year attendance whereas in Table 9.8 VR *group* explains 2.8%. Rutter generally seems to use the expression VR band when he is referring to his three-fold classification and VR group when he is referring to the seven-fold one.

9 Rutter presumably uses these broad categorisations because of his commitment to log-linear analysis. The conventional wisdom is that in log-linear analysis the numbers in each cell need to be kept relatively large, and hence a few broad categories may be preferred to a large number of fine ones.

10 Halsey, *et al., op. cit.* The same kind of picture emerges if we use the material presented in Peaker, W. *The Plowden Children Four Years On* (Windsor, National Foundation for Educational Research).

11 These calculations are based on the correlation matrix presented in Halsey *et al., op. cit.,* p. 170. Certain assumptions are required in order to make these

calculations (notably those of linear regression) and no particular significance should be attached to the absolute figures. It is the overall *pattern* which we wish to illustrate.

12 What we have done is to calculate the variance explained when school-leaving age is regressed on the following four sets of independent variables: father's class and son's IQ; father's class, son's IQ and school type; father's class, son's IQ and father's education; father's class, son's IQ, father's education and school type. The variance explained was 29.9, 45.3, 32.9 and 46.5%. The additional variance explained by school type is calculated accordingly. The assumptions of linear regression were again employed.

13 For an account of the adjustment procedure it appears that we should refer to Rutter, M. (1977) Prospective studies to investigate behavioural change. In: Strauss, J.S., Babigian, H.M. & Roff, M. (1979) (eds) *The Origins and Course of Physchopathology* (New York, Plenum Publishing).

14 Preece, P.F.W. (1979) 'Fifteen taus and rhos,' *Research Intelligence* (BERA Newsletter), August, pp. 16–17.

15 Sherif, M., Harvey, O.J., White, B.J., Hood, W.R. & Sherif, C. (1961) *Intergroup Conflict and Cooperation: the robbers' cave experiment* (Norman, Oklahoma, University of Oklahoma Book Exchange). This is one of the main studies cited by Rutter.

16 See Peaker, *op. cit.*, and Kalton, G. (1966) *The Public Schools: a factual survey* (London, Longmans).

17 One possibility is that there are some interesting non-linear effects which verbal reasoning has on examination results, and that the technique of linear regression used for Table 9.4 has failed to capture these. This of course does not absolve Rutter. Alternatively the definition of the dependent variable may have changed in a way that we have not understood.

Part II

1979–1986 Conservative Government, Margaret Thatcher and slow change

9   The educational consequences of Mr Norman Tebbit*

Stuart Maclure

Source: 'The educational consequences of Mr Norman Tebbit', *Oxford Review of Education*, 8(2): 103–120, 1982.

The present mood of public education is glum and oppressed. Educational finance dominates the schools, the further education colleges, and all institutions of higher education. The fall in the birthrate from 1965–77 is now hitting the schools and threatening the universities. With it has come a reaction against the liberal ideas and the optimism of the 1960s, as successive Secretaries of State have sought to articulate what they believe to be the views of a critical public.

Worse than any of the particular ills which beset the education system and all who work in it, are the ills which beset Britain and the British economy—ills which go beyond the confines of these islands to the world economy and the world recession.

One thing distinguishes the depression of the 1980s from that of the 1930s as far as education is concerned. In the 1930s there was a fairly clear idea of what needed to be done in regard to education. The school leaving age had to be raised. Grammar school fees had to be abolished and secondary education opened to everyone. Day continuation schools had to be introduced. Access to higher education had to be opened up. The messy arrangements for Church schools had to be tidied up. When, in 1941 it became possible to start planning for a post-war future, all that the officials of the Board of Education in their Bournemouth Hydro had to do was to write down on the proverbial back of an envelope a shopping list which commanded general support.

Today's melancholy does not cloak any such consensus for future reform among the educators. There is no new 1944 Act waiting in the wings.

What there is, is something rather different, but in its way not much less significant. Now, in the middle of the recession and without waiting for another war and another peace, a major social advance of an educational nature is about to be made. But this time, the moving spirit is not education at all, but Employment—or, to be more accurate, Unemployment.

Table 9.1 The Tebbit White Paper

Target groups:	(1) 16-year-old school leavers with no employment experience
	(2) 16-year-olds unemployed after some period in work
	(3) 17-year-old school leavers with no employment experience
	(4) 17-year-olds unemployed after some period in work
Guarantee:	One year traineeship for (1)
	Six month course for (2)
Hope to offer: (no guarantee)	Similar arrangements for (3) and (4)
Time-table:	
1982–83	Build up to 100,000 one-year traineeship places
September 1983	Guarantees come into operation, YOP replaced by Youth Training Scheme
Trainee support	
Youth Training Allowance	£750 a year to 16-year-olds, £1250 a year to 17-year-olds
Supplementary Benefit	Not eligible until September in the year following minimum leaving age
Child Benefit	Paid in respect of unemployed up to September of the year following minimum leaving age
Total numbers expect to pass through the scheme in one year	300,000 from September 1983 at a cost of £1000 million
Other measures to be extended	
Unified vocation preparation: 1984–85	For those under 18 in employment 50,000 places rising from the 3500 filled places in 1980–81
Apprenticeship	
1982	ITBs to submit clear plans for training to standards
1982–83	MSC to fund 35,000 first year apprenticeships, an increase from the 25,000 supported in 1980–81
1985	MSC support to be confined to training to standards previously agreed
Development schemes	£16 million for types of scheme not included above in particular localities and sectors

Needs must, they say, when the Devil drives. And youth unemployment, which threatens to leave 60% of school leavers without jobs, is the driving force behind the Tebbit White Paper[1] and the MSC's New Training Initiative (Table 9.1).

The Tebbit scheme guarantees a one-year traineeship to all jobless 16-

year-old school-leavers with a training allowance paid by the Manpower Services Commission.

A White Paper is, of course, no more than a declaration of the Government's intent. How the scheme actually develops will be determined by the pressures, now building up in the TUC and the CBI, which will influence the 'high level task force' set up by the MSC to make further proposals. There are many doubts about the size of the programme—is it too small to tackle the problem or too large to put through in the time?—and about the wisdom of guaranteeing only the first year, about the amount to be paid by way of training allowance. There are those who would like to see more emphasis on training across the board—not just at the 16–18 level—and others who would prefer to put the emphasis on subsidising ordinary employment, believing that this is the first necessity for meaningful training.

All the signs are, however, that the line of development initiated first by the Youth Opportunities Programme, and now extended by the White Paper and the large financial backing it carries, will move forward towards the removal from the labour market of, first, the 16-year-olds and later the 17-year-olds and the extension of the traineeship period to two years. The logical expectation must be to see the ordinary employment of under-18s disappear. The school-leaving age will remain unchanged but the new concept of a minimum age for completing 'traineeship' will have been established alongside and beyond the school system.

There is, therefore, every reason now to hope for the achievement of an aim which has more than once been adopted and relinquished since it was put forward more than 60 years ago by the Lewis Committee which in 1917 urged that "the conception of the juvenile as primarily a little wage-earner be replaced by the conception of the juvenile as primarily the workman and the citizen in training".[2]

Notwithstanding many questions about detail and practice which still have to be answered, the White Paper deserves at the outset to be warmly welcomed. It has profound consequences for education, however, and these need to be closely examined. The initiative which it provides will shift the log-jam: how to take the greatest advantage of it is now what should be occupying the attention of the education world. It is quite easy to see how the great stride forward could lead to unintended difficulties.

What, then, are the characteristics and the implications for education of the new forms of social organisation which the White Paper betokens?

I propose to start by examining the origins of the scheme and the formative influences which shape it. I then want to consider the activities which it will give rise to, and their impact on the colleges of further education and the schools. I want to look at other ways of achieving the same objective by incorporating more of these activities within the education system. And I want briefly to touch on the financial arrangements and how they stand to affect public education.

Origins and formative influences

Unemployment

I have referred already to the political impact of youth unemployment, and the fact that this is the driving force behind the Tebbit scheme. It is now clear that the argument which has been going on since the mid-1970s about the nature of youth unemployment can be stated, and set aside.

For a while it was the prevailing view among government economists that youth employment would bounce back, once the economy recovered and the large age-groups born in the early 1960s had moved up the ladder. It was difficult to get any agreement about the relative significance of structural, demographic, social and cyclical factors in pushing up the jobless figures. But ever since the 1960s, each succeeding economic cycle has produced higher youth unemployment at the low point, and each recovery has been less complete at the top. Many jobs traditionally done by young people have disappeared or been taken over by older workers, including married women. Legislation designed to protect employment may well have benefited those already in work at the expense of newcomers.

The demographic curve has only made things worse. Only now is the number of 16- and 17-year-olds beginning, marginally, to go down. Over the next 10 years, the number of men and women under 30 seeking jobs will remain very high, though by the end of the decade the number in the upper teenage bracket will have fallen substantially (Figure 9.1).

An upturn in employment, generally, would undoubtedly cause the number of openings for young people to jump, and go some little way towards reviving traditional apprenticeship. Because youth employment has been especially bad during the recession, the number of young people without jobs could well fall faster than unemployment as a whole when the economy turns up. But even so the expectation must be that it will not return in the foreseeable future to the very low levels of the 1960s and early 1970s. And it is clear that it would take a major change-around in Britain's fortunes to bring about a marked improvement.

So Britain seems set to follow, a bit belatedly, the example of other advanced countries of the West which, by one means or another, keep most young people off the labour market until 18 or 19. For what it is worth, this is what the European Community is likely to push. Mr Ivor Richard and his staff are shortly to bring foward their 'Youth Guarantee' proposals and have received every encouragement from the European Employment Ministers. There must be a long way to go and many obstacles to overcome before an EEC initiative in the field could become Community law, but this is the ultimate aim of the Commission. It is sensible to try to act together on this because it might well have implications for international competition, and for international companies operating throughout the EEC.

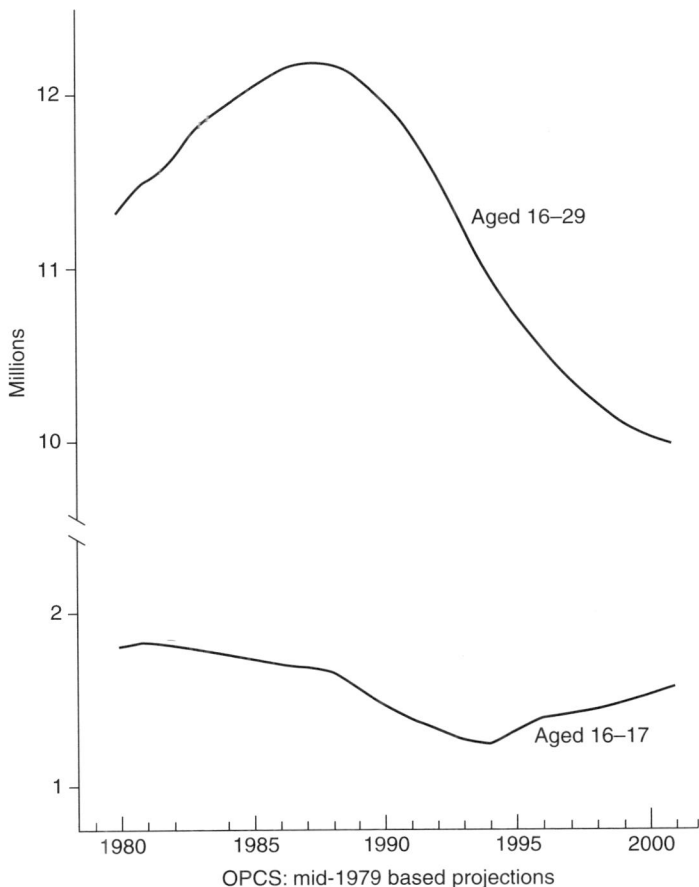

Figure 9.1 Working population in Great Britain under 30: 1980–2001.

Department of Employment and the Manpower Services Commission

Because it is the political importance of unemployment which unlocks the money bags and summons up the will to act, it is the Department of Employment and its executive agency, the Manpower Services Commission, which occupy the driving seat. The Tebbit proposals and the MSC's New Training Initiative reflect a set of concerns which originate within the field of industry and employment. The White Paper bears the name of the

Secretary of State for Education and Science and his Scottish and Welsh counterparts, but the voice is the voice of employment.

The way in which the MSC and the Department of Employment have taken over leadership in this area is a matter of almost paranoid anxiety for the educational world. The evidence is not in question. The Manpower Services Commission has grown with amazing rapidity over the past eight years from nothing to its present imposing strength, with a 1981–82 budget of £992 million. It has proved to be versatile and flexible in improvising successive increases in the Youth Opportunities Programme to mop up the growing army of young unemployed. It is easy to brand YOP as being mainly concerned with doctoring the unemployment statistics, but this does the MSC an injustice. For several years, the Youth Opportunities Programme was remarkably successful in providing the element of breathing space and initiative needed to usher many young people into jobs. The trouble is that as unemployment rises the breathing space needs to be extended. During the past 18 months the proportion of young people ending a spell in YOP without getting an ordinary job has risen to disconcerting heights, and the programme has come under increasing criticism as a form of subsidised, cheap labour, which fails to provide adequate training.

The traineeship scheme is emerging as a kind of super-YOP, building on the experience gained, but reckoning to guarantee a much more structured programme of training and planned experience. I will return to what this might comprise shortly.

The origins of the Tebbit traineeship, therefore, ensure that it is conceived and operated within the conventions of the world of industry and commerce. The MSC is controlled by a Board dominated by the representatives of the Confederation of British Industry and the Trades Union Congress. (Under a Tory Government, the CBI is on top; under a Labour Government, the TUC calls the tune.) The essential doctrine is that industrial training is the responsibility of industry—largely paid for by employers and reflecting their specific production requirements. Any educational contribution is subsidiary to this main philosophical principle. And because training is industry's responsibility, it is subsumed within the field of industrial relations and bargaining between employers and unions.

All these considerations have played their part in the evolution of the traineeship scheme. Within the government itself the Department of Employment is powerful and its responsibility for politically sensitive measures aimed at combatting unemployment adds still more strength to its arm. The large funds provided for the MSC are administered directly from the centre. They can be brought to bear quickly on specific targets. They require the minimum of consultation and democratic control. The policy and its execution are in the hands of a single agency.

In almost every respect this contrasts with the formation and execution of education policies. Successive Secretaries of State for Education have been frustrated by their limited powers over money. Cash has to be channelled to the local authorities in a block grant-in-aid, which covers all the local services. Ministers sponsoring particular services have little or no control over how it is spent. Within the upper reaches of government, Ministers and civil servants from the DES have repeatedly been unable to answer for education as a whole or to guarantee that if funds were provided for the 16–18s through the education system the money would find its way to the intended recipients. Their apparent impotence is held against them when it comes to considering how new services should be delivered and who should provide the central government control. The long tradition of democratic control and consultation, built up over decades, has hamstrung the education interest in the face of the challenge from employment. There are, of course, many good reasons for entrusting education to democratic institutions and for engaging in careful consultation with all the interests concerned. But these count for little with brash new bodies like the MSC, in the face of a crisis of youth unemployment and stricent demands for government action.

Financial support systems

The link between the new programmes and employment (and unemployment) is also emphasised by the assumption that all participants must be paid a wage. The White Paper envisages a training allowance of the order of £750 a year. This represents a sharp reduction from the present YOP figure of £25.00 a week for 16-year-olds, and there is now some lively (and somewhat synthetic) argument about the merits of ending potential trainees' entitlement to supplementary benefit, if they should decide to reject a training place. No doubt this will eventually simmer down.[3] But what will remain will be the sharp distinction between those in the traineeship scheme and those who elect to remain in full-time education in the ordinary way.

The significance of this cliff edge has already been fully recognised. It provided the stimulus for Mrs Shirley Williams' abortive attempts to introduce realistic educational maintenance allowances in 1978–79. (The present EMAs, uneven and haphazard and harshly means-tested, only provide about £3.7 million a year for all the 16–18s who remain at school—about 19p a head a week. It is difficult to see how the contrast between the guarantee of an un-means-tested training allowance for all 16-year-old leavers and the absence of any such guarantee for all who stay in full-time education can fail to become a more and more damaging anomaly in the coming years. This, too, is something I shall return to later.

Education and training considerations

If the rise in youth unemployment is the mainspring behind the new initiative, and the administrative and financial mechanism reflected in the balance of power within the government explains its orientation, there are also important influences which relate directly to education and training.

As things now stand, two inter-linked weaknesses stand out:

— the failure of the school system to develop an effective vocational element;
— the failure of British industry to modernise its training, and in particular, its hidebound apprenticeship arrangements.

The first is part and parcel of the wider malaise of the English academic tradition and the low esteem traditionally accorded within the culture of modern Britain to commerce and industry. Because training has been consigned to the responsibility of the employers and their bargaining with the unions, large tracts of vocational education have been effectively limited to meeting specific demands of employers. The apprenticeship system, with all its built-in restrictions, has determined the volume of vocational education in respect of a whole range of craft skills.

College-based courses in some fields have grown up more recently, but it is broadly true to say that many of industry's weaknesses in industrial training have been reflected in the failure of vocational education to surge forward in the past 20 years.

No less to the point, the close connection between vocational education and the specific requirements of employers has not encouraged the development of vocational education within the school system. Vocational education has been positively discouraged by the broader aim of extending, and opening up access to, general education. (It has often been pointed out that the technical school is the one part of the old tripartite system which has sunk without trace in the comprehensive school.) The result has been to prevent the emergence of a general education based on a vocational orientation, of the kind which has formed an important part of the educational provision in a number of European countries. There may well have been some good reasons for this—*premature* vocational education has been under fire in many European countries in recent years—but what is now taking place via the MSC for the 16–18s seems to be an attempt to make up for the failure to develop the kind of vocational education system which the Europeans are now modifying.

All this is now coming together. It is to be seen as part of a more general failure on the part of the schools to do a good job for the least successful 40% of the system—the 40% for whom the Dutch or the French would be providing vocational education, or who would be ending up in the German *Berufeschulen*.

This failure—part, undoubted fact; part, a prejudiced fiction—is now being used by Ministers within the DES to justify the decision to hand the initiative over to the MSC—'the schools have had their chance and failed', the argument runs; 'now it's time to give someone else a chance'. The half-truths on which this is based are less important than the function which the myth is being made to serve, which is to rationalise decisions taken on quite other grounds. Unfortunately the same myth justifies the sharply contrasting financial treatment meted out to the schools and to the MSC.

As to the failure of industry to put its training house in order, and in particular to modernise apprenticeships, this is one of the most depressing stories of post-war England, as first one and then another attempt to break out of the rut has been thwarted. Now the Tebbit proposals hold out the real possibility of broadening the base of skill training and replacing time-serving with the assessment of competence. But there are still many hurdles to clear. Already there are signs that the unions are closing ranks in defence of many traditional aspects of apprenticeship. It is not by any means obvious that the task of reform will be made any easier by the decision to chop down most of the Industrial Training Boards.

Education and training under the traineeship scheme

Events have already moved fast to bring into the colleges of further education large numbers of students on courses arranged for the Manpower Services Commission.

Various modes for future development have been put forward by such bodies as the Further Education Curriculum Review and Development Unit, the Industrial Training Boards and the Youth Skills Project at the Institute of Manpower Studies, University of Sussex, where Mr Christopher Hayes, a former senior member of the MSC staff, has been working on the curriculum and content of industrial training.

The Tebbit White Paper indicates the magnitude of the educational element: it is estimated that an extra 80,000 full-time equivalent places in the colleges of further education are needed. The courses will vary from one to five days a week and from instruction in traditional vocational subjects to the new schemes of vocational preparation developed by the FEU. Some of these courses are likely to contain a good deal of straightforward remedial education. Others, though firmly intended to be provided in what Mr Jack Mansell, the director of the FEU, would call "an occupationally-relevant context", bear a recognisable connection to the kind of general education which was once envisaged for day continuation colleges and later for county colleges. 'Life Skills' has a splendidly non-academic ring to it, and so too has 'Vocational Preparation', but the 'Common Core Objectives' identified by the FEU as basic to many of these courses include many aims which relate much more directly to personal development and social education in citizenship than to the practice of any particular occupation. Let me give some examples:[4]

— to bring about an ability to develop satisfactory personal relationships with others;

— to provide a basis on which the young person acquires a set of moral values applicable to issues in contemporary society;
— to bring about a level of achievement in literacy and numeracy appropriate to ability and adequate to meet the basic demands of contemporary society;
— to bring about sufficient political and economic literacy to understand the social environment and participate in it;
— to bring about a flexibility of attitudes and willingness to learn sufficient to manage future changes in technology and career.

(Judging from the ghastly language in which these grandiose objectives are set out, it is not surprising to find no mention of learning to write plain English.)

Of course, setting out basic objectives in cant phrases and jargon terms—even if you read the small print which is meant to elucidate the main headings—does not necessarily tell us much about what will actually happen. But there is enough here to indicate that vocational preparation is going to provide a wide field of social studies in which college lecturers can gambol to their hearts' content. Of course, the objectives also include others relating to career choice, study skills and physical and manipulative skills, and it is unfair to dissociate the basic aims from the underlying assumptions of occupational relevance and work experience.

And here, the studies initiated by Hayes may come to have a direct bearing. He has sought to develop an approach to industrial training now widely used on the Continent, dividing the skills which have to be learnt into process skills and product skills.[5] The product skills are those which relate directly to a work task, while process skills

> do not normally lead to clearly definable outcomes but a capability for inter-acting effectively with a person's environment through, for instance, listening, planning, working in a team, problem-solving, learning. Process skills also range from the highly job specific to the more general, but more of them are relevant to a wide range of activities which include work as well as life in the family and community. They also span a range of levels of complexity. Because of their more abstract nature, they cannot be learnt by rote nor can they be tested by examinations which require reproducing information or by repeating learnt manual or mental procedures. The key to becoming better in their use lies in the way in which tasks are learnt and mastered. An assessment of the effectiveness with which they are used must relate to a person's management of a process in which she or he is involved.

Alongside an examination of the skills to be instilled goes an analysis of the occupational structure aimed at dividing the labour market up into 'occupational training families' so that "an individual's training, experience and further education planned as an entity within a broad framework of a cluster or group of related jobs, skills or occupations". (Western Germany comes up with 13 families; Denmark, eight; the Netherlands, 11. The Swedish vocational training plans provide for three 'routes' and 21 lines; Luxembourg plans to unify vocational education and training into nine families of occupations.)

The aim is to construct a traineeship framework which will

> make it possible to strike a balance between conflicting demands: the widest choice and opportunities for a young person to acquire competence and, more specifically, to be able to apply for work available in his or her locality; the needs of local employers; and the acquisition of skills in a way which will help the young person to embrace future change and cope with life in the community and during unemployment ... based on planned work, training and education.

Just how the product and process skills are to be married to the occupational clusters, and to the peculiarities of the many local labour markets which the new industrial training and vocational education set-up will have to serve, remains to be seen but it is clear that there is a great deal more to be done on the curriculum and in staff development. It is not at all clear where the teachers and instructors for the new-style further education are going to come from or who is going to train them. I get the impression that the last people the MSC wants to let loose on these young people are conventionally trained teachers. A college principal of my acquaintance when seeking staff for some of these courses makes a point of choosing people who look as unlike teachers as possible. MSC staff speak with admiration of the contribution made by instructors whose experience and training has been obtained on the shop floor. The teacher training institutions would love to get into this work and they could make an important contribution as Iolo Roberts[6] has pointed out, but only if they can overcome a mighty prejudice against them in the world outside, and only if they can show some reasons why they should be supposed to have any special expertise to offer.

If it is by no means clear where the staff will come from, it is difficult to doubt the strength of the momentum behind these developments. Already it is being argued in the FEU—and I have heard its chairman, George Tolley, argue this with passion and eloquence—that it will require a new structure, to give coherence to the disparate courses, and this means enabling one course to link up with another. Coherence is something which further education has always lacked and it is not going to be easy to introduce it now. One element in a coherent system is 'progression'—the provision of the ladders and bridges needed to enable successful passage through the training and vocational education provided under the MSC rubric to count for credit and for merit elsewhere in the labyrinth of the further education system. The implications here go very far indeed and point unmistakably towards more open access to higher and continuing education and to the closed world guarded by the professional institutions.

The case for a new legal framework for further education and a new tertiary administrative frame covering the upper reaches of secondary education and the 16–18s in FE is getting stronger every day. This might be interpreted as meaning a new Ministry spanning education and training. The argument for changes in the machinery of government, however, is liable to obscure the more important question of how the system is to develop after the machinery has been changed. Rough edges will remain, however the departmental responsibilities are carved up. But if not a new Ministry, at least there may need to be a new agency to work jointly with Education and Employment, and, as Barry Taylor, the Somerset CEO, suggested at the 1982 North of England Conference,[7] new local education and training authorities, with strong industrial and trade union representation, to administer the tertiary stage. And, of course, a new financial mechanism which would enable the government to channel funds into this area of activity without going through the Rate Support Grant.

The object of such a structural change would be to remedy what is the most obvious weakness in the Tebbit White Paper, and indeed, in the whole approach to 16–18 adopted by the present Government and its Labour predecessor.

This is the refusal to look at the 16–18s as a whole. It is perfectly obvious why this has happened, given the political and institutional pressures. But now is undoubtedly the time to look again at the fundamental weakness of the English educational system—its high attrition rates and the unsatisfactory deal it offers the least successful 40%, which arise from this. It is a major point to the credit of the Labour Party's recent discussion document[8] that it recognises this, even if it fails to come up with a complete set of realistic proposals.

School leaving patterns

As I see it, the present pattern of school-leaving and staying on is the result of two things: (1) the now falsified expectation that jobs (and wages) will be available for two-thirds of the age group at or soon after the age of 16; (2) the mechanics of the secondary education system itself—the system of valves and overflows which are operated by the examination system and the curriculum to filter the inflow at 11 down to the trickle which emerges at 18.

It occurs to me that all those arithmetical problems which used to be set to my generation of schoolboys to give an illusion of practical problem-solving (relevant to future plumbers if to no-one else)—which involved calculating the rate at which cisterns fill or empty, given supply pipes of one dimension and waste pipes of another—were really meant to be parables of the education system. The system has lived so long with the expectation of early leaving that most of the mechanisms which make sure it happens are valued parts of the educational tradition which affect assessment and educational guidance from the primary school onwards. Teachers and pupils alike learn who goes down which plug-hole. At appropriate points along the way, the necessary valves are opened and closed and the 100% of 5-year-olds, who enter on the flowing tide, are reduced 13 years later to the 12 or 13% who go on to higher education. The high drop out and low retention rates do not, in any sense, represent a failure of the system, but a vindication of it. This is the way it has been designed. It would be perverse to expect it to lead to other results than those which are systematically programmed by the complicated mixture of institutional and cultural traditions which society bequeathes to the schools.

A change in the employment situation which destroys the expectation of jobs at 16 calls into question the systematic operation of all the exclusion mechanisms in the education system.

What we should now be doing is asking what changes would be needed to retain within the education system some 60% of the age group—that is to say we should examine our secondary education arrangements *as a system* and consider what systematic changes in curriculum and examinations at various levels would be needed to 'qualify' a much higher proportion of young people.

I take it that the necessary changes would all be interdependent—that it would be no good, for example, pursuing a policy aimed at keeping more 16-year-olds in full-time education beyond the leaving age by financial incentives and changes in the examination system, while restricting the curriculum in such a way as to emphasise rigorous and exclusive academic requirements. It would be no use changing the 16-plus examination to provide success for more 16-year-olds if the 18-plus exam was made even more demanding.

There is already mounting evidence that more young people are continuing beyond 16, as a response to the present state of the labour market; evidence also that schools and further education colleges are introducing courses geared to their needs. More young people would stay on now, if there was more vocational education available for them. It is not a matter of setting out from scratch to make a revolutionary change: rather, it is a question of reviewing a number of policies, some of which are favourable, and others hostile, to this development and, for once, attempting to be consistent. In the end, it would add up to something like a revolutionary change, but one which could be seen to be a direct and logical response to equally radical changes in the job market. There is no suggestion here of raising the minimum legal leaving age. It would have to depend on encouraging more to stay on of their own volition.

Curriculum

To incorporate a larger fraction of the teenage population in education beyond 16 would mean reviewing the curriculum with this specific end in view.

The secondary school curriculum still has a very restricted notion of success. The usual measure is taken to be five 'O' levels or CSE grade 1s—which more or less corresponds to the old matriculation level which used to incorporate the old grammar school tradition. Only 25% of young people in England leave school with five or more 'O' levels or better. This compares with the 38% who stay on in full-time education (school and FE) beyond 16 and the 14½% who achieve two or more 'A' levels.

The object of the curriculum exercise, therefore, would have to be to devise a set of examinations and curricula in which a much higher proportion can succeed. This would be the equivalent of adjusting the valves to make sure fewer young people get sluiced away at the earliest opportunity.

There are obviously very great difficulties. Standards of attainment, though by no means immutable, become an ingrained part of an educational tradition.

It does not automatically follow that if 'pass' levels were lowered and more pupils of average and below average ability were allowed to succeed, the levels of attainment of the brightest and best would necessarily fall. But in essence, the problem of achieving a more diverse secondary education is just that fallacy writ large. So long as the Secretary of State can, with a straight face, tell the House of Commons Select Committee that reducing the number of students going on to higher education is a way of raising standards, there is no easy way of broadening the conception of worthwhile secondary education and vocational preparation. It must make sense to put the emphasis on broadening the range of courses and interests covered rather than on the dilution of the traditional academic tradition.

Some of the changes needed if there were to be a genuine diversification of the secondary school curriculum would, no doubt, point in the same direction as the FEU and the MSC are beginning to point. Sir Keith Joseph has begun to talk about the need for more vocational orientation from 14 onwards—this theme is mentioned in the Tebbit White Paper.

While it would be quite essential to provide a better method of vindicating children in the middle range of ability who are now expected to drop out at 16, it would be necessary to develop the kind of education for capability and competence which might be made the basis of certificated courses of a more practical kind than those which have hitherto dominated the secondary school. It would also be essential to establish a link between courses in the last years of the compulsory school and the kind of examination which is now planned at 17 for those engaged in vocational preparation.

It goes without saying that all this would suggest a very different kind of 16 plus examination reform from that now being attempted. It might even suggest the abolition of exams at 16 plus, and the postponement of the first external examination until 17 at the earliest—to act, in itself, as a carrot for those who might otherwise leave at 16.

Sixth-form studies

Any attempt to raise the staying-on rate would also imply a much wider range of activities beyond 16. It is in this context that it makes sense to think in terms of a new tertiary structure, provided this is clearly seen as extending beyond 'tertiary institutions' to the upper secondary school as well. It is not reasonable to think of a wholesale change to tertiary colleges, but it would be quite reasonable to require local education and training authorities to make coherent plans for the whole of the age group, and incorporate within the tertiary structure the kind of vocational preparation envisaged by the MSC *and* the progression to further education and training envisaged by the FEU. The aim has to be nothing less than to raise the status of vocational education and its close relative, professional education. This cannot be done in school alone: it depends on changes in society at large and in industry in particular. It is dependent on the seriousness with which other questions of industrial training are tackled. And it must depend, too, on a broadening of opportunity for vocational education in adult life.

There is a great apprehension in some quarters—it is clearly stated in the Labour Party discussion paper—that the diversified programme which is essential to any serious attempt to provide for the full range of ability and aspiration, will end up by re-creating at the tertiary level the unacceptable status gradations of the tripartite system of secondary education, with the 'new, new sixth form' and those in various kinds of vocational preparation cast in the role of rejected secondary moderns.

This may well come to dominate the political discussion—with what could be disastrous or tyrannical results. It is already possible to hear otherwise mild-mannered Hampstead intellectuals cheerfully insisting on the destruction of the academic sixth form, and the banishment of those destined for intellectual pursuits to a stint in the salt mines for the good of their souls.

It is clearly not possible to impute high status within the education system to activities which do not enjoy high status in society as a whole. But the best hope is not to make sure status differences are hidden by making everybody do the same thing—which would be impractical as well as pointless—but to capitalise on the diversity of the economic activities around which the divisions of labour are formed, and to keep the lines open for re-routing when individual opportunity and motivation change.

The acceptance of diversity must be better than the preservation of the semblance of a unified curriculum by simply watering it down more and more for the less able. The need is for real choices and a range of different goals along the line. Recent Scandinavian experience suggests that, provided access to higher education is broadened, and the range of acceptable entrance qualifications is extended, the traditional biases against vocational education can be greatly reduced.

Higher education

All of which leads on, briefly, to the observation that any successful attempt to extend the range of students in upper secondary and further education would, in due course, have implications for higher education. So far, 38 years on from the 1944 Act, Britain still does not have mass secondary education; if this is now going to come, would it still be compatible with elite higher education?

A good deal of the pressure which builds up behind the outflow of pupils at 16 results from the narrow entry to higher education at 18–19, and the narrow definition of what justifies full-time education at the post-secondary stage.

It seems absurd to talk of the North Americanisation of British higher education, now, when the Government, and the University Grants Committee are actively restricting entry and refining the academic gold in search of even greater purity. But if the schools and the universities are truly interdependent, then a major expansion of secondary education is not conceivable without a consequential expansion, later on, at the higher education level, and (it may be) a major expansion of secondary education is, in itself, dependent upon loosening those outlet valves at the top of the system and releasing some of the pressure which otherwise forces students out lower down.

A much larger system of post-secondary education would, of necessity, imply a wider range of institutions, activities and centres of quality. It might involve deliberately choosing cheaper models, with a wider range of staffing levels and a further erosion of student grants (whoever, in the West, heard of mass higher education going hand-in-hand with full mandatory student grants?) It would also, certainly, require something like the Swedish 24+5 scheme under which adult students age 24 and over with 5 years of employment behind them are entitled to enter university without the regular qualifications.

The institutional mix would also change, with the colleges of further education coming into their own as real Community Colleges, bringing within the higher education network forms of education and vocational training, not hitherto held in high esteem, and developing new, full-time adult courses combining general education with very specific vocational skills.

It is, of course, easy to float off on a comforting cushion of hot air and uplifting talk of *éducation permanente*. I have no illusions about this: I do not believe that life-long education is going to come quickly, nor yet that returning adults provide an easy answer to demographic decline over the next 10 years.

But I do believe that there will be a great deal more retraining and updating of skills, some of which will take place within the context of a broadened higher education. Because the universities have been able to content themselves with their traditional patterns of teaching and research they have had little occasion to look at what they could offer in other forms or to other groups. It is interesting to note how present economic stringency is causing institutions like LSE to reconsider these traditional patterns and to look at ways of stepping up other kinds of course for other client groups.

What is clear is that a more diversified pattern of secondary education and industrial training—however it is provided—will create new demands at a later stage—and this will be true even if the articulation between the various parts of the system is less than perfect.

The cost of such an expansion belongs to the future. A larger population in post-secondary education will be another consequence of the higher productivity which advanced technology will bring along with upheavals in the labour market. It will have to be seen against a background of a continuing surplus of labour and the desirability—indeed the necessity—of absorbing more young people and adults within the education system, rather than watching them swell the dole queues.

Financial support for trainees and students

And so I come back again to the question of financial support for trainees and students, to which any attempt to consider the needs of the 16–18s as a whole, rather than piecemeal, returns. So long as the financial support system forms a high cliff-edge between the full-time students and the trainees there can be no pretence to an equitable approach across across the board.

Clearly, all that can be done here is to consider the costs implicit in the Tebbit White Paper and ask whether there is no way of distributing this money more fairly. When I speak of the costs implicit in the White Paper, I mean not just those involved in meeting the first, limited guarantee but of extending it to the whole of the 16- and 17-year-olds who have left school. In the case of those who remain in full-time education there is the cost of Educational Maintenance Allowances, a marginal sum, and Child Benefit allowances paid to the parents of such students.

What I have done is to set out these costs, together with the costs of providing traineeships and the cost of full-time education for 16–17s (with some cautious guesswork) as they would be if such a scheme operated in 1983 (Table 9.2).

A year ago an exercise was undertaken by a Cabinet working group which investigated the possibility of introducing a means-tested allowance

Table 9.2 1983: support payments for trainees and students aged 16 and 17

Assumptions:	Present rates of staying on in full-time education
	10% are in ordinary employment
	All not in full-time education receive training allowance
Size of age group:	1,794,000 in Great Britain

Youth Training Scheme

(i) Not in full-time education	Number on Scheme (000s)	% of age group %	Allowance £ pa	Annual cost £m	
Aged 16	431.4	48.2	750	323.6 m	
Aged 17	567.9	63.2	1250	709.9	
	999.3	55.7			£1033.5 m

Full-time education

(ii) In full-time education	Numbers (000s)	% of age group %	EMAs £m	Child Benefit £m	Annual cost £m	
Aged 16	374.1	41.8	2.3	102.1	104.4 m	
Aged 17	241.2	26.8	1.5	65.8	67.3	
	615.3	34.3	3.8	167.9		£171.7 m

(iii) Other public expenditure costs		
MSC administration and grants to sponsors[a]	£1824.5 m	
Education: net recurrent institutional cost[b]		
—410,200 in school @ £1340	549.7	
—205,100 in FE @ £1760	361.0	
Total: 1983		£3940.5 m
Total per capita cost, 1983	£2440.48	

Notes

a Norman Tebbit told the House of Commons on 15 December 1981 that the total cost of the training scheme would average £55 week for each trainee, including the training allowance.

b P.Q. 2 June 1981.

c These figures (and those in Table 9.3) are calculated on the basis of a 52-week year for the payment of allowances.

for those who remained in education and for those unemployed on Supplementary Benefit. Using 1980 figures for the numbers in the various groups, they calculated that it would be possible to pay a new Young Persons' Benefit replacing both Child Benefit and Supplementary Benefit, at a flat rate of £5.65 a week. Another option, preferred by the working group, provided for a basic allowance of £4.74 (the Child Benefit rate) plus a means-tested supplement of up to £10.50 (raising the maximum payment to the then Supplementary Benefit rate of £15.25).

For many reasons, this got nowhere in the face of opposition from the Department of Health and Social Security and the Department of Employment. It did not take account, however, of the money paid out for YOP allowances (at a higher rate than Supplementary Benefit).

If the YOP allowances were taken into account in the share-out the levels of the youth benefit could be increased, though the working group concluded that the YOP payment would have to continue to be about £8 a week more than the top of the Supplementary Benefit scale to preserve its necessary lead.

The introduction of the £15 a week traineeship allowance alters many of the basic figures in the working group calculations. So does the rise in unemployment (and the expansion of YOP) since the figures were used.

Let us, therefore, now see what the figures would look like for 1990, given a reversal of the proportions of those in full-time education and those who have left and entered traineeship (Table 9.3). I have also included various assumptions about means-testing, based on the distribution of gross incomes for households with children from the 1979 Family Expenditure Survey. To preserve the idea of a lead for the heirs and successors of YOP, I have assumed that their allowances are not means-tested, while those of the student group are. (The Cabinet working group used the Family Income Supplement Means Test which is unreasonably steep for this purpose. I have used the more generous Means Test laid down for the Assisted Places Scheme).

These are not wholly frivolous calculations, though they obviously leave a lot to be desired. It is quite plain that the matter of student support is central to any equitable and effective scheme for the 16–18s: that the present imbalance should not be built into a permanent scheme. It is equally true that the imbalance between mandatory and discretionary student grants at the 18 plus level is totally unjustifiable and makes a nonsense of the 1944 Education Act. The trouble is that by aggregating anomalies you present the politicians with more than they can stomach. The latest flirtation with student loans is another attempt, doomed to failure, to break out of this circle. I do not suggest that there is any special logic behind the idea of paying training allowances *without* a means test and EMAs *with* one, but it might enable the money to be spread a little farther.

Conclusion

This paper has turned into a highly speculative exploration of an idea. The details of the exploration are much less important than the underlying propositions: that we should look at the needs of the 16–18-year-olds as a whole—those in education as well as those in (and out of) work;

Table 9.3 1990: support payments for trainees and students aged 16 and 17

Assumptions:	*Staying on rate in full-time education at 67% of 16-year-olds and 45% of 17-year olds*
	10% are in ordinary employment
	All not in full-time education receive training allowance
Size of age: group:	1,467,000 *in Great Britain*

Youth Training Scheme

(i) Not in full-time education	Number on scheme (000s)	% of age group %	Allowance £ pa	Annual cost £m	
Aged 16	164.8	23.3	750	£123.6 m	
Aged 17	338.4	44.5	1250	423.0	
	503.2	34.3			£546.6 m

Full-time education

(ii) In full-time education	Numbers (000s)	% of age group %	Allowance Means Tested £ pa	Annual cost £m	
Aged 16	470.6	66.7	750	200.3 m	
Aged 17	346.5	45.5	750	147.5	
	817.1	55.7			£347.8 m

(iii) Other public expenditure costs		
MSC administration and grants sponsors	£892.6 m	
Education: net recurrent institutional costs		
—408,550 in school @ £1340	547.5	
—408,550 in FE @ £1760	719.0	
Total: 1990		£3053.5 m
Total per capita cost, 1990 £2312.73		

(a) That we should not be stampeded by the opportunism of the Department of Employment and the power of youth unemployment to command public funds, into policies which fail to do justice to the needs of young people.

(b) That we should look beyond crisis measures designed to take two age groups off the labour market to the long-term needs of the post-industrial society, which will certainly require a much broader attitude to higher education and personal development.

(c) That we should recover confidence in what education can offer to the nation as a whole, not just to those who are good at those things which education has traditionally valued most.

It is obvious that at the present time, the Department of Employment is pushing forward with a training scheme which could represent the most important educational development since the mid-1960s. It is equally obvious that the DES is watching from the sidelines, while at the same time pursuing other policies—with regard to examinations and to higher education—which run totally contrary to the logic of the Tebbit initiative.

A new legal, administrative and financial structure is needed for the tertiary stage in general, and for further education in particular. If we could agree on this within the wider fraternity of education, we might at least have the basis of a consensus on which to build a brighter future when the recession is over.

Note

* Text of an Inaugural Lecture given by Stuart Maclure as honorary professor in the Department of Education of the University of Keele, February 8 1982.

References

1 Department of employment (1981) *A New Training Initiative: a Programme for Action*, Cmnd. 8455, December (London, HMSO). Since this address was given the MSC task group proposals have been accepted and the £1,000 million earmarked in the White Paper will now be used to extend the concept of traineeship over a larger section of the 16–18 population, while still maintaining guarantees for unemployed school-leavers. The underlying assumption that full admission to the adult employment market will increasingly be delayed till 18 or 19 remains.

2 Report of the Departmental Committee on Juvenile Education in Relation to Employment after the War (the Lewis Report), 1917. Quoted in Maclure, J.S. (1979) *Educational Documents, England and Wales, 1816 to the present day*, 4th edn, pp. 167–170 (London, Methuen).

3 In adopting the MSC task group's proposals, the Government have decided to accept the higher figures, and retain the Supplementary Benefit entitlement.

4 Further Education Curriculum Review and Development Unit (FEU), *Vocational Preparation*, January 1981.

5 Institute of manpower studies (1981) *Occupational Training Families*, report of a pilot study for the Youth Skills Project, University of Sussex, April. See also their report for the MSC, *Foundation Training Issues*, January 1982.

6 Roberts, Iolo (1981) 'Time to fill the vacuum,' *The Times Educational Supplement*, 11 December.

7 Taylor, Barry (1982) 'The contribution of the professional educator,' *North of England Conference*, Leeds, 5 January.

8 '16–19: *Learning for Life*,' A Labour Party Discussion Document, January 1982.

10 Reconciling the irreconcilable: declining secondary school rolls and the organisation of the system

W. F. Dennison

Source: 'Reconciling the irreconcilable: declining secondary school rolls and the organisation of the system', *Oxford Review of Education*, 9(2): 79–89, 1983.

Fewer children

As the Education Act, 1980 only affects secondary school entry from 1982, and because the numbers of 11-year-olds will fall most rapidly from then until 1988,[1] actual experience in the new circumstances of the implications for secondary schools of fewer children is minimal. However, even before 1982 there were sufficient indications that a scarcity of pupils, as opposed to the shortages of places which characterised much secondary education up to the later 1970s, was likely to have as profound an impact in many districts as the imposition of tripartite arrangements after 1944, or the transition to a comprehensive system. Essentially it is an urban problem; in most rural areas schools will be relatively unaffected, apart from the fewer pupils and less resources.[2] By contrast in many towns and cities parents will have two, three or four schools available for selection. Whether these schools like it or not, perhaps initially without even realising it, they are in competition for pupils; and in situations in which one school's gain is inevitably another's loss.

Paradoxically, too few places present less problems than a surplus. Temporary accommodation can be pressed into service, and most parents will be reasonably happy—if only because they have no other option—about the decisions made on their behalf in the name of scarcity. There will be those who will complain and criticise, but adverse comments not entirely generated by self (child)-interest, are potentially convertible into a lobby for new premises; a possibility over which the LEA can claim, quite rightly, it has limited direct control. However, once a facility of additional school places has been established (in terms of space, staff expertise, etc.) any under-usage introduces elements of client choice, unless, of course, the LEA takes extra places out of use exactly in line with the fall in pupil numbers. In practice this is highly impracticable, and LEAs are already discovering that either of their own volition; as they wish to retain surplus places, or because closures present so many problems, that in numerical terms potential facilities are greater than roll-sizes; and the opportunities for client choice are substantial and likely to continue increasing.[3]

What, then, are the possible outcomes from this increasing divergence between school size and pupil attendance; and, more important, why is it likely to have such an effect on the organisation and functioning of the system? To answer these questions a number of interrelated issues associated with the statutes, working practices, case-law, and traditions of the system have to be considered.

Consumers, the law and selection

The legal position is dominated by the Education Acts of 1944 and 1980. The substantive Act placed the duty of ensuring suitable education firmly with the parent, and while the phrase "by regular attendance at school or otherwise"[4] may have had a 'hollow ring' to the small number of parents who tried to convince the courts of their ability to educate their children at home,[5] the obligation on the parent—as the legislation intended—is clear.[6] To some extent this specification of parental duty is subsumed and contradicted by a later section of the Act, which adopting the dual assumption (proven correct) that most parents would delegate their responsibilities to the LEA and schools would be full, develops the general principle that:

> so far as is compatible with the provision of efficient instruction and training and avoidance of unreasonable public expenditure, pupils are to be educated in accordance with the wishes of their parents.[7]

Taking these sections together, there are obviously two separate routes by which an interested parent could intervene to fulfil his/her obligations. The first of these, by affecting the curriculum, syllabus or teaching methods of the school, is unattainable because of professional practice. It is the headteacher and staff who determine the curriculum, and attempts to introduce even some element of parental influence into the process of school decision-making have been strongly resisted by the teaching profession.[8] The second route therefore—the choice of a school with a curriculum and characteristics which the parent approves—has to be sought if the parent is to have any impact on the child's formal education; and in the main this mechanism remained underdeveloped because of the lack of spare places and the exigencies of the 11+. The story of how the concept of allocating the individual child to the most appropriate school in a bipartite/tripartite system of equal but different secondary schools became, in practice, a rigorous selection procedure is well known.[9] In these circumstances, exacerbated by the shortage of space (the building programme was almost entirely concerned with replacing old schools or coping with additional children), the parent had little or no choice. In the main, if the child was selected, the parents were happy; if they were concerned about a LEA non-selection decision the courses of action available were minimal. Invariably the selective schools were over-subscribed, and if the authority defined the academic selection criteria rigorously it needed a resourceful parent to demonstrate, if need be via the courts, that a place in a selective school for a non-selected child was "compatible with the provision of efficient instruction and training".[10] In other words with a selective system and full schools the exercise of consumer freedom was a 'non-issue'.

It is interesting to speculate what might have happened had falling rolls occurred while most LEAs retained selection at 11+. In what ways might the selection procedures have been modified? Would the level of demand for selective school places have changed? If the assumption is made—and it seems to be demonstrably true—that the consumer demand for selective places considerably exceeds supply, then even with a pupil decline of a third most selective schools would remain full. Obviously, with this order of reduction in the number of available children entry criteria would be modified, but the very act of selection, and therefore by implication the categorisation of non-selected as rejected, would be sufficient to maintain full selective schools. Conversely, even in percentage terms, that is, ignoring for the time being the whole range of adverse educational economic and social factors, the potential effects on the non-selective schools is catastrophic.

If in an area of annual pupil intake of 1000 with a selective entry of 250, there is an overall decline to 600 pupils, and numerically the selective schools are unaffected, the actual reduction for the non-selective schools will be from 750 to 350—in excess of 50%.

Of course, with the consolidation of non-selective secondary education in most LEAs these figures are little more than speculation. However, by the late 1970s, even with secondary re-organisation, the need to readjust the legislation, as a result of falling rolls, was obvious.[11] The interests of both the LEA and the parent had to be protected in this new situation. The LEA must plan pupil numbers, school by school, in a rational way, if it is to avoid situations both educationally unsound and economically inefficient; the parent has to be convinced that the opportunities for choice presented by the excess of places over pupils are realisable, not in general terms but in his or her individual circumstances.

LEA logistics

From a LEA perspective perhaps the most important consideration is logistical. Functioning within tight budgetary constraints, a large authority has to devise arrangements so that several thousand 11-year-olds enter a large number of staffed and resourced schools, with the expectations of minimal disruption, certainly up to age 16. It may well be completing secondary reorganisation, almost certainly it will be trying to reduce entries to previously over-full schools and taking old buildings out of service; it will also have to consider transport problems and factors such as actual and projected population movements. In these circumstances it is hardly surprising that the planning of pupil-numbers, school by school, can be seen as a series of complex issues, to be solved with the use of computer programs, flow-charts, path-scheduling etc., and whatever sophisticated tool of management science seems appropriate.[12] It is not the technical efficacy of these techniques which is in doubt, but their suitability in the decision-making environment of the LEA. In the main they were devised and refined for problems in which the basic units were commodities, and their adaptation to situations involving the circumstances and perceptions of individuals is never easy and sometimes highly inappropriate. In fact, it is probably impossible to over-state the importance of the personal dimension. No matter how large the authority, or how complex the plans for distributing children to schools, it is not the effectiveness or the rationality of the total scheme which impresses a parent, but the potential effect of the decision on the future of his/her child. Stated as simply as this it may sound trite, but it is relatively easy for an administrator, responsible for a complete package of arrangements, to ignore the overwhelming priority given by individuals to the likely effects upon them and their families, in preference to the totality of which they are a very small part.

Without defending individualism and self-centredness in this context, and accepting that in time by example, persuasion and education they may be reduced, it would still be unwise for LEAs to overlook or ignore them when defining and implementing policy as schools empty. If the LEA, for example, decides to reduce entry to a popular school then parents denied a place, a must, in their individual cost-benefit analyses, rank a high cost (their child denied entry) against negative benefits; and that will be their assessment irrespective of the equation of educational, economic or social costs and benefits constructed by the authority for the community as a whole. In addition, there is the evidence empirically and, probably as important, from common experience that the more important a situation is perceived to be by an individual, and the greater the competitive element, the more likely that he/she acts and thinks to fulfil self-interest. On this basis, with perceptions of life chances closely linked to qualifications and continuing high levels of youth unemployment, it would be fallacious for LEAs to assume that, at least for a substantial number of its parents, school choice would not be an important issue.

Of course for most LEAs, while logistical considerations might dominate, these will be expressed through educational, financial and, occasionally, social arguments. A decision to close a school, for example, could be claimed to have educational advantages (the transfer of the children to another school with a broader curriculum), financial savings and social costs (a local community would not have a focus for activities based on the premises). The authority then completes a cost-benefit calculation—

invariably, and probably inevitably, qualitative—and, if the decision is for closure, the implicit assumption is that while some individuals will be aggrieved it is the optimum choice for the whole community. In this context the dilemma is that the general principle, that on occasion decisions taken to benefit the majority in the knowledge that they will be to the detriment of a minority, fits uneasily alongside the exercise of consumer preference; particularly if parents whose wishes are not met have the means and the ability to exploit the political environment.

It would, of course, be misleading to imply that all parents are equally committed to the role of selective consumer. Some, even when choice possibilities are available, will be unaware, and, if alerted, show minimal interest. As far as the LEA is concerned, if all parents were in this category it could pursue a logistical approach to declining rolls with few hindrances. Alternatively, if all parents were highly committed and fully aware of the choices available, the LEA would have more difficulty in implementing policy, but these problems would be limited in comparison to the actual situation in which levels of involvement include the two extremes and every possible category in between. As a result, the LEA has a responsibility both to sustain the interest and involvement of the most concerned parent—for there are many potential advantages in such high commitment—and protect the education of the child whose parents are apparently unwilling to accept consumer responsibilities; recognising that these represent two ends of a spectrum and that all other spectral positions are occupiable and might—and, in an ideal world, should—require individual attention.

Theoretically, of course, the interrelated and possibly conflicting interests of parent, child and community are safeguarded because all LEA decision-making is subject to democratic scrutiny and, if there is a major dispute, legal processes. It is not as if decisions are made by an anonymous board of directors responsible to an equally anonymous group of institutional shareholders. Whether it is the determination of general policy (school amalgamations, changes in catchment areas, etc.) or the resolution of an individual parental request then the Education Committee, and possibly the main Council, have a very substantial role in initiation and implementation of whatever is decided. In many situations the Education Committee is the ultimate arbiter, and the plans and decisions of the professional administrators are subject to the normal constraints of a political environment. Lobbies can be established (to safeguard a school threatened by closure, for example), individual councillors, who may not be members of the Education Committee, can be persuaded to support an aggrieved parent, so that policies promoted by administrators as rational and sensible—with, to them, educational, financial and social advantages—have to be foregone. In other words, schemes to reduce pupil numbers which to an outsider appear valid and reasonable, with high benefits and low costs, might well be unsustainable if they ignore the political dimension; and general recommendations to LEAs about procedures have to be contingent upon individual circumstances.[13]

Closures and reductions

School closures are the clearest examples of how a LEA strategy can be diverted by an adverse climate. The administrators suggest and the committee approves a policy of closures, both to save money and to avoid attendance at schools with few children and a restricted curriculum. What has been overlooked are the social costs to the community now without a school, and the extent to which these can be used as a focus to mobilise support and provoke criticism. Quite possibly there are many non-educational factors in the protest, but the potential loss of the school is so pivotal, so major a step, that it may appear to be the only ingredient in the community complaint. It is, for example, extremely difficult to convince parents that the financial savings are worth having when they are so insignificant in comparison to total authority spending, and the educational benefits of attendance at a larger school, probably with increased travelling, are not easily explained or demonstrated.[14] Faced with hostility, there are many political attractions to the LEA in compromise, and a reversal of the original decision to close, placing the total strategy of reducing pupil-places in jeopardy. Ultimately, the rational scheme can be replaced by a series of political expediences. The nub of the problem is that the time schedule involved in closures, amalgamations etc. must be considerably longer than that of the politician subject to re-election. It would be far too cynical to suggest that politicians want to be liked, but if they are to continue to do their jobs they require re-election, and this is unlikely if for a long time they are associated with unpopular measures. Given the time-scale, therefore, the sustainment of a consistent contraction policy may just not be feasible.

Closure represents the extreme; if a school shuts there can be no compromise, the decision cannot be disguised, and it is the situation which most easily arouses community hostility. Nevertheless LEAs continue to close schools; with much of the strategy depending on how vociferous and well organised is the opposition, the logicality of the argument of the LEA and any opponents, the use made of the media, and the nature of the local politics. In practical terms, when faced with a difficult closure situation, the position of the LEA is unaltered by the Education Act, 1980. True, they have more freedom in theory, as a decision to shut has now only to be approved by the Secretary of State if it is opposed by ten local electors, but if a group are to mount effective opposition then gaining this level of support is no more than a starting point.[15] However, as pupil numbers reduce, it is the more sophisticated procedures and subtle changes associated with consumer preference which become more significant.

Even with full schools it was often difficult for a LEA to demonstrate that the addition of one extra pupil made a school over-full except when, with selection, unambiguous academic criteria were available. As a result, for the individual parent, the Education Act 1944 was interpreted quite liberally, to a certain extent because the marginal cost to the school of taking one additional pupil was, and remains, so minimal. Therefore, articulate or awkward or over-concerned parents could often reverse a LEA decision; particularly if they were prepared to utilise the political environment and achieve the backing of local councillors, favourable media coverage etc. However, for most parents such levels of activity did not occur, most probably because the potential benefits were thought not to warrant them. They were reasonably happy, although possibly not in total agreement, with the school choice made for them and they could see no feasible alternative. For the most affluent there was always the option of moving house to a preferred catchment area, or opting out of maintained education; for the great majority, aspirational levels became attuned to what was available and consumer freedoms remained under-developed.

In the new circumstances of less pupils than places, and the possibility of substantial vacancies, then it is unlikely that previous expectations will hold. Parents may well be satisfied with decisions made in their name when they perceive there are few alternatives; it is improbable that this will remain so when real choice opportunities prevail. On this basis alone the idea of Planned Admission Levels, or artificial restrictions on school entries, is a strategy beset with problems. To assist with their planning, and to inform parents, LEAs must now publish a maximum pupil-entry for every school; in addition they are allowed to reduce the number of admissions to a school by 20% of the base figure (normally the entry in September 1979) without having to ask for DES permission.[16] The rationale is indisputable. If pupil-numbers are to decline by a third, say, and the LEA thinks it inappropriate, or is unable, to close schools then substantial reductions in the annual intakes to all schools is a logical method of allocating pupils to schools; both safeguarding their education and avoiding too wasteful a use of resources. However, it is one thing for a scheme to be rational and logical, in practice it may be another for it to become generally acceptable.

As it plans admissions, and even if it does this publicly only a year at a time in a contracting situation, a LEA has to reveal arrangements to reduce school sizes. For most LEAs it will only be a short time before non-controversial opportunities to take clearly unsatisfactory accommodation out of service are used up. Then it is a matter of Education Committee agreement to make arrangements containing unpopular elements, and the probability that sectional interests will become agitated. Nevertheless, because of the pressures on it to reduce surplus places, and overall financial constraints, each LEA will have to decide something about admissions, and whether this is done on a short-term basis (perhaps to avoid the development of what might be thought too contentious a policy), or involves a long-range scheme for reducing entries, closing schools, etc., with resultant problems (many stemming from the difference in this time-scale to that associated with the political process), a key issue will be how rigorously the detail of the adopted scheme is pursued. Take, for example, a decision to reduce the pupil intake of a school from 180 to 150 (a choice a LEA is perfectly entitled to make). Irrespective of the time horizon of the planning schedule, the substantive item is how staunchly this decision will be defended if strongly criticised. Clearly the school can accept 180 children, or perhaps more, because it has previously done so.

Who, then, are likely to be opposed to such a scheme? In the first place, if it is a popular school, the parents of at least 30 children, denied a place. Why should this happen, when, in their perception, a main reason is to sustain numbers in another school, less popular, less effective and not offering the education they want for their child? Even the basest of arguments, having paid taxes and rates why should they be disadvantaged, is not without substance in this context. For with the new legislation LEAs have to make their own arrangements so that each parent can express a preference, authorities have a duty to comply with these preferences, and dissatisfied parents a right to use the specially constituted appeals procedure. In this example, therefore, the LEA has to go both through a political process of convincing parents, local councillors, etc. that a reduction in pupil-entry to the school is desirable, and a judicial process of specifying and applying criteria which will stand up to the scrutiny of an appeals committee. It can, of course, attempt to limit entry to exactly 150 pupils, by claiming that even the admission of one more child would 'prejudice the provision of efficient education or the efficient use of resources', although the supportive logic is rather dubious on both educational and financial grounds. However, were it to do this, how should the 150 children be chosen, if the LEA rejects, as most of them do, selection according to 'ability or aptitude'? What happens if the specified criteria, based perhaps on primary school membership or some residential qualification, produce 155 or 145 potential attenders? In the former case either new guidelines have to be invented to eliminate five pupils or the 'full at 150 rule' must be breached (and if the school can accept 155 pupils why not 156, 157 etc?); in the latter case how does the authority select five more children to 'top-up'? The possibilities that these situations present to the aggrieved parent are clearly substantial. Probably by gaining the support of local councillors, less often by exploiting the media, it will not be difficult to show that the LEA and its administrators have devised an inflexible policy, which is insensitive to the wishes of local people. Now, if only a handful of parents feel mistreated this will be a gross misinterpretation of the impact of LEA arrangements, but it cannot divert attention from the developing opportunities, particularly for the articulate parent who knows something about the system. Whether it is checking on school curricula to justify the original preference, or presenting a case to an appeals committee, it is more than likely that a determined parent will be successful; and the strengthening of school attendance provisions in the Education Act 1980 will have minimal effect, for it was only a tiny minority of disaffected parents who were so aggrieved that they prevented their children attending any school.[17]

In the context of changed legislation the attitudes of school staffs and headteachers towards admission limits and parental preferences is clearly important. Many, as professionals, will have a wider concern for education in the area than for factors limited to their own school, but in a contracting situation, with size of staff dependant upon the number of pupils, it would be surprising if the first priority were not seen as maximising roll-size. This is not over-cynical: it does not imply that teachers will do anything to attract pupils nor suggest that the advantages of job-saving will be viewed more favourably than the broader curriculum which can be offered to more children by additional staff. Nevertheless, there can be no doubt that, in the example, the staff would be strongly opposed to the idea of arbitrarily reducing the entry limit from 180 to 150 pupils. In terms of job-protection, alone, for teachers (and the support from non-teaching staff is likely to be equally powerful) 30 less children per year during the five years of secondary schooling is the equivalent to 150 pupils and up to 10 posts, if the PTR is held constant.

Therefore, the institutional stance likely to be adopted by popular schools is obvious. They offer an education which is in demand and they need to protect that position—indeed if they fail to do this they might not be able to sustain the elements which apparently makes them attractive. As far as less popular schools are concerned their main thrust must be towards situations in which they themselves have to resist arbitrary reductions in entries; in other words to convert into popular schools. The role of the headteacher is particularly interesting. As far as staff, pupils and parents are concerned, he/she has a measure of responsibility for interpreting and implementing LEA policy. Yet, with regard to the allocation of pupils to schools it is impossible to be neutral, and extremely difficult to balance school and LEA interests. For a whole range of reasons—staff jobs, curriculum protection, prestige (far better to be running a school which is in demand than one few people want to know about)—a main objective of each headteacher must be, at worst, to minimise reductions in pupil numbers; even to the extent of attracting pupils from other LEAs. The scope for a well-placed entrepreneurial headteacher is very real. The school has something good to offer, which consumers with their new found freedoms are demanding, and therefore it is worthwhile opposing LEA attempts to limit entries or supporting efforts by individual parents to gain an admittance at variance with LEA arrangements.

In many situations, therefore, the interests of school, headteacher and consumer apparently coalesce, but often to the detriment of LEA arrangements for pupil allocations intended to limit the adverse affects of falling rolls. There are still other factors which make the LEA task more difficult. It is highly probable, for example, that LEAs with popular schools will exploit opportunities to offer places to children from neighbouring authorities.[18] There is the kudos of appearing to have the better schools, more chance of maintaining established curricula, enhanced job-prospects for staff because of the additional pupils, and the financial advantages of spending at marginal rates while recovering the higher average cost from the child's home authority. Even within their own areas LEAs have the real problems posed by special agreement and, particularly, voluntary aided schools. They have a different administrative relationship with the LEA from other maintained schools, a majority of non-LEA governors, and whatever overall plans the LEA has for contraction those parts which affect these schools, whether it is amalgamations, entry limitations or closures, have to be separately agreed with individual governing bodies, many of whom can rely upon substantial community support. In these circumstances, given the time constraints on LEA decision-making—the scarcity of attention available for any problem—there must be a temptation to evolve arrangements for county schools alone as this, although difficult, is easier to achieve than unanimity of purpose with a number of independent governing bodies and church authorities. If the voluntary schools are popular, however, the resultant developments will not be dissimilar to those outlined earlier for selective and non-selective schools, with the county schools taking a disproportionate reduction in pupil numbers and the voluntary schools continuing relatively unaffected.

Reconciling the irreconcilable

So long as there are more places than pupils there will be tension between the LEA and parents over allocations; and, irrespective of whether 5 or 95% of parents are sufficiently concerned to make sure that their wishes prevail, the nature of the problems presented to the LEA, and the overall concerns of the parents, will be the same. The LEA has to deploy resources to maximum effect so that the education of all children is protected, not just the 95 or 5% with overtly committed parents; the parents need to convince themselves that they are doing the best for their child. Additionally, it is not a tension which will evaporate of its own accord. This present government wishes for more elements of parental choice to be introduced,[19] and while other administrations may be elected less supportive of the principle of consumer freedom, it is improbable that at local level a reduced commitment by DES would be translated into practical situations much different from those currently developing. Therefore, until the early 1990s, while secondary school rolls decline, the exercise of choice will be a dominant influence on the evolution and structure of the system. Many schools without a captive audience will have to attract potential pupils in competition with others. Those that are successful may even become larger, if the LEA has a sufficiently flexible admissions policy, or at least maintain entry levels; those that are less successful will obviously decline more rapidly. The paradox is, of course, that schools able to attract the most pupils will by this very attractiveness appeal to yet more parents; conversely the unpopular school may well be rejected by some parents simply because of its apparent unpopularity—possibly having to close eventually through a shortage of pupils.

In a structural sense the probable impact of less and smaller schools is obvious; but also in organisational, social and pedagogical terms the influence of fewer pupils will be only slightly more disguised. One of the main issues established by the empirical work of the 1950s and 1960s on educational opportunity and social class was the relationship between parental interest and occupational status.[20] On the assumption that this connection remains, there will be social bias among parents attracted by a popular school (and able to ensure that their children attend), and conversely among the children who continue to attend a rapidly declining school. Already, given some parental freedom, there is evidence that these skews in commitment are reflected in the children's ability measures.[21] More directly, popular schools will not only attract extra children but a greater share of able pupils. Examination performances will benefit, providing yet another factor in the attraction of additional children. This is not to suggest that good examination results are the only item the concerned parent requires of a secondary school, but they meet an important need. The response of the school, if it is to maximise pupil numbers—for job-security, prestige or whatever reasons—has to be commensurate and therefore, because of the demands of the examination supportive infra-structure, pedagogically and attitudinally the school is affected almost as much by the possibility of fewer pupils, or what it must do to limit this occurrence, as the actual reduction in children on roll.

This unavoidable competition among schools for extra pupils epitomises the problems of the LEA. In this context there are many potential benefits in inter-school rivalry. It is a useful motivator in reviewing practice; the successful will try to capitalise on their strengths, the less-so are more likely to be spurred to new activity and greater effort by the threat of failure than the words of some innocuous HMI or local advisory report. In many ways fewer pupils can be used as a vehicle for holding the school and its staff accountable to, at least, some of the consumers, if not the LEA. On the negative side the competition is rarely, if ever, fair. Even before falling rolls, schools had different reputations, some good, some bad, and these can be difficult to change in the public mind. Not only this, but schools have moved into rivalry situations from variable vantage points. Indisputably, an ex-grammar school, generously provided for over many years in staff, buildings and other resources, is going to appear more attractive than a recently established ex-secondary modern school which has never had an opportunity to accrue demonstrably sufficient experience, expertise and materials, irrespective of the inherent quality of the educations offered by the two schools.[22] In other words, consumer judgments may well be based on what has gone before as opposed to current performance and practice. More generally, consumer knowledge can never be perfect; obviously because some parents do not wish to know about the choices they could make, but also as those who want to select cannot possess the necessary myriad of up-dated detail about a range of schools. In fact, it would be misleading to imply that the statutory obligation upon LEAs to publish information about schools can do anything more than partially ameliorate the situation;[23] indeed, some of what it appears, may well exacerbate the difference in attractiveness between popular and unpopular schools, further extending the unfair competition.

From the perspectives of parent, school and LEA, the problems and opportunities presented by falling rolls are very different. The school, for the first time, may well have to adapt its objectives and practices, not in line with professional judgments but on account of consumer preferences if it is to attract sufficient pupils. Even with appeals committees, some parents will be most unhappy with the school their child has to attend—to the extent that they question whether they have any choice at all.[24] That this can occur, while simultaneously LEAs perceive consumer choice as prejudicing their ability to plan and organise the system, symbolises the dichotomy in needs and interests. The parent has a legitimate concern for the education of the child; the LEA has to arrange for the optimum education of all children—perhaps with spare capacity and differential attractivenesses the two factors are irreconcilable. Parental commitments will not disappear—in many ways the LEA and the school need to cultivate them—and the LEA can do no more than tamper and modify existing arrangements as they evolve. Positive discrimination in favour of unpopular schools is made difficult by inter-school rivalry; some control over travel arrangements is possible but in some disadvantaged areas may exaggerate the unpopularity of neighbourhood schools; linking primary with secondary schools in catchment areas will further heighten geographic variations and create a pecking order among primary schools; and all are no more than minor palliatives. It could be of course that what appears irreconcilable in theory turns out differently as practice develops during the middle and later 1980s. More likely, however, with varying degrees of covertness, LEAs will allow scarcity of attention orthodoxy to prevail, except when they have no alternative but to intervene. The attractive schools, adapting willingly or not, some of the measures preferred by consumers, will prosper, the unattractive schools will find themselves still more disadvantaged.

Notes and references

1 DES (1982) *Report on Education, Number 97: Pupil and School Leavers: future numbers* (London, HMSO).

2 Cmnd. 8494. *The Governments Expenditure Plans 1982–83 to 1984–85*, April 1982 (London, HMSO).

3 *Education*, 4.12.81, p. 426 on the Association of County Councils' response to DES Circular 2/81.

4 Education Act, 1944, s. 36.

5 Taylor, G. & Saunders, J.B. (1976) *The New Law of Education* (London, Butterworth).

6 Dent, H.C. (1968) *The Education Act 1944*, 12th edn, pp. 33–34, 8th edn, p. 129 (University of London Press).

7 Education Act, 1944, s. 76.

8 The reception given by representatives of the teaching profession to the Taylor Report (DES, *A New Partnership for our Schools*, 1977, HMSO) on School Governors, in particular the recommendations of lay participants in curricular matters, illustrates this point.

9 For example in Parkinson, M.H. (1970) *The Labour Party and the Organisation of Secondary Education 1918–65* (London, Routledge & Kegan Paul).

10 Education Act, 1944, s. 76.

11 In this context it is significant that the clauses in the Education Bill of the last Labour administration dealing with falling rolls issues were not markedly different from those in the Education Act, 1980 of the Conservative government.

12 For an example of a large LEA plan see *City of Birmingham Education Department: Secondary School Profiles 1981–1990*, 17.7.81.

13 The general recommendations resulting from the DES sponsored research study on secondary school falling rolls (reported in Briault, E.W.H. & Smith, F. (1980) *Falling Rolls in Secondary Schools*, NFER) would appear to lack this dimension.

14 If a LEA spends £50m then a projected saving even of £50,000 (0.1% of the total) following a school closure must seem, to those committed to keeping the school open, quite trivial; particularly when so much of the detail of the £50,000 projected saving is debatable.

15 Education Act, 1980, s. 12 (3).

16 Education Act, 1980, s. 15 (1).

17 Education Act, 1980, s. 10 & 11.

18 Education Act, 1980, s. 8 (3) (d).

19 *Education*, 8.10.82, p. 265. Address to Conservative Party Conference by Secretary of State for Education and Science.

20 For example in Central Advisory Council for Education (England) (1967) *Children and their Primary Schools: a report* (London, HMSO).

21 Fiske, D. (1978) 'Parental Choice—For How Many' *Where*, No. 136, March, pp. 71–73.

22 Byrne, E.M. (1974) *Planning and Educational Inequality* (Slough, NFER).

23 Education Act, 1980, s. 8.

24 *New Society*, 26.8.82, p. 339.

11 Educational attainment in secondary schools

John Marks and Caroline Cox

Source: 'Educational attainment in secondary schools', *Oxford Review of Education*, 10(1): 7–31, 1984.

Since 1964 the proportion of British secondary schoolchildren in comprehensive schools has risen from about 10% to approximately 90%. A major influence in this process was *Circular 10/65*,[1] issued by Anthony Crosland when he was Secretary of State for Education. This rapid changeover to comprehensive schools has been called "... one of the most significant developments in secondary education since 1902, that is, from the time when the state first supported secondary education".[2]

Once under way, the change to a system consisting wholly of comprehensive schools has been widely regarded as inevitable—see, for example, the book *Halfway There*,[3] published in 1970.

Even so it was recognised as long ago as 1969 that comprehensive education "... is a gigantic experiment with the life chances of millions of children. The results will not be known for years".[4]

An experiment suggests the collection of evidence and its evaluation. While recognising that there is much more to education than examinations, this paper will take it as axiomatic that public examination results are *one* important kind of evidence which can help to evaluate changes in the secondary school system.[5]

In attempting to assess the rapid movement towards a comprehensive system it is also important to appreciate that many other factors affect secondary education. It makes no sense to try to compare the present primarily comprehensive system with the selective system[6] which existed 20 years ago. The 'ideal' comparison would be between the comprehensive system as it is now with what the selective system would be *now* if *Circular 10/65* had not been implemented, given all the other changes of the last 20 years such as increasing resources, greater equalisation of resources between pupils in different schools, the raising of the school leaving age, the rise of CSE and the increasing proportion of girls succeeding in public examinations.[7]

In the real world such 'ideal' comparisons can rarely be made. There is also an additional problem: much research in the social sciences can interact with and change its subject-matter and educational research has repeatedly influenced educational policy through many post-war studies.[8]

However, the absence of systematic monitoring of "the most important reform in secondary education since 1902"[9] has been remarkable. Eighteen years have now elapsed since *Circular 10/65* and it should be possible to assess some of the evidence which is now available. In this paper we will first consider the kinds of evidence provided by five recent and very different studies, comparing in turn the sample, the data, the types of analysis, and the results for each study.[10] Then we will discuss the way those studies have been received; this topic is important because, in an open democratic society, how research is perceived by the public may significantly affect future policy. Finally we will suggest how reliable information about secondary schools can be made more widely available.

Standards in English schools by Marks, Cox & Pomian-Srzednicki[10]

This study analyses information on examination results which has to be made publicly available to comply with regulations made under the 1980 Education Act. All state schools, both maintained and voluntary, and all schools accepting pupils under the Assisted Places scheme are required to make available to parents on request their full 'A' level, 'O' level and CSE examination results, subject by subject and grade by grade; the numbers who are unclassified or who fail do not have to be published.

Sample

The main sample used had a very broad coverage including 54 of the 96 LEAs and more than half the pupils in England; examination results for 1981 were collected for 1897 schools with more than 349,000 fifth-year pupils.[11]

The sample was designed to include LEAs with different types of school organisation, with different social class and other socio-economic characteristics and from all parts of the country. Counties were included from the North, the Midlands, East Anglia, the West Country, the South and the South-East, as were LEAs from all the Metropolitan Districts—Greater Manchester, Merseyside, Tyne and Wear, West and South Yorkshire, the West Midlands and London. The response rate was very high—nearly 100% for LEAs sending their results *en bloc* and around 90% when schools were approached individually.

Results were also collected from three LEAs in Wales and from 125 independent schools with more than 12,000 fifth-year pupils.

Data

For each school the number of passes in each grade at 'A' level, 'O' level and CSE is recorded for eight major subjects—English, French, history and geography (arts subjects) and mathematics, physics, chemistry and biology (science subjects)—and for all other subjects taken together.

For each school information was also collected about school size, the size of the fifth-year and seventh-year cohorts, school type (comprehensive, grammar, secondary modern, other; mixed, boys, girls; maintained, voluntary or special agreement), religious denomination (if any) and age range. In addition information was collected about the type of entry to the school (comprehensive, grammar or secondary modern) when the 16-year-old cohort taking 'O' level or CSE examinations in 1981 were entering their secondary schools (normally 1976 for entry at age 11) and when the 18-year-old cohort taking 'A' level examinations in 1981 were entering secondary school (normally 1974 for entry at age 11).

For each LEA data were obtained for pupil-teacher ratios for secondary schools and for expenditure per secondary school pupil for 1980–81 from the information published by the Chartered Institute of Public Finance and Accountancy (Education Statistics, 1980–81 Actuals).

Two socio-economic indicators were used. The proportion of children living in households whose head is a semi-skilled or unskilled manual or farm worker (social classes IV and V) was used as a measure of the social class composition for each LEA; these data were taken from the DES *Statistical Bulletin* 8/82 (July 1982) and had been derived from the 1978 National Household and Dwelling Survey carried out by the Department of the Environment. *Bulletin 8/82* also gives for each LEA the percentage of children born outside the United Kingdom or belonging to non-white ethnic groups and these data were used in some analyses. The other socio-economic indicators for LEAs given in *Bulletin 8/82* were found to be fairly closely correlated with the social class indicator and with each other; in addition they were found to be less highly correlated with examination results. Consequently they were not used in the main analyses.

Types of analysis

Indicators:

The primary examination results data are used to construct five major indicators of examination performance:

(i) the number of 'O' level and CSE grade 1 (OC1) passes per pupil (all the indicators are expressed as proportions of the total fifth-year cohort—either nationally, for each LEA or for each group of schools or school, as appropriate—and not as passes per entrant; in this way problems caused by differences in entry policy are minimised and fairer comparisons are possible);

(ii) the number of CSE passes at grades 2 to 5 (C2–5) per pupil;
(iii) the quality of 'O' level and CSE (O/C) passes is estimated by calculating the O/C points per pupil using a 7-point scale devised by ILEA (the scale ranges from 7 points for an A-grade at 'O' level to 1 point for a CSE grade 5);
(iv) the number of 'A' level passes per pupil;
(v) the number of 'A' level points per pupil using the 5-point scale devised by UCCA (ranging from 5 points for an A-grade to 1 point for an E).

Indicators (i), (ii) and (iv) are based on the *numbers* of passes while indicators (iii) and (v) refer to the quality of passes. Each of these indicators is analysed for all subjects together and for the eight main subjects together. The 'O' level and CSE indicators are also studied for each of the eight main subjects separately with particular attention being given to mathematics and English. The 'A' level indicators are also studied for the four main arts subjects taken together and science subjects taken together. *Standards* therefore uses 30 separate indicators of performance at 'O' level/CSE and eight separate indicators of performance at 'A' level.

National averages

National averages for maintained schools in England are calculated for all 30 'O' level/CSE indicators and for all eight 'A' level indicators. The same indicators are used in nearly all the analyses and they have always been averaged over the number of pupils in the appropriate cohort. This means that data of similar type are presented at all levels from the individual schools, through groups of schools of various kinds right up to local authority and national level.

Local authorities

Averages are given for 57 LEAs in England and Wales for 10 'O' level/CSE indicators—OC1 passes, C2–5 passes and O/C points per pupil for all subjects and main subjects and OC1 passes and O/C points for mathematics and English—and for all eight 'A' level indicators.

Multiple regression analyses were carried out for eight of the indicators of examination performance as outcome measures—OC1 passes and O/C points per pupil for all and main subjects, OC1 passes per pupil for mathematics and English and 'A' level passes and points per pupil for main subjects. Five input variables were used in each case—pupil/teacher ratio, expenditure per pupil, low social class, selectivity and ethnicity (see above for definitions). The regression equations and the correlation matrix are given.

Since the correlation and regression analyses confirmed many earlier studies in showing a strong correlation between social class and examination results, LEAs were divided into three more homogeneous groups with respect to the low social class variable—Group A with 7–13% in social classes IV/V, Group B with 14–18%; and Group C with 19–31% (national average 16%; national range 7–31%). National averages are calculated for LEAs in each of these groups for 'O' level/CSE and 'A' level indicators and the appropriate social class group is indicated for each LEA in the tables for separate LEAs.

Types of school

National averages are given for pupils at comprehensive schools (293,200 pupils), secondary modern schools (33,000 pupils) and grammar schools (19,900 pupils) for all 30 'O' level/CSE indicators and for all eight 'A' level indicators. All these 'O' level/CSE indicators and the four main 'A' level indicators are also given for each type of school in each social class group.

In addition, for the eight main 'O' level/CSE and the four main 'A' level indicators, these results for different types of school were used to estimate the values of these indicators for a wholly selective system of schools with either 25 or 30% of pupils at grammar schools. These estimated values for a selective system of schools were calculated for all the schools in the sample and also for each social class group separately and were then compared with the corresponding values for comprehensive schools. For the national sample of comprehensive schools, it was also possible to estimate a correction for the 'O' level/CSE indicators for those comprehensive schools with very few pupils in the top 20% of the ability range; this was done using data from the HMI report *Aspects of Secondary Education in England* (HMSO, December 1979).

Variations between and within schools

Some data are given for the variations on some major indicators which are found *between* schools of the same type in the same LEA. In addition details are given of the full results for 15 individual schools and the implications of some of the differences between them are discussed. In addition, individual school profiles are described which set out all 30 of the 'O' level/CSE indicators and enable them to be compared with the average results for schools of the same type and social class group. These profiles also enable some analysis to be made of the considerable variations between the results for separate subjects *within the same school* and in some cases allow inferences to be made concerning strengths and weaknesses of different departments within the same school; this possibility arises because many of the same pupils are involved, particularly in cognate subjects, and thus the influence of differences in ability and social class between pupils is much reduced.

Results

National averages

Table 11.1 summarises some of the results for four 'O' level/CSE indicators—O/C points per pupil for all subjects and OC1 passes per pupil for main subjects, English and mathematics. These data are first given for all schools, comprehensive schools, secondary modern schools and grammar

Table 11.1 Data from *Standards*

	No. of schools	No. of pupils	O/C points All subjects	OC1 passes per pupil		
				Main subjects	English	Maths
England						
All	1,897	349,000	22.7	1.53	0.50	0.27
C	1,200	253,000	21.4	1.34	0.45	0.23
M	236	33,000	19.4	0.89	0.32	0.17
G	162	19,900	39.0	4.44	1.35	0.72
S1=0.25G+0.75M			24.3	1.78	0.58	0.31
CF			21.9	1.44	0.48	0.24
Social class Group A						
All	578	103,000	25.1	1.84	0.60	0.33
C	306	64,000	23.8	1.64	0.55	0.29
M	87	13,000	20.6	0.97	0.33	0.17
G	63	7,800	41.6	4.91	1.48	0.81
S1=0.25G+0.75M			25.9	1.96	0.62	0.33
Social class Group B						
All	851	159,000	22.3	1.42	0.48	0.25
C	521	111,500	21.2	1.28	0.43	0.22
M	101	14,700	19.9	0.95	0.36	0.18
G	60	7,300	39.4	4.53	1.38	0.73
S1=0.25G+0.75M			24.8	1.85	0.62	0.32
Social class Group C						
All	468	87,000	20.8	1.31	0.44	0.22
C	373	77,000	20.3	1.22	0.42	0.21
M	48	5,200	15.3	0.54	0.19	0.10
G	39	4,800	34.0	3.53	1.13	0.53
S1=0.25G+0.75M			20.0	1.29	0.43	0.21

Key
C—comprehensive; M—secondary modern; G—grammar; S—selective; CF—full range comprehensive (see text). A school is classified as C, M or G according to its status and the entry it received in 1976 when the cohort taking 'O' level/CSE in 1981 were entering their secondary schools. All schools include schools whose 1976 entries did not fall clearly into one of these three categories together with other schools such as bilateral, technical, former independent schools etc.

schools in England and then for each of the categories for social class Groups A, B and C. In addition the number of schools and fifth-year pupils is given for each category.

These data are examples of some of the many national averages—all for a very large number of pupils—which are given in *Standards*; these figures provide national norms which can be used as benchmarks in assessing the results of individual schools or groups of schools.

Local authorities

Results for separate LEAs show wide variations. For example the average number of OC1 passes per pupil for all subjects ranges from 3.05 to 1.15 (England mean 2.14), for main subjects from 2.23 to 0.73 (mean 1.53), for English from 0.74 to 0.26 (mean 0.50) and for mathematics from 0.42 to 0.15 (mean 0.27).

Considerable variations were also found between LEAs within the social class groups described above. For example, for LEAs in Group B, which are near the national average for proportions of pupils from classes IV or V, OC1 passes per pupil for all subjects range from 2.69 to 1.34 (mean 2.05), for main subjects from 2.04 to 0.91 (mean 1.42), for English from 0.63 to 0.31 (mean 0.48) and for mathematics from 0.34 to 0.16 (mean 0.25).

The correlation and multiple regression analyses of the 'O' level/CSE indicators for separate LEAs all showed a consistent pattern. For example, OC1 passes per pupil for main subjects was negatively correlated with expenditure (correlation coefficient −0.49), low social class (−0.64) and ethnicity (−0.53) and positively correlated with pupil/teacher ratio (0.34) and selectivity (0.52); similar correlations of comparable magnitudes are found for the other 'O' level/CSE indicators. The multiple regression equations for all six 'O' level/CSE indicators also showed a consistent pattern—the outcome measures were all negatively correlated with expenditure, low social class and ethnicity and positively correlated with selectivity.

Of the input variables, pupil/teacher ratio and expenditure were highly correlated (−0.79) and both were highly correlated with ethnicity (−0.61 and 0.71 respectively). However low social class and selectivity were fairly weakly correlated with each other (−0.29) and with the other output variables.

Consequently it was decided to investigate these two variables further by analysing separately the results for different social class groups and for different types of school (selective and comprehensive). Such analyses also had the advantage that large and small LEAs would not be treated as equivalent, as they were in the correlation analyses, but would contribute to the overall averages in direct proportion to the number of pupils involved.

Social class

All the 'O' level/CSE indicators involving OC1 passes and O/C points show a consistent pattern; they are highest for Group A and lowest for Group C with the Group B data in the middle at levels a little below the national averages for England. OC1 passes for Group A are about 40% higher than those for Group C and O/C points are about 25% higher; Table 11.1 shows some examples of these data. By contrast C2–5 passes per pupil are very similar for all three groups.

Types of school

Table 11.1 gives some examples of results for comprehensive, secondary modern and grammar schools both nationally and for each social class group.

For comprehensive schools, all the indicators involving OC1 passes and O/C points are consistently somewhat below the averages for all schools—both nationally and within social class groups (see Table 11.1). However C2–5 passes per pupil are consistently a little above the national average for all schools. The national averages for all comprehensive schools are virtually identical to the average results for all those LEAs in the sample which were fully comprehensive in 1976 (17 LEAs; 330 schools; 72,000 fifth year pupils).

Secondary modern schools have very few pupils considered to be in the top 20% of the ability range—for which 'O' level examinations were originally intended. Given this, their pupils' results on 'O' level/CSE indicators are very good. On average pupils at secondary modern schools obtained 1.39 OC1 passes per pupil and 19.4 O/C points per pupil compared with figures for comprehensive school pupils of 1.91 and 21.4 respectively. The results for secondary modern schools in Group B are even closer to those for comprehensive schools in this group; however in Group C the differences are rather greater.

Secondary modern pupils also achieved particularly good results in the core subjects of mathematics and English; for example, they obtained more O/C points per pupil in mathematics than *all* the pupils in seven LEAs and more in English than *all* the pupils in no less than 17 LEAs—almost a third of those studied.

The results for grammar school pupils are uniformly high (see Table 11.1 for some examples) as would be expected given that they only admit pupils considered to be of high ability. Pupils at grammar schools in social class Group A obtain better results on average than those in Group C with Group B in between at levels slightly above the national average.

Comparisons between comprehensive and selective systems of schools

The national averages for comprehensive (C), secondary modern (M) and grammar school (G) pupils are used to compare the results, both nationally and within social class groups, which might be expected from a wholly selective (S) system of schools compared with a wholly comprehensive system. For the latter the national averages for comprehensive schools are used (see above). These data are compared with two estimates of the average for a selective system; the lower estimate S1 is calculated by assuming that 25% of pupils attend grammar schools (S1 = 0.25G+0.75M) and the upper estimate S2 by assuming 30%. Estimates are also made of the results to be expected from comprehensive schools with pupils from the full ability range CF; however these estimates could only be made for the national averages since the data from HMI on which the corrections are based are only available in this form.

Comparisons of national averages are made for the eight main 'O' level/CSE indicators and are remarkably consistent. They show that the estimates S1 and S2 for a fully selective system are considerably higher than the figures C and CF for a fully comprehensive system. The differences are higher for OC1 passes per pupil ranging from 27 to 35% for S1 compared with C and from 19 to 29% for S1 compared with CF. For O/C points per pupil the differences range from 14 to 18% for S1 compared with C and from 11 to 16% for S1 compared with CF (see Table 11.1 for examples of these data). The differences are, of course, greater for S2. The magnitudes of these differences are also consistent with those estimated from the coefficients in the multiple regression equations described above.

These differences are even larger for social class Groups A and B but for Group C the differences are not so great (see Table 11.1 for some examples of these data); in one case, O/C points per pupil in mathematics, the comprehensive system has a 7% advantage for S1 which drops to 2% for S2.

Variations between schools

Comparisons between individual schools are difficult to make without detailed knowledge of the particular circumstances of the school and of its intake. Nevertheless two points are worthy of comment. First, large differences are found between different comprehensive schools even within the same wholly comprehensive LEA; these differences are often greater than the substantial differences between LEAs discussed above. In some LEAs, pupils at some comprehensive schools obtained, on average, about four times as many OC1 passes and $2\frac{1}{2}$ times as many O/C points as pupils at other comprehensive schools within the same LEA which may not be surprising given differences of intake and social class within LEAs.

However, such wide differences have important implications for parental choice and for policies involving neighbourhood schools.

Secondly, some secondary modern schools obtained results which were not only well above average for schools of their type and social class group but were above national averages for *all* pupils too. For example two such schools obtained 3.00 and 2.88 OC1 passes per pupil (national average 2.14 for *all* pupils) and 29.9 and 29.2 O/C points per pupil (national average 22.7) respectively. The achievement of pupils at these secondary modern schools, and schools like them, may give some indication of the extent of under-achievement of pupils at other schools.

Variations within schools

The patterns of variation of all 30 'O' level indicators within schools are analysed using the school profiles described above. A *school ratio average* is defined as the ratio of the average for main subjects for the particular school to the average for main subjects for all schools of that type and social class group. This school ratio average can be compared with the same ratio for separate subjects and this comparison can sometimes show interesting differences. For example, in one school, the school ratio average for OC1 passes in main subjects was 1.40—showing that the school was achieving results on this index which are 40% above the national average for schools of the same type and social class group. However, the ratios for OC1 passes in mathematics and English are 1.18 and 1.23 respectively, whereas those for most other subjects, both arts and sciences, were 1.50 or greater; similar patterns were found for O/C points and C2–5 passes per pupil. These results possibly indicate weaknesses in English and mathematics at this school since many of the same pupils will be taking cognate subjects.

Such analyses are inevitably tentative but nevertheless only come within the bounds of possibility if detailed data, like those described in *Standards*, are analysed for individual schools and for groups of schools.

Other results

The results using all the 'O' level/CSE and 'A' level indicators of examination performance, with one exception, show all the same trends as those described above: variations between LEAs; with social class and amount of selection; between systems of schools; between schools of the same type and between schools within LEAs. These same trends are found for all subjects together, for the eight main subjects together and for the eight main subjects separately. Therefore the findings are, in this sense, robust. The exception is C2–5 passes per pupil which, in most analyses, do not vary in any systematic way; this may be because high attainment in these grades can be due to any combination of under-achievement by pupils of high ability, satisfactory achievement by pupils of about average ability or very good achievement by pupils of below average ability.

We now turn to the other major studies in the field in order to highlight relevant points of comparison and contrast.

Studies for the National Children's Bureau by Steedman[10]

The National Children's Bureau (NCB) has published two major reports, *Progress* and *Examinations*, which attempt to draw conclusions about secondary schooling. Both were based on the National Child Development Study (NCDS) which followed the lives of all the 16,000 or so people born in Great Britain in one week of March 1958. We will consider these reports in turn.

Progress in secondary schools

Sample

The NCDS cohort normally entered their secondary schools in 1969 at the age of 11 and reached the age of 16 in 1974. The NCB analyses therefore refer to the effects of schooling during a relatively early stage of the change to comprehensive schools. In addition, the results may be exceptional because the school leaving age was raised from 15 to 16 in 1973.

The actual numbers used in most analyses were considerably less than the 16,000 or so in the original NCDS cohort. The analyses did not include individuals from Scotland and Wales, those who went to independent or direct grant schools, those who changed secondary school and those for whom information about a number of background variables was lacking. The result is that many analyses involve only 4056 pupils—912 in grammar schools, 1765 in secondary modern schools and 1379 in comprehensive schools. However, sometimes a further 2000 or so pupils are included from transitional schools which became comprehensive between 1969 and 1974.

These low remaining numbers could mean that the residual sample used may not be fully representative. In addition, since all the individuals were born in the same week in March, they were all in the middle of their school year group. Their experiences may therefore not be fully representative of the whole year group.

Data

The main data used in *Progress* were obtained from follow-up surveys of the cohort at the ages of 11 and 16. Three tests of attainment were used at 11—a general test of verbal and non-verbal skills and tests of reading comprehension and mathematics. At the age of 16, two tests of attainment were used—the *same* reading comprehension test used at 11 and a mathematics test originally designed for 15-year-olds. In addition some information was gathered about other matters including behaviour, truancy and parental satisfaction.

The reading test was a sentence completion test of the type criticised in the Bullock report;[12] it showed a significant ceiling effect for 16-year-olds.[13]

Type of analysis

Progress does not give any unadjusted data for the tests used at 16 although some unadjusted data are given at 11. All the outcome measures at 16 are analysed using multiple regression. In each analysis five input variables are always included: scores on one or more of the tests taken at age 11; sex of pupil; age range of school; social class of father (classes I or II; III non-manual; III manual or IV or V); parental interest. In some analyses additional input variables were also used. The results presented are the residual scaled differences remaining after adjustments for input background variables had been made. No correlation matrices for the various input and output variables are given. Nor is there any indication of the size of the adjustments which were made as a result of the regression analyses.

Results

MATHEMATICS

The average attainment, after adjustment, of grammar school pupils was by far the highest with secondary modern pupils scoring a little below those in comprehensive schools. The average for grammar and secondary modern pupils together was slightly higher than that for comprehensives. Pupils from early comprehensives (established before 1966, mostly in purpose-built accommodation) scored significantly lower than either those in more recent comprehensive or those in transitional schools which became comprehensive between 1969 and 1974.

READING

The average attainment, after adjustment, of grammar school pupils was clearly higher than that of pupils in either comprehensive or secondary modern schools; the secondary modern adjusted mean was marginally lower than that of the comprehensives. There was little difference between pupils from the grammars and secondary moderns taken together compared with comprehensive pupils; the ceiling effect, mentioned above, may have contributed to this finding. Nor were there any major differences between comprehensives which had been in existence for different periods of time.

OTHER OUTCOME MEASURES

The adjusted results for behaviour in school, truancy, and parental satisfaction all showed a consistent pattern—the combination of grammar and secondary modern schools performed better than comprehensive schools. In each case too the longer established comprehensives were worst of all.[14]

Examinations in selective and non-selective schools

Sample

The sample used in this report was even smaller than that used in *Progress* because examination results could not be traced for all the pupils concerned. For most analyses involving direct comparisons between selective and comprehensive schools, the maximum size of the sample was 2896 pupils—747 in grammar schools, 1213 in secondary modern schools and 936 in comprehensive schools. In some analyses the sample was even smaller—for example, the 772 pupils with an 'O' level grade in mathematics.

Since there were less than 3000 pupils in this residual sample, the numbers in some important subgroups were very small indeed. For example, there were only 127 pupils in comprehensive schools in the top 20% of the ability range as shown by tests at 11.[16] When these 127 pupils were further subdivided, there were 63 pupils with fathers in non-manual occupations (30 in early comprehensives and 33 in recent comprehensives) and 64 with fathers in manual occupations (15 in early comprehensives and 49 in recent comprehensives). The numbers involved in some subdivisions within the top fifth—used, for example, in some reliability corrected regressions—are not given but must be even smaller.

Data

The main data used in *Examinations* are the data used in *Progress* from the follow-up studies of the NCDS cohort at 11 and 16 together with information collected separately about 'A' level, 'O' level and CSE public examination results, subject by subject and grade by grade.

A number of outcome measures were constructed from the detailed examination results. Six of these involved the attainments by the age of 16 of the whole of the residual sample:

 (i) the proportion of pupils with no graded 'O' level or CSE result in any subject;

(ii) the mean number of higher grade 'O' level or CSE grade 1 (OC1) passes per pupil;

(iii) the proportion of pupils with five or more OC1 passes;

(iv) the proportion of pupils with an OC1 pass in mathematics;

(v) the proportion of pupils with an OC1 pass in English Language;

(vi) the mean number of 'A' level passes per pupil (by 1976).

A number of other outcome measures concerned with the quality of passes are also used but these only relate to subsets of the residual sample.

Types of analysis

A small amount of unadjusted data concerning examination results is given for pupils at different kinds of schools. However the overwhelming majority of analyses used multiple regression in almost exactly the same way as in *Progress*. The results presented are the residual scaled differences remaining after adjustments had been made for background variables—the five usual variables in each case plus others in some cases. Again no correlation matrices for the input and output variables are given.

Results

The differences, after adjustment, between grammar and secondary modern schools taken together and comprehensive schools were found not to be statistically significant for all six of the main outcome measures described above (i–vi). The mean grade for English, after adjustment, for pupils obtaining a graded result in English (2130 pupils) was statistically significantly higher for grammar and secondary modern pupils compared with comprehensive pupils; however this was not true for mathematics (1719 pupils).

However for *all* these eight measures, after adjustment, pupils at grammar and secondary modern schools performed *better* than pupils at comprehensive schools. Only one of these differences was statistically significant but the direction of all the differences was not random, as would be expected if there were genuinely no differences between the two groups of pupils, but was consistently in favour of the selective schools. It is therefore possible that the differences would have been statistically significant if the total sample had been larger.

The unadjusted results showed considerably greater differences between pupils at selective compared with comprehensive schools; in all cases the selective schools had the better results. Table 11.2 gives some of these results which are for 2896 pupils in 1974; they are clearly compatible with those from *Standards*, shown in Table 11.3, for 306,000 pupils in 1981 given the large differences in sample size and year and the fact that the English results are for English Language only in 1974 and for both Lan-

Table 11.2 Examination results for 1974 (from *Examinations*; 2896 pupils)

	G	C	M	G+M unadjusted	S 0.25G+0.75M	S/C
OC1 passes	5.12	1.60	0.98	2.56	2.02	1.26
>5 OC1 passes	0.63	0.15	0.07	0.28	0.21	1.40
OC1 English	0.80	0.27	0.16	0.41	0.32	1.19
OC1 maths	0.64	0.18	0.09	0.31	0.23	1.28

Table 11.3 Examination results for 1981 (from *Standards*; 306,000 pupils)

	G	C	M	S 0.25G+0.75M	S/C
OC1 passes	5.51	1.91	1.39	2.42	1.27
OC1 English	1.35	0.45	0.32	0.58	1.29
OC1 maths	0.72	0.32	0.17	0.31	1.35

Key to Tables 11.2 and 11.3.
G—grammar school; C—comprehensive school; M—secondary modern school; S—selective schools; note that the English results are for Language only in Table 11.2 and for both Language and Literature in Table 11.3.

guage and Literature in 1981. The OC1 results for pupils at both secondary modern and comprehensive schools seems to have increased between 1974 and 1981 which may be partly due to the rise in the school leaving age and to the increase in the numbers obtaining grade 1 in CSE examinations.

Reconstructions of secondary education by Gray, McPherson & Raffe[10]

This study surveys the whole development of secondary education in Scotland since 1945; the comparisons which it makes between the public examination results of selective and comprehensive schools form only a relatively small part of the book. However, it is these comparisons which will be primarily considered here.

Sample

The sample used in the comparisons of examination results is based on a postal survey of 40% of the school leavers during 1975–76 in four of the nine regions of Scotland.[17] The total number of respondents was 16,926 which represents about 20% of all the school leavers in Scotland in 1975–76.

Data

Information was collected for results from the Scottish Certificate of Education (SCE) Highers and O-grade examinations and for the social class of father according to the Registrar-General's six main categories (see earlier section, 'Studies by the NCB'). A school was defined as comprehensive or selective in terms of the intake it received when the members of the sample entered the school.

No information was available about the ability or attainment of pupils when they entered secondary school.

Types of analysis

An 18 point scale was used to describe the SCE examination results attained by each pupil—1 point for no SCE awards; 4 points for D or E awards only at O-grade; 7, 8, 9, 10, 11, 12 points for 1, 2, 3, 4, 5, 6 or more O-grade A–C awards respectively; 13, 14, 15, 16, 17, 18 points for 1, 2, 3, 4, 5, 6 or more Highers passes respectively.

Schools were divided into two groups called the 'uncreamed comprehensive sector' and the 'selective sector'. All comprehensive schools which were near to a "selective school in any of the maintained, grant-aided or independent sectors" were defined as 'creamed' comprehensive schools. Nearly 50% of the pupils in the sample attending comprehensive schools were in such 'creamed' comprehensives and were thus included in the 'selective' sector which then comprised 11,615 pupils. The remaining 5236 pupils in comprehensive schools in primarily rural areas comprised the 'uncreamed comprehensive sector'. Thus all the pupils at comprehensive schools in Dundee, Edinburgh and Glasgow, together with those at a few schools elsewhere, were included in the 'selective sector'. Between 4000 and 5000 comprehensive school pupils were transferred in this way and they comprise about 40% of the pupils in the 'selective sector'. It therefore seems likely that this 'selective sector' contains a lower proportion of grammar school pupils than there would be in a fully selective system. This throws doubt on the validity of using this study to assess the performance of a fully selective system and as a baseline for comparison with other research.

Comparisons are made between the two sectors thus defined for the mean scores on the 18-point SCE scale both for all pupils and for pupils in each of the six social class groups. In addition the proportions in each sector attaining specific scores on the SCE scale are compared.

All the analyses included involve comparisons between different groups using the 18-point SCE scale. No analyses involving multiple regression were reported.

Results

The mean score per pupil was 7.53 in the 'uncreamed comprehensive sector' compared with 7.15 in the 'selective sector'. For middle class pupils (social classes I, II and III non-manual), the 'selective sector' mean was higher—11.6 compared with 10.9—while for working-class pupils (social classes III manual, IV and V), the 'uncreamed comprehensive sector' mean was higher—6.5 compared with 5.9.

The 'selective sector' had a higher proportion of pupils with three or more Highers passes but also had a higher proportion with no SCE awards. The 'uncreamed comprehensive sector' had a higher proportion with a few A–C O-grades.

The authors tentatively attribute this relative equalisation of attainment in the 'uncreamed comprehensive sector' not to comprehensive reorganisation but to "a continuation of the equality already established by the omnibus-school tradition" in Scotland.

School standards and spending: statistical analysis by DES[10]

In their *Statistical Bulletin 16/83*, the DES investigate the substantial variations in the public examination performance of pupils in maintained secondary schools in the 96 LEAs in England and try to relate these variations statistically with some socio-economic characteristics of the LEAs.

Sample

The sample used in *Bulletin 16/83* is based on the annual DES 10% sample survey of school leavers. This survey only gives reliable annual information for the larger LEAs which is why the DES only publish annual information on examination attainments for the 63 LEAs in England with more than 4000 school leavers. In order to include all the 96 LEAs in England, *Bulletin 16/83* averages the examination results for leavers over three years—1979, 1980 and 1981. The number of pupils in the annual survey is roughly 70,000 each year giving a total of about 200,000 pupils for the three years together.

Data

Four measures of examination performance are analysed—the proportions of pupils in each LEA gaining:

 (i) no graded GCE or CSE result;
 (ii) one or more OC1 passes;
 (iii) five or more OC1 passes;
 (iv) one or more 'A' level passes.

The background variables for each LEA included two measures of social class. (*Bulletin 16/83* uses the term socio-economic group (SEG) rather than social class but we shall follow the normal usage and refer to social class throughout.) One was a measure of high social class—the proportion of household heads in non-manual social classes (I, II, and III non-manual) taken from the 1971 Census; the other was a measure of low social class—the proportion of children living in households whose head is a semi-skilled or unskilled manual or farm worker (social classes IV or V) taken from the 1978 National Dwelling and Household Survey (NDHS).[18]

A number of other socio-economic and demographic variables are also used. These include the five socio-economic variables used in addition to the low social class variable (see above) in estimating additional educational needs (AEN) for the Grant Related Expenditure calculations: the proportions of children living in poor housing conditions, one-parent families or large families; the proportion of children who were non-white or born abroad (all from the 1978 NDHS survey); and the proportion of children receiving free school meals (1979 DES survey). Measures of population density and unemployment are also included (taken from Department of Employment statistics, 1977–79).

The expenditure measure used is the secondary school expenditure per pupil expressed at a common price base and averaged over four years—1977–78 to 1980–81; an adjustment for London weighting is included.

No data were available concerning the abilities or attainments of pupils when they entered secondary school.

No attempt was made to include any measure of the type of school attended or of the proportion of pupils in grammar, secondary modern or comprehensive schools. This variable was not mentioned in a discussion of the factors which might influence examination performance.

Types of analysis

Each of the four measures of examination performance was analysed using multiple regression in two ways:

(i) against four selected background variables—high social class, low social class, sum of AEN categories and expenditure; a number of runs are reported in which the four background variables are selected in different orders and combinations;

(ii) against all background variables; variables were included in the order which maximised the value of R^2 at each stage. Regression equations involving the first few variables (three, four or six) were used to calculate fitted values of each examination measure for each LEA; these fitted values were then compared directly with the actual values for each LEA. The correlation matrix for all variables and lists of values for each LEA are given.

Results

Social class variables

The strongest correlations for the two 'O' level measures and the no graded results measure are with the low social class variable ($R^2 = 0.60$, 0.58 and 0.45 respectively) whereas the 'A' level measure is most strongly correlated with the high social class variable ($R^2 = 0.68$). However the differences between the correlations with these two social class measures are not large; this might be expected since low and high social class are themselves closely correlated ($R = -0.77$) and each can thus, to a considerable extent, be regarded as a proxy for the other.

The social class variables were clearly the most important socio-economic variables used in the analyses and the low social class variable was the single most important variable.

Other socio-economic variables

The correlations between the 'A' level and 'O' level measures and other socio-economic variables was not as high as for the social class variables and on the whole the addition of these other socio-economic variables to the regression equations did not add much to R^2. The additional variable which seemed to be most important was the population density of 16–18-year-olds; in every case higher population densities were associated with lower examination results.

Expenditure per pupil was not found to be an important factor in most analyses with the exception of some analyses with the 16 LEAs with the highest additional needs. In some analyses with this group, greater expenditure was associated with lower examination results; however, the small number of LEAs involved means that these results should be treated with caution.

Public reception of research reports

The reception given to the four studies of examination results discussed here has been very different. *Examinations, Reconstructions* and *Bulletin 16/83* have been largely reported on their own terms. Considerable space has been given to uncritical reporting of their findings in the educational press and their results have been widely quoted as being 'authoritative'.

However the reception given to *Standards* has been different. The *Times Educational Supplement (TES)* gave a very brief account of its findings and then published in the two succeeding weeks (July 8 and 15 1983), two articles by Gray and Jones (one headed *Disappearing Data*) which claim to vitiate the results of *Standards*. Gray and Jones purport to show that the considerable variations between different LEAs can be 'explained' almost exclusively in terms of social class differences, although no details are given of their analyses. Gray and Jones carry out their critique using a different and much cruder data base than that used in *Standards* and one which is seriously unbalanced and unrepresentative. It is unrepresentative because it is based on the DES data for the proportions of school leavers (not 16-year-olds) with five or more or one or more 'O' levels in different LEAs in 1981; these data are published for only 63 LEAs since they are based on the annual DES 10% sample survey of school leavers which can only give reliable information for the larger LEAs. These 63 LEAs form an extremely unrepresentative sample since they include 38 of the 39 counties but only 25 of the 57 metropolitan boroughs. These DES data used by Gray and Jones are also much less detailed than those analysed in *Standards*—giving only four fairly crude measures of examination performance for a sample of school leavers in the larger LEAs. No information was available about the examination results of individual schools or about the numbers of pupils in the fifth-year cohorts in individual schools of different kinds.[19] Consequently Gray and Jones were not able to calculate the wide range of indices of examination performance used in *Standards;* in particular, they had no measure which included CSE grades 2–5, which indicated the quality of passes or which related to individual subjects. Moreover, they could neither calculate the selectivity index used in *Standards* nor perform the more detailed analyses in which the results for a wide range of indicators were calculated for pupils at all the comprehensive, grammar and secondary modern schools in the sample and for groups of these schools from LEAs with different social class characteristics.

The *TES* also published an article by Professor E. Wragg which implied that the authors of *Standards* had no direct knowledge of comprehensive schools—which can be seen to be false from the biographical note in *Standards*—and which claimed, *inter alia*, that the authors did not "actually understand the difference between a correlation or a carpet, or between multiple regression and ludo..."

The *TES* refused to give the authors of *Standards* comparable space to reply to Gray and Jones and in total published over 170 column inches of critical and largely adverse comment about *Standards* compared with just over 20 column inches describing the findings of the research.

In September 1983, the DES prepared an internal commentary (dated 14/9/83) which was intended to remain confidential but which was later leaked to the press. This commentary was in three parts—an annex written by Statistics Branch, comments by Schools Branch based largely on this annex, and a short summary of advice to the Secretary of State. The annex by Statistics Branch criticised *Standards* on two main grounds—that the sample of LEAs used was unrepresentative and that better allowance for social class could have been made if a high social class variable rather than a low social class variable had been used.

Both these criticisms by Statistics Branch contain major errors. The claim that the sample was unrepresentative was made because the DES statisticians misread *Standards* by mistaking 1976, the year in which pupils entered their secondary schools, with 1981, the year in which they took their 'O' level and CSE examinations. Consequently Statistics Branch compared the percentage of grammar school pupils in the NCES sample (6.5%) with the figure for the DES school leavers sample for 1981 (3.6%) and concluded that the NCES sample incorporated all the LEAs with selective schools which remained in 1981 but only just over a quarter of the other LEAs and was thus a very unrepresentative sample. This chain of reasoning is invalid and the conclusion false because *Standards* had clearly stated that a school was classified according to its status and the entry it received in 1976. Comparison of the appropriate figures for 1976 shows that the NCES sample was fully representative. This error was admitted by the DES statisticians at a meeting with NCES on November 23.[20]

The second error in the commentary by the DES statisticians concerns the use of high and low social class indicators. The DES commentary states that:

> The work by Statistics Branch on standards and spending also adjusted the LEA results by socio-economic variables. Several possibilities were tested and it was found that the proportions of the populations in the higher socio-economic groups were *much more strongly associated with O-level passes than the low socio-economic variable used in the Report*.
>
> (Annex 1 by Statistics Branch, paragraph 10, p. 4; our emphasis)

This statement is flatly contradicted by the data given in *Bulletin* 16/83 (published in December 1983; see above) which clearly shows that it is the low social class variable—the same indicator of social class used in *Standards*—which correlates most highly with 'O' level examination results.

The comments by Schools Branch in the DES commentary repeated and amplified these errors by Statistics Branch and introduced many other errors which are too numerous to specify here. One example is the comment that "... the Department's own work on expenditure has shown that the real correlation is between high social class and good exam results rather than low social class and bad exam results". Again this statement is flatly contradicted by the data in *Bulletin* 16/83.

Schools Branch concluded that *Standards* contains 'serious flaws'. However the DES statisticians subsequently stated at their meeting with NCES on November 23 that at no time did they or would they have used this term to describe *Standards*.

On September 28 there began a series of leaks from the DES concerning the confidential commentary of September 14. This process started with a press release from Frank Dobson, the Labour Party spokesman on Education, which claimed that the DES statisticians had 'rubbished' the NCES research. Subsequently a large number of press reports appeared, primarily in the *Guardian*, the *TES*, the *Sunday Times* and the *Teacher*, the weekly newspaper of the National Union of Teachers (NUT). All referred to the contents of the DES commentary with the comment concerning 'serious flaws' being frequently mentioned. It was suggested that the Secretary of State for Education was preventing the publication of the DES commentary. At this stage the authors of *Standards* had not seen a copy of the DES commentary and at no stage have they officially been given a copy.

On October 14 the *Guardian* quoted directly from the DES commentary and on October 19 the NUT published its own analysis of *Standards*. The main 'criticism' made by the NUT was that the sample used in *Standards* was very unrepresentative. The NUT arrived at this erroneous conclusion by making the *very same error* as the statisticians at the DES—that is, they confused 1976 with 1981 (see above).[21] However, unlike the DES statisticians the NUT have neither acknowledged their error nor retracted their allegation that the NCES sample was unrepresentative.

Numerous press reports criticising *Standards* continued to appear even after the meeting between NCES and the DES statisticians on November 23 and the subsequent statement to the House of Commons on November 28.[20]

Apart from the inaccuracy of the allegations of errors in the NCES report, there has been another common feature of many of these reports and of the DES commentary on *Standards*. This is the absence of comparably detailed criticisms of other research on examination results. There has therefore been little careful comparison between *Standards* and these other pieces of work. This omission is academically unsound and seriously impoverishes the public debate about education policy. Hence, in the next section of this paper, we will briefly compare and contrast the main features of the studies discussed in the previous sections.

Comparison of research on examination results

Four recent studies of examination results have been described in the earlier sections. In this section we will attempt to compare these studies in order to see to what extent—either separately or taken together—they enable some evaluation to be made of that "... gigantic experiment with the life chances of millions of children" (see the first Section).

Table 11.4 summarises the main characteristics of the four studies; it clearly shows that these studies are very different indeed. They differ in:

    (i) the size and type of sample;
   (ii) the year(s) and even the country involved;
  (iii) the type of data about examination results;
   (iv) the type(s) of analysis;
    (v) the level(s) of analysis (national, LEA, school, etc.);
   (vi) the definition of type of school;
  (vii) the allowance made (if any) for ability/attainment at entry;
(viii) the allowance made (if any) for social class and other socio-economic factors.

Table 11.4 Summary of comparisons

| | Sample | | | | | | | | |
	Size	Type	Year	Country	Pupils per school	Data	Types of analysis	Definition of type of school	Levels of analysis
Examinations (Steedman/NCB)	2897	Cohort	1974	England	About one or two	'A', 'O' & CSE all subjects all grades	Multiple regression	Type of entry at 11 *if* not changed by 16	Types of school
Reconstructions (Gray et al.)	16,926	Leavers	1976	Scotland	20% on average for each school	SCE Highers & 'O' grades; passes per pupil	Tabulations for numbers of passes	Type of entry at 11	2 sectors— 'selective' versus 'uncreamed comprehensive'
Bulletin 16/83 (DES)	200,000 (70,000 per year)	Leavers (3 years)	1979–81	England	10% for all schools	Proportions passing zero; 1+ & 5+ 'O' & 1+ 'A' levels	Multiple regression	Not applicable	LEAs
Standards (Marks et al./ NCES)	349,000	Cohort	1981	England	All pupils in schools included	'A', 'O' & CSE all subjects all grades	Tabulations for numbers and quality of passes; multiple regression	Type of entry at 11	National averages; LEAs; types of school; individual schools; within schools

However, there are some aspects of these studies for which direct comparisons can be made.

Years studied

Examinations and *Reconstructions* deal with examination results for 1974 and 1976 respectively and therefore they are concerned with secondary schools during the years 1969–74 in England and 1970–76 in Scotland which were periods when many secondary schools were being reorganised as comprehensive schools. For this reason, the results of these studies may be untypical of the present situation as the authors themselves recognise.

According to *Examinations*:

> ...the pupils studies were all of a particular year group and at school during a period of rapid change in school organisation. So results from this study may not generalise to any other era of the history of educational provision, past, present or future. Moreover, 1974, the year in which these children were sixteen, was an unusual year in that the school leaving age was raised.
>
> (p. 8)

And according to *Reconstructions*:

> ...the sample relates to a specific stage in the early development of comprehensive education in one country; one should be cautious about drawing general conclusions from this sample concerning the effectiveness of comprehensive education at other times and in other countries.
>
> (p. 250)

Bulletin 16/83 is concerned with a later stage in secondary reorganisation; it analyses the examination results for school leavers in LEAs averaged over the period 1979–81. It is difficult to make any adequate allowance for selectivity when results are averaged over three years of school leavers (and therefore, in effect, over at least five years of entry: 1972–76) since the pace of reorganisation was very rapid during these years.[19] In any case, no attempt is made to consider selectivity in *Bulletin 16/83*, perhaps for this reason.

Standards analyses the results for 1981 for a single cohort of pupils who entered secondary school in 1976. Its results are thus the most recent of the four studies as well as the most detailed; furthermore it is relatively easy to establish the relevant degrees of selectivity for a single cohort.

Allowances for social class

All four studies use one or more measures of social class as a major factor in their analyses of examination results. It seems to be accepted that social class indicators are more useful in these analyses than are other socio-economic indicators. Where reasonably direct comparisons are possible between the four studies, similar values for correlation coefficients are found. For example, both *Standards* and *Bulletin 16/83* found that a low social class variable (proportions of children in classes IV and V) for LEAs was highly correlated with 'O' level results, even though these studies used different 'O' level measures; in *Standards* the correlation coefficient was –0.67 for OC1 passes per pupil while in *Bulletin 16/83* the coefficients were –0.77 and –0.76 for the proportions passing five or more and one or more 'O' levels respectively. For 'A' level results, these correlations were also very similar; in *Standards* the coefficient was –0.74 for 'A' level passes per pupil while in *Bulletin 16/83* it was –0.76 for the proportion passing one or more 'A' levels. The size of the correlations between examination results and social class in *Standards* was thus very close to that found in other studies despite statements to the contrary by Gray and Jones in the *TES* and in the DES commentary on *Standards*.

Use of multiple regression

Three studies used multiple regression. *Examinations* and *Bulletin 16/83* used it as their major tool of analysis while *Standards* used it primarily to indicate how subsequent more direct analyses could best be planned. This difference was partly due to choice and partly dictated by the differences in the data bases used in these studies. In particular, the very small sample size in *Examinations* and the lack of reliable information about individual schools in *Bulletin 16/83* made it difficult for these studies to carry out detailed analyses of subsets of their data. This limitation did not apply to *Standards* because of its very large sample and the detailed information available about individual schools.

Each study carried out multiple regression analyses for some 'O' level measures. *Examinations* found values of R^2 of 0.59 for OC1 passes per pupil (seven input variables—class, sex, age range, parental interest and three measures of attainment at 11) and of 0.80 for the proportion passing five or more 'O' levels (five input variables—class, age range, parental interest and two measures of attainment at 11). *Bulletin 16/83* found values of R^2 of 0.77 for the proportion passing five or more 'O' levels (six input variables—low and high social class, 16–18-year-old population density, poor housing, unemployment and one-parent families) and of 0.73 for the proportion passing one or more 'O' levels (eight input variables—as previously plus population density, free school meals and large families but minus unemployment). *Standards* found values of R^2 of 0.85 for OC1 passes per pupil and 0.87 for O/C points per pupil (five input variables in each case—low social class, selectivity, pupil-teacher ratio, expenditure and ethnicity). These examples indicate the range of input variables used in these studies. It should be emphasised that the size of the multiple correlation coefficient R^2 gives the proportion of the variation of the examination measure which can be *statistically associated* with the *combination* of input variables used in each analysis. Unless these input variables are uncorrelated with one another (and in these analyses, as in most analyses of complex social situations, this is not the case), there is no way of unambiguously deciding on the contribution which each input variable makes to the total variation. Nor can statistical association imply unambiguously the existence of causal relationships.

Directions for future research

The four studies discussed in this paper provide different kinds of evidence (see earlier Sections) about the changes in secondary schools since *Circular 10/65*. However, the evidence they present is very limited and only applies to particular specific periods of time. It is clear that the "gigantic experiment with the life chances of millions of children" has not been adequately monitored in the crucial matter of standards of attainment as measured by examination results or in other ways. There has been no systematic collection and evaluation of evidence concerning "one of the most significant developments in secondary education since 1902".

There is therefore an overriding need for more and better information concerning standards of attainment in schools for at least three purposes:

(i) to facilitate academic research both into long-term trends in attainment and into more immediate educational issues;
(ii) to inform policy decisions at both national and local levels, particularly since there are likely to be major changes in secondary schools in the next decade; this is because the fall in the birth rate during the 1970s means that whereas about 700,000 11-year-olds entered secondary school in 1982, only 500,000 will do so in 1989;
(iii) to enable parents to make better informed choices between schools.

Sources of information

There are at least four possible sources of information concerning examination results which could be made more readily available:

(i) The data which schools now have to publish under the 1980 Education Act could be made more readily available.[22] This could be achieved by a simple amendment of the School Information Regulations so as to require LEAs, and schools participating in the Assisted Places scheme, to send to any person, on request, copies of the examination results for *all* the schools, both maintained and voluntary, within their jurisdiction. This would facilitate an accurate annual census of the examination results of all schools supported partly or wholly from public funds.

Alternatively, or in addition, the DES could be required to compile such an annual census and to make the results available to any interested persons. This would be a relatively easy task, given modern methods of data processing, and, for the years from 1981 onwards, would provide an invaluable data base for research of all kinds.

(ii) The data collected by HMI during their major secondary survey (1975–78) for the full examination results for all fifth-year pupils in a 10% sample of secondary schools in England.

(iii) The data collected by the DES in their 10% sample of school leavers. These data would need to be processed so that they referred to age cohorts rather than leavers (because pupils leave at different ages) and so that information was available about school type at entry as well as at leaving and about 'A' level, 'O' level and CSE results, subject by subject and grade by grade. All this information is collected annually and should therefore be available for a large number of past years as well as in future.

(iv) The data collected by the NCB for *Examinations*;[23] these data are primarily for 'O' level and CSE examinations taken in 1974 and 'A' level examinations taken in 1976. Further data concerning attainment which could be made more readily available include those collected by the NCB on mathematics and reading for *Progress* and those collected by the Assessment of Performance Unit.

Methods of analysis

In analysing complex social processes like the development of secondary education, it is clearly useful to have as many different sources of information as possible and to analyse these in a variety of ways. When the terrain to be mapped is relatively uncharted, there is much to be said for triangulation.

There is a place for sophisticated statistical methods of analysis like multiple regression but these should always be used with care and their limitations recognised. Such analyses are beset with problems of at least two kinds—analytic and mathematical.

Problems of the first kind include deciding which variables to include in the analyses and in what form—in other words, they are problems of deciding on an appropriate and simplified mathematical model for analysing a complex real world situation. The decisions concerning which variables to include are inevitably bound up with the view we take about what is important in the real world situation we are attempting to model— in this case, our system of secondary schools. Such decisions are therefore, almost inevitably, value-laden and open to question and debate.

Problems of the second, mathematical kind include disentangling the effects of intercorrelations amongst the independent variables, of deciding on the most appropriate order to enter variables into regression equations and of interpreting the multiple correlation coefficient, the coefficients in the regression equations and the magnitudes of the residuals.

All these problems provide fertile areas for dispute and legitimate disagreement as the literature shows. It must therefore be recognised that there is no *single* correct method of analysing a complex social situation, of using multiple regression or any other statistical technique or even of deciding how to incorporate a single factor, say social class, into analyses.

There is therefore a strong case for using simple methods of analysis alongside complex ones and for presenting analyses in ways which retain as much contact as possible with the primary data. If this is not done, there is a risk of confusing the educational issues by submerging the primary data, which often have major limitations of various kinds, in a complex mathematical analysis which may be incomprehensible to all but a relatively small number of experts. There is a tendency to build an inappropriately sophisticated statistical edifice on an inevitably relatively crude primary data base.[24]

It also needs to be recognised that all corrections and adjustments to primary data are approximate and that there will always be arguments about their validity. Hence the need to set out clearly what the primary data are and to describe corrections and their underlying assumptions as precisely as possible. These considerations are particularly important in presenting data to parents, teachers, school governors and other members of the public but are also desirable in presenting research to an academic audience.

International comparisons

Further useful data concerning attainment can be obtained by the careful evaluation of evidence from other countries.

An obvious possibility is to compare England and Wales with Northern Ireland. Two interesting statistics here are the proportions of school leavers obtaining five or more 'O' levels and one or more 'A' levels given by the appropriate school leavers surveys. For England and Wales, these proportions rose during the 1950s and 1960s but since 1970 have been fairly static. The proportions for Northern Ireland show a very different pattern—the rise there during the 1950s and 1960s continued throughout the 1970s and the figures there are now well above those for England and Wales. Two relevant factors here may be that Northern Ireland has retained a fully selective system of grammar and secondary modern schools and that many more schools there are religious schools.

Another recent study[25] has compared the standards achieved in mathematics in German and English schools for pupils at various levels of ability. This study concludes that standards of attainment in England and Germany are roughly comparable for those at the top of the ability range but that the average level of attainment for all pupils is appreciably higher in Germany. In particular:

> Attainments in mathematics by *those in the lower half of the ability-range in England appear to lag by the equivalent of about two years' schooling behind the corresponding section of pupils in Germany.*
>
> (p. 42; emphasis in original)

Some important differences between Germany and England noted by this study include:

Germany has three different kinds of school—the *Gymnasium, Realschule* and *Hauptschule*—each of which caters specifically for different levels of ability;

each of these types of school has a specific school-leaving certificate designed for its particular ability range;

each certificate requires pupils to study and pass a specified number of subjects including some compulsory subjects of which mathematics is one.

The case seems unanswerable for more studies of this kind in which attempts are made to compare absolute standards of attainment, where this is feasible, using as many different sources of information as possible to cross-check the results.

The same principles need to be applied to the evaluation of the attainments of pupils in secondary schools in this country both in the future and, in so far as this is possible, to make good the lack of such evaluation in recent decades.

Notes and references

1 *Circular 10/65*, issued in 1965, was the first statement of national policy which requested all LEAs to reorganise their secondary schools along comprehensive lines.
2 Neave, G. (1979) 'Sense and sensitivity: the case of comprehensive education,' *Quantitative Sociology Newsletter*, No. 21.
3 Benn, C. & Simon, B. (1970) *Halfway There: Report on the British Comprehensive School Reform* (London, McGraw-Hill).
4 Ford, J. (1969) *Social Class and the Comprehensive School* (London, Routledge & Kegan Paul).
5 Public examination results were widely used in the early debates about the merits of comprehensive schools; see, for example, the influential and much reprinted Pedley, R. (1963) *The Comprehensive School* (Harmondsworth, Penguin). Public examinations, for all their problems, are the major external and independent check on teaching and learning in schools.
6 Grammar, secondary modern and technical schools.

7 Or perhaps the 'ideal' comparison should be with a comprehensive system as it would be if *Circular 10/65* had been fully implemented.

8 See, for example, Douglas, J.W.B. (1964) *The Home and the School* (London, MacGibbon & Kee) and Floud, J., Halsey, A.H. & Martin; F.M. (1957) *Social Class and Educational Opportunity* (London, Heinemann).

9 See 2.

10 Marks, J., Cox, C. & Pomian-Srzednicki, M. (1983) *Standards in English Schools* (London, National Council for Educational Standards); Steedman, J. (1980). *Progress in Secondary Schools* (London, National Children's Bureau); Steedman, J. (1983) *Examinations in Selective and Non-selective Schools* (London, NCB); Gray, J., McPherson, A.F. & Raffe, D. (1983) *Reconstructions of Secondary Education* (London, Routledge & Kegan Paul); DES (1983) *Statistical Bulletin 16/83—School Standards and Spending: Statistical Analysis* (London, DES); hereinafter these publications are referred to as *Standards, Progress, Examinations, Reconstructions* and *Bulletin 16/83* respectively.

11 The original aim of the research was to conduct a census of the results of *all* schools in England and Wales. This did not prove possible because many LEAs either could not or would not cooperate by sending the results for all their schools *en bloc*. Therefore in order to achieve a representative sample, schools in many LEAs had to be approached individually. In addition some LEAs sent us their results only on the condition that the identity of the LEA and of individual schools would not be disclosed. Consequently *Standards* does not refer to individual schools or LEAs by name both for this reason and because many LEAs and schools have been extremely helpful to us in our work and we do not wish to make their results the focus of public attention. This would, perhaps, discriminate against them when they have been kind enough to help us in our research—particularly when other schools and LEAs have not been cooperative. This problem could be overcome if *all* LEAs were required to make *all* their results easily available, thus enabling an annual census of all schools to be made (see section, 'Directions for Future Research').

12 Report of the Bullock Committee (1975) *A Language for Life* (London, HMSO).

13 Start, J.B. & Wells, B.K. (1972) *The Trend of Reading Standards* (Slough, NFER) used a parallel reading test and found it too easy for the "brighter *fifteen year olds* with a consequence that their test scores do not adequately reflect their reading comprehension ability" (p. 16; our emphasis).

14 For further discussion see Cox, C. & Marks, J. (1980) *Real Concern* (London, Centre for Policy Studies) and Steedman, J., Fogelman, K. & Hutchison, D. (1980) *Real Research* (London, NCB).

15 Some analyses included a further 1479 pupils from transitional schools which became comprehensive between 1969 and 1974.

16 This is the group for which 'O' level examinations were originally intended.

17 These regions—Fife, Lothian, Tayside and Strathclyde—contain three-quarters of the population of Scotland.

18 This low social class indicator is the same indicator of social class used in *Standards*.

19 This information is difficult to collect because the examination results data are for school leavers in 1981 and not for the 16-year-old cohort in 1981; these leavers may have entered secondary school in any year from 1973 to 1976 (assuming entry at 11)—a period when many schools were being reorganised.

20 Following this meeting, the DES agreed to an unprecedented statement to the House of Commons (November 28 1983) which welcomes the pioneering work undertaken by NCES, retracts the DES allegation that the NCES sample was unrepresentative and states that, contrary to some press reports, the

Department does not regard the research as 'seriously flawed'. In addition the Department recognises that many complex problems are involved in allowing for socio-economic factors and in using multiple regression techniques.

21 Estimation of the odds against two major educational institutions like the DES and the NUT *independently* making *exactly* the same elementary error is left as an exercise to the reader.

22 This is the information on which the analyses in *Standards* are based.

23 These data were collected at public expense but very little unadjusted data have been published by the NCB.

24 Compare for example the complex reanalysis of the data from Bennett, N. (1976) *Teaching Styles and Pupil Progress* (London, Open Books) by Aitkin, M., Anderson, D. & Hinde, J. (1981) 'Statistical modelling of data on teaching styles,' *Journal of the Royal Statistics Society*, 144, pp. 419–461, with the much simpler reanalysis by Prais, S.J. (1983) 'Formal and informal teaching: a further re-consideration of Professor Bennett's statistics,' *Journal of the Royal Statistics Society*, 146(2), pp. 163–169; note also the different conclusions reached by these two reanalyses.

25 Prais, S.J. & Wagner, K. (1983) *Schooling Standards in Britain and Germany: some Summary Comparisons Bearing on Economic Efficiency*, Discussion Paper No. 60 (London, NIESR).

12 Problems in comparing examination attainment in selective and comprehensive secondary schools

Ken Fogelman

Source: 'Problems in comparing examination attainment in selective and comprehensive secondary schools,' *Oxford Review of Education*, 10(1): 33–43, 1984.

Writing yet more on the question of examination attainment in different types of secondary school is not a task which one undertakes with any relish. The political nature of the context and potential implications of such research has always been apparent. Less acceptable has been the descent to a political style of debate, with accusations and counter-accusations of bias, smear and conspiracy.

Furthermore, one senses an increasing disenchantment in many quarters. Teachers feel that such research is of little relevance to their everyday classroom concerns; researchers and academics point out that it does not contribute to our attempts to understand the learning process. Reactions in the media and in parliament suggest that the topic is still of burning importance to the general public and to politicians, but they are understandably confused and frustrated by the apparent inconsistencies and contradictions among the studies which have reported their findings in the past year.

Nevertheless, the nettle has to be grasped. However irrelevant the question is to educational theory or pedagogic practice, society has a right to know whether the major educational change of recent years has had any effect on the children leaving our schools. Attainment is only one area in which we might look for such effects, but one which many people would argue to be the most important; and examination performance is only one of the possible measures of attainment, but one which is generally accepted and a major determinant of opportunities for employment and continued education.

The three studies

During 1983 three reports appeared which, entirely or in part, were concerned with comparing the examination results of pupils from comprehensive schools with those of selective schools. Each reached somewhat contrasting conclusions. In the remainder of this paper I shall consider some of the major differences among the three studies in an attempt both to clarify some possible reasons for the contrasting interpretations, and to illustrate some of the major difficulties in research of this kind.

This is not the place for a detailed account of the findings. Each study used more than one examination measure and each attempted to look in some way at the differential performance of children of various ability levels and social background. Nevertheless the general pattern of results can be seen in the following quotations:

> ...the data would suggest that comprehensive education had a levelling effect on attainment, raising fewer pupils to the highest levels of attainment, but helping more of them to progress beyond the minimum. It appears to have raised *average* attainment...
>
> (Gray, McPherson & Raffe, 1983)

> It did not seem likely, from these results, that pupils' exam attainments were differing systematically in a way that would permit the conclusion that going to comprehensives as against the 'alternative' grammar and modern combination, explained examination performance.
>
> (Steedman, 1983)

> The results of these conclusions show, consistently and coherently, that substantially higher O-level, CSE and A-level examination results are to be expected in a fully selective system than in a fully comprehensive system.
>
> (Marks, Cox & Pomian-Srzednicki, 1983)

So, we have one ringing declaration of the superiority of the selective system, one cautious 'no difference,' and one equally cautious, and qualified, slight advantage to comprehensive pupils. Where might the explanation lie?

Political affiliations

I mention this only to dispose of it. Much has been made in some quarters of the political associations, real or imaginary, of the researchers concerned. However, this paper is concerned with the competence of the three pieces of research and the validity of their findings. There is sufficient evidence within the three publications to enable judgement on those issues, without recourse to any discussion of political beliefs.

Secular differences

The data drawn upon by Gray *et al.* were taken from a postal survey of people who left Scottish schools in the academic year 1975–76. Thus they relate mainly to pupils who entered secondary schools in 1970 or 1972 and took either O-grades in 1974 and H-grades in 1976, or O-grades in 1976, although there will presumably have been a small proportion taking one or both levels of examination early. Steedman's study was based on the National Child Development Study, and so was of children born in one week in 1958. Most will have entered their secondary schools in 1969. In the study under consideration here, the results were analysed of CSE and 'O' level examinations taken by 1974 and 'A' levels by 1976.

Marks *et al.* used the results of examinations taken in 1981. Again some departures from the common pattern can be expected, but for the majority this will mean that CSE and 'O' level results are for those entering secondary schools in 1976 and 'A' level candidates will have transferred in 1974.

Thus the first two studies are broadly of the same vintage, but the third relates to examinations generally taken between five and seven years later. It does not seem likely, but the possibility cannot be discounted, that the situation had changed so significantly during this period. Certainly the proportion of secondary-age pupils in England who were attending comprehensive schools had increased from some 60% to over 80%. If anything, this might have been expected to improve the relative average performance of the comprehensive pupils, but there are no means of assessing this independently of the three studies under consideration and this question must be left open.

National differences

As already indicated, one study was carried out in Scotland and the other two in England. Gray *et al.* describe at some length the contrasting history of secondary reorganisation in Scotland. Given this, and also the differences in the examination systems of the two countries, it would not be altogether surprising if this were to result in different patterns of exam attainment between different types of school in Scotland and England.

However, the conflict in the results of the three studies is not on national lines, so we must look elsewhere for the explanation, at least for the contrast between Steedman and Marks *et al.*

Definition of school-type

There are two distinct issues here. The first concerns the correct and consistent application of administrative labels for schools of different kinds; the second is about the extrapolation of findings for schools as they actually were to statements about what the findings would be for the 'ideal' of a fully comprehensive or fully selective system.

The second point is important because we are not in fact dealing with two systems—the comprehensive and selective—which are fully independent of each other. In many areas comprehensive and selective schools exist alongside each other. To some extent the former will be 'creamed', and not contain the same proportion of more able pupils as under a fully comprehensive system. Similarly, the intakes of the grammar and secondary modern schools may well not be exactly as they would be under a fully selective system. While statistical adjustments can attempt to ensure that we are comparing like with like, that is the attainments of pupils of, for example; similar ability or social background, it is not possible to adjust the school environment. If the ability range within a school has an effect on the attainment of pupils within that school, then we cannot claim that the results of schools as they were at a particular time can be adjusted to represent the results of a notional fully comprehensive or selective system.

Steedman is carefully clear on this point:

> This was not therefore, a test of two systems, the selective and the comprehensive, still less a test of the ideal of those systems, but simply a presentation of some information on the operation of the English secondary school system at a particular historical stage in its piecemeal reorganisation along comprehensive lines.

By contrast, as we have already seen in the quotation above, Marks *et al.* do apparently feel able to assert that their findings represent what would be expected in a fully selective system and a fully comprehensive system.

Even if one accepts, as surely one must, the limitation that these studies are about schools as they were, rather than ideals, there is still the question of accurate classification of schools as they were. The approach of Gray *et al.* to this is different from that of the others. Their 'comprehensive' group does not consist of all those schools which were called comprehensive at the time of the study, but only of those which were 'established' by 1970— that is, offered a full range of SCE courses and had a non-selective intake. Comprehensives whose proximity to selective schools made it likely that their intakes were 'creamed' were classified as part of the selective sector together with senior selective and junior secondary schools. In other words this is an attempt to define a fully comprehensive group of schools to compare with a selective group. If the judgement as to creaming was correctly applied then the result will have been a comparison of schools containing the full ability range, at least as represented in their catchment areas, with schools which contained selected high ability pupils only or in which the most able pupils were either absent or under-represented. Whether the latter group can be taken to represent a fully selective system is somewhat problematic. Gray *et al.* do report that the two groups of schools were virtually identical in their social class composition, but are properly cautious about inferring from this that they were "identical with respect to the pupils' ability or other determinants of behaviour".

On the other hand, the starting point for both Steedman and Marks *et al.* is the administrative designation of the school. In Steedman's case this was as at 1974, when the children in the study were aged 16, but she also had available data on when the school became comprehensive and was thus able to identify a 'transitional' group whose schools changed while the study pupils were there. These pupils of transitional schools were in fact the majority of those attending schools called comprehensive in 1974, and were treated in analyses as a separate group and did not figure in the major comparison between selective and comprehensive schools. This is justified in that some proportion of these pupils' secondary schooling will in fact have been in a grammar or secondary modern school. Indeed, depending on how the comprehensive was created, their own year group may have remained selective throughout.

Marks *et al.* state that they classified schools according to their status in 1976, i.e. the year of entry for the majority of pupils who took CSE or 'O' level in 1981 (footnote, p. 49). As no further information is given it must be assumed that their selective schools contain an unknown number which were comprehensive by the time pupils were taking examinations in 1981.

Not only will some schools have changed their status during the relevant period but in addition some pupils will have changed schools and in doing so may have moved from one type of school to another. Among the National Child Development Study data at age 16 was a question on how long pupils had been at their current school, and those who had not been at the same school throughout were excluded from analyses. Neither Marks *et al.* nor Gray *et al.* appear to have been able to make similar exclusions, so that, in both cases, some of the pupils whose results were taken to represent either selective or comprehensive schools will in fact have experienced both types of schools.

Sampling

All three studies attempted to obtain samples of pupils or schools which were nationally representative of maintained schools at the appropriate time.

Gray *et al.*'s findings were derived from a postal survey of school-leavers in four Scottish regions (Fife, Lothian, Tayside and Strathclyde) which contain three-quarters of the population of Scotland. Response was high, at 82%, but a careful exploration of biases by the authors does suggest that the less academically successful were more likely to be omitted. Subsequent analyses, it is reported, were weighted to compensate for "biases associated with sex and SCE attainment".

Steedman's initial sample, as mentioned above, was all children in the country born in one week in 1958. It is difficult to conceive of any way in which this could be systematically related to the type of secondary school attended 11 years later. However, there is also sample attrition to be considered. Analyses reported elsewhere (Goldstein, 1976) are generally reassuring about the overall representativeness of respondents at 16. It is not possible to test so directly the relationship between response and type of school attended, but the proportions in schools of different kinds at 16 do correspond closely with DES figures.

Marks *et al.*, by approaching either local authorities or individual schools, attempted to obtain information from all maintained secondary schools in England, and succeeded for about half. Early commentators on this study have queried the representativeness of the ensuing sample because of discrepancies between the distribution of schools in the study and the national figures for 1981, the year in which the examinations considered were taken. However, the authors have pointed out that as schools were classified according to their status in 1976, that is the relevant year of comparison. They are also reported to have presented information to the DES to support their claim that the sample was representative for that year. I am not able to comment on that information, but have difficulty in reaching a similar conclusion from what has been published. Table 12.1 compares the proportions of schools of the three main types in Marks *et al.* (taken from table 16, p. 53) with those in the DES Statistics of Education for 1976.

Although these figures do raise some questions, I do not believe the apparent discrepancies are of major importance. A representative sample of secondary schools in England will not produce a sample of comprehensives and of selective schools which are equivalent in their intakes. It is how that problem is tackled, how differences in intake are allowed for, which is crucial. The sample on which that is done is only of importance if it is so severely biased that *the relationship* between the characteristics of the intakes and subsequent examination attainment is unrepresentative of such schools in general. That does not seem likely for any of the three studies.

Intakes

As we have seen, Gray *et al.* classified their schools in such a way that the comprehensive and selective groups were similar in their intakes, at least as

Table 12.1 Proportions of schools of different types in 1976

	Comprehensive	*Secondary modern*	*Grammar*
Marks *et al.*	75%	15%	10%
Statistics of education	66%	23%	11%

far as could be judged from their social composition. They then proceeded to straightforward comparisons of the examination results of the two groups of schools, but acknowledged that this may not have taken full account of differences in intakes.

By their use of the designated status of the schools, the other two studies are in a very different situation. Only Steedman was able to look at intakes directly, because of the availability of National Child Development Study data at the age of 11 in the final year of primary schooling.

As Table 12.2 shows, those children who were subsequently to attend comprehensive schools were far from being equivalent to the combination of those who were to go to grammar or secondary modern schools. Indeed they were barely distinguishable from the secondary modern pupils alone.

Although Marks *et al.* did not have data on intakes, they do acknowledge their likely pattern and the need to take this into account. As they write:

> We cannot make direct comparisons of the examination results of different kinds of schools because this would be misleading. For example, the schools vary in their pupils' social backgrounds—and, as we have already noted, social class correlates with educational attainment. Also schools vary in the academic ability of their pupils...

This represents considerable progress from their reactions to the earlier National Children's Bureau study (Steedman, 1980) when they apparently perceived such an approach as 'doctoring the data' (Cox & Marks, 1980).

Before discussing the specific techniques for allowing for intake differences used in the two studies, two further points should be made. Firstly, both studies attempted to allow for such differences in terms of social class and ability (Steedman additionally took into account a measure of parental interest in schooling). Of the information likely to be available in large-scale studies of this kind, these are undoubtedly the most appropriate variables to use for this purpose, in that both are powerful predictors of subsequent attainment. However, this is not to say that they are the only relevant variables. A number of studies have shown how other factors, such as family situation, family size, housing circumstances, are also

Table 12.2 Intakes of schools (Steedman, 1983)

	Mean test scores at 11			Percentage with fathers in non-manual occupations
	Maths	*Reading*	*General ability*	
Grammar	29	22	60	57
Secondary modern	13	14	39	27
Comprehensive	14	15	40	26

related to attainment. Although each is, in turn, correlated to some extent with social class, the latter alone will not account for all their separate effects. Thus, although allowing for social class and ability is a necessary minimum, there may well still be further differences in intakes which could explain some part of any differences found in outcomes.

Secondly, a careless reader of Marks *et al.* might be left with the impression that they have undertaken analyses which allow for differences in both social class and ability. This is not the case. What is presented is one set of analyses which attempt to allow for social class alone, and a separate set of analyses which incorporate an attempted correction for ability. Thus there are no analyses in this report which take proper account of the authors' own remarks quoted above.

Allowing for social class differences

The central analyses presented by Steedman are analyses of variance in which social class, 11-year attainment test scores and type of school (and also sex and parental interest) are entered as independent variables, with the examination measures as the dependent variable. The fitted constants (or, for some analyses, ratios) which result in relation to type of school essentially summarise the average differences between the comprehensive and selective schools for pupils who are of the same social class, initial attainment etc. The unit of analysis is the *individual child*, that is to say each measure used as an independent or dependent variable is a measure of the individual's social class, attainment etc.

Cox & Marks (1980) were formerly critical of this kind of analysis. They have now apparently been converted to a belief in its usefulness, as they use it elsewhere in their latest report (e.g. p. 48). However, they could not do so for the comparisons of the exam results of selective and comprehensive schools, as they did not have the relevant information for individual children. Given the nature of their examination data, it would have been possible for them to adopt the *school* as their unit of analysis, if they had had information on the social composition of each school. However, they did not. What they have done is to compare the examination performance of pupils of different types of school within *groups of local authorities* which they claim to be socially homogeneous. The DES social class measure which they use is extremely crude for this purpose, identifying as it does only three groups or 'clusters' of local authorities, based on the proportions within them of social classes IV and V, that is the semi-skilled and unskilled manual groups. Others have pointed out how, *a priori*, this is hardly likely to be sensitive to the social differences between authorities and, empirically, it results in such seemingly disparate authorities as ILEA and Gloucestershire, or Lincolnshire and Liverpool being treated as identical (NUT, 1983).

Even more important, though, than the detail of the measure used is the patent absurdity of this approach. It would be valid only if it did indeed allow for the differences in the social composition of schools, that is, if within each group of local authorities the intakes of comprehensive and selective schools were closely similar. Common sense suggests that this is extremely unlikely, but data are not available either nationally or within Marks *et al.* to check this. It is possible, however, to use National Child Development Study data to shed some light. We do not, of course, know exactly which authorities contributed to Marks *et al.*, but it is possible to identify for all authorities into which of the DES clusters they fall. Table 12.3 is based on the National Child Development Study data for 1974, and shows the proportions of children who went to selective or comprehensive schools, whose fathers were in semi- or unskilled manual occupations, within each of the three groups of local authorities. I am grateful to my colleague Dougal Hutchison for providing these figures.

As can be seen, within each cluster of local authorities, the social composition favours the selective schools. It is interesting to note that the contrast is relatively small within cluster C, which is also where Marks *et al.* found only small, if any, differences in the exam results of selective and non-selective schools. The possibility that the greater constrasts which they found within clusters A and B are simply the result of inadequate allowance for social class can hardly be ruled out.

Allowing for ability difference

Having no information on the ability levels of individuals, or schools, or groups of local authorities, Marks *et al.* adopt an even less direct method of allowing for differences in the ability range of the intakes of selective and comprehensive schools.

They apply a 'correction factor' by which the 'adjusted' results of the comprehensive schools are the actual results increased by 0.23 of (the actual comprehensive results minus the secondary modern results).

$$0.23 \text{ is } \frac{1-0.81}{0.81},$$

with 0.81 "being the proportion of comprehensive school pupils in schools with full ability range".

Table 12.3 Percentage in social classes IV and V, by sector, for three local authority groups (NCDS unpublished data)

	Selective	Comprehensive
Cluster A	12.8	17.9
Cluster B	17.6	20.3
Cluster C	21.3	22.5

In other words the results of the 'missing' comprehensive pupils are represented by a proportion of the results of those comprehensive pupils who got better results than the secondary modern pupils, on the assumption presumably that these pupils were equivalent to those above the ability range for secondary moderns (i.e. to those in grammar schools). But it is obvious that any 'creaming' from the comprehensive schools will not be, as this assumes, randomly from among the most able 20 or 30% who would have gone to grammar schools under a selective system, but disproportionately from among the most able of these. Thus they could be expected to obtain better examination results on average than the most able of those pupils who remain in comprehensive schools, and this will not be adequately reflected in Marks *et al.*'s correction factor.

Additionally, closer scrutiny is necessary in order to judge whether the figure of 0.81 as the proportion of full ability comprehensive schools is correct. They state that they were able to arrive at this estimate from figures reported in the HMI (1979) survey, but do not offer any detailed explanation. It is therefore necessary to examine that report for further information.

The Inspectorate surveyed a total of 236 comprehensive schools and found that 163 were 'full range', 45 were 'restricted range' and 28 were transitional. Evidently 0.81 is

$$\frac{163+28}{236},$$

and the transitional schools have been counted by Marks *et al.* as full range. The HMI report states that

> Transitional schools were almost all restricted range comprehensive schools formed from existing secondary modern schools with a non-selective intake working up the school from the first year. There were only two cases of transitional schools stemming from grammar schools.

Thus the correct proportion of 'full range' schools was

$$\frac{163+2}{236},$$

or 0.7, which leads to a value of 0.43 for Marks *et al.*'s correction factor. When applied to the results this would of course give a significantly greater adjustment in favour of the comprehensive schools.

But would even this revised adjustment be adequate? An adequate adjustment would be one which produced a weighting which was equivalent to the comprehensive schools having their full share of the most able pupils, that is equivalent to the proportion in the selective schools. Marks *et al.* carry out their calculations as if this were the case, but even a careful reading of their own words is enough to raise doubts. A restricted range comprehensive, they say, is one with "very few or no pupils from the top 20% of the ability range". In other words a full-range comprehensive, by their definition, is not necessarily a school with its *full* share of able pupils, but rather one with more than 'very few or no' such pupils.

To assess what this means in practice it is again necessary to look in more detail at the actual criteria employed in the HMI report. The question which was put to the headteachers in the survey (Form 1, Appendix 1, pp. 278–279) was: "Enter the approximate range of ability, in percentiles, within which all but exceptional pupils lie."

Further instructions or explanations in the main text make it clear:

(i) That the headteachers completing the form were asked to round to the nearest 10. Answers were of the form, for example, '100–0' for a 'fully comprehensive school', or 100–80' for a typical grammar school.

(ii) That in arriving at the classification relied upon by Marks *et al.*, only those schools replying 80 (or lower)-0 were counted as restricted range. Those indicating 90–0 were combined with 100–0 as being 'full range'.

Thus:

(a) An unknown number of schools with no pupils whatsoever in the top 10% of the ability range are counted as 'full range'.

(b) Because of rounding, an unknown number of schools with no pupils whatsoever in the top 14–15% are counted as 'full range'.

(c) It is unlikely that, in arriving at their answers to this question, heads will have compared the distribution of ability in their school with the normal distribution curve. Those with more than a very few 'exceptional' pupils in the top 20% will have described their ability range as 100–0 or 90–0. This cannot be taken to mean that the top 10%, or second 10%, were represented in the same proportions as in the grammar-secondary modern combination.

The exact extent of each of these problems cannot be estimated from the data available, but it is clear that they could be very substantial.

In summary, even if we accept that the use of a correction of this kind is valid, the version applied by Marks *et al.* is quite inadequate. Firstly, it incorporates a misreading of the HMI figures taken at their face value. Secondly, it is not necessary to delve far below the surface of the HMI data to conclude that they do not provide the basis for a realistic estimate of the appropriate correction. The minimum value of the factor to be used is 0.43, rather than the 0.23 used by Marks *et al.*, but its correct value is some unknown number greater, and probably considerably greater, than this.

Conclusion

The foregoing has identified some of the major problems associated with attempting to compare the performance of pupils in comprehensive and selective schools, and in particular those inherent in making indirect adjustments for the differing social composition and ability of the intakes of schools of different type.

The only satisfactory solutions are either to be able to compare groups of schools which are similar in their intakes, or to have available sufficiently detailed information on pupils or schools (depending on which is the unit of analysis) to enable proper statistical adjustments. In fact, the first solution also requires adequate data on intakes in order to be able to demonstrate that the groups of schools are comparable.

In England, at least, it is not the case that selective and comprehensive schools are similar in their intakes, and it is not likely to become so, given the continued coexistence of the two sectors and the political and social characteristics of those authorities which adopt one system or the other.

The national data now available, as used by Marks *et al.*, are not sufficient for this purpose. There might be scope for some locally based studies, but most authorities do not routinely collect, and still fewer would make publicly available, detailed information on school intakes.

However, this is not intended as a prescription for abdication from the area by researchers. The debate continues and the decision-makers and the general public have every right to look to researchers to provide evidence which is as objective and valid as possible, as one element in their considerations.

None of the evidence already available is completely satisfactory. The National Child Development Study data relate to pupils who entered secondary schools in 1969 and took examinations in 1974 or 1976. Gray *et al.*'s data are from the same period. We cannot be confident that the patterns found in the first half of the 1970s apply equally to the present day. Moreover there are dangers in assuming that the Scottish findings can be generalised to England (and equally, for Scottish readers, the NCDS findings cannot be taken to apply to Scotland).

The examinations on which Marks *et al.* is based are more recent, but in view of the methodological weaknesses discussed above, it is clear that this is just about the only virtue of that study.

The time-table of a study starting now, with a survey of 11-year-olds, and which would therefore produce results in five or six years time, would clearly be unacceptable. However, it is not necessary to wait that long. There already exists a national cohort study of children born in 1970 (e.g. Osborne, Butler & Mossis, 1984) which holds data collected at the end of primary schooling. These children will be taking CSE and 'O' level (or whatever version of them then exists) in 1986. It is very much to be hoped that the opportunity will be taken to collect the relevant information, in order to make possible what would probably be the first worthwhile comparative study of selective and comprehensive schools in the 1980s.

References

Cox, C. & Marks, J. (1980) *Real Concern* (London, Centre for Policy Studies).

Goldstein, H. (1976) A study of the response rates of sixteen-year-olds in the National Child. Development Study. In: Fogelman, K. (ed.) *Britain's Sixteen-Year-Olds* (London, National Children's Bureau).

Gray, J., McPherson, A.F. & Raffe, D. (1983) *Reconstructions of Secondary Education* (London, Routledge & Kegan Paul).

HMI (1979) *Aspects of Secondary Education* (London, HMSO).

Marks, J., Cox, C. & Pomian-Srzednicki, M. (1983) *Standards in English Schools* (London, National Council for Educational Standards).

National Union of Teachers (1983) *A Question of Standards* (London, NUT).

Osborne, A.F., Butler, N.R. & Mossis, A.C. (1984) *The Social Life of Britain's Five-Year-Olds* (London, Routledge & Kegan Paul).

Steedman, J. (1980) *Progress in Secondary Schools* (London, National Children's Bureau).

Steedman, J. (1983) *Examination Results in Selective and Non-selective Secondary Schools* (London, National Children's Bureau).

13 Selection does make a difference

Peter Clifford and Anthony Heath

Source: 'Selection does make a difference', *Oxford Review of Education*, 10(1): 85–97, 1984.

British secondary education has been subject to continual change and reorganisation. The major reforms of the 1944 Education Act were followed by a period of gradual change as the tripartite system of grammar, technical and secondary modern schools was slowly modified, the number of grammar schools increasing as the number of technical schools declined. In 1965 the pace of change quickened as a result of the Labour Government's policy of support for comprehensive schooling. In theory, selection at the age of 11 would end and selective schools would be replaced by comprehensives in which children of all abilities were to be educated under a single roof. However, these changes have come very slowly and nearly 20 years later there is still a hybrid system.

In its crudest terms the question before us now is whether this move towards comprehensive schooling has worked. Can we say that the reform has been a success? Three studies have recently appeared which address this question—Gray, McPherson & Raffe's (1983) *Reconstructions of Secondary Education*, Steedman's (1983) *Examination Results in Selective and Nonselective Schools*, and Marks, Cox & Pomian-Srzednicki's (1983) *Standards in English Schools*. They reach different conclusions. In this paper we shall argue that the answer to the question 'has it worked?' can be 'yes' or 'no' depending on the selection of data and of statistical techniques. It is in this sense that selection undeniably makes a difference. The three studies use different sources of material and employ different statistical strategies. Even if they had used the same data, their selection of statistical methods might well have led to different answers nonetheless.

This can happen not because of statistical incompetence but because there are inherent technical problems in the question being asked. We do not yet understand the sources of variation in schools' examination results (exams being the main criterion of success used in these studies). Until we do so, we are likely to confuse the effects of selective education with those of other social and educational processes. It would be foolish to make firm policy decisions based on our present state of knowledge.

We argue, therefore, that the primary task at the moment should be to understand what makes one school 'better' than another. If we wish to improve educational standards, there is more mileage to be made from discovering how to improve the worst schools, be they grammar, comprehensive or secondary modern, than by discovering whether the move towards comprehensive schooling 'has worked'. This is because, on our reading of the evidence on examination results, the difference between the comprehensive and selective systems is not very great whereas that between the 'best' and 'worst' schools within each system is in comparison quite substantial.

The three studies

The three studies use different types of data, collected at different periods and relating to different populations. *Reconstructions* is based on postal questionnaires answered by nearly 17,000 individual school-leavers in Scotland in 1975–76. *Examination Results* is based on data from a longitudinal study originally of 16,000 children born in England and Wales in March 1958 and followed up at intervals since then; much of the material reported in *Examination Results* relates to the 'O' level and CSE results obtained by 2896 of these children in 1974, when they were aged 16. *Standards* is based on returns from 1897 English schools covering 349,000 fifth-year pupils in 1981. We thus have a cross-sectional study of Scottish school-leavers; a longitudinal study of a particular group of English and Welsh children; and a cross-sectional study of English schools and educational authorities.

The authors of these three studies naturally ask a variety of questions of their data sets. We shall not attempt to summarise all their answers here but will concentrate on the ones which relate to our central issue 'what has been the effect of comprehensive reorganisation on examination results?'

In *Reconstructions* Gray and his colleagues concluded that:

> …comprehensive education had a levelling effect on attainment, raising fewer pupils to the highest levels of attainment, but helping more of them to progress beyond the minimum. It appears to have raised *average* attainment, although the definition of this average clearly depends on the relative importance of different levels of attainment implied by our scale.
>
> (Gray *et al.*, 1983, p. 256)

This conclusion was based on a comparison of the attainment of school-leavers from 'uncreamed' comprehensives with those of leavers from the remaining schools. That is to say, they compared schools in regions which had become completely comprehensive with those in regions where comprehensive reorganisation had come more slowly and where some element of selection remained. The comparison is thus between a fully comprehensive sector and a 'selective' sector that included creamed comprehensives and grant-aided schools as well as junior and senior secondary schools (the Scottish equivalents of secondary modern and grammar schools).

As well as higher average attainment, Gray *et al.* (1983) also found a lower level of social class inequality in the fully comprehensive sector.

> Children from social classes I and II achieved rather better SCE results at schools in the selective sector than at schools in the comprehensive sector. Children from each of the three manual classes, and unclassified children, did better in the comprehensive sector than in the selective sector. As a result, the gap between the middle and working-class average scores was narrower in the comprehensive sector than in the selective sector.
>
> (p. 257)

They then went on to say:

> Our conclusions ... have supported many of the optimistic claims made by advocates of comprehensive education. However, the form of comprehensive education that sustains these claims is not the one introduced by the post-1965 reorganisation, but one arising out of an older and traditional form in Scottish education, the omnibus school. The relative equality of opportunity in the comprehensive sector was not the result of reorganisation, but a continuation of the equality already established by the omnibus-school tradition.
>
> (p. 266)

In *Examination Results* Steedman began by comparing the results of pupils in three different types of school—established comprehensives, secondary moderns and grammar schools. She found that the 'raw' or uncorrected results placed grammar schools well in the lead with 5.12 'O' level equivalents per pupil; comprehensives came next with an average of 1.60, and secondary moderns came last obtaining 0.98 'O' level equivalents (Steedman, 1983, p. 78). However, after making allowances for differences in intake—that is, after taking account of differences in attainment at age eleven, in social class background and in parental interest—the differences in examination results were much reduced. The ranking of the three types of school remained the same, but the difference between the grammar and comprehensive schools was reduced to 0.92, and that between comprehensive and secondary modern schools to 0.28 (measured as before on the basis of 'O' level equivalents).

Next Steedman put the results of the grammar and secondary modern schools together and compared the overall average for this combination of schools with that of the comprehensives alone. Again she found that, before correcting for differences in family background and initial attainment at age 11, the grammar/modern combination obtained the better overall results. However, after correcting for intake, the now tiny difference between the sectors was found not to be statistically significant. Steedman concluded that "There was no sign from these results that selection, in the sense of having a mixture of grammars and secondary moderns, could be said to have made a difference to examination performance" (Steedman, 1983, p. 133). We should note, however, that this comparison between 'sectors' (our term, not Steedman's) is rather different from Gray's. Gray's *selective* sector included creamed comprehensives, but Steedman placed these schools in her *comprehensive* sector so long as they were already established as comprehensives when her sample entered them. Transitional schools, namely those which had been in the process of reorganisation while the study's pupils attended them, were excluded from most of Steedman's sector comparisons but included in Gray's selective sector.

In *Standards in English Schools* Marks *et al.* did not have data about individual pupils but about schools and LEAs. They found substantial differences in examination results both within and between schools. "For example, pupils at some comprehensive schools obtained on average about *four times* as many O-levels and CSE Grade 1 passes as those at other comprehensive schools *within the same LEA*" (Marks *et al.*, 1983, p. 19; italics in original). They found further substantial differences—differences of the order of a factor of 2—between LEAs even after taking some account of the social class composition of the LEAs.

Marks *et al.* then attempted to explain these differences between LEAs. They found that "both social class and selectivity were consistently related to examination results—higher examination results being related to more selection and to lower percentages of pupils in classes 4 and 5" (p. 47). They measured selectivity "by calculating the fraction of the whole age cohort in that LEA which entered grammar schools in 1976" (p. 42), while social classes 4 and 5 represent semi- and unskilled manual workers.

Finally, they estimated what results might be expected in a fully comprehensive system as compared with a fully selective system. They proceeded somewhat as Steedman did, comparing the average results in comprehensive schools with those in the combination of grammars and secondary moderns. They adjusted or reweighted the average for the grammar/secondary modern combination to take account of the likelihood that in a fully selective system between 25 and 30% of pupils would be in grammar schools. (Like everyone else they ignored the fact that historically the English selective system contained around 10% of pupils in technical schools.) They concluded that the resulting estimates "show that the examination results to be expected for pupils in a fully selective system are considerably higher than for pupils in a fully comprehensive system" (Marks *et al.*, 1983, p. 57).

Even from this highly abbreviated summary it should be clear that not only are the conclusions rather different but the methods of analysis are very different as well. All three research groups are clear about the methodological difficulties they faced in tackling the central question. They all entered caveats at various stages of their reports. They all also tried out a variety of different procedures within the confines of each study. Where they were able to adopt the same procedures, they in fact got much the same results. For example, both Steedman and Marks would agree that the *uncorrected* results for grammar schools were superior to the uncorrected ones for comprehensives, which in turn were superior to those for secondary moderns. It is in the choice of technique for making corrections that the studies differ and the results start to diverge.

Corrections for intake

The need to make corrections for intake is well known and is the cornerstone of educational sociology. The intakes of pupils to different types of school will differ in all kinds of educationally relevant ways, and we must take account of this if we are to make valid inferences about the effect of school organisation and to disentangle it from the effects of intake and social background. The three studies differ in the ways they made these corrections. Gray *et al.* made no correction at all. They were in the fortunate position of discovering that the intakes to their comprehensive and selective sectors were almost identical in their social class distributions according to the OPCS five-class schema. They did, however, appear to find some differences between the two sectors when these social classes were disaggregated into a more detailed schema of 38 occupational groups of their own devising (of which they do not give details). In comparing class inequality in the two sectors they reweighted in order to take account of these detailed differences in occupational distributions, but they do not appear to have done so when comparing overall examination results (Gray *et al.*, 1983, p. 259).

Aside from social class, Gray *et al.* do not appear to have had information on other educationally relevant aspects of family background. Nor did they have information on the ability of the pupils. Naturally, then, they could not check whether the intakes were alike in these respects nor control for any differences. They entered an appropriate caveat. Since pupil ability and parental interest are correlated with, but not identical to, social class, it is clear that the intakes to the two sectors could differ in these other ways, and that such intake differences could account for the examination differences that Gray *et al.* discover between the sectors, or indeed could generate differences that at present remain hidden.

There is another interesting problem even with social class, however. Gray *et al.* pointed out, as we summarised earlier, that the relation between social class and educational attainment is different in the two sectors, the selective sector having the greater class inequality. This means that, if the class profiles of the two sectors were to change, the pattern of their examination results would change from those observed in 1976. Suppose, for example, that the social class distributions in the two sectors gradually changed, manual work perhaps contracting and non-manual expanding, but changed *equally* in the two sectors. The greater class inequality in the selective sector would mean that it would tend to pull ahead as the class structure became more 'top heavy'. The fact that "children from social classes I and II achieved rather better examination results at schools in the selective sector than at schools in the comprehensive sector" would give the selective sector an advantage in a society with a larger middle class than that which obtained in Scotland in 1976. If we accept the assumptions implied, the findings of Gray *et al.* are consistent with the notion that comprehensive schooling would deliver better examination results in a working-class society but selective schooling would do better in a middle-class society.

We do not accept this inference ourselves for it is based on the assumption that the relation between social class and educational attainment would remain the same as the social structure changed its shape. This is an assumption that would need to be checked carefully. But the point does bring out the difficulty of drawing policy implications from comparisons which simply, and necessarily, compare systems as they happen to be at a particular time in a particular place. As Heraclitus said, "You cannot step into the same river twice". Conditions will be different on a later occasion.

The problem of drawing policy implications might be even more complex than this. It is quite possible, for example, that the relationship between social class and educational attainment varies not only between sectors but also between types of school within a sector. Thus it might be the case that the attainment of pupils exhibited sharper class inequalities within senior secondary schools than within junior secondary or creamed comprehensives in Scotland. Gray *et al.* do not tell us about this, and it does not affect their comparison between sectors as it stands, but it might be important as soon as we wished to draw conclusions about policy. If there is a different relation between class and attainment in the senior secondary schools from that in the other types, the average for the selective sector as a whole will change as the proportions of pupils at the various types of school changes. (And we may note that in Scotland in 1976 the selective sector contained relatively few senior secondary schools—apparently only about 13% of pupils in the selective sector attended such schools.[1])

It follows that we must be careful in extrapolating from these results to what would happen in a fully selective system, and Gray *et al.* wisely do not attempt to do so. The naive observer might believe that, since the fully comprehensive sector of uncreamed schools did better than the selective sector of junior, senior, grant-aided and creamed comprehensive schools, it would therefore perform better still than a fully selective sector. But she/he might be wrong. We might in fact change the overall results equally well by moving in a selective direction as by moving in a comprehensive direction. Which result we predict will depend upon which particular statistical model we assume about the relation between class, school and attainment. We do not know enough at the moment to go beyond description to policy recommendation.

In contrast to Gray *et al.* Steedman has much more information about intake, having data on ability and parental interest as well as social class. And she has need of this information because of the peculiarities of her sample—her comprehensive and selective sectors having very different social class and ability profiles from each other. The comprehensive schools in Steedman's sample have a social class intake that is very similar to that of the secondary modern schools while their ability profile comes somewhere in between those of the grammar and modern schools.

Despite the richness of the data, there are some difficulties with Steedman's controls for intake. In the first place it is disturbing to find that the sample has been reduced from its original size of around 16,000 children to less than 3,000. Some of the reductions are quite proper—the restriction to England, for example, or the exclusion of children who attended independent schools. However, there is the worry that there has been some distortion in the sample over and above these deliberate exclusions.

There are always going to be some biasses in the response to surveys, and we have to check whether these might affect the conclusions reached. Dougal Hutchison considers this in the statistical appendix. He reports that there was a fairly high non-response rate of approximately 30% between the 11-year-old sample and the 16-year-old exam sample. In other words only 70% of the children for whom there were full data at age 11 were still 'present and correct' with full educational and examination data at age 16. As might be expected, the children who remained in the sample were somewhat biassed towards the middle class and towards grammar school education. However, Hutchison is also able to report that this 'non-response bias' did not significantly affect the relationships between variables (that is, on relationships between the 11-year-old variables since these were naturally the only ones that could be checked in this way).

Hutchison's report is encouraging, but there is a further possible source of bias. Hutchison shows in his table A5 that 12.6% of the exam sample at age 16 attended grammar schools, and this appears to be closely in accord with national DES figures for 1974. However, although table A5 has been reduced by the 30% non-response between ages 11 and 16, it still covers 11,068 children. Steedman's analyses on the other hand are carried out either on 4,375 children (when those who attended transitional schools are included) or on 2,896 children (when the transitional schools are excluded) (see Steedman, 1983, table 1a). Steedman points out that grammar school pupils make up 17% of the 4,375 children and 26% of the 2,896 children.

As Hutchison points out, this is not necessarily a problem, providing that the relationships between the variables remain the same and are not affected by the reduction in sample size. If they are of the conventional linear type, the relationships probably will remain unchanged, but curvilinear ones will be more of a problem. Consider, for example, Table 13.1. This shows a clear non-linear relationship between social class and the acquisition of 'O' level. If we were to omit a substantial fraction of, say, working-class children from the sample, a linear estimate of the relationship between class and 'O' level would give highly misleading results. If we wished to extrapolate from such a truncated sample to the full one, we would fall into error.

Steedman is in fact very careful about this and does not herself make such extrapolations. She makes it clear that she is simply describing the relationships that held true within a particular subsample drawn at a particular time and place. It is only if we are willing to assume that the same relationships would hold true between these variables at other times and with other distributions of children that any policy implications might begin to follow. It would be unwise to make this assumption.

Next we come to Marks *et al.* They *do* want to make policy recommendations, so the general points we have already made about Gray's and Steedman's work must apply to theirs as well, although their methods of adjusting for intake are rather different. They neither have Gray's good fortune in finding sectors with similar social class profiles nor Steedman's wealth of family background and ability data. What they have are data about the social class composition of the LEAs. More specifically they adjust LEAs examination results by considering the percentage of children in each LEA living in class IV and V households.

Table 13.1 Social class and educational attainment[2]

Father's occupation	% obtaining 'O' level or SCE	N
Professional	81	36
Managerial	76	49
Junior non-manual	71	34
Self-employed	43	37
Skilled manual	29	146
Semi-and unskilled manual	30	77

Source: British Election Survey 1979.
Sample: men and women aged 18–30 and on the electoral register in Britain in 1979.

This method of controlling for social class is inadequate if some other aspect of social class (such as the percentage in classes I and II) is correlated with examination results and with selectivity. As Table 13.1 shows, it is the children who are in higher social classes who are more likely to obtain 'O' level. It is thus the proportion of children from these social groups in an LEA which is likely to be most strongly associated with examination success. There is a different conclusion if we turn our attention to the children who fail to obtain any qualifications at all. These children are more likely to be drawn from classes IV and V. Hence the relationship between social class and attainment will vary depending on which criterion of attainment we take. In estimating the effect of selectivity on attainment, therefore, it will be important to use the control for social class which is appropriate for the criterion of attainment being employed. Marks *et al.* fail to do so.

Nevertheless, the use made of correlations and multiple regression in *Standards* to analyse differences between LEAs is in principle an illuminating way of exploring our question 'has comprehensive reorganisation worked?' The controls for intake relate to the same unit of analysis as the outcome variables, namely to the LEA, and so we can begin to discover whether an LEA's degree of selectivity 'makes a difference' or not. However, the comparison of school types *within LEA groupings* which Marks *et al.* also attempt is more difficult to justify. This is because the controls for intake relate to the LEA as a whole not to the catchment area of each school. What they do is to divide LEAs into three groupings which contain authorities with similar percentages of children in classes IV and V. They then compare examination results at grammar, secondary modern and comprehensive schools within each of these three groupings. But within a particular LEA or group of similar LEAs the grammar schools will have different social class intakes from the secondary modern or comprehensive schools, and this must be controlled in the statistical analysis.

Marks *et al.* did not have the right kind of data to make adjustments for the intakes of different types of school in the way that Steedman could. It seems to us that they were therefore wrong to attempt comparisons between school types or to use these comparisons to estimate what would happen in a fully selective system. Given the data available to them, the comparison of LEAs was the appropriate way to proceed.

We might add that it is a pity that Steedman did not also try to compare authorities in the way that Marks *et al.* did. She could have grouped her pupils into those attending schools in selective LEAs, mixed LEAs, and fully comprehensive LEAs. She might then have carried out an analysis using the LEA as the unit of analysis, controlling not only for its social class composition but also for the ability of its children. Sample size permitting, such an analysis would be illuminating. It is somewhat paradoxical that Marks *et al.* chose to use one technique—comparison of school types—that was inappropriate for their data while Steedman failed to choose a technique—comparison of authorities—that might have been appropriate.

Corrections for schools

The general need to control for intake is now very well established and familiar. There is, however, another set of less familiar controls that need to be made when attempting to discover whether comprehensive reorganisation has been a success. These are controls for *which* schools have been reorganised. Just as children are not randomly assigned to schools, so schools were probably not assigned at random to sectors. We doubt very much whether it is a random selection of grammar schools that has survived the general movement towards comprehensives. We might expect the weaker schools to be the first candidates for reorganisation and for the schools with the best reputations to survive longest. This of course will only be important if the quality of a school is a relatively stable attribute that persists from year to year despite its ever-changing mix of pupils and staff. There is some evidence that this is the case, but it must be admitted that our information about such phenomena is rather scant compared with the knowledge we now have about pupils.

The central point is that, if we want to make policy inferences from our data and predict what would happen in a fully comprehensive or fully selective system, then we must either assume that the schools to which the data currently relate are 'representative' of, say, grammar schools as a whole, or we must make some correction for any lack of representativeness which we believe to occur. Most arguments for preferring selective schools to comprehensives are based on the implicit assumption that selective schools are more effective, with respect to examination results, than are comprehensives even after controlling for intake. (There are of course other reasons for preferring a particular system of schooling which have nothing to do with examination results but more to do with parental choice or social justice.) Our point is that, even if this is true of the selective schools remaining in existence to be studied, it might not be true of selective schools in the past or future, or at any rate not to the same extent. If as a result of reorganisation only the best grammar schools are retained, then obviously our estimate of grammar school effectiveness will be correspondingly inflated.

This kind of argument can in principle be checked from a data set such as Steedman's. We could investigate whether, after controlling properly for intake, grammar schools exhibited a greater superiority over other types of school in authorities which had retained the fewest (and therefore we assume the best) grammar schools.

This kind of problem arises in interpreting the results of all three studies. Gray *et al.* are very clear that their array of uncreamed comprehensives are not a random selection and cannot be regarded as representative. They write:

...the schools that had become 'established comprehensives' by 1970 (in the sense that a full range of SCE courses was already available by that date, and that the intake was entirely non-selective) did not do so at random. Many had already been omnibus schools before Circular 600; and others may have been reorganised quickly because they presented fewer problems (of size, staffing siting) than schools which took longer to reorganise...

(Gray *et al.*, 1983, p. 250)

They rightly conclude therefore that "one should be cautious about drawing general conclusions from this sample concerning the effectiveness of comprehensive education at other times or in other countries" (p. 250). To be sure, Gray *et al.* are suggesting a different model from ours—they suggest that their sample of established, uncreamed comprehensives may have been atypically effective rather than the reverse. But the point is that we know very little about the selective processes operating on schools as opposed to pupils. Either model could be advocated with plausible argument but meagre evidence.

Steedman is even more cautious than Gray in drawing inferences from her data. The caveats loom large in her text, and she emphasises that her results pertain only to a particular historical period that was atypical in many respects. She wrote:

This study was of a particular period (1969 to 1974) in the piecemeal changeover to comprehensive schooling, at which time there was no fully comprehensive system ... It must, however, be emphasised at the start that the findings of this study concerning schools called comprehensive may not generalise to present day comprehensive schools. They are observations of how pupils were faring in schools which were not true comprehensives but which coexisted with selective schools.

(Steedman, 1983, p. 3)

Unfortunately, Steedman did not have sufficient information about the schools to distinguish pupils at creamed from those at uncreamed or 'true' comprehensives, but the research could in principle be done. It is astonishing that we still have many LEAs which cream their comprehensives and yet the research which would tell us the consequences of this practice has yet to be carried out.

In *Standards* Marks *et al.* also recognise the importance of creaming. Their strategy is to construct a model which assumes that pupils in 'restricted range' comprehensives will obtain the same results as those in secondary modern schools. In principle this seems to be a sensible model, although in the absence of actual evidence on the effects of creaming a range of different assumptions can always plausibly be made. All we can do is to select a particular model and set of assumptions and hope that hindsight will one day prove it sound.

Aside from creaming, however, there are still serious problems for Marks *et al.* As we have said before, they do want to generalise to what a fully selective or fully comprehensive system would be like. We do not criticise them for this. Indeed, one could question the value of social science research if it were always so hedged around with caveats that policy implications could never be drawn. But to make policy recommendations one always has to go beyond description of the current state of affairs to construct a model based on specifiable assumptions. The assumption that Marks *et al.* make is that currently existing grammar and secondary modern schools are typical, with respect to their effectiveness, of future grammar and modern schools in a fully selective system. A number of alternative models with different assumptions and implications for policy could equally well be constructed. Thus even if they dealt satisfactorily with the problems of controlling for intake and still found that selection 'made a difference', the policy implications would still depend on debatable assumptions. For example, if we made the assumption that an atypically good grammar school, if reorganised, will make an atypically good comprehensive, then the implication might be that we should have more comprehensives. We need to know more about the determinants of school effectiveness if we are to be confident of our recommendations.

The determinants of school effectiveness

That schools vary in their effectiveness is widely agreed. There is little dispute that, after controlling for intake, grammar schools achieve better examination results than comprehensives, which in turn have better results than secondary moderns. But why? It cannot just be a matter of having different names. But unless we know what the causes are we cannot sensibly decide whether grammar schools should be expanded in number or not. The argument for selection must surely assume that whatever it is that makes for grammar school success is unique to a selective system and cannot be exported to comprehensives. It is not a self-evident proposition and ought to be checked.

That school effectiveness is not related in a simple manner to size, expenditure or pupil:teacher ratio is also broadly agreed. Some of the major candidates remaining are: history, tradition and ethos; the quality of the teaching staff; the 'balance' of the intake. They can be used to illustrate the difficulties in choosing policy.

Consider first history, tradition and ethos. Gray *et al.* produced some evidence that comprehensive schools which had previously been junior secondary schools within a selective system achieved worse results than other uncreamed comprehensives. They concluded that:

It seems that the previous organisation of a school and, more important, the meaning of its organisational history in the context of the educational policy of the local authority, may continue to influence the
performance of the school over and above factors associated with the
characteristics of its intake.

(Gray *et al.*, 1983, p. 291)

They do not tell us whether comprehensives which had previously been
senior secondary schools fared better than the average, but this could also
be true. At any rate the possibility is there that, although existing grammar
schools may get better results than existing comprehensives, turning grammars into comprehensive schools will not have any adverse effects since
the schools may retain their traditions and ethos despite the change of
name and intake. Equally, comprehensive reorganisation of yet more secondary moderns might not have the desired effects. Measured purely in
terms of examination results, it might simply pull the comprehensive
average down as these schools brought their less exam-orientated traditions with them.

On this line of argument the implications of the existing differences in
school effectiveness might be somewhat more limited than appears at first
sight. Still, it need not be grounds for total inertia. Traditions come from
somewhere and can perhaps be encouraged, although they may take time
to emerge. The implication would be that comprehensives must be given
time, as with the omnibus schools in Scotland, to develop their traditions.
A fair test of comprehensives will not be possible until they have been
around for a considerably longer period.

Next, consider teacher quality. Marks and his colleagues produced
some interesting evidence on this which they summarise as follows:

Results *within* individual schools often show striking differences. As
many of the same pupils take examinations in related subjects, differences in attainment are likely to reflect the quality of teaching.

(Marks *et al.*, 1983, cover)

That teachers vary, and that their pupils' results vary in consequence, is
on the face of it a plausible suggestion, and the evidence presented in *Standards* is consistent with it. Moreover, it is also plausible that teacher quality
will vary not only *within* but also *between* schools. If teachers were allocated randomly, we would expect that by chance alone some schools would
end up with more than their 'fair share' of good teachers. In practice, too,
some catchment areas or some schools' reputations will be more attractive
to teachers and thus generate a larger pool of applicants for teaching posts
from which the head can select. This is in principle yet another researchable
topic: in explaining school effectiveness perhaps we should look not at the
pupil:teacher ratio but at the ratio of applications to posts.

There is no need to stop here. Teacher quality could also account for differences in the effectiveness of the various types of secondary school. Perhaps grammar schools historically have had the best fields of applicants for their posts and the relative effectiveness of grammar, comprehensive and secondary modern schools is to be explained simply in terms of the recruitment of teachers. On this line of argument, changing the teachers' quality becomes more important than changing the type of school or the system of secondary education. Reorganisation of secondary schooling might merely redistribute the existing stock of teachers without any improvement whatsoever in overall standards. An LEA which retained a large number of grammar schools might be able to recruit better teachers and boost its examination results relative to other LEAs, but the national gain would be zero.

Yet another possibility is that the 'balance of intake' accounts for differences in school effectiveness. Having a nucleus of able children in a school might pull its standards up generally as their ability 'rubs off' on the less able. There is some evidence for this. In our reworking of Rutter's statistics we found that 'balance' was the best predictor of school effectiveness once the usual allowances for family background had been made (Heath & Clifford, 1981).

In principle balance could explain differences between grammar, comprehensive and secondary modern schools as well as between individual schools. It might be the mechanism which explains why selection 'makes a difference'. Thus the concentration of very able pupils in grammar schools might pull up the standards of the borderline ones, and the absence of very able pupils in the secondary moderns might operate in the reverse direction. It could also explain why the old Direct Grant schools had such good records at 'A' level and Oxbridge entry (see Halsey, Heath & Ridge, 1984). It makes sense of quite a wide array of educational findings.

The balance thesis, unlike the teacher quality hypothesis, could well have implications for the system of secondary education. For example, if a nucleus of very able pupils pulls up the standards of the slightly less able but not of the average or below average, grammar schools might well be the best institution to capitalise on the effects of balance. If, on the other hand, the 'rub off' effects of the able pupils are diffused right across the spectrum of ability, comprehensives might be a more effective system of organisation. Again, these are eminently researchable hypotheses but ones on which we remain at present quite ignorant.

Conclusions

Our three studies provide valuable material on the recent history of British secondary education. But in moving from description to causal inferences and policy recommendations we face serious problems. In answering our question 'has comprehensive reorganisation improved or worsened examination results?' we have to take account of the fact that children are not randomly allocated to schools and that schools were not randomly allocated to sectors. Our three studies have chosen different strategies for correcting for these processes, and it is their selection of statistical technique which largely accounts for the differences in the conclusions which they reach. They use radically different methods for controlling for intake and for dealing with 'creamed' comprehensives. It is not surprising that they disagree.

But even if our authors agreed on their choice of statistics and reached a unanimous conclusion, it is not clear that any policy recommendation would automatically follow. Suppose they found that the move to comprehensive education had not improved exam results. Our policy should still depend on the answer to the further question 'why is selection superior?' Do grammar schools succeed because they attract the best teachers, because they have had the time to develop academic traditions, or because the concentration of able pupils rubs off on the less able? We cannot begin to answer this question at present.

It is clear, then, that we know very little about what makes for an effective or ineffective school. We know a lot about the determinants of pupils' attainment and so can sensibly control for intake variables like cognitive ability and social class. But we have very little knowledge of the equivalent determinants of school effectiveness. Presumably there are such determinants, or at least people must believe there to be such determinants, since otherwise there would be no point to these heated debates. If schools do not vary in their effects, and it is all simply a matter of home background, there is no point in worrying about selection and comprehensive reorganisation. But until we know what it is that determines their effectiveness, educational policy is helpless. The need for serious research into the factors affecting school effectiveness is clear. Could it be, to reduce the argument to its absurd extreme, that a change of name is sufficient? Should we call all schools grammar schools and sit back and enjoy the resulting higher standards? Obviously not, but it is scandalous that our present state of ignorance should (almost) lead us to such a conclusion.

Notes

1 In table 14.1 Gray *et al* show that 9% of all school-leavers in their sample came from schools that were still selective in 1972. Since less than a third of school-leavers were taken to come from the comprehensive sector, it follows that the leavers from the selective schools would amount to roughly 13–14% of the selective sector.

2 In Table 13.1 occupations have been grouped according to a collapsed version of the OPCS schema of socio-economic groups. This provides greater discrimination than the usual schema of five social classes used by the three studies discussed in this paper.

The collapsed version is constructed as follows:
professional—SEGs 3, 4, 5.1;
managerial—SEGs 1.2, 2.2, 5.2;
junior non-manual—SEGs 6, 7;
self-employed—SEGs 1.1, 2.1, 12, 13, 14;
skilled manual—SEGs 8, 9;
semi- and unskilled manual—SEGs 10, 11, 15.
See OPCS (1970) *Classification of Occupations 1970* for further details.

References

Gray, J., McPherson, A.F. & Raffe, D. (1983) *Reconstructions of Secondary Education: Theory, Myth and Practice since the War* (London, Routledge & Kegan Paul).

Halsey, A.H., Heath, A.F. & Ridge, J.M. (1984) The political arithmetic of public schools. In: Walford, G. (ed.) *British Public Schools: Policy and Practice* (London, Falmer Press).

Heath, A.F. & Clifford, P. (1981) 'The measurement and explanation of school differences,' *Oxford Review of Education*, 7, pp. 33–40.

Marks, J., Cox, C. & Pomian-Srzednicki, M. (1983) *Standards in English Schools: An Analysis of the Examination Results of Secondary Schools in England for 1981* (London, National Council for Educational Standards).

Office of Population Censuses and Surveys (1970) *Classification of Occupations 1970* (London, HMSO).

Steedman, J. (1983) *Examination Results in Selective and Nonselective Schools: Findings from the National Child Development Study* (London, National Children's Bureau).

14 The expansion of special education

Sally Tomlinson

Source: 'The expansion of special education', *Oxford Review of Education*, 11(2): 157–165, 1985.

This article advances the argument that special education is expanding as part of a restructuring of the education-training system to deal with large numbers of young people who are now defined as unable or unwilling to participate in normal education. The expansion is occurring as attempts are made to change education to fit the perceived needs of a technologically-based society in which a large social group will be partially or permanently unemployed. Evidence for expansion is examined, professional interests in an expanding clientele are noted, and the dilemmas inherent in comprehensive schooling and a disappearing youth labour market are discussed. The concept of special needs is thought to have become an ideological rationalisation which obfuscates the educational, political and economic needs actually served by the expansion.

Special education in Britain, as in other advanced technological societies, is expanding. In changed forms and rationalised by changed ideologies, notably the ideology of special needs, it is becoming a more important mechanism for differentiating between young people and allocating some to a future which, if not as stigmatised as in the past, will be characterised by relative powerlessness and economic dependency. It is expanding primarily as part of a political response to a crucial dilemma facing education systems in late twentieth-century technological societies. This dilemma is centred round restructuring the education-training system to deal with the increasing number of young people who are defined as being unable or unwilling to participate satisfactorily in a system primarily directed towards producing academic and technical elites. Adequate achievements in normal school education or educational training are becoming more important in gaining any sort of employment or income above subsistence level, or exerting any influence on the wider society.

The expansion of special education is linked to the question of what sort of education—or preparation for future life-style—can or should be offered to a larger social group who are likely to be partially or permanently non-employed, and thus in traditional industrial-society understandings are not economically profitable or 'useful'. As special education expands it is likely to provide both a rationale and a justification for the economic and social position of at least a part of this social group. Although presented in ideological terms as catering for the 'needs' of pupils, the expansion of special education is the result of rational action on the part of those who control and direct education and training, to restructure the education system to fit the perceived needs of a post-industrial, technologically based society.

This article examines evidence for the claim that special education is expanding and discusses three reasons for the expansion—professional vested interest, comprehensive school dilemmas and the declining youth labour market—and asserts that the ideology of 'special needs' directs attention away from the social, economic and political concerns which have led to the expansion.

Evidence for expansion

Legally, special education is defined as the curriculum and pedagogy offered to pupils who pre-1981 had a 'disability of body or mind' calling for special educational treatment, and post-1981 have a learning difficulty which calls for special educational provision. The number of such children rose from nil in the early 1870s—at the beginning of compulsory state education—to some $1\frac{1}{2}$ million in 1981.[1] This argues that a sub-system of special education has been successfully established and has become an important structural component of the educational system. The expansion can be largely accounted for by the number of children who have no physical or sensory handicap, but who are educationally defined as being incapable of participating or unwilling to participate in what is currently defined as the 'normal' curriculum, and being incapable of 'adequate achievements' via this curriculum. Such children have, over the past 100 years, been variously described as feeble-minded, educable defective, educationally sub-normal, those having moderate learning difficulties, dull and backward, remedial, and maladjusted and disruptive.

The expansion is linked to enhanced definitions of 'achievement'. There is increasing pressure on schools to raise standards and to credential more and more pupils. This has led to pressures on schools to devise more and more courses leading to lower-level credentials and to seek ways of separating out those who are unable or unwilling to achieve even these lower-level qualifications. In this way the sub-system of special education appears capable of seemingly indefinite expansion. For example, the number of pupils considered to have a disability of body or mind in 1946 was 2% with a further 8% to 9% likely to be unable to achieve adequately in schools.[2] In 1978, the number in need of special provision was considered by the Warnock Committee to be 20% of the school population. By 1982 the Secretary of State was expressing his concern about the less able 40%, and a DES-sponsored programme for lower-attaining pupils was instigated. The ideological differences between the 20% of pupils needing special provision owing to learning difficulties and the learning difficulties of the bottom 40% are problematic, and in practice the programme appears to fill a gap between school definitions of 'special needs' and 'CSE material' (NFER, 1984). In Scotland the system may be expanding faster. A Scottish Inspectorate comment on learning difficulties in 1984 noted that since "there is a whole range of difficulties faced by very many pupils in the lower half of the ability range ... the progress report was thinking in terms of up to 50%".[3] Accurate numbers of those in special education provision, or 'in need' of this kind of provision have always been difficult to quantify. One reason for this have been the changing definitions of special education. Another reason is that LEAs have always differed in the kinds and amount of special provision they offered. Perhaps of more interest are the proportional and percentage increases.

Post-war, Booth has worked out that in 1950 2402 pupils per million were categorised as ESN-M; by 1977 the proportion had risen to 5763 per million. Similarly, in 1950, 93 pupils per million were officially maladjusted, by 1977 this had risen to 1416 per million (Booth, 1981, p. 295). In another entertaining comparison Squibb (1981, p. 47) estimated that in 15 years (1961–76) there was an increase of 150% in pupils classed as ESN, a 237% increase for those classed as maladjusted, a 1332% increase for those classed as speech defective and an infinite increase (from no pupils in 1961 to 951 in 1976) in those classed as autistic. As Squibb has noted "we may all be autistic soon" (1981, p. 48). Further evidence of percentage increases of pupils segregated into special schools and classes under the pre-1981 system of classification by handicap has been provided by Swann who worked out that despite assumptions that integration was occurring and fewer pupils were being physically removed from mainstream schooling, the proportion of pupils segregated in special schools actually increased by 4.8% between 1977 and 82 and he particularly noted the increased segregation into ESN-M and maladjusted provision (Swann, 1984).

From its beginnings special education was concerned to take in those with obvious and definable physical and sensory handicaps and behaviourally troublesome pupils, but from 1889 the most likely candidates for inclusion in an expanding system were those originally classed as feeble-minded or educable defectives—their heirs being the dull and backward, educationally sub-normal, remedial, moderate learning and behavioural difficulties, the less-able, etc. I have argued (Tomlinson, 1982) that the persistent connection of this expanding group—and of learning and behavioural problems—with the children of the manual working-class is perenially resilient. The 'social problem' class that worried Cyril Burt continues to worry educationalists from the Secretary of State downwards. Connections between lack of intelligence, inability to learn, bad behaviour, low socio-economic status and a variety of undesirable social attributes continue to ensure that it is largely the children of the lower working class and the unemployed who are candidates for the expanding special education sector. The story of Bill and Daisy included by A.F. Tredgold (1914) in his *Textbook of Mental Deficiency* may still be pertinent:

> Bill, we will suppose, had been a pupil in a special (educationally subnormal) school up to the age of 16 ... and has since been employed in a number of jobs, starting as an errand boy and graduating to simple machine-minding in a factory. Daisy went to an ordinary school but was very backward and like Bill, is scarcely able to read and write. Daisy, before her marriage to Bill, has held a variety of jobs mainly assembling or varnishing small electrical parts.
>
> After joining a gang for acceptance and a sense of importance Bill was ... impelled to seek a girl friend, but was so unprepossessing that his only chance would be with a girl equally unattractive who might be available. Daisy was unattractive but simple and compliant and an easy date. Between the pair a bond of sympathy grew up. They each provided for the other what had been lacking all the years—comfort and appreciation. (Daisy became pregnant and they married and went to live in an attic room in an overcrowded house—going down four flights of stairs for water and six for the WC. Daisy had to give up her job, the couple lacked foresight and planning.)
>
> After the baby's birth, Daisy went out cleaning, Bill lost his job—they had another baby but fear of further pregnancies led Daisy to fail to give Bill comfort and solace. Bill took to staying away from home and he became ripe for any criminal exploitation that might come his way. The children will have a natural backwardness at school, will play truant and delinquent practices will follow. Thus history will have repeated itself.
>
> (p. 394)

Tredgold's documentation of two ESN school-leavers who found semi-skilled work, married and had a family could be read as a eugenist's warning, or as a libel on a couple who lacked an adequate wage, decent housing and contraceptive advice.

Expansion and professional interests

Much of the expansion of special education has been ascribed to accident, spontaneous adjustment, progress and benevolence. These explanations have always proved a stumbling block to the analysis of the emergence and expansion of a special subsystem of education. Archer's (1979) contention that educational structures are the result of the *interests* of those social groups who manage, as a result of conflicts, to achieve educational control, is a more useful starting point. The development and expansion of special education is the result of a variety of conflicting interest groups, both inside and outside education. Indeed, an understanding of the competition and alliances among interest groups in special education is crucial to understanding its expansion.

Pre-1945 (as I have documented in Tomlinson, 1982) educationalists, psychologists and medical practitioners all had vested interests in expanding the numbers of pupils in special education, and government had an interest in the control and direction of numbers of pupils who might prove 'troublesome' in their post-school careers in a variety of ways (principally by unemployment, crime or by requiring resources). Ordinary teachers' interests in the removal of special pupils—who originally interfered with payment-by-results and filled the standard 'O' classes—has proved an enduring and crucial force behind expansion. Then, as now, the public status of ordinary teachers was dependent on their ability to 'raise standards', which called for the removal of defective and troublesome children. This removal coincided with the interests of the new sub-profession of special school teachers who had a vested interest in obtaining clients for their schools. It also coincided with the interests of the eugenists who were concerned to identify and isolate defectives who threatened the 'racial stock'. Psychologists had a crucial interest in developing the tools of assessment for special education, which have proved to be so important in their professional development and claims to specialist expertise. The enduring medical influence in special education has also been well documented (Pritchard, 1963) and the recorded conflicts of educational and medical personnel over the control of access to special education post-1908 provides a good example of the strategic power-play that ultimately determines control of the education system.[4]

Post-1945, medical and psychological interests took precedence over education in vying for control of assessment processes for special education, psychologists partially reaching parity of esteem by 1975 and certainly by 1981. However, by this time all professional interests were becoming united by a suspicion that central and local administrators had annexed control of special education via distribution of resources, control of assessment procedures, parental appeals and decisions on provisions. The 1981 Act did, however, place more control of the expanding sector of special education in the educationalists' area, as its major location became the ordinary school. In particular the expanding sub-profession of 'special needs' Heads of Departments, teachers and support staff in ordinary schools now has power to shape and control large sectors of special education and in particular to decide who the special clients in the ordinary school will be and what sort of 'special' curriculum and pedagogy they will be offered. The ideology of 'special needs' is currently penetrating the secondary school curriculum and conflicts of interest are developing between 'special needs' specialists and their colleagues. In addition it was not to be expected that teachers in special schools would willingly give up their special expertise or clients as the location changed, and there are currently conflicts of interest between special and ordinary schools over the retention or movement of pupils, particularly in areas where segregated provision was well established.[5] But by the late 1970s 'special' teachers in both segregated and integrated provision had, to some extent, realised that their common interest lay in enhanced professional claims to special expertise. These claims are currently being strengthened and the expansion of special education has created the opportunity for more expert special teachers, support staff, advisers and inspectors to be employed.

Comprehensive school dilemmas

The expansion of special education cannot be understood without reference to developments and changes in the whole education system, particularly changes since the establishment of state comprehensive education during the 1970s. A common school, underpinned by egalitarian ideologies and attended by middle and working class children, was envisaged by comprehensive supporters, but comprehensive education is now dogged by a series of dilemmas. One dilemma which was slowly realised during the 1970s was that if selection by ability was inadmissible, so was selection by disability or inability. The 100-year-old principle of segregation gave way to notions of integration and comprehensive schools were expected to incorporate many non-conformist and troublesome children who would previously have been candidates for exclusion. Other dilemmas included the promise to offer equality of opportunity, while explaining away unequal outcomes in what Shaw has termed "our incorrigibly competitive and hierarchical society" (Shaw, 1983, p. 37); the pressure to raise standards and credential more pupils by expanding the examination system while offering a suitable curriculum to the 'less able'; and the pressure to incorporate a subject-orientated traditional grammar school-type curriculum while incorporating secondary modern-type pupils.

Reynolds & Sullivan (1979) have argued that initially comprehensives were left relatively free to develop their own curriculum, pedagogies and forms of control with little outside interference, and one response to dilemmas posed by the 'less able' and the 'unwilling' (pupils with learning and behavioural problems) whose numbers increased after 1973 and the raising of the school-leaving age, was to segregate them internally within the schools. The rapid development of behavioural units for disruptive pupils from 1974 and the development of large remedial departments created an unofficial expansion of special education in secondary schools. This expansion was noted by the Warnock Committee which recommended that "children previously regarded as disruptive" and "children who have hitherto been seen as requiring remedial rather than special education" should be deemed candidates for special education (Warnock Report, 1978, p. 47). Thus the unofficial expansion was given official recognition. Up to the beginning of the 1980s there was little evidence that comprehensive schools had solved the dilemma of providing a curriculum for the 'less able' or the 'remedial-special'. Evidence (HMI, 1979; Reid *et al.*, 1981) indicated that most comprehensives preferred streaming, setting and banding to mixed-ability teaching, and their curriculum for the less able was narrow and inappropriate. Given the pressures to concentrate on the able and the examinable, this is perhaps not surprising.

The incursion of the new vocationalism and MSC activities into secondary schooling and the blurring of the education-training divide has created more dilemmas for comprehensive schools—one of which is how far 'special needs' pupils will be incorporated into technical and vocational courses, or how far they will be offered watered-down palliatives of 'work experience' and 'social and life skills'.

The disappearing youth labour market

While the comprehensive school curriculum has increasingly become a matter for pressures from political and economic interest groups outside school, a major focus has been on the curriculum for the 'less able'. The DES 14–16 'lower attaining pupils programme', for example, is a direct but little publicised political incursion into this curriculum. DES criticism of the inappropriate curriculum offered to the less able up to the early 1980s was largely a criticism of the apparent slowness of schools to realise the social and political consequences of the disappearance of the youth labour market for less able and special leavers. The pupils to whom the DES and other vocational and educational programmes for the less able are aimed are those who, up the mid-1970s, could be minimally motivated to learn and behave at school by means of the carrot of possible employment. Programmes designed for the less able and special adolescents are part of a political response to the problem of dealing with larger numbers of young people who, despite new vocational initiatives, will probably never acquire employment. The expansion of special education to embrace larger numbers of young people, particularly at post-16 level, may provide both a rationale and a justification for the subsequent economic position of this group. I suggested in 1982 that 'to have received a special education—with its historical stigmatic connotations, even a non-recorded special education in an integrated setting, may be regarded unfavourably by potential employers' (Tomlinson, 1982, p. 177). However, this kind of assertion now needs much more careful elaboration. The role of special education in preparing large numbers of young people for a workless future or at least one of sporadic, low-skilled employment needs research and analysis.

Any discussion of the relationship between the expansion of special education and the economic situation must start from the premise that to have 'special needs' is not an individual characteristic; it is the product of interaction between individuals and their social environment. It has been an underlying theme of this article that special education expands, not because of intrinsic qualities or lack of qualities in pupils, but because of the social or educational criteria currently being applied. *Similarly, whether or not the handicapped or the special find employment depends on the current economic conditions rather than on the possession of suitable abilities or skills.* Thus, while the economy was in need of low-skilled labour, the majority of special school leavers found employment, even though their mental or physical capacities were judged to be low. It has been an enduring characteristic of the 'handicapped' (as Barnett (1984) has recently elaborated in an interesting discussion of the economics of mental retardation) that they have often been considered retarded or problematic at school, but not outside school, particularly in employment. In Britain one careers officer wrote in 1974 that in his experience "the majority of special school leavers found jobs with comparative ease ... these included polishing, assembling, building, painting, canteen work and even office work" (City of Birmingham, 1977). A major task of special education has always been to prepare pupils for routine manual work, and some employers came to prefer special school leavers who were often more docile, obedient and punctual than others (see Collman, 1956; Atkinson, 1981). By 1975, however, the same careers officer was noting that "many special school leavers are affected by the recession and those requiring routine or semi-skilled work found most difficulty". In this, of course, special school leavers were joined by the less able and also leavers with school-leaving certificates. In 1974 80,000 under-20-year-olds were unemployed; by 1981 this number was 532,000 (although 360,000 were in government schemes or work experience programmes). The kind of work those who had received a special education formerly undertook has now virtually disappeared, although some low-skilled manufacturing or service jobs may continue to be available for them. Although the question of "specially educated for what?" can only be answered by empirical investigation of the post-school careers of those leaving special education, an examination of some post-16 college courses for special needs students suggests that for those pupils with severe sensory, physical or mental handicaps traditional supervised provision, usually at Adult Training Centres, is envisaged after they have undertaken college courses to the age of 19 or 21. For those with moderate learning difficulties (as the description now runs) further special courses, including special YTS schemes, transfer to a normal YTS place, or even low-skilled employment is the aim, while for more able but handicapped students transfer to mainstream college courses, YTS or particular kinds of employment is the aim. The courses usually include a large component of 'social and life skills', 'coping and independent living' and 'adult responsibility' as well as college or employer-based introductions to basic manual skills. The expansion of special education may have brought more young people in its orbit but the aims of special education may not have changed too drastically over 100 years. Training for self-sufficiency and controlled social behaviour, and training for low-skilled productive work are traditional aims in special education. The major future difference may be that disappearance of low-skilled work will lead to more and more extensive special courses and more carefully planned supervision for those who will never achieve work. The next expansion of special education will undoubtedly be into 'adult special needs' courses.

The ideology of special needs

To study ideology, as Thompson (1984) has recently pointed out, is to study the ways in which the meaning of particular words or ideas serves to sustain relations of domination. The concept of 'special needs' has become an ideological rationalisation for those who have the power to shape and define the expanding special education system and have vested interests in this expansion. Those who can define the 'needs' of others and give or withold provision have great power, yet the benevolent image with which the notion of 'catering for special needs' has become imbued precludes discussion of the supposed needs, or criticism of provision and practice. This, however, is the purpose of ideology—'ideology is, as it were, the linguistic legislature which defines what is available for public discussion and what is not' (Thompson, 1984, p. 85).

The concept of special needs began to be applied to particular groups of pupils in the 1960s—most notably to ethnic minority pupils whose language and cultural needs were 'special', and to 'disadvantaged pupils'. The liberal child-centred pedagogies of the 1960s focused on children's supposed needs, as did egalitarian programmes to compensate for social disadvantages. The concept was applied to special education in 1965 when a DES report described such education as "education that is specially well adapted to meet a child's needs". The Warnock Committee in 1978 adopted the concept both as a rationale for an expanded system of special education ("broader provision", p. 36) and as a more positive description of the clients of special education than description by handicap or disability. While the concept appears to have done the former, all sorts of expansion is now taking place with no further justification than "the pupil has special needs", the descriptive problem has not been overcome. The child with special educational needs has become the SEN or the SNARC pupil who needs a SNAP![6] The extension of the concept to cover 'gifted' pupils, or indeed *all* pupils, has led Mary Warnock to repudiate the use of the concept for those pupils her report had dealt with (*TES*, 12.11.82, 11.11.83).

The whole concept of special needs is ambiguous and tautological. It has become part of a rhetoric that serves little educational purpose. While it does mainly focus on negative psychogenic properties of individual pupils – their difficulty, disability, incapacity or lack of intelligence, it does not provide any mechanism for deciding who has these properties. The current desperate search for improved assessment procedures is an indication that the concept of special needs is no actual help in deciding who the clients of special education should be. At the same time the concept, with its humanitarian overtones, precludes discussion of the needs and interests actually being served by the expansion of special education. Those who find difficulty in moving beyond humanitarian rhetoric, and insist that "all children have special needs" still have to explain why a whole sub-system of special education has developed and expanded, which is backed by legal enforcement and caters largely for the children of the manual working class. To do this, attention must turn from the psychogenic focus on individual 'needs' to the social interest groupings, the educational, political and economic 'needs' which an expansion of special education is serving. At the present time the ideological obfuscation provided by the focus on the 'child's special needs' prevents an adequate analysis of this expansion.

Notes

1 In 1981 approximately 200,000 pupils were excluded from mainstream education in special schools and classes plus those unofficially counted and excluded in disruptive units. The Warnock Report's suggestion that remedial and disruptive pupils be officially counted as needing special provision—implicitly accepted by the 1981 Act, and that 1 in 5 children may need special provision, brought the number to 1½ million in 1981—a fifth of the (then) 8 million pupils in education.
2 *Special Educational Treatment*, Ministry of Education pamphlet no. 5, 1946, pp. 22–23.
3 In *The Concept of Special Educational Needs* by J.H. Thompson HMCI, paper given to the Conference on Special Educational Needs, Dundee, February 1984.
4 See *Report of the Royal Commission on the Care and Control of the Feeble-minded*, Vol. 1, 1980, HMSO.
5 See, for example, the conflicting evidence offered to the Fish Committee, set up in 1984 to examine segregated special provision in the Inner London Education Authority.
6 Some schools now have Special Educational Needs (SEN) departments, at least one school has a Special Needs and Remedial Children (SNARC) Department and many schools are adopting the Special Needs Action Programme (SNAP) produced in Coventry.

References

Atkinson, P. *et al.* (1981) Labouring to learn: industrial training for slow learners. In: L. Barton & S. Tomlinson (eds) *Special Education Policies, Practices and Social Issues* (London, Harper & Row).

Archer, M.S. (1979) *The Social Origins of Educational Systems* (London, Sage).

Barnett, W.S. (1984) *The economics of mental retardation*, unpublished PhD thesis, (State University of Utah).

Booth, A. (1981) Demystifying integration. In: W. Swann (ed.) *The Practice of Special Education* (Milton Keynes, Open University).

Collman, R.P. (1956) *The employment success of ESN pupils, American Journal of Mental Deficiency*, 60, pp. 247–51.

Fish, J. (1985) *Committee of inquiry into ILEA Special Schools* (London, ILEA).

HMI (1979) *Aspects of Secondary Education: an HMI survey* (London, HMSO).

National Foundation for Educational Research (1984) *Lower attaining pupil programme newsletter*, November (Slough, NFER).

Pritchard, D.E. (1963) *Education of the Handicapped 1760–1960* (London, RKP).

Reid, M.I. *et al.* (1981) *Mixed Ability Teaching: problems and possibilities* (Slough, NFER).

Reynolds, D. & Sullivan, M. (1979) Bringing school back. In: L. Barton & R. Meigham *Schools: pupils and deviance* (Driffield, Nafferton).

Shaw, B. (1983) *Comprehensive Schooling; the impossible dream* (Oxford, Blackwell).

Squibb, P. (1981) A theoretical, structuralist approach to special education. In: L. Barton & S. Tomlinson, *op. cit.*

Swann, W. (1984) 'Statistics of Segregation,' Childright, 8, pp. 18–19.

Thompson, J. (1984) *Studies in the Theory of Ideology* (London, Polity Press).

Tredgold, A.F. (1914) *Text-book of Mental Deficiency*, 2nd edn (Tindall, Balliere & Cox).

Tomlinson, S. (1982) *A Sociology of Special Education* (Henley, Routledge & Kegan Paul).

Warnock Report (1978) *Special Educational Needs* (London, HMSO).

Warnock, M. (1982) 'Personal column,' *The Times Educational Supplement*, 12.11.82, p. 72.

Warnock, M. (1983) 'Personal column,' *The Times Educational Supplement*, 11.11.83, p. 64.

Part III

1987–1997 Conservative Government, the Education Reform Act and after

15 Evolution or revolution: dilemmas in the post ERA management of special educational needs by local authorities

Catherine Clark, Alan Dyson and Alan Millward

Source: 'Evolution or revolution: dilemmas in the post ERA management of special educational needs by local authorities', *Oxford Review of Education*, 16(3): 279–293, 1990.

The management by local education authorities (LEAs) of provision for special educational needs has long proved problematical, especially in mainstream schools. In the period following the 1981 Education Act, many LEAs sought to develop a 'continuum of provision' by the central direction of resources into the mainstream, but with limited success. In the wake of the 1988 Education Act, LEAs will need to pursue a more collaborative approach to the development of special needs policy. Examples of such approaches are studied and a model of an interactive relationship between schools and LEAs is proposed. Finally, the implications for LEA support services are discussed together with suggestions of a distinctive role for institutions of higher education.

The management of special needs provision by LEAs has never been particularly easy. Certainly, in relation to segregated and separate provision, that process has been significantly easier than it has in relation to mainstream schools. Not only have such schools always enjoyed a certain degree of autonomy, but their principal concerns have inevitably tended to be with issues other than the special needs of a minority of their populations. Hence, while LEAs have been able to create 'bolt on' facilities such as special classes and units in order to create the appearance of a unified provision, there must be significant doubts as to their ability to bring about the internal developments in mainstream schools which are necessary in order to make that unity meaningful. In this and other respects, the recent history of special education policy formulation highlights unresolved dilemmas in the relationships between LEAs, their special schools and services and the mainstream sectors; dilemmas which are likely to become even more acute in the 'new dawn' of the 1988 Education Act.

Whilst the pre-Warnock era was characterised by clearly delineated relationships between the LEAs and the segregated special schools, with established boundaries, practices and bureaucratic processes, the impact of the 1981 Act in particular, and of the integrationist movement in general, was to disturb dramatically what had until then been a fairly tranquil situation. Charged with establishing a 'continuum of provision', LEAs responded by systematically enhancing their capacity to manage an 'expanded notion of special needs', appointing more (or often appointing for the first time) advisers, increasing the Schools Psychological Service, and developing peripatetic services. By strengthening the centre the intention was to create the services and structures to direct the periphery, in the expectation of influencing individual teachers in classrooms. This strategy was given legislative force via the statementing process which gave LEAs, in theory at least, the capacity to affect what happened in respect of individual pupils with special educational needs.

Whilst the intent was clear the actual response naturally varied between LEAs (Goacher *et al.*, 1988). What remained constant was the intent to manage centrally the provision to create this elusive 'continuum of need', in respect of special education. Within LEAs themselves, this represented something of a problem, for here, often for the first time, was an example of one of their sectors—special schools, previously operating to all intents and purposes in an hermetically sealed vacuum—demanding an influential role in policy formulation in the field of mainstream education where previously it had expressed at best only a passing interest. If this was an issue at LEA level, then at school level even more potential existed for conflict. The structural coherence and administrative neatness of the newly developed responses to Warnock and the 1981 Act would be as nothing if they failed to bring about the change at school level necessary for the establishment of this 'continuum of provision'. Traditionally the LEAs had managed their special schools through centralist techniques: the manipulation of resources, the operation of management hierarchies, the division of responsibilities between the various 'caring' agencies and so on. In doing so they had been able to command respect and ensure that their influence and policy stipulations were, to a significant extent, implemented. The question was whether such central manipulation of resources in the mainstream sector would be adequate to bringing about the fundamental changes in practice at school and classroom level that the concept of a continuum of provision demanded.

The Somerset experience (Taylor, *TES*, 6.2.87) provides a typical example of this. Barry Taylor, writing in his role as CEO for Somerset, describes a situation where an LEA progressively increases its financial contribution to the special education budget in pursuit of a policy that was integrationist in intent. He talks, as we might expect, in terms of transferring special school staff to outreach work, appointing additional Educational Psychologists and developing peripatetic support services. Yet he appears somewhat surprised that this policy is fraught with difficulties, amongst which he instances: "the universal law of rising expectations", for, "as halting advances are made, so identified needs become greater". Apparently he sees no alternative to pumping yet more resources into special needs provision, while realising that political and economic realities were making this increasingly unrealistic. Taylor identifies a further problem, a failure to prepare adequately mainstream schools and teachers for working with pupils from special schools. For Taylor this is yet another dimension of the management of resources requiring, in this case, a focusing of attention on both initial and in-service training in respect of special education. The Somerset situation of "144 mainstream schools sharing 23 teachers with a qualification in special educational needs" is typical both of the staffing situation in most LEAs at the time and of the belief in many authorities that provision for special educational needs in mainstream schools simply meant the direction of more specialist resources into those schools.

Taylor offers no other firm analysis of this failure than a passing reference to the need to reorientate the focus of agents such as Educational Psychologists who were charged with the primary delivery role in respect of managing this process. He comments, "training—and change are expensive". So we must address the key problem of trying "… to put 'special education' resources increasingly into mainstream schools." What Taylor fails to address, although it is implicit in his analysis, is that the resources at the LEA's disposal were largely targeted towards the supposed special needs of individual children. We would suggest that there is a fundamental contradiction in the idea of developing complex organisations such as mainstream schools by the centralised direction of resources towards individuals. It may in fact be that the primary task is not one of trying "to put 'special education' resources increasingly into mainstream schools", but of ensuring that mainstream schools are encouraged by the LEA to develop their own problem-solving responses.

The 1988 Act

Within this context the 1988 Act can be seen as no more than the blocking off of an alley that was always blind, by severely restricting the capacity of the LEA to engage in this sort of centralised direction. The question now is whether any significant role remains for the LEAs in developing this elusive continuum of provision for special needs. Certainly some authorities seem only too ready to jettison their responsibility in respect of developing mainstream provision. Surrey LEA, for instance, has declared its intention to remove children with moderate learning difficulties from mainstream schools by the age of eight, in order to maintain the special schools sector over which it retains direct control:

If you want a structure of special schools, you really do need children to fill them.

(R Collett, *TES*, 10.6.88 p. 1)

LEAs with strong traditions of directive management may well have developed no strategies for influencing mainstream provision other than via central manipulation and control. They are now faced with the problem of identifying alternative means of achieving, if they still retain it as a principle, this continuum of provision. It might be worth their while to examine the nature of the new relationship that exists, which, we will argue, can be conceived of as a continuum of reciprocal power and influence along the following dimensions:

1. Directive powers

LEAs will still retain some of their directive powers with regard to special educational needs in the mainstream school, in particular their capacity to control statementing policy and their new inspectorial duties. However, these directive powers may well prove to be largely negative in their impact if conceived narrowly. As inspectors they have no obligation to provide positive guidance as to good practice, and as gate keepers in the statementing procedure they have no *obligation* to assist schools in dealing with their most problematic pupils.

2. Influence

In addition to these directive powers the LEAs will retain limited control over: the INSET budget, manipulation of LMS formulae, and deployment of probably reduced ancillary and support services. These resources can be conceived of as giving the LEAs some measure of influence over schools by enabling and facilitating initiatives the LEA may choose to support.

3. Nurturing of good practice

A final dimension of LEA influence is through its capacity to be responsive to instances of good practice emanating from individual schools. The mechanisms which will sustain this include personal contact between schools and officers, the inspectorial role conceived of in its broadest sense as the identification, sustaining and dissemination of good practice, and the LEA's continuing ability to formulate policy in terms of statements of philosophical position and in terms of generalisation of existing good practice.

The limitation of the LEA's power and influence in mainstream schools would seem to suggest that increasingly it is this latter role which will become pre-eminent if LEAs are desirous of retaining any say in the formulation of special needs provision along the continuum of need. What is of significance in this new climate is that the process is in practical terms dependent more on persuasion and negotiation than on the direct exercise of power. Clearly this will require LEAs to examine fundamentally how they structure their relationships with mainstream schools.

Can LEAs learn from a situation which they were instrumental in creating in the aftermath of the 1981 Act—that is, the situation which faced many special needs co-ordinators in mainstream schools throughout the 1980s?

Appointed to create a continuum of provision these co-ordinators found themselves bereft of power and frequently misunderstood by their colleagues (Bines, 1986 & 1988, provides an interesting account of these problems). They could no more bring about change in the classroom practice of colleagues by central direction than could LEAs. Some of them persisted in seeing the development of the 'whole-school approach' as requiring simply the direction of resources—support teachers, teaching materials and so on—into mainstream classrooms, and were surprised to find that the resources ran out before any lasting change had been effected. As Bines (1986) puts it, they often found that, "although the 'goods' of support are being provided, the 'price' of sharing decisions or instituting change is not being paid" (p. 120). How similar is this to Somerset's experience of pumping resources into the seeming 'black hole' of mainstream provision? The more successful special needs co-ordinators realised that change was about more than blanket resourcing. Accordingly, they resolved the dilemma by adopting collaborative strategies, identifying good practice in colleagues' classrooms, resourcing promising developments and formalising successful initiatives into school policies. In many cases, this process was facilitated by the creation of management structures which allowed mainstream teachers to participate in decision-making in matters relating to special needs provision, often through some sort of inter-departmental steering group (Dyson 1981, Luton 1986).

An additional analogy of equal interest in these times of the National Curriculum is to consider the Australian experience of curriculum development. Kennedy (1985) argues that the centre-periphery model has had no more than minimal impact in both the Australian and the United States context. He points out that centralised initiatives are vulnerable to both political and economic pressures—in other words, precisely those pressures which have overtaken LEA centralised development in the form first of strict expenditure controls and then of the Education Reform Act. However, Kennedy identifies a third reason for the relative failure of central initiatives—their inability to bring about observable change in practice 'on the ground'. This he attributes to their "cultural alienation of teachers who were never able to feel that the resulting products were designed for their specific teaching situations Thus what was planned to be the great strength of externally developed products—the use of eminent scholars and educators along with reliance on the latest technology—turned out to be a positive disadvantage when it came to actual classroom use of the materials" (p. 55). Again, the parallels with the relative ineffectiveness of LEAs' direction of 'alien' special needs resources into mainstream schools seem obvious.

Kennedy goes on to describe how the Australian Curriculum Development Centre (CDC) resolved this problem. Granted the ineffectiveness of the centre-periphery model—particularly in a federal system where the centre, like the English LEA, has very limited power over its periphery—the CDC evolved a collaborative approach to curriculum development:

> There are a range of client groups—state systems, independent school systems, professional associations, community groups, teachers and students all of whom have a stake in curriculum. The task of CDC was and still is to operate in such a way that clients are involved in national intiatives and come to feel a sense of ownership over them. This means determining strategies for development and decision-making that break down the centre-periphery emphasis.
>
> (p. 56)

These strategies were, in practice, threefold—the identification and dissemination of exemplary local practice, the construction of a national consensus, and the identification of issues of national concern.

What emerges is a model of curriculum development which depends on continuous interaction and interchange between centre and periphery. The role of the central agency is not to use its position at the centre as a power-base from which to develop materials or direct resources into schools. Rather, its central position enables it to respond to and facilitate local developments by providing various forms of support and by setting those developments in a broader context of national practice and issues. As Kennedy says,

> national curriculum development ought not to be based on the assumption that national needs can be superimposed on local needs. Rather, the emphasis should be on generating support for national initiatives by targeting activities towards identified local needs.
>
> (p. 60)

What also emerges equally clearly is that while such a model depends on the development of appropriate attitudes within the central agency, those attitudes alone are unlikely to be effective without the creation of appropriate structures for facilitating and protecting the centre-periphery interaction. Structures for a directive, centralised model of curriculum development can afford to be very simple—a central research and development team with appropriate channels of distribution to the periphery.

However, the equivalent structures in an interactive model are necessarily more complex. Alongside the central agency and 'expert' teams, for instance, Kennedy identifies a series of review conferences securing input from practising teachers, and project teams establishing support networks which ensure continuing involvement in the project from teachers.

If the analogy between the CDC and English LEAs in the post-1988 era is valid, then this would seem to suggest that the relatively simple structures of development and direction which LEAs currently operate will need to be rethought in favour of apparently more complex structures which loosen LEA control so that schools and teachers can be involved in decision-making.

It may be interesting to set alongside Kennedy's model an example of developments in an English LEA's special needs provision which might perhaps be seen as similar in some important respects. The Oxfordshire experience with regard to special needs provision is well documented. The LEA has been criticised by Booth (1982) and Galloway & Goodwin (1987) for having been insufficiently proactive and directive and therefore having fallen prey to 'policy drift'. According to the critics the LEA did not do more than offer limited support to isolated initiatives developed by individual headteachers. In fact when we examine the process of change in Oxfordshire more carefully, we see a pattern emerging which is neither centralised direction or decentralised drift, but is more akin to the complex interactive model employed by the CDC.

Jones (1983) provides a fascinating account of the Oxfordshire experience from an LEA perspective. He concedes, with the authority's critics, that early initiatives came principally from individual innovative headteachers. However, the LEA was not passive in its response to these initiatives, but sought rather to identify examples of good practice, and to monitor and evaluate their impact in order to seek generalisations which were useful to other schools. Hence, a limited initiative at Carterton School was monitored, supported, and refined, so that the lessons learned from it could be generalised to other situations. This process ultimately bore fruit in the far more wide-ranging Banbury Special Needs Project which extended to a whole area within the LEA and demanded considerable commitment from the authority to make it possible. This process is, it would seem, not dissimilar to the CDC policy of identifying local needs, supporting local initiatives, and building central policy on the basis of local experience.

The Banbury project, therefore, was neither an entirely local nor an entirely central initiative. Hence, like the Australian curriculum projects, it required a complex and interactive management structure, "to handle not only problems in specific schools, but also those issues that spanned schools, their links with support services, and the LEA administration". (p. 246) The resultant formation of 'sector management units' based on a comprehensive school, its feeder primaries, and its support service personnel has precisely the effect that we outlined earlier of weakening the LEA's ability to 'line manage' schools in order to increase the involvement of those schools in decision-making. As Jones points out:

> As changes have taken place and new initiatives have emerged, the need has arisen for some kind of forum where ideas, and reactions to them, could be handled. Line management across the LEA hierarchy through administrators and advisors is often not adequate to secure the level of confidence needed to keep services running well whilst at the same time the debate for change takes its course.
>
> (p. 251)

This shift in management style can be seen most clearly in the way in which Oxfordshire moved towards a special needs policy statement. The ability to formulate and impose policy has been one of the LEA's traditional means of managing the education system. However, Jones freely admits that, in Oxfordshire, "planning was *adhoc*, and nowhere was there explicitly a policy, written or by practice" (p. 246) with regard to special needs. The first moves towards a policy came after rather than before the Carterton initiative, and arose directly out of an evaluation of that experience. Moreover, that evaluation took the form not of a fully-fledged policy, but of a "discussion document" constituting a "prototype for a county policy" (p. 246). The Banbury project, therefore, was established not simply to *implement* an already-formulated policy, but explicitly in order to 'investigate the management and organisational problems inherent" in the prototype. It was, in other words, part of a cycle of action research in which tentative conclusions and formulations of policy were subjected to refinement through reflection on practical experience.

Reflections on experience

In our attempt to shed light on the dilemmas currently facing LEAs with respect to their management of special needs provision, we have looked at three apparently diverse case studies—special needs co-ordinators managing whole-school approaches in the post-Warnock era, the Australian CDC operating as a national curriculum development agency within a decentralised federal system, and Oxfordshire LEA evolving a whole-authority approach to special needs through the experiences of particular schools.

Despite the diversity of these case studies, they do have certain important features in common, which we will now attempt to summarise:

(1) Centre-periphery models of management and development are disappointingly ineffective in bringing about change in practice at school and classroom level.

(2) A more collaborative and interactive relationship between centre and periphery seems likely to be more effective in securing the desired changes.

(3) Such a relationship implies a conscious and structured attempt to learn from experience and to formulate policy as a response to the needs and initiatives of the periphery rather than as a means of maintaining central direction of the system.

(4) Such a relationship requires the creation of structure which will allow the periphery to participate in decision-making and policy-formulation that has hitherto taken place more or less exclusively at the centre.

Above all, what all three case studies, together with the Somerset experience, highlight is that change in schools and teachers cannot be brought about simply by flooding them with resources which may in reality be alien to their professional culture. The focus has to be on the development of the potential inherent within that culture itself.

Prospect for the future

Having considered the various examples above which can inform our understanding of the future prospects for the planning and implementation of special needs policy it is now incumbent upon us to offer a substantive model which can contribute to policy formulation. Our starting point is a conceptualisation of the relationship between Policy and Practice which we see in dynamic terms; the development of practice at a school level contributing to the formulation of policy at the centre and the two interacting to produce a motor of continual development. Policy then, is the result of a reflection on practice, just as practice is an interpretation of policy in terms of the specifics of a given situation. We are describing here a relationship which is reciprocal in nature, in which power and coercion act only as limits to the evolution of praxis and policy. It is in the recognition of this equivalence that the LEA has its primary task in ensuring a continuity of the dynamism which is the potential at the heart of this process. For this process to be functionally dynamic, in other words for it to have a creative evolutionary dynamic rather than mere circularity, we have to conceive of it as a process in which learning and by implication growth and development take place. The starting point of this process is the desire to take action. If this action is seen as at all problematical, then it has within itself the potential for a creative tension which is the basis for a problem solving process. The continuing cycle of practice and policy thereby becomes a progressive refinement of the search for a solution to the problem. This opens up the possibility of the problem as originally framed presenting itself as being in need of reframing, or revealing new problems not initially conceptualised. We can represent this diagrammatically in Figure 15.1.

POLICY

Reflection

Implementation

Springboard for:
further refinement,
reframing or new
problems

Problematical
position

PRACTICE
Increasing refinement

of solutions

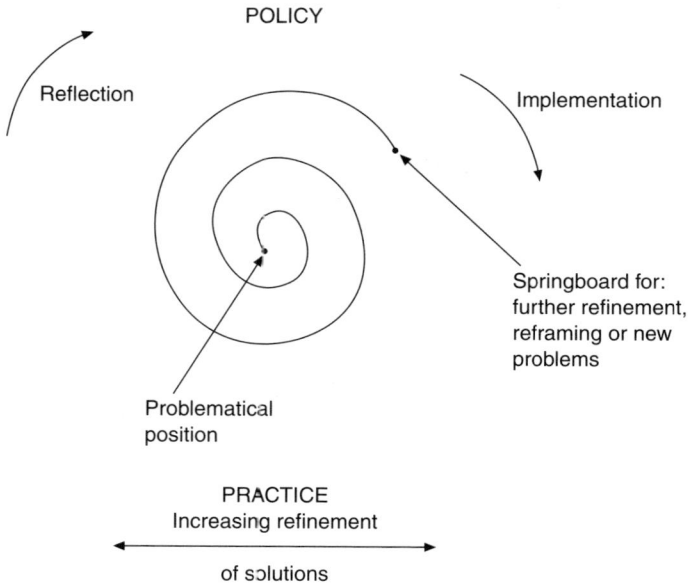

Figure 15.1 The continuing cycle of practice and policy.

We would claim theoretical support for this model from the growing understanding within the educational community of how teachers and schools learn and develop. Underlying the model, for instance, is Schon's (1983) notion of the 'reflective practitioner'. Schon is concerned by the apparent failure of professionals such as teachers to implement the findings of authoritative research, and therefore by the apparent failure of researchers to influence practice. This is, of course, precisely the problem which confronts the LEA seeking to effect change in schools, the CDC seeking to foster curriculum development from the centre, or the special needs co-ordinator seeking to influence the practice of his/her mainstream colleagues.

Schon argues that professionals are not simply technicians implementing the received wisdom of 'experts', but are themselves problem-solvers engaging with the unique characteristics of the situations within which they practise their profession. Externally-imposed precepts are always likely to prove irrelevant or inapplicable to those unique situations. The enhancement of practice, therefore, depends on the enhancement of the practitioner's ability to problem-solve within the unique dimensions of his/her own experience—in other words on his/her ability to reflect on that experience. It follows that development and change must be led by practice, though they will not be constrained by current practice since reflection upon experience presupposes the ability to stand outside of that experience.

A similar view of the relationship between practice, reflection and change underlies emerging conceptions of leadership in education. In a series of essays, Smyth *et al.* (1989) argue that traditional conceptualisation confuse leadership with the technical management of a particular system, with personal 'charisma', or with the simple exercise of power. Such leadership, they argue, is profoundly anti-educational since it denies the possibility of precisely the sort of reflective practice that Schon describes. They argue that leadership, properly understood, involves both articulating the experience of the practitioner and facilitating reflection upon that experience. There is a very real sense, therefore, in which the leader is led by the practitioner, in which s/he is not the teller, but the articulator. It follows that leadership:

> does not necessarily lie with those who have been hierarchically anointed, or with those deemed to possess some special or inalienable qualities or traits.

On the contrary,

> whatever leadership acts are, they probably have more to do with processes of communicating understanding, developing a sense of community and reconstituting the power relationships which get in the way of educative processes in schools.

> (p. 4)

At a more fundamental level still, Schon, Smyth and our own model are underpinned by an epistemology, owing much to Freire, Gramsci and, ultimately, to Marx, which questions the dichotomy between thought and action. It proposes instead the concept of thinking-in-action in which every act implies a conceptualisation of the world, and in which thinking is itself an act which constitutes the world. Such an epistemology sees the world as problematical rather than given, so that thinking-in-action is necessarily provisional, a testing of hypotheses in experience and a refinement of those hypotheses in reflection. In the same way, our model posits a relationship between policy and practice in which policy constitutes a provisional response to a problematical situation and in which practice is not simply the implementation of policy but is an experimental testing of policy with a view to its reformulation or reframing. It follows from this that there is no place for policy as an apparently authoritative definition of reality which is implemented non-reflectively by schools and teachers.

We can ask at this point what tasks are there for the LEA in this type of relationship. Firstly, the LEA has actively to engage in the dynamic of this process; it has to sustain this development by dedicating its efforts towards maintaining the interaction of policy and practice. This means it has to withdraw from its traditional role of sole policy maker, "key arbiter of reality" (Sharp & Green, 1975), in favour of a more collaborative approach. It has to create an environment in which action is seen as problematical, and therefore the interaction between practice and policy seen as a problem solving process. It has to encourage and enable collaborative reflection on practice in ways which will lead towards the development of policy. It has to contribute to policy formulation a perspective which is not constrained by the unique features of a specific situation, whilst at the same time encouraging the perception of practice as the active re-interpretation of policy within individual contexts. Finally, it has to encourage the search for ever more appropriate solutions to already-identified problems, for more illuminating framings of those problems, and for new problems, not hitherto identified.

Facilitating the process

Having described the principles which underpin this process we must now specify more precisely ways in which LEAs can facilitate this process. Initially this can be instigated through the adoption of a stance towards special needs provision which has at its basis the concept that policy formulation is itself a problematic process, one in which there are no longer fixed tenets of belief but merely starting points which lead to the generation of hypotheses to which individuals can respond. For example, it is now interesting in retrospect to consider how Cleveland LEA initially responded to the 1981 Education Act. Unlike many other authorities, although Cleveland may well have held to an integrationist philosophy, it did not follow the pattern of a wholesale reorganisation of its special schools.

It would appear that two strategies emerged: on the one hand it identified certain limited areas where it could or should intervene directly, chiefly in terms of the building of new facilities which would make integration practicable; on the other hand it encouraged experimentation between its mainstream and special schools. Only after the LEA and schools had had the opportunity of evaluating the outcomes of these two strategies did the LEA seek to formalise its policy, firstly by stating firmly its intention to promote integration and secondly by examining systematically the role of its special schools.

In 1986 Cleveland published a document entitled "Focus on Integration" setting out major elements of its policy on special needs. Significantly much of the document is concerned with describing various initiatives, the majority of which had been instigated by schools themselves. It resists the temptation to describe the policy as a definitive statement. The policy instead concerns itself with:

a number of general implications which we would feel need consideration when any integration programme is envisaged. We would be
reluctant to describe these as 'conclusions' or 'recommendations';
rather they should be seen as a series of guidelines based on our
experiences so far.

(p. 25)

Moreover, the document envisages future initiatives as emerging from
schools rather than the authority. It suggests strongly that "appropriate
officers of the LEA need to be involved in the planning of an integration
project from its inception" but there is no implication that such projects
can be centrally imposed. As a result the role of LEA officers is to "act as
consultants in the early stages" and to "advise on the viability and appropriateness of any projected scheme" (p. 26).

This experience is in direct contrast to those authorities which sought to
impose centrally a total reorganisation of their special needs provision in
the light of the 1981 Act. Retaining a regional perspective on this issue, it
is interesting to examine how Newcastle LEA responded to this situation.
We can characterise their strategy as being one of central policy formulation followed by a period of 'intensive selling and telling'. In stark contrast
to Cleveland's attempt to foster and learn from an evolutionary approach,
Newcastle opted for a wholesale reorganisation from a fixed point in time
to the extent that all special schools were formally closed one day and
reopened in their reorganised form the next day.

If policy is to be seen as problematic then LEAs have—as in the Cleveland and Oxfordshire experience—to concede to schools the role of acting
as 'Action Research Stations' where findings feed directly in to the
formulation of policy. In this sense early school-led integration initiatives
in Cleveland contributed to later authority-led initiatives such as the building of two physically handicapped provisions alongside mainstream
schools. In the same way the Banbury Special Needs Project was based on
the learning experience of Carterton and other initiatives. Implicit in the
success of this is a particular relationship between LEA officers and the
schools. The Cleveland document refers to this in the following way:

LEA administrators, advisers and support services such as the CPS are
all in a position to act as consultants in the early stages and will be able
to advise on the viability and the appropriateness of any projected
scheme. The role of the Special Education Adviser can be of critical
significance. If that person is seen to appreciate all the extra-mural ramifications of a project, the schools will feel supported and understood.

(p. 26)

The notion of consultancy is now an accepted part of the rhetoric of
special education. But for the agencies of the LEA this represents a significant

reorientation of their traditional role as interpreters of policy and deliverers of centrally-directed resources to sustain that policy.

Again the literature highlights two contrasting notions of how this might operate; in Cleveland we have the rhetoric of consultancy and collaboration, whilst for Taylor writing in respect of Somerset it is a process of 'putting special education resources into mainstream schools'.

Doubtless many advisers currently see themselves as being in a position which is the best of both worlds, being able to balance their power-relationship as agents of the authority against their supportive role to individual schools and teachers. With the onset of the requirements of the inspectorial role, this balance may well be threatened and if advisers wish to have any influence in the development of special needs initiatives at a school level then they will be required to re-examine their *modus operandi*.

We see two possible models in respect of the inspectorial role. The first is what Jo Stephens, Oxfordshire CEO calls: "The looking at and reporting on syndrome" (cited in Tim Brighouse, *TES*, 26.3.89, p. 15).

By which she has in mind an assumption that practice is not problematical but is simply the more or less competent implementation of centrally prescribed policy. She contrasts this with a "looking with, planning with and implementing with approach" which sees practice as a continuing search for solutions to complex problems. Inspection in this sense is seen as the means by which the LEA identifies, develops and disseminates the more promising solutions and keeps reformulating problems where promising solutions do not emerge.

Some LEAs are already beginning to develop relationships with their schools which are based on this extended view of the inspectorial role. Margaret Maden, Warwickshire's CEO, for instance, argues for a form of inspection which will lead to a 'collegial' relationship between school and authority that seems to have much in common with the 'educative' style of leadership proposed by Smyth *et al.*:

> Even the large school which is held in high esteem in its locality has a need to recognise its place in a larger system. Self-managing institutions (like self-managing learners) are characterised by a capacity to review their own performance against both their own goals and those of a larger system of which they are part ... In education the value of the collegial model is especially significant as is the capacity to combine assessment and monitoring with support and encouragement; this applies to the individual teacher in relation to pupils, to the headteacher in relation to staff and to the local authority in relation to schools and colleges.
>
> (*TES*, 1.9.89, p. 10)

Hence, Maden sees no contradiction between either the local authority's inspectorial and its 'nurturing' roles or the local authority's responsibility for developing coherent provision and its loss of direct central control. The inspectorial role leads directly into policy-formulation, not simply by providing information on the performance of the system to the system-managers at the centre, but as the mechanism by which schools can articulate their needs and hence participate in the decision-making process. The relationship between authority and school, therefore, is not that of inspector and inspected, but is a dialogue between different viewpoints:

> A clearer and more productive partnership or 'compact' should emerge through a needs assessment and policy review system based on reports from schools and colleges, the observations of inspectors and officers and the experience and knowledge of councillors with regard to the needs and aspirations of wider constituencies.

She therefore envisages a role for the local authority which is very similar to that proposed in our model, a role in which the authority on the one hand responds to and nurtures its schools, and on the other provides them with a perspective that is different from and broader than their own:

> Gone will be detailed direction and control; the successful authority of the 1990s will be characterised by its operational efficiency, its responsiveness and, not least, by its networking function based on a credible understanding of what constitutes high-quality education. In Warwickshire, we believe that the essential role of the authority is to create the right climate and structure for the promotion and celebration of educational quality.

What is emerging from our model, therefore, is a relationship between authority and schools in which the school acts as an action-research station testing out and contributing to the formulation of local authority policy. In its turn, the local authority feeds into the school a wider perspective and articulates the school's needs and experiences in terms of that perspective. This process is facilitated by structures within which dialogue between the two participants can take place—principally by an extended form of inspection, but perhaps also by means of specially-constituted forms of management structure (Jones), project teams (Kennedy), or other 'networking' mechanisms (Maden).

All of this applies equally to mainstream and special needs provision. However, in respect of special needs provision the LEA has additional means of access to the mainstream school in the form of its psychological and support teaching services. We have already alluded to the problems of bringing about change in mainstream provision by means of targeting additional resources towards individual pupils, and these problems are sufficiently well-recognised to have led over a number of years to some attempts at 'restructuring' these services (Gillham, 1978). The question is, of course, if psychological and support services are not effective in the role for which they are designed and trained, then what, if anything, can they usefully do?

Our model would seem to suggest a number of possibilities. First, if schools are operating as action-research stations, then they will need tangible support in carrying out their experimental role. Such support, in terms of teacher time and technical advice can be provided by the supportive services. But, it should be noted, that support is targeted at the school with a view to facilitating innovation, not at the individual pupil within the school with a view to remediation or maintenance.

Second, these services are usually peripatetic, and therefore have a role to fulfil in what Maden calls 'networking'. They are ideally placed to identify and disseminate good practice, and to relate a particular school's concerns, needs and innovations to a wider pattern within the authority. Third, and for a similar reason, these services can play a part in the wider inspectorial role of the local authority. While they may not have the skills or credibility within the schools to stand in quite the position that adviser-inspectors do, they nonetheless occupy a position that is different from that of the school's own teachers. They can reflect back to those teachers their concerns and encourage them to consider their practice from a somewhat different, and perhaps broader, perspective.

However, these possibilities will only become realities where the support services accept the model of school and local authority relationships that we have outlined above, and hence accept, along with their line-managers in the authority, a diminution of their direct control over schools and their own working practices. If they are genuinely to support and to 'look with' rather than 'look at' schools, then they cannot remain what they so often are—sole arbiters of major aspects of the education of children with special needs. They cannot, for instance, work with children in segregated settings, retaining control over the content of their teaching. Neither can they determine which children will be offered additional provision when and where. Neither, indeed, can they arbitrate on behalf of the authority on which children shall or shall not be offered special school places. Above all, they have to be prepared to abandon their role as experts delivering a version of reality legitimated both by their own expertise and by their role as agents of the local authority.

Fortunately, some initial formulations for the detailed methodology which might be employed by support services operating such a model are already beginning to emerge. Denise Taylor (1985) for instance, describes a systems approach to analysing the school-consultant relationship and advocates the use of an action research process to facilitate school development. This process, she stresses:

> ...is a *collaborative* endeavour. ... The task of the action researcher is to help the client organisation to ask answerable questions, to generate

valid information and to assist in the making of informed and reasonable choices.

(p. 164)

Although Taylor's 'action researcher' is conceived as less interested in contributing a particular perspective than an LEA as a whole legitimately might be, the parallels with our model mould would seem to be clear.

Similarly, and significantly, Jones (1989) suggests that educational psychologists will, in future, need to concentrate less on the psychology of the individual than on what he calls the 'psychology of schooling'. His analysis of the role of psychological services in school development is one of the first to emerge in the wake of the 1988 Education Reform Act and the Elton Report (1989), and is a logical extension of his earlier analysis of LEA policy making, which has so fruitfully informed our own thinking.

Conclusion

In describing ways in which we believe LEAs can respond to this new situation, we have highlighted a complex process within which there are many variables; in these circumstances it is understandable why many LEAs may wish to retain the surface simplicity of the Centre-Periphery model. But as in all situations of change it is perhaps those who are prepared to risk most that are likely to emerge with the most coherent, and ultimately most stable, relationship between themselves and schools. We would advocate that central to the success of what we are now prepared to describe as a symbiotic relationship between schools and LEAs are the skills, attitudes and abilities of those who must enact this relationship. In particular this relates to: LEA administrators, advisers, and support services, for whom the opportunity to examine their own development at an interpersonal, professional and philosophical level becomes crucial. This is not to advocate a prescriptive form of training for those people which would be against the spirit of the relationships we have outlined above, but to conceptualise this as a process of consultancy with marked similarities to the consultancy between LEA officers and schools. This then becomes one of the "distinctive contributions" which University Departments of Education can make in addition to that concerned with training at either an initial or in-service level.

References

Bines, Hazel (1986) *Redefining Remedial Education* (London, Croom Helm).

Bines, Hazel (1988) Equality, community and individualism: the development and implementation of the 'whole school approach' to special educational needs. In: L. Barton (ed.) *Politics of Special Educational Needs* (London, Falmer).

Booth, Tony (1982) *Special Needs in Education: national perspectives*, Course E241 (Milton Keynes, Open University Press).

Brighouse, Tim (1989) 'Dodgy Cocktails,' *Times Educational Supplement* 23.6.89, p. 15.

Cleveland LEA (1986) *Focus on Integration: theory and practice* (Middlesbrough, Cleveland LEA).

Department of Education and Science and the Welsh Office (1989) 'Discipline in schools,' *The Elton Report* (London, HMSO).

Dyson, Alan (1981) 'It's not what you do—it's the way that you do it: setting up a curriculum for less-able high school pupils,' *Remedial Education*, 16(3), pp. 120–123.

Entwistle, Harold (1979) *Antonio Gramsci: conservative schooling for radical politics* (London, Routledge & Kegan Paul).

Freire Paulo (1985) *The Politics of Education: culture, power and liberation* (London, Macmillan).

Galloway, David & Goodwin, Carole (1987) *The Education of Disturbing Children* (London, Longman).

Gillham, William Edwin Charles (ed.) (1978) *Restructuring Education Psychology* (London, Croom Helm).

Goacher, Brian, Evans, Jennifer, Welton, John & Wedell, Klaus (1988) *Policy and Provision for Special Educational Needs: implementing the 1981 Education Act* (London, Cassell).

Jones, Neville J. (1983) 'Policy Change and Innovation for Special Needs in Oxfordshire,' *Oxford Review of Education*, 9(3).

Jones, Neville J. (1989) The psychology of schooling: supporting the curriculum. In: N. Jones (ed.) *School Management and Pupil Behaviour* (London, Falmer Press).

Kennedy Kerry J. (1989) 'Reconceptualising efforts at National Curriculum development,' *Journal of Education Policy*, 4(1).

Luton, Kathleen (1986) 'Learning by doing: the development of a whole school approach,' *Support for Learning*, 1(4).

Maden, Margaret (1989) 'New Networks for Old,' *Times Educational Supplement*, 1.9.89.

Schon, Donald A. (1983) *The Reflective Practitioner: how professionals think in action* (New York, Basic Books).

Sharp, Rachel & Green, Anthony (1975) *Education and Social Control: a study in progressive primary education* (London, Routledge & Kegan Paul).

Smyth, W. John (ed.) (1989) *Critical Perspectives in Educational Leadership* (London; Falmer).

Taylor, Barry (1987) 'Wanted—a sense of direction,' *Times Educational Supplement*, 6.2.87.

Taylor, Denise (1985) Schools as a target for change: intervening in the school system. In: Emilia Dowling & Elsie Osborne (eds) *The Family and the School: a joint systems approach to problems with children* (London, Routledge & Kegan Paul).

16 Equality fifteen years on

Mary Warnock

Source: 'Equality fifteen years on', *Oxford Review of Education*, 17(2): 145–153, 1991.

An enormous amount has happened in the last 15 years, both politically and ideologically, and nowhere has this change been more marked than in the world of education. In the early 1970s, as well as in the 1960s, school education had come to be widely regarded as primarily an instrument of social engineering. There was an accurate perception that our education system, totally unlike that of all other countries, was somehow to blame for the social ills we suffered, and especially the class divisions which seemed to stifle growth. It is true that such a concept of education was subject to a great deal of criticism and indeed aroused deep hostility among many. There were those who demanded, unrealistically, that politics should be kept out of education. There were others who, though they realised that education was inevitably a political issue, wanted to be allowed to stand back and consider what went on at school in a purely educational way, putting the class war low on the agenda. Nevertheless because as a country we recognised our obsession with class it seemed to many that the only logical step we could take towards the classless society was through the education system.

The Welfare State after the war had promised education, free, to everyone. But real equality, though it was the inspiration of the welfare state, had not materialised, and the only step forward seemed to be to educate all, or nearly all, children in the same kind of school, teaching them as far as possible together when they got there. The expansion of the comprehensive system, originally introduced as an experiment, and mixed ability teaching within the system seemed necessary for equality. Those who opposed such measures believed that equality must be abandoned as an ideal, and something more properly educational substituted for it.

Three things have changed this emphasis on social engineering, and have made the old objections to equality as an ideal seem somehow misdirected and off-target. The first was the so-called Great Debate, which began in 1977. This event has been fairly widely discussed, and I do not want to go into the story again in detail. What happened was not a debate at all but a series of rather tedious meetings where local education officers and a handful of politicians spoke at various venues all over the country, airing their often very strong views. What is now of interest is the motivation for setting it all up. Increasingly it had become clear that education was failing. Children were leaving school as soon as they could legitimately do so (or rather before), and in many cases they were illiterate and innumerate when they left, 11 years of school appearing to have helped them in no way at all. They were virtually unemployable, except as unskilled labourers. Employers complained ceaselessly about educational standards. Parents, fearful of unemployment for their children began to be vociferous in their demands that their children should be better served. The emphasis shifted with dramatic speed from the structure of the system (what sorts of schools there should be) to its content (what should be taught).

James Callaghan, the then Prime Minister, set the Great Debate in motion in a speech at Ruskin College, the workers' college just outside Oxford. This was October 1976. Already before this concern had been mounting, James Hamilton, a Permanent Secretary at the DES had said, in June of that year, "I believe that the so-called secret garden of the curriculum cannot be allowed to remain so secret after all, and that the key to the door must be found and turned" (Annual Conference of the Association of Education Committees, 25 June 1976). His was by no means a lone voice. Increasing numbers of parents, joined by industrialists, began to demand that the curriculum itself must be changed so as better to serve both children themselves and the economy.

It was in 1975 that the notorious case of the William Tyndale primary school in Islington hit the headlines. This was a school where relations between teachers and management appeared to have broken down completely. Teachers were accused by the governors and some parents of having become so 'progressive' in their methods that children were learning nothing at all. The headmaster was said to have asserted that learning to write was outdated; and at least one teacher was supposed to have refused to teach reading, and sent children off to play or watch television instead. There was an enormously long drawn-out formal enquiry into the case, and a report on it was published in 1976.

The recommendations of the report were soon forgotten, but the effect on the public attitudes to education were permanent. There was an overwhelming demand for a central curriculum which could be delivered to all children at school. They must not be short-changed. Their own futures and that of society demanded that they should, all of them, be taught what it would be useful for them to know. A new concept of equality was beginning to emerge in embryo: there should be a common curriculum, mandatory for all state schools, and this would ensure that all children equally were provided, educationally, with what they would need in their future lives. Sadly the teachers emerged from the Great Debate as the villains. It was thought to be they who had been so much carried away by their waging of the class war that they had, it seemed, become totally political, and forgotten about the educational needs of their pupils. Their reputation has hardly recovered.

The second event of the later 1970s was in some ways closely connected with the Great Debate, though at first sight quite different in its motivation. In the early 1970s responsibility for those children hitherto designated 'ineducable', the severely mentally handicapped, was transferred from the Department of Health to the Department of Education and Science. This was an event not much noticed at the time, and probably too little noticed by social historians. It was nevertheless a profound change. One man can take a large measure of responsibility for the outcome, and that is the energetic and ebullient Stan Segal, who ceaselessly lobbied every MP, including Mrs Thatcher when she was Secretary of State for Education, and who wrote an influential book called *No Child is Ineducable*. The immediate response from government was to set up a committee of enquiry into the education of the handicapped; and, after a change of government, this committee finally started work in 1974, publishing its report in 1978, while the Great Debate was still in progress. Committees of enquiry are on the whole strange creatures, partly innovative, partly following sheep-like where civil servants lead. This committee, of which I was chairman, was no exception. We did not know at the time quite what we were doing, because, as soon as we started to look into it, so many problems arose in the matter of educating children with handicaps in vast variety, temporary or permanent, that our task seemed overwhelmingly hard. But in the end what arose out of this committee, by genuine consensus, was a belief that education was a track along which *every* child and adult had a right to walk, a *right of way*. For some it was a relatively smooth and easy track, for others it was set about with obstacles. These might arise from a variety of causes, and might in some cases be terribly daunting. It was the duty of the education service, we thought, to enable children as far as possible to progress along this track, by helping them to overcome the obstacles. To provide such help was to provide for those children's *special needs*. And thus the concept of educational need, always latent in educational thinking, and certainly by no means new, came to have prominence in the late 1970s and early 1980s, and was incorporated in the 1981 Education Act.

The notion of need is one that is essentially relative to some end. Thus if you are to live you need food and water and air. If you are to become a top-class ballet dancer you need not only the right physique, but time to practise, and the development of a sophisticated ear for rhythm. If we as a committee were prepared to talk about educational need we had to be able to specify what end constituted and created that need. We had thus to state in our report, however briefly, what we thought the proper goals of education were, such that in order to move towards them children needed to have certain services provided, needed to be allowed access to a curriculum which would advance them towards these goals. We set out the goals, perhaps dogmatically, as independence, the ability to do useful work and the ability to enjoy life, by imaginatively understanding it and participating in it. Now these were, in our view, common goals. The very severely handicapped might advance only a very short way to their achievement. But, for them, each step was of immense importance. Thus, for example, a child who had been for years doing nothing but sitting in a corner waiting to be fed, and who could exercise no choice of any kind, could, as we discovered, by patient teaching learn how to point to things, to choose whether to accept chocolate or raspberry flavoured instant whip, to indicate that she wanted to have the radio to play with rather than the teddy bear. Such advances in the ability to choose seem incredibly small to those of us who have been choosing since infancy. But to the individual who can make and communicate such preferences for the first time the advance is enormous. The quality of her life has vastly improved. Such communication is a step towards independence, even though for some children independence will never get much further than this; and choice, however limited, is a step towards enjoyment.

The committee had considerable difficulty in persuading people, especially, at first, members of the medical profession, that severely handicapped people could be educated. Surely what they needed was what they had hitherto had, namely care or, perhaps, therapy, treatment, or at best training. We were fortunate in this matter to be able to rely on the law. All children were now entitled by law to education, not just care. However, if the concept of education was to be made to apply in reality as well as in theory and in law to all, we had to try to show that the purpose of education was the same for everyone. With regard to education all were equal in the eyes of the law, a law that had been made specifically with equality of provision in mind.

To say that education is, as to its purpose, common to all is entirely different from saying that education must be the same for all. For once you embrace the project of educating everyone, the most severely disabled as well as the potentially brilliant, within the context of *meeting their educational needs* then this becomes obvious, for the idea of an educational need is, and must be, extremely flexible.

Up till 1981 it had been assumed that about 2% of those who were at school were so disabled one way or another that they must have special education in special schools. A different sort of education altogether with different goals could then be given to the remaining 98% of children who were normal. Once it was recognised, however, that the goals of education were the same for all, that there was only one kind of education, that which was designed to meet a child's needs, and that everyone had educational needs which had to be met, the picture changed. It began to be seen that there were far more children than the 2% in special schools who had educational needs for which a school ought to lay on something special if their needs were to be met. At any one time there might be as many as 20% of children (and in some schools far more) who would need special help if they were to be able to overcome the obstacles in their way and progress down the educational road. Many of these special needs were temporary and could be met by a bit of extra help to catch up with lessons missed through illness or for other reasons; or, say, a place in the front of the class for a child deaf after an infection. Some were permanent and could be met only by long-term provision. It was the duty of teachers to be alert to such needs and spot them early. Schools increasingly became aware that they must make provision for this kind of flexibility. For it was the duty of a school to ensure that as far as possible everyone could make educational progress whatever their abilities. In the light of the concept of need, then, equality was seen as equality of entitlement, not identity of provision.

The 1981 Education Act incorporated these ideals. They were not realised in practice (though the Act had considerable influence). It would doubtless have been impossible at any time to realise them completely, because of the costs involved, as well as the need for changes in attitude. Nevertheless attitudes *did* change, not only to the disabled but to equality itself. It began to seem possible to marry the idea of equality with that of variety, within a common framework of provision. To some extent then the ideal embodied in the Act was accepted.

What really made it inevitable that the 1981 Act should be more or less still-born was the financial crisis. This gave birth to a new ideal in education, that of cost-effectiveness. This has been the third great change since 1975. At first what we saw seemed entirely negative. We saw nothing but 'the cuts', savage measures inhibiting the realisation of any ideals whatsover. Gradually, however a new philosophy began to be received behind the cuts, the positive philosophy of the market. We were beginning to see the rise of Thatcherism, the ideology that will be forever associated with the 1980s.

For Thatcherism, inefficiency is the major sin. Whatever is must be cost-effective and what is not cost-effective must either be cut away, or allowed to wither away for lack of support. All the metaphors of education which in the 1960s were notoriously drawn from the garden and the greenhouse were suddenly changed, deriving now from industry and the management schools. Indeed the language of industry became more than metaphorical. Schools and universities were not simply to be run like businesses; they were businesses.

Thus in education one could no longer afford to be soft. Whatever could not be shown to be efficient must go. The thought that the education service was meant to satisfy educational needs was held to be paternalistic and was therefore condemned. The admired 1980s person was in no need of a father, nor even a father-figure. He had an independence, born of having risen from the bottom, pulled up by the strength of his own boot laces, not by any help given him by the State. There were to be no more hand-outs, no free lunches, no assumption that free education was a right. Nothing except the spirit of self-reliant independence, nothing but a determination to get on, better yourself and make money (in order to own your own house, buy your own car, send your children to fee-paying schools) would qualify you for admiration. In the market economy, people would be free, it was held, to decide what they wanted and pursue it. The 'Nanny State' would not dictate to them what it was they ought to want. Intellectual educational theorists could shut up shop. They had always been in the business of trying to influence policy, and even to deliver, through the maintained system, what they thought children should have in the way of education. Now, instead, people untainted by theory, parents, were to be able to decide. They would put up with no nonsense. Had they not already, in the William Tyndale case, shown that they could stand only so much, and in the end could call the tune? And it was assumed that parents would always choose for their children schools where they would be prepared for gainful employment, and where they would learn only what was useful.

The market philosophy thus assumed that schools would become more efficient in response to parental demands and that this would be true both of independent and of maintained schools. In both categories, those schools which failed to deliver would ultimately simply disappear.

That this philosophy was widely accepted was shown by the enormous increase in the number of parents prepared to pay for private education in the last decade: and the trend continues. Very large numbers of parents who did not themselves go to independent schools are anxious to pay for their children to do so, on the grounds that in this way they will get on. They will get an education that fits them either for employment immediately after school, or for higher education and a degree, and thence the glittering prizes. Parents cannot and should not be blamed for this determination to do what they see as best for their children, often at considerable cost to themselves. But of course there are numbers of parents who cannot take action or who are too ignorant or apathetic to do so. Many of them are simply too poor. For them there is a new idea: that of the safety net. The safety net is meant to pick up the real no-hopers whether by giving them a social services hand-out, or by ensuring that their children get educated somehow, even if they do not go to the successful and competitive schools. It was for some of these children that the new City Technology Colleges were invented, schools intended to be set up by industry and then funded by direct grant from the DES. They were supposed to be for those children who would benefit by a high-powered technological education and whose parents were prepared to guarantee that they would stay at school till their course was concluded and would work extra hard for extra long hours as long as they were at school. In the event those CTCs that have come into existence have not turned out quite like that. They seem to be selective; few are in inner cities, and they are mainly established by government funds. They certainly do not seem much of a safety net for the disadvantaged.

I shall return to the safety net in a moment. First it is worth commenting in more detail on the concept of utility on which the Thatcherist educational philosophy is founded. That education must be useful to those who are being educated would hardly ever have been denied. Only extreme fanatics for a concept of purity in education would ever have refused to allow that we educate people 'for' something—if only for a more satisfactory life after education is over. Certainly the concept of educational needs implied as much. For an educational need, as I have argued, is determined by the non-educational goals a child is aiming for, goals which are described in terms of what the child wants to do, or how he wants to live. And it has been generally supposed that usefulness to the individual will add up in the end to usefulness to society. The educated person would serve society the better for his education.

However, in the late 1970s the idea of utility took on a narrower aspect. The country was failing commercially and economically. We were quite manifestly being overtaken by our European neighbours and by Japan. It was generally held that our failure was caused by our lack of skilled technologists. And so usefulness in education came to be identified with what was confusingly lumped together as 'science and technology'. It was an assumption of Thatcherism that parents and employers would agree that education should be technology-orientated. It was necessary only to set market forces loose, and the desired vocational education would overtake all other forms. Producer and consumer would work together in harmony. The invisible hand would ensure it.

This new concentration on applied science and technology was far from all bad. The scientific and mathematical incompetence of the average British school child had become notorious. They were often genuinely unemployable without a further course in basic arithmetic, because without it, they could not even begin to master the technological skills they were supposed to be able to use in industry or commerce. Such incompetence is by no means yet a thing of the past.

The trouble was that the concentration on applied science and technology went too far. It began to mean that every element of education not obviously usable or not technological would be thrown away. Even the universities, traditionally thought to be centres of scholarship and learning, of theoretical science, fundamental research and philosophy were told that they must sell their services to industry, or close their departments. There are still threats in the air. It has become a matter of urgency and ingenuity to defend the humanities and theoretical science in such a way as to make it seem that these disciplines too are worth funding, even though industry cannot be expected to fund them. We have to make them seem in some way as useful as the rest. A liberal education cannot any longer be defended on the grounds that it leads to a civilised or enjoyable life, nor on the grounds that people continue to want it. It must also be shown to produce value for money, in a market economy.

Fortunately, the narrow notion of utility is gradually being abandoned by many industrialists in favour of something wider and more realistic. It is recognised that employers want people who can communicate and co-operate with one another as well as solve problems on their own. They need people who can explain things as well as do them. Above all they need people who can communicate in more than one language. Moreover it is perhaps slowly being recognised that intelligent decisions about the future cannot be made, whether in politics or in industry, without some understanding of how we got to the position we are in, how the past is related to the present and future. The more truly we are parts of Europe the broader this understanding will have to be. Thus history, literature and the history of ideas will gradually have to be let into the concept of the useful. The National Curriculum, mandatory for all maintained schools and in some form voluntarily adopted by almost all independent schools will in the end contain the elements of a liberal or humane as well as a technological education. Reading, writing and thinking historically are there, to be taught to all children, and so are modern languages.

There is, however, a bleak consequence of the new market-led concept of education and that is the inescapable fact that in the market-place some are losers. Some schools, we are told, will simply turn out to be too bad, and will either have to improve or close. But what if such a 'bad' school fails to come up with the proper examination results because it has a lot of 'bad' pupils who cannot pass examinations? What will happen to such pupils in the future? We are already told that schools may 'exempt' certain pupils from the National Curriculum tests. There is a real danger that such pupils may also be 'exempted' from the national curriculum itself. Moreover if a school, or its teachers, are to be judged efficient by the percentage of children entered for tests who pass, there will be a strong temptation to 'exempt' as many potential failures as possible, in order to make the results look good. This is a moral issue which brings us back at last to the idea of equality.

Since 1944 and until the 1980s it had been a matter of genuine consensus that everyone is entitled to the best, or, if they cannot get the best they are entitled to a *chance* of it. Thus in the case of education, a child had a right to be educated, and there was a real commitment to making that education as good as possible. In the health service, though what one got depended inevitably on where one lived, in areas with good hospitals it was a matter of pride that everyone could get the best possible service. The welfare state, though it did not always work, was thus founded as I have already suggested on the concept of equality. The revolution of the 1980s cannot be presented too starkly. Consensus has become in general despised; and consensus with regard to welfare is despised more than any other. The word 'wet' was hijacked to describe those who clung to the ideal of equality, and who found it hard to stomach the 'safety net' for the helpless as a true alternative.

In the market the underdog does not have his day. There is no place for him. So, educationally, there is no place for the dim, the disadvantaged, the disabled, or the slow. We may be sorry for them and perhaps at Christmas give a little to a charity that helps them. But they are no longer entitled to the best. In the 1981 Education Act, as I have argued, there was an implicit assumption of equal entitlement to education within a global concept of meeting educational needs. Now, though education is to be vocational in order to meet the needs of society, the notion of a pupil's needs has disappeared. For that would entail that in some cases more had to be spent on those whose needs were greatest; and this could never in any circumstances be cost-effective. The handicapped as a group cannot, or not in any obvious sense, as a group be educated efficiently if this is measured in terms of a result valuable to industry for the least possible cost. (There is a different argument, to the effect that educating the disabled for independent living and, where possible, employment, is more cost-effective than not educating them and having to maintain them all their lives. But this argument has never as far as I know found much favour, for it involves spending money first, and saving later.)

If choices are left to parents, only those parents with handicapped children of their own will choose a school which makes good provision for children with special needs. Most parents will continue to choose schools with good test scores and then good A level results. In principle these schools might be the same schools; but when funds are low, and so, within a school, something has to be sacrificed, it will inevitably be the special needs provision that will suffer, especially now that schools manage their own budgets. Thus the position of children with special needs will revert to what it was in the 1960s: they will hardly be thought worth educating. No one will be prepared to spend money on them; little research will be initiated into new innovatory ways of teaching them. The great step forward of placing them under the auspices of the DES will have been wasted. The safety net, whatever form it takes is no substitute for entitlement to education. Neither is the concept of 'caring'. The disabled and disadvantaged do not need 'care'; they need education on a basis of *equal rights*.

Thus I would argue that the idea of equality as an educational ideal must be reinstated in a different form. But my argument does not rest solely on the case of the disabled. We have, very properly, been told by Government that we must increase the numbers of those who stay on at school and proceed to further or higher education. This is an essential aim whether we think of education as primarily vocational or as useful in the wider sense for which I have argued. But it cannot be achieved as long as we set up a series of obstacles in the path of people at school, such as to deter or defeat them. Children tend to think of school as a kind of puissance competition, with the last, vast wall represented by A levels, examinations regarded with awe or simply refused by a vast majority of school children. If we are to increase the number of people going on to higher education, we need as a matter of urgency to abolish A levels. In their place we need a whole series of graded tests, up to the highest standard we can devise, both practical and written in every subject. These tests could serve, in the early stages of school, to test the National Curriculum. But unlike the tests currently envisaged, they would not be taken by groups of children of the same age. They would be taken by anyone, child or adult, when he was ready. In this way both the high and the low flyers would be involved in the same system of examinations. Everyone would leave school with some test success (even if it were only grade 1 practical reading or grade 2 practical car maintenance), and institutions of higher and further education would have a profile of the candidate, showing what he could do. I have no doubt that devising these graded tests would be difficult. But it has already been done in modern languages and some of the sciences as well as music. I believe that with good will the system could be extended. And if it were, it seems to me that, beyond doubt, everyone would be better served, as the goal of having pupils aged between 16 and 21 in education would be achieved.

Moreover it would be a *practical* triumph for the idea of equality. I am not arguing that equality should be the only educational ideal; nor that, as our ideal, it is compatible with *all* the other things we want and need from education. But we are becoming, I believe, more accustomed to the notion that we may quite sincerely embrace more than one ideal, and in order to get our policies right, in education and other fields, we have a struggle not to forget any of the things we think worth pursuing, however hard a compromise may be.

Let me quote Noel Annan's book *Our Age* (1990, p. 361). Writing of the twentieth century he says

> Like Faust, Our Age discovered that *Zwei Seelen wohnen ach! in meiner Brust*. The first soul, the soul of justice, wanted more children to stay on and work in the sixth form, far more to enter higher education, wanted the disparities between the public school pupils and the children who before the war left school at fourteen to be diminished, wanted them to be taught about things that make life worth living ... music, literature and art. This was the soul that, analysing statistics, was shocked to see how the scales were weighted against the poor and later the blacks. The other soul, the soul of excellence, wanted the standards of entry to universities raised, and sixth-form studies to multiply but remain as rigorous as ever. This soul dreamed of a society

where merit replaced privilege, longed for boys and girls to study whatever subject stirred their imagination, and admired the high standards achieved by early specialisation. In all the reports on education ... in all the sapient articles ... you can see the two souls wrestling for mastery. The very documents that called for the expansion of education upheld principles that curtailed it.

It is, in my opinion, our duty as educationalists, to find a way to marry the ideal of equality of entitlement with that of cost-effectiveness. This is partly a political task; but, more, it is a task for which the teaching profession itself, along with the universities and polytechnics, must now give their formidable and foreseeing minds.

17 'British schools for British citizens'?

Barry Troyna and Richard Hatcher

Source: ' "British schools for British citizens"?', *Oxford Review of Education*, 17(3): 287–299, 1991

This article explores the contention that the National Curriculum (NC) for 5–16 year olds in England and Wales provides 'entitlement' to all pupils. We interrogate the culturalist impulses in the NC and argue that they are anathema to the development and legitimation of anti-racist education. After exposing the limitations of the Labour Party's alternative policy package for education we indicate how the concept of culture might be reconstructed in ways in which anti-racist, anti-sexist and associated social justice principles could be effectively realised.

The nostalgia factor

"In recent years", lamented Norman Tebbit in *The Field*,[1] "our sense of insularity and nationality has been bruised by large waves of immigrants resistant to absorption, some defiantly claiming a right to superimpose their culture, even their law, upon the host community" (Tebbit, 1990, p. 78). As one of seven (white, male) 'eloquent citizens' invited to contribute to the magazine's series, *Fanfare On Being British: Seven Britons Speak Out*, Tebbit simply rehearsed the essence of what might be termed a 'Little Englandism' ideology. That is, "the peculiarly English combination of racism, nationalism and populism" (Mercer, 1990, p. 53). But he has not stopped there, of course. His re-enactment of this perspective, prefigured and popularised in some of the pronouncements of the Conservative politician, Enoch Powell, in the late 1960s (Nairn, 1977; Seidel, 1986) was diffused to a wider audience in April 1990 with his remarks about the efficacy of a 'cricket test' of British citizenship. Then, it may be recalled, he posed the rhetorical question to a reporter from the *Los Angeles Times*: "Which side do they [i.e. citizens of Afro-Caribbean and South Asian background] cheer for? Are you still harking back to where you came from or where you are?" At the dawn of a new decade, then, with the imminent establishment of a single European community we are witnessing the endorsement of a restrictive conception of British citizenship which draws its legitimacy from tacitly accepted inclusionary and exclusionary conditions. It promotes a Little Englander ideology predicated on a racialised view of citizenship which crystallises around seemingly inviolable and prescriptive views of what is, and what is not, 'acceptable'.[2]

After ten years of Conservative party rule under Mrs Thatcher, Tebbit's indelicate, some might say abrasive, declaration of 'Little Englandism' did not come as a surprise. After all, it provided the ideological lynchpin for three of the milestones of Thatcherism in the 1980s: the 1981 Nationality Act, the Falklands conflict and, in the run-up to the 1983 General Election, the copy line of a campaign poster depicting a black businessman: "Labour says he's black, Tories say he's British". In each, the tenets, if not the tenor, are the same: a recognition and celebration of 'us' and 'our' national identity; a consolidation of 'our' shared values; and, as a corollary, encouragement to racialised 'outsiders' (defined primarily by their distinctive phenotypical features) to blend in, or be forcibly returned to their supposed 'homelands' in the Caribbean, South Asia and elsewhere. What is constructed in this scenario, then, is a picture of a nation characterised historically by its cultural and political unity and seemingly threatened by the settlement and growth of black communities. Kobena Mercer summarises the effects of this impulse in Thatcherism: "... the brutalising neo-conservative reassertion of competitive individualism and archaic 'Little Englandism' has hegemonised the common-sense terms in which the British are invited to make sense of and live through the vertiginous experience of displacement and decentring that these processes entail" (Mercer, 1990, p. 50). On these grounds, assimilation has been resuscitated under Thatcherism as a vigorous and legitimate policy imperative. But assimilation is a one-way process. The 'only if' conception of citizenship which it promotes and defends means that for black people acquisition involves loss. "Being British in this version", as Ellis Cashmore and Barry Troyna (1990, p. 8) observe, "is instead of, not as well as, being an ethnic minority group member".

In our previous writings on the 1988 Education Reform Act (ERA) we have argued that the systemic and institutional changes it brings will inhibit the development of racial equality in education (Hatcher, 1989; Troyna, 1990; Troyna & Carrington, 1990). Without wishing to lose sight entirely of the broad structural framework which defines and confines what takes place in schools we want to centre our attention here on the extent to which the Tories have been successful in infusing the 'Little Englandism' ideology into the new National Curriculum. Let's begin by sketching out the imperatives of the National Curriculum as conceived and promoted by that loosely structured ensemble of conservative journalists, academics, policy-makers and politicians popularly referred to as the New Right.[3]

The New Right is engaged in a cultural struggle against the previously dominant liberal social-democratic ideology. For New Right ideologues the crisis of British society is fundamentally the result of a breakdown in cultural transmission. Their project, then, exemplified by a series of articles in *The Salisbury Review* in the 1980s, has been the construction of a new ideology of 'nation' based on the restoration of an in fact mythical relationship between society and history, elaborating themes first brought to prominence by Enoch Powell. In a critique of E.P. Thompson in the first issue of *The Salisbury Review*, Roger Scruton argued that the important social forces are "language, religion, custom, associations and traditions of political order— in short, all those forces that generate nations" (quoted in Seidel, 1986, p. 109). Two things follow from this conception of nation for the project of the New Right. One is the centrality of 'race', defined in cultural terms: the threat that the 'British character' might be rather swamped by people with a different culture', as Mrs Thatcher put it in an interview on *World in Action* in 1978. The second is the centrality of education as a terrain of cultural struggle. It is in the schools that the process of cultural reproduction takes place, and where it has been contested by 'progressive education'. Arguably, the sharpest challenge to the government's promotion of cultural continuity as an educational and social policy imperative has been posed by antiracist education, and it is that issue that has attracted the most sustained and vehement attacks from the New Right. This is how John Quicke represents New Right opposition to antiracist education:

> a denigration of the cultural heritage and therefore, a deprecation of the very framework of tolerance which permits radical critique of existing British institutions. It is anti-educational and illiberal.
>
> (Quicke, 1988, p. 10).

It is therefore no accident that many of the key cultural battles that New Right activists have engaged in during the last decade have been around issues of 'race' and education: the Honeyford affair in Bradford; the McGoldrick case in Brent; parental choice in Dewsbury; the aftermath of the murder of Ahmed Iqbal Ullah at Burnage; and disputes over religious worship in Bradford and elsewhere.[4] In all these, wider cultural struggles over 'race' and nation are being fought out on the stage of education. They exemplify the close relationship between cultural struggle and political struggle in the Tory project. And, as a perusal of speeches by Conservative Party spokespersons indicates, the offensive against antiracist education was a central part of the successful campaign waged against left Labour councils in the 1980s.

It is clear, therefore, that this debate has not remained the property of a group of intellectuals on the right of the Conservative Party. It is a measure of their success that these themes have been adopted by the two principal architects of the Tories' counter-reformation in education, Sir

Keith Joseph and his successor as Secretary of State for Education, Kenneth Baker. Consider, for instance, Sir Keith Joseph's valedictory speech as Secretary of State for Education in which he extolled the virtues of a "British school for British citizens" and then proceeded to insist that education should "transmit to all its pupils a sense of shared values and traditions" (1986). Reflecting on the ground (allegedly) lost to the left in the 1960s and '70s, Kenneth Baker echoed these sentiments at the 1987 Annual Conference of the Conservative Party. He told delegates that he regretted the "introduction of irrelevant subjects into the curriculum" and the provision of "anti-family, anti-police and anti-competitive values". He was determined to reverse the trend by encouraging the diffusion of those allegedly universalistic values, traditions and beliefs which define British-ness. In a revealing phase of his speech he noted:

> But you know my friends, education is not just only about acquiring academic and technological skills. It's also about a return to the underlying values of our society.
>
> (Baker, 1987, p. 14)

The 'commonality that defines us'

The National Curriculum figures prominently in the reaffirmation of 'Little Englandism', prompting some critics to prefer the epithet, Nationalist Curriculum (e.g. Raynor, 1989). In any case, National Curriculum is a misnomer; neither independent schools nor the newly formed City Technology Colleges are statutorily obliged to adopt this provision.

Introduced progressively since autumn 1989 for pupils aged between 5 and 16 in state schools, the National Curriculum (NC) consists of three core subjects (English, Maths and Science) supported by seven foundation subjects: History; Geography; Art; Technology; Physical Education; Music and, from the age of 11, a Modern Language. It is generally agreed that the NC will comprise at least 80 per cent of the school timetable. Pupil attainment in all areas of the NC will be assessed at 14 and 16 whilst testing of attainment in the core subjects is likely to take place also at the ages of seven and 11.

Much of the debate around the NC has arisen from the conflict over culture. Indeed, Kenneth Baker informed his audience at Manchester University in September 1987 that fear of 'our' children losing "any sense at all of a Common culture and a Common heritage" provided an important impetus to the development of the NC. Its main function, according to Baker, was to play "a cohesive role" in providing "our society with a greater sense of identity" (cited in Ball & Troyna, 1989, p. 27). The dispute over 'culture' as it articulates with Conservative ideology in the NC has generated the fiercest heat in five areas: history, geography, religious education together with acts of worship in assemblies, community languages, and English. We will exemplify our arguments by referring to two of these, History and English.[5]

"Identities today", argues Raphael Samuel, "are typically asserted not through similarity but through difference" (1989, p. xx). Needless to say, you can't have one without the other. The interpretive structure of the History and English subject reports derives from an illusory, contrived vision of national identity and cultural superiority. Whilst stopping short of a virulent assimilationist perspective, both reports legitimate Anglocentric convictions and eschew critical reflection on what 'we' and 'our' achievements might denote and connote. Indeed, the History working group was criticised by Kenneth Baker's successor as Secretary of State, John MacGregor, for failing to emphasise sufficiently 'the British experience' in its 1989 interim report. The group was asked to rectify this in the publication of its final report.

MacGregor's injunction corresponded closely with the views of his immediate predecessors. For instance in his address to the Historical Association conference in 1985 Keith Joseph nailed his colours firmly to the mast of teaching a 'national history' in which "that commonality that defines us as a society" would be heavily stressed. Kenneth Baker was less circumspect in identifying the role of history in the inculcation of "Little Englandism'. In sharp contrast to historians such as Raphael Samuel and Christopher Hill, who have advocated a more critical, 'warts and all' approach to the teaching of British history (Samuel, 1989), Baker told colleagues at the 1988 Conservative Party conference that he was "not ashamed of what we have done. Britain has given many great things to the world. That's been our civilizing mission".

What emerges from the programme of study developed by the History Working Group is Britain as the epicentre in which an aggregated, rather than reconstituted, national history prevails. In a subject area which in Baker's words provides "the foundation-stone of citizenship and democracy" (cited in Gill, 1989/90, p. 69) room for manoeuvre was always likely to be constrained.

Much the same can be said for the English working group. The straightjacket effect of the Secretary of State's brief needs little commentary from us:

> The Working Group's recommendations on learning about language and its use should draw upon the English Literary heritage; should promote the reading of great literature and the knowledge and appreciation of literature; and should indicate the types of literature which all pupils should cover in the course of their studies.
>
> (Cited in Troyna & Carrington, 1990, pp. 105–6)

The working party (chaired by a former contributor to the Black Papers, Brian Cox) was charged with developing programmes of study and attainment targets for English congruent with a conception of the subject as conservational and preservational. To all intents and purposes, this definition of the discipline of English articulates with the project of cultural hegemony which, as we have indicated, can be discerned more generally within the Conservative party's curricular reforms. Whilst Cox and his colleagues make occasional genuflections towards some of the liberalising features which have characterised the teaching of English in schools over the last decade or so, these are little more than perfunctory. Its orientation is consensual rather than dissident and it is imbued with transmissionist not transformative impulses.

These brief insights into the ideological and political themes governing the National Curriculum highlight the sharp contrast with the critical approach developed by teachers and educationalists committed to multicultural and antiracist education: imperialism and resistance in history; World Studies in geography; multi-faith approaches in RE. But it is important to stress another dimension to the debate about culture, and that is the cultures that children and young people themselves bring to the classroom. Child-centredness, starting from where the child is, has been one of the basic tenets of progressive education. Many teachers have given this approach a more radical edge by making the cultures of children, conceived in terms of social class, gender and 'race', the focus of classroom work aimed at developing their critical understanding of their own identities and the social relationships that form them. It is within English teaching that this work has been developed furthest (e.g. Kean, 1989; see also Jones, 1990).

This is of course anathema to the New Right, but what is significant is how DES documents too have ignored this critical tradition of English teaching (Jones, 1990). Instead, a national curriculum embodying a supposedly 'universal' culture is counterposed to the particularities of 'race', gender and class. The purpose of the National Curriculum, it is claimed, is

> that all pupils, regardless of sex, ethnic origin and geographical location, have access to broadly the same good and relevant curriculum and programme of study…
>
> (Department of Education and Science, 1988)

Relevance to pupils' own experience is sought, but 'regardless of' signifies that it is the experience of abstract individuals taken out of the ensemble of social relationships.

The successes of the New Right in inserting their culturalist concerns into the government's agenda for education are quite clear. Is the picture then one of unrelieved gloom? Two more optimistic interpretations may be heard.

The first is that the National Curriculum documents themselves contain many statements which positively endorse multicultural education and racial equality. Multicultural education has official status as a 'cross-curricular dimension' of the National Curriculum. The National Curriculum Council itself has a multicultural working party whose policy document is, at the time of writing, still awaited. The argument is that these will ensure that progress on racial equality continues, with the advantage that it is now integrated into statutory provision (Anderson, 1989).

The second argument is that there still remains sufficient space within the National Curriculum, and elsewhere in the non-statutory part of the curriculum, for example in Personal and Social Education, for teachers to continue to develop anti-racist work even if overall government education policy is unfavourable to it.

There is of course an important element of truth in these arguments. There is space, even if it is much reduced, and certainly those committed to racial equality as a priority in education will make maximum use of every favourable reference to it in the NCC documents. But we do not mistake these opportunities for the overall import and effect of the introduction of the National Curriculum, seen in the context of the ERA as a whole, and in conjunction with other relevant policies, including increasingly restrictive guidelines for the use of Section 11.[6] The overall trend whatever the gains made in some areas and by a minority of teachers and schools, will be to further marginalise racial equality in education. It is possible to adduce three main reasons for this more pessimistic prognosis.

To begin with, as Madeleine Arnot has argued, racial (and gender) equality was marginal to the process of policy formation of the National Curriculum, and therefore is not integral to it (Arnot, 1989/90). References to equality apply at the stage of implementation, not formation. The result is that they are bolt-on afterthoughts which stand in contradiction to the central thrusts of the National Curriculum: namely the 'universal' (or 'entitlement') curriculum not rooted in pupils' real experiences of 'race'; the notion of blanket testing based on a spurious hierarchy of attainment objectives and the inevitable increase in streaming to which it will give rise.

Secondly, the squeezing out from teachers' time of work such activities as anti-racist curriculum and policy development, which are not central to the National Curriculum, as a result of a combination of 'innovation overload', and new tighter management techniques borrowed from industry.

Thirdly, the fear of a 'white backlash', particularly after the introduction of open enrolment and Local Management of Schools, which make schools much more vulnerable to racially discriminatory pressures from parents, whether expressed through governing bodies with enhanced powers or through the removal of pupils and hence funding. The decision of white parents in Dewsbury, Cleveland and Wakefield to move their children away from multicultural schools is only the tip of the iceberg of widespread, unpublicised 'white flight'. The New Right project bases itself on a genuine popular sentiment among a section of the white population, as is indicated by a survey carried out by London Weekend Television in 1987 which showed that more than 40% of white parents in the south-east pre-ferred and supported racially segregated schools. Against this backgound, the decision of the then Secretary of State for Education, John MacGregor to give precedence to 'parental choice' (enshrined in the 1980 Education Act) over the statutory duty of LEAs and their education institutions not to discriminate in carrying out any of its functions under the Education Acts 1944–1981 (Section 18 of the 1976 Race Relations Act) may give encouragement to an increasing number of white parents to select schools for their children on racial grounds. So is it our conclusion that the dominance of the New Right in education is now secure, that it has established a new hegemonic cultural agenda which is guaranteed to be translated into practice as the provisions of the ERA come on-stream? In our view that judgement is premature. To assess the success of the Cultural Right we need to look at the overall current situation of the Tories' project, and at existing and potential opposition to it.

It is important to note that the National Curriculum is not simply the education programme of the cultural restorations, as Ball (1990) calls them, translated into government policy. There is another powerful strand in government thinking about education, whose imperative is not the restoration of an imaginary cultural heritage but the modernisation of British capitalism.[7] For the modernisers the problem of British education is that it reflects the anti-industrial orientation of the British cultural establishment. Their aim is not cultural continuity but a break with the culture of the past. Elements of the programme of the cultural restorationists are at best irrelevant and at worst actually dysfunctional for the regeneration of British capital: for example, the promotion of Christianity in schools, and the hostility to vocationalism. Now that the cultural restorations have cleared the ground, and as the pressure of the Single Market becomes more acute, the modernisers' influence will become stronger at the expense of the culturalists'. It would be wrong, however, to place confidence in the likelihood of the modernisers' education programme significantly reducing racial inequality. While it differs from that of the culturalists in emphasising an abstract individualism oriented to vocationalism, rather than cultural cohesion, and has incorporated some of the vocabulary of progressive education, it shares the culturalists' hostility to egalitarianism as an educational aim.

There are also serious doubts about the extent to which the ERA will actually work. The fundamental problem is the attempt to implement a radical reform of education while under-funding it. The points of strain are apparent: a shortage of some of the subject specialists needed to put the NC into practice; a widespread shortage of primary and certain subject specialist teachers. It is also gradually becoming apparent that national assessment as envisaged in the ERA may be quite impractical, as the retreat announced by MacGregor from testing foundation subjects in the primary school demonstrates.[8]

Nor have the Tories been successful in gaining general public support for their education reforms. A survey of parents reported in the Times Educational Supplement in December 1989 showed widespread support—about 9 out of 10—for a national curriculum and national testing, though that does not necessarily mean such universal support for the specific versions that the Tories advocate once their implications are demonstrated in practice. But in spite of this, education is not a vote-winner for the Tories, and that is a political disaster for them after they have invested so much political capital in it. An opinion poll reported in the Guardian (15.2.90) showed education to be the second most important policy issue, after health. But when asked which party had the best education policies, 43% chose Labour, as against 27% for the Tories. Subsequent opinion polls reported in the press towards the end of 1990 confirmed this pattern. Thus, in November 1990 the *Daily Telegraph* reported the findings of an opinion poll showing that nearly three quarters of sample voters believed that the quality of education was declining and two thirds of this sample blamed the Government. It also showed the Tories trailing Labour on this issue by an increasingly wide margin (7 November).

Taken in the context of the Government's electoral decline in the early years of the decade, it seems very possible that the programme of the cultural restorations will not be put into practice, as the ship on which they were travelling, already heavily listing, heads for the rocks of the next General Election.

However, it does not follow that the end of the Tory government means the end of Tory policies. Perhaps it is the case that the Tories have established an ideological dominance over the whole political field, and especially on 'race' and education set an agenda which does command wide popular support? The question then is, to what extent would an incoming Labour government break from that agenda and offer a new perspective for racial equality in education?

The Labour Party and racial equality in education[9]

The most authoritative statements of the position of the Labour Party leadership are three policy papers published in 1989: *Multicultural Education*; the education section of the Policy Review adopted at the 1989 party conference, entitled *Good education for all*; and an accompanying document, *Children First: Labour's policy for raising standards in schools* (1989).

Multi-cultural Education: Labour's policy for schools situates itself within the framework of the Swann Report (1985). In that context there are some positive proposals: LEAs will have to produce action programmes for tackling racial inequality; extra funding will be made available to institutions to improve Black access to teaching education courses; Indic languages will have parity within the national curriculum. But its adoption of Swann's definition of the problem as one of cultural conflict prevents it from offering an effective response to processes of racial discrimination. It is against cultural bias in the curriculum, but avoids mention of anti-racist teaching. It is aware of how Section 11 marginalises provision but refrains from a commitment to incorporate it into mainstream funding. It acknowledges the need to be sensitive to non-Christian religions, but speaks of "monitoring the effects" of the 1988 Act, not of removing its pro-Christian bias. It promises to increase access to Black student teachers, but doesn't propose the concrete measures that will ensure that schools, still under local management, appoint them and promote them.

What is most revealing is what happened to the issue of racial equality when the Labour leadership elaborated their perspective for education as a whole in the Policy Review Document. *Good Education for All* is based on two principles: education for social justice and education for the economic development of British capitalism. It claims they go hand in hand; there is no notion in the policy document that there might be some tension, let alone a fundamental contradiction, between them. But the two principles are not given equal weight. The overwhelmingly dominant theme of the document is education's economic role, to which its social role is subordinate and ancillary. Labour's clear intention is to occupy the same terrain as the Tory modernisers. The consequence is that racial equality achieves only a token reference. Racial inequality is subsumed into the general argument that higher standards can be achieved if schools are 'effective'. There is no mention of anti-racist teaching. It is as if the experiences of the last ten years of anti-racist education had never happened.

The token and marginal status of the issue of 'race' in education is confirmed by the third and much more detailed document, *Children First*. The models of education that it offers are the education systems of the most successful capitalist economies, West Germany and Japan. Equality in education is defined in terms of equality of opportunity and diversity of provision to meet diverse needs. The rhetoric here closely parallels that of the Tory modernisers, as does the abstract individualist conception of the pupil that underlies it—without any reference to gender, class or 'race', in the 42 pages of the document. Inequality is to be removed by providing 'effective schools'. The priority attached to the 'effective schools' scenario in the promotion of equality of opportunity in Labour party policy demands our attention. Can this movement be seen as a realistic route towards the mitigation of racial inequality in education?

The credo of the 'school effects' movement can be stated simply: different schools are able to achieve significantly different results with children who are comparable in terms of their background and attainment at point of entry to the school. What is more, it is possible to identify specific in-school characteristics which are causally linked to pupil progress and attainment levels. The movement can therefore be contrasted with the conviction of educationists such as James Coleman and Christopher Jencks in the USA and Halsey and Plowden in the UK. They have argued that the variation in educational outcome can be accounted for primarily by structural factors. The 'school effects' argument is a popular one, of course, and has relied heavily on the positivist methodology of researchers such as Michael Rutter (1979), Peter Mortimore (1988) and, most recently, David Smith & Sally Tomlinson (1989). It is salutary to note, however, that Smith & Tomlinson, whose sophisticated and complex statistical analysis of the internal processes of 20 urban, multiracial comprehensive schools has been championed not only by the Labour party but also by leading exponents of the New Right (e.g. Flew, 1989), do not claim that inequalities within an 'effective' school are reduced. Their argument is that: racial inequalities in performance are small and that "what school a child goes to makes far more difference (in terms of exam results) than what ethnic group he or she belongs to" (1989, p. 305). Nevertheless, the relative nature of racial inequalities remains, even if everyone's standard in the 'effective' school rises. Smith & Tomlinson again: "... some schools are much better than others, and the ones that are good for white people tend to be about equally good for black people" (1989, p. 305). The logical conclusion to be drawn from this analysis, however, is that 'effective schools' would tend to make these racial inequalities more salient.

The positivist paradigm which underscores the 'effective schools' movement prevents researchers from addressing issues such as identity and meaning which, if ignored by schools, reinforce, even exacerbate racial inequalities. Why? Because it gives priority to the provision of a curriculum which, though formally universal, positions different groups of children unequally. In short, the analysis of what takes place in (in)effective schools is privileged above, and dislocated from the delimiting social, economic and political influences on racial equality in education.

In any case, the movement draws its rationale from an (implicit) commitment to the credibility of meritocratic principles. That is to say, they promote the view that, to paraphrase James Murphy (1985), the difference school makes, makes a difference. But does it? The tenuous link between educational and occupational success, especially for young blacks, women, and working class students, demonstrates the limits of this exclusive focus on educational attainment and progress.

Towards an alternative

We have explored the central role of culture in the educational politics of the right, and the failure of the Labour Party's response to offer a radical alternative to it. For some suggestions as to what such an alternative might consist of, we want to refer to the 'Burnage report' (MacDonald *et al.*, 1989), *Murder in the Playground*, which was finally published in 1989.[10] The Burnage Report differs from the coverage of other well-publicised 'critical incidents' that have marked out the debate about 'race' and education, in that it is a critique of multicultural education, of what it calls "moral or symbolic antiracism", "from the left". (The initial attempt by the popular press to co-opt it for the right was sharply repudiated.) It is also the only major report on 'race' and education the majority of whose authors have been black.

The current orthodoxy within liberal education counterposes multiculturalism to the New Right's monoculturalism. The Burnage Report rejects both:

> A central tenet of multi-cultural education, and one of the theories underpinning it, is that racism and racial conflict in Britain are caused by some sort of cultural misunderstanding. If only people understood each other's cultures, then racial conflict would be unnecessary and would wither away ... In this scheme of things, nothing need be said about such disturbing and controversial things as power relations as they have to do with sex, race or class ... As a result, multi-culturalism does not in fact deal with or assist in the understanding of the complexity of people's lives and histories and does not draw upon the lives and experiences of the students who are being taught. In fact multi-culturalism has been much criticised for not effectively coming to grips with the racism and racial harassment experienced in school and the wider community.
>
> (MacDonald *et al.*, 1989, pp. 344–345)

The Tories' cultural project aims at reinforcing the segmentation of the working class. In a mirror-image of the Tory approach, 'moral antiracism' is also divisive, both because it isolates 'race' from class and gender and because it denies any validity to the experience of the white working class. The inquiry panel spoke to white parents who had formed the Parents English Education Rights (PEER) group.

> After hearing the evidence of the PEER group in Manchester, one gets the sense of white working class parents who have little basis on which to root their own identity, and whose education has given them little or no conception of the value of their own experience as English working class.
>
> (pp. 344–345)

This distinctive focus on the cultures of the oppressed has implications for the curriculum of schools. As an illustration, the Report comments on a drama project, based on the life of Len Johnson, a local boxer and black activist, in which pupils from Burnage and another school participated.

> What struck us was that the students were using the play and its themes as a metaphor for their own lives and were learning about

their own culture and the significance of friendships and relationships with each other at school and at home, and in particular about attitudes to women, race and class. In the course of the play they unpack and lay bare the content of a sexist and racist culture.

(p. 404)

There is another aspect of culture which the Burnage Report develops, the culture of democracy. In implicit counterposition to the imposed culture of the National Curriculum the authors of the report stress the importance of the empowerment of pupils and parents. Their concern, like that of the New Right, is social cohesion, but posed within an entirely different perspective. "We believe", they write, that "self-organisation amongst students and parents ... may well prove to be the only guarantor of social cohesion in the inner-city schools of tomorrow. But it will mean change" (p. 373).

The elements we have identified in the Burnage Report seem to us to be central to a rethinking of the concept of culture in the face of its aggressive reconstruction by the right. There is evidence that such re-thinking is taking place across the anti-racist movement: for example, the Black Agenda published by Black Sections, the Charter for Anti-Racist Education produced by the Campaign Against Racism in Education in conjunction with the Socialist Teachers Alliance in the National Union of Teachers, and debates within the Socialist Movement. The question is: can they develop and build support for a radical programme for education within the context of the struggles that are now breaking out against the Tories, which goes beyond the new realism of Labour's alternative.

Notes

An earlier version of this paper was presented to the conference: 'New Issues in Black British Politics', Centre Conference 1989/90, Radcliffe House, University of Warwick, 14–16 May, 1990.

1 We would like to thank Harbhajan Brar for bringing this reference to our attention, and Andrew Dorn for his help in preparing this article.
2 Robert Miles (1988, p. 246) has defined racialisation as a political and ideological process by which particular populations are identified by "direct or indirect reference to their real or imagined phenotypical characteristics" in such a way as to suggest that the group can only be understood as a supposed biological unity.
3 Andrew Gamble argues that the New Right ideology comprises both neoconservative and neo-liberal tendencies. However, they converge in their commitment to securing a free economy. Where they differ is in their prioritisation of approaches: "Neo-liberals put the objective of a free economy first; the strong state is a means of achieving this. The state is not valued in itself. Just the opposite is true for neo-conservatives" (1985, p. 22). See also Ball (1990), Demain (1990) and Quicke (1988) for discussion about New Right ideology and its impact on educational and social policy.
4 Clearly, there is insufficient space here to document the details of these dis-

putes. They have been analysed extensively in Halstead (1988), Macdonald *et al.* (1989) and Troyna & Carrington (1990). For a thorough critique of New Right discourse and its application to the debate about 'race' and education see Oldman (1987).

5 More exhaustive, though complementary, analyses of subject working parties, their composition, reports and associated principles of assessment have been carried out by Arnot (1989/90), Ball (1990), Burton & Weiner (1990) and Troyna & Farrow (1991).

6 This refers to the section of the Local Government Act (1966) which empowers the Home Secretary to make payments to Local Authorities who "in his opinion are required to make special provision in the exercise of any of their functions in consequences of the presence within their areas of substantial numbers of immigrants from the Commonwealth whose language and customs differ from those of the community". Andrew Dorn & Paul Hibbert (1987) provide an incisive critique of the legislation, its underlying ideology and implementation at both central and local government levels. They argue that the allocation of Section 11 monies is limited and limiting because of its reliance on a cultural and linguistic definition of what constitutes 'special needs'. Home Office circular 78/1990 on Section 11 grants reinforces and extends the restrictions on how LEAs and their educational institutions may use this source of finance.

7 We have drawn here on Ken Jones' analysis of strands within Tory thinking (1989).

8 At the time of writing (November 1990) there are indications that plans to give seven-year-olds formal tests in science might be abandoned by the Secondary Examination and Assessment Council (SEAC).

9 For further discussion of this theme see Hatcher (1990).

10 For a detailed analysis of the events leading to the murder of Ahmed Iqbal Ullah at Burnage High School and the aftermath of the tragedy see Macdonald *et al.* (1989) and Troyna & Hatcher (1991).

References

Anderson, B. (1989) 'Education and antiracism: strategies for the 1990s,' *Multicultural Teaching*, 7, pp. 24–27.

Arnot, M. (1989/90) 'Conservation or legitimation? Race and Gender politics and the making of the national curriculum,' *Critical Social Policy*, 27, pp. 20–38.

Baker, K. (1987) *Speech to the Annual Conference of the Conservative Party*, 7 October, Blackpool.

Ball, S.J. (1990) *Politics and Policy Making in Education: Explorations in Policy Sociology* (London, Routledge).

Ball, W. & Troyna, B. (1989) 'The dawn of a new ERA? The Education Reform Act, "Race" and LEAs,' *Educational Management and Administration*, 17, pp. 23–31.

Burton, L. & Weiner, G. (1990) 'Social justice and the National Curriculum,' *Research Papers in Education*, pp. 203–227.

Cashmore, E. & Troyna, (1990) *Introduction to Race Relations: Second Edition* (Lewes, Falmer Press).

Demaine, J. (1990) The reform of secondary education. In: B. Hindess (ed.) *Reactions to the Right*, pp. 78–98 (London, Routledge).

Department of Education and Science (1985) *Education for All* (London, HMSO).

Department of Education and Science and Welsh Office (1987) *The National Curriculum 5–16: A Consultative Document* (London, DES).

Dorn, A. & Hibbert, P. (1987) A comedy of errors: Section 11 funding and education. In: B. Troyna (ed.) *Racial Inequality in Education* pp. 59–76 (London, Tavistock; reprinted by Routledge, 1989).

Flew, A. (1989) 'The school effect,' *Ethnic Enterprise*, November/December, pp. 21–22.

Gamble, A. (1985) 'Smashing the state: Thatcher's radical crusade,' *Marxism Today*, June, p. 22.

Gill, D. (1989/90) 'Indoctrination, curriculum and the law,' *Critical Social Policy*, 27, pp. 56–72.

Halstead, M. (1989) *Education, Justice and Cultural Diversity* (Lewes, Falmer Press).

Hatcher, R. (1989) 'Anti-racist education after the Act,' *Multicultural Teaching*, 7, pp. 26–7.

Hatcher, R. (1990) 'What difference will a Labour Government make?' *Multicultural Teaching*, 9, pp. 41–42.

Jones, K. (1989) *Right turn: The Conservative Revolution in Education* (London, Hutchinson).

Jones, K. (1990) *The National Curriculum: Working for Hegemony* (Unpublished listed paper presented to the BERA conference).

Joseph, K. (1986) *Without Prejudice: Education for an Ethnically Mixed Society* 20 May (unpublished).

Kean, H. (ed) (1989) *English Teaching and Class* (London, ILEA).

MacDonald, I., Bhavnani, T., Khan, L. & John, G. (1989) *Murder in the Playground* (London, Longsight Press).

Mercer, K. (1990) Welcome to the jungle: identity and diversity in postmodern politics. In: J. Rutherford, (ed.) *Identity: Community, Culture, Difference*, (London, Lawrence and Wishart), pp. 43–71.

Miles, R. (1988) Racialization. In: E. Cashmore (ed.) *Dictionary of Race and Ethnic Relations: Second Edition*, (London, Routledge), pp. 246–7.

Mortimore, P., Sammons, P., Ecob, R. & Stoll, L. (1988) *School Matters: The Junior Years* (Wells, Open Books).

Murphy, J. (1985) 'Does the difference schools make, make a difference?' *British Journal of Sociology*, 36, pp. 106–115.

Nairn, T. (1977) *The Break-Up of Britain: Crisis and neo-nationalism* (London, New Left Books).

Oldman, D. (1987) Plain-speaking and pseudo-science: 'New Right' attack on Anti-Racism. In: B. Troyna (ed.) *Racial Inequality in Education* (London, Tavistock; reprinted by Routledge, 1989).

Quicke, J. (1988) 'The "New Right" and education,' *British Journal of Educational Studies*, 36, pp. 5–20.

Raynor, J. (1989) A National or Nationalist Curriculum? In: B. Moon, P. Murphy & J. Raynor *Policies for the Curriculum* (London, Hodder and Stoughton), pp. 45–50.

Rutter, M., Maughan, B., Mortimore, P. & Ouston, J. (1979) *Fifteen Thousand Hours* (Shepton Mallet, Open Books).

Samuel, R. (1989) Introduction: exciting to be English. In: R. Samuel (ed.) *Patriotism: The Making and Unmaking of British National Identity: Vol. 1 History and Politics* (London, Routledge), pp. xviii–lxvii.

Seidel, G. (1986) Culture, Nation and 'Race' in the British and French New Right. In: R. Levitas (ed.), *The Ideology of the New Right* (Cambridge, Polity Press).

Smith, D.J. & Tomlinson, S. (1989) *The School Effect: A Study of Multi-Racial Comprehensives* (London, Policy Studies Institute).

Tebbit, N. (1990) 'Fanfare on being British,' *The Field*, May, pp. 76–78.

Troyna, B. (1990) 'Reform or deform? The 1988 Education Reform Act and racial equality in Britain,' *New Community*, 16, pp. 403–416.

Troyna, B. & Carrington, B. (1990) *Education, Racism and Reform* (London, Routledge).

Troyna, B. & Farrow, S. (1991) Science for All? Anti-racism, science and the primary school. In: A. Peacock (ed.) *Science in Primary Schools: The Multi-Cultural Dimension* (London, Macmillan), pp. 111–132.

Troyna, B. & Hatcher, R. (1991) 'Racist incidents in schools: a framework for analysis,' *Journal of Education Policy*, 6(1), pp. 17–32.

18 Specialisation and selection in secondary education

Tony Edwards and Geoff Whitty

Source: 'Specialisation and selection in secondary education', *Oxford Review of Education*, 23 (1): 5–15, 1997.

In the 1992 White Paper on 'Choice and Diversity', the British government identified specialisation rather than selection as the main direction for secondary education. Four years later, its latest Education Bill was promoting both. Yet it had earlier distinguished between them on the grounds that specialisation gave choice to parents whose demand for different kinds of secondary schooling had been suppressed in Local Authority 'monopolies', whereas selection gave (or returned) choice to schools. In this paper, the extent to which specialisation is the acceptable face of selection is explored through an analysis of government initiatives from the Assisted Places Scheme and its recent expansion to the current encouragement of schools to 'select by ability or by aptitude for particular subjects'. It is argued that in the English system of secondary schooling, both the causal relationship asserted between choice and diversity and the likelihood of specialisation without selection are highly questionable.

Introduction

On his appointment as Secretary of State for Education in 1992, John Patten promised that specialisation rather than selection would be the relevant 's' word in the shaping of government policy. In his subsequent White Paper, those terms were officially differentiated by defining selection as giving choice to schools and specialisation as giving choice to parents. In line with the main theme of that policy statement, specialisation was presented as a consumer-driven response to the aspirations of parents for particular kinds of schooling (DES, 1992, pp. 9–10). Its declared policy at that time was neither to encourage nor discourage schools from becoming academically selective.

Four years later, a return to academic selection appears firmly on the

Conservative government's agenda. Despite some tactical manoeuvring, the Opposition Parties remain opposed to it. But a shift from 'common' secondary schooling to variously specialised versions has become the orthodox approach for both Conservatives and New Labour. Is specialisation the 'acceptable face' of selection, or as clearly distinguishable from it as advocates claim? In this paper we explore the various forms which both have taken under the Thatcher and Major governments in England and Wales, and consider what existing evidence indicates about their effects.

Restoring academic opportunity: the assisted places scheme

Even in its earliest education legislation, the Thatcher government began to relegitimate conventional forms of academic selection. In 1979, it removed any requirement for local education authorities (LEAs) to proceed with comprehensive reorganisation of secondary schools. More positively, it created through the 1980 Education Act a new publicly funded 'scholarship ladder', making it possible for 'able children from less well-off homes' to attend academically selective private schools which their families could not otherwise afford.

Although this Assisted Places Scheme was identified retrospectively in the 1992 White Paper as a first step towards greater diversity, it was initially presented much more as an escape route from neighbourhood (especially inner-city) comprehensive schools deemed unable to provide 'real' academic opportunities. The schools to which assisted places were allocated had therefore to 'prove' their fitness for that purpose by meeting entirely traditional academic criteria—high pass rates in public examinations, high entry rates to universities, and a wide choice of academic subjects in the sixth form. Those schools which passed scrutiny, and many did not, might therefore be considered specialist schools for the academically gifted. Certainly the Scheme's introduction was a considerable success for the powerful private education lobby in its efforts to associate academic excellence with independent status. It was a particular success for the pressure group within the private sector which represented the highly academic former direct-grant grammar schools. For many of those schools, as for some other day schools in the private sector, the Scheme has made possible a more academically selective entry than reliance on fee-paying is likely to produce. To that extent, it has enhanced their competitiveness by securing an intake more likely to 'deliver' high attainments and high levels of entry to university. Certainly the relative success of assisted place holders in public examinations has been prominent in the private sector's annual reports on the Scheme, and in its more general publicity (for example, Marks, 1992).

It has long been argued in defence of grammar schools that they can compensate 'poor but able' children for an otherwise limited educational and cultural inheritance. Although introduced on a smaller scale than some of its advocates had hoped for, the Scheme represented a traditional scholarship 'ladder' improved by means-testing the assistance provided. The preceding direct-grant system had been increasingly criticised, even from within the private sector, for being indiscriminate in its subsidising of fees. The facts that around 40% assisted-place holders have qualified for free places and around 80% have parents with incomes below the national average are therefore cited often in ministerial accounts of the Scheme's success (for example, in the Secretary of State's speech on 12 June 1996 reviewing the government's educational achievements). But while our own research indicated a predominance of low-income families among those we interviewed, it also indicated a very different clientele from that envisaged in the Scheme's early publicity—which was composed largely of working-class 'embers' to be lifted from the 'ashes' of failing inner-city comprehensive schools. Although less socially selected than the fee-paying intake of the same schools, our sample of such pupils came predominantly from homes with relatively high levels of cultural and educational capital located in the catchment areas of comprehensive schools which had demonstrated their capacity to provide for academically able children (Edwards *et al.*, 1989). In the absence of more recent evidence indicating greater success in reaching those most in need of 'rescuing', it is reasonable to question what place holders are being rescued from. Yet the government has begun a doubling of this 'investment' in private education, adding 4000 new entry places from September 1996 to 5700 already available. Expansion on this scale raises doubts about whether the 60 schools newly admitted to the Scheme are sufficiently and demonstrably 'excellent' within its particular terms of reference to justify a further diversion of public money into the private sector. Nor has any evidence been offered that the 226 schools whose allocations have provided increased places are being rewarded for their effectiveness.

It was, however, asserted by the Secretary of State that all schools participating in the Scheme 'achieve outstanding GCSE and A-level results and maintain strong sixth forms' (29 February 1996). Those schools are thereby being encouraged *not* to change. As grammar schools began to disappear rapidly from the public sector, a traditional academic model of secondary education provided at least the leading private schools with an obvious means of market differentiation and an obvious marketing strategy (Edwards & Whitty, 1997). The Assisted Places Scheme both emphasises and reinforces that model. Indeed, some schools which might otherwise have felt constrained to diversify in order to attract more fee-paying customers were sponsored by the government to remain the same. Certainly the Scheme gave no encouragement to innovative schools, or even to those claiming particular excellence in (for example) science or technology.

An alternative form of specialised secondary education

In sharp contrast to that deliberate conservatism, the City Technology College (CTC) programme announced at the 1986 Conservative Party Conference was a conscious attempt to create a 'new kind of school' oriented explicitly towards an enterprise culture driven forward by high technology. Though limited to 20 even in the initial programme, and then to 15 by the failure to obtain sufficient private sponsorship, they were intended not only to provide a modern alternative to traditionally academic secondary education but, more ambitiously, to point the way towards a system of self-governing schools freed from the compromises and mediocrity associated with Local Authority 'control'. Some commentators presented them as a version of the American Magnet Schools, which would similarly attract a socially diverse intake through the market appeal of a specialised curriculum (for example, Sexton, 1987). But in the English case, the magnetic pull was pre-defined by the government. A combination of vigorous publicity, new or transformed buildings and richly resourced information technology was intended to *create* consumer demand for previously low-status 'technical' education. Certainly the schools presented themselves as being distinctively different. Their brochures promised (for example) 'a new concept in educational thinking', that they were 'designed to take advantage of latest developments in education and building design', and that they offered prospective clients 'the school of the future', 'a school for tomorrow for the children of today', 'a high-tech school for the twenty-first century', and the use of 'the very latest equipment and teaching techniques' to 'meet and go beyond the challenge of tomorrow' (cited in Whitty *et al.*, 1993, p. 96).

Yet evidence from our own and other studies indicated that CTC's main appeal was neither an especially direct relevance to employment (even though their sponsorship by influential local employers or large national companies was often stressed in promotional material) nor the unusually high-level provision for information technology. Parents were more inclined to see them as at least partly selective, and more likely than neighbouring comprehensive schools to uphold traditional values and discipline (Gewirtz *et al.*, 1991; Walford, 1991; Whitty *et al.*, 1993, pp. 82–89). This evidence suggests a market still stratified in relation to a traditionally academic model of secondary education and to the selectiveness which that is seen to entail, with consequent pressures on CTCs to move away from their designated role as centres of excellence in technology (Walford & Miller, 1991). It seemed that parents were identifying private and grammar schools with a better education and with 'getting on', and then inserting CTCs near the top of the existing hierarchy rather than perceiving them as a 'new choice of school' not directly comparable with others. Typical comments from our research included: 'I think you can class the CTC, just like that, as a grammar school' and 'I couldn't believe our luck when she got in, because it's just like getting a private education' (Whitty *et al.*, 1993, pp. 87–88).

This evidence, which was collected early in their development, may underestimate the emerging novelty of the CTCs once they have established their viability. Yet whatever parents' and pupils' reasons for choosing them, their entry procedures have been both uniquely complicated and yet illustrative of general difficulties in matching supply with demand. First, the government stipulated what aptitudes and attitudes should be looked for. Then, in what has appeared from within the CTC 'movement' an illogical departure from the government's belief in 'open' enrolment, they were also required to admit intakes representative of the local population in ability, social class and ethnic identity. The result was what an early study of the process described as 'an impossible task' of implementing 'collectively unworkable criteria' (Murphy *et al.*, 1990).

The predictable part of the process was that applicants were supposed to demonstrate their 'readiness to take advantage of' a distinctive curriculum. Some of those charged with recognising that 'readiness' doubted the feasibility of doing so, one CTC project director telling us that because 'there is no way on earth that anybody can take children at the age of 11 and determine unequivocally any kind of aptitude bias they have', he simply ignored the instruction (quoted in Whitty *et al.*, 1993, p. 74). But their parents had also to display at interview their commitment to full-time education extended beyond the age of 16, to the bias towards science and technology, and to an ethos constructed from 'qualities of enterprise, self-reliance and responsibility'. Assessment of *family* suitability is therefore unusually overt. The inclusion of parents in the interviewing process provides an opportunity to enquire into attitudes which have traditionally acted as a substantial social filter, and to remind them and their children of the CTC's longer working day and longer school year. Perhaps foreshadowing the suggestion in the 1996 White Paper that over-subscribed schools might insist on home-school contracts as a condition for admission, the working definition of merit goes far beyond that employed in selecting pupils for assisted places. It seeks to exclude those (of whatever 'ability') who might 'waste' a place because they lack a family background endowed with attitudes strategic for educational success (Dale, 1990). The approach was clearly articulated by a main sponsor of one CTC in our study, who argued that testing and interviews were designed to elicit 'ability to benefit from what's on offer, and a willingness [on the part of parents] to be involved' (quoted in Whitty *et al.*, 1993, p. 82). Such social and cultural selectivity was made explicit by the Principal of Dixon's CTC in Bradford when he justified a high acceptance rate for Asian applicants on the grounds that 'the strong work ethic associated with such families is exactly the sort of quality which we are looking for' (letter in *Education*, 1 June 1990).

Some CTCs quickly attracted many more applicants than they could take, prompting the then Chief Executive of the CTC Trust to consider using stratified random selection—a lottery within each required social and ability category until that 'quota' had been filled—and for at least one CTC to experiment with the method. But these new schools also had to survive in a competitive market supposedly driven by pupils' performance in public examinations. That some of the more inner-city CTCs have done rather badly in their local league tables has made their principals strong advocates of value-added measures of school effectiveness, an issue subsequently taken up by the CTC Trust itself (Elkin, 1995). In sharp contrast to the marketing of modernity mentioned earlier, other CTCs have seen the way forward in more conventional ways of attracting 'suitable' custom. Certainly an awareness of the benefits of appealing to traditional, as well as modern conceptions of excellence, has produced some complex discursive positioning in the educational marketplace. One CTC claimed in its prospectus to be promoting 'values appropriate to the Christian ethos of the College within the framework of total quality management'. Another was lauded by a local newspaper under the headline 'Experimental college makes the grade with old values', the ensuing report giving prominence to a parent's view that it offered—'a return to old-fashioned teaching standards, school as the way it was when we were young, and the children love it' (cited in Whitty *et al.*, 1993, pp. 48, 126).

Grant-maintained schools: opting for diversity?

Potentially the largest move towards a market of autonomous and differentiated schools has been the creation of grant-maintained status, a status which takes a school out of its Local Authority through the exercise of a collective consumer voice in favour of self-government. From the market perspective exemplified by Chubb and Moe (1990), schools should thereby be enabled to play to their particular strengths by escaping the compromises inherent in being controlled from above. In their later analysis of British progress towards an educational market, it was this reform which they particularly commended; it was 'a revolutionary idea' which 'attacks the system head on' (Chubb & Moe, 1992, p. 28). As the key move towards deregulating educational supply, it is also the reform which dominates the 1992 White Paper (DFE 1992).

Presented in that policy statement as the vanguard of diversification, grant-maintained schools were also suspected from the outset of being a mechanism for restoring academic selection. Doubts about the political acceptability of doing so too openly led to an initial restriction on changing the 'character' of a grant-maintained school within five years of its achieving that new status. In effect it was a check on schools returning rapidly to what the 1996 White Paper terms 'full grammar school status'. That restriction was then removed as an inappropriate constraint on self-governing schools, and as an obvious impediment to that diversity of provision which their relative freedom to play the market was intended to produce. But while many grant-maintained schools have used their additional financial resources to market themselves more energetically, that marketing has been more obviously of a 'traditional' than of a 'modern' image. There is an obvious analogy here with the market appeal of past status as a selective school (Echols *et al.*, 1990). Evidence so far shows them more as enhancing choice by preserving an existing option than as adding something distinctively new, and being perceived as 'better' because they conform more closely to traditional academic standards (Power *et al.*, 1994). Evidence of a tendency to be more academically and socially selective in their intakes comes from the other main study of grant-maintained schools, a main conclusion of which is that they facilitate a two-tier system of chosen and unchosen schools (Bush *et al.*, 1993). To the extent that popular schools can select from among their applicants, then that local market is much less consumer-driven than is often assumed by advocates of parental choice. This is especially so when both parents' choice of schools and schools' choice of parents remains heavily influenced by a dominant academic model of schooling. Nor is the sifting limited to the point of entry. Grant-maintained schools have been identified as among those with the highest rates of exclusion of their existing pupils and among the least willing to cater for pupils with special educational needs (Feintuck, 1994).

In the spirit of the times, Labour policy also highlights greater organisational diversity (Labour Party, 1995). By offering grant-maintained schools a new status of 'foundation schools', it is hoped to encourage them to re-enter their local educational system (a change which Chubb and Moe would surely regard as an anti-reform reform). They would thereby lose their present freedom to control admissions, and so have no greater freedom than other public schools to specialise and then shape their intake accordingly. But that new label might still sustain an 'exclusive' image, differentiating them in status as well as governance from the main category of 'community schools'.

Specialist schools

The belief that grant-maintained schools will use their relative freedom to diversify the system seems to rest on assumptions about a consumer demand for different kinds of secondary school which the Local Authority 'monopoly' had suppressed. If consumers were now free to choose, then schools would be obliged to seek out custom, securing their niche in the market by developing some distinctive appeal. The now extensive research into parents' and children's reasons for choosing a secondary school shows no evidence of choice being shaped by curriculum preferences. This might be explained by market advocates as reflecting the uniformity they deplore because, as with early Ford cars, there has been no colour but black. Yet the causal connection which they assume between choice and diversity remains to be shown (Edwards & Whitty, 1997).

In the 1992 White Paper, assisted places and city technology colleges were portrayed as an enhancement of consumer choice and as first steps towards deregulating supply. We have argued that neither has done much to break the mould. The first reinforced an established model. As an attempt at government sponsorship of a new model, the second was open to objections that allowing schools to change and new schools to emerge 'of their own accord' in response to consumer demand was ideologically and practically preferable to top-down innovation (Chubb & Moe, 1992, p. 28). However more extensive government sponsorship of specialisation has followed, beginning with the 1991 Technology Schools Initiative. This gave one-off capital payments to secondary schools (including those maintained by LEAs) willing within the limits of an extensive and prescriptive National Curriculum to specialise in science, technology or mathematics. The government's promotion of 'technology colleges' and other specialist colleges in the following year had three declared objectives—to extend choice and diversity by encouraging schools to specialise in particular subject areas; to raise the standards of teaching and learning of technology, science, mathematics or foreign languages by placing a special emphasis on such subjects in the school's identity and mission; and to strengthen links between schools and the business community. In return for meeting conditions which included having to find £100,000 of private funding, schools would receive from the government a further £100,000 in capital funding and an extra £100 per pupil per year. That the opportunity to do so was initially restricted to voluntary-aided and grant-maintained schools indicated a fourth and undeclared objective—that of further undermining local authorities by adding to the inducements of non-LEA status. Following the removal of that restriction, nearly half the successful applications in the first two bidding rounds of 1995 were from maintained schools. By mid-1996, 151 technology colleges and 30 specialist language colleges had been designated and continuing growth at that rate would produce by 1997 well over 300 specialist secondary schools, or around 10% of English secondary schools. But schools which are not LEA-maintained remain highly over-represented among the successful bidders, while individual schools are of course very differently placed to attract the necessary £100,000 of private sponsorship.

Partial selection

Government encouragement of schools to specialise has generally been presented not as a return to academic selection but on the basis of 'giving parents greater choice on deciding the type of school that will best meet their children's interests and needs'. As Benn and Chitty (1996, pp. 322–325) observe, schools may indeed specialise in some area of the curriculum without attempting to identify that aptitude or interest at the point of entry. But they may also seek to position themselves—in market discourse, to find their niche—so as to attract a particular clientele. In fact, comprehensive schools have never been as 'inter-changeable' as critics of LEA 'monopoly' provision have asserted. At the systemic level, the 'testing' of their effectiveness has always been impeded by the survival of various types and levels of selection. Some grammar schools have survived; some voluntary aided schools have used their freedom to maintain a distinctively Christian character to shape their intakes academically; school endowments and public funds assist attendance at private schools; and some popular comprehensive schools have been able to attract a disproportionate share of the ablest children in their area. That these attenuating circumstances have been much less evident in Scotland helps to explain the relative success of Scottish comprehensive schools in reducing social class inequalities (MacPherson & Willms, 1987).

The Scottish system appears rather closer to that model of comprehensive secondary education—socially balanced intakes following a common curriculum—which has been portrayed by critics as imposing both uniformity and mediocrity. Many of these critics have supported openly a return both to selection and *un*common schooling, and have seen these reforms as necessarily related. Thus Stuart Sexton recognises that an over-subscribed school will give preference to applicants 'who demonstrate a greater ability and aptitude to learn what it teaches'. He then advises less popular schools to consider what they do best, market their strengths energetically, and so try to become similarly selective but in relation to different aptitudes and abilities (Sexton, 1992, p. 15).

Just as problematic is the advocacy of specialisation with selection which is more a 'diagnostic' matching of demand and supply than a matter of admitting or excluding aspirants for the same product. A recent comparative study of parental choice (OECD, 1994) concluded that more choices can be satisfied—that is, without the imposed rationing inherent in selection—if preferences can be spread around a wide range of alternatives. And schools cannot then be arranged in a single hierarchy, determined for example by conformity to and success in implementing a traditional academic curriculum—because their appeal will be assessed against different models of excellence. Yet we have suggested elsewhere (Edwards & Whitty, 1997) that English conditions make it more likely that competition between schools will foster similarity than diversity (see also Walford, 1996), even though government encouragement of specialisation has assumed a long-suppressed consumer demand for variety.

Since 1992, it has been possible for comprehensive schools to select up to 10% of their intake by aptitude for and interest in that part of the curriculum which the school regards as its particular strength. By 1996, 42 out of 1053 grant-maintained schools had received approval to do so. Such selection by specialisation may encourage schools to pursue real diversity. It may also enable the more popular schools to choose specialisms as a cover for or legitimation of social and academic selection, a charge made against some Magnet schools in the US.

Concern about the implications of selection by interest and aptitude have already been expressed on the basis of experience in the few areas where such measures are well advanced. Gewirtz *et al.* (1995) suggest that 'unusual talent' in music and dance, for example, is being used to enhance the entry of children from middle-class families with high academic ability. Such partial selection may also make some inner-city comprehensive schools more academically comprehensive than they are at present. But what the Director of Education for an inner-London borough describes as the 'sting in the tail' of recent government permissiveness about selection is that it allows oversubscribed schools to decide which pupils it takes after interviewing them with their parents, thereby enabling them to have 'an intake balanced by ability which has, however, weeded out any child/family that the school considers might be "problematic" or a drain on its resources' (Whatford, 1996, p. 18). This echoes the charge made in the 1970s that some voluntary aided schools which adhered to the Inner London Education Authority's banding system were able to secure intakes very different in their composition from LEA-maintained schools nearby. Complaints centered on the right of governors in those schools to manage admissions, and the consequent opportunity to use interviews designed to explore religious affiliation to assess academic suitability (Williams & Murphy, 1979).

Conclusion

The policies we have outlined have produced a 'trend in reverse', a move back from the 10% of schools describable as selective, non-comprehensive or private in 1979 to the 21% identified in 1996 (Benn & Chitty, 1996, p. 88). Even without including the prime ministerial vision of 'a grammar school in every town', the 1996 White Paper represents a further substantial step back towards selection (DFEE, 1996). Schools wishing to achieve or return to 'full grammar school status' will be able to do so. Since such selectiveness excludes all children regarded as unable to cope with an 'academic' curriculum, it apparently signals a return to the 's'-word regarded in the 1992 White Paper as being incompatible with 'choice and diversity'. But the main thrust of the White Paper is towards diversity through partial selection. To a greater or lesser extent, all schools are to be enabled to create a 'grammar stream' within an otherwise comprehensive intake or to shape their entry according to a particular curriculum strength. If the proposals are implemented, LEA-maintained schools will be able to select up to 20% of their intakes either by 'general' ability or by special aptitude, without needing ministerial approval and with a right to appeal against LEA disapproval. That the figure is 30% for technology and other specialist schools might seem a logical recognition of their already specialised character. That the proportion is as high as 50% for grant-maintained schools may be further evidence of a government wish to use these schools to advance a national policy, although it also assumes a wish to become more largely selective which most of them have not yet revealed. How far and how they do so would be a matter for them.

It is the 'Tory crusade to restore grammar schools' (to quote the *Birmingham Post* headlining of the White Paper, 25 June 1996) which has attracted most attention and been widely deplored. As we noted early in the paper, however, selection by specialisation has received significant support. It may be with an eye to that support that the White Paper refers to 'a pattern of diversity' going far beyond the 'outmoded division' into grammar, technical, and secondary modern schools. And it is support which comes from several sources. Arguing that notions of 'common' schooling are impractical, Hargreaves (1996) opts for diversity as 'a means of eluding both the return to selection and the hierarchies of schools based narrowly on league tables'. He believes that it can be made consistent with the 'comprehensive principle' which opposes selection by general ability into schools with a limited ability range. Recognising that this will require supply-side initiatives to increase the range of choices, he nevertheless gives little indication how this will overcome the widespread presumption that a traditional academic style of education is best. Marketing different versions of educational excellence has not so far proved to be a progressive alternative in a context where few parents see the alternatives as being different but equal, and where the entrenched prestige of a traditionally academic education has produced a persistent devaluing of alternatives on the part of those schools able to dominate the market (Edwards & Whitty, 1997). Indeed, recent research found no evidence to date of choice producing greater diversity in the school system, some evidence of a tendency towards greater uniformity, and no significant movement in the traditional hierarchy of types of school (Glatter *et al.*, 1997). The only exception was where there had been additional government funding to foster the development of specialist technology schools. In other words, it was government intervention rather than parental choice that had brought innovation on the supply side. And despite some reduction in the extent and prescriptiveness of the National Curriculum following the 1994 Dearing review, there is little evidence that either schools or parents have yet been persuaded that there is parity of esteem between different models of educational excellence. It is more likely, therefore, that privileged producers and consumers, those with real choice, will continue to search each other out in a progressive segmentation of the market (Ranson, 1994). The 'free' interplay of market forces may in theory produce a system diversified horizontally in a variety of 'equal but different' forms. We have argued on present evidence that it is more likely to create a highly stratified system in which the élite private schools and those public schools which most resemble them still provide the model against which other schools are judged.

Hargreaves' confidence that this prospect can be avoided seems to be shared by the current leadership of the Labour Party, which has espoused the idea of specialist schools with increasing enthusiasm while continuing to oppose on principle 'any return to selection through the 11-plus' (Labour Party, 1995). Having moved from seeing them as a threat to comprehensive education to a grudging welcome of the extension of specialist school funding to LEA schools, a recent announcement of specialist schools was warmly welcomed by the Party (*Times Educational Supplement*, 24 May 1996). However, there is some confusion about Labour's position. In a talk to the Social Market Foundation on 27 February 1996, David Blunkett, the Shadow Education Secretary, argued that aptitude for a particular subject could be grounds for admission to particular schools, though he did recognise the dangers of possible abuse of the system through the use of particular specialisms as a means of covert selection. But he has also seemed to espouse an alternative way of viewing such schools which might reduce such dangers. In a subsequent television appearance (*On the Record*, BBC Television, 14 April 1996), he emphasised that schools which had developed a specialism would be expected to share their expertise with other schools in a local network, presumably through the provision of specialist classes, in-service support for staff, etc. This was echoed in the Labour Party's welcome for the latest batch of specialist schools, when it argued that they 'could promote expertise throughout a community' (*Times Educational Supplement*, 25 May 1996). Such an approach is reminiscent of a model that we have suggested as a way of reintegrating CTCs into the mainstream system and recouping for the general good some of the huge public investment in them (Whitty *et al.*, 1993).

What is not clear from current Labour thinking is why, under such a system, specialisms would need to be an element of admissions policies. With a cooperative network of schools, children could surely gain the benefits of the specialism while being enrolled in any school in the network. This would allow admissions policy to be based on other rules less open to abuse. These would reduce the possibility of covert academic and social selection and be more clearly consistent with the comprehensive principle. It would also be more consistent with what we know about the difficulties and dangers of choosing a specialism on the basis of aptitude and/or interest at age 11 and give children a real opportunity to change their minds during the course of their secondary school career. Much of the current debate suggests a calculated collective amnesia about why selection became in the 1960s both unpopular with parents and widely regarded as unacceptably wasteful of ability.

References

Benn, C. & Chitty, C. (1996) *Thirty Years On: is comprehensive education alive and well, or struggling to survive?* (London, David Fulton Publishers).

Bush, T., Coleman, M. & Glover, D. (1993) *Managing Autonomous Schools* (London, Paul Chapman Publishers).

Chubb, J. & Moe, T. (1990) *Politics, Markets and America's Schools* (Washington, Brookings Institution).

Chubb, J. & Moe, T. (1992) 'The classroom revolution: how to get the best from British schools,' *Sunday Times*, 19 February, pp. 18–36.

Dale, R. (1990) 'The Thatcherite project in education: the case of the city technology colleges,' *Critical Social Policy*, 9, pp. 4–19.

Department for Education (1992) *Choice and Diversity: a new framework for schools* (London, HMSO).

Department for Education and Employment (1996) *Self-government for Schools* (London, HMSO).

Echols, F., MacPherson, A. & Willms, D. (1990) 'Parental choice in Scotland,' *Journal of Education Policy*, 5, pp. 207–222.

Edwards, T. & Whitty, G. (1997) Marketing quality: traditional and modern versions of educational excellence In: R. Glatter, P. Woods & C. Bagley (eds) *Choice and Diversity in Schooling: perspectives and prospects* (London, Routledge).

Edwards, T., Fitz, J. & Whitty, G. (1989) *The State and Private Education: an evaluation of the Assisted Places Scheme* (Lewes, Falmer Press).

Elkin, S. (1995) *Adding Value and Improving Performance* (London, City Technology College Trust).

Feintuck, M. (1994) *Accountability and Choice in Schooling* (Buckingham, Open University Press).

Gewirtz, S., Ball, S. & Bowe, R. (1995) *Markets, Choice and Equity* (Buckingham, Open University Press).

Gewirtz, S., Walford, G. & Miller, H. (1991) 'Parents' individualist and collectivist strategies,' *International Studies in Sociology of Education*, I, pp. 173–192.

Glatter, R., Woods, P. & Bagley, C. (1997) Diversity, differentiation and hierarchy: school choice and parental preference. In: R. Glatter, P. Woods & C. Bagley (eds) *Choice and Diversity in Schooling: perspectives and prospects* (London, Routledge).

Hargreaves, D. (1996) 'Diversity and choice in school education: a modified libertarian view,' *Oxford Review of Education*, 22, pp. 131–142.

Labour Party (1995) *Diversity and Excellence: a new partnership for schools* (London, The Labour Party).

MacPherson, A. & Willms, D. (1987) 'Equalisation and improvement: some effects of comprehensive re-organisation in Scotland,' *Sociology*, 21, pp. 509–537.

Marks, J. (1992) *The Assisted Places Scheme* (London, Independent Schools Information Service).

Murphy, R., Brown, R. & Partington, J. (1990) *An Evaluation of the Effectiveness of City Technology Colleges' Selection Procedures* (Nottingham University, Report to the Department of Education and Science).

OECD (1994) *School: a matter of choice* (Paris, Centre for Educational Research and Innovation).

Power, S., Halpin, D. & Fitz, J. (1994) 'Parents, pupils and grant-maintained schools,' *British Journal of Educational Research* 20, pp. 209–226.

Ranson, S. (1994) Towards education for democracy. In: S. Tomlinson (ed.) *Educational Reform and its Consequences* (London, Institute of Public Policy Research).

Sexton, S. (1987) Foreword. In: Cooper, B. *Magnet Schools* (Warlingham, Institute of Economic Affairs Education Unit).

Sexton, S. (1992) *Our Schools—Future Policy* (Warlingham, Independent Primary and Secondary Education Trust).

Walford, G. (1991) 'Choice of school at the first City Technology College,' *Educational Studies*, 17, pp. 65–75.

Walford, G. (1996) 'Diversity and choice in school education: an alternative view,' *Oxford Review of Education*, 22, pp. 143–154.

Walford, G. & Miller, H. (1991) *City Technology Colleges* (Buckingham, Open University Press).

Whatford, C. (1996) 'Interviews with comprehensive pupils are the sting in the tail,' *Times Educational Supplement*, 2 February, p. 18.

Whitty, G., Edwards, T. & Gewirtz, S. (1993) *Specialization and Choice in Urban Education: the City Technology College experiment* (London, Routledge).

Williams, P. & Murphy, T. (1979, revised 1984) 'The dual system: end it or mend it,' *Teaching London Kids*, 14 (and 22, 1984).

19 Choice and diversity in education: a defence

James Tooley

Source: 'Choice and diversity in education: a defence', *Oxford Review of Education*, 23(1): 103–116, 1997.

Choice in education is desirable for the sake of, *inter alia*, equity, because it acts as a check on monopoly power; and a diversity of educational opportunities is likely to arise if sympathetic account is taken of human differences. The paper first examines the objection that recent 'choice' and 'diversity' educational reforms do not satisfy equity. This is conceded, but it is argued that three rather obvious reforms could make the current system equitable, in terms of the arguments and definitions of critics of choice. However, it is recognised that this depends upon an assumption about the desirability of choice in general. Choice is examined from first principles, and the peculiar powers it has for the promotion of human good are identified. Given this, an argument for a broader understanding of 'choice' in a more authentic market in education is offered, and objections to this countered.

I Introduction

This paper sets out to defend choice and diversity in education, in a way which challenges two fundamental assumptions which have emerged in recent debates. The first assumption stems from Hargreaves (1996a,b), who, arguing from a libertarian[1] perspective, suggests that: 'If it is a matter of choice or no choice, diversity or uniformity, people will favour choice and diversity, other things being equal' (1996a, p. 11, 1996b, p. 132). But this is not prima facie obvious, even from a libertarian viewpoint. For as Dworkin (1988), for example, argues: '[t]he proliferation of products, services, and so forth, hailed with much enthusiasm as the chief virtue of competitive markets, brings with it the need to know more and more in order to make intelligent choices' (p. 66), and this need for information is often burdensome, a significant *personal* cost (i.e. over and above any social costs) to be weighed against any purported benefits. It is interesting that, while in his exchange with Hargreaves, Walford does challenge him on this issue, he does not seem to object to the notion that on a personal level we might prefer more choice to less choice. His challenge stems from the concern that as far as *social* costs are concerned, more choice might be undesirable (Walford, 1996, p. 144). While accepting the importance of separating out the personal and social costs (and benefits) of choice, this paper will seek to defend choice and diversity without Hargreaves' assumption that people will necessarily (at least prima facie) prefer more choice to less choice, even on a personal level. This will be explored in Section III, when we look at choice from first principles in other goods and services to ascertain if lessons can be learnt for the case of education.

The second assumption challenged here, found in much of the educational literature, is that defenders of choice and diversity necessarily will support the 'choice and diversity' reforms which are currently being introduced into the education systems of England and Wales and elsewhere. This 'choice system' has as its chief characteristic that parental choice is permitted within a heavily regulated, state provided and funded schooling system. But defenders of choice and diversity in areas other than education do not normally have in mind that the state should be so heavily involved—choice and diversity in the market, where goods and services are not state provided or funded, is what is seen as desirable. It is of course the case that many educationists call the current state schooling system, with parental choice thrown in, 'a market', but this is unhelpful—for if we call the state provided and funded system 'a market', what term is there left to describe an education system which is not state provided and funded? The reason for raising this issue will become apparent in the discussion in Section III, where we point to the parameters of an education system which might be more appropriate for supporters of choice and diversity to defend. Meanwhile, in order to avoid any confusion, I will resort to the philosopher's trick of indicating as 'choice$_s$' the system where parental choice exists within heavy state regulations, funding and provision of schools (and, at most, use of state funds for a small minority to opt-in to private schools); and 'choice$_m$' to indicate a different system, the parameters of which will be described in due course.

These two issues take up much of the latter part of this paper. However, we have already noted that any defence of choice and diversity must take cognisance of both personal and social costs (and benefits), so in Section II, the biggest social cost objection to choice, that it does not satisfy equity, will be examined. It will be argued that there are modifications to the system which could make the system equitable. However, it is recognised that these depend upon an assumption about the personal desirability of choice in general. Section III questions this, and points to the way choice does seem to have desirable properties in areas of our lives where we take choice somewhat for granted. It is suggested that analogous arguments could be applied to defend 'more authentic' choice in education. Section IV then explores objections to this kind of choice in education, looking at the justifications for state intervention, while Section V draws the arguments together.

II Is choice_s inequitable?

The biggest single objection to choice, in the literature is that it is inequitable. Parents' responses to choice_s will vary across social class and ethnicity; hence choice, reinforces social division (Ball, 1993; Bowe et al., 1994; Edwards & Whitty, 1992; Gewirtz et al., 1993, 1995; Krashinsky, 1994; Ranson, 1993; Walford, 1994; Woods, 1992). For our purposes here, we will adopt something like the 'needs-based' definition of Gewirtz et al. (1995), that 'educational resourcing should favour those with greater educational need and those with fewer private resources in the home and community to be able to meet educational needs' (p. 181). The problem of inequity, then, is when 'individuals receive less than others because of factors *beyond their control*' (Le Grand, 1991, p. 86); a remedy for this in educational terms is for the educationally disadvantaged to be given greater educational priority.

Now, the arguments of the researchers cited above do seem plausible. Choice_s does seem to have a differential impact on people. While some are clearly advantaged by the system, it is likely that others will be made more disadvantaged than they were before—although because there are both winners and losers, it is hard to say whether the system pre- or post-choice_s is the more inequitable (although of course, it is accepted in all the literature cited above that the system pre-choice, *was* inequitable). Indeed, given the strength of this research, the a priori argument that many of us in the 'pro-choice' lobby found convincing at one time or another does not now seem persuasive: low-income, disadvantaged parents and their children were trapped in inferior schools. Give them choice_s, in the form of open access to other state schools or, through something like the Assisted Places Scheme, to private schools, and they will break free from these poor schools, or the threat of breaking free will influence the school management to raise quality. But there is a large body of empirical work to suggest that, in practice, things have not quite worked so smoothly. Of course, it could be argued that the choice, system in England and Wales has hardly been in place long enough to offer conclusive evidence either way, and that the longer it is in place, the more beneficial the outcomes. However, there seem to be clear reasons emerging, outlined below, as to why the reforms are unlikely to benefit all in this way, however long they are given to work through.

Nevertheless, although it is agreed that choice_s does have this differential impact, it may be that critics of choice_s are far too pessimistic about room for potential improvement. My reading of the literature is that the outlook need not be so bleak; for, in principle at least, it would seem that three fairly obvious reforms would be needed in order to ensure that choice, (as it occurs in England and Wales, with ramifications for similar systems elsewhere) could be made equitable.

How do I arrive at this position? My reading of the evidence is that an important distinction is neglected in most of the literature. For example, Fuller and Elmore (1996) summarise their collection of (American) research papers by stating that: 'Choice appears to have a stratifying effect, by social class and ethnicity, even when it is explicitly designed to remedy inequality' (p. 189). However, this is not quite what the papers collected together in their volume actually did show. What is revealed, rather, is that there are considerable numbers of 'low-income and minority families' who *are* in favour of, and able to take advantage of, choice when it is offered (for example, see Lee *et al.*, 1996, p. 87; Witte, 1996, p. 119; Blank *et al.*, 1996, p. 167). What this shows is that the social classes do not remain static when choice, is brought in. Some who were previously in the least advantaged social groups are able to use the mechanisms to their advantage.

Similarly, Gewirtz *et al.* (1995) summarise their findings thus: 'First, choice is very directly and powerfully related to social-class differences. Second, choice emerges as a major new factor in maintaining and indeed reinforcing social-class divisions and inequalities' (p. 55). Again, my reading of their research is that it doesn't quite support this summary. What they have argued is that people can be classified in terms of three 'ideal types' of 'chooser': the 'privileged/skilled', the 'semi-skilled', and the 'disconnected'. In general they point out that most in the first group are middle-class, and in the latter working class, but, crucially, there are 'exceptions to the general pattern' (p. 24), the class categories are in any case fluid, and that, to use Bourdieu's phrase, 'a network of secondary characteristics' (quoted, p. 24) also impact on determining in what category of 'chooser' people fit. But what seems of importance to investigate, and what the authors seem to ignore, is just what *are* the relevant 'secondary characteristics' which allow a person of whatever social class to become a 'privileged/skilled chooser'.

The crucial point is that social class is not static in the way that using words like 'maintaining' and 'reinforcing' suggest. If there are exceptions to the 'middle class: skilled; working class: unskilled' dichotomy of Gewirtz *et al.* (1995), which they acknowledge there are, and if these exceptions are anything like the numbers found in the surveys cited above, then we need to know what enables some of the previously disadvantaged to benefit from choice.

Actually, two sets of factors are clearly revealed in the research. The first are material factors. For example, Gewirtz *et al.* (1993) point to the way the choices of the 'disconnected' were frequently hindered by both poverty and *time* poverty (p. 23). Similarly, it is clear that some, who were otherwise disadvantaged, were able to benefit from the Milwaukee Choice Program because they were given financial assistance in order to attend and travel to private schools (Witte, 1996).

The second set of factors refer to 'cultural capital'. To isolate these factors, we ideally need studies which have random samples of 'choosers', linked with a control group of 'non-choosers', matched for socio-economic status and ethnicity. Several studies have achieved this. For example, while all who participated in the Milwaukee Choice Program were of low socio-economic status (Witte, 1996, p. 119), the 'choice' group was characterised by several statistically significant factors in comparison with a matched group of families of similar socio-economic status: they had higher education levels of parents; higher educational expectations for children; significantly more involvement with children's schooling before choice, became available; significantly more involvement with children's education at home; slightly fewer children per family; and greater dissatisfaction with the existing school the child attended (p. 122–125).

In combination, then, these two sets of factors, material and 'cultural capital', allow parents to participate in, and benefit from, choice$_s$. These factors will enable parents of any class or ethnic background to benefit from choice$_s$; if either or both factors are missing, then children are unlikely to benefit. In what follows, for ease of exposition, we will use the term 'educationally responsible' as shorthand, to denote those with the appropriate 'cultural capital' and 'inclination' to take advantage of the choice, system. So effective choice requires 'educational responsibility' *and* sufficient funds.[2]

Now, the critics contend that, if the choice$_s$, mechanisms will benefit those whose parents have the requisite 'cultural capital', they are in turn likely to further disadvantage those whose parents do not. For while without the choice$_s$ mechanisms in place, in a deprived area both 'educationally responsible' and 'educationally irresponsible' (to use our new shorthand) disadvantaged people would patronise the local school, under choice, at least some of the 'educationally responsible' are likely to take their children away from the school. Moreover, the argument that was given a priori by many of us, that failing schools would be forced to close, does not seem to have been borne out by the evidence, and there are, again, good reasons why not. For schools have, to a certain extent, a captive market; enough young people are likely to stay, given inertia and 'educationally irresponsible' parents, and, of course, given compulsory schooling. In the failing school, too, staff are paid on similar pay-scales to staff in successful schools, so there are few, if any, financial incentives to do much about the problem, although of course, there may be other incentives. In this way, failing schools are quite unlike failing businesses, and there are not genuine 'market disciplines' which can easily take effect. So when Hargreaves writes: 'Bad schools do not, as the political right has theorised, die of their own accord *through market forces*: bad schools have to be murdered' (Hargreaves, 1996, p. 135, emphasis added), my suggestion is that they do not 'die' because of the lack of 'market forces', rather than their presence. We will return to this point in Section III below.

To summarise: choice, does have differential impact on people and, in particular, on the disadvantaged. Some have the 'cultural capital' to be able to take advantage of it; but others do not.

Given this, we can see the three 'fairly obvious' reforms noted earlier which could make choice, equitable. First, the current allocation of extra material resources to the disadvantaged must be made more obvious to all concerned. At present schooling is free at the point of delivery, with many 'special educational needs' and disadvantaged groups allocated more resources, so this in itself goes some way to satisfying our definition of equity. However, it would be far better if the parents and/or children were made more aware of their added 'purchasing power'. One way of doing this would be along the lines of the learning accounts being proposed by Labour and Liberal Democrats (see for example Tooley, 1996, chapter 6). In addition, increased material resources would be needed to ensure that the disadvantaged young people had required funds for travel, uniform and other extras. Such families would also need funds to ensure that child care was not an issue in preventing school choices being made.

Secondly, government-promoted league tables would have to be reviewed. At present they give crude indicators based on performance, which clearly prevents those schools with fewer academically able students from competing effectively with selective schools or schools in prosperous catchment areas. So, to aid equity, the league tables should be abolished; if necessary, some government incentives could be given to encourage the setting up of independent agencies to advise on choice of schools, perhaps along the lines of *Which?* or *Consumer Report*, the consumer magazines.

Finally, measures are needed to ensure that failing 'sink' schools are identified quickly, and remedial measures enforced. This would involve, presumably, some early-warning inspection system and 'emergency squads' of experienced managers and educationists to turn around 'sink' schools, similar to those proposed by the current government.

In other words, with a 'weighted voucher' type scheme (see Coons & Sugarman, 1978; Jencks, 1972), with genuine, not contrived, consumer information, and with remedial measures for failing schools, choice, could become equitable. Hargreaves has observed how there seems an unwillingness among those opposed to choice, to explore whether their objections could be met within the choice, system (Hargreaves, 1996b, p. 137); my conclusion seems to support his notion that choice, can in fact be salvaged from its detractors. The baby does not, it would seem, have to be thrown out with the bath-water.

Or does it? The solution to the problem of inequity in the choice, system depends upon one major assumption, and has one major problem. The major problem concerns the solution to the problem of 'sink' schools. For it depends on government-promoted inspection to find the failing schools, and government-promoted 'hit squads' to go in and solve the problems. But some might not be happy with the way this could politicise the process of failure. For example, a government vulnerable to claims of being educationally incompetent may be reluctant to use these draconian measures, or a government interested in proving the opposite might become too trigger happy. Moreover, the feedback mechanisms would inevitably be slow and cumbersome, relying on indicators which may not reveal the true extent of the educational experiences taking place, or which are out of date by the time they are acted upon.[3] It is also, of course, unsatisfactory for those children left in the school, who not only have disadvantaged backgrounds to contend with, but now have the added uncertainty of being in a failing school which may be closing, subject to political wrangles, and so forth.

The major assumption is that 'choice' is worth salvaging in the first place. Even if these solutions to the problem of inequity under choice, work, if it is not in itself desirable nor desired, then this argument is all rather beside the point. As was noted in the introduction, Hargreaves' (1996a,b) assumption that, *ceteris paribus*, people will always favour choice over no choice, and diversity over uniformity does not seem to be widely shared. However, could it be that there are arguments, which do not depend on libertarian assumptions, that choice is desirable, even when it is not actually desired?

III The personal costs, and the peculiar power, of choice

Dworkin (1988) does seem to have a valid point: he argues that the making of choices 'is not a costless activity, and the assessment of whether one's welfare is improved by having a wider range of choices is often dependent upon an assessment of the costs involved in having to make these choices' (p. 66). He notes three significant personal costs of choice, involving: costs in time and money of acquiring information to make reasonable choices; costs in time and effort in making the judgement after appropriate information has been acquired; and 'psychic' costs, of accepting responsibility for whether the right decision has really been made. These costs seem particularly relevant in the case of choice of education, where the informational requirements to make school choices seem huge, and where so many life options depend on getting the choice right. Indeed, others go so far as to argue that 'parents have ceded authority in education to a professional élite because of the simple realities of the division of labour' (Krashinsky, 1994, p. 123), that it is rational for parents *not* to want to make choices in education. Moreover, the testimony of many, if not all, of the parents in Gewirtz *et al.* (1993, 1995), skilled and unskilled choosers alike, describing how choice is puzzling and confusing, supports the suggestion that the demand for choice$_s$, is not a demand for choice *per se*, but rather a demand for better schools; if these could exist without the distressing realities of choice$_s$, so much the better. *Ceteris paribus*, if choice in schooling could be avoided, it could be argued, this would not be wholly undesirable.

But things are not otherwise equal, as we shall see. To address the issue of the personal costs, let us examine what it is about choice that makes it desirable in other areas of our lives, and ask if these are also true in terms of education.

One of Dworkin's examples concerns choice in consumer goods. Many people, he argues, find it completely undesirable to have choice in goods such as shirts and shoes, because it brings too many costs in terms of time and effort, worries about being unfashionable, and so on. Many of us, according to Dworkin, would be far happier if there were no choice in these consumer goods. But would we really? A simple thought experiment shows the 'peculiar' power of choice in protecting consumers from unscrupulous suppliers and manufacturers.

Suppose there were a monopoly supplier of an essential consumer good (a pair of shoes, for example). How can the consumer respond if, say, the good is of poor quality, or if its price dramatically jumps, or if the quality of sales service is poor, or there are other similar complaints? With a monopoly supplier one can do very little, for without choice any power to influence the goods is severely undermined. The consumer has nowhere else to go for those goods, and the supplier knows it, and can abuse this position.

How does having choice change anything? Once competition between suppliers and manufacturers is brought into the picture, then whole new sets of incentives emerge. If I buy a particular good from supplier A and am not satisfied, I can go to supplier B next time. It is in supplier A's interest, then, to ensure that I don't go to B; hence there are pressures on her to ensure that my goods are satisfactory. It is not that I have to go to A, feel dissatisfied, and then go on to B—the suppliers themselves conduct this hypothetical reasoning, and strive to keep me as a customer. Competition between manufacturers will ensure that the quality of the good is kept high, and that technological innovations are introduced (bringing new materials and process into production, to lower prices and improve quality, to keep up with other manufacturers); competition between suppliers would help keep price low (provided that the monopoly manufacturer didn't set the price too high) and improve service (through 'relationship marketing', loyalty cards, special ancillary offers, and so on).[4]

With consumer goods, choice is desirable, even if not desired, in order to protect the customer from complacent and corrupt monopoly suppliers and manufacturers. It is consumer choice which keeps them on their toes. Moreover, diversity is likely to arise as an inevitable concomitant of choice, given a range of human tastes and preferences. Walford challenges the notion that 'diversity and choice' are as ' "natural" as fish and chips or love and marriage' (Walford, 1996, p. 146). However, in consumer goods at least (and we will return to education shortly) it does seem that they do go together, given diverse human needs and interests. The supplier and manufacturer who first provides a range of sizes, styles and colours for the consumer is likely to be patronised more, since human diversity points to the likely demand for a range of sizes, styles, etc. Such suppliers and manufacturers are also likely to be imitated by other suppliers, anxious to maintain their market position. What is interesting, however, and perhaps what Walford is pointing to, is that diversity of goods does not necessarily imply a diversity of kinds of outlets; indeed, the majority of suppliers could all become rather uniform, as they imitate the most innovative. Diversity is made apparent in catering for the range of human tastes and preferences, but not necessarily in the type of institutions which supply them.

I suggest similar arguments could be applied to the range of goods and services available in the market. One other example is worth considering, which will be of relevance to the educational case below, namely that of newspapers. It is sometimes said that the poor quality of much of the press in Britain leads many to wonder whether it is a good thing to have choice in newspapers at all. However, even here, the peculiar power of choice becomes apparent—although it also becomes apparent that it is not a panacea, that it is at most a necessary but not sufficient condition for high quality. For I have lived in a country, Zimbabwe, where choice in newspapers was progressively taken away by the government, and then it soon became apparent why choice was desirable. Without it, it was much more difficult to gain an opportunity to hear alternative viewpoints about current affairs, and to have the opportunity to weigh different arguments against one another. With a monopoly in the media, it is hard to avoid the propaganda of the 'hegemonic' classes. Similar considerations would apply to having no choice in book publishers, or film makers, and so on; in the realm of ideas, consumer choice becomes an important foundation for the avoidance of indoctrination.

Two other factors need to be noted from this discussion before we return to education. First, if I do not want to be bothered to choose, then as long as there are a significant number who *are* discriminating choosers, the suppliers and producers cannot take the risk that I am not one of them. I might patronise a particular supplier just because I am lazy, or whatever; but the supplier and producer cannot assume this about me. So good service and good quality goods must be ensured, in case I am one of the discerning buyers. In a sense, the 'irresponsible' can 'free ride' on the responsibility of others.

Second, subjecting the producers and suppliers of consumer goods and services to the rigours of genuine competition does not in practice lead to the type of situation we highlighted when discussing choice, and schooling above—where there are failing schools limping along, perpetuating disadvantage for those trapped in them. Even in disadvantaged areas, there are usually competing supplies of goods available, offering products from competing manufacturers. But if one of the suppliers or producers should start to go into decline, it is either quickly replaced by another (often the new business will take over the same premises, and indeed, one might not even realise that the business has changed hands), or other businesses quickly expand to take demand away from it. Genuine competition and choice do not lead to poor quality suppliers limping along; they are quickly and easily forced out of business, and the consumer does not suffer. It is not that there are no failing restaurants, say; simply that they cannot exist as failing restaurants for very long: the market is too unkind to let them.

Let us sum up. We have looked at these other goods to see what it is about choice that is desirable: we found that, without choice, there could be no checks on the monopoly power of the supplier, and hence severe risks of poor quality, poor service, high prices and technological stagnation. Moreover, in the realm of ideas, choice in suppliers and producers was important to avoid the problem of propaganda and indoctrination. Diversity moreover arose as a necessary concomitant of choice, given the likelihood of differences in human needs and preferences. In areas where choice is taken for granted, by factoring it out, we have suggested that choice is better than no choice, even for those who, like Dworkin, thought they might not *want* to have to choose. Choice has costs, as noted, but the crucial benefits greatly outweigh these costs.

Now, are these arguments applicable to the educational case too? If we could come to education with an open mind, free of preconceptions about the way it is currently organised, then I suggest that these same considerations should apply. The desirability of having a choice of suppliers of educational opportunities should be abundantly clear, since all the dangers of a monopoly supplier listed above seem to apply, *a fortiori*, to something as important as education. Of course we would want to avoid a monopoly supplier who could be complacent and corrupt; insensitive to individual differences in needs, interests, abilities, aptitudes and aspirations; not responsive to community pressures; and disregarding of appropriate technological innovation. Moreover, because education is at least in part concerned with the communication of ideas, similar considerations to those discussed under the newspaper example apply: if there was a danger of 'hegemonic' forces corrupting us, undermining our critical thinking, and so on, then absolutely the last thing we should want would be a monopoly supplier. And of course, the desirability of having diversity in educational opportunities should be apparent too. For individual and cultural differences which emerge in our preferences for different types of consumer goods and services would apply, *a fortiori*, to education, where differences in learning aptitude and interests are so clear. Again, this diversity would not necessarily be expressed in terms of a diversity of institutions, but may well arise as a diversity of experiences offered within rather uniform institutions.

Although we started out on this course of argument in order to defend the underlying motivation behind the choice, system, we have arrived at a position looking to a defence of a much stronger form of choice—choice between competing suppliers, with a supply-side opened up so that the same peculiar, beneficial properties of choice noted above can be brought into the education system. We can call this system choice$_m$—choice in the 'market'—the market of the economists, where the state is not the monopoly supplier and funder.

Importantly, we see how this system has the potential to tackle the major difficulty with the solution to choice$_s$ in terms of equity noted above, the problem of 'sink' schools, and the questionable efficacy of government intervention to solve this problem. Granted, the choice$_m$, system, in order to satisfy equity, would need something akin to the weighted voucher, so that all could be able to partake of educational opportunities (see Tooley, 1996, chapter 4). But under choice$_m$, there would be new incentives to ensure that 'sink' schools would not limp along in the destructive way that they can under choice$_s$, and government 'hit squads' would not be needed to ensure that these improved. For choice$_m$ would ensure, just as it does for other goods and services, that suppliers are able to take over failing enterprises, or easily expand to cater for unsatisfied demand. 'Educationally irresponsible' parents would be able to 'free ride' on the responsibility of others.

Of course, it could not be argued that under choice$_m$ there would be no failing educational settings. However, under these more authentic market mechanisms, such settings would be forced out of business quickly. Wouldn't that be terrible for the children involved with them, however? Not necessarily, if there were genuine market mechanisms operating, and in particular, an open supply-side. For then the failing educational settings could be taken over by more successful businesses even before any of the customers noticed the failure, or other businesses could step in very quickly to ensure that the demand for educational opportunities (expressed through the weighted voucher in areas of poverty) was taken up if the setting were forced to close. But it can be categorically asserted that, under choice$_m$, there would not *be* the problem of 'sink' schools that occur under the state system, that is, failing schools able to limp along indefinitely, causing indefinite suffering to their 'captive' students. Again, the market is far too unkind to tolerate such aberrations. A choice could be desirable, even when not desired, in education for precisely the same reasons that it is desirable in other areas of our lives.

Many readers will not concur with the argument thus far. While choice and competition may be an obvious mechanism for consumer protection (and diversity an inevitable concomitant of that) in consumer goods and services, education requires the intervention of the state to ensure quality. Government became involved in education for benign reasons, intervention is maintained for equally benign reasons, state intervention is effective, and any alternative much worse.

I beg to differ on all these counts. A complete defence of choice obviously requires that the justifications for state intervention in education are addressed—but there is not space here to do this. Instead, I can briefly mention three broad areas of justification for state intervention, and point to other literature which challenges these, before summarising the defence that has been mounted here in favour of a stronger form of choice.

IV Justification for the state overriding choice

First, it is argued that without the state there would not be educational opportunities at all, or at least not for the great majority. West ([1965] 1994), however, argued that the great majority of working people were very much concerned about, and able to provide for, the educational needs of their children, and that the state intervened in order only to keep that education under surveillance, to use a Foucauldian expression. His position has been subject to a barrage of criticism. However, I argue (Tooley, 1996, chapter 3) that his argument emerges largely unscathed, with obvious implications for the debate about the need for the state to provide educational opportunities (see also High & Ellig, 1992; Richman, 1994).

Second, there are justifications based on the 'social dimensions' of education, that education is 'a public good' (e.g. Grace, 1989), or that there are 'collective action' problems in educational provision (e.g. Ranson, 1993). Conversely, I have argued that education is not a public good in the economist's sense, although clearly it could have desirable externalities, including all the ones commonly listed, such as education for democracy and social cohesion, equality of opportunity or equity, law and order and economic development. However, there is nothing in the public goods literature which shows that these externalities need state intervention in order to ensure their provision, and I have pointed to the various ways in which, without the state, it seems much more likely that they will be provided more successfully than with the state (Tooley, 1994, 1995a, 1997).

The key point is that the solutions to collective action problems do not 'depend necessarily upon cooperative and deliberative public action for their resolution' (Ranson, 1995, p. 37). For there are clear examples of collective action problems which are solved by cooperative action within markets, rather than deliberative action within democracies. For example, an adequately fed population is as much as 'public good' as an adequately educated one; but this does not rule out choice and diversity in the market as the way of providing for this public good.

The debates about the prisoner's dilemma (see Jonathan, 1990; Ranson, 1993; Winch, 1996) try to formalise these collective action problems—indeed, they are the fall-back position for all who try to demonstrate that these problems arise and need the state to intervene. But I have argued (Tooley, 1992; 1995b; 1997) that the prisoner's dilemma model is unlikely to be applicable in general to the educational process, because education has private as well as public benefits and, moreover, there are cooperative and contract solutions to the prisoner's dilemma which can move us away from its sub-optimal outcomes (see Schmidtz, 1991; Taylor, 1987).

The third set of justifications concerns the 'nature of education', and how this makes it not amenable to 'commodification'. Such arguments tend to have three major shortcomings. First, they suffer from what might be called a 'category error', conflating different conceptual levels; secondly, they use *petitio principii* in order to argue the case for the difference in the nature of education; thirdly, they tend to conflate 'education' with 'schooling'. For example, McMurtry (1991) argues that the aims and processes of 'the market' and 'education' are not compatible, because there are 'contradictions' between them in terms of their respective 'goals', 'motivations', 'methods', and 'standards of excellence'. Agents in the market, he says, have 'profit' as their main goal, while 'educational agents' have as their goal educational aims such as the advancement and dissemination of knowledge (1991, p. 211); similarly, excellence in markets is measured by the success in making a product-line sell; in education, however, excellence is measured by 'how disinterested and impartial its representations are' (p. 213). These oppositions show for McMurtry the incompatibility of education and markets. However, this argument is far too quick. Take any service or good which is normally accepted as being amenable to market mechanisms, say air transportation. We can easily find differences between the goals, motivations, methods, and standards of excellence of 'air transportation' and 'the market'. The goals of air transportation are, say, getting people from A to B quickly, whereas that of the market is, still, profit; the standards of excellence of 'air transportation' might be in conveying the greatest number of people in the greatest comfort with minimum accident; excellence in markets is, still, the number of sales notched up. This sort of discussion tells us nothing about whether or not the market can satisfactorily deliver air transportation. Nor does it tell us anything about markets and education.

To avoid this sort of error, it is necessary to distinguish 'education' from 'the delivery of educational opportunities', and hence 'educational agents' (in McMurtry's language), from 'agents who ensure the opportunities are delivered'. Educational agents have overriding educational goals, while bursars and finance managers are concerned with overriding financial goals. There is no necessary divergence of interests between these two. One can be concerned with profit, the other education, and each can complement, not undermine, the other.

But this brings us to the second shortcoming of these sorts of arguments, that they often beg the question by pointing out that (the delivery of) education is different from other commodities because educational institutions are, in fact, not concerned with making a profit. Winch (1996), for example, argues that '*Most* educational activities, being largely sponsored through taxation, do not need to make a profit in order to survive in the way commercial companies do' (p. 13, emphasis added), and that, 'in education', there is no price mechanism operating (p. 100). In both cases *petitio principii* is at work: if we are considering whether (the delivery of) educational opportunities should be part of the state's remit, then it is begging the question to point to qualities of schooling which are the case because schooling is provided by the state. We want to know if the lack of profit motive or pricing mechanism in schooling is intrinsic to education, not simply that this is the way schooling is now. McMurtry (1991) goes even further in this way, ruling out private education, it would seem, by definition. He writes: 'The place of education ... remains a place of education only in so far as it educates those whose motivation is to learn, independent of the money-demand they exercise in their learning' (p. 212).

Finally, the third main shortcoming of these arguments is in the conflation of education and schooling. It might be that (most) schooling is currently funded through taxation, but it is not clear that most educational activities are. For example, the educational process can arise through reading books, going to the cinema, visiting zoos, walking in the countryside, talking with family, watching television, etc. Most of these are already in the private (i.e. non-state) sector. Hence the simplest challenge to the 'commodification' argument lies in pointing to these everyday counter-examples. Anyone committed to the destructive impact of commodification would have to argue that the reading of books, zoo trips, etc. were harmful and undermining of educational aims. I wait for such an argument to appear.

V Conclusion

Education is, of course, different from other goods and services. But these differences do not rule out the similar ways in which real choice and competition in the delivery of educational opportunities is desirable, on the grounds of equity. It is not that we, as individuals, necessarily prefer to have more choice than less, as Hargreaves suggests, but simply that choice is there for our protection. Nor should the possibilities for choice be considered exhausted by the current reforms in England and Wales and elsewhere. For if we wish to have the same sorts of protection as choice affords us in other goods and services, then we need to consider the potential of a stronger version of choice in a more authentic market.

Choice$_s$—the system of heavily state regulated, state-provided and state-funded education, with parental choice thrown in—was agreed to have a tendency to inequity, but its critics were being too pessimistic about its potential for reform. Three reforms were outlined which would make the system of choice, equitable. However, it was agreed that such reforms would only be worthwhile if it was accepted that choice itself was desirable—which many of its critics clearly did not accept. Discussion of consumer goods and services pointed to the 'peculiar power' of choice in protecting us from the corruption and complacency of monopoly suppliers, and from the danger of indoctrination; diversity of provision followed as an inevitable concomitant of this, given human differences, and the desirability of avoiding monopoly power over the expression of tastes and preferences. It was then argued that these principles could be applied to education too. All the dangers of monopoly supply, and monopoly control over diversity, seemed even greater when applied to something as important as education.

But it was conceded that not many would be willing to go down this route, instead pointing to the way education is different from other goods and services. Some of these arguments—justifications for state intervention in education—were very briefly surveyed, and further literature highlighted. It was suggested that the weight of arguments elsewhere could lead to the undermining of these justifications for state intervention in education. If this was upheld, then not only could we defend choice$_s$, but also a much stronger version, choice$_m$, choice in more authentic educational markets, with a liberated supply-side.

Fundamentally, the issues here converge on the question of 'who controls education?'. Choice—choice$_m$—is a way of ensuring that whoever does is mercilessly subject to the needs and desires of the people, and not able to dictate to them what their interests and aspirations should be.

Notes

1 It is refreshing to read Hargreaves' argument, for generally discussions about choice tend to be framed as if *equity* was the only important value, and liberty is consequently neglected. An example of this is in Gewirtz *et al.* (1995, p. 21), where it is pointed out that greater freedom was one of the justifications given for increased choice, but this is then not mentioned again in the text—it is not challenged, just ignored.

2 Gewirtz *et al.* (1995) might object to this definition, for they assert: 'Differences in choice-making are not a matter of relative deficiencies or of social pathology in which certain parents are less responsible, or efficient or effective choosers' (p. 24). Instead: 'use of the term "skill" is intended to denote particular cultural capacities which are unevenly distributed across the population but which are valorised by the operation of the education market' (p. 24). There seems to be only one significant difference between these two statements: for the latter surely implies that under choice, those with the requisite cultural capacities *will* become more 'efficient or effective' choosers, as in the first statement; the only addition there is the word 'responsible', which perhaps carries a value judgement which the authors do not wish to endorse. I am not sure when one can escape this value judgement. But in any case, in what follows, the term 'educationally responsible' can be taken simply as a shorthand to refer to those qualities described, and any implicit value judgement ignored.

3 It was said by some, for example, that when the government 'hit squad' closed the notorious Hackney Downs School in north London, the school actually was beginning the process of reversing its decline, although this had not yet filtered through to its test results.

4 If the different suppliers are simply outlets of the same overarching company, then competition between them will probably not be as great as if the different suppliers are themselves competing companies; hence the latter is greatly to be preferred.

References

Ball, S.J. (1993) 'Education markets, choice and social class: the market as a class strategy in the UK and the USA,' *British Journal of Sociology of Education*, 14, pp. 3–19.

Blank, R.K., Levine, R.E. & Steel, L. (1996) After 15 years: Magnet schools in urban education. In: B. Fuller & R.F. Elmore (eds) *Who Chooses? Who Loses? Culture, institutions and the unequal effects of school choice* (New York, Teachers College Press).

Bowe, R., Ball, S. & Gewirtz, S. (1994) ' "Parental choice," consumption and social theory: the operation of micro-markets in education,' *British Journal of Educational Studies*, 42, pp. 38–52.

Coons, J.E. & Sugarman, S.D. (1978) *Education by Choice: the case for family control* (Berkeley, Los Angeles, London, University of California Press).

Dworkin, G. (1988) *The Theory and Practice of Autonomy* (Cambridge, Cambridge University Press).

Edwards, A. & Whitty, G. (1992) 'Parental choice and educational reform in Britain and the United States,' *British Journal of Educational Studies*, 40, pp. 101–117.

Fuller, B. & Elmore, R.F. (1996) (eds) *Who Chooses? Who Loses? Culture, institutions and the unequal effects of school choice* (New York, Teachers College Press).

Gewirtz, S., Ball, S.J. & Bowe, R. (1993) 'Parents, privilege and the education market-place,' *Research Papers in Education*, 9, pp. 3–29.

Gewirtz, S., Ball, S.J. & Bowe, R. (1995) *Markets, Choice and Equity in Education* (Buckingham & Philadelphia, Open University Press).

Grace, G. (1989) 'Education: commodity or public good?' *British Journal of Educational Studies*, 37, pp. 207–211.

Hargreaves, D.H. (1996a) Diversity, choice and excellence: beyond the comprehensive school. In: F. Carnie, M. Tasker & M. Large (eds) *Freeing Education: steps towards real choice and diversity in schools* (Stroud, Hawthorn Press).

Hargreaves, D.H. (1996b) 'Diversity and choice in school education: a modified libertarian approach,' *Oxford Review of Education*, 22, pp. 131–141.

High, J. & Ellig, J. (1992) The private supply of education: some historical evidence. In: T. Cowen (ed) *Public Goods and Market Failures: a critical examination* (New Brunswick, Transaction Publishers).

Jencks, C. (1972) *Inequality* (New York, Basic Books).

Jonathan, R. (1990) 'State education service or prisoner's dilemma: the 'Hidden Hand' as source of education policy,' *British Journal of Educational Studies*, 37, pp. 321–338.

Krashinsky, M. (1994) Why educational vouchers won't help Johnny read. Commentary in: B.W. Wilkinson (1994) *Educational Choice: necessary but not sufficient* (Montreal, Institute for Research on Public Policy).

Lee, V.E., Croninger, R.G. & Smith, J.B. (1996) Equity and choice in Detroit. In: B. Fuller & R.F. Elmore (eds) *Who Chooses? Who Loses? Culture, institutions and the unequal effects of school choice* (New York, Teachers College Press).

Le Grand, J. (1991) *Equity and Choice: an essay in economics and applied philosophy* (London, HarperCollins).

McMurtry, J. (1991) 'Education and the market model,' *Journal of Philosophy of Education*, 25, pp. 209–217.

Ranson, S. (1993) 'Markets or democracy for education,' *British Journal of Educational Studies*, 41, pp. 333–352.

Ranson, S. (1995) 'Public institutions for cooperative action: a reply to James Tooley,' *British Journal of Educational Studies*, 43, pp. 35–42.

Richman, S. (1994) *Separating School and State* (Fairfax, VA, The Future of Freedom Foundation).

Schmidtz, D. (1991) *The Limits of Government: an essay on the public goods argument* (Boulder, CO, Westview Press).

Taylor, M. (1987) *The Possibility of Cooperation* (Cambridge, Cambridge University Press).

Tooley, J. (1992) 'The prisoner's dilemma and educational provision: a reply to Ruth Jonathan,' *British Journal of Educational Studies*, 40, pp. 118–133.

Tooley, J. (1994) In defence of markets in educational provision. In: D. Bridges & T.H. McLaughlin (eds) *Education and the Market Place* (London, Falmer).

Tooley, J. (1995a) 'Markets or democracy for education? A reply to Stewart Ranson,' *British Journal of Educational Studies*, 43, pp. 21–34.

Tooley, J. (1995b) *Disestablishing the School: debunking justifications for state intervention in education* (Avebury, Aldershot).

Tooley, J. (1996) *Education Without the State* (London, Institute of Economic Affairs).

Tooley, J. (1997) Cooperation without deliberation: the market solution. In: K. Watson, C. Modgil & S. Modgil (eds) *Educational Dilemmas: debate and diversity*, Vol. 3 (London, Cassell).

Walford, G. (1994) *Choice and Diversity in Education* (London, Cassell).

Walford, G. (1996) 'Diversity and choice in school education: an alternative view,' *Oxford Review of Education*, 22, pp. 143–154.

West, E.G. ([1965] 1994) *Education and the State* (Indianapolis, Liberty Fund).

Winch, C. (1996) *Quality and Education* (Oxford, Blackwell).

Witte, J.F. (1996) Who benefits from the Milwaukee choice program? In: B. Fuller & R.F. Elmore (eds) *Who Chooses? Who Loses? Culture, institutions and the unequal effects of school choice* (New York, Teachers College Press).

Woods, P. (1992) 'Empowerment through choice? Towards an understanding of parental choice and school responsiveness,' *Educational Management and Administration*, 20, pp. 204–211.

20 Through the revolution and out the other side

Stuart Maclure

Source: 'Through the revolution and out the other side', *Oxford Review of Education*, 24(1): 5–24, 1998.

This offers an overview of the revolutionary changes in education in England and Wales in the decade following the Education Reform Act of 1987. After an introductory section on the background to the new dispensation, the perception of failure which galvanised the politicians, and the attack on the 'education establishment' which under-pinned it, the article looks at the elements which came together to form a comprehensive re-working of the education system and its power structure. Major changes in higher education and in teacher training began well before the Education Reform Act appeared on the scene and continued throughout the period under discussion, informed by the same mixture of ideology—the release of market forces—and managerialism.

This account goes on to discuss the changes as they affected the school curriculum and regular testing, the role of local authorities and school governors in the management of the education system, the re-invention of inspection and the publication of information for parents on performance. It concludes that the revolution which took place under the Thatcher and Major governments is more likely to be consolidated than overturned by their Labour successors who, having changed some of the rhetoric while keeping the impetus for reform, have begun to mobilise the maligned education establishment behind the new order.

Hyperbole is never far from the discussion of education in these islands. There is an apparently irresistible temptation to brand every setback a disaster, every custom a hallowed tradition, every change a revolution. But the events of the past decade have turned many aspects of the world of education upside down. It is no exaggeration to say that the English education system has indeed passed through a revolution in the decade since the passing of the 1988 Education Act.

The title suggests that the 1997 general election brought this particular revolution to an end. In a sense it did. The revolution has been consolidated without relaxing the pressure for change. Its history deserves careful study.

A few powerful ideas dominated the thinking of the New Right reformers:

- Distrust of local democracy and the institutions of local government.
- Distrust of the Educational Establishment—the teachers' unions, the local education authority leaders and professional staff, the university authorities, the teacher trainers.
- Distrust of professional autonomy and the ideals of public service.
- Belief in market mechanisms as applied to public sector activities such as education and health.

The great post-war expansion had taken place within the framework of an Education Act passed in 1944 by the war-time coalition—a carefully prepared piece of legislation which had enjoyed the widest political and public support. This was swept away by an 'education reform' Act which made no attempt to gather cross-party backing—which was, in fact, calculated to divide rather than unite; a major plank in a radical Conservative manifesto for the general election of 1987.

There was no attempt to disguise the far-reaching nature of the challenge it presented to what had gone before. The old dispensation was to pass away and another take its place. The changes which were enacted laid down new ground-rules for the education profession and the way education is managed. They set out to change attitudes and expectations, altering the power structure—the relations between the teachers, the local education authorities and the central government—injecting new life into governing bodies and promoting them as a more authentic expression of democratic participation than the elected bodies set up by the creaking machinery of local democracy.

Moreover, in doing this, they maintained enough ideological drive to give consistency to the revolution. The radical Right set out to remove any ambiguity about the locus of power by formally abandoning the century-old idea that authority should be shared between central and local government. The related ambiguity about who was responsible for the curriculum was also removed: the introduction of a National Curriculum made Parliament the arbiter of what is to be taught.

The ideology provided a strategy for on-going improvement: elements of an internal market were to promote competition and choice. The system was to be made more transparent: more information would be fed to parents, as consumers, making their own decisions. Management responsibility was moved down to the level of the individual school, subject to a rigorous regime of inspection, assessment and examinations to monitor the managers.

Distrust of professional independence was a dominant Thatcherite idea in many areas of policy, but seen nowhere more clearly than in dealings with the teachers. Teacher training and even teaching methods in basic subjects have been brought under central control. A similar distrust has governed policy towards higher education where a massive expansion has been accompanied by a ruthless determination to cut unit costs.

Finally, there are the changes which have been introduced to give greater recognition to vocational and technical education within mainstream secondary and further education and in industrial training. Here the clarity which has driven forward the reform of school management has been lacking in attempts to reconcile the 'competence-based' ideology of the National Council for Vocational Qualifications—a creature of the former Department of Employment—with the more traditional curriculum concerns of the Department for Education. In their contribution, Michael Young and Ken Spours thread a path through this tangled story.

The purpose of this introductory essay is to offer an overview of the revolution as a whole. Other writers will discuss particular aspects in more detail, using the experience of what has happened to inform consideration of where we go from here. Peter Downes helped to pioneer local management and lived through the period as a head of a large secondary school. Christopher Tipple observed the changes as director of education for a large county. Paul Black had the impossible task (and bruising experience) of trying to design an assessment regime which combined the educational need for formative feed-back with the Government's demand for rigorous summative judgements. Eric Bolton describes how Her Majesty's Inspectorate fell victim to the radical critique of the educational establishment. Eric Hoyle and Peter John consider what has happened to teacher training.

Chris Pierson reviews the structural changes from the perspective of a political scientist concerned with the governance of education as a public service. And two contributors look at what has been happening in higher education. John Roberts contributes an autobiographical account of what it was like for one vice-chancellor in what he calls the pre-revolutionary period when the UGC was on its last legs. Martin Trow gives an outsider's view of the impact of ideology and bureaucracy on the universities since the early 1980s. In this, he draws in part on his on-going research with Oliver Fulton into the impact of current changes on academics and administrators.

The background

Change on this scale must be assumed to reflect profound political dissatisfaction with what went before. There are still many PhD theses to be written on how the perception that schools were 'failing' became a commonplace in the media and among politicians, particularly, but by no means exclusively, among politicians on the right. It is right to talk about perceptions rather than facts because the evidence of success is as substantial as that of failure. But it is the perception of failure which has influenced policy.

The same commonplace perception has dominated the discussion of primary and secondary education in the USA since the 1960s. State after state has brought forward ambitious plans for reform, backed with state-prescribed curricula and tests, and financial incentives to improve practice. But no matter what changes are introduced the assumption of failure persists, having by now entered into the common currency of public discussion and become a necessary political cliché.

In the UK the turning point came towards the end of the 1960s when post-war optimism began to turn sour. The signals included student unrest spreading from continent to continent and culminating (for Europe) in 'les évènernents de 1968'. Concern about unruly students was extended to schools when the first of the so-called Black Papers appeared in 1969. The media response to what was in fact a not very good collection of polemical articles showed that the authors had struck a nerve: the quality of their argument was less important than the public's eagerness to believe what they said. What began as a reaction against progressive education and wrong-headed teachers soon developed a party political dimension as Conservative MPs like Rhodes Boyson broadened the attack.

The intervention of James Callaghan in a major speech at Ruskin College in the autumn of 1976 was a deliberate attempt to prevent anxiety about education from becoming an exclusively Conservative issue—it ushered in a ten-year period of more or less consensual reform. Shirley Williams under Labour began, and Mark Carlisle and Keith Joseph under Mrs Thatcher continued, a programme of incremental change aimed at clarifying the curriculum, modernising the examinations and tightening the management of the education system. Most of these reforms came to fruition under Keith Joseph as legatee of the work started rather ineffectually after the Callaghan speech.

The undercurrent of dissatisfaction continued throughout the period, strengthened rather than diminished by on-going reform. International comparisons came to the fore in the early 1980s. English education had enjoyed a high reputation in Europe and the English primary school was believed to be universally admired. The English, for their part, had taken it for granted that their way of doing things was better than the Continental and had been brought up to regard direct state control of education in countries like France as inherently repugnant: decentralisation, like the English Channel, was assumed to be a protection against totalitarianism.

All these verities came under attack as England's record of economic decline cast doubt on all received wisdom. Although international comparisons are notoriously difficult, Sig Prais and his colleagues at the National Institute for Economic and Social Research started to look in detail at syllabuses and examinations in Britain and West Germany[1] and reached disturbing conclusions. People began to take more seriously the league tables produced in the 1960s by the International Educational Achievement study. The over-confident mood changed to one of excessive gloom as evidence mounted that in key subjects such as mathematics, English students performed less well than their opposite numbers in Germany and France, not to mention Japan and the Pacific rim.

By the mid-1980s, the immediate cause of public dissatisfaction was a protracted dispute between the teachers and the local authorities on pay and conditions of service which caused much disruption and public inconvenience. The quarrel was deeply damaging to the teachers as a group, and to the local authorities; in so far as it made it obvious that something had to be done it paved the way for radical measures. Keith Joseph was replaced by Kenneth Baker. The dispute with the teachers was disposed of by a short Bill removing their collective bargaining rights—a body blow for the unions—and the decks were cleared for the general election of 1987 and the Education Reform Bill.

I suspect that in England, as in the USA, public dissatisfaction about education is here to stay. It has become part of the cultural furniture—one of the things people think when they are not thinking about anything in particular—a belief which they can hold even if they are (as poll after poll shows) well satisfied with the schools their own children attend.

There is no escaping the contradictory nature of the evidence.[2] Since the introduction of the General Certificate of Secondary Education, the schools appear to have forged ahead—the percentage of students achieving five A-C Grades at GCSE is now above the 50% mark—up from around 30% under the GCE and CSE in the mid-1980s. These remarkable figures are reflected in staying on at school beyond 16, the rise in the number of successful A-level entrants, and the explosion of numbers entering higher education.

But there is the equally clear evidence of failure—the long tail—the bottom 40% over whom Sir Keith Joseph used to agonise—who emerge from 11 years of schooling with little to show for it, not even a sound grasp of basic literacy and numeracy.

Whether the improvement apparent in the examination figures is all it seems remains a matter for continuing debate—nobody knows the extent of grade inflation (if any). Changes in the system of examining at 16-plus opened the gates to many who would not have passed through before. The General Certificate of Education had been devised when it was assumed that 'academic success' was likely to be the prerogative of the brightest third of the school population. Its task was to act as a sieve at the end of the compulsory school period to filter out those thought capable of benefiting from further study. The General Certificate of Secondary Education made different assumptions, with a measure of criterion-referencing and an attempt to test what students could do rather than what they could not do. Comparing standards in two different kinds of examinations at different times is endlessly complicated, but what is certainly true is that the GCSE has proved to be an examination in which many more students achieve success. More success in GCSE meant fewer leavers at 16. Quite quickly it ceased to be the norm for students to break with education as soon as they reached the minimum legal leaving age: and once those who stayed on became a majority, the social pressures changed.

As for the rapid increase in the numbers going on to higher education, it is not clear how far this can be used as evidence of improvements in the school system. It seems much more likely that quite different factors were at work—notably the powerful financial incentives given to institutions in the 1980s to maximise their income by filling up their marginal places.

The perception of 'school failure' and 'falling standards' was a political fact made all the more potent because it was based on populist intuitions rather than analytical research. The radical Conservatives targeted the 'liberal educational establishment' which was in no position to resist a populist attack and quickly lost credibility by becoming excessively defensive.

The anatomy of an educational revolution

All sectors of the education system have been called into question. The Education Reform Act of 1988 was mainly concerned with schools. It was the flagship of radical Conservative reform, bringing in its wake a flotilla of Bills on other related matters. But before Mrs Thatcher and her colleagues decided to put education in the forefront of the 1987 general election campaign, major changes were already under way in higher education and teacher training.

Higher education

The revolution in higher education has been no less comprehensive than that which has overtaken the schools, but the time-scale covers a longer period and the policy considerations and unforeseen events which have brought it about are different and more complex.

The sequence of events began in the early 1980s when the University Grants Committee got into difficulties which proved fatal and the ground was prepared for the removal of the polytechnics from the local authority sector. High inflation in the 1970s had already undermined the UGC regime. When the Conservatives took office in 1979, their main policy objective for higher education was to curb expenditure. This, inevitably, impacted on the UGC whose task it was to distribute the limited funds available. Government dissatisfaction with the way they did this hastened the end of the UGC era and the new funding arrangements introduced by the 1988 Act.

Keith Joseph, a former Fellow of All Souls, was a devotee of high standards and rigour and appeared to believe that standards could be raised by limiting entry. He sought to make distinctions between 'wealth creating' fields of learning like engineering and the applied sciences, and others such as the humanities, of which (like grand opera) we could only have as much as we could afford.

From speculating quite seriously about making entry to universities more difficult, the ministerial mood changed dramatically when Kenneth Baker succeeded Joseph. Baker was an unashamed expansionist. By making marginal students more financially attractive to universities, the Government stumbled on a way of funding expansion while at the same time reducing unit costs—an aim which was maintained till the mid-1990s when curbs were imposed to limit overall numbers and costs.

After a quarter of a century, the division of higher education between an autonomous university sector and a 'public' polytechnic sector was ended by the 1991 Education Act. The change was made with the minimum of consultation and no forward planning. The creation of a single funding agency for both former higher education networks has created a quango which distributes more than £3 billion a year. The emphasis is of necessity on accountability and value for money—a dominating obsession which quickly drives out trust and encourages new forms of academic fraud. The Higher Education Funding Council's relationship with universities and colleges is very different from that of the University Grants Committee—both more distant and more intrusive. Its bureaucracy is still developing suitable performance indicators against which to measure efficiency in different areas.

Changes in the financial regime have successfully forced universities to be more commercially-minded and fund more of their activities from non-governmental sources. As unit costs are brought remorselessly down—and university teachers' salaries are tightly controlled—the universities take on a depressed air and claims that standards are not suffering sound less and less convincing.

What is clear is that the expansion of higher education was long overdue and if there was to be a move to mass higher education there had to be a sharp reduction in what each student cost the state. But the way the expansion was engineered was governed by an ideological hostility to planning which got in the way of any serious attempt to face the consequences. Jointly and severally, universities began to consider the need to levy supplementary fees from students to make up for under-funding from the Funding Council.

As the 1997 general election loomed the Conservatives and Labour colluded in keeping higher education out of the campaign by appointing Sir Ron Dearing to head a group (with minority academic representation) to look forward and report after the election. It remains to be seen how the unified university system will become stratified to take account of differences in quality and function, and what will be the consequences for élite, international universities like Oxford; how higher fees will be introduced and paid for; how—or whether—university programmes will be linked in any formal way to employment and the needs of commerce and industry.

It begins to look as if a massive programme of educational reform, embarked upon to raise educational standards all round, is going to be accompanied (by accident or oversight) by disaster for the universities.

Teacher training

For teacher training, too, the reform process goes back well before 1988. Teacher training outside the universities has been in a state of flux for most of the period since the end of the Second World War.

In the 1960s the then teacher training colleges went through a series of major expansions geared to the increasing school population and the extending of the period of training to three years: numbers in training doubled— from 60,000 to 120,000—in the decade. In the 1970s came the restructuring and the redundancy, the mergers and the changing relations with universities and the Council for National Academic Awards. The promise of an all-graduate profession began to be realised with most would-be teachers receiving their higher education in universities and in colleges which had become part of polytechnics. The content of their professional studies reflected changing academic priorities, with the philosophy, psychology, sociology, and history of education competing for time alongside teaching practice.

The process of tightening control on the education and training of teachers began in 1983 when Keith Joseph discovered how to use existing regulations to intervene directly. He laid down criteria which teacher training institutions must meet, and set up a Council for the Accreditation of Teacher Education to oversee their imposition; a relatively gentle intervention but one which gave the Secretary of State wide indirect powers over the professional formation of teachers.

In the wake of the education changes initiated in 1988, Ministers were determined to go further. They tried with limited success to open up school-based avenues to a teaching qualification which by-passed regular teacher training. The underlying aim was to minimise the influence of the people and institutions—the teacher training establishment—which they most distrusted by handing more responsibility over to the schools. Universities like Sussex and Oxford had pointed the way with internship and the development of a mentorship role for practising teachers: the reformers saw in these schemes— stripped-down—a way of cutting the university contribution down to size.

In 1994, the creation of the Teacher Training Agency (TTA) brought together responsibility for recruitment and staffing, the content and practice of training, and funding. The role of the universities in teacher training became that of agents, employed to carry out specified functions for the TTA. This was underlined when the TTA and OFSTED, the new body set up to manage school inspection, were instructed by the Secretary of State to prepare a national curriculum for teacher education.

It would be absurd to suggest that teacher training had been so well ordered under the old arrangements that there was no room for improvement, but the way in which tight supervision was imposed sent a chilling signal to university education departments as well as to the then colleges of education. Central control of teacher education has become a fact which will long survive the revolution.

The debate has been carried on at two levels. Superficially it is about the technical aspects of teacher training—how best to equip teachers for life in the classroom, with the emphasis on practice rather than theory. But the underlying questions are much wider: they concern the culture of teaching—the conscious and unconscious attitudes which teachers derive from their higher education and teacher training. The New Right sub-plot was to change the culture, and break free from the progressive philosophy which was held to have undermined teachers' effectiveness as instructors.

The criticism of the present teaching culture is easy to caricature—a mixture of the serious and the trivial, the absurd and the disturbing. It features teachers, beguiled by notions of 'child-centred' education, who tolerate classrooms where children express themselves while minimal learning takes place. It deplores the lasting influence of John Dewey, and the progressive voices which link the Hadow report of 1931 and the Plowden report of 1967. It echoes familiar complaints of a more practical nature—about the reluctance of some teachers to use phonic methods and make children learn their tables; their reluctance to teach standard English grammar and the Victorian classics and give children a nation-building overview of English history; their sloppy dress and failure to instil moral standards.

Caricature or no caricature, all or some of these perceptions about the culture of teaching are widely held among otherwise intelligent people who are not part of the education establishment. The same perceptions underpinned the Black Papers a quarter of a century ago. The fact that they were latched on to by a body like the Centre for Policy Studies did not mean that Dr Sheila Lawler[3] and her colleagues invented them.

No one could dispute the existence of a culture of teaching in the public education system which is different from, say, the culture of teaching in the independent schools. Education as an academic study seems to be prone to fads and fashions—a characteristic which suggests that if government ministers (and the TTA) try hard enough they could succeed in changing the culture. No future minister, of whatever political hue, will be prepared to leave teacher education (and the intellectual baggage which teachers bring to their job) to the discretion of the teacher trainers.

The education reform act, 1988

The legislation drew on two separate strategies for change:

- The first is the conventional top-down approach based on the Government's view of what needs to be done, and direct legal provisions to make this happen.

- The second is the rearrangement of the incentives within the system to create a simulated market in which consumer choice will force the providers to compete for custom and therefore raise their standards.

At times, the two strategies have been in conflict—ministers (and the Department) have wanted to manage things which (in theory) might have been left to the market. As Chris Pierson points out in his contribution, rigging the market became a management tool.

Separately and in conjunction, these strategies were applied to

- Curriculum policy
- Competition and choice
- Management

and, as we have seen, Teacher Training and Higher Education.

Curriculum policy

The National Curriculum is, perhaps, the most extreme example of the top-down method of educational reform. Its impact was all the greater because it brought ministers back into an area of education from which they had largely excluded themselves for more than 50 years.

It is easy to forget how deep-seated was the orthodoxy which Kenneth Baker challenged when he propounded a State-prescribed curriculum. Only a year earlier, Keith Joseph had issued a White Paper, *Better Schools*,[4] in which he expressly rejected the idea of a legally enforced National Curriculum, and restated his intention to go ahead with a negotiated framework in which curriculum control was shared between central government, local education authorities and school governors.

Even so, when the new policy was announced with a characteristic flourish by Kenneth Baker in the autumn of 1986, there was next to no protest. The National Curriculum seemed like an idea whose time had come. The National Union of Teachers demurred; *The Times Educational Supplement* objected; but the educational world at large seemed to heave the kind of collective sigh of relief which often greets decisive action. Admittedly, this was followed shortly after by well-founded apprehension about how it would be implemented and policed but a national curriculum was accepted in principle with little fuss. After Labour's landslide election victory in May 1997, the hands on the controls changed but the revolutionary transfer of power was consolidated, not challenged.

There could, in any case, have been no going back to the situation before 1988, when custom and practice had veiled the general confusion about who was responsible for what. Legal control of the curriculum rested with the local education authorities and the voluntary school authorities. The Secretary of State had no direct power to intervene, he had to act through them. But the local education authorities and voluntary school authorities had long since informally delegated their responsibilities to the heads and staffs of schools.

The proverbial visitor from Mars—or even from somewhere like Sweden which puts a premium on neatness and tidiness—would have found the pre-Education Reform Act situation hard to credit. Curriculum control in primary schools rested largely with headteachers; only where selective secondary schools remained, were the primary schools constrained in part by 11-plus tests. As comprehensive education spread, this constraint disappeared and primary headteachers used their own judgement, tempered by the guidance of advisers and inspectors, to determine what should be taught and how.

In the secondary schools, external examinations came into play. But it was up to the schools to decide who should be entered for what examinations. What they did in practice varied widely according to local circumstances and the strengths and weaknesses of the teaching staff. The two years or so before the examinations were due were mainly devoted to examination courses, but this affected some pupils more than others. It was possible for pupils to drop essential subjects before the examination stage if they were thought to lack aptitude or motivation—or if the school lacked qualified specialist staff to teach all pupils.

The extent of the diversity which resulted had been documented by the local education authorities in their responses to a Circular (14/77) issued by the Department of Education and Science some years before Kenneth Baker published his Education Reform Bill. But attempts to bring about more coherence and offer children and their parents some kind of curriculum guarantee made slow progress. Such attempts depended on local education authorities taking back some of the powers which had passed by default to teachers, who resented anything which could be described as political interference. Their touchiness was not altogether unreasonable because among the authorities most eager to intervene were a few with strong left-wing majorities who wanted to use the curriculum to press policies on race, gender and sexual orientation. One of the acknowledged besetting weaknesses of the English education system remained its patchiness—the wide gap between the best and the worst—and to tackle this there was a growing belief that there had to be agreement on what common core schools should try to make available to all pupils.

The legal provisions for Kenneth Baker's National Curriculum were laid down in the opening sections of the Education Reform Act. They went far beyond a common core. Going into remarkable detail, they enumerated the nine subjects to be taught at primary level in England, and the ten (including a modern language) at secondary level—to which was added religious education which, though not part of the 'national' curriculum, was legally required as part of the 'basic' curriculum. The relevant sections of the Act went on to deal with assessment and testing and the publication of results.

No one could describe the way in which these legislative provisions were carried out as an unmitigated success. The creation of a broad and balanced National Curriculum was undertaken at break-neck pace without adequate time for preparation and planning. It is easy to see why the rapidly-changing succession of Ministers—Baker, MacGregor, Clarke, Patten—forced the pace. Given the pressures of confrontational politics, they did not feel they had time for pilot projects and careful evaluation. They were reluctant to discuss their plans in advance with experienced educational administrators. To do this would have given the old guard educational establishment the opportunity to re-group and counter-attack. The momentum had to be maintained if there were to be any quick political dividends.

So the whole thing was rushed. Wholly predictable pressures fell on the schools where time-consuming curriculum development had to be undertaken alongside existing work. There were big in-service training requirements: the testing and assessment demands alone meant that teachers had to learn new skills if they were to relate the assessment techniques back to the process of teaching.

The story of mismanagement does not need to be told in detail. The two advisory councils set up under the Act to advise the Secretary of State on curriculum and testing were intended to draw on a wide range of expertise and to consult widely. But the time-table was extremely tight and the machinery was placed effectively within the control of the Secretary of State whose civil servants kept the councils on a tight rein, determined to head off anything the Department opposed.[5] The first two chairmen—one a former senior civil servant in the Education Department, the other a former chief education officer, were people who were well qualified to do the job and could not be described as placemen. But neither served out a full term; both were succeeded by people who had had little direct connection with education but were political insiders.

The National Curriculum Council set up parallel working parties on the different subjects in the curriculum without any clear idea of how they would achieve a coherent whole. Even before the first meeting of the council it was obvious there would be difficulty in making a nine or ten subject compulsory curriculum fit into the time available.[6] There were simply not enough periods in the week to accommodate what each subject group wanted. Few people wanted the prescribed National Curriculum to bespeak every minute of the timetable—there were other subjects (the most quoted being the classics and the separate sciences) which some schools would want to teach and which the Secretary of State was believed to wish to see taught. But this ideal, like the important cross-curricular themes which were not otherwise programmed, became increasingly difficult to defend.

The Act also required all children to be assessed and tested at the end of each key stage—that is at about the ages of 7, 11, 14 and 16. Here again nothing had been thought through before Parliament was invited to legislate. The result was overload; the testing regime threatened to get in the way of good schooling.

The combination of overloading the content and demanding excessive external testing brought about the crisis in March 1993 which persuaded the then Secretary of State, John Patten, to call in a trouble-shooter. The appointment of Sir Ron Dearing marked the belated recognition that the National Curriculum could not follow precisely the form set out in the Education Reform Act. Sir Ron (who laid claim to no prior knowledge of curriculum matters) looked and listened and drew his own conclusions: he pruned the subject content and the assessment procedures. The full ten subject curriculum was effectively ended at the end of Key Stage 3—that is when pupils start the two-year run up to GCSE; it then becomes more differentiated and problematical and overlaps with the attempts to tackle the intractable problems of the general-vocational divide which Michael Young and Ken Spours write about elsewhere (pp. 83–97).

The remarkable success of Sir Ron has been due to his willingness to listen to, and accommodate, a range of views; his practical common sense and feeling for what is and is not acceptable and possible. His second venture—with the 14–18 age-range—was more difficult than his first and left more loose ends. The success of his work on the school curriculum owed a lot to the gratitude of all concerned to someone who could get schools and ministers out of the mess which had been created by six years of bungling. Dealing with curriculum matters in the future will require a robust institutional framework which does not rely so heavily on the emollient good sense of a high-grade fixer. A number of points emerge for further consideration.

Narrow or broad?

The Act requires a National Curriculum which is broadly defined: a core of mathematics, English and science (plus Welsh in Welsh-speaking schools); plus the 'foundation' subjects of history, geography, technology, music, art, physical education (and a modern language at the secondary stage) and Welsh in schools in Wales which are not Welsh-speaking (Education Reform Act: Section 3[1] and [2]). Kenneth Baker adopted the widely held view that if you were going to prescribe anything you had to prescribe everything—that once you set up a National Curriculum anything not written into it was liable to go by the board.

He took an equally broad view of the testing required to back up the extensive subject base of the curriculum. Indeed, from the start the way the curriculum was to be tested influenced the way it was defined; many of the problems which followed arose from this.

Kenneth Baker accepted the proposals of Professor Black's Task Force on Assessment and Testing which provided a format which combined moderated assessment by teachers with Standard Assessment Tasks set by external bodies. He may not have fully understood what such a scheme would cost in time and money if fully and imaginatively implemented. At all events, he did not carry it out—instead he used it selectively, picking and choosing the bits he found convenient.

Baker[7] has described how he and Margaret Thatcher disagreed on these matters—she arguing for simple pencil and paper tests concentrating on a core of basic subjects like mathematics and English, and he for a testing programme extending across the whole curriculum. Baker fought his corner, and the planning went ahead on the basis of a broad curriculum backed up by a broad and oppressive testing regime. In the end, when it fell to Sir Ron to pull the chestnuts out of the fire, he came down nearer to Thatcher's view than Baker's—he had to if he was to do the pruning which was needed. At the same time he gained universal support for a five-year moratorium on further change. This has provided a breathing space, but in two or three years' time these issues will be revisited by Tony Blair's government with a different set of prejudices.

Experience suggests that on grounds of sheer practicality, Kenneth Baker (not to mention the Department of Education and Science) got it wrong. The belief that the curriculum must be defined and policed in detail seems to be based on a sub-professional view of the teachers—a view which may also stunt the possibility of professional growth. But it is a widely held view—one shared by many specialist teachers who despair of their colleagues and feel obliged to protect their own subjects at all costs.

Politicisation

By its very nature, a national curriculum raises questions about political intervention in academic matters with potentially Orwellian overtones of State-imposed political correctness. This was one reason why some of us were opposed to what we saw as a particularly undesirable form of nationalisation. When, therefore, the Secretary of State gave key jobs on the curriculum and assessment advisory bodies to his friends, there were protests from the world of education echoed by the Opposition in Parliament. It seemed to many obviously unsatisfactory to let party politics loose on the content of school subjects like English and history.

But such protests missed the point. The change in the law had its origin in the perceived need to take the public curriculum back into the public domain. If this meant anything it meant giving the elected representatives of the people the chance to get their hands on the controls-that is, Parliament, and the Secretary of State as the responsible minister. This was bound to lead to a clash. If, as ministers believed, the educational establishment was corrupted by such liberal errors as a belief in child-centred education, they had to do more than just keep the unions at bay. They had to be on their guard also against the leaders of the subject associations—

they too were thought to reflect attitudes and practices which had contributed to failure. (The National Association for the Teaching of English (NATE) had long been regarded as a hotbed of 'progressive' ideas.) If Ministers wanted to change the curriculum, not perpetuate its faults, they could not afford to hand the advisory councils over to functionaries of the status quo.

English and history raised these questions in the most acute form, on both pedagogic and political grounds. There were arguments between those like Kenneth Baker, who wanted the emphasis on hard facts, and those whose rejection of a *1066 and All That* approach had led them to regard history as training in the skills of handling evidence. The latter approach, which had a wide following, was distrusted by right-wing critics who saw history as a necessary way of instilling a sense of national identity.

English gave even more trouble when Brian Cox, one of the joint editors of the original Black Paper, who had been brought in to chair the working group on English, proved a disappointment to the radical Right. The Order which resulted from the work of his group was attacked by right-wing critics before the ink was dry and a brand new Secretary of State, John Patten, was prevailed upon to sanction an instant review. This absurdity—and the uncertainty and confusion it brought to people in schools trying to teach English—was a contributing factor to the decision to call in Sir Ron Dearing.

Sir Ron managed to draw a line under these episodes but it is still going to be necessary to come to terms with the on-going reality of the political control of the curriculum. Every change of government must now be assumed to imply a change of curriculum emphasis. A minister who intervenes will not be doing something outrageous—simply his or her job; inevitably all ministers want to make their mark and in future the National Curriculum will be somewhere to do this.

It would, of course, be intolerable if history had to be re-written every time a new government came in, or if, like John Patten, every new Secretary of State felt obliged to revise the English literary canon to demonstrate his political virility. One might speculate that new conventions will come into existence to limit the extent to which it is deemed proper for ministers to intervene—the educational establishment will, no doubt, find ways of domesticating the revolution. Parliament may need to look again at the consultative machinery. But so long as the National Curriculum is enshrined in Parliamentary Orders, it will represent the policy of the government of the day and ministers (urged on by their Department) will insist on being in charge of what they have to defend.

Competition and choice

The attempt to release the power of parents as consumers within a simulated educational market-place brought a number of related measures, some designed to strengthen parents, some to increase the ability of individual schools to respond to the pressures which empowered parents might bring to bear.

This was wrapped up in a strong ideological package. Behind it was a formula which was being applied to many other aspects of public policy. The shades of Adam Smith were invoked to endow market forces with a unique wisdom, benign and all-pervading. Privatisation and deregulation would release profit-oriented enterprise. The power of professions—like those of trade unions—had to be curbed to allow the market to operate freely. Public service ethics had to give way to competition and marketing. It was the same ideology which underlay the introduction of an internal market in the health service. It was about turning clients, patients, parents and passengers into customers, armed with the power of the purse in a consumer society. It was the quintessence of Thatcherism and what it stood for in electoral terms.

The populism released by the Conservatives has successfully changed the background to future policy as well as the policy of the past decade. Education has become part of the consumer society. The taste of power which parents have enjoyed under the Conservatives has created an appetite which will only grow with feeding. Many of the changes which have been introduced under a right-wing rubric have ceased to be controversial and become familiar features of the education system as it prepares to enter the 21st century. The creation of 'New Labour' has been a recognition of this.

Open enrolment

Competition depends on parents being able to choose between schools. For obvious reasons parents can never be given absolutely free choice. All they can be offered is the chance to express a preference; such a right was enshrined in weak form in the 1944 Act. But each local education authority was allowed to develop admissions policies which, in effect, shared the pupils out among their schools. There being a surplus of places overall, authorities were allowed at their discretion to cut the planned admission to any school to 80% of its physical capacity. In this way they ironed out differences in intake from year to year and area to area, keeping large numbers of places at popular schools out of the 'market'—and denying parents the opportunity to send their children to the school of their choice. The Education Reform Act rectified this by removing the authorities' discretion, and requiring all schools to accept children up to the full limit of their physical capacity.

How much difference this makes in practice varies from place to place and school to school. Parents have certainly exercised their preferences but for obvious reasons some have been more successful than others. Admissions have become a major issue, as can be gauged by the number of appeals (where children have not been admitted to the school of their parents' choice) running at more than 50,000 a year. Local authority education staff have argued that open enrolment distorts sensible planning and leads to some schools being inefficiently overcrowded while others are underused.

It has probably increased parents' influence to some degree in some places and, taken together with other changes, made heads and governing bodies more eager to make their schools attractive to parents. But a major study by the Audit Commission concluded that across the country as a whole, logistics decree that there is very little real choice.[8] The rhetoric is necessary to support market theories, but to give reality to it would be costly. The economic pressure is to relate the number of school places more closely to the number of children. There is an obvious conflict between ministers' wish for parents to have more choice of school, and their concern to reduce the number of 'surplus' places. The more successful they are in persuading local authorities to take empty places out of service, the less choice there can be for parents.

Local management of schools

If schools were to be more responsive to parents as consumers, they had to have more control over their own affairs and be less dependent on the local authorities. This meant giving them their own budgets and letting them decide how to spend them—making local authorities distribute most of the total sum available for primary and secondary schooling on the basis of a weighted per capita formula.

Peter Downes' contribution describes how this has changed the way schools are run and transformed the job of the headteacher. Some of the services schools formerly received as a matter of course from the local education authority, they now have to pay for (or buy from some other source). The schools have moved into the driving seat as their relationship with the LEAs has changed. Instead of being dependent institutions, unable to put in hand minor repairs without the approval of some official in the education office, the schools have become clients and customers whose business the authority has to cultivate.

This has to some extent overshadowed the monitorial responsibilities which the authorities have retained. When schools run into difficulties for some combination of reasons, pedagogic and managerial, it is still up to the local education authorities to support them, but as a result of LMS the authorities have fewer resources with which to carry out a supervisory function.

Governors

Governing bodies have taken over many managerial functions which once fell to the local authority. Governors decide how many teachers to employ and who to appoint. It is their responsibility to see that the National Curriculum is taught and that religious education is given according to law. The fate of the school depends in large measure on the combined skills of the head and the chair of the governors, and on their seeing eye-to-eye on essentials.

Local Management of Schools has been a popular way of getting value for money while giving schools more control over their own destinies. Few governing bodies would now voluntarily surrender the responsibilities they have taken on. From the Conservative Government's point of view LMS has been a means of deliberately cutting back the local education authority function. The opportunity for local authorities to impose their own political priorities on the schools has been removed. The Act has severely reduced the authorities' education functions and all but eliminated their strategic role. The new Labour Government gives local authorities a bigger role in monitoring and support services but does not challenge the principles of local management.

Grant-maintained schools

The Act created a new class of schools directly funded from central funds and independent of the local authorities. To achieve GM status governors had to ballot parents and seek the Secretary of State's approval. The scheme was extremely controversial and fewer schools applied to become grant-maintained than the Government hoped. As time passed, the number of schools applying to go GM tailed off and of those which decided to ballot, fewer voted 'yes'. Notably the church school authorities—both Anglican and Roman Catholic—urged their schools not to seek GM status which they regarded as having a divisive effect among maintained schools as a whole.

Schools which chose to apply for GM status did so for a variety of reasons beside the desire to benefit from the access of independence which it brought. When the scheme was launched there were significant financial advantages to schools which opted out. Ministers hoped it would provide an escape route for schools in areas run by left-wing Labour education authorities. In the event few schools in such areas have taken the GM route. Most local education authorities—and all Labour authorities—have done their best to discourage opting out.

Nothing has been more likely to prompt a move to opt out than a proposal to close a school or merge it with another. GM status has represented such a school's best chance of reprieve. Local authorities have responded by bringing forward fewer reorganisation schemes and weighing carefully the possible consequences in terms of GM defections—if only because if one school is allowed to opt out, the balance of a reorganisation scheme may be radically altered.

Encouraging choice means encouraging parents to discriminate between one school and another. What many critics feared was that, given the Government's enthusiastic backing, GM schools would be seen as having a higher status than schools maintained by local authorities and therefore attract more middle-class pupils. Such sociological concerns never being far from the centre of the discussion of education in England, these fears were almost certainly justified; the perception that one kind of school is going to have a higher status than another is enough to make it so.

At the centre of the GM school policy were two conflicting theories. The scheme as launched was for a network which would give parents, wherever they lived, a choice of sending their children to a GM school, a County school or a Voluntary school. But before long another scenario emerged: that the ultimate aim should be for all schools to become grant-maintained and for the Funding Agency for Schools (the quango set up to fund GM schools) to take over from the local education authorities responsibility for all primary and secondary schools. If all schools were to become grant-maintained arguments about whether one category of school had a higher status than another would disappear. But by the same token, the claim that a new category of schools gave parents a wider choice would also fall to the ground.

The GM mechanism was also seen as a means of enabling new schools to come into the system, to take in minority groups as yet unrepresented— evangelical Christians, Muslims, humanists, etc. In fact this never happened, though as the 1997 election approached there were some signs that, given a renewed mandate, the idea might have taken off.

The Labour Party never hid its dislike of the GM scheme, notwithstanding the Blairs' choice of school for their son, and promised a new category of 'foundation' schools which would bring the GM schools back under the local authority umbrella without depriving them of the benefits of self-management.

Though not part of the GM school story, there are other initiatives aimed at increasing choice and diversity—the move towards specialist schools, spear-headed by the City Technology Colleges and the schemes for schools to specialise in technology, languages and other academic areas. These have been tied up with attempts to get money and sponsorship from industry. There were also suspicions that this was to be a way of re-introducing grammar schools by the back door. John Major talked in general terms of a grammar school in every city and more control for GM schools over their admissions. But by the time Labour took over, little had been done to give reality to such talk. Labour had adopted the idea of encouraging comprehensive schools to specialise in languages, technology or whatever, as a way of doing something positive for morale and aspirations in urban and suburban slums.

Management

The National Curriculum now provides a job description to which the schools can be held to account. The enforcement of accountability is now a key management function. There are also clear signs that those who think they can prove short-comings (bullying, bad teaching) on the part of the schools will try to take their grievances to court. The more precisely the schools' obligations are spelled out, the greater the chance that the courts will intervene and build up case law on which future litigants can rely.

The Education Reform Act took many decisions about how money was to be spent away from local authorities and gave them to school governors, but the size of local budgets (and the grant LEAs receive from central government) vary widely, as much for historic as for objective reasons. One piece of unfinished business concerns the attempt to find a common funding formula. Pilot schemes have shown the difficulties but the quest will continue. One factor working in favour of the status quo is the opportunity it gives to central government to rig the distribution formula in favour of their friends.

Information

Ensuring a free flow of information has an obvious populist appeal, especially against a background of assumed public anxiety about standards. It has also been seen as fundamental to the creation of choice and competition: markets depend on consumers having enough information on which to make rational choices. Schools now have to tell parents how they have spent their funds; authorities must show how they have allocated the aggregated schools budget and give school-by-school figures for expenditure per pupil.

The results of assessment and testing at 7, 11 and 14 are meant to provide parents with consistent information of their children's progress through the first three key stages. League tables compare the results, school by school; GCSE and A levels follow—all published and ranked. Add to these regular inspection reports and the full measure of the information explosion becomes apparent. No previous generation of parents has been so fully served with facts and figures about pupil and school performance.

There remain fierce arguments about the value of the figures and the need to find a way of measuring value-added. This provides a fertile field for researchers but it is the crude figures which make the immediate impact. The potentially misleading nature of the 'raw' results are plain for all to see; so are the credibility problems which would follow from attempts to 'cook' them. Bringing all this information out into the open is one of the most significant changes of this education revolution. The toothpaste being out of the tube, there is no way of putting it back.

If there are very obvious limitations on the flow of information—and therefore on the quality of the simulated market—the significance of the changes is not in question. The desire for openness extends far beyond those who think in terms of subjecting schools to market forces; it is now a permanent and popular feature of the educational scene.

A lot of anecdotal evidence suggests that the management of schools has been directly affected by the league table culture. Schools are acutely concerned about their examination results; they have become more achievement-oriented. This is said to be reflected not only in better examination results but also, less commendably, in the way some schools respond to pupils with special needs whose presence threatens the examination scores.

Market forces can be seen at work most clearly in the independent schools where the league tables have a direct impact on recruitment and viability. These schools are already in a real, not simulated, market place. In all schools the publication of results has focused attention on teaching, intensifying pressure on heads and heads of departments in secondary schools whose performance is put on the line annually by the external examination of their students. Most parents welcome being able to compare the relative performance of schools and believe it is legitimate to use this information to hold teachers accountable.

Inspection

Ministers also believed that to hold the school accountable there had to be a reorganisation of the arrangements for school inspection.

Her Majesty's Inspectors of Schools—480 in number—were an élite group drawn from the upper reaches of the teaching profession, who spent their time going into schools, advising teachers and gathering information, preparing surveys and reports. Full inspections were an important part of their job but their resources were so limited that only a small sample of schools could ever be subject to a full inspection in any one year.

They also had an important role to play inside the Department of Education, working alongside the other civil servants who advised the Secretary of State, feeding in first-hand information of what happened at school level and providing an invaluable departmental memory. The Senior Chief Inspector held the civil service rank of deputy secretary and had access to policy-making at the top level.

But when the Thatcher government set out to shake up the education system, it included HM Inspectorate in the educational establishment which had to be by-passed in the interests of reform. Many of the progressive ideas now under attack were thought to have been espoused by HMI. The Inspectorate had many extremely able and distinguished members, but the radical Right believed that enough of them had 'gone native' to make them part of the problem rather than the solution. Moreover, the traditional (though limited) independence of the Inspectorate, as appointed by Royal Warrant, gave them an unwelcome critical status inside the Department. As Eric Bolton's article shows, the Inspectorate was put on the defensive, aware that its methods of working were in question and its future was under threat.

Quite apart from such doubts about the Inspectorate's ideological correctness, there were practical reasons for making major changes. If all schools were to be regularly inspected—once in four years—there would have to be many more inspectors; there was no way the existing Inspectorate could be expanded to the extent required and still retain its character and quality. The Education (Schools) Act 1992 set up an Office for Standards in Education (OFSTED) outside the Education Department, with a remit to concentrate clearly on the task of inspecting (unlike HM Inspectorate which had combined inspection with advice). It began life with a nucleus of 175 HMIs, sub-contracting the work of inspecting to 'registered' inspectors who (after training) would be invited to tender for inspection jobs. This commercial consultancy model was intended to bring in a new breed of independent observers with fewer preconceived ideas. Some commercial consultancies have been among the bidders but a large share of the work has gone to local authority inspectors, semi-privatised in the wake of LMS.

The inspection programme began in the autumn of 1993 with the secondary schools. Progress with the primary inspections took longer to get started and will take longer to complete. In the long term the time between inspections is likely to be six years or more.

In the managerial scheme of things, it is OFSTED's function to verify that the National Curriculum is being taught and to assess the quality of teaching and learning; to look at the management of resources—value for money—and to report on the spiritual, moral, social and cultural development of the pupils. More controversially, inspectors are expected to grade lessons and teachers on the basis of their snapshot visits. Whereas HM Inspectorate relied on a strong collegiate tradition and shared experience (as well as internal guidelines) to achieve reliability and common practice, OFSTED has formalised procedures in the OFSTED Framework and Handbook, setting out how registered inspectors should carry out an inspection and construct their reports. This serves as a Bible for inspectors and a guide for schools to what they can expect when the inspectors call.

It was Keith Joseph, a decade earlier, who had broken with tradition and decreed that HMI's school inspection reports should be published. This caused a brief flurry of indignation and excitement which quickly subsided. OFSTED's reports were to be published from the start, and backed up by the requirement that school governors should produce an action plan dealing with matters raised by the inspectors within 40 days of receiving their report.

Inspectors' reports now add considerably to the information available to parents when applying for schools. On balance, schools say they appreciate the value of a visit from the inspectors—the effort required to prepare the paper work for an inspection, though often resented, is seen as having a salutary effect. But the scheme has not been going long enough for any reliable evaluation, and sceptics point out that schools generally approve of the inspection process if they have come out of it reasonably well.

But there are obvious questions to be asked about the consistency of the judgement of large numbers of inspectors whose individual experience may be limited. Given the importance which may be attached to the gradings of lessons and the effect they may have on the professional lives of particular teachers, it is not surprising that there are calls for the inspectors to be inspected and their methods checked. When inspectors attempt to put numbers on their judgements they quickly stray into the field which educational researchers consider their own. Increasingly the inspectors can expect their findings to be subjected to rigorous analysis. The traditional strength of HMI was to base every conclusion on the experienced observation of the connoisseur. The more OFSTED offers statistical analysis, the more attention will focus on the flimsy and subjective nature of much of the information they collect.

One of the tasks which fall to the HMIs at OFSTED is to monitor the work of the registered inspectors. Another is to follow up inspection reports which identify 'failing' schools and make their own assessment. The ultimate sanction in the case of a 'failing' county school is for the Secretary of State to send in a team of trouble-shooters with power to make such staff, and other, changes as may be needed to get a school back on the rails. Labour has adopted the idea, while changing the detail.

The role of the Senior Chief Inspector (SCI) has always been somewhat exposed—increasingly so in the last decade of the old regime, when the SCI and the Inspectorate found themselves being asked to pass professional judgements on matters which were politically sensitive, like the level of funding needed to maintain standards of provision. Running OFSTED was first entrusted to a distinguished academic, Professor Stuart Sutherland, who left to became Principal of the University of Edinburgh before the heat was turned up. His successor, Chris Woodhead, who moved across from the National Curriculum Council, proved tough and combative, taking up a controversial public role as candid critic of the schools. He did not hesitate to show his head above the parapet, not least when he drew media attention to the short-comings of the least competent teachers.

Former SCIs worked hard to avoid giving the appearance of being politically *parti-pris* for fear of compromising their professional independence; even so, they found themselves in the eye of the storm. OFSTED has from the outset been a much more political animal. It was created with the trappings of independence but its function is to implement the Secretary of State's policy. The nationalisation of the curriculum has made an independent Inspectorate at worst an unsustainable anachronism, at best an endangered species. It came as no surprise that under Woodhead the office of SCI was politicised; anyone in that position was on a hiding to nothing: if he or she told ministers what they wanted to hear, people would say the SCI had sold out; to challenge ministers' received wisdom, would put the job on the line. The moral will not be lost on future ministers; they may disguise their intentions but will certainly expect cooperation from anyone appointed to this sensitive post. Under Labour the Secretary of State intends to intervene directly on matters of school improvement, bringing his own academic experts into the Department to mastermind new programmes. How soon such in-house activities clash with those of OFSTED and the Teacher Training Agency remains to be seen.

Conclusion

There is a sense in which Labour's massive election victory in May 1997 completes the revolution—because in re-shaping Labour policy to make Labour electable, Tony Blair and his colleagues were forced to come to terms with the achievements of the Thatcher and Major Governments, not least in education, and to build on them rather than reverse them.

The structural changes, the centralisation of authority and strategy, the nationalisation of the curriculum, the enforcement of accountability—all these will remain and be used by Labour ministers to impose their vision. Labour will be no less interventionist but because they do not share the Conservatives' faith in the market, they will be less likely to antagonise the functionaries of the system.

Conservative reformers never lost their hostility to the educational establishment. Their hostility forced the educational establishment into opposition—when the Opposition became the Government the educational establishment heaved a collective sigh of relief and welcomed the chance to move from confrontation to cooperation. It was open to Labour to enlist the teachers, the local education authorities and the education officers and to re-invent the notion of partnership on which the success of the education service depends.

The time had come for a change of style—for an approach which assumes the education service is driven by goodwill and a sense of duty, not trendy idleness. The irony is that Labour can capitalise on the establishment's goodwill while making good use of the revolutionary changes introduced by the Conservatives—changes which, in their time, all the partners energetically opposed.

Notes

1 For a review of research on Germany, France, Japan, the USA and Britain, see Green, A. & Stedman, H. (1993) *Educational Provision, Educational Attainment, and the Needs of Industry* (National Institute for Economic and Social Research, London).

2 Barber, M. (1996) *The Learning Game* (Gollancz, London).
3 Lawler, S. (1990) *Teachers Mistaught* (Centre for Policy Studies, London).
4 (1985) *Better Schools*. White Paper from Department of Education and Science.
5 Graham, D. & Tytler; D. (1992) *A Lesson for Us All: the making of the National Curriculum* (Routledge, London).
6 (July 1987) *The National Curriculum 5–16*, A Discussion Document from the DES.
7 Baker, K. (1996) *Turbulent Years: my life in politics* (Faber, London).
8 The Audit Commission (1996) *Trading Places* (HMSO).

21 14–19 education: legacy, opportunities and challenges

Michael Young and Ken Spours

Source: '14–19 Education: legacy, opportunities and challenges, *Oxford Review of Education*, 24(1): 83–97, 1998.

This paper begins with an analysis of the changes in 14–19 education from the beginning of the 1980s until the last government's White Paper *14–19 Education: Learning to Compete*, which appeared in March 1997. It then considers the tensions in this legacy before exploring some of the issues that might be involved in realising the Labour Party's aims as set out, before the General Election, in their policy document *Aiming Higher*. Finally, the authors speculate, in light of developments since the Labour Party's victory on 2 May, on a possible scenario for the next decade and outline the kind of 14–19 system that we might be wanting to try to develop in the future.

Introduction

The middle of 1997 is a particularly appropriate time to assess public provision for 14–19 education in England and Wales. In March 1997 the Conservative Government published *Learning to Compete* (DFEE, 1997). It was the first ever White Paper on 14–19 education, as the foreword by the then Secretary of State, Gillian Shephard, proudly reminds us. Despite its claim to have at last recognised the strategic importance of seeing the 14–19 phase of education as a whole, the White Paper was disappointing; it had many of the characteristic features we came to expect from the previous government; it was unreflective, self-congratulatory and little more than a collection of past policies with little overall coherence. It remained firmly convinced that a framework for future progress for 14+ education was already in place, based on a combination of national regulation, local diversity and individual choice. It floated the idea of further marketisation of 14+ education and training through a voucher scheme and accepted, without question, the triple-track qualifications system set in place by the 1991 White Paper *Education and Training for the 21st Century*.

Little happened as a result of the White Paper and within three months there was a new Labour Government. Though 14–19 education was hardly mentioned in the general election campaign, the Labour Party has an official policy document, *Aiming Higher* (Labour Party, 1996a), which charts a very different direction for 14–19 education than that expressed in the March White Paper. While not eschewing choice or diversity, *Aiming Higher* argues that choices for individual students, as well as decisions taken by schools and colleges, must be seen within an overall framework and direction for the future. The direction proposed is towards a more unified system within which A Levels are broadened, vocational qualifications are upgraded and progression is enhanced for all students through a strengthened work-based route. Much debate and discussion will be needed to flesh out the details of the broad sweep of the proposals in *Aiming Higher*. This paper is a contribution to that debate. It begins by reflecting on the changes since the beginning of the 1980s that led up to the last government's White Paper. It then considers some of the tensions in this legacy before exploring some of the issues that might be involved in realising the aims of *Aiming Higher*. Finally, it speculates on a possible scenario for a decade ahead and the kind of 14–19 system that we might be wanting to try to develop.

14–19 education: the Conservative legacy

The legacy of Conservative policies on 14–19 education and training is a mixed one. Far more students participate in 14–19 education than did at the beginning of the 1980s, attainment levels at 16+ and 18+ are significantly higher in the 1990s than they were a decade ago, there are the elements of a national qualifications framework in place and we have a further education (FE) sector which has grown by a third since colleges were incorporated in 1993 with significantly lower costs than schools. Yet despite this progress a sense of crisis does not go away. Participation and attainment trends appear to have peaked and we are in real danger of not reaching the relatively modest National Education and Training Targets by the end of the century. Moreover, we do not appear to be closing the performance gap between us and other advanced industrial countries. We are a long way from a genuinely inclusive national 14–19 system of the kind found in the Nordic countries or in the German combination of gymnasia and a dual system of vocational education that includes all students up to 18 or 19. The English system at 16+ is still firmly focused on a minority of the cohort. The crisis is a reflection of the complex and contradictory character of the legacy of Conservative policies. This legacy can be examined in relation to three areas in which the present government will have to make policy decisions—participation and achievement, the national qualifications system and organisation and funding.

Raising participation and achievement

During the 1980s and early 1990s, the 14–19 education and training system moved from what can be termed a 'low-participation system' to a 'medium-participation system'. This expansion was largely unplanned; government policies were dominated by responding to rising youth unemployment and, later, to unexpected rises in full-time participation (Hodgson & Spours, 1997). By the mid-1990s, however, both participation and attainment trends were showing signs of flattening out (Spours, 1996). Only 70% of 16-year-olds now stay on in full-time education and this declines to 40% for 18-year-olds. Drop-out begins pre-16 and a significant minority of 16–19 year olds do not participate in any form of education and training or do so only for very short periods.

This halt to the steady increases in 14–19 participation and attainment of the ten years up until the mid-1990s poses severe challenges for the new government. We identify three of these challenges; one is concerned with inclusion, one with expectations and one with finance. The issue of inclusion refers to the situation of the young unemployed, the disaffected and those who have turned their backs on the education and training system. It is this group of young people, which stretches well beyond the 14–19 age group, to which the 'Welfare to Work' proposals financed by the proceeds of the 'Windfall Tax' on the privatised utilities are directed. It is a challenge of entirely different proportions to the problems of youth unemployment in the early 1980s. It involves reaching out to engage these young people in developing their learning capacities and not just 'warehousing' them for a couple of years as was the outcome of so many YTS and YT schemes.

The second challenge is less visible but no less important. It is to raise the expectations and therefore the levels of attainment of the 50% of 'average' students in the two middle quartiles of the ability range. Arguably, the key must involve a triple strategy that shifts the balance of priorities of the national qualifications system from a predominant focus on selection to a focus on progression. It also means creating incentives that encourage schools and colleges to maximise their capacities to support student learning (Hodgson, 1997). Thirdly, and crucially, there is a need to develop new pedagogic strategies that strengthen the learning capacities of individual students (Guile & Young, 1998).

The third challenge is financial. The expansion of participation in the late 1980s and early 1990s took place when other factors were leading to a reduction in the costs per student. The demographic down-turn and the declining size of the national cohorts of 14–19 year-olds meant that, for the years 1987–1994, increased participation often involved filling empty places in schools and colleges. Expansion could therefore take place without *pro rata* increases in capital or current expenditure. Also, during this period, increases in participation tended to be short-term (one to two years). Finally, increased numbers in schools and, particularly, in colleges were accompanied by a sharp reduction in course hours as part of a drive for greater efficiency. A decade later, many of the most efficient institutions are running at full-capacity and cannot expand further without new investment (Lavelle, 1997).

The new government is faced with a dilemma. It cannot now rely on the factors which allowed increased participation at reduced cost as in previous years. At the same time, it wants to increase participation amongst those sections of the cohort that are 'harder to get' and, therefore, who are more expensive. The new government wants students to stay on longer in order to achieve more and it aspires to increase study hours in order to broaden the curriculum. None of these goals can be achieved on existing resource allocations and taken together they point to the need for significant increases in investment in post-compulsory education in future years.

Restructuring the national qualifications framework

The existing qualifications arrangements were set in place by the 1991 White Paper *Education and Training for the 21st Century*. It established a formal tracked system based on distinctions between the academic track (A levels), the broad vocational track (GNVQs) and the occupationally-specific track (NVQs). Following the 1991 White Paper, there were some attempts to align A levels and GNVQs into levels and units to encourage mixed study programmes. However, the different tracks embody quite different and largely incompatible assessment and learning methodologies. One of the results of these incompatibilities is that only 15% of the early cohorts of GNVQ advanced students took an A level (IOE *et al.*, 1994) and even fewer students on A-level programmes took GNVQ units.

By the mid-1990s, it was becoming apparent that the triple-track system established by the White Paper had not overcome the problems of low performance that it had been designed to tackle. Nearly a third of those taking A Levels were failing to complete their studies successfully and this rose to nearly 50% in the case of GNVQs (Spours, 1995). The up-take of NVQs continued to remain very low (Robinson, 1996) and NVQs were frequently accused of narrowness (*Financial Times*, 1996). It was the accumulation of such problems that persuaded the Conservative Government, in 1995, to set up the Dearing Review of 16–19 qualifications. At the same time, and under pressure from employers as well as the government, NCVQ initiated the Capey Review (1995) of GNVQ assessment and the Beaumont Review (1995) of the 100 most popular NVQs and SVQs. These reviews can best be seen as attempts to retain the triple-track system at the same time as making it more effective. The Modern Apprenticeship Scheme can also be seen, alongside the reviews, as a measure to upgrade the work-based route and disassociate it from the poor image and low qualifications outcomes that characterised Youth Training (Unwin, 1997).

The immediate challenge facing the new government is to identify the positive proposals made in the three qualification reviews. All were compelled to consider measures to combat the narrowness, excessive bureaucracy and rigidity of the triple-track system. At the same time, they were heavily constrained by Conservative dogmatism. This consisted of preserving A levels unchanged, maintaining a dominant role for external assessment regardless of what it actually achieved, treating modularisation as a threat to standards, despite all the research and evaluation to the contrary, and a continuing belief in voluntarism, market forces and the efficacy of narrow forms of occupational competence.

The challenge for any genuine reform of the qualifications system, however, is far more complex than discarding a series of outdated dogmas. Broadening A levels is a fine slogan which has a 40-year history. However, in that period they have shown themselves remarkably resistant to actual change (Young, 1997a). Similarly, the period since the early 1980s is littered with attempts to establish a credible system of vocational qualifications of which the outcomes-led approach adopted by NCVQ is only the latest. None of these attempts has shown signs of offering routes to genuine vocational specialisation of the kind found in many countries in continental Europe. Furthermore, the design of qualifications, though important, is far from the only issue. Whatever the flaws of existing qualifications, there are institutional interests associated with preserving all of them. In some cases this is simple 'innovation fatigue' (Spours, 1996). In others cases it is either schools which have benefited most from unreformed A levels, employers who accept the narrow and low-level competence-based NVQs or teachers who have invested time and effort to develop GNVQs and who are suspicious of further change.

Organisation and funding regimes

A major legacy of the Conservative years is a marketisation strategy linked to untried and, as it has turned out, crude funding mechanisms. The FE sector, in particular, has been subjected to a far-reaching experiment in funding methodologies and marketisation (Spours & Lucas, 1996).[1] Measured in terms of 'average levels of funding', the sector is more efficient than it was four years ago with far less difference between levels of efficiency of the 460 colleges and with more students being taught for the same amount of money. On the other hand, it is estimated that about 20% of colleges are in financial difficulties, staff morale is low, student retention rates are often poor and course hours have been reduced to a point at which quality and attainment is difficult to sustain. The funding and organisational legacy which is the outcome of marketisation policies is fraught with tensions. There are questions of stability arising from the encouragement of, and then halting of, demand-led funding in the FE sector. Furthermore, marketisation and competition has encouraged new divisions—between colleges and schools, between high-cost and low-cost colleges and between educational institutions and TECs. Not only is new funding needed, but also a more common funding system, designed to encourage, through local partnerships, a more co-operative climate between the institutions. Most promising are the proposals from the Kennedy Committee on participation which was set up by the FEFC. Initially it appeared that the Kennedy Commission would suggest shifting funds, which currently support university students who are, by and large, from relatively well off families, towards the much more disadvantaged students found in further education colleges. However, the final report limited its recommendations to a more general plea for more funding for FE (FEFC, 1997).

Responding to the Conservative legacy, on each of the issues considered, will be far from straightforward. It will involve decisions on at least two fundamental questions. The first is the nature of a long-term approach to the future of 14–19 education, the continuing relevance of such Labour Party documents as *Aiming Higher* (Labour Party, 1996a) and *Life-Long Learning* (Labour Party, 1996b) and the strategies that might be involved in planning a ten-year period of government or two terms of office. The second question concerns which of the elements of the Conservative legacy can be taken forward and built on in the process of addressing the underlying weaknesses of our present 14–19 system. These questions require an understanding both of where the system has come from and the direction in which the new government is aiming. The next section of the paper provides a framework for understanding the Conservative legacy by setting current tensions in different periods of change over the last 20 years.

Stages of development of a national 14–19 system

In making sense of the legacy of 18 years of Tory education policies and the many dramatic and both quantitative and qualitative changes in that time, it is useful to see the period as a series of phases beginning with the election of the Conservative Government in 1979. Elsewhere we have suggested that in the period from 1979 to 1997, developments in government policy on 14–19 education can be divided into four distinct, but related, phases (Spours & Young, 1996a; Howieson *et al.*, 1997). The four phases are:

Phase 1 (1979–1986). Adhoc expansion and incremental prevocational and academic developments.
Period 2 (1987–1991). Establishing a national framework for vocational qualifications (NVQs).
Period 3 (1991–1995). Establishing a national triple-track framework for all qualifications.

Period 4 (1996–). Reviewing the national framework and developing 'linkages' between the tracks.

A number of words of caution are in order in relation to this periodisation. First, it is based solely on qualification policies, when many of the factors effecting the delivery of 14–19 education and training (such as funding and the role of LEAs), are not concerned with qualifications as such. We justify our focus in the case of England, because of the extent to which 14–19 policy has been qualification-led. Secondly, there is significant overlap from one period to another; a point dealt with later in this section. Thirdly, the periodisation is primarily internal, in that it focuses on changes in the education and training system, not the wider social and political system within which educational changes take place. Nevertheless, the periodisation serves a useful analytical purpose in highlighting both the historical development in the 14+ national qualifications framework as well as barriers and resistances to change. Any future-oriented policy for 14–19 reform that does not take account of the past as well as the extent to which different issues and different barriers become significant in different times is, as has so often been said in relation to broader policy issues, doomed to repeat past mistakes.

However, in order to link the discussion of periodisation of 14–19 education policy both to the conservative legacy and possible policy alternatives for the new government, it is necessary to shift the analysis from 'end-on periods' to 'overlapping lines of development'. The first line of development was the expansion in post-16 (and therefore 14–19) provision that took place through a range of *ad hoc* national and local innovations from 1979 to 1991. The second line of development, to establish a national system of qualifications, began with the Review of Vocational Qualifications in 1986 and continued throughout the life of the previous government. The third line can be broadly characterised as the attempt to create a unified 14–19 system which, arguably, began in 1990 with the publication of *A British Baccalaureate* (Finegold *et al.*, 1990).

An era of ad hoc innovation (1979–1991)

The period 1981–1991 constituted a decade of what has been termed the 'New Vocationalism' (Dale 1985). The early 1980s, beginning with the New Training Initiative (MSC, 1981), reflected a systematic attempt to shift 14–19 education towards more explicit economic priorities through an increasing role (via the Youth Training Scheme and the Technical and Vocational Education Initiative) for the MSC and the Employment Department. It was also a period preoccupied with the effects of rising youth unemployment and the need to provide post-16 qualifications for low-achievers which culminated in the innovative, if problematic, Certificate of Pre-Vocational Education (CPVE). A further development of the 'new vocationalism', though still based on supporting local innovation, was the extension of TVEI from 14–16 year-olds to those over 16. TVEI Extension represented the first educational initiative that covered the whole 14–19 age range. During the same period, GCSE was launched and later identified as a key factor in stimulating, in the late 1980s, higher staying-on at 16 (Gray *et al.*, 1993). By the end of the decade, modular syllabuses, internal assessment strategies and a growing number of locally-inspired experiments in institutional collaboration and bridging the academic and vocational divide at 16+ were developed. A decade which had started with widespread criticism of forced government-led vocational initiatives (Holt, 1987) ended with a stronger sense of the potential of innovation at local level. A dominant professional experience of the period was of a variety of forms of local innovation based on different, and sometimes competing, concepts of vocationalism and lacking any clear sense of the role of 14–19 education as a whole.

It is clear, in retrospect, that by the end of the 1980s the Conservative Government of the time was faced with three choices. The first was to allow the locally-inspired innovations to continue. In earlier periods of English educational history this would have been the likely response. However, the political context at the end of the 1980s was new. We had an aggressively directive government that believed in the 'political' role of education and was not prepared to 'allow things to muddle on'. From the perspective of such a government, diversification was perceived as a threat to standards and the primary selective role of upper secondary education. The experience of local innovation and development, which had been given such a boost by TVEI, needed to be given a national coherence and direction which it had lacked. A second more strategic choice could have built on successful local innovations and given them a direction. Such an option was articulated through a series of publications including the IPPR's *A British Baccalaureate* (Finegold *et al.*, 1990), the Royal Society's *Beyond GCSE* (1991) and culminated in the National Commission on Education's proposals in *Learning to Succeed* (1993). These enjoyed considerable support from professional opinion and even business, albeit in a somewhat guarded fashion, but the Conservative Government of the time had another agenda and opted for a third approach. It chose to curb the innovations by restricting internal assessment in A levels, controlling modularisation and by developing a competence-based GNVQ to challenge and replace traditional vocational qualifications such as the BTEC National Diploma. The 1991 White Paper which enshrined a three-track system, and sought to raise standards by encouraging institutions to compete, also symbolised the end of an era of *ad hoc* innovation. From now on qualifications, though locally delivered, were to be nationally designed.

establishing a National Qualifications Framework (1986–)

Unlike the period of support for *ad hoc* local innovation discussed in the previous section, the line of development associated with creating a National Qualifications Framework in England is far from ended. It has, up to now, fallen into three phases—the 'NVQ phase' which began with the setting up of the Review of National Qualifications in 1986; the 'triple-track phase', initiated by the 1991 White Paper's attempt to establish a three-track framework inclusive of all qualifications; and what might be called a 'flexible framework phase' which grew out of the Dearing Report (1996) as an attempt to overcome the rigidities of the three tracks. In the first phase, establishing a national framework for vocational qualifications did not exercise a widespread effect because NVQs did not grow rapidly and only constituted a small part of the overall education and training system. Not only did academic qualifications remain outside the framework but, despite the hopes expressed in the Review of Vocational Qualifications, there was no attempt until after 1991 to incorporate other vocational qualifications within the NVQ framework. However, the NVQ framework had three features which have shaped and are likely to continue to shape the future development of 14–19 qualifications. Two features were negative: its voluntary nature and its narrow definition of learning outcomes. The system of qualifications levels, on the other hand, was a positive development because levels offered the opportunity to align different types of qualifications within the system. Bringing different qualifications into close proximity for comparison has accentuated issues of parity of esteem between academic and vocational awards. The system of levels also creates further pressure to bring more qualifications into the National Framework. Both of these factors increase pressures for system inclusion and coherence.

It is inconceivable, however, that a truly coherent national qualification framework will emerge if the negative aspects of the NVQ framework are not, at the same time, addressed. The voluntarism of current arrangements whereby Awarding Bodies, Industrial Training Organisations or Industrial Lead Bodies have been allowed to offer qualifications outside the framework with no agreed rules guiding employer recruitment practices except the exigencies of the labour market, will have to be tackled. It will be interesting to see whether the newly-formed Qualifications and Curriculum Authority (QCA) will move towards a more expansive regulatory position.

A number of problems have also emerged as a consequence of the NVQ definition of learning outcomes. For example, instead of being a framework for kite-marking qualifications, as the RVQ intended, NVQs have, in effect, become a niche market qualification with little relevance for 14–19 education and training or many sectors of commerce and industry. This has meant that vocational qualifications that pre-date NVQs have continued, the number of qualifications has proliferated and a potentially progressive development such as Modern Apprenticeships has been forced into offering a far from coherent combination of old and new qualifications. Secondly, the NVQ competence model has been the basis for developing GNVQs on the assumption that this would facilitate links between the two. In effect, the rigidities of the GNVQ design have made combinations of vocational and general education difficult, and created the need for more bridges across the general/work-based vocational qualification divide.

The second phase of establishing a National Qualifications Framework followed the 1991 White Paper. It had widespread effects, not only upon qualifications, but also upon further education and institutional competition between schools and colleges. However, by 1994, the steady increases in both participation and attainment began to slow and the reality of 14–19 provision, which was a culmination of the variety of piecemeal changes of the previous 15 years, proved too complex to fit into a rigid three-track framework. National Targets, developed initially by the Confederation for British Industry and then adopted by government, pulled in the opposite direction to attempts to make A levels more rigorous; the Department for Education and the Employment Department pulled in opposite directions over GNVQs and the compromise over modular A levels was overwhelmed by the demand from the schools and colleges for modular syllabuses (Young, 1997a). GNVQs were meant to replace older vocational qualifications such as BTEC National but many colleges continued to offer the latter. In the field of work-based qualifications, NVQs only really took off in government training schemes and in low-skill areas, and colleges increasingly offered programmes to adults based on accreditation through the Open College Network. As a result of these contradictions, the proliferation of qualifications continued and, by the mid-1990s, over 50% of qualifications offered by FE colleges lay outside the formal triple-track framework (FEFC, 1997). By 1995 it was becoming clear, even to the previous government, that the 1991 White Paper had created as many problems as it had solved.

Dearing's review of *Qualifications for 16–19 Year Olds* (1996) can be seen as the beginning of a response to the rigidities of the triple-track framework. This we refer to as the 'flexible framework phase'. It was an attempt to consolidate the tracked system while at the same time making it more flexible (Spours & Young 1996b; Young 1997b). The Review sought to offer something to everyone. A levels were to be made more difficult but a new one-year AS would offer an exit point for those who could not achieve them. Core (now Key) Skills would be encouraged by way of voluntary 'National Certificates' and an 'Advanced Diploma' which would encourage breadth. GNVQs would be made more rigorous with an increase in the proportion of external assessment and more mixing of academic and vocational study would be encouraged by aligning A, AS levels and Advanced GNVQs into blocks of six and three units. As the implementation strategy for the Dearing recommendations began to emerge, the unworkable nature of many of the proposals became increasingly apparent. Renaming GNVQs, a new AS in core skills, and the National Certificates all disappeared and even the new Advanced Diploma, at least in the form proposed by Dearing, looked an unlikely starter. The whole review process, constrained from the start by extremely narrow terms of reference (Young, 1997b), looked more and more like window dressing for a policy of no change. By mid-1997, what was left of the Dearing reform process was the rationalisation of A level syllabus cores, further restriction on modular A levels, the development of 'families' of qualifications, voluntary key skill units, more external assessment in GNVQs and some further alignment of GNVQ and A level structures. What many hoped would be an expansive review process was reduced, in the implementation phase, to the logic of the 1991 White Paper with an emphasis on track-based qualifications with limited forms of 'linkage'.

Creating a coherent and unified 14–19 system (1990–)

The period of unification, at least in England, originated in 1990 with the publication of *A British Baccalaureate* (Finegold *et al.*, 1990). Unlike in Scotland, where a unifying strategy is represented by a White Paper *Higher Still* (Scottish Office, 1994) and will be implemented from 1998 or 1999, unification in England has been essentially a legacy of opposition, reflected in the debates and policy documents of think-tanks and professional organisations often explicitly in opposition to Conservative Government policy. Ideas for unifying academic and vocational learning only influenced the previous government insofar as it sought to incorporate them, in voluntary and truncated forms, in proposals, later dropped, for an overarching Advanced Diploma and National Certificates in the 1991 White Paper and later, in the Dearing Report.

To understand this particular legacy, it is important to see unification, not as a monolithic idea but as an emerging set of debates and strategies (Howieson *et al.*, 1997). In England during the early 1990s two related types of ideas on unification have emerged. The first was based on a 'baccalaureate' concept which evolved around the idea of an advanced diploma to replace A levels and existing vocational qualifications (Finegold *et al.*, 1990; Royal Society, 1991; NCE, 1993). The second was a looser framework based on unitisation and credit which could contain existing qualifications without changing them and which would retain sufficient flexibility to be applicable to adults (APVIC, 1991; FEU, 1992; AfC *et al.*, 1994). The baccalaureate concept prioritised breadth of learning and focused primarily on provision for 14–19 year-olds while the 'framework' approach emphasised curriculum flexibility and stressed the importance of being inclusive of all learners. Within the professional education community it can be observed that the baccalaureate approach tends to be favoured more by those representing schools and those largely concerned with A levels whereas the framework approach tends to be supported by those associated with further education.

In 1995, the *Learning for the Future Initial Report* (Richardson *et al.*, 1995) suggested that these two tendencies could be reconciled into a single strategy by a phased approach to unification. The authors argued that a first phase of 14–19 reform could focus on flexibility through developing modular syllabuses and a shift in the balance between internal and external assessment. A later stage could build on this greater flexibility and concentrate on broadening the 14–19 curriculum (Spours & Young, 1995). The Labour Party's policy document, *Aiming Higher*, though lacking essential detail, reflects such a phased strategy for reforming the 14–19 curriculum and the possibilities of synthesising the baccalaureate and framework approaches.

As we suggested at the beginning of this paper, 1997 is undoubtedly another watershed for 14–19 policy. We have a complex legacy of reforms which are the result of a combination of dogma and pragmatism. On the other hand, there are relatively undeveloped alternative possibilities forged in opposition. In the final section of this paper, therefore, we identify some of the challenges that this situation presents to the Labour government and chart a possible direction that could lead to a coherent, high quality and inclusive system of 14–19 education and training. As we suggested earlier, two broad issues need to be addressed. The first is the kind of vision of a future 14–19 provision that we are aiming for, and the second is a reform strategy that might build on the legacy we have analysed.

14–19 education: a vision and a strategy for the next decade

An article like this which is written in the aftermath of the 1997 General Election, but before the new government has made any public statement on 14–19 education, can only consider principles underlying a possible vision. However, the principles of a future system are important as they alone can provide the aims and direction to shape any short-term measures that may be introduced, and prevent these being, as so often in the past 20 years, merely reactive responses. Such a vision of 14–19 education will need to be one of rising and enhanced standards attainable in diverse and flexible ways. It will need to take into account the new demands for skill and knowledge that young people are likely to face in the 21st century and balance economic and technical demands with a far greater stress on moral, civic and spiritual values. Above all, it will need an awareness that the most important outcome of a young person's experience of 14–19 education will be a willingness and capacity to continue learning. The vision will need to be for a system that is inclusive of all young people, holds together their different needs and does not let these differences become a basis for new divisions. It will need to continue to take into account the

20% 'high fliers' who aim at 16 to gain entry to one of the top 20 or 30 universities in two years time; the next 30% 'hard workers' who can reach A level before they leave school or college but who may need three years of post-compulsory education to do so; the slow learners who are unlikely to reach A level by the age of 19 but can see it and beyond as goals during their working life, and those with special learning needs to feel that they can make progress in a meaningful way and are not shuttled into some *cul de sac* at 14 or 16 that takes them nowhere.

The underlying principles of a 14–19 system of the future must be that it is flexible in how it encourages participation, attainment and breadth of study and that it is connective between all learners and types of learning (Guile & Young, 1997). These principles have implications for qualifications, the curriculum, funding and organisation and can only be hinted at here. At the centre of 14–19 provision that might be fully in place a decade from now must be an Advanced Level Diploma which might be taken by some at 18 but which should be achieved by 70–80% by the age of 19 or later. It is likely by then that there will be some overlap with higher education and some young people will have begun degree level studies during the 14–19 phase of their education. GCSE, as a left-over from a time when the majority finished full time education at 16, would be phased out and students would progress at different rates between Foundation, Intermediate and Advanced levels of the Diploma. The Diploma could have a number of variants designed to suit the range of full-time 14–19 students, as well as providing a ladder for those on the work-based route and Modern Apprenticeships; it could also be a framework for credit transfer and APL possibilities for adults to build on their experience and their attainment level at 18. For such a vision to be realised, the new government will have to make strategic decisions, not only about qualifications and funding, but about how to involve institutions in local collaborative networks and feel a real involvement in the reform process. Decisions about the reform of TECs to establish a more proactive role for employers will also be needed as well as assurance that any reform of qualifications for 14–19 year-olds articulates with the needs of older learners and supports the increasingly important priority of promoting life-long learning.

Schools and colleges are looking for leadership in a context where they are having to plan an A-level curriculum, decide which AS exams to offer, whether to offer GNVQ Part Ones at 14+, and, at 16+, which GNVQs to offer and at what level. They are also looking at ways of broadening the post-16 curriculum but without the essential signposts of a national policy and confronting a number of areas of uncertainty in their curriculum decision-making (Spours, 1996). They do not know what aspects of the Dearing Review will be implemented, they are unsure of the implications of Labour's vision in *Aiming Higher* and they are often uncertain as to whether they will have the staff to deliver the courses and students to take them up. It is little wonder that the idea of a year's pause in the Dearing of any reform process has been greeted with almost universal approval. The future success of any reform strategy will be decided not only by the quality and coherence of the design of the qualifications but by the ability of institutions to relate to the reform process. At present, schools and colleges are under acute funding pressures and teachers have experienced 'innovation overload'. There is a real danger that the genuine reform programme that might emerge from *Aiming Higher* could be blocked by institutional 'conservatism' rooted in day-to-day problems rather than any intellectual opposition to the reform ideas themselves. Based on our consultations with practitioners (Spours, 1996), there is only space here to indicate how such 'conservatism' might be overcome or at least minimised. There is considerable professional agreement with the broad principles espoused in *Aiming Higher*. We think this broad sympathy could be transformed into practical support, if a reform strategy was based on the following broad principles:

- a one-year pause in implementing 14–19 changes,
- continuing post-Dearing SCAA development work with the accent on dissemination to and dialogue with schools and colleges,
- a ten-year vision of improvement, based on broadening A levels and up-grading vocational qualifications within an increasingly unified framework,
- a recognition of the interdependence of qualifications, funding and developing institutional capacity in any successful reform,
- strengthening the work-based route to increase participation and achievement and facilitate movement between full and part-time study,
- finding ways of involving HE more directly in 14–19 reforms especially in the development of alternative routes at advanced level,
- developing ways of linking 14–19 provision to lifelong learning,
- a regional policy that encourages new forms of collaboration between schools and colleges and with employers.

Since we first wrote this paper, the government has announced plans for a 'pause' in implementing the Dearing recommendations. So far they have adopted a more cautious and less visionary approach than we have advocated, perhaps leaving more radical reforms to a hoped for second term of office. However, without a longer term vision and without a conscious attempt to establish the building blocks for a more unified system in the future, a second Labour government is likely to face much the same legacy as the present one and could fail to provide the leadership that practitioners so badly need. We must hope that when the terms of the consultation are announced that scope will be left not only for a practical debate with practitioners as to what is possible, but for a wider debate about what kind of 14+ system might be needed in the future.

Conclusion

This paper has reviewed the legacy of the past government's policies for 14–19 education as a complex mixture of rigidity and dogma, confusion and pragmatism and genuine possibilities for the future. It has suggested that a reform strategy that goes beyond the dogmas and builds on the possibilities needs to have four fundamental components, all of which are vital if schools, colleges and workplaces, where the actual learning takes place, are to play the part that they need to. The first component is a vision, which in a period dominated by choice and markets, has been sadly missing. Leaving curriculum decisions entirely to individual institutions, when they do not have the basis for knowing the full implications of the decisions that they make, is not the answer. They are looking for leadership in what is still the new area of an all-through 14–19 curriculum. We have indicated some of the principles that should underlie such a vision. The second component of a strategy is the implementation process itself. We have outlined what might be involved in taking account of both the legacy of previous policies and the situation in which schools and colleges find themselves. The third component is a phased strategy, lasting initially for a ten-year period, in which the 14–19 system develops an evolutionary capability and which is the most likely to secure a lasting consensus. The final component is financial. An expanded system, both in terms of participation and curriculum, will require significant additional resourcing—if not immediately, certainly within five years. These components of an overall strategy for 14–19 education constitute just the beginning of a long-haul process to create a more inclusive and coherent National Qualifications Framework.

Acknowledgements

The research on which this article is based is part of the ongoing work of the Unified Learning Project funded by the ESRC (L123251039) as part of the Learning Society Programme. The Unified Learning Project is a two-year project which ends in April 1998. The aim of the project is to contribute to the debate about the need to unify academic and vocational learning which was begun in the UK with the publication of *A British Baccalaureate* (Finegold *et al.*, 1990) by comparing recent policy developments in Scotland and England and Wales. The Unified Learning Project is a joint project of the Centre for Educational Sociology, University of Edinburgh and the Post-16 Education Centre, Institute of Education, University of London.

Note

1 By marketisation we mean the way that government policy has forced colleges to compete for students with each other and, in many cases, with schools. This has

meant that the short term need to maintain student numbers has increasingly come to shape the curriculum offered by colleges. One result, as indicated in the National Survey of GNVQs (Institute of Education *et al.*, 1994), has been the expansion of courses in Business Administration, Leisure and Tourism, Health and Social Care and Art and Design, and the very small numbers in technical and scientific fields.

References

Association for Colleges. The Girls' School Association, The Headmasters' Conference, The Secondary Heads Association, The Sixth Form Colleges' Association, The Society for Headmasters and Headmistresses in Independent Schools (1994) *Post-Compulsory Education and Training: a joint statement* (London, AfC).

Association of Principals of Sixth Form Colleges (1991) *A Framework for Growth: improving the post-16 curriculum* (Wigan, APVIC).

Beaumont, G. (1995) *Review of 100 NVQs and SVQs* (London, DfEE).

Capey, J. (1995) *GNVQ Assessment Review, National Council for Vocational Qualifications* (London, NCVQ).

Dale, R. (ed.) (1985) *Education, Training and Employment: towards a new vocationalism?* (Oxford, Pergamon).

Dearing, R. (1996) *Review of Qualifications for 16–19 Year Olds* (London, Schools Curriculum Assessment Authority).

Department for Education and Employment (1997) *Learning to Compete: education and training for 14–19 year olds* (London, HMSO).

Department for Education/Department for Employment/Welsh Office (1991) *Education and Training for the 21st Century* (London, HMSO).

FEFC (1997) *Student Numbers at Colleges in the Further Education Sector and External Institutions in England on 1 November 1996* (Coventry, FEFC).

Financial Times (1996) 'Vocational Training Needs Serious Evaluation: a letter from 14 experts,' *Financial Times*, 17 January.

Finegold, D., Keep, E., Miliband, D., Raffe, D., Spours, K. & Young, M. (1990) *A British Baccalaureate: overcoming divisions between education and training* (London, Institute for Public Policy Research).

Further Education Unit (1992) *A Basis for Credit? Developing a Post-16 Credit Accumulation and Transfer Framework: a paper for discussion* (London, FEU).

Gray, J., Jesson, D. & Tranmer, M. (1993) *Boosting Post-16 Participation in Full-Time Education: a study of some key factors in England and Wales, Youth Cohort Study No. 20* (London, Employment Department).

Guile, D. & Young, M. (1998 forthcoming) The question of learning and learning organisations. In: M. Kelleher (ed.) *Understanding Organisations* (Dublin, Oak Tree Press).

Hodgson, A. (1997) Building institutional capacity for national education reform: the case of the formative value-added system. In: A. Hodgson & K. Spours (eds) *Dearing and Beyond: 14–19 qualifications, frameworks and systems* (London, Kogan Page).

Hodgson, A. & Spours, K. (1997) From the 1991 White Paper to the Dearing Report: a conceptual and historical framework for the 1990s. In: A. Hodgson & K. Spours (eds) *Dearing and Beyond: 14–19 qualifications, framework and systems* (London, Kogan Page).

Holt, M. (1987) (ed.) *Skills and Vocationalism: the easy answer* (Milton Keynes, OUP).

Howieson, C., Raffe, D., Spours, K. & Young, M. (1997) 'Unifying academic and vocational learning: the state of the debate in England and Scotland,' *Journal of Education and Work*, 10, 1, pp. 5–35.

Institute of Education, Further Education Unit & Nuffield Foundation (1994) *GNVQs 1993–94: a national survey report; an interim report of a joint project 'The Evolution of GNVQs: enrolment and delivery patterns and their policy implications'* (London, FEU).

Kennedy, H. (1997) *Learning Works: widening participation in further education* (Coventry, FEFC).

Labour Party (1996a) *Aiming Higher: Labour's proposals for the reform of the 14–19 curriculum* (London, Labour Party).

Labour Party (1996b) *Lifelong Learning* (London, Labour Party).

Lavelle, D. (1997) *The Cost Implications of Dearing at Level 3: a case study of Winstanley College* (Wigan, Winstanley College).

Manpower Services Commission (1981) *A New Training Initiative—An Agenda for Action* (London, Manpower Services Commission).

National Commission on Education (1993) *Learning to Succeed: a radical look at education today and a strategy for the future*, Report of the Paul Hamlyn Foundation National Commission on Education (London, Heinemann).

Richardson, W., Spours, K., Woolhouse, J. & Young, M. (1995) *Learning for The Future, Initial Report* (Post-16 Education Centre, Institute of Education, University of London/Centre for Education and Industry, University of Warwick).

Robinson, P. (1996) *Rhetoric and Reality: Britain's new vocational qualifications* (London, London School of Economics Centre for Economic Performance).

Royal Society (1991) *Beyond GCSE: a report by a working group of the Royal Society's education committee* (London, The Royal Society).

Scottish Office (1994) *Higher Still: opportunity for all* (London, HMSO).

Spours, K. (1995) *Post-Compulsory Education & Training: statistical trends* (Working Paper No 7, Learning for the Future Project, Post-16 Education Centre, Institute of Education, University of London/Centre for Education and Industry, University of Warwick).

Spours, K. (1996) *Institutional Responses to Dearing and Aiming Higher* (Post-16 Education Centre and Essex Advisory and Inspection Service, Post-16 Education Centre, Institute of Education, University of London).

Spours, K. & Lucas, N. (1996) *The Formation of a National Sector of Incorporated Colleges: beyond the FEFC model* (Post-16 Education Centre Working Paper No 19, Institute of Education, University of London).

Spours, K. & Young, M. (1995) *Post-Compulsory Curriculum and Qualifications: options for change* (Learning for the Future Working Paper 6, Post-16 Education Centre, Institute of Education, University of London/Centre for Education and Industry, University of Warwick).

Spours, K. & Young, M. (1996a) Academic and vocational learning: division, framework or unified system. In: J. Lasonen (ed.) *Surveys of Strategies for Post-16 Education to Improve Parity of Esteem for Initial Vocational Education in Eight European Countries*, Interim Report of the Leonardo Project Strand III 2.a (Finland, University of Jyväskylä).

Spours, K. & Young, M. (1996b) 'Dearing and beyond: steps and stages to a unified system,' *British Journal of Education and Work*, 9, 3, pp. 5–18.

Unwin, L. (1997) Reforming the work-based route: problems and potential for change. In: A. Hodgson & K. Spours (eds) *Dearing and Beyond: 14–19 qualifications, frameworks and systems* (London, Kogan Page).

Young, M. (1997a) From A levels to an advanced level curriculum of the future. In: A. Hodgson & K. Spours (eds) *Dearing and Beyond: 14–19 qualifications, frameworks and systems* (London, Kogan Page).

Young, M. (1997b) The Dearing Review of 16–19 qualifications: a step towards a unified system? In: A. Hodgson & K. Spours (eds) *Dearing and Beyond: 14–19 qualifications, frameworks and systems* (London, Kogan Page).

Part IV

1997–2005 Labour Government, change and continuity

22 From City Technology Colleges to sponsored grant-maintained schools

Geoffrey Walford

Source: 'From City Technology Colleges to sponsored grant-maintained schools', *Oxford Review of Education*, 26(2): 145–158, 2000.

During the 18 years of Conservative government in Britain, only two attempts were made to stimulate the 'supply side' of the quasi-market of schools. These were the introduction of City Technology Colleges and sponsored grant-maintained schools. This paper draws comparisons between the two initiatives. It is shown that, while the CTCs were largely a 'top down' policy, and the sponsored grant-maintained schools might be seen as the result of 'grass roots' pressure group activity, there were many similarities between the two programmes.

In practice, both initiatives stalled at just 15 schools, but it is argued that their significance is far greater than their numerical strength would indicate. Both can be seen as examples of increased privatisation and selection, and it is shown that what may develop from them is a greatly changed education system.

Quasi-markets and the supply of schools

Within England and Wales the 1988 Education Reform Act has come to be seen as the crucial legislation that introduced elements of the market into state-maintained schooling. That Act significantly restructured state-maintained schooling by creating more devolved management structures for schools, giving them greater autonomy, allowing families the right to express a preference for any state-maintained school they wish to use, and funding schools largely according to the number of students each attracts. Together, such changes made the state-maintained schooling system more like that of the private sector. A 'quasi-market' was encouraged, where a greater emphasis was given to market forces and private decision-making (Le Grand & Bartlett, 1993). It was a 'quasi-market' rather than a free-market, because the state retained many powers over schools and gave itself several new ones.

Such developments have been common within the education systems of industrialised countries around the world (Walford, 1996; Whitty *et al.*, 1998). During the 1980s and 1990s, many countries introduced schemes that were supposedly designed to increase choice of school and to enhance the efficiency and effectiveness of state-maintained schooling through school-based management. However, in common with the schemes introduced in other countries, the 1988 Education Reform Act did nothing to encourage the supply-side of that market. The Act provided no new ways by which interested charitable or religious bodies could establish new state-maintained schools.

That this is true is not immediately obvious, for the 1988 Act included legislation on grant-maintained schools and City Technology Colleges. Both of these would appear to be supply-side developments, but the reality is different. While the concept of grant-maintained schools was certainly new, the reality was that existing local education authority schools were simply removed from the control of their Local Education Authorities (LEAs) and became funded by central government (eventually through the Funding Agency for Schools) instead. Much research has shown that grant-maintained schools generally offered little that was distinctive and rarely went beyond cosmetic changes such as smarter uniforms for students (Fitz *et al.*, 1993; Power *et al.*, 1994; Halpin *et al.*, 1997). Local management of schools (LMS) within the LEA sector has meant that the grant-maintained schools differed only slightly from LEA schools in their degree of autonomy and hardly at all in the day-to-day experiences of staff or students.

On the other hand the City Technology Colleges were certainly an attempt to increase the supply side of schooling. They were designed to be a significant new way of sponsoring and funding schools. But, as will be discussed further below, the 1988 Act's legislation on City Technology Colleges was merely making minor adjustments to a programme that was already under way—and which was already under pressure and liable to fail. The City Technology College programme had been launched in 1986 and the first CTC was announced in February 1987. So, while the 1988 Act is often seen as being the centrepiece of the British Conservative government's quasi-market for schools, it actually included no new methods whereby potential sponsors could start new schools.

Although the Conservative Party trumpeted its belief in the superiority of the market, during their long term in government from 1979 to 1997 there were only two separate attempts to encourage the establishment of new schools—the City Technology Colleges, announced in 1986, and the sponsored grant-maintained schools contained within the 1993 Education Act. This second initiative enabled groups of sponsors or existing private schools to apply for state funding by joining a new category of school—sponsored grant-maintained schools. This paper examines and compares these two initiatives and draws some conclusions about their significance.

The City Technology College initiative

The initial public announcement of the City Technology Colleges was made during a speech by Kenneth Baker (then a new Secretary of State for Education) on 7 October 1986 at the Conservative Party Annual Conference. He outlined how a pilot network of 20 City Technology Colleges was to be created which would be jointly funded by central government and industrial sponsors. The initiative was explicitly presented as one of a number of new measures that were intended to 'break the grip' of left-wing local education authorities, and one designed to offer new hope and opportunity to selected young people and parents. As the name suggests, City Technology Colleges were to provide a curriculum rich in science and technology, but they were also designed for a specific group of 11–18-year-olds from the 'inner city'. One major feature was that they were to be private schools, run by independent charitable trusts, with the sponsors having a major influence on the way in which the Colleges were managed. These sponsors were also intended to provide substantial financial and material support. While central government would provide recurrent funding on a scale similar to that of local authority schools, additional funding was expected to be provided by the private sponsors.

More details of the plan were made available in a brochure published by the Department of Education and Science a week after the speech (DES, 1986), which was sent to about 2000 leading industrial and commercial organisations asking them to support the venture. As these details have been discussed in detail elsewhere (e.g. Walford & Miller, 1991; Whitty *et al.*, 1993), only a selective account will be given here. According to that booklet, it was in the cities that the education system was under the most pressure and where the government's aims and parents' aspirations 'often seem furthest from fulfilment'.

> There are many examples of good schooling offered by committed teachers in the cities. But many families living there who seek the best possible education for their children do not have access to the kind of schools which measure up to their ambitions. The government believes that there is, in the business community and elsewhere, a widespread wish to help extend the range of choice for families in urban areas.
>
> (DES, 1986, p. 3)

The City Technology Colleges were thus firmly linked to the idea of widening and improving educational provision in urban areas, particularly the disadvantaged inner cities, where the government believed the local authority system was often failing children. The attack on the Labour councils which controlled practically all of the inner-city local education authorities was not made explicit in the booklet, but was plain from many political speeches at the time.

The reaction to the announcement of CTCs was not as the government would have wished. Apart from the expected negative reactions from the teacher unions, the local education authorities and the Labour opposition, there were very few industrialists who showed their 'wish to help extend the range of choice for families in urban areas', and many who were openly hostile to the idea. Several directors of major companies already involved with state schooling rejected the idea of sponsoring a single school, and argued the benefits of wider sponsorship. It took until February 1987 for the first site and sponsor to be announced. The northern part of Solihull which bordered on Birmingham was to have a College sponsored by Hanson plc and Lucas Industries. A little later, just before the General Election, two more sponsorships were made public. All of these sponsors were regular supporters of the Conservative Party, but even they were unprepared to donate anything like the proportion of the funds that had been originally envisaged. While the intention was that practically all of the capital expenditure would be provided by sponsors, they refused to give more than about 20%, leaving the government with a large, and unexpected, bill.

This reluctance to fund the CTCs accounts for their mention in the 1988 Education Reform Act. As the CTCs are officially independent schools they required no new legislation; the government could simply use its existing powers to give funding to private schools as it wished. However, the ease with which funding could be granted had both positive and negative features, for it meant that another government could equally quickly cease to fund the CTCs if it wished. Even after the 1987 re-election of a Conservative government, fears of what a future Labour government might do led to clauses in the 1988 Act that began to protect the investment of sponsors. In practice, even with this safeguard, the scheme rapidly stalled. As is well known, the considerable difficulties in attracting sufficient sponsorship and in finding appropriate sites for the CTCs continued (Walford & Miller, 1991; Whitty *et al.*, 1993). The programme stalled at 15 CTCs with about only 20% of capital funding having been provided by sponsors and the bulk of the capital expenditure and practically all of the current expenditure being provided direct by central government.

Sponsored grant-maintained schools

It was not until the 1993 Education Act that any further changes were made to increase the supply-side of the quasi-market. As a result of that Act it became possible for groups of parents and charitable, religious or independent sponsors to apply to the Secretary of State for Education in England or the Secretary of State for Wales to establish their own grant-maintained schools. According to the Government White Paper that preceded the Act, the explicit intentions behind such developments were to widen choice and diversity of schools and to allow new grant-maintained schools to be created 'in response to parental demand and on the basis of local proposals' (DFE, 1992, p. 26). If the Secretary of State approved individual proposals, the way was opened for England and Wales to have state-funded schools that aimed to foster, for example, Muslim, Buddhist or evangelical Christian beliefs, or that wished to promote particular educational philosophies. Groups of sponsors could propose either an entirely new school or that an existing faith-based or other private school for which they were responsible should be re-established as a grant-maintained school.

These sponsored grant-maintained schools differed from existing grant-maintained schools in that sponsors had to pay for at least 15% of costs relating to the provision of school buildings and some other capital expenditure. In return for this financial contribution, through the school's Trust Deed and Instrument of Governance, the sponsors could ensure that the school retained the purpose for which it was established. The composition of the governing body allowed the sponsors to ensure that the religious objectives of the school were maintained and that the religious beliefs and practices of teaching staff were taken into consideration in appointments.

Technically, it was already possible for LEAs to support new religiously-based schools through voluntary aided status. But the vast majority of these schools are supported by the Church of England and the Roman Catholic church, with a small number of Methodist and Jewish voluntary schools. None are owned by any other religious minorities. Over the years several existing Muslim and evangelical Christian private schools had applied to their LEAs to become voluntary aided, but all such requests had been rejected. Usually this happened at the LEA level, but occasionally the LEA agreed to support a new voluntary aided school and central government refused the request. The fact that many Muslims have particular minority ethnic origins makes such refusals highly politically charged. The 1993 Act removed any barriers to the support of faith-based schools erected by local authorities, and passed the decision directly to the Department for Education.

Within England, the process that potential sponsors of grant-maintained schools had to follow was gradually developed over a period of several years by the Funding Agency for Schools (FAS) and the Department for Education (DFE). In respect of new sponsored schools, the FAS provided advice and had to be officially 'consulted' by the sponsors. The FAS was one of several bodies (in fact, the most important body) that gave its opinion about the proposal to the DFE before the Secretary of State made a decision (Walford, 1997b).

Various schools or sponsor groups had made some initial contact with the FAS since April 1994 but, by the time of the General Election in May 1997, only 20 full proposals in England had been published. Only seven of these proposals had been successful—all but one were from existing private Roman Catholic secondary schools, the exception being an existing private Jewish primary school. Four of the successful secondary schools were part of a group owned and run by the Order of Christian Brothers. At the time of the Election, only one application had been rejected by the English Secretary of State for Education, but two had been withdrawn and there were still ten applications outstanding. Some of these had been with the Secretary of State for over a year. At the same time, a further 15 or so promoters were in serious discussion with the FAS.

In Wales the number of applications and approvals was even smaller. By May 1997 only one existing private school had become grant-maintained, and this was a small Roman Catholic school in Denbigh, Clwyd, which at that point had only 150 pupils. Two other applications had been made to the Secretary of State for Wales. Strangely, these two were separate proposals to establish a new school in Usk, near Cardiff, where a single group of proposers broke into two groups following disagreements between them and submitted competing bids for a comprehensive secondary school. Both of these proposals were rejected in early 1998.

Since the General Election the Labour government has produced its own White Paper, *Excellence in Schools* (DfEE, 1997), and the *School Standards and Framework Act* 1998 has introduced a new organisational structure for schools. All grant-maintained schools have been brought back into a revised local education authority system, and the Funding Agency for Schools has been abolished. However, somewhat incongruously, the new Labour Secretary of State for Education and Employment has made decisions on several proposals that had been with the past Secretary of State for many months. In England, seven schools have been allowed to proceed, including two Jewish primary schools (one entirely new), and a small school for disaffected students. Crucially, two existing private Muslim primary schools and one secondary Seventh Day Adventist school have also been accepted as grant-maintained schools. All of the remaining three schools were rejected (one Jewish primary, one Catholic secondary and one Transcendental Meditation primary school). No new applications for sponsored grant-maintained status were accepted.

The result is that in numerical terms the overall policy has thus not been as successful as the original supporters of the 1993 legislation had hoped. Very few schools or sponsors have managed to meet the demands made on them during the application process. Many have fallen by the wayside before their applications were passed to the Secretary of State for consideration, and only 14 schools in England and one in Wales have successfully become grant-maintained under these new regulations. All but one of the sponsored grant-maintained schools involved the transfer of an existing private school into the state-maintained sector. The one entirely new school opened in September 1999, after grant-maintained status had been abolished.

Continuities and discontinuities

Just six years separate Kenneth Baker's Party Conference speech of 1986 in which he announced the CTCs and the 1992 White Paper by John Patten (Secretary of State for Education) which included proposals for sponsored grant-maintained schools. In terms of encouraging the supply-side of the quasi-market, both initiatives must be seen as failures. Both the CTCs and the sponsored grant-maintained schools stalled at just 15 schools. Yet, in both cases, the significance of the initiatives is far more important than the numbers of schools would indicate. What are the similarities and differences between these two initiatives? And what is their long-term significance?

Origins

As with many policy initiatives, it is impossible to determine exactly which groups and individuals had the most influence on the development of the City Technology College idea and what they saw as the main objectives for the programme. The policy was not developed in an ideological vacuum, but in a context where a multitude of pressure groups and social, cultural and economic influences jostled for attention. Personal careers and private prejudices intertwined with local and national priorities and perceptions as to how these priorities might be met.

At first sight, the CTCs appear to be a top-down initiative that went wrong. What seemed to be a 'back-of-the-envelope' idea faltered at the first fence and later stalled completely. There appears to have been little consultation with potential sponsors from industry before the announcement, and their support was (incorrectly) assumed. The plan led to a great deal of controversy with local authorities and an unexpectedly large bill for government. In practice, of course, although the degree of consultation was certainly inadequate, the CTC idea did not just appear from nowhere.

Whitty *et al.* (1993) trace what they call the 'ideological ground-clearing' for the attack on local education authorities and the promotion of the market back to the foundation of the Institute of Economic Affairs in 1957, but it was not until the mid-1970s that pressure began to build for a greater role for market forces in schooling provision. The last two of the infamous *Black Papers on Education*, for example, included papers that called for educational vouchers (Boyson, 1975) and greater choice and diversity within the schooling system (Sexton, 1977).

More direct influences on the CTC initiative came from a variety of sources. When Kenneth Baker was appointed in May 1986 he found 'very little which could be described as worked up anywhere in the whole range of educational performance ...' (quoted by Whitty *et al.*, 1993, p. 19). According to Whitty *et al.*, there had been some pressure from Bob Dunn (then Schools Minister) for something resembling magnet schools and he was credited in late 1985 with a specific proposal to create 16 to 20 'technical schools in main urban centres', outside LEA control and funded by the taxpayer. These were to select children who would benefit from a special emphasis on 'science, business studies, and computer programming'. Dunn was also co-author of a Department of Education and Science briefing paper in late 1985 which called for the creation of new, directly government-funded schools. The other author was Stuart Sexton who had been political adviser to the two preceding Secretaries of State for Education—Keith Joseph and Mark Carlisle.

For Stuart Sexton, the technological aspect was of minor importance compared to his desire for per capita funding of new schools outside the LEA system (Sexton, 1987, 1992). But the technological emphasis was matched by those industrialists who attended a Centre for Policy Studies conference organised by Cyril Taylor in January 1986 and called for the creation of 100 technical secondary schools to be funded by central government on a direct grant basis. Interestingly, again, these were to be initially focused on the 'deprived inner-city areas' and were to act as 'beacons' for other secondary schools (Taylor, 1986, p. 20). Taylor, a businessman running an education company and an ex-Greater London Council Councillor, went on to become the Chief Executive of the Technology Colleges Trust which helped establish specialist schools. The challenge to the LEA system echoed Margaret Thatcher's views and also those of Brian Griffiths who was the head of the Prime Minister's Policy Unit at that time and had considerable influence. He was a firm advocate of education being opened to the rules of supply and demand and of business-school partnerships (Griffiths, 1990). In the end, it seems that it was Kenneth Baker himself who contributed the idea of sponsorship of schools by business and industry. He saw sponsorship as a way to display a unique commitment and to create a 'direct relation between local employers and their schools' (Whitty *et al.*, 1993, p. 21).

Whitty *et al.* (1993, p. 27) argue that it is simply wrong to see the American magnet schools as an explanation of the origins of CTCs, and it is certainly correct that Kenneth Baker's visit to magnet schools in New York and Washington in September 1987 followed his announcement rather than preceded it. Baker brought back from that visit a new discourse of justification and the DES paid for the Principal of the first CTC and others to visit magnet schools (Walford, 1991). However, it would be wrong to ignore completely the influence of the magnet schools on the CTCs. While they probably had little effect on the direct framing of CTCs, they were part of the ferment of ideas about choice, diversity and specialisation that led to the CTC initiative. In the mid-1980s there were some fierce advocates of magnet schools. For example, Caroline Cox (1986), a strong supporter of selective education, proposed 'specialist comprehensives' based on the magnet schools and, after the announcement of the CTCs, as a prominent member of the informal Conservative Hillgate

Group (1986), she advocated that all schools should be run by independent trusts, that the CTC concept should be expanded to other specialisms, and that schools of proven merit should be singled out to act as magnets.

While the CTCs initially had nobody from business or industry wishing to sponsor them, the sponsored grant-maintained schools had very many potential sponsoring groups and existing private schools who were interested. Whereas the CTC can be seen as a 'top down' initiative, the sponsored grant-maintained schools initially appear to be a 'bottom-up' initiative from the 'grass roots'. It is certainly true that a long and very specific campaign by a diversity of pressure groups and individuals preceded the announcement of these sponsored grant-maintained schools (Walford, 1995a,b,c); what is of great interest is that many of those involved with CTCs were also highly influential in the campaign for sponsored grant-maintained schools. Of particular importance were Stuart Sexton, Caroline Cox and Brian Griffiths.

A full account of the campaign has been given elsewhere (Walford, 1995a), but one of the major pressure groups involved represented several small private evangelical Christian schools. These schools had formed in the 1970s and 1980s as a result of dissatisfaction with the state sector, and they wished to obtain state funding on the same basis as Church of England and Roman Catholic schools. Several of those involved with the schools had developed links with active Christians within the House of Lords, House of Commons and in other prominent places. One who had a particularly close relationship with some of the schools was Baroness (Caroline) Cox, who had made several visits to the schools and had even been the official guest at one of the schools' prize days in the mid-1980s. As early as 1981 she was arguing for the right of religious minorities to establish their own schools funded by the state (Marks & Cox, 1981).

The intervention of Brian Griffiths was also crucial. When the Education Reform Bill was published in November 1987 a few of the heads arranged to see Brian (now Lord) Griffiths who was at that time Head of the Prime Minister's Policy Unit. Their hope was that the government itself might add an amendment to the Bill or support amendments that were due to be put forward in the Lords. Lord Griffiths is a firm Anglican who believes that extending choice in education is an essentially Christian activity (Griffiths, 1990). When he met with the heads of these schools, he asked for more information and that a report on the schools be submitted to him. This report was prepared and was later published in a modified form by Ruth Deakin (1989). More importantly, it would appear that the eventual establishment of a separate pressure group resulted from this meeting with Brian Griffiths, for he accepted that there appeared to be some injustice but argued that there was a need to generate a campaign before the government could be expected to act. Griffiths believed that it was too late for anything to be included in the 1988 Education Reform Act, but that the schools should look to the longer term and try to change public opinion. The best way forward would be to launch a campaigning organisation which would produce news and information on the schools and which would work towards the introduction of a further Bill.

As a direct result of this suggestion, after the 1988 Education Reform Act had become law, the heads of the new Christian schools acted to set up a campaigning organisation. At the beginning of 1989 the Christian Schools Campaign was established with the long-term goal of obtaining public funding for the schools. When it was formed 47 schools were involved, at least 13 of which had made unsuccessful initial applications to their LEAs for voluntary aided status.

The Christian Schools Campaign became the fronting organisation for a Private Members Bill that was introduced into the House of Lords by Baroness Cox in November 1990 and debated in March 1991. The Bill sought to amend the 1988 Act such that certain categories of independent school would be eligible to apply for grant maintained status. It also aimed to amend the 1980 Act to make it easier for independent schools to obtain voluntary aided status against the wishes of the relevant LEA. Of considerable importance is the fact that the Bill was written for the Christian Schools Campaign by Stuart Sexton. Over the years Sexton (1987, 1992) has made clear his desire for a fully privatised education system, preferably financed through vouchers which can be 'topped-up' by parents. In 1987 he set out his 'step-by-step approach to the eventual introduction of a "market system", a system truly based upon the supremacy of parental choice, the supremacy of purchasing power' (Sexton, 1987, p. 11). Helping the Christian Schools Campaign with the drafting of this Bill thus fitted well with Sexton's long-term aims. His interest was not in supporting Christian schools as such, but in the wider policy of which he saw them to be a part. In the end, for complex reasons, the Bill was withdrawn rather than being voted on, but only after a vociferous four-hour debate. The debate received considerable publicity both at the time and in the months following (O'Keeffe, 1992), for it raised many important questions about the nature of schooling and the government's understanding of parental choice of schools.

Baroness Cox also played a crucial part in moving amendments to the 1993 Education Act. As the Bill was originally drafted, it was only possible to apply for sponsored grant-maintained status where the FAS already had some control over the supply of school places within the LEA. This meant that it would not have been possible for new GM schools to have been established until there were already 10% of primary or secondary pupils in an LEA already in GM schools. Again, much of the political activity took place in the Lords and amendments were put by Lord Skidelsky and Baroness Cox to change the 10% threshold. There was also considerable behind-the-scenes lobbying such that on 10 June 1993 Baroness Blatch (the Education Minister who was guiding the Bill through the Lords) announced that she had been persuaded by the arguments that the threshold was an unnecessary impediment and that a Government amendment would remove it. In her response to the announcement, Baroness Cox thanked Baroness Blatch for her acceptance of the change and said more about some of the schools that the change might effect.

> I know that a number of the new schools already set up by parents making great sacrifices—not the kind of parents who could normally pay independent school fees but those wanting a good education in areas where that was not necessarily available—would have fallen foul of the 10 per cent trip-wire. They will now be able to apply for grant-maintained status. For example, I was speaking today to the head of Oakhill school in Bristol, which is a new independent Christian school. It is an excellent school. [S]he said that the freeing of the 10 per cent trip-wire will enable that school to go ahead with an application. It would never otherwise have been able to do so. It will potentially save the life of that school if it is able to make a successful application.
>
> (Lords' Debates, Hansard, 10 June 1993, cl. 1160)

Oak Hill School in Bristol is the school where Ruth Deakin, ex-Director of the Christian Schools Campaign, was formerly headteacher. As Avon had no GM schools at this point, a 10% limit would have prohibited her school from applying. The change allowed Oak Hill to be one of the first schools to submit its application once the Funding Agency for Schools for England had been established in April 1994. That it was also the first application to be rejected does not reduce the significant part that Caroline Cox, Stuart Sexton and Brian Griffiths played in the legislative process.

Selection

Selection of specific children for specific provision has been a central feature of both the CTC and sponsored grant-maintained schools initiatives. It must be remembered that when the CTCs were introduced in 1986 most children were still allocated to schools through some form of catchment area system. In contrast, the CTCs were required to select children from a defined catchment area drawn so that about one in five or six of the relevant age population could be accommodated. They were explicitly not to be 'neighbourhood schools taking all comers', but the Head and governing body were to select applicants on the basis of:

> general aptitude, for example as reflected in their progress and achievements in primary school; on their readiness to take advantage of the type of education offered in CTCs; and on their parents' commitment to full-time education or training up to the age of 18, to

the distinctive characteristics of the CTC curriculum, and to the ethos of the CTC.

(DES, 1986, p. 5)

Academic selectivity and a direct attack on comprehensive schooling, which might have acted as a vote-loser in the soon expected next General Election, was thus replaced by selection on a broad range of less easily measurable criteria which would include parents' characteristics as well as those of their children. For a child to be accepted by a CTC, families need to know about the Colleges and be able and prepared to negotiate the entrance procedures (which usually include a test and interview). Further, the children have to agree to work a longer school day, to attend for longer terms and have to state that they intend to stay in education until the age of 18. Thus, the CTCs were specifically selective schools, designed to benefit children from 'deserving' working-class families. In short, those families who can show themselves to be 'deserving' are far more likely to gain a place than others. Those children from families with little interest in education are ignored. This form of selection allowed the 'deserving' to be selected from the 'undeserving' and, just as importantly, helped to justify and 'normalise' the fact that some children *should* be selected to benefit from special facilities that are not available to those who are not selected (Walford, 1997a).

Selection has also played a major part in the sponsored grant-maintained initiative. In this case the results of the initiative have been to a large extent dependent upon the particular sponsors and schools that have applied. Yet, although the total is only 15 schools, many more schools and sponsors showed an initial interest. Some were encouraged and some not. Of the seven schools that were given sponsored grant-maintained status by the Conservative government, six of these could reasonably be called 'grammar schools' while the other one was a co-educational Jewish primary school. The six were all Roman Catholic schools and all had existing financial support from the state—either through Assisted Places or through the LEA paying for RC 'grammar school' places to match the selective places available for non-RC children in the area.

The first two successful applications for sponsored grant-maintained status are a good illustration. These two were existing Roman Catholic grammar schools in Birkenhead, Merseyside. About a third of the population in the area is Catholic, and the key aspect of these two proposals was that for many years the local education authority had bought grammar school places within the schools. Following the local authority reorganisation of 1974, the Wirral was left with a complex system where most of its schools were comprehensive, but there remained some selective secondary schools in one small area. The policy of the Catholic Diocese was that all Catholic secondary schools should be comprehensive, and all voluntary aided or controlled RC schools in the whole area are indeed comprehensive. Thus, in order to have some equity between the non-Catholic and the Catholic provision, the LEA bought places at two private schools—St Anselm's College and Upton Hall Convent School—to provide the selective part of Catholic provision.

In 1994 Upton Hall Convent School had an intake of about 90 girls each year. Forty of these had places paid for by the LEA, and a further 30 girls had help from the Assisted Places Scheme. Only about 20 paid full fees, and these were low. The school would have liked to have become a voluntary aided grammar school, but this was not possible without support from the LEA and the Diocese. Neither would sanction such a move as both favoured comprehensive education. When the 1993 Act was passed the school rapidly acted to make what eventually became a successful application.

The application for grant-maintained status for St Anselm's College was conducted in parallel with that of Upton Hall Convent School. Their situations were very similar, as St Anselm's provided Wirral's Roman Catholic selective provision for boys while Upton Hall did so for girls. The school had once been Direct Grant, but became fully private again from 1976. By 1993 the LEA paid for about 40 places for nominated children, and there were about 30 boys on the Assisted Places Scheme. Thus, in a similar way to Upton Hall, St Anselm's had only a low number of full-fee payers—25 out of 96 places per year. The fees for St Anselm's were higher than those for Upton Hall, and the staffing ratios and salaries more generous. In order for the school to show itself ready for grant-maintained status and the reduced funding that would be available, the number of staff had to be cut by about seven and new contracts had to be introduced which reduced some salaries by about 10% and enforced a longer working year. In both cases the school buildings were leased to the new school from the religious Order for 99 years on a peppercorn rent and the Orders also won the right to reconsider their position if grant-maintained status were abolished.

A similar 'pair' of RC school to be given sponsored grant-maintained status in Trafford was St Ambrose and Loreto, while St Edward's, Liverpool and St Joseph's, Staffordshire brought the total to six. Of these six, four (St Anselm's, St Joseph's, St Ambrose, and St Edward's) were schools run by the Order of the Christian Brothers whose central body indicated that all of the schools in its care should carefully consider this option. St Edward's is technically not a grammar school, but is certainly viewed as such in the neighbourhood and is oversubscribed. The direct result, however, is that there has been an expansion in the number of grammar schools in the state-maintained sector. The five schools classified as grammar schools brought the total number of grammer schools to 166, and so the addition was far from insignificant.

Whether they are academically selective or not, religious schools introduce another layer of selection. The admissions process for sponsored grant-maintained schools can give preference to children from families with particular beliefs in the same way as existing Roman Catholic or Church of England voluntary schools. While the two Muslim primary schools would not see themselves as selective schools, they may well soon find that they have far more applications than they have places available. These schools are allowed to ensure that the children come from homes where Islam is taken seriously, and are thus able to select on this basis from the families that apply. In the same way, John Loughborough, the Seventh Day Adventist school in London that has been given sponsored grant-maintained status is able to select on the basis of adherence to Seventh Day Adventism. At present the school is an all black school, for Seventh Day Adventism has a largely black following in Britain. While the school is unable to charge fees, the church has agreed to give it substantial and continuing funding. There are echoes here of places and funding being provided for the 'deserving'. In all cases the schools, parents and community have made substantial financial, work and time donations, and they have now been rewarded.

Privatisation

Privatisation was one of the major policy priorities of successive Conservative governments since 1979, and its extension to education has been strongly supported by the New Right (e.g. Sexton, 1989, 1992). It has taken many different forms (Walford, 1997b) but may be seen as supporting the private sector financially and ideologically, while also encouraging private investment in the state-maintained sector to replace Government funding which is gradually withdrawn. Thus, the state maintained sector has seen, for example, contracting out of services, increasingly inadequate funding, and a growing need for schools to beg for support from industry, parents and the local community.

The CTCs can be clearly seen as a privatisation measure within schooling. One of the major aims of the initiative was that sponsors would fund a substantial part of the initial capital costs and continue to make a contribution to recurrent expenditure. The fact that sponsors actually only contributed about 20% of the initial costs and have only made small further additions does not change the nature of the policy. But the private nature of the CTCs had broader effects than just the directly financial. Their private school status allowed the colleges considerable flexibility in staffing, curriculum and management issues (Walford, 1991). Staff were not necessarily employed on standard national salaries, not were unions necessarily recognised. Further, non-teacher-trained staff could be employed as teachers and as other employees with teaching and managerial responsibilities. It also allowed the Colleges to have Governing Bodies that excluded parents and, of course, there was no link with the local education authorities. Accountability was imprecise.

The sponsored grant-maintained schools can be seen as a further case of privatisation. While building new schools with the support of sponsors can easily be seen as a special case of privatisation, bringing existing private schools into the state-maintained sector might be seen initially as the very opposite. In practice, however, both processes have elements of privatisation and may add to inequities associated with such processes.

Upton Hall Convent School's application is a good example which can be seen as having elements of privatisation. Central to this interpretation is that the LEA already bought many places at the school, and the Assisted Places Scheme paid for many more. The total new expenditure involved in giving grant-maintained status was relatively small. Further, although private, the school was not entirely dependent upon fees or local and government grants. Since 1982 the school had managed to build a sports hall and six additional classrooms and had undertaken major repair work. This had been supported by the local Catholic community and had not come from fee income. The school kept its fees low and was seen to be efficient. Most significantly, the sisters were handing over a site and buildings for a peppercorn rent. This, then, was a new school for the state sector at very low cost to the Government.

The various attempts by groups of sponsors to start entirely new schools also illustrate the covert 'privatisation' aspect of the policy. Sponsors of new schools had to provide substantial financial start-up costs and to have the energy and enthusiasm to establish the school and make it successful. Moreover, it became clear that the larger the proportion of the capital costs the sponsors could provide the more likely they were to be successful. If they could provide continuing recurrent financial support, so much the better. In the end only one entirely new school was established through this process—a Jewish school where the majority of the capital costs were found from an independent Trust.

Conclusion and speculation

It is important to recognise that when Kenneth Baker took over from a rather tired Sir Keith Joseph in May 1986 there was little firm planning for the 1988 Education Reform Act. Baker clearly wished to make rapid changes. He also had an interest in technology in schools as he had been the minister responsible for computers in schools when in the Department of Trade and Industry. In the end, the CTC initiative, as such, must be judged a failure. Even the target of 20 pilot schools was never reached. But, in practice, the CTCs' importance can be seen in what they were precursors to—local management of schools, delegated budgets, per capita funding, decreased roles for LEAs, grant-maintained schools, increased emphasis on selection for inequitable provision, and greater specialisation between schools. All these aspects can be seen in embryonic form in the CTC initiative. More directly, the CTCs led briefly to the Technology

Schools Initiative (where support was given to certain schools for technology) and then to the Technology Colleges and sports, arts and modern languages specialist colleges (where schools have to raise funding from commercial sponsors and are rewarded with additional substantial funding from government). There are now several hundred such Colleges.

In a similar way, in numerical terms, the sponsored grant-maintained schools initiative must be judged a failure. Very few schools or sponsors managed to meet the demands made on them during the application process. Many fell by the wayside before their applications were passed to the Secretary of State for consideration and, coincidentally, this initiative also faltered at just 15 schools. All but one of the sponsored grant-maintained schools involved the transfer of an existing private school into the state-maintained sector. The one entirely new school opened in September 1999, after grant-maintained status was abolished. The number of children involved is minute.

However, as with the CTCs, the significance of the sponsored grant-maintained schools initiative far outweighs the limited number of schools and children that have been involved. The acceptance for state funding of schools run by Muslim and Seventh Day Adventist sponsors marks a turning-point in the way schools are provided within Britain. Private schools for religious minorities are now able to apply for state funding and become Aided schools, as did a Sikh school in December 1999. The decision thus marks a crucial change in policy towards the education of religious and ethnic minority children and may come to be seen as one of the most important educational decisions made during Labour's first five years in office.

References

Boyson, R. (1975) The developing case for the educational voucher. In: C.B. Cox & R. Boyson (eds) *The Fight for Education. Black Paper 1975* (London, Dent).

Cox, C. (1986) Specialist comprehensives: one answer to curriculum problems. In: D. O'Keeffe, (ed.) *The Wayward Curriculum* (London, Social Affairs Unit).

Deakin, R. (1989) *The New Christian Schools* (Bristol, Regius).

Department for Education (1992) *Choice and Diversity* (London, HMSO).

Department for Education & Employment (1997) *Excellence in Schools* (London, The Stationery Office).

Department of Education & Science (1986) *City Technology Colleges: a new choice of school* (London, DES).

Fitz, J., Halpin, D. & Power, S. (1993) *Grant Maintained Schools: education and the market place* (London, Kogan Page).

Griffiths, B. (1990) The Conservative quadrilateral. In: M. Alison & D.L. Edwards (eds) *Christianity and Conservatism* (London, Hodder & Stoughton).

Halpin, D., Power, S. & Fitz, J. (1997) Opting into the past? Grant-maintained schools and the reinvention of tradition. In: R. Glatter, P. A. Woods & C. Bagley (eds) *Choice and Diversity in Schooling* (London, Routledge).

Hillgate Group (1986) *Whose Schools? A radical manifesto* (London, Hillgate Group).

Le Grand, J. & Bartlett, W. (eds) (1993) *Quasi-markets and Social Policy* (London, Macmillan).

Marks, J. & Cox, C. (1981) Education allowances: Power to the people? In: Flew, A, Marks, J., Cox, C. Honey, J. O'Keeffe, D., Dawson, G. & Anderson, D. (eds) *The Pied Pipers of Education* (London, Social Affairs Unit).

O'Keeffe, B. (1992) A look at the Christian schools movement. In: B. Watson, (ed.) *Priorities in Religious Education* (London, Falmer).

Power, S., Halpin, D. & Fitz, J. (1994) Underpinning choice and diversity? The grant-maintained schools policy in context. In: S. Tomlinson, (ed.) *Educational Reform and its Consequences* (London, IPPR/Rivers Oram).

Sexton, S. (1977) Evolution by choice. In: C.B. Cox & R. Boyson (eds) *Black Paper 1977* (London, Temple Smith).

Sexton, S. (1987) *Our Schools—A Radical Policy* (Warlingham, Surrey, Institute for Economic Affairs Education Unit).

Sexton, S. (1992) *Our Schools—Future Policy* (Warlingham, Surrey, IPSET Education Unit).

Taylor, C. (1986) *Employment Examined: the Right approach to more jobs* (London, Centre for Policy Studies).

Walford, G. (1991) City Technology Colleges: A private magnetism? In: G. Walford (ed.) *Private Schooling: tradition, change and diversity* (London, Faul Chapman).

Walford, G. (1995a) 'The Christian Schools Campaign—a successful educational pressure group?' *British Educational Research Journal*, 21, 4, pp. 451–464.

Walford, G. (1995b) 'The Northbourne Amendments: is the House of Lords a garbage can?' *Journal of Education Policy*, 10, 4, pp. 413–425.

Walford, G. (1995c) *Educational Politics. Pressure groups and faith-based schools* (Aldershot, Avebury).

Walford, G. (1995d) 'Faith-based grant-maintained schools: selective international policy borrowing from The Netherlands,' *Journal of Education Policy*, 10, 3, pp. 245–257.

Walford, G. (ed.) (1996) *School Choice and the Quasi-market* (Wallingford, Oxfordshire, Triangle Books).

Walford, G. (1997a) Privatization and selection. In: R. Pring & G. Walford (eds) *Affirming the Comprehensive Ideal* (London, Falmer).

Walford, G. (1997b) 'Sponsored grant-maintained schools: extending the franchise?' *Oxford Review of Education*, 23, 1, pp. 31–44.

Walford, G. & Miller, H. (1991) *City Technology College* (Buckingham, Open University Press).

Whitty, G., Edwards, T. & Gewirtz, S. (1993) *Specialisation and Choice in Urban Education. The City Technology College Experiment* (London, Routledge).

Whitty, G., Power, S. & Halpin, D. (1998) *Devolution and Choice in Education. The school, the state and the market* (Buckingham, Open University Press).

23 Faith-based schools and state funding: a partial argument

Harry Judge

Source: 'Faith-based schools and state funding: a partial argument', *Oxford Review of Education*, 27(4): 463–474, 2001.

It is frequently asserted that some public services, including the provision of schooling, might with advantage be committed, together with appropriate financial assistance, to voluntary faith-based bodies. There are however serious disadvantages in this particular mingling of 'private' and 'public' provision. The arrangements currently in force in the various parts of Britain are the result of complex historical compromises and any further extension of state aid to faith-based schools is likely to lead to an unwelcome fragmentation of society and a diversion of resources from schools committed to developing a common culture, while respecting a diversity of cultural identities.

The argument of this essay is that, in the circumstances of the contemporary world, state funding and support should not be extended to schools which base themselves explicitly on a specific religious faith—whether that faith be Christian in some broad sense, Jewish, Protestant, Islamic, Catholic, Hindu, or Scientologist. It mines and exploits the careful analysis embedded in the studies which follow, entering a note of dissent from what now appears to be the dominant transatlantic consensus that public welfare services, and notably those associated with the great enterprise of schooling, may safely and more effectively be entrusted to religious bodies of all kinds. Underpinning this consensus is a morose recognition that publicly provided and bureaucratically managed services have failed to deliver what was idealistically expected of them. Such disillusionment reinforces the conclusion that schools based on firm religious principles (regardless of the nature of that religion), and welfare services linked to a religious imperative (including an aspiration to convert those receiving such assistance), are appropriate recipients for large subsidies from the public coffers. In educational terms, such a proposition is a wounding contradiction of the claims made for those common schools which are open to all irrespective of religious or ideological allegiance, publicly funded, and dedicated to inculcating the values of pluralism and comprehensiveness.

The argument here presented is partial in both of the common meanings of that word. No attempt is made to disguise it as an objective summation of the evidence presented and expertly discussed in the articles that follow. On the contrary: most of the distinguished authors would draw from their own work conclusions diametrically opposed to the line of advocacy outlined in this introductory essay. Most, although possibly not all, of them would be more disposed to take an opposed view and therefore argue for the maintenance and extension of state financial support for faith-based schools. The argument in these pages is however unashamedly partial, for some even partisan, and based on a long reflection upon the cumulative implications of the specific studies which follow, as well as upon material drawn from other countries not reviewed in these pages. It follows that the argument is partial in a second sense, since it relates only to the situation in the United Kingdom (although not just England and Wales), whereas a more inclusive discussion of these matters would embrace many other societies—including those set in profoundly different cultures (notably the Islamic), as well as a range of traditionally defined 'Western' societies (notably the United States, Australia and a number of sharply different European nations). This extensive international and comparative work has yet to be undertaken.[1] The argument elaborated here applies therefore particularly (but not exclusively) to the United Kingdom, just as the papers which follow address the situation (but not exclusively) throughout the same nation.

In its crudest form, this is an argument about money. At no point does it question the rights of parents to educate their children as they see fit, and to bring them up in accordance with the religious and moral principles which distinguish each particular family. (It could of course be objected that these same children themselves have in these matters rights which are similarly worthy of protection by the State, and that resonant appeals to the values of the family become increasingly problematic as that institution itself becomes both fragile and provisional. Assertions in 19th-century France of the rights of 'the father of the family'—by secular republicans as much as by ultramontane catholics—sound a little misplaced in the 21st century. But that is not the point at issue here.) Let it be readily conceded that just as parents may instruct their own children entirely at home, so they also enjoy the right—except where the most elementary rules of safety and public order are offended—to educate their children in schools of their choice and for which they pay. The State may have residual rights and duties in these matters, but few would now assert that it has the right to an exclusive monopoly. The central question in present circumstances is whether the public should be expected or required to pay for such schooling. That, as the last paper in this issue makes clear, is now the critical issue. It is therefore the only one directly addressed in this argument.

Nor is it necessary, or indeed relevant, to question the quality of the schooling provided in very many of the publicly recognised and financially assisted denominational schools in the UK—be they Anglican, Roman Catholic, Jewish or Islamic. In the following pages adequate evidence is deployed, sometimes perhaps with a hint of apology, to demonstrate that Voluntary schools—to give them their technically correct title, and like Catholic and other religious schools in the United States—do achieve remarkable academic success, and (hence the subdued Christian apology) do outstandingly well in the competitive league tables which now disfigure and distort public education in the United Kingdom. Faith-based schools are successful—a simple fact which does much to explain the obvious affection for them manifested by many politicians already disposed to prefer the 'private' to the 'public'. Two comments nevertheless intrude themselves. There is an obvious danger in conducting an educational system, as clearly distinguished from an educational institution, on the Jeffersonian principle of raking over the rubbish, or plucking brands from the burning. Although educational policies which help to make some public schools avowedly 'better' than others may be cosmetically attractive, and even solve some acute local difficulties, they leave unresolved—in the United Kingdom as in the United States—a host of major systemic problems and indeed sometimes exacerbate them.[2] Moreover, while it may be true that denominational schools, broadly defined, do as a general but not universal rule achieve good results as measured in a variety of ways, there is no agreement among sympathetic observers and researchers about the extent to which such achievement is related to the religious character of the schools in question. Any school granted the exceptional and remarkably attractive privileges of being able to choose its own teachers, to depart from bureaucratically defined procedures, to develop its own sense of mission and—this above all—in the last analysis to select its own pupils, whether by admission or through the ultimate sanction of exclusion, is almost certain to succeed. Such a truism does not of itself constitute sufficient justification for the public funding of religious schools.

This exploratory critique of the extension of public funding to religious schools is, therefore, partial in that it is obviously based on an incomplete body of evidence, and makes no pretence whatsoever to represent a balanced appraisal of the arguments on both (or all) sides. Still less does it presume to summarise the conclusion of the papers which follow it. Nor is it a criticism, actual or implied, of the quality of the work done by faith-based schools or of the dedication and skill of those who work in and for them. Nor does it question the rights of parents in a free and open society to choose the general character of the upbringing their children should receive—whether Christian, secular, Islamic, humanist, Jewish, Amish, or Mormon. Personal preferences are not at issue. Funding, and all that it implies, are. If one clear and universal conclusion does emerge from all eight of the papers which follow, it is that agreements on such funding have always been the product of a particular history, of specific negotiations, of changing social and political circumstances (dramatically manifested on both sides of the Atlantic by patterns of mass immigration). Such arrangements for public funding therefore always incorporate delicately balanced compromises. The public funding of religious schooling for these reasons differs significantly from one part of the United Kingdom to another: in important senses, as will appear, England, Scotland and Northern Ireland have relatively little in common with one another. This is what makes the three case studies in this volume so illuminating of the issues central to Church and State relationships in the field of education. Some might argue, although I would not, that such compromises—being the product of circumstances which have long since vanished—should be abandoned in favour of some simpler and apparently more rational set of agreements. These might require—at the two extremes—either the formal abolition of all public funding for religious schools (as, in principle but hardly in practice, in the United States), or the effective dismantling of the framework of publicly administered schooling and its replacement by a patchwork of schools based on communities of faith and other preferences (as, in principle and sometimes in practice, in The Netherlands).

The much more narrow argument here is, however, not for the abolition of present arrangements, but more simply for a careful consideration (which, I repeat, has not yet been evidenced) of the consequences of any further *extension* of those arrangements—an extension, that is to say, either in the sense of magnifying their importance within the public system by funding more and more religious schools belonging to the historically entrenched groups, or by adding to the number of groups entitled to receive such public funding. The present arrangements are purely the result of unique historical circumstances and developments. It may be as undesirable (although one or two of the authors might question that) as it would be impracticable to reverse the history of the last two hundred years. It is certainly not necessary to extend that history without seeking to inflect its course.

The Church of England stands at the centre of the stage in any discussion of the public funding of religious schools in England, and indeed in the United Kingdom as a whole. This is not primarily because of the scale and quality, in the past and in the present, of its contribution to education in that kingdom. The reason for its centrality to this exposition is that nothing else makes any sense without an understanding of it, and for that reason the article dedicated to the Anglican perspective is placed first. The close association, even identification, of the English nation with a Church of England established to eliminate foreign domination was deeply rooted in English history and sentiment. Thinkers like Hooker were able to argue that to be English was to be a member of the Church of England by law established. The parish was as much a civil as an ecclesiastical jurisdiction. Given that education is an integral part of the mission of any Christian church, Protestant or Catholic or Orthodox, parish schools, albeit on a small scale, were established whenever resources sufficed and there was a demand. Against this assumed background, two factors were of great importance in the development during the 19th century in England of an uneven pattern of public schooling for the poorer classes. The first, frequently but fruitlessly lamented by reformers, was the persistent disinclination of the State—in the shape of Parliament or of the government of the day—to take any direct initiative in the extension of public education. Such a disinclination, reflecting deep prejudices conspiring to limit the field of action open to the State, stood in marked contrast to the policies and practices of other European states. A vacuum was in effect created. Of equal importance, in the early years of the century, was the shift of the emphasis in religious and philanthropic effort from the local to the national level. National societies, and notably the dominant one associated with the Church of England, were established in an attempt to stimulate and support the efforts of the local clergy and laity to provide schooling for the general public, especially in the countryside. A confessionally based, and predominantly Anglican, system of 'national' education, wide in scope but geographically uneven in provision, therefore began slowly to take shape. The State began to make modest grants in aid of such efforts, at the same time insisting on minimal rights of inspection and control, which were gradually to be extended. At the same time, a Protestant interdenominational body made similar, albeit smaller, provision and it soon became politically impossible, and morally indefensible, to deny similar support to Catholic and Jewish schools. It is for this reason that the historical position of the Church of England remained the dominant factor in determining the contours of the frontier between faith-based schools and the State.

Such provision inevitably proved inadequate, and more comprehensive State provision and engagement came to be recognised as inevitable. By that late hour however, the scale of Anglican (and other) provision was such that—even if the risks of confrontation had been deemed politically acceptable—a dual system became in effect inevitable as complex compromises, not to be rehearsed here, emerged. Deep dissatisfactions persisted, not least in those places where the only provision—unacceptable to nonconformists of all kinds—was in the hands of the established Church. The great legislative compromises of the last century, in 1902 and 1944, secured for the Church of England an indispensable but perennially ambivalent place in the educational firmament. On the one hand, its (so called 'domestic') purpose was to nurture children and young people in the faith of the Church of England, or at the very least of the mainstream Christian traditions. At the same time, its complementary (so called 'public') purpose was and is to serve the needs of the whole population, regardless of creed or confessional affiliation. The divergence of these two traditional purposes is evident in an increasingly secularised and pluralist society. It is, however precisely this dual characteristic of much of State-supported faith-based education in England which has encouraged the recent enthusiasms for committing to the 'national Church' a good deal more of the public education of the country.

Other faiths and denominations, given that their initial entry into financial and juridical relationships with the State was deeply conditioned by the Anglican precedent, have nevertheless evolved in quite different directions. Their predominant purpose, always influencing the terms on which they have sought and accepted State funding, has with remarkable consistency been to preserve the distinctiveness and integrity of the religious traditions in which they are grounded. This conclusion emerges with arresting clarity from the narratives and analyses which run through to the contemporary Islamic scene from the classic account of the relationship between the Roman Catholic community and the British State. In all the situations reviewed in these pages, and even more plainly in such cases as that of the United States, one of the problems for religious minorities in previous centuries has been the capturing of the public system of schooling by Protestants, as the dominant social and political group. For example, when the British government imposed (as it had every right to do) conditions on those establishments receiving public grants, it required that not only should they accept inspection of their work and standards but also provide for the daily reading of the Bible in the translation of 1611, the so-called King James version. Such a requirement obviously excluded Catholics who, before the mass immigrations from Ireland, represented only a small minority in England, enjoying very little political power. Circumstances changed and, although some Catholics leaders remained firmly opposed to accepting public money (on the grounds that it would inevitably compromise the integrity of their schools in proclaiming the Catholic faith), a deal was struck. Although government inspectors were accepted, they had to be Roman Catholics who could inspect the teaching only of secular subjects; the Bible could be read in the version approved by the Catholic church.

The distinctiveness of Catholic schooling in England was therefore preserved just as that of its Protestant counterparts was steadily eroded: no attempt was made to provide Catholic schooling for those who were not Catholics. Even when, in the later years of the 19th century, overtly non-denominational (but not inherently non-Christian) schools were directly provided with public money and under public control, the Catholics were not tempted to relinquish their own schools, but jealously defended their right to continue to provide Catholic education in England at public expense. Many Protestant nonconformist and some Anglican schools were, by contrast, willingly relinquished to the emerging State system, in which a general background of non-denominational Christian beliefs and values was more or less generally taken for granted. Catholics had entered the lush pastures of state patronage through the gate which had been freely opened to the Anglicans, and had no intention of ever again being excluded. The growing size and influence of the Cathlic population, and the slow erosion of popular hostility towards it, ensured that the State-funded Catholic schools assumed a significant, and soon to become logistically indispensable, part of the publicly funded provision of education. Their firmly defined separateness was further clarified by the 1944 Act, when no Catholic schools (or to be precise, only one, and in anomalous circumstances) accepted the status of Voluntary Controlled schools. Their choice was clear.

The implications of that choice remained unproblematic until the major shifts in educational policy, and in the underlying ideologies, which occurred in the 1980s. Those shifts challenged the Catholic schools in their efforts to offer to the Catholic population an integrated and systematic pattern of Catholic education, and prompted some Catholic schools to move into the world of academic competitiveness and away from a full participation in a locally planned Catholic system. In spite of subsequent changes in the political climate of the country, the persisting emphasis on academic competition among schools of all types and a generalised preference for 'private' over 'public' providers ensure that the challenges to the integrity of that Catholic system survive into the 21st century. The dilemma can be presented in an oversimplified form: If Catholic schools are exclusively for Catholic children and for preserving the historic faith of the Church, why in a modern society should they be publicly funded? If they are not distinctively Catholic, why should they be supported differently from, and be subject to rules different from, those applying to all publicly funded schools?

The case of the day schools provided for and by the Jewish community in England, and subsequently receiving a full measure of State support, is interestingly if unsurprisingly different. It too has been much affected by the waves of immigration into these islands. For the most part, the Jewish community and its leaders seemed for many years to favour a generous measure of integration within the mainstream public schools, on the clear understanding that such integration should not be confused with or degenerate into assimilation. Many large public schools in the East End of London in effect became schools with a predominantly Jewish character, respectful and observant of Jewish norms. Great importance was at the same time attributed to an extensive supplementary education, provided through the synagogues and protecting the perpetuation of the Jewish tradition. Alongside such extensive Jewish education supplementing the publicly funded provision of secular education, and within a few years of Catholics securing just treatment from central government, the Jewish community also secured State financial support for a small number of day schools which it then wished to maintain. Interest in and commitment to those schools nevertheless steadily declined, in part no doubt because most Jews wished for good reason to be regarded as fully participating members of British society. More recently, however, and under pressure from the growing conviction that Jewish identity is now itself seriously at risk of dilution, there has been a marked revival of interest in Jewish day schools and in securing for them support from public funds. Since the numbers involved are small, and the general public remains ignorant of many of the issues central to contemporary Jewry, such developments have aroused little general comment or interest. The same cannot be said of the Muslim community in England. This close link between funding (without which schools for religious minorities would inevitably struggle to survive), and schooling, and the deeply valued sense of identity cultivated by a minority community is of fundamental importance in the case of education for Muslims in England. This example seems likely to prove the test case—the limiting case, as it were—for the robustness and the acceptance by the public at large of the historically well-established principle that religions commanding the allegiance of a substantial minority of citizens should have extended to them the same rights of support from public funds as have long been enjoyed by the Church of England, and by those Christian groups who have reasonably and successfully claimed equitable treatment alongside that (still) established church.

The education of Muslims in England is yet another example of the profound and long lasting effects of immigration on the delicate relationships between the State on the one hand and faith-based communities on the other. As in the case of Roman Catholics and of Jews, immigrants of the Muslim faith tended to be (and to remain) concentrated in particular cities and districts. In some, perhaps even most, cases strenuous efforts were made by the local education authorities and the schools to accommodate respectfully the beliefs and practices of these new populations. This was never a simple task, requiring adjustments in nearly every aspect of the life of a school, ranging from the provision of meals prepared in acceptable ways to the management of the rhythms of the day and of the year. Equally important and contentious of course—and not least in a society which proved anxious to preserve Christian traditions and morality without taking too seriously the commitments which they entailed—was the teaching of religion. The law requires such teaching to be of a predominantly Christian character, while allowing a range of exemptions. Muslims and their community leaders, confronted with a system which already bestowed generous funding upon the main Christian groups and (albeit on a smaller scale) Jews, soon claimed the same rights for themselves. Heroic efforts in establishing from their own resources their own schools, in communities which were generally underprivileged, strengthened their case, in reason and justice, for securing an equitable measure of State support for some of those schools. That support has now been secured for a few well established schools, and is likely to be extended. Good Muslim schools nurture, and were indeed founded to develop, a focused sense of Islamic identity. They articulate firm and cogently expressed concepts of the role of the teacher as a model of Islamic behaviour and belief, of the nature of knowledge as based on revelation, of the role of women in society. Such emphases impose on a westernised (if post-Christian) state the duty of defining the limits which such a state should impose on its own willingness to fund—not, be it noted, simply to permit—forms of education which may prove to be fissiparous. It is altogether too easy, and quite unhelpful, to dismiss such questions as proof of Islamophobia. Sometimes, no doubt, they do reflect such unlovely prejudices—but not necessarily. There are powerful and potentially dangerous tensions between the (publicly funded) nurturing of distinct cultural identities within a heterogeneous society, and an orderly process of integration. Some advocates of state funding for Muslim schools might of course argue that although faith-based schools represent an inherently flawed and anachronistic ideal, it is incontrovertibly a fact of life that Christians already have them, and therefore ... That is, however, an argument with dangerously open, but not wholly unforeseeable, consequences. If it is accepted (reluctantly by some) that it would be impracticable to reverse the course of history, and somehow disentangle the historic partnership (effectively, between the State on the one hand and its two quite different partners, the Catholics and the Anglicans), then the only serious public policy question which remains is whether those arrangements—rooted in compromises—should now be widely extended. And if it is concluded that, as matter of public policy, they should *not* be extended, it follows that a contraction of the present arrangements is to be preferred to *any* measures having the effect of diverting additional funds from publicly maintained and managed schools to those schools attached to particular faiths or denominations. The choice is both simple and fundamental, and certain to be powerfully illuminated by a careful reading of the articles which follow. That is not to say, as has already been emphasised, that every reader (or every author) would draw the same conclusions as those espoused in this partial argument.

If government, buttressed to some extent by public opinion, continues to favour the extension of State funding for faith-based schools, it will encounter problems which are at present occluded by the cloudy and fashionable belief that 'public' has failed and that 'private' will resolve all difficulties (even those of the London Underground). Confidence in the extension of faith-based schools, in England at least, seems to be based on the unspoken assumption that most of the new state funding will go to the 'mainstream' Christian groups, and (given its historic commitment to a public mission and its latitudinarian attitude to denominational affiliations) especially to the Anglicans. It does not appear that those promoting such developments have yet given a great deal of thought to the broad implications of a significantly wider extension of such financial support, including support for groups which have not yet asserted themselves. There is no possible justification for supposing that, in the course of the coming century, no other religious groups of an unpredictable character will emerge, and in their turn claim equal access to the State coffers in order to provide their own schools. Scientology schools with support from public funds already exist in other countries. Is that possibility to be contemplated with equanimity? What would be the consequences of imposing on the State the duty of distinguishing between good (or acceptable) and bad (or unacceptable) faiths? Nor will the demand for funding for schools belonging to faiths not yet in receipt of State support be confined to non-Christian groups. The rise—in Britain as in America—of evangelical Christian schools, supported by parents distressed by what they perceive as the secularisation and low academic standards of the public schools, has already led in England to demands for such support. Those attempts have not so far been successful, but dealing with them will become increasingly problematical if state support for faith-based schools is extended, while welcoming them will raise awkward questions related to the conflict between biblical fundamentalism and contemporary scholarship, between ecumenism and sectarianism, in some cases possibly between racial segregation and pluralism, between the values of conviction and those of (educational) neutrality. Experience in The Netherlands, where two-thirds of the population of school age attend 'private' schools enjoying full state support suggests that, whereas the difficulties of gaining approval for the opening of new evangelical schools may have been minimised by English advocates of similar developments in their own country, there is in that civilised society dedicated to the principle of widespread support for schools based on a religious faith—or indeed any other shared conviction—no sustainable objection in principle to the extension of official support for such new schools. State support is already available for a wide variety of schools—including Catholic, Protestant, Jewish, Sikh, Seventh Day Adventist, Muslim, Hindu, and schools based on the principles of Transcendental Meditation. The difficulties in establishing new 'faith-based' schools relate primarily to logistic and economic objections to multiplying surplus provision of school places. But all that needs to be demonstrated in terms of the general policy of public funding is that such new schools, deliberately departing from those principal religious traditions of the country which are already amply represented in existing schools, can show that they are indeed themselves based on significantly distinctive theological (or philosophical) principles. In other words, a virtue is made of the magnification of differences, and therefore of fragmentation. Policy makers must judge whether, in a contemporary British society already threatened by divisive strains, such longer term developments are to be welcomed.

The problems associated with the continued encouragement of faith-based schools are, perhaps, even more evident in Scotland and in Northern Ireland than in England. The Scottish settlement of 1918 is a fine example of a (generous) compromise, accepting the inescapable fact that—for reasons of cultural and political history—the public system itself had in effect been colonised by dominant Protestant groups, and that separate 'public' provision therefore had to be made for the rapidly growing Catholic population which immigration from Ireland had generated. The tensions implicit in that historic settlement (itself viewed enviously by some advocates of faith-based schooling south of the border) remain substantial and deep. So do the contradictions which lie in the generalised criticism of the privileged power of the Catholic church in Scotland, which is at one and the same time accused both of exercising a dangerously divisive influence and—as a result of being subject to the controls entailed by public funding—of surrendering the core identity of mainstream Catholic schools. Scotland has in effect a public education system openly divided between Catholics (more or less committed) and Others (historically Calvinist, but now secular with a Protestant flavour). That is unlikely to prove a stable mixture, especially as it seems to allow no legislative margin for the funding of Muslim schools, the demand for which is already growing. But, within the United Kingdom, it is no doubt in Northern Ireland that the most vivid illustration is provided of the inescapable perils of directly linking schools to the divisions of an unhappy society. Faith-based schooling quite obviously did not of itself manufacture the tragic divisions of that society: but nobody has yet argued that it has in any sense helped or is helping to heal them. The slow but steady growth of the movement towards integrated schools, now with public financing available to them, is an eloquent commentary on that truism.

It is against the background of these reflections on the situation in England (with which, in the present context only, Wales may be identified), Scotland, and Northern Ireland—contrasted effectively with the very different solutions developed in The Netherlands—that the experience of the United States may prove to be most instructive.[3] The United States is a large and complex society, profoundly affected by successive waves of immigration, characterised by a powerful commitment to making a multicultural and multi-faith society work effectively and peaceably. It is also, by almost any measure, the most religious—or at least religiously observant—nation in the western world. Its public schools, often characterised or caricatured as being—especially in the inner city—deeply troubled, remain nevertheless deeply committed to the ideal of the common school, on which the reformers associated with Horace Mann made so deep and lasting an imprint. As in Britain, that public school system was in the 19th century in effect colonised by the Protestant establishment, and certainly proved to be inhospitable to Catholic immigrants. The Catholics therefore built, with no support and little encouragement from public authorities, their own system of Catholic schools. Alongside those schools, and now beginning for the first time to rival them in the scale of their influence, have more recently grown many new establishments best characterised as evangelical Christian. Naturally enough, parents dissatisfied with what the public schools offer them (in terms of ideological commitment, or moral standards, or academic achievement, or all three) have been eloquent in arguing for some form of financial assistance, whether through vouchers or otherwise. The issues flowing from the relationship between 'Church and State' remain far from resolution.

Meanwhile, and in spite of some closely fought battles, the Supreme Court (where such matters may ultimately be resolved) has so far in its First Amendment judgments, maintained the wall of separation between Church and State, even if the elevation of that allegedly impregnable wall can be shown to be of more recent origin than has often been maintained. There is, moreover, in the United States a greater sensitivity than in Britain to the dangers as well as to the attractions of committing public funds and official support to the benevolent activities, in the social services as in education, of voluntary faith-based bodies. The recently elected President and his allies were disconcerted to discover that their proclaimed enthusiasm for an extension of faith-based provision was questioned not only by traditional defenders of the wall of separation, but also by sincere and traditionally minded Christians who were dismayed by the thought that the public funding which they obviously deserved might also be extended to supporters of the Unification Church or of Scientology. And that, surely, is the whole point.

The concluding words of the last contribution to this issue of the *Oxford Review of Education* read:

> The right of parents to educate their children in religious schools of their choice is a precious one, and one which is—at this point in American history—beyond legal challenge. The right of parents to choose such schools does not, however, mean that others in society must be compelled to fund that choice. The demand of religious-school advocates that the public fund religious schools on a par with secular ones ignores the fact that religion and politics constitute a volatile mixture which tends to undermine the atmosphere of tolerance upon which all religiously diverse societies depend. To believe that the United States is exempt from this truth is to believe that we (as individuals) are exempt, somehow, from one of the most consistent lessons of human history.[4]
>
> (Underkuffler, 2001: 588)

Would it not be an even greater error to suppose that any society is, somehow, exempt from learning this lesson?

Epilogue or epitaph?

As the preceding essay and the articles which follow it were going to press, the world did not stand still. On 5 September 2001 the British Government published a White Paper proposing a significant extension of funding for new faith-based schools[5]. On 25 September, the Supreme Court of the

United States announced that it would review the decisions made by the courts of Ohio on the public funding, through vouchers, of religiously affiliated schools.[6] In Northern Ireland, sectarian violence again erupted as Protestants protested against the route taken by children on their walk to their Catholic school. These were significant events of limited impact, dwarfed by the horrors of the destruction in New York on 11 September of the World Trade Center. It may seem presumptuous, to some even blasphemous, to link such events. In the first issue of this *Review* in 1975, the historian Alan Bullock wrote:

> Education has come to play so large and important a part in society— or at least in our thinking and talking about it—that many people who have never thought of themselves as educationalists are drawn or driven into taking an active interest in it.[7]

Occasionally, the often placid meanderings of educational policy collide with tragic events in world history. In the last issue of *The Economist* for September 2001, the following article appeared. In the context of this special issue it requires no comment.

> The day before the terrorist atrocities in America, pupils arrived for the first day of the new term at Feversham College in Bradford, Britain's first state-funded Islamic secondary school for girls. Might the two events, however remotely, be connected? Some people fear that they are.
>
> Relations between the country's 2m Muslims and the rest of the population have never been so tense. September 11th has already sparked a small backlash against Muslims. And the terrorist attacks came at the end of a summer of rioting between Muslim and white youths in several towns in the north of England.
>
> Yet the government still wants to press on with its plans to open more religious schools like Feversham. It is encouraging different religions to start up single-denomination schools with taxpayers' money. The Church of England wants to open 100 more such schools. The first Sikh school opened in 1999, and there are already three other Muslim schools.
>
> The events of September 11th have deepened critics' worries about this policy. Lord Alii, a Muslim Labour peer, has already asked the government to think again.
>
> Critics fear that single-faith schools will institutionalise segregation. Children will be brought up ignorant of or hostile to other religions. And this could be a breeding ground for the rioters, or terrorists, of the future. After this summer's riots in Bradford, a report on the city's racial divide was published. The report, by Sir Herman Ouseley, a former chairman of the Commission for Racial Equality, warned that

people's attitudes appear to be hardening and intolerance to differences is growing.

Growing differences between Muslims and Christians are not the only source of worry. The dreadful scenes in Northern Ireland in recent weeks of Protestants baying at children going to a local Catholic primary school have also highlighted the dangers of segregated schooling.

Some Muslims in Bradford say they would prefer their children to go to multi-cultural schools, but that the poor standard of schooling in the city has condemned their children to a cycle of low achievement, unemployment, poverty and crime. Religious schools, which have higher academic standards and better discipline, offer a way out of this trap and, possibly, into another one.[8]

Notes

1 I hope shortly to publish a contribution to such a study, examining and comparing the relationship between the State and Catholic schools in France, the United States, and England. This study, from which are derived some of the reflections offered here, was generously supported by the Spencer Foundation of Chicago.

2 The term 'public schools', unavoidable in any international or comparative context, refers of course to publicly provided and funded schools (in England and Wales technically called 'maintained schools', even where the providing body is a religious denomination). The misleading use in England alone of the term 'public school' to describe an independent school is, in the interests of clarity, to be avoided.

3 No bibliography is offered for this article, as the necessary references will (for obvious reasons) all be found in the notes to the articles which follow it. Fuller references will be found in the case study of the relationship of Catholic schools to the State in France, England, and the United States (mentioned above). Meanwhile, the reader may find it useful to relate the comments made here on the United States to the following recently published works.

4 Underkuffler, this volume, pp. 579–594.

5 Department of Education and Skills (2001) *Schools Achieving Success* (London, The Stationery Office).

6 *New York Times*, 26 September 2001.

7 *Oxford Review of Education*, 1, 1975, p. 1.

8 Reproduced with permission from *The Economist*, September 26-October 5, 2001, p. 36.

References

Bryk, A.S. *et al.* (1993) *Catholic Schools and the Common Good* (Cambridge, MA, Harvard University Press).

Carter, S.L. (1993) *The Culture of Disbelief: how American law and politics trivialize religious devotion* (New York, Basic Books).

Doerr, E. *et al.* (1991) *Church Schools and Public Money* (Buffalo, NY, Prometheus Books).

Formicola, J. (ed.) (1997) *Everson Revisited: religion, education and law at the crossroads* (Lanham, Rowman and Littlefield).

Glenn, C.L. (2000) *The Ambiguous Embrace: Government and faith-based schools and social agencies* (Princeton, NJ, Princeton University Press).

Hunt, T.C. *et al.* (1992) *Religion and Schooling in Contemporary America: confronting our cultural pluralism* (New York, Garland).

Levy, L. (1994) *The Establishment Clause: religion and the First Amendment* (New York, Macmillan).

Morris, C.R. (1997) *American Catholic: the saints and sinners who built America's most powerful church* (New York, Times Books).

Nord, W.R. (1995) *Religion and American Education* (Chapel Hill, University of North Carolina Press).

Underkuffler, L.S. (2001) Public funding for religious schools: difficulties and dangers in a pluralistic society, *Oxford Review of Education*, 27, 4, 577–592.

Wills, G. (1990) *Under God: religion and American politics* (New York, Simon and Schuster).

Youniss, J. *et al.* (2000) *The Catholic Character of Catholic Schools* (Notre Dame, IN, University of Notre Dame Press).

Youniss, J. *et al.* (2000) *Catholic Schools at the Crossroads* (New York, Teachers College Press).

24 School admissions and 'selection' in comprehensive schools: policy and practice

Anne West, Audrey Hind and Hazel Pennell

Source: 'School admissions and 'selection' in comprehensive schools: policy and practice, *Oxford Review of Education*, 30(3): 347–369, 2004.

This article examines secondary school admissions criteria in England. The analysis revealed that in a significant minority of schools, notably those responsible for their own admissions—voluntary-aided and foundation schools—a variety of criteria were used which appear to be designed to select certain groups of pupils and so exclude others. Specialist schools were more likely than nonspecialist schools to report selecting a proportion of pupils on the basis of aptitude/ability in a particular subject area but voluntary-aided/foundation schools were far more likely to select on this basis than community/voluntary-controlled schools. Criteria giving priority to children with medical/social needs were given for nearly three-quarters of schools; however, community/voluntary-controlled schools were more likely to include this as a criterion than were voluntary-aided/foundation schools. Nearly two-fifths of schools mentioned as an oversubscription criterion, pupils with special educational needs; these were predominantly community/voluntary-controlled schools as opposed to voluntary-aided/foundation schools. The evidence reported here reveals that despite attempts by the Labour Government to reform school admissions, considerable 'selection' takes place. Implications for policy are addressed.

Introduction

A 'quasi-market' in school-based education resulted from the education reforms introduced by Conservative Governments in the 1980s. One of the consequences of these reforms is that twice as many state secondary schools than in 1988, the year of the Education Reform Act, now determine their own admissions: in January 1988, 15% of schools were their own admission authority whereas now this figure is 30% (West & Pennell,

2003). Schools that are their own admission authority are in a position to 'cream skim'; that is, they can, if they choose to do so, select pupils who are likely to maximise their examination 'league table' results or, conversely, not select those who are likely to have a negative impact on school examination results. However, only oversubscribed schools that are their own admission authorities are in this position, namely foundation and voluntary-aided (in the main religious) schools.[1]

This paper focuses on reforms to secondary school admissions made by the Labour Government since 1997 and, more specifically, the impact they have had on policy and practice. The following section examines the policy context and in particular the changes that have been made in an attempt to make the process of admissions fairer and more transparent. It also reports on objections made to, and decisions by, the schools adjudicator—a new system of quasi-regulation. The research methods are also outlined. The next section examines admissions criteria in place in English state secondary schools (excluding academically selective grammar schools), and presents examples of ways in which individual admissions authorities 'select in' or 'select out' particular types of pupils via these criteria and other admissions policies. The final section concludes with a summary of the main findings and their implications for policy and practice.

Policy context

Under the previous Conservative Government a variety of commentators expressed concerns about the administration of school admissions in various parts of the country. These included the lack of policy co-ordination and equity issues surrounding admissions policies and practices, particularly those used by the former grant-maintained schools (now mostly foundation) and voluntary-aided (mostly church) schools[2] (see Gewirtz *et al.*, 1995; Audit Commission, 1996; West & Pennell, 1997; West *et al.*, 1997, 1998).

The Labour Party in its 1997 election manifesto committed itself to a fair system of admissions to schools: 'We support guidelines for open and fair admissions ...' (p. 9). The 1998 School Standards and Framework Act and accompanying regulations set a new legal framework for admissions. Associated with the legislation is a Code of Practice on School Admissions. This legislative framework can be seen as an attempt to alleviate problems created by the development of a largely unregulated market as regards school admissions. It also provides a new mechanism—the adjudicator— for resolving local disputes in relation to, amongst other issues, school admissions.

The first Code of Practice came into force on 1 April 1999 (DfEE, 1999) and applied to arrangements leading to admissions from September 2000. A new Code of Practice came into force on 31 January 2003 (DfES, 2003). Key aspects of the Code of Practice relate to the provision of information for parents and guidance concerning the admissions process. Information on oversubscription criteria that admission authorities (LEAs, voluntary-aided and foundation schools) should use is also provided: where more parents have expressed a preference for a particular school in a given year than it has places available, the admission authority must apply the oversubscription criteria in its published admission policy in deciding which parents' preferences it should meet.

Specific reference is made to partial selection that is permitted in some circumstances but not others. The first Code of Practice addressed the issue of interviews stating that schools or admission authorities should not interview *parents* at any part of the application or admission process, although church schools may do so, but only in order to establish a person's religion, including religious denomination or practice. There was no mention of interviewing children. It is significant that the revised Code of Practice (DfES, 2003) states that for the admission round leading to September 2005 intakes and subsequently, '*no parents or children* should be interviewed as any part of the application or admission process, in any school except a boarding school' (s3.15) [our emphasis]. The Code also notes that 'auditions which are part of objective testing for aptitude conducted by a school with a specialism in a prescribed subject' may be carried out in accordance with the school's published admission arrangements.

Turning specifically to oversubscription criteria, the Code of Practice (DfES, 2003) states:

> The admission authority has a fairly wide discretion in deciding what these oversubscription criteria should be, provided that:
>
> - The criteria are not unlawful
> - The admission authority has considered the factors which it believes to be most important in ensuring that children receive an efficient and suitable education and has had regard to guidance in the Code
> - The criteria are clear, fair and objective and are published.
>
> (sA.51)

One of the mechanisms introduced by the Labour Government was the 'schools adjudicator', designed to resolve local disputes in relation to, amongst other issues, school admissions. Objections can be made to adjudicators by admission authorities; by community and voluntary-controlled schools (since 2003); and in the case of certain existing partially selective arrangements, by parents.

West and Ingram (2001) investigated objections to school admission decisions made to the Office of the Schools Adjudicator during the first 13 months of its operation (July 1999 to the end of July 2000). Over this period, the adjudicators ruled on 57 objections relating to admissions. Objections related to admissions policies in different parts of the country, but the vast majority were in London and the South East of England. In almost all cases these were in local education authorities (LEAs) where there is a 'highly developed' market in operation (West *et al.*, 1998), with a variety of school types co-existing—foundation schools, voluntary-aided schools, fully selective schools, partially-selective schools and so on.

Objections to the Office of the Schools Adjudicator concerned different aspects of the admissions process but in the main related to partial selection by ability/aptitude, interviews, whether employees/children of former pupils should have priority for places, concern about the testing procedures, and feeder schools to secondary schools (see West & Ingram, 2001). The majority of objections relating to partial selection were not upheld by the schools adjudicator. In some cases the objection was upheld in part (e.g. by partial selection being reduced) but in only two cases was the objection fully upheld. In both these cases the partial selection by ability was deemed unlawful on the grounds that it had been introduced after the cut off date, namely the 1997/98 school year.

Interestingly, across all the examined adjudications, none of the objections to priority being given to children of former pupils of the school provided evidence showing specific examples of adverse effects, but each time the adjudicator decided that such admissions criteria were unfair and objections were thus upheld. In several cases an admissions criterion referred to priority being given to children with a parent employed at the school; this, it was reasoned could discriminate against traveller and refugee children who had moved to the area and was thus contrary to the Race Relations Act 1976. Objections to the practice of interviewing pupils prior to admission were made in relation to one voluntary-aided school for non-religious places. The school claimed that it was not breaking the law, as the (first) Code of Practice did not explicitly state that interviews with pupils were not allowed. However, the adjudicator upheld the objection. Other objections to interview-like processes (e.g., sports trial, musical audition) were similarly upheld (West & Ingram, 2001).

As noted above, the use of interviews is not permitted in the *revised* Code of Practice. Moreover, the Code (DfES, 2003) also specifically addresses some of these issues raised in rulings made by the adjudicator:

> Bearing in mind the provisions of the Sex Discrimination Act 1975, the Race Relations Act 1976 (as amended by the Race Relations (Amendment) Act 2000), and the Disability Discrimination Act 1995 (as amended by the Special Educational Needs and Disability Act 2001), admission authorities should carefully consider the possible impact, direct or indirect, on equal opportunities of their proposed oversubscription criteria. For example, criteria which give preference to children whose parents or older siblings had previously attended the school or whose parents followed particular occupations, such as teachers, could disproportionately (even if unintentionally) disadvan-

tage ethnic minority, Traveller or refugee families who have more recently moved into the area. In such cases, the criterion could be unlawful unless objectively justified. Such criteria have been determined by the Schools Adjudicator not to be in the interests of all local children and have been ruled out when the subject of an objection. It would not be good practice for admission authorities to set or seek to apply oversubscription criteria that had the effect of disadvantaging certain social groups in the local community, including disabled pupils. Examples would be explicit or implicit discrimination on the basis of parental occupation, employment, income range, standard of living or home facilities.

(s3.12)

We now turn to our own investigation of admissions criteria, which augments and complements earlier research carried out by White *et al.* (2001), who analysed secondary school admissions arrangements relating to 40 LEAs in England and Wales.[3] Their analysis was at the LEA level, and so focused on *community schools* and in some cases voluntary-controlled schools, not on voluntary-aided and foundation schools. One of their key findings was the considerable variation between LEAs in terms of the criteria they used for allocating places.

Our study, by way of contrast, focused on admissions criteria used for state secondary schools—community, voluntary-controlled, voluntary-aided and foundation. The research involved setting up a database of criteria to individual state-maintained secondary schools for pupils entering in Year 7 (age 11) in September 2001. In a minority of cases criteria for September 2002 were used. The schools in the sample were secondary schools (or high schools in the case of those LEAs with middle/high schools). Data were collated for the vast majority (95%) of secondary/high schools in England (N = 3013) (excluding the 15 city technology colleges that are officially classified as 'independent'). Data were obtained from LEA brochures and from individual admission authority schools (voluntary-aided and foundation schools) where information was not provided in LEA brochures. The missing schools were foundation/voluntary-aided schools that were not included in LEA brochures and did not provide us with admissions information when we contacted them to request details. The sample consisted of 69% community schools, 14% voluntary-aided schools, 14% foundation schools and 3% voluntary-controlled schools. As certain voluntary-aided and foundation schools did not provide information our sample under-represents these school types. Full details of the research findings are provided by West and Hind (2003) and West *et al.* (2003). This paper, which draws on these, focuses specifically on admissions criteria for non-selective secondary schools in England (N = 2862) (and not the 164 grammar schools in England that select all pupils on the basis of ability).

Key findings

Admissions—overall picture

Some admissions criteria were used by a high proportion of secondary schools. Table 24.1 gives those reported most frequently.

A high proportion of schools reported giving priority to siblings and to distance; medical or social needs were frequently referred to; and catchment areas were also widely used.

Comparisons were made between schools of different types. Some statistically significant differences were found between community/voluntary-controlled and voluntary-aided/foundation schools; these included more community/voluntary-controlled schools reporting the following admissions criteria: siblings (98% versus 90%); distance (91% versus 71%); medical/social need (80% versus 52%); catchment area (67% versus 43%); first preference (48% versus 22%); and pupils with special educational needs (48% versus 15%); however, more voluntary-aided/foundation than community/voluntary-controlled schools reported admissions criteria mentioning feeder schools (32% versus 26%).

A wide variety of other criteria were used by admission authorities in order to prioritise who should be offered places (see Annex A). These included: religious criteria (13% of schools); children of employees (9%); a difficult journey to another school (6%); children of former pupils (5%); travel time (4%); 'banding' by ability (3%); partial selection by ability/aptitude in a subject area (3%); compassionate factors (3%); children from other religions (3%); children in public care (2%); children with a family connection (2%); and partial selection by general ability (1%).[4]

We now move on to examine a range of criteria that provide opportunities for particular categories of pupils to be 'selected in' and 'selected out' during the admissions process. The criteria considered include: partial selection by ability or aptitude, which has been the subject of intense debate in recent years; giving priority to children of employees or former pupils; the use of religious criteria; the use of 'banding' to obtain a 'bal-

Table 24.1 Most frequently used admissions criteria

Criteria	Percentage of schools (N = 2862)
Siblings	96
Distance	86
Medical/social need	73
Catchment area	61
'First preference'	41
Pupils with special educational needs	39
Feeder schools	28

anced' intake; and criteria giving priority to children who have special educational needs or who have particular medical/social needs.

Admissions criteria and opportunities to select

In this section we investigate criteria that may be considered to be 'unfair' because, for example, they give preference to pupils with certain abilities or aptitudes or because they could contravene current legislation. Some of these criteria could be considered to be forms of covert, if not overt, selection.

Criteria relating to ability/aptitude

The 1998 School Standards and Framework Act defines 'ability' as 'either general ability or ability in any particular subject or subjects'. It does not define aptitude, but the Code of Practice notes that a pupil with aptitude is one who 'is identified as being able to benefit from teaching in a specific subject, or who demonstrates a particular capacity to succeed in that subject'. It is not clear how demonstrating a 'capacity to succeed' differs from 'ability'. However, given the complexity we have included partial selection by either ability or aptitude, although we have excluded 'general ability'. Thus our focus was on partial selection by ability or aptitude in *particular subject areas* (e.g. technology, music, dance, art, languages). The distinction between aptitude, ability and achievement is not at all clear. For example, one school made reference to selecting up to 10% of pupils on the basis of 'proven aptitude in music'; the accompanying notes state that children applying under this criterion 'must have achieved at least Grade III of the Associated Board ... in an instrument or voice'. This can be construed as a measure of ability or aptitude or achievement—or all three.

It is noteworthy that the relevant subjects, set out in regulations, are: physical education or sport or one or more sports; the performing arts or one or more of those arts; the visual arts or one or more of those arts; modern foreign languages or any such language; design and technology and information technology (DfES, 2003). Amongst the schools in our sample, we found examples of schools selecting pupils on the basis of these subjects, but also on the basis of science and mathematics.

Some schools had more than one criterion relating to pupils' aptitude. One foundation school, for example, had three such criteria: 10% of places for pupils by aptitude for music by audition; 5% of places for pupils by aptitude for dance by audition; and 10% of places for pupils with technological aptitude (see also Annex B).

The legislation governing partial selection by aptitude is not straightforward, as certain pre-existing partial selection (i.e. partial selection that took place prior to the election of the Labour government in 1997) is allowed to continue. New partial selection (introduced after 1997/98) is permitted for schools with a specialism (including specialist schools) and in these cases schools may select up to 10% of pupils on the basis of aptitude in the subject(s) in question.

Given the debate about specialist schools selecting pupils on the basis of ability/aptitude (see West *et al.*, 2000; Flatley *et al.*, 2001; Gorard & Taylor, 2001; Fitz *et al.*, 2002) we examined whether designated specialist schools were more likely than non-specialist schools to be selecting pupils by ability/aptitude in a subject area. As our database related to admissions in October 2001, we compared specialist schools in operation in September 2001 with non-specialist schools (our sample included 90% of specialist schools in operation at that time[5]).

Overall, in our sample, 3% of secondary schools were found to select a proportion of pupils on the basis of ability/aptitude in one or more specific subjects; just 2% of these schools were non-specialist schools, whilst 6% were specialist. This difference was statistically significant (chi-squared = 27.8, p < 0.001). One might therefore assume that the reason that more specialist schools are selecting is as a result of their 'specialist' status (which allows such schools to select up to 10% of pupils on this basis).

However, it can also be argued that as the early specialist schools were either grant-maintained or voluntary-aided (see West *et al.*, 2000; Gorard, 2003), partial selection by ability/aptitude might be more a function of school type than specialist status—with schools in control of their own admissions being more likely to select on this basis than other schools. This is confirmed by our data. If we look at the percentage of schools of different types selecting a proportion of pupils on the basis of ability/aptitude in a subject area, we find that the highest percentage of schools selecting in this way are foundation schools, followed by voluntary-aided schools, then community and voluntary-controlled schools (see Table 24.2).

It is clear from this table that the schools in our sample that were selecting a proportion of pupils by aptitude/ability were predominantly those that were their own admission authority. Looked at another way, 8.7% of voluntary-aided/foundation schools and just 0.3% of community/

Table 24.2 Percentage of secondary schools selecting a proportion of pupils by aptitude/ability

Type of school	Percentage of schools selecting by ability/aptitude	N
Foundation	11.2	357
Voluntary-aided	6.5	401
Community	0.3	2023
Voluntary-controlled	0.0	81
All schools	**2.5**	2862

voluntary-controlled schools selected pupils on this basis.[6] Moreover, within specialist schools, we found that 0.7% of community/voluntary-controlled schools were selecting pupils in this way compared with 16.1% of foundation/voluntary-aided schools. This difference was statistically significant (chi-squared = 56.8, p < 0.001).

To see if there were *independent* effects of specialist school status and school type (community/voluntary-controlled versus voluntary-aided/foundation) on whether schools partially selected pupils by ability or aptitude we carried out a logistic regression. The results are shown in Table 24.3.

Table 24.3 shows that there was a statistically significant association between school type and partial selection (with voluntary-aided/foundation schools selecting more than community/voluntary-controlled schools). The odds ratio revealed that voluntary-aided/foundation schools were over 27 times more likely to be partially selecting pupils by ability/aptitude than community/voluntary-controlled schools. Specialist schools were about three times more likely than non-specialist schools to be partially selecting pupils on this basis. Thus, both factors had a statistically significant association with partial selection by ability/aptitude but the odds ratio was greater for the 'school type' variable (voluntary-aided/foundation versus community/voluntary-controlled) than for specialist school status.

Finally, whilst only 1% of schools selected a proportion of pupils on the basis of *general ability*, we again found that such selection was not observed in voluntary-controlled schools and was exceedingly rare (0.2%) in community schools. More voluntary-aided and foundation schools (2% and 4% respectively) selected a proportion of pupils on this basis. In some cases, selection by aptitude was combined with selection on the basis of general ability; in one voluntary-aided school 10 places were allocated for 'pupils demonstrating musical aptitude' and 65 places for pupils with high levels of general ability (measured by verbal reasoning test scores and additionally tests of English and mathematics).

Banding

The School Standards and Framework Act 1998 permits secondary schools to select pupils in order to gain a balanced intake of pupils based on their

Table 24.3 Logistic regression analysis of partial selection

Model	Odds ratio	Probability
School type	27.64	<0.001
Specialist school status	3.2	<0.001

Note
School type: voluntary-aided/foundation versus community/voluntary-controlled.
Specialist school status: specialist school versus non-specialist school.

ability; this is commonly referred to as 'banding'. Overall, 3% of secondary schools in our sample reported the use of some form of banding (2% of community/voluntary-controlled schools compared with 5% of voluntary-aided/foundation schools).

Under the legislation (s101), banding is allowed so long as no level of ability is 'substantially over-represented or substantially under-represented'. The meaning of 'substantially' is open to debate, but our research revealed examples of schools banding in a way that gives rise to an intake 'skewed' towards higher ability pupils. Below we give two examples:

> Places are offered in the following ratios: Band 1 [the highest]: 40%, Band 2: 40%, Band 3:20%.
>
> (foundation school)

> The girls chosen for admission will be drawn from across the ability range, i.e. above average, average and below average ... The Governors' expectation is that the ... entrants to the school will be approximately made up of [27% of] girls of above average ability, [56%] of average and [18%] of below average. These proportions are in no way rigid... .
>
> (voluntary-aided school)

A different approach was adopted where community schools used banding (predominantly in London, see West *et al.*, 2003); this involved the LEA allocating places rather than individual secondary schools:

> A quarter of the total places available at each of these schools are allocated to each of the four reading bandings [25% in each].[7]
>
> The main purpose of the [mathematics and reading] tests[8] is to make sure that each secondary school has, as far as is possible, an even balance of pupils of different abilities and is therefore a truly comprehensive school. [There are five bands of ability with 20% in each.] Children with the greatest difficulty in the tests will be in band 3 and those with a high score will be in band 1a. The rest will be in bands 1b, 2a or 2b.

There are two main reasons why 'banding' systems used by LEAs can be construed as being fairer than those used by individual schools. First, the LEA-wide system involves all pupils attending primary schools within the LEA (and those applying from outside the LEA), whilst a school-based system involves only those primary pupils who *apply* directly to the secondary school in question. This is important, as there may be particular reasons why some parents may be deterred from applying to a particular school—for example, there may be a perception that there is little chance of success (see Noden *et al.*, 1998). Second, if the admission authority is the LEA the system is more likely to be clear and transparent as the LEA has no vested interest in the process. Evidence indicates that where banding takes place on an LEA-wide basis, its introduction was an attempt to obtain a fully comprehensive intake to schools in the area, whereas in the case of *some* school-based systems, as we have noted above, the banding system could be skewed in favour of those of higher ability. It is also noteworthy that banding at the LEA level appears to be associated with decreases in school segregation over time (Fitz *et al.*, 2002), suggesting that it also serves a 'social justice' function.

Criteria giving priority to children of employees/former pupils etc.

The Code of Practice on School Admissions makes specific reference to admission authorities giving priority to certain categories of pupils such as the children of former pupils or employees, stating that these should not be used as they may contravene the Race Relations Act 1976. Nevertheless, we found that 9% of secondary schools in our sample were giving priority to the children of employees/governors: 5% community/voluntary-controlled schools versus 20% voluntary-aided/foundation schools. An example is given below:

> Children of present school staff who are normally employed for a minimum of 10 hours per week. Headteachers will have the discretion to include children of other staff employed at the school.
>
> (community schools in one LEA)

Overall, 5% of secondary schools in our sample gave preference to the children of former pupils (2% of community/voluntary-controlled schools versus 11% voluntary-aided/foundation schools). A small percentage of schools (2%) gave preference to pupils with a 'strong family connection' or equivalent (1% community/voluntary-controlled schools versus 4% voluntary-aided/foundation schools). Altogether we found that 11% of schools were giving priority to one or more of these categories of pupils (priority to employees, the children of former pupils or some other family connection).

Religious schools, criteria used and 'other' faiths

Just over one in ten secondary schools (13%) in our sample made reference to religious criteria. As might be expected, over nine out of ten (92%) voluntary-aided schools had such criteria as did 16% of voluntary-controlled schools.

Just under a quarter (23%) of voluntary-aided schools made explicit reference in their admissions criteria to pupils from other faiths or another 'World Faith'. Below is one example:

If after considering applications made which meet any of the above criteria or a combination of one or more of the same, there remains a shortfall in the planned admissions, then the governors will consider all applications made by parents of children of other Christian denominations. It would be necessary for such parents to have expressed a genuine desire for them to be educated in a Catholic School and to be fully supportive of its Catholic ethos. Such admissions will be limited to 5% of the relevant age group (such an application would need to be supported, in writing, by the appropriate Minister of Religion. Also parents of such applicants may be required for interview).

It is noteworthy that some voluntary-aided schools did not even mention pupils from other Christian denominations. However, we found an example of a school that not only had a criterion relating to those who were not Christians, but also provided details of the proportion of 'non-Christians' admitted the previous year. An unusual example, was a voluntary-aided school that used the same admissions criterion as the LEA (which was very rare) but also noted: 'However, in addition, as we are a Church and a multi-faith school, we request that students are sensitive to, and respectful of, religious worship and prayer' (voluntary-aided school).

Admissions criteria and 'social justice'

In this section, we examine a number of criteria, the presence of which might be construed as indicating that the admission authority has considered issues related to what we have called broadly 'social justice'. This does not mean that these categories are, in practice, used in an equitable manner, however.

Criteria relating to medical/social need

Nearly three-quarters (73%) of schools in our sample had an admissions criterion relating to medical or social needs of the child. However, as can be seen from Table 24.4, community/voluntary-controlled schools were more likely to specifically include such a criterion than were voluntary-aided/foundation schools (80% versus 52%, chi-squared = 229.6, p < 0.001).

Interestingly, medical/social need did not necessarily need to be supported by a professional, so leaving the possibility of administrative discretion being used by an admission authority to admit certain categories of pupils and exclude others—who may, in terms of social justice considerations, have more 'need' for a place.

Below we show the admissions criterion for one foundation and one community school in one LEA. As can be seen, the former allows discretion as to what constitutes 'personal or medical need' whilst the latter is less likely to be amenable to administrative discretion:

Table 24.4 Percentage of schools with admissions criteria referring to medical/social needs

Type of school	Percentage of schools with medical/social need criterion	N
Community	80	2023
Voluntary-controlled	80	81
Foundation	69	357
Voluntary-aided	35	401
Total	73	2862

> Where there are special medical/social grounds for admitting the girl.
>
> (foundation school)

> In exceptional circumstances, the Director of Education has discretion to give a higher priority where a parent provides professionally supported evidence, at the time of application, that their child has an acute personal or medical need for a place at the college.
>
> (community school)

Special educational needs

Nearly four out of ten schools in our sample (39%) had an admissions criterion making reference to pupils with special educational needs (or 'special needs', 'physical or psychological conditions' etc.). As shown in Table 24.5, more were community/voluntary-controlled schools than voluntary-aided/foundation schools (48% versus 15%, chi-squared = 245.3, $p < 0.001$).

It thus appears that children with special educational needs may be less likely to be admitted to secondary schools that are their own admission authority than to schools where the LEA is the admission authority.

Table 24.5 Percentage of schools with special educational needs admissions criterion

Type of school	Percentage of schools with SEN criterion	N
Community	48	2023
Voluntary-controlled	44	81
Foundation	20	357
Voluntary-aided	11	401
Total	39	2862

However, in some LEA brochures and individual schools' admissions information, the admission of children with special educational needs and more particularly for those with statements of special educational need[9] is not explicitly mentioned as an admissions criterion. This information therefore needs to be treated with caution. It is also important to note that where a school is named in a statement of special educational need, the pupil concerned is required to be admitted to that school.

However, when we examined admissions brochures from LEAs where special educational needs was included for community schools it was generally not included as an admissions criterion for voluntary-aided or foundation schools. In one LEA, for example, the first admissions criterion for community schools was: '[Children] for whom a statement of special educational needs has been made under the Education Act 1996 and for whom the school has been named in that statement'. By way of contrast, none of the foundation or voluntary-aided schools in this particular LEA had such a criterion and only 16% of the schools in this category mentioned 'special needs' as either an admissions criterion or in the admissions information provided to parents.

Support for the hypothesis that 'faith' schools are not accepting their 'fair share' of pupils with special educational needs comes from recent government data (House of Commons, 2001) revealing that in January 2000, pupils with statements of special educational need accounted for 2.2% of the population of Church of England secondary schools, 1.9% of Roman Catholic secondary schools, 1.5% of Jewish secondary schools and 2.6% of all other secondary schools.

Children in public care

Just under 2% of schools in our sample (1.7%) had children in public care as an admissions criterion. More of these schools were community/voluntary-controlled than voluntary-aided/foundation (2.3% versus 0.1%).

Idiosyncratic practices to 'select in' and 'select out' pupils

We found a wide range of idiosyncratic criteria and practices that are potentially unfair. These included interviews, imprecise, unclear criteria, and reference to the pupil's academic record or the record of siblings.

Interviews

The first Code of Practice (DfEE, 1999) stated that 'Church schools may carry out interviews, but only in order to assess religious or denomination commitment' (s5.25). In 2% of secondary schools in our sample, parents were reported to be interviewed. All of these schools were voluntary-aided; overall, 10% of voluntary-aided schools reported interviewing parents (27 were Roman Catholic schools, 11 Church of England and 4 other religions or denominations).

We also found that 2% of schools in our sample reported interviewing pupils. The vast majority of these schools were voluntary-aided; overall 16% of voluntary-aided schools reported interviewing pupils (of these 45 were Roman Catholic, 13 Church of England and 11 other religions or denominations). In addition, one voluntary-controlled school and three foundation schools reported interviewing pupils.

In some cases, the interviews were to assess religious commitment, for example: 'An interview to confirm Catholicity' or to determine religious commitment. In other schools, however, this was not their sole aim:

> Applicants and their families making a Foundation application will be invited to come for interview. *The function of the interview is to assess whether the aims, attitudes, values and expectations of the applicant and her family are in harmony with those of this Anglican school* as detailed in the school prospectus ... and to explore further the family's commitment to their faith [our emphasis].
>
> Catholicity of home and *pastoral benefit to be derived by child* [our emphasis].

Moreover, in some schools, no reference was given to 'religion':

> Admission criterion 1: The outcome of an interview with the pupil to ascertain their *potential to contribute to or benefit from a small school with a caring family atmosphere* [our emphasis].

In the case of this criterion, it is hard to see how any child would not benefit from a 'small school with a caring family atmosphere'.

Criteria that are not clear, objective or fair

Some criteria were not clear or fair in that they were vague and allowed administrative discretion. One, used by a voluntary-aided school was 'compassionate factors'; another, also used by a voluntary-aided school was 'any pastoral, social or educational benefit to be gained'.

Other criteria related to the behaviour of siblings, which again would seem to be unfair, enabling schools to 'select out' some pupils on account of the behaviour of others, for example:

> Whether the candidate has a brother or sister with a satisfactory record at the school and whose parents have supported the school (for this purpose, a pupil's record will be regarded as satisfactory if she or he has: (i) consistently achieved A or B grades for effort in all subjects, general attitude to work and school, and conduct (as shown in interim

and annual reports); (ii) good records of punctuality and attendance; and (iii) taken part in extra-curricular activities or made a contribution to the school in another way).

[(voluntary-aided school)]

Although not an 'admissions criterion' some schools as part of their admissions procedure reported taking up references from pupils' primary schools:

> The school will also require each application to be supported by a reference from the applicant's primary headteacher ... The purpose of taking [this] up is to give the primary heads the opportunity to show that the applicant and her family's attitudes, values and expectations are in sympathy with this ... school.
>
> (voluntary-aided school)

Finally, in one case the criteria relating to religious commitment appeared to be unachievable:

> Baptised fully practising children of families where at least one Catholic parent/guardian is a Baptised fully practising member of the Catholic Church, *whose first priority is a Catholic education for the child where both child and parent/guardian have attended Saturday evening/Sunday Mass every week since the child started Primary School.* This must be supported by:
>
> • An interview at the school to confirm Catholicity
> • A signed statement by the parent/guardian stating that they have not applied nor taken steps to apply (including the sitting of a selective test) to a non-Catholic school. (voluntary-aided school)

The requirement to have attended Mass every week is likely to be unachievable, with childhood illnesses and holidays. Moreover, the requirement for parents to confirm that a non-Catholic school has not been applied to would appear to be unreasonable as there is no guarantee that an application to *any* Catholic school would be successful; such a requirement could leave parents without a school place for their child.

Conclusions

Our analysis has revealed that the admission criteria used by the majority of schools in England appear to be fair in that they do not seem to have been designed to select any specific categories of pupils at the expense of others. This is particularly the case with those for community schools. However, a significant minority of schools, notably those that are their own admission authorities, use a variety of criteria that appear to be designed to select certain groups of pupils but exclude others—there are thus clear opportunities for schools to 'select in' and 'select out' pupils. It is important to stress that the results reported here almost certainly under-estimate the amount of 'selection' that takes place as our sample did not include *all* voluntary-aided and foundation schools in England. The missing schools were foundation/voluntary-aided schools that neither appeared in local education authority admissions brochures, nor responded to our request for information about their admissions criteria. Our sample therefore under-represents those schools that are more likely than others to have 'selective' admissions criteria.

The fact that certain types of schools have lower levels of poverty than others lends support to the notion that some schools are more likely than others to 'select out' certain groups of pupils. For example, in England in January 2001, the percentage of pupils known to be eligible for free school meals was 11.4% for Church of England schools, 15.6% for Roman Catholic schools, 6.2% for Jewish schools and 6.5% for Sikh schools, compared with 16.1% for all other maintained secondary schools in England (House of Commons, 2001).

Given the links between social background, prior attainment and later examination performance, various selective practices enable some such schools to obtain higher positions in examination 'league tables' than others. Indeed, an analysis of the overall increase in terms of the percent-age of pupils gaining five or more General Certificate of Secondary Examination (GCSE) passes at grades A* to C between 1997 and 2000 found an increase of 3.6 percentage points across all types of maintained secondary schools in our database.[10] However, this figure was only 2.8 for voluntary-controlled schools and 3.4 for community schools, whilst for voluntary-aided schools it was 4.3 and for foundation schools 4.4 percentage points (both of which are in control of their admissions).

Schools that are their own admission authorities are clearly placed in a favourable position compared with other schools, particularly in urban areas where the 'quasimarket' is most highly developed. Such schools are in a posi-tion to 'cream skim' as we have demonstrated. There is also the question of the complexity of the admissions system (e.g. multiple preferences) which is likely to affect parents who are less well versed in the education system, for example, those from minority ethnic groups (see West *et al.*, 1997).

Although the Labour Government has made attempts to reform school admissions, there is still considerable room for improvement. Some admis-sions criteria that are not objective, clear or fair continue to be used and some may contravene legislation, for example the Race Relations Act, 1976. The new Code of Practice reiterates the concerns raised in the previ-ous version about oversubscription criteria that are potentially discriminat-ing, but were nonetheless in operation at the time of our study (e.g. criteria giving preference to children whose parents or older siblings had previously attended the school, or whose parents followed particular occupations, such as teachers). Guidance is not being adhered to by certain admission authorities and the body that has been set up to regulate school admissions—the Office of the Schools Adjudicator—needs more power if it is to have the impact that is needed for unfair admissions policies and practices to be removed.

One issue raised in the Code of Practice, but addressed by very few admission authorities, relates to children in public care, who are a particularly disadvantaged group. The Code recommends that 'all admission authorities give these children top priority in their oversubscription criteria'. It remains to be seen which admission authorities will take up this recommendation.

Another issue that is mentioned in the Code of Practice relates to children with statements of special educational needs; where a school is named in the statement, pupils are required to be admitted to that school: 'It is good practice for LEAs to mention this in their composite prospectuses' (s7.20, DfES, 2003). This is another area where current practice could be improved. The admissions criteria and brochures we analysed were not consistent in terms of what was reported. It would be in the interests of the parents of children with special educational needs to have information about this issue. In our view, the secondary transfer process needs to be further reformed so that some groups of parents and pupils—and schools—do not continue to benefit at the expense of others. By encouraging academically and socially-mixed schools that do not give unfair advantages to some categories of pupils, policy makers have an opportunity to improve educational outcomes for the majority at the same time as promoting social justice (see West & Pennell, 2003).

Additional problems will arise with the advent of academies (formerly known as city academies); although subject to the Code of Practice they are nonetheless responsible for their own admissions (and will also be able to select a proportion of their pupils on the basis of aptitude in subjects in which they specialise). Thus, they may be more likely than, say community or voluntary-controlled schools, to seek to select higher performing or more motivated pupils. The advent of such schools will also add to the complexity of the admission process for parents in the urban areas where they are to be located and where the admission process is already at its most complex (see Flatley *et al.*, 2001).

Various changes could be made to school admissions to overcome some of the problems we have identified; for example, the adjudicator could adopt a more proactive role, which would regulate school admissions more effectively (see also West & Ingram, 2001). This would require legislation. However, we feel it may be necessary to go much further. The House of Commons Education and Skills Committee in a recent report that examined secondary admissions as part of an investigation into the diversity of types of schools noted:

Legislation now requires coordinated admissions arrangements both within and between LEAs. This change calls into question the whole issue of schools retaining the role as their own admissions authorities.

(House of Commons, 2003, p. 35)

We would concur and urge that a thorough investigation be conducted to consider whether the admissions problems that have been examined in this paper and elsewhere would be better addressed by removing the rights of schools to act as their own admission authority rather than by the current method of quasi-regulation via Codes of Practice and the schools adjudicator. To date, these reforms do not appear to be working and more radical steps may well be needed in order to deliver an admissions system to parents that is fair and equitable.

Acknowledgements

The research reported here was undertaken in conjunction with the Research and Information on State Education (RISE) Trust. Thanks are due to all those who provided information for this research, in particular the local education authorities and schools concerned. We would like to thank all those who provided research and administrative support, in particular, Matthew West, Laura Bracking, John Wilkes and Dabney Ingram. Thanks are also due to the two anonymous reviewers of an earlier draft of this paper.

Notes

1 Admission authorities are legally required to admit children, on demand, up to the physical capacity of the school except in the case of selective or religious schools; religious schools will be required to admit children up to this limit from 2004/05 (DfES, 2003).
2 Following the School Standards and Framework Act 1998, grant-maintained schools either reverted to voluntary status or were, in the main, designated foundation schools.
3 There are currently 150 LEAs in England.
4 This list is not exhaustive. For examples of other criteria see Annex B.
5 613 out of the 676 specialist schools that were not special schools—the remainder did not provide information. Of the specialist schools, 69% were community/voluntary-controlled and 32% voluntary-aided/foundation.
6 In the main, for purposes of simplicity, percentages have been rounded; in some cases, for clarity, they are reported to one decimal place.
7 A reading comprehension test, taken in Year 6 (age 10 to 11 years) of primary school, is used to allocate pupils to bands.
8 The English Qualification and Curriculum Authority's optional mathematics and reading tests for children in Year 5 (age 9 to 10 years) are used.
9 A statement of special educational needs is associated with additional funding.
10 This is of significance as school performance tables published by the Department for Education and Skills have as a key indicator the percentage of pupils achieving five or more GCSEs at grades A* to C.

References

Audit Commission (1996) *Trading places: the supply and allocation of school places* (London, The Audit Commission).

Department for Education and Employment (1999) *Code of Practice on school admissions* (London, DfEE).

Department for Education and Skills (2001) *Statistics of education: schools in England 2001* (London, The Stationery Office).

Department for Education and Skills (2003) *Code of Practice on school admissions* (London, DfES). Available online at: http://www.dfes.gov.uk/sacode (accessed 18 February 2004).

Fitz, J., Gorard, S. & Taylor, C. (2002) 'School admissions after the School Standards and Framework Act: bringing the LEAs back in?' *Oxford Review of Education*, 28(2/3), 373–393.

Flatley, J. Connolly, H., Higgins, V., Williams, J., Coldron, J., Stephenson, K., Logie, A. & Smith, N. (2001) *Parents' experiences of the process of choosing a secondary school* (London, DfES). Available online at: http://www.dfes.gov.uk/research/data/uploadfiles/RR278.PDF (accessed 18 February 2004).

Gewirtz, S., Ball, S. J. & Bowe, R. (1995) *Markets, choice and equity in education* (Buckingham, Open University Press).

Gorard, S. (2003) Verbal evidence to the House of Commons Education and Skills Committee, 34–35. House of Commons, Secondary Education Diversity of Provision. Fourth Report of Session 2002–3 (London, House of Commons).

Gorard, S. & Taylor, C. (2001) 'The composition of specialist schools in England: track record and future prospect,' *School Leadership and Management*, 21(4), 365–381.

House of Commons (2001) *Hansard written answers for 22 October 2001*.

House of Commons (2003) Secondary Education: Diversity of Provision. Fourth Report of Session 2002–3, House of Commons Education and Skills Committee (London, House of Commons).

Noden, P., West, A., David, M. & Edge, A. (1998) 'Choices and destinations at transfer to secondary schools in London,' *Journal of Education Policy*, 13(2), 221–236.

West, A. & Hind, A. (2003) *Secondary school admissions in England: exploring the extent of overt and covert selection* (London, Research and Information on State Education Trust). Available online at: http://www.risetrust.org.uk/admissions.html (accessed 18 February 2004).

West, A. & Ingram, D. (2001) 'Making school admissions fairer? Quasi-regulation under New Labour,' *Educational Management and Administration*, 29(4), 459–473.

West, A. & Pennell, H. (1997) 'Educational reform and school choice in England and Wales,' *Education Economics*, 5, 285–306.

West, A. & Pennell, H. (2003) *Underachievement in schools* (London, Routledge-Falmer).

West, A., Hind, A. & Pennell, H. (2003) *Secondary school admissions criteria in London secondary schools: examining the extent of cream skimming* (London, Research and Information on State Education Trust). Available online at: http://www.risetrust.org.uk/london.html (accessed 18 February 2004).

West, A. Noden. P. Kleinman, M. & Whitehead, C. (2000) *Examining the impact of the specialist schools programme* (London, DfEE).

West, A., Pennell, H. & Noden, P. (1997) *Secondary school admissions: towards a national policy?* (London, Research and Information on State Education Trust).

West, A., Pennell, H. & Noden, P. (1998) 'School admissions: increasing equity, accountability and transparency,' *British Journal of Educational Studies*, 46(2), 188–200.

White, P., Gorard, S. Fitz, J. & Taylor, C. (2001) 'Regional and local differences in admission arrangements for schools,' *Oxford Review of Education*, 27(3), 317–337.

Annex A. Secondary school admissions criteria

Data in the following table relate in the vast majority of cases to admission in September 2001. Information was obtained from LEA composite prospectuses and from individual schools for those voluntary-aided and foundation schools not included in prospectuses (in some cases information relating to admission in September 2002 was provided); not all such schools provided data. Data were available for 3013 state-maintained secondary schools out of 3165 secondary schools in England (excluding middle schools and city technology colleges) (DfES, 2001). Of these, 151 were designated grammar schools (out of 164 in England) and 2862 were not. The latter are the focus of this paper.

Table 24.A1 England: secondary schools admissions criteria practices (excluding grammar schools)

Criterion	Percentage of secondary schools N=2862
Siblings	96%
Distance	86%
Medical/social need	73%
Catchment area	61%
'First preference'	41%
Special educational needs	39%
Feeder school	28%
Religion	13%
Children of employees	9%
Difficult journey	6%
Children of former pupils	5%
Banding	3%
'Other faiths'	3%
Ability/aptitude in subject area	3%
Pupil interviews	2%
Strong family connection	2%
Parent interviews	2%

Note
This table does not provide an exhaustive listing of admissions criteria/practices used.

Annex B. Examples of admissions criteria

Community school

1. Applicants who have a brother or sister already at the school.
2. Applicants who live nearest to the school. Nearness to the school will be measured on a large-scale map of the area. For this purpose measurement will be over the shortest reasonable walking route and accessibility by private or public transport will be disregarded.
3. In exceptional circumstances the ... Director of Education ... will admit children on grounds of particular medical or social need for [named school].

Community school

Priority for places will be allocated strictly against the following criteria in the order listed.

1. A proven medical need relating to your child (the requirements are strict and need certification by an appropriate doctor or psychologist).
2. The attendance of a brother or sister at the time of admission.
3. Children living in the area served by the following [five named] primary schools.
4. The desirability of maintaining relationships while transferring from primary to secondary school.
5. The distance from home to school and the ease of access.

Voluntary-aided school

Where there are more applications for places than the total of 120 places available, places will be offered according to the following order of priority:

1. Roman Catholic children baptised into and practising their faith, whose parents can produce a letter of priestly support.
2. Other Roman Catholic children baptised into the faith.
3. Christian children whose parents wish their daughter to attend [named school].
4. Non-Christian children whose parents wish their daughter to attend [named school].

Voluntary-aided school

The Governors consider that it is reasonable to ensure that prospective pupils can demonstrate their clear wish to be educated within an environment that has clear and strong emphasis on nautical activities and seafaring traditions. The criteria to be applied in rank order are:

1. Demonstration of a clear commitment to [the school's] nautical ethos, and a wish to pursue a nautical career. (The Governors would assess this through an interview in which prospective pupils are given the opportunity to demonstrate their interests and ambitions with regard to the school, and express how they would take full advantage of the specialist education offered. The assessment criteria used for the interviews will be available from the school.)
2. Sibling links.
3. Geographical distance.

Voluntary-aided school

(a) Pupils will be admitted at age 11 without reference to ability or aptitude. Clear priority will be given to pupils drawn from the former [named Urban District Council area] as at 1972. The children of staff have a right to attend the school.
(b) Where applications for admissions exceed the number of places available, the following criteria will be applied, in the order set out below, to decide the children to admit:-

1. Where the child has a sister or brother currently attending the school;
2. Where there are medical grounds (supported by a doctor's certificate) for admitting the child;
3. Proximity of the child's home to the school, with those living nearer being accorded the higher priority.

Voluntary-aided school

Group A

1. Children of worshipping members of the Church of England including those worshipping at the Cathedral (up to 58 places).
2. Cathedral day choristers (up to 8 places).
3. Children of staff currently at the school at the time of application.
4. Brothers and sisters of children attending the school at the time of application.
5. Children of other worshipping members of other Christian denominations and faiths.
6. Children of any other applicants to the limit of the places available, according to proximity to the school.

Group B

Pupils selected by ability as measured by the school's assessment procedures in merit order for a maximum of 15 places.

1. 12 of these places will be selected on overall academic ability.
2. 3 of these places will be selected on musical ability.

Voluntary-aided school

Category A1

i.   Children of families ... actively involved in local RC communities (max 118 places).
ii. Children of families ... actively involved in Anglican Church Communities (min 40 places).

Should the numbers in any one sub-category exceed the number of places the following criteria will be applied

(a) evidence of significant involvement ... in the church...
(b) evidence of some involvement...
(c) number of years the family has been involved...

Category A2
Children of families who are members, but not active members of the local RC and Anglican Church communities ... with reasons ... which deserve priority.

Should the numbers in this category exceed the number of places the following criteria will be applied:

(a) evidence of some involvement...
(b) number of years family involved...
(c) weight of reasons...

Category A3
Notwithstanding all of the above ... special consideration ... child with special educational needs, medical problems, or exceptional domestic or social problems ... with appropriate evidence.

Category A4
...applications from parents of other Christian denominations ... supported in writing

    ...
    Tie break

i.   brother or sister attending
ii. greater number of years the siblings would be part of the same school
iii. weight of reasons...

Foundation school

1. Residents within [three named] parishes.
2. Children with a brother or sister attending the school.

3. Children who have benefited from a period of residence outside the UK leading to experience of a language/culture other than English.
4. Children influenced by the culture/language of another country as a result of residence there of one or more parents.
5. Children influenced by the culture/language of another country as a result of work/interests of one or more parents.
6. Children with a proven interest in language/culture outside the UK.
7. Children whose parents work/interests are connected with other countries.
8. Proximity of home to school, those living closest being accorded higher priority.

Foundation school

Allocation of places will follow the criteria in order as published:

* Siblings of pupils at present on roll at the School
* 10% places for pupils by aptitude for Music by audition
* 5% places for pupils by aptitude for Dance by audition
* 10% places for pupils with Technological Aptitude
* Pupils whose parent works at the School
* Remaining places-allocated by geographical proximity to the School.

Foundation school

1. Children with a brother or sister currently attending the school.
2. A number of children, up to a maximum of 21, who have high levels of ability and aptitude in music and/or drama—proportions in each subject to be determined by the Applications and, if there are sufficient, in the ratio of 2:1 respectively, i.e. 14 children of high ability in music and 7 in drama. Preference will be given to those who have high abilities and aptitude in both subjects.
3. Medical grounds (supported by a doctor's certificate) for admitting the child.
4. Proximity of the child's home to the school, with those living nearer being accorded the higher priority.

25 Labour government policy 14–19

Richard Pring

Source: 'Labour government policy 14–19', *Oxford Review of Education*, 31(1): 71–85, 2005.

The paper, first, outlines the official policy regarding education and training 14–19, second, picks out five areas within which that policy might be assessed, and, finally, raises questions about the educational thinking which underlies the policy.

14–19[1]

Any division of education into phases must have a certain degree of arbitrariness about it. Young people develop at different rates; they have different aptitudes and aspirations. But divisions there have to be, howsoever rough and ready. It was once believed that 'a tide begins to rise in the veins of youth at the age of 1—they call it adolescence' (Norwood Report, 1943). And so, for most parts of the United Kingdom, the age of 11 was when primary schooling ended and secondary schooling began.

There is no such psychological backing (valid or invalid) for a change at 14. But, almost by stealth, various changes are taking place at that age which marks it off as a time for rethinking both the curriculum and the institutional provision and support. It is the end of Key Stage 3, when all young learners will have been tested and graded. Choices are made for the first time in their educational career about the subjects to be studied—in preparation for GCSE. Parts of what, in 1988, was a National Curriculum for all can at 14 be disapplied (history, geography, modern languages, the arts), a measure which was particularly directed to students who were less academically able or disengaged. Students are obliged between the ages of 14 and 16 to have work experience. They have the opportunity to study full or part-time in colleges of further education—and over 100,000 do so. Careers guidance is offered, and in many schools becomes part of the timetable. And what are referred to as 'vocational options' are introduced.

Furthermore, as an increasing number of young people remain in education and training beyond the compulsory school age of 16, so does the 'break' at 16 seem incongruous. Greater continuity is sought across the 16 age divide.

It is as though the educational programme has to change direction somewhat—to shift from a programme before the age of 14 of learning 'for its own sake', and for the acquisition of 'basic skills' in literacy and numeracy, to a programme after 14 which is 'more relevant' to the world after school—the world of work or of further training or of higher education. Choices have to be made which affect one's life—choices concerning further studies, further training, employment and career. And so schooling has to be 'more relevant'. And 'lack of relevance' is often seen by both learners and employers to be a matter for criticism. Students become disengaged from learning because they do not see the point. Employers say that the educational system is not providing the future employees with the knowledge, skills and attitudes necessary for successful economic performance.

There are several assumptions in what has been said which need to be questioned, and indeed they are questioned in the penultimate section of this paper. However, such assumptions do seem to lie beneath many of the changes which are currently taking place—and which seem to have been endorsed by the Labour government since its election in 1997.

Labour policy 14–19

Assessing the achievements of the Labour Government's policy 14–19 is complicated for the following reasons. The aim of that policy (reflected in the series of policy papers summarised below) would seem to be threefold: social inclusion, higher standards and greater relevance to economic performance. But each of these terms (and thus the policies they describe) is open to different and contested interpretations. What count as appropriate standards, the most appropriate ways of including all young people, and the relation of different kinds of learning to economic success are not universally agreed. Indeed, they are extremely controversial, in particular since they embody wider moral debates, seldom acknowledged, concerning the aims of education and the values which the system ought to be both embodying and promoting.

Social inclusion

As soon as Labour was elected, it produced a Green Paper *Excellence for all children: meeting special educational needs* (1997),[2] which declared the commitment to inclusion in mainstream schools of 'all children who will benefit from it'. Subsequent Green and White Papers extended the idea of greater social inclusion. *The learning age* (1997) sought to remove barriers to participation through Individual Learning Accounts and through improved guidance and information (for example, the 'learning direct' telephone helpline). *Learning to succeed: a new framework for post-16 learning* (1999) focused careers service provision on 'those in greatest need'—which led eventually to the establishment of ConneXions. A major aim of policy has been to increase participation and retention, especially of the rather long tail of young people who leave education and training opportunities as soon as possible. Many join the ranks of the NEET's (Not in Education, Employment or Training). This is seen partly as a curriculum matter – to be solved by increased choice and the availability of more vocational and work related courses. But it is seen also as partly a financial matter—hence, according to the 2004 document *Opportunities and Excellence Progress Report*, Educational Maintenance Grants will be available nationally for 16 to 18 year olds from 2004 onwards.

Therefore, any assessment of policy must look carefully at participation and retention of young people across the social spectrum, not only in numbers and proportions, but also, more subtly, in terms of distribution across courses and institutions.

Higher standards

Following the 1997 White Paper, *Excellence in schools*, a Standards Task Force was established as well as a Standards and Effectiveness Unit at the DfEE. Education Action Zones were created which targeted support and resources where it was most needed, especially in the inner cities. To raise standards, so it was understood, required, first, a clearer definition of what those standards are, and, second, a set of targets for the proportion of young people who should reach those standards. The first is a notoriously difficult task. Standards logically relate to the aims which one is seeking to pursue. Change the aims and you change the relevant standards. As the policy of greater social inclusion is pursued (and thus encouragement to remain in full-time education), so aims of a more vocational nature are recognised, requiring different definitions of standards. Therefore, there has been a lot of work undertaken by the Quality Assurance Agency (QCA), and, within the QCA's framework, by the examination boards, to create vocational qualifications with their own distinctive standards. There has been the further task of establishing 'equivalence' between these different qualifications—to locate the differences within the same overarching framework of 'levels'.

Of primary concern has been the emphasis upon basic standards of literacy and numeracy at Key Stages 3 and 4. The Moser Report (1999) showed the very high proportion of adults with low standards of literacy, despite their '15,000' hours of schooling. And poor literacy would have profound effect upon the personal and social lives of young people as well as upon the economic well being of the community. The Smith Report (2004), *Mathematics counts*, reported that the overwhelming number of teachers, university academics and employers thought that the curriculum and assessment in mathematics was quite inadequate, that the present mathematics curricula were demotivating for the less able and that the subject was in crisis.

Economic relevance

There has been a prolific output of policy documents concerning the 'skills revolution', in particular, the need to provide a more skilled workforce through a transformed educational and training system. The most significant was the 2003 White Paper issuing jointly from the DfES, the Treasury, the Department of Trade and Industry and the Department for Work and Pensions, entitled *21ˢᵗ century skills: realising our potential*. It is difficult to summarise in a few words the grandiose captured within this paper (see Pring 2004 for a detailed account and critique). Its aim is to provide the framework in which Britain might prosper economically in a highly competitive world. The essential ingredient is a skills revolution—ensuring that many more people acquire relevant skills. Educational providers play a crucial role in this, but that role must be seen within the wider context of a partnership with employers, the Regional Development Agencies, the (occupational) Sector Skills Councils and the local Learning and Skills Councils. The precise way in which all these interrelate is not clear, but it is assumed that it is possible: first, to identify in some detail the skills required at different levels, in different occupations and in different regions; second, to match these *demands* for different levels and kinds of skill with educational and training *supply*; third, to create the partnerships between schools, colleges, universities, employers, private learning providers and funding agencies for the most efficient delivery of the required skills.

These different but interconnected aims could, of course, be pursued without any reference to a distinctive 14–19 phase. But they were seen to have a distinctive 14–19 flavour. The Green Paper *14–19: Extending opportunities, raising standards* (2002) addressed particularly social inclusion and the raising of standards. It anticipated a new framework of qualifications which would include—and give greater value and status to—vocational qualifications (including work based learning) from the age of 14 upwards. By proposing an overarching diploma at different levels, the document indicated that almost all learners would receive a qualification which reflected both the content of what had been learnt and the level at which that learning had been completed. Though there would be different pathways, there would be a common strand of literacy, numeracy and ICT. To achieve the more flexible, multi-pathway through the system from 14 to 19, elements of the National Curriculum, previously compulsory, could be 'disapplied'. Participation would be improved, so it was believed, if there were greater choice of learning pathways and if those choices included more vocational and work based (or work related) courses, leading to vocational GCSEs and eventually advanced vocational qualifications at 18 or 19.

After a period of consultation, most of the Green Paper proposals became firm policy in the (2003) White paper *Opportunity and excellence*. Furthermore, the 2004 document *Opportunities and excellence progress report* budgeted for £60 million for 'Enterprise Education Entitlement' from 2005/6 to provide all 15/16 year olds with the equivalence of five days enterprise activity, including the employment of 250 enterprise advisers. Enterprise is a further skill required in the 'skills revolution' and the fight for economic prosperity. As a prime aim of education is increasingly seen to be about economic achievement both for the individual and for the wider community, so 'enterprise' becomes the new educational virtue. But it would be a mistake to understand all these developments simply in terms of economic success. Following the Crick Report (1998), education for citizenship has also been seen as an important educational aim. Not only is a skilled workforce required. That workforce must also be equipped with the understanding and attitudes and dispositions to be responsible citizens. Citizenship is now a compulsory part of the curriculum post-14.

Subsequently, the Tomlinson Working Group was established to review and make proposals for the framework of qualifications which would encourage greater participation and retention and would define standards at different levels of achievement. It reported in October, 2004. It was important to provide a framework which would give greater flexibility of choice, which would encourage a greater number of young people to remain in education and training and which would provide clear and guided lines of progression.

In sum, the Labour government, concerned about the underachievement of a large minority of young people and about the comparatively low participation rate post-16, has put forward measures to increase the interest of young people in remaining in some form of education and training and to make that financially possible for them. It has broadened the understanding of what would count as appropriate standards of achievement by opening up more vocational routes and by seeing the value in work related and work based learning. It has seen, too, the importance of guidance and counselling, giving careers guidance a higher profile and creating a ConneXions Service which addresses particularly the needs of the most vulnerable and disengaged. It has emphasised the importance of the key skills of literacy and numeracy as necessary conditions for progress in any other aspect of education or training. Finally, it has insisted upon the need for the educational system to produce the kind of skills, knowledge and qualities which will serve the economy in a very competitive global market. 'Inclusion', 'relevance' and 'standards' have been the watchwords, and policies and funding have been applied to ensure that these aims are achieved.

Assessment of the policy

These aims (namely, social inclusion, higher standards and economic relevance), howsoever operationalised, must in many ways be seen as long term. It may be the case that 'reforms' put in place might not bear fruit within a few years, or be reflected in short term targets. They are laying the foundations for improvement. There is, for example, as much faith as there is science in the reform of qualifications or in the creation of foundation degrees.

None the less, evidence there is as to whether these aims are being achieved, if only slowly and stealthily. In examining this evidence, I shall focus upon five aspects of government policy, namely:

- Reform of qualifications
- Participation and retention
- Work-based learning
- Institutional provision
- Equality of esteem

Reform of qualifications

One way of meeting the aims would be to reform the examination system to make sure that a wide range of achievement (both academic and vocational) is acknowledged and that there might be progression through the various levels and varieties of study. Following the Dearing Report (1996), the government introduced *Curriculum 2000*. According to Hodgson and Spours (2003), the

> primary aim [was] of making all advanced level qualifications more accessible and more equally valued, thus providing learners with greater flexibility to move between the qualifications tracks and to build programmes of study based on different types of qualifications.

To achieve this, students would be encouraged to take a wider range of subject post-16. These subjects would be selected from both academic and vocational pathways or indeed from a mixture of both. Modular, rather than linear, courses would be the norm, with assessment at the end of the first year of advanced level study.

The subsequent National Qualifications Framework had three broad categories: (a) the general (or academic), namely, a two-part General Certificate of Education (GCE) A Level, with Part I being taken at the end of Year I; (b) the 'vocationally related' school or college based course, formerly the Advanced General National Vocational Qualification (GNVQ); and (c) the occupationally specific National Vocational Qualification (NVQ). There was also the attempt to introduce the Advanced Extension

Award, so that greater discrimination might be made between the increasing numbers who were obtaining top grades at A Level.

There were some well known difficulties in the introduction of Curriculum 2000. Originally the A Level Subsidiary subjects (Part I) were to be five (preferably contrasting) with a view to broadening the post-16 experience which, for a long time had been criticised as too narrow. However, in fact, few schools, logistically, were able to teach five subjects at that level, and the norm reduced to four. Furthermore, in a disproportionate number of cases the fourth subject was complimentary rather than contrasting, thereby not providing the greater breadth of learning which originally had been envisaged. Finally, many students used the results at Part I to decide upon the subjects to be taken at Part II. One major victim was mathematics. According to the Smith Report (2004), already referred to, Curriculum 2000 'reform' led to a 15% fall in entry to Part II—with consequent follow-on problems for matriculation to mathematics based courses in universities. One important lesson from these curriculum reforms is that, such is the interrelationship of different parts of the system, that changes in one part have unforeseen consequences in other parts.

There is a wider concern, not the result of government reforms, but seemingly not helped by them, over the decline in certain key subjects taken at A Level. The number of sixth formers studying French and German has halved since 1992. Those taking physics fell from 46,000 in 1985 to 31,000 in 2002. The Smith Report (2004) pointed to the decline in the numbers taking mathematics.

However, it would be wrong to dwell solely upon these failures. Curriculum 2000 was a serious attempt to respond to the changes in schools and colleges, and to reflect the increasing number of young people, of different levels of achievement and of different aspirations, remaining in education and training. By creating the Advanced Certificate of Vocational Education, it went some way towards creating greater equality of status, although the strong tendency has been for students to opt for the more academic route rather than for the vocational A Levels. The Tomlinson proposals have built on the experience of Curriculum 2000.

Participation and retention

Participation is often seen to compare unfavourably with that in other countries of the developed world, and indeed remains below average for OECD countries. In 2001, 75% of the 15 to 19 age group participated in some form of education and training in the UK, compared with approximately 90% in Belgium and Germany. What is clear from the data is that the successfully increased participation achieved between 1986 and 1993 has not been maintained, although there are very significant variations according to locality, gender and occupational sector.[3]

The early success was reflected in the growth of qualifications which related to the more vocationally related courses introduced—including those of the City and Guilds of London Institute (CGLI) and the Business and Technical Education Council (BTEC). On the other hand, there would now seem to be lower retention rates within the full-time vocational pathways. But the significance of this is always difficult to assess. It could be the case that the 'drop outs' are in fact 'dropping in' to employment, made possible by the experience gained on the (unfinished) course.

One might look at the data in a slightly different way, namely, in the proportion of young people gaining different sorts of qualification. Thus, there was an increase of young people in England gaining Level 2 qualifications from 32.8% in 1989 to 51.2% by 2002, but these figures hide the discrepancy in achievement between boys and girls, the girls doing quite a lot better (see Nuffield Review, 2004, Part III).

On the other hand, research also shows that Britain compares well with other countries in raising the proportion of the population obtaining qualifications at Levels 2 and 3 (see Steedman *et al.*, 2004) This success is helped by the inclusion of qualifications of those over the age of 19. None the less, it reflects the success of the effort to improve qualifications, of which the participation of young people is one key aspect.

There has for many years been a sizeable majority of young people who are disengaged from education. Possibly as many as 7% of the 16/17 year olds join the ranks of the NEETs (Not in Education, Employment or Training) when they leave school. An emphasis of recent government policy has been to ensure that this group is included in education and training. To this end, there has been created the Increased Flexibility Programme, which tries to link the learning experience much more closely to their every day lives. There has also been a stress upon work based learning, especially through the renewed apprenticeship system. It is too early yet to evaluate the results of the Flexibility Programme.

But it is important to see the problem of 'disengagement' in perspective. There is little evidence that the UK is different from other countries with large urban areas. Serious efforts have been made through the Education Action Zones and now Excellence in Cities to break the mould—to re-engage often alienated youth. It is difficult to assess the success of such initiatives. Excellence in Cities is new and replaces but builds upon Education Action Zones. But the problem perhaps needs to be tackled by a more radical appraisal of the curriculum for many young people and of the cultural influences upon the decisions they make (see Ball, 2004).

The Nuffield Review is addressing this problem. It has tentatively concluded, in the light of the evidence it has reviewed, that the reasons for either remaining in or dropping out of education and training are much more complex than many policy initiatives would assume—the availability of unskilled employment, financial hardship, peer pressure, sense of failure at school, and so on (see Hodkinson, 2004).

Work based learning

The government believes that the more practical and work based learning experience is, for many young people, especially those disengaged from school or college, a more effective and motivating way of learning. Therefore, work experience (or work related learning) has been made a requirement for all young people aged 14–16. Indeed, parts of the National Curriculum have been 'disapplied' for those for whom work based learning is thought to be more appropriate. Furthermore, work based learning is strongly promoted through what were originally called Modern Apprenticeships.

It is difficult to assess the value of work based learning (see West, 2004). What we do know is that there has been a reduction of about 12% in the uptake of work based learning amongst 16–17 year olds. Not enough is known about the quality of that learning. It is organised mainly by Private Learning Providers, of which there are over 1000. There is no doubt that many provide an excellent service, but the evidence would point to a rather patchy quality across the many kinds and locations of work based learning. In 2002/3, the Adult Learning Inspectorate (ALI) judged 46% of work based learning provision to be inadequate. But that showed considerable improvement on the previous inspection (see ALI, 2003)

Modern Apprenticeships (see West, 2004) were established in 1993. The purpose was to create a work based learning experience which would deliver world class standards in occupational skills at Level 3. These were seen to be an alternative pathway into employment for young people who could reach Level 3—and thus access to higher education. But there did seem to be some confusion in policy. The aim was to recruit up to 28% to such apprenticeships at the same time that the target for entry to university was set at 50%. Was not a target of over 75% for Level 3 rather too ambitious?

By 1997, Modern Apprenticeships were divided into Advanced Modern Apprenticeships (AMA), which were at Level 3, and Foundation Modern Apprenticeships (FMA), which were at Level 2. The 'Modern' was dropped from the title. Even then the achievements were nowhere near the targets set. In 2002/3, only 23% of those leaving the FMA completed the whole framework (which included key skills); only 36% achieved the National Vocational Qualification (NVQ) part of the framework. Only 33% achieved the whole framework of the AMA; only 43% reached NVQ Level 3.

One criterion for assessing the actual as opposed to the claimed importance attached to work based learning is the amount of funding allocated to it. The Association of Learning Providers reported to this year's Spending Review that, out of the Learning and Skills Council's budget of £8.6 billion, only 6% is spent on work based learning (*Times Educational Supplement*, 26 March 2004).

Institutional provision

In pursuit of these policies certain institutional changes were deemed to be necessary.

First, the system needed to be made more accountable in relation to the targets which central government defined (for example, minimum perform-ance levels for GCSE attainment by 2006, according to *Excellence in schools*, 1997). Overall targets were cascaded down to local education authorities (LEAs) which would now be inspected by Ofsted and assessed in relation to those targets. And *Success for all: reforming further educa-tion and training* (2001) tied funding of colleges of further education (CFE) to college development plans and improved targets. Target setting was not new, but it has taken on a more vigorous role under Labour, despite the failure in many cases to reach what often appear to be arbit-rarily set targets. As Keep (2004) argued, 'target chasing is the dominant focus of management activity as targets for learning achievement are cas-caded down from the Treasury to the DfES'. Only one in six of the targets set by the National Advisory Council for Education and Training for 2002/3 were met; only one in four for 2002 was met.

Second, following *Learning to succeed: a new framework for post-16 learning* (1999), the funding of all post-16 education and training was to come from the newly established Learning and Skills Council (LSC)—including that for sixth forms, previously under the control of the LEAs. Subsequently, the LSC, through its 47 local councils, launched Strategic Area Reviews (StARs) to ensure, according to *Success for all: reforming further education and training* (2001) 'the right mix of provision ... to meet learner, employer and community needs' and to further ensure that there would be collaborative networks throughout the country. Again, col-laboration between schools, colleges and training providers was emphas-ised by the 2002 Green Paper *14–19: extending opportunities, raising standards*.

Third, the system of education and training provision which Labour inherited was itself rather complex. On the one hand, schools were responsible to the local education authorities. On the other hand, colleges of further education were 'incorporated' and funded, not by the LEAs, but by the Further Education Funding Council. The colleges, in turn, had a history rooted in vocational preparation, especially for part-time students. But, in recent years, they had increasingly encroached upon the traditional 'academic' areas of study of the sixth forms of schools. Similarly, the schools, in encouraging young people to remain in education, were increasingly offering vocational courses traditionally associated with the colleges, even though they may not be properly equipped for doing so (e.g. in hotel and catering or in business studies). But even that is a simplistic picture. In 'further education', there were colleges which provided a wide range of vocational and non-vocational courses, at different levels, both full-time and part-time. There were also the sixth-form colleges, which generally focused only on A Levels, and Tertiary Colleges, which provided all education and training post 16 for a given area. Schools were similarly heterogeneous (11 to 16 and 11 to 18)—mainly comprehensive, but with a substantial number of grammar schools in certain parts of the country, City Technology Colleges and Grant Maintained Schools directly funded by government. How, with such a complex and competitive system (competitive both between schools and between schools and colleges), could Labour create a coherent system 14 to 19 which has flexible routes through the system and where choice of subject or pathway depends, not on the particular institution one happens to be in, but upon ability and aspiration? The promotion of partnership was the answer—especially between schools and colleges and across schools. And there are now many examples of such partnerships. But much militates against them, in particular the ways in which schools and colleges are still funded on a different basis and the way in which each institution, for purposes of accountability, is treated as an autonomous unit.

Fourth, despite the frequent reference to partnership in order to meet the aims of greater social inclusion, higher standards and economic relevance (reflected in the Strategic Area Reviews), there was also a policy of expanding specialist schools to increase diversity within the secondary system (*Schools: building on success*, 2001) and finally to create mainly government funded City Academies within the private sector (*Schools: achieving success*, 2001). A difficulty in understanding Labour policy at the secondary phase lies in reconciling the greater autonomy, competition and fragmentation of the system, on the on hand, with the recognition of the need for cooperation and partnership, on the other.

Fifth, this paper has given passing reference to the changing funding arrangements. Funding according to targets successfully achieved has become one of the 'levers' or 'drivers' of the reformed management of the education system. But, as 14 to 19 comes to be seen as a whole, the differential funding between different institutional providers becomes an anomaly.

Finally, as has already been mentioned, 14–19 education and training has to be seen within a wider framework of the 'skills revolution', in which the DfES is one of several government departments trying to construe and then manage a much bigger cooperative venture. That involves (i) Regional Development Agencies, identifying the training needs of each region; (ii) Sector Development Councils for each major occupational group, identifying the skill needs nationally for that kind of occupation; (iii) the Learning and Skills Council (and its local branches) which funds the education and training post-16 (school and college and work based) and, in doing so, will take into account the regional and sector analyses; (iv) the LEAs, still responsible for funding education up to 16; (v) the incorporated colleges which remain essential for the provision of further education and colleges;

(vi) the employers whose cooperation is essential to the provision of work based and work related education and training; (vii) higher education which not only takes on the products of the 14 to 19 system but also is a major economic force in each region, and (viii) the various examination boards which need to respond to all this in creating the assessment system which will be credible in the eyes of the users.

Equality and esteem

'Equality of esteem' between different pathways—the more general or academic, on the one hand, and, on the other, the more vocational—is understandably seen as a major policy aim. There is a deep rooted disdain within the educational system for the more practical and vocational modes of learning. This is long standing and was trenchantly analysed some time ago (see Wiener, 1985, and Barnett, 1986). But as was found in the past (see Olive Banks, 1955, *Parity and prestige in English secondary education*) such esteem cannot be bestowed. The reforms of a qualification system can go some way to redress the balance, and it is a commendable aspect of the reform of qualifications outlined above that the government is seeking to put vocational qualifications within the same diploma framework as the more academic and traditional ones.

However, the attainment of such parity of esteem depends on other factors, some of which are not within the easy grasp of government. Parity of esteem depends largely upon the 'currency' of the qualifications—what they will 'buy' in terms of entry to employment, further training or higher education. But also the complex institutional framework outlined above is unhelpful. Different sorts of institution specialise (even if not by choice) in particular kinds of course. In 2001, sixth form colleges (many of which had formerly been grammar schools) admitted fewer than 7% of those with less than five GCSEs at grade C; 70% of those studying for Level 2 qualifications went to Colleges of FE; only 22% remained in school sixth forms. There are wide differences between institutions, some evidence of selection, and thus a strong chance that many are forced into 'selecting' courses which are less prestigious and not their first preference. This re-enforces the argument, in the previous sub-section, that, to achieve its aims, the government needs to reform the institutional framework so that co-operation rather than competition (on an unequal playing field of funding and prestige) might prevail (see Stanton, 2004).

In conclusion, therefore, the new Labour government in 1997 wanted to address the low participation and retention rate (as that compares with other countries); it wanted to make closer links between the system of education and training and the economic needs of the country and the individuals learners themselves; and it wanted to raise standards generally. In part, this might be seen as essentially a curriculum and teaching matter—

to be solved by greater subject choice, the creation of more practical, work-based and vocational courses and the reform of the framework of qualifications.

However, the government saw that this required much more than a reform of learning styles, of curriculum and of qualifications. There needed to be a change of attitude towards more vocational studies. There needed to be a reform of funding and of institutional provision. There needed to be much closer partnership between educational and training provision, on the one hand, and, on the other, the needs of employers within the different occupational sectors and the different regions. Many of the changes which have taken place have tried to address these institutional issues. But at times it seems rather half-hearted and even contradictory, reflected particularly in the encouragement of partnership, on the one hand, and the encouragement of fragmentation of and competition between schools, on the other, through the establishment of City Academies (now, simply 'academies') and the expansion of specialist schools. Funding issues remain to be addressed so that institutions, providing the same service, might be on a level playing field. Much closer links, not just voluntary partnerships, between institutions need to be established if all young people are to receive the same opportunity to pursue the course which they want and which most suits them and if such courses are to be properly resourced and staffed. Above all, there are serious questions to be asked about the capacity of central government or its agencies (LSC, Regional Development Agencies and Sector Skills Councils) to manage such a massive inter-related system on the evidence which is available

Education, education, education: where is it?

There is no doubting the determination of the Labour government since its election in 1997 to transform the educational and training opportunities for all young people. In its view, far too many exited from the system as soon as they could, thereby being excluded from opportunities which education and training afforded them. Furthermore, the country needed what is often referred to as a highly skilled workforce in a very competitive world. The government brought together a moral drive for greater social inclusion and an economic drive for greater prosperity. There was also a deep concern about the lack of basic skills of literacy, revealed in the Moser Report (1999), and numeracy. Add to that the perceived importance of ICT. There was, therefore, a renewed emphasis at the political level, but also at the very practical level of resources and assessment, upon these three 'key skills'.

To achieve these broad aims, quite radical changes were judged to be needed within a much more coherent and integrated progression from the period of compulsory schooling through to further and higher education and training and into employment. What previously had been seen as sharp divisions—between education and work, between pre and post 16, between secondary, further and higher education, between academic and vocational, between those capable of further education and those unable to benefit from further study—were no longer seen to be so. Indeed, the more blurred the division became the more would one be able to provide appropriate opportunities for all—not just for the privileged few.

And yet, in all the documents referred to and in all the practical measures put in place, there is no clear statement of *educational* aim or purpose, hardly any reference (except in the introduction of citizenship) to the kinds of qualities and values which make young people into better human beings, no vision of the kind of society which a more skilled workforce should serve, no idea of the kind of learning which one should expect of an educated person in the present economic, social and environmental context. The policy is trapped in a language which militates against the broader moral dimension of education—the language of skills and targets, of performance indicators and audits, of academic studies and vocational pathways, of economic relevance and social usefulness.

What is worth learning? Certainly, young people need to learn those skills and attitudes which will enable them to earn a living and to contribute to the economic well-being of themselves and of the wider society. But not all learning is judged to be worthwhile in such a limited sense of utility. We have inherited a world of ideas through which we have come to understand the physical and social and moral worlds in a particular way. It is an inheritance, and it is the job of education to enable the next generation to gain access to that inheritance, to grasp and understand those ideas and to gain a deeper understanding of the world in which they live. And there are pressing problems which beset us all and which need to be understood and grappled with—problems of the environment, of social and ethnic relations, of violence and injustice, of the exercise of power, of the prevalence of poverty. And such issues and problems are the very stuff of literature and the arts, of drama and of history, which did have and should retain a central place in the education of all young people.

Furthermore, we do not live by bread alone; there is the need to introduce young persons to ideals which enable them to transcend immediate wants and desires, to be inspired to make the world a better place, to persevere when the going gets tough. The teaching of the arts and the humanities at their best are precisely that—an introduction to that perennial discussion of issues, which affect us deeply, and to different visions of what is good and worth pursuing.

However, in all the documents, the importance of the arts and the humanities, of drama and poetry, or of modern languages, receive no mention—except as subjects, which unlike mathematics and science, can be 'disapplied' at the age of 14. It is believed, without evidence, that the unmotivated will become motivated once that which is to be learnt is seen to be 'vocational'. Those, however, who have seen good drama teaching in schools will know how false that assumption is. Drama and the arts generally have the capacity to engage all young people, precisely because they address those matters which are of deep personal concern, and yet do so through a means which transcends the uniqueness of each person's particular life.

The pity is that we have been here before and yet, having no educational memory, the Labour government seems unable to learn from the past. When the school-leaving age was raised to 16 in the early 1970s, it was felt by many that the resulting disillusion of those forced to stay on would be resolved by a strong dose of practical and vocational studies. It was, however, a tribute to Lawrence Stenhouse (see Stenhouse, 1975) and others that a different philosophy prevailed. The humanities and the arts, far from being downgraded to an option for those who wished to study them, became central to an exploration of what it means for each young person to be human and to how society might itself become more human. The themes of Shakespeare were also the topics which most concerned young people—the use of violence, relations between the sexes, ambition and jealousy, injustice and poverty, racism and tolerance, relations with parents and authority. The job of the teacher was to make the links between the personal concerns of the young people and the literature, poetry, drama, art and narratives of other people and other times. Highly disciplined discussion was at the centre of the learning experience, lacking therefore precise targets to be attained. For who can set precise targets to a well informed and vigorous conversation?

In raising the status of the 'vocational pathways', from the very best of motives, is not the Labour government reinforcing the dubious distinction between the academic and the vocational—a distinction which leaves little space for those areas of learning which fit into neither category and yet are an essential part of an *educational* experience?

Conclusion

The threefold aim of the government policy is higher standards, greater social inclusion and economic relevance.

Many of the reforms which the government has put in place can be assessed only in the long term—for example, the establishment of such agencies as the Leaning and Skills Council and the Sector Skills Councils, or the creation of a more unified framework of qualifications, or the steps taken to increase participation and retention in different forms of education and training, or the creation of a better trained work force.

The evidence so far is mixed. The state of mathematics education and levels of numeracy are a matter of grave concern. There remains a large minority of young people unaffected by the measures taken to engage them in education and training. Work based learning remains patchy in quality, although improving. There are clear tensions in policy between the advocacy of co-operation and partnership, on the one hand, and policies which create fragmentation and competition, on the other. The development of further institutions under different regulations and funding arrangements exacerbates the inequality of status and opportunity. And, finally, there is an absence of debate on the broader aims of education, of an historical grasp of the issues which have been tackled in several initiatives within the last two or three decades, of the links between the provision of education and training, on the one hand, and deliberation over the kind of society and worthwhile form of life we should be introducing young people to. Hence, so many of the government documents and of the connected discussions are, trapped into an impoverished language of skills and qualifications without the deeper consideration of the kind of learning which should be promoted.

Notes

1 Many papers referred to for evidence were commissioned by the Nuffield Review of Education and Training 14–19 for England and Wales. These can be found on the website 'www.nuffield 14–19review. org.uk'. Thanks are due to all those who have contributed to this large scale, three year review, the first year of which is summarised in the Annual Report (Nuffield Review, 2004).
2 See the detailed list of policy documents in the appendix of the Nuffield Review Annual Report, 2003/4 (Nuffield Review, 2004) upon which these sections draw. It was compiled by Alis Oancea and Susannah Wright, research officers for the Review.
3 See Part III of the Nuffield Review Annual Report, 2003/4, compiled by Geoff Hayward, for a very detailed analysis of the data on participation and retention.

References

ALI (2003) *Chief Inspectors Annual Report, 2002–3* (London, DfES).
Ball, S. (2004) Participation and Progression in Education and Training 14–19: Working Draft of Ideas, Discussion Paper for Nuffield Review Working Day 6.
Banks, O. (1955) *Parity and prestige in English secondary education* (London, Routledge & Kegan Paul).
Barnett, C. (1986) *The audit of war* (London, Macmillan).
Crick Report (1998) *Education for citizenship and the teaching of democracy in schools* (London, DfEE).
Dearing Report (1996) *Review of qualifications for 16 to 19 year olds* (Hayes, Middlesex, SCAA).
Hodgson, A. & Spours. K. (2003) *Beyond A Levels* (London, Kogan Page).
Hodkinson, P. (2004) *Learning careers and career progression*, Nuffield Review Working Paper 12.
Keep (2004) *The multi-dimensions of performance: performance as defined by whom, measured in what ways, to what ends?* Nuffield Review Working Paper 23.
Moser Report (1999) *Improving literacy and numeracy: a fresh start* (London, DfES).

Norwood Report (1943) *Secondary schools curricula and examinations* (London, SSEC).

Nuffield Review (2004) *Annual Review 2003–04* (copies from University of Oxford, Department of Educational Studies).

Pring, R. (2004) 'The skills revolution,' *Oxford Review of Education*, 30(1), 105–116.

Smith Report (2004) *Making mathematics count* (London, The Stationery Office).

Stanton, G. (2004) *The organisation of full-time 14–19 provision in the state sector*, Nuffield Review Working Paper 13.

Steedman, H., McIntosh, S. & Green, A. (2004) *International comparisons of qualifications: skills audit update* (London, DfES).

Stenhouse, L. (1975) *Introduction to curriculum instruction and research* (London, Heinemann).

Tomlinson Report (2004) *14–19 curriculum and qualifications reform*, Final Report of the Working Group on 14–19 Reform (London, DfES).

West, J. (2004) *Work-based education and training for 14–19 year olds*, Nuffield Review Working Paper 14.

Wiener, M. (1985) *English culture and the decline of the industrial spirit, 1850–1980* (Harmondsworth, Penguin).

26 Reinventing 'inclusion': New Labour and the cultural politics of special education

Derrick Armstrong

Source: 'Reinventing "inclusion": New Labour and the cultural politics of special education', *Oxford Review of Education*, 31(1): 135–151, 2005.

New Labour has placed inclusion at the centre of its educational agenda. Its policies have been characterised by an attempt to include disabled children, together with others identified as having 'special educational needs', within the ordinary school system and the shifting of responsibility for meeting their needs to teachers in the ordinary classroom. Policy on inclusion has also been formulated under the wider policy goal of improving educational quality as measured by narrowly conceived performance criteria. Yet, New Labour's policies have failed to engage with the issue, identified in particular by the disability movement, of the cultural politics of special education and exclusion. In consequence, New Labour's policy on inclusive education is beset with contradictions and there is little evidence of real change in the system, even in terms of the government's own ambitions. What is distinctive about New Labour policy on inclusive education is how the language of inclusion has been mobilised as a central normalising discourse of governance. State intervention is advanced in pursuit of technical 'solutions' to social exclusion as a moral rather than as a political problem.

Introduction

Special education is rarely seen as a contentious area of public policy, except perhaps by those families whose lives are directly touched by it and those professionals and administrators with responsibility for managing this resource-hungry sector. Special education is generally seen as a charitable, humanitarian concern rather than as a politically constructed domain that defines the nature and limits of 'normality'. Thomas and Loxley (2001) point out that the discourse of special education is deeply ingrained and it is one which has led to generosity becoming the hallmark of educational funding. Throughout its history, this humanitarian discourse has been a significant factor in securing additional resources for children who have experienced serious failure within the mainstream education sector, or who have been excluded altogether from that system. Yet, beneath the surface of this humanitarian consensus there have always been rumblings of dissent and the 'dark side' of special education as a system of regulation and control of troublesome populations is one that has been widely exposed and critiqued by sociologists (Ford, *et al.*, 1982; Tomlinson, 1982; Armstrong, 2003a), historians (Pritchard, 1963; Hurt, 1988; Copeland, 1999), psychologists (Galloway & Goodwin, 1987; Sigmon, 1987), parents (Murray & Penman, 1996, 2000; Murray, 2004) and by disabled people (Mason & Rieser, 1990).

It is, of course, easy to oversimplify the nature of special education, both as a humanitarian resource and as a system of control. Recent developments in this field, in particular, are suggestive of the complexity of the system and of the discourses underpinning it. In this respect, much has been made of the inclusive 'third-way' philosophy of New Labour. In special education, this philosophy is represented in terms of policy goals of the integration of children with special needs in mainstream schooling, of the provision of high quality education for all, and of a responsibility shared by all teachers for children with special needs. Yet, as will be argued in this paper, the New Labour vision of inclusion is one that reconstructs inclusion within the traditional framework of special education and in so doing reinforces its traditional purposes. This involves a conceptualisation characterised by what Slee (2001a, p. 117) has described as 'a deep epistemological attachment to the view that special educational needs are produced by the impaired pathology of the child'.

I begin this article by outlining the key features of New Labour's early Green Paper on special and inclusive schooling, *Excellence for all children* (DfES, 1997a), which provided the framework upon which policy has subsequently been developed. I will then look more closely at three key initiatives on inclusive education introduced by the New Labour government over its two terms of office: the 2001 Revised Code of Practice (DfES, 2001a); the Special Educational Needs and Disability Act (HMSO, 2001); and the SEN Strategy, *Removing barriers to achievement* (DfES, 2004) which aims to bring special educational services under the broader strategy of child protection. In the third section of this paper I will argue that, despite the rhetoric of 'inclusion' in which these policies have been cloaked, it would be quite misleading to represent 1997 as a turning point for 'inclusive education'. The statistics on the identification, statementing and placement of children with special educational needs during the period of New Labour's term of office do not suggest any radical transformation of the social practices of inclusion/exclusion. Indeed policy on inclusion is characterised by incongruities with the broader, reconceptualisation of educational values in terms of the values of performativity, uncritical notions of 'academic standards' and the role of education as a producer of human capital. This model of inclusive education is one that has allowed the recreation of the special educational industry under the banner of 'inclusion'. What is distinctive about New Labour policy on inclusive education, however, is how the language of inclusion has been mobilised as a central normalising discourse of governance. State intervention is advanced in pursuit of technical 'solutions' to social exclusion as a moral rather than as a political problem.

Year zero—the end of ideology and beginning of an inclusive society?

Robin Alexander (2003), writing in the *Times Educational Supplement*, argued that, for Tony Blair and New Labour, 1997 represented 'year zero' in education: 'The strategy is part of a political world view in which history and enlightenment began in 1997'. The 'enlightenment' of educational policy was grounded in the school-effectiveness and school improvement movements. The language of individual pupil needs was ostensibly rejected and replaced by a policy focused upon failing schools and the actions required to transform institutional failure into success and by this means into individual pupil achievement. The White Paper *Excellence in Education* (DfEE, 1997a) set out the broad agenda of the government as it started upon an educational 'crusade'. Emphasis here was placed upon the improvement of 'standards' and the accountability of schools, setting out six policy principles:

- Education will be at the heart of the government.
- Policies will benefit the many, not just the few.
- The focus will be on standards in schools, not the structure of the school system.
- We will intervene in underperforming schools and celebrate the successful.
- There will be zero tolerance of underperformance.
- Government will work in partnership with all those committed to raising standards.

Shortly after publication of this document the government brought out its consultation paper *Excellence for all children—meeting special educational needs* (DfEE, 1997b) which signalled its commitments to improving the quality of education for children with special educational needs.

The relationship between these two documents is of course important, with the latter being firmly embedded in the philosophy of the former, as David Blunkett, the first New Labour Secretary of State for Education, made clear in his Foreword (p. 4), 'There is nothing more important to the Government than raising the standards children achieve in our schools'. Yet, he was also to maintain that this vision of school improvement and rising standards was, at least for children with special educational needs, 'an inclusive vision' (p. 4). What he wanted to know was why it was that mainstream schools were identifying 18% of their children as having special educational needs and almost 3% of children had statutory statements of special educational needs which set out additional special educational provision that they required. For Blunkett, this said something very telling about the quality of education being provided within the mainstream school sector and this led him to argue for the benefits of high expectations and standards being established in the mainstream sector with the implication that many more pupils with special educational needs would benefit from an inclusive system of education: 'Where all children are included as equal partners in the school community, the benefits are felt by all. That is why we are committed to comprehensive and enforceable civil rights for disabled people. Our aspirations as a nation must be for all our people' (DfEE, 1997b, p. 5).

Blunkett went on to set out the six principles underpinning the strategy. First, there would be high expectations for all children, including those with special educational needs. Second was the promotion of inclusion of children with special educational needs within mainstream schooling wherever possible. This would not only involve the removal of barriers to participation but also a redefinition of the role of the special school in terms of a network of specialists. A place was to remain for special schools but this place was one that was itself framed by the broader objective of educational inclusion. Moreover, the somewhat sterile debates about the 'integration' of children with special educational needs into mainstream schooling were to be overridden by an emphasis not merely upon the educational advantages of inclusion but also of the social and moral benefits of this policy. Third, a commitment was given to providing parents of children with special educational needs with effective services from the full range of local services and voluntary agencies. The fourth principle was concerned with ensuring value for money which would mean 'shifting resources from expensive remediation to cost-effective prevention and early intervention' (p. 5). This, he argued, would entail a review of the statementing procedures for special educational needs. Local education authorities were by this time spending one-seventh of their budget (£2.5 billion) on special education and the costs of statementing, in particular, had been rising quite staggeringly during the earlier part of the 1990s. Fifth, Blunkett promised to boost opportunities for staff development in special education. Finally, he stated an expectation that in the future provision locally would be based on 'a partnership of all those with a contribution to make' (p. 6).

This was a document claiming very explicitly that change *would* happen. The target setting agenda of the first term of the New Labour government has been well documented, as have some of the spectacular failures to meet the targets set. This document was no exception with a total of 31 policy targets being set, with an implementation date of no later than 2002. Yet, in practice some of these specific targets were achieved with greater success than others. Targets, as New Labour came to recognise, are a hostage to fortune. In the setting, if not in their realisation, they do suggest a dynamic programme of transformation. However, such a transformatory agenda may be characterised by the rhetoric of change rather than by any substantive transformation of values and practices. Of more interest is the rationale that underpinned those targets. The document certainly adopts the language of 'inclusion', yet, despite so doing, its focus is entirely upon individual pupils' needs and improving the efficiency and cost-effectiveness of systems for managing those needs. Thus, the targets that are set out in *Excellence for all children* are grouped into eight sections which can be summarised as follows: improving efficiency to reduce expenditure; maximising parental involvement and therefore responsibility; refining early assessment procedures to reduce statementing; encouraging integration of children with special educational needs in mainstream schools; improving national and regional planning and support for children with special educational needs; training teachers and support staff; maximising interagency collaboration; and building teacher skills and support systems for managing pupils with emotional and behavioural difficulties. Nowhere does the strategy talk about the barriers that create educational disadvantage; nowhere does it talk about the institutional and social discrimination experienced by pupils from certain minority groups (e.g. children of Caribbean heritage and children of Irish heritage, to name but two); nowhere does it talk about the principles of an inclusive society and the role of educational as a tool of social policy for supporting social cohesion and inclusion. The list could go on. Policy, as Tony Booth (2000, p. 91) has forcefully argued, 'remains locked into a response to difficulties in learning experienced by children and young people which predates the Warnock Report of 1978'. The rhetorical emphasis upon mainstream schools as the point of delivery for special educational support was hardly new. Given the continuing reliance upon special schools for the more disabled and troublesome pupils the reality did not represent such a radical departure from the past as it was claimed to be. The replacement of a discourse of individual failure by a discourse of school failure based upon the promotion of academic excellence for those identified as having special educational needs did little to challenge the underlying conceptualisation of individual deficits.

This basic approach remained unchanged as a torrent of policy documents and legislation for special education flooded from Westminster. All of this strengthened the rights of children with special educational needs to a mainstream education but said little about the nature of that education, other than the promotion of the universal mantras of 'high expectations', 'standards', 'school improvement'. Thus, for instance, while *Meeting special educational needs—a programme for action* (DfEE, 1998), which set out the strategy for achieving the objectives of the earlier Green Paper, strengthened the rights of children and parents to mainstream schooling, there was little recognition of the wider social barriers to inclusion that inhibited inclusion within the environment of mainstream education. Again, those barriers that were recognised were merely those of low expectations and standards. The wider context of discrimination, segregation and exclusion, some of which was promoted by the very policies of 'inclusion' themselves, were at best unanalysed and more commonly ignored.

Policy, policy, policy!

Despite concerns about the level of sophistication underpinning New Labour's approach toward inclusive education, the Green Paper on special education and inclusion did give rise to a number of significant initiatives in furtherance of the broad policy objective of making educational opportunities more widely available to disabled children and young people. Indeed, the extent of policy intervention by this government in the field of special and inclusive education for outstrips that of any previous government. However, in this second part of the paper I want to look in detail at three initiatives that highlight both the interventionist trend and the substantive thrust of policy in this area: the Special Educational Needs Code of Practice (DfES, 2001a); the 2001 Special Educational Needs and Disability Act (HMSO, 2001); and New Labour's most recent Strategy for SEN, 'Removing Barriers to Achievement' (DfES, 2004).

A new code of practice

The 2001 Code of Practice was not in itself new. It revised an existing Code of Practice on the Identification and Assessment of Special Educational Needs introduced by the previous Conservative government in 1994. The 1994 Code of Practice arose out of the 1993 Education Act which made a number of significant amendments to the landmark 1981 Education Act. The latter had introduced the statementing procedure for children with special educational needs, but was perhaps more renowned for its introduction of the notion advanced by the Warnock Report (DES, 1978) of a continuum of special educational need. At the time, this conceptualisation of special educational needs, rejecting as it did the idea of categories of handicap based on individual deficits, was widely seen as promoting a charter for the integration of children with special educational needs into the mainstream sector. In retrospect, such claims were massively overstated. Not only were there significant 'let-out' clauses in this legislation (and in the Warnock recommendations that underpinned it) but, in practice, the subsequent difficulty in specifying what constituted a 'special educational need' led inexorably to a growth in statementing and special school placements as this meaning was negotiated in practice by powerful pressure groups and Local Education Authorities struggled to manage and restrain the professional judgements that had been empowered by the 1981 legislation. The 1993 Education Act made provision for a Code of Practice on the identification and assessment of special educational needs to be introduced which would direct attention towards early assessment and intervention rather than at the far more costly statutory assessment procedures. This Code of Practice (DEE, 1994) introduced a five stage procedure ranging from initial classroom monitoring at stage 1 to statutory assessment at stage 5 and created the new role in each school of the Special Educational Needs Co-ordinator, or SENCO. SENCOs were to have special responsibility for the school-based elements of the procedure and in particular for individual education plans (IEPs) which were to include information on such things as short-term targets, teaching strategies, special resources, review dates, etc.

In 2001 a revised Code of Practice was introduced by the Labour government (DfES, 2001a). This replaced the five stage assessment process with two pre-statutory stages: 'School Action' and 'School Action Plus'. The former is to be initiated where there is evidence of poor progress linked to emotional and behavioural difficulties, sensory or physical problems, or communication difficulties, despite the child having received normal differentiated learning opportunities in the classroom. The action to be taken is to be specified in an Individual Education Plan. School Action Plus involves a request for help from external services and follows upon continued lack of progress on the part of the child, despite the measures taken at the School Action stage. Whereas, in the past, a referral of a child with special educational needs to outside agencies generally resulted in a statement of special educational needs and, frequently, placement in a special school, the procedures introduced by the Code of Practice were designed to avoid this by ensuring a clear record of assessment, intervention and review at each stage. By implementing such procedures it was intended to avoid the crisis management of children who experience difficulties with learning.

One of the major impacts of the Code of Practice has been to give greater responsibility to mainstream schools and to ordinary classroom teachers for pupils with special educational needs. Yet, teachers may be encouraged to represent different sorts of issues under the banner of special educational needs simply because the Code provides a convenient system for organising the management of pupils who experience difficulties with learning and behaviour in their schools. Deeper seated problems such as bullying and discrimination can easily be reconstructed under the procedures of the Code as individualised learning and behaviour deficits. In this way, the Code may perpetuate long-standing and institutionally embedded practices such as racial and gender stereotyping which lead to distortions in the gender and racial profiling of special educational needs (Armstrong, 2003b).

Revisions to the Code of Practice introduced by New Labour have done nothing to address these disturbing features associated with the 'distribution' of special educational needs. Indeed, it could be argued that in some respects these features have become more damaging with the emphasis placed upon a rhetoric about children's involvement in decision-making. Thus, the revised Code of Practice (*Section 3:2*) states that:

> Children and young people with special educational needs have a unique knowledge of their own needs and circumstances and their own views about what sort of help they would like to help them make the most of their education. They should, where possible, participate in all the decision-making processes that occur in education including the setting of learning targets and contributing to IEPs, discussions about choice of schools, contributing to the assessment of their needs and to the annual review and transition processes. However, there is "a fine balance between giving the child a voice and encouraging them to make informed decisions, and to overburdening them with decision-making procedures where they have insufficient experience and knowledge to make appropriate judgements without additional support."

The purpose of this involvement is made clear in the following section where we see the same series of assumptions about 'accessing voice' and the value of children's voices to professional decision-making that characterised the original Code of Practice. Thus *section 3:3* maintains that:

> the principle of seeking and taking account of the ascertainable views of the child or young person is an important one. *Their perceptions and experiences can be invaluable to professionals in reaching decisions.* (My italics)

Absent from this discussion of inclusion is any reference to the protection of children's rights against the discriminatory practices that may arise from the process of assessment itself.

The apparently 'inclusive' principle of children's involvement in decision-making continues under the new Code of Practice to be subordinated to the practical value of the child's involvement for those professionals who are managing the child's learning, emphatically asserting the purpose of the Code, not as a tool of empowerment for children but rather, as a mechanism for channelling troublesome voices into safe waters. At root, the rhetoric of inclusion is based upon the assumption that to be 'just' the education system must accommodate children whose individual disadvantages place them at risk of exclusion. It palpably fails to appreciate how the language of 'special educational needs' is a socially constructed response by adults to troublesome behaviour that is located in wider-reaching social inequalities. In other words, ironically, it fails to appreciate how the language and policies of inclusion, as presently represented in educational policy, are part of the problem and not part of the solution.

The 2001 Special Educational Needs and Disability Act

At first sight, at least, a much wider reconceptualisation of special educational needs is suggested by the 2001 Special Needs and Disability Act (HMSO, 2001). Part I of this Act applies specifically to special educational provision and is concerned with relatively minor 'tweaking' of previous legislation: for example, requiring local education authorities to provide and advertise parent partnership services and tightening up the workings of the Tribunal system to reduce delays. Part II of the Act, however, extends the power of the Disability Discrimination Act (1995) to education, ensuring that discrimination against disabled students is unlawful. Thus, a duty is placed on schools not to discriminate against disabled pupils, either in the provision of education and associated services or in respect of admission to and exclusion from mainstream schooling. Moreover, schools are required to have regard to the Disability Rights Commission Code of Practice when identifying the 'reasonable steps' they must take to avoid discrimination. Section 316 of the Act states that a child who has a statement of special educational needs must be educated in the mainstream school unless this would be incompatible with: a) the wishes of the child's parents; or, b) the provision of efficient education for other children (HMSO, 2001). 'Mainstream education cannot be refused on the grounds that the child's needs cannot be provided for within the mainstream sector' (DfES, 2001b). However, the fact that mainstream education can be refused on the grounds that the educational interests of other children would be adversely affected by the presence of a disabled child continues a qualification on inclusion that has a long legislative history.

Government policies on special education have historically shied away from linking special educational needs to the politics of disability. For this reason, the linking of special educational needs with disability issues by New Labour in the 2001 Special Educational Needs and Disability Act is significant. This has been a position advocated for many years by the Disabled People's Movement (Oliver, 1996; Barton & Oliver, 1997; Oliver & Barnes, 1998) but it is one that in the past has been largely ignored by politicians and professional agencies working with children in educational settings.

For disability activists, there have been two broad arguments in favour of conceptualising inclusive policies in education in the context of society. The first of these has focused upon the ways in which disability, including learning difficulty, is a social construction, created by the social relations and power structures in society. On this argument, impairment does not of itself give rise to disadvantage and social exclusion. Physical and mental impairments are factors reflective of the diversity of the human condition. What turns diversity (and therefore impairments) into disabilities is the way in which people are disadvantaged and mistreated because of those differences. Special education, and particularly segregated special educational institutions, belongs to the social relations of oppression through which people are disabled. The second strand of argument advanced by disability activists has been that the struggle against the disabling features of social life should focus upon removing the barriers that disabled people face in accessing participation in social life. These barriers include those barring physical access to social spaces as well as the discriminatory practices of public policy and private prejudice. These two aspects are inextricably linked and this has informed the writing of a new generation of disability activists and inclusive education theorists. Sadly, few lessons have been drawn by policy makers from this rich critical tradition.

The disability legislation introduced by New Labour has focused almost exclusively on issues of physical access to public spaces. Legislation in this area is, of course, to be welcomed and removing these physical barriers to access in many ways does represent an ambitious and difficult objective to achieve. On the other hand, the policy is one that implies a technical solution to the problem of how to achieve educational equity. It suggests that if only disabled people can physically access educational spaces the barriers to participation will be dissolved. At best this is idealistic and at worst disingenuous. The radical thrust of the argument of disability activists that disability is not a product of impairment but rather a social act of discrimination embedded in the power relations of society is muted by this legislation. The political concept of inclusion, and the wider social question that asks why discrimination and disadvantage are so embedded in the system, is lost in legislation that represents inclusion in terms of 'impairment friendly' schooling. Similarly there is no consideration of how the relations of power that support discrimination against disabled people can be transformed as a necessary basis for an inclusive society. Yet schooling, as Slee (2001b) has argued, was never really intended for everyone. 'The more they have been called upon to include the masses, the more they have developed the technologies of exclusion and containment' (p. 172). Special education, however, has been historically characterised by the pathologising of young people who are represented as troublesome. An analysis of the processes and mechanism of exclusion, such as that advanced from within the disability movement begins to unpack the 'disablement' of people on the basis of their impairments, social class, gender, ethnicity and their willingness, or not, to conform to state-imposed systems of child management. The most important contribution of the disability movement of the framing of debates about inclusive education has been to politicise disablement in terms of these broader processes of cultural representation and social exclusion. The disability legislation of New Labour however, fails even to acknowledge the politics of exclusion. A policy promoting inclusive education that remains constrained by the goal of assimilating those with impairments into mainstream schools without addressing the exclusionary character of a disabling society is doomed to reinforce the very exclusionary process that it seeks to overcome.

'Removing barriers to achievement': the government's strategy for SEN

The most recent New Labour initiative in support of inclusive schooling has been the Strategy for SEN, 'Removing Barriers to Achievement' (DfES, 2004). The significance of this strategy is that it contextualises special education within the broader policy initiative of the Green Paper *Every child matters* (The Stationery Office, 2003) and as such offers the most complete articulation of inclusive education policy within New Labour's wider ideological vision of the inclusive society. *Every child matters*, which had its origins in the Victoria Climbie Report (DOH/Home Office, 2003) speaks to a commitment to reform children's services to prevent vulnerable children 'falling through the cracks between different services' (p. 5) and the need to recognise that 'child protection cannot be separated from policies to improve children's lives as a whole' (p. 5). The Government's Strategy for SEN (DfES, 2004, p. 9) attempts to represent inclusive education within a similar framework of child protection by targeting attention toward four areas of activity which are seen as essential for the protection of vulnerable children in schools and the promotion of learning opportunities for children with special educational needs. These are:

- Early intervention—to ensure that children who have difficulties learning receive the help they need as soon as possible and that parents of children with special educational needs and disabilities have access to suitable childcare.
- Removing barriers to learning—by embedding inclusive practice in every school and early years setting.
- Raising expectations and achievement—by developing teachers' skills and strategies for meeting the needs of children with SEN and sharpening our focus on the progress children make.
- Delivering improvements in partnership—taking a hands-on approach to improvements so that parents can be confident that their child will get the education they need.

Pursuing this child protection model of inclusion, the Strategy for SEN locates special educational interventions within the broader context of social disadvantages experienced by young people whose origins lie within 'risk factors' associated with educational failure, community breakdown, parenting inadequacies, school disorganisation and individual and/or peer group difficulties. These risk factors have been widely proclaimed as giving rise to concerns for the welfare of young people across the domains of education health, social welfare and youth justice (Lupton, 1999; Bessant *et al.*, 2003). The risk factor model is one that has been instrumental in promoting an interventionist strategy of risk reduction to be delivered by cross-agency childhood services.

Dyson (2001, p. 103) has argued that notions of risk and resilience 'offer the sort of "hook" that is now needed ... [for] "reconnecting" educational difficulty to wider issues in social and economic disadvantage'. This view is certainly shared by the Strategy for SEN (DfES, 2004, p. 8) where we are told:

> We have never been so well placed to deliver such a wide-ranging strategy to transform the lives and life chances of these children. The reform of children's services set out in Every Child Matters, with its focus on early intervention, preventative work and integrated services for children through Children's Trusts, will deliver real and lasting benefits to children with SEN and their families. And our commitment to reducing child poverty, investing in early years education and childcare and targeting support at areas of social and economic disadvantage will enable us to address the underlying causes of children's difficulties.

Thus it is maintained that we are historically now at a juncture at which an intervention strategy can transform the lives of children with special educational needs. This transformation is possible because child services have been integrated in ways that make early intervention and prevention capable of delivering real benefits. Moreover, such a strategy will have the significant impact of reducing child poverty because early intervention and support can now be targeted at areas of social and economic disadvantage, thus addressing 'the underlying causes of children's difficulties'.

Herein lay a set of important ideological claims. First, that poverty is the underlying cause of educational disadvantage. Second, that the effects of poverty can be transformed through social interventions aimed at those most at risk. Third, that we now have the technical skill and organisational structures to maximise the impact of such interventions. Implicit in the first two of these claims is a view that poverty is a consequence of the inadequacies of those individuals who are placed at risk by it. If this is not what is being claimed then what would be the purpose of intervening at the individual level rather than at the macro-economic level to reduce poverty and its effects? The third claim advanced in the quotation above maintains that elimination of the disadvantages of poverty can be achieved through early interventions with children because the technical skill exists to identify and target those most at risk. The reduction of poverty and disadvantage (as well, presumably, as its creation) is represented as possible through technical solutions aimed at the individual child.

Susser (1998) has argued that there are serious problems about extrapolating from factors identified at the group level to assessments of individual
risk. Moreover, despite the apparent linkage between individual risk and
social disadvantage, what this model proposes is a focus upon protecting
those individuals who are at risk from the micro-social factors of 'disadvantaged' families, schools and communities that are correlated with risk.
What is lacking in this approach is any theorisation of the ways in which
risks are situated historically in cultural and social formations in relation
to the construction and negotiation of individual identities as 'normal' or
'abnormal' and of how social power is exercised both in the social construction and academic theorisation of what constitutes risk (Armstrong,
2004). An illusion of scientific objectivity is also created which implies that
these risks and the likelihood of their effect upon future behaviour can be
measured and therefore controlled by appropriate early interventions.

Inclusion, governmentality and the interventionist state

Gillian Fulcher (1989) has argued that written policy is but one element of
the policy-practice equation. Written policy may speak to social aspirations
but it also gives voice to a political conceptualisation of social problems.
Similarly, enacted policy reflects the implementation of policy aspirations
but it also constitutes a continuing rearticulation and contestation of the
meaning of policy as an expression of power, normalising views of how the
world *is*, whilst at the same time marking the limits of power by the ambigu-
ities of policy as practice. In this section of the paper I first consider what
difference New Labour policies have actually made to the construction of
children's educational experiences. Statistics are useful in this respect
because they reveal the extent to which the old labels of 'special educational
needs' remain active in defining the character of educational failure. Moreover, they point to the ways in which special education operates as a
mechanism suppressing alternative cultural representations of disempowered
identities. Second, I will explore the contradictions within the policy agenda
of New Labour to suggest how these contribute to the reinvention of the
special needs industry in inclusive education (Slee, 2001a). Third, I will
discuss how New Labour's policies on inclusion reflect the processes and
contradictions of governmentality in late modern societies.

Are more children included?

Looked at in its own terms, the successes of New Labour policy on inclusion have been limited. Statementing has in fact very slightly increased
since the New Labour special educational strategy was set out in 1997.
Between 1999 and 2003 a 1% increase to 250,500 pupils with statements
of special educational needs in England was recorded (DfES, 2003a). Over
the same period a similarly modest decrease of 1% (from 97,700 to

93,000) was recorded in the numbers of children receiving their schooling in special schools. Yet, these figures conceal more worrying indications of the failure of inclusive schooling to be realised. Apart from wide local variations in statementing and placement policies that have been a characteristic of the special education system throughout its history, there continue to be significant differences in statementing practice between the primary and secondary sectors (in 2003 2.4% of secondary school pupils having statements compared with 1.6% of primary pupils); and between year groups within each sector (e.g. in 2003, 53% of statements of special educational needs in England were held by children aged 11 to 15 year-olds compared with 37% held by children aged 5 to 10 years). Gender differences continue to show the most striking disparities with boys accounting for 71.7% and 77.9% of all statemented pupils in primary and secondary schools respectively in 2003. Differences between ethnic groups continue to be pronounced despite a long history of concern about discrimination and institutional racism (Blyth & Milner, 1996; Gillborn & Youdell, 2000), with travellers of Irish heritage and Roma/Gypsy children having the highest percentage of children with statements of special educational needs. In 2003 1% of primary schools still accounted for 10% of pupils with statements and 0.5% of secondary schools accounted for more than 10% of pupils with statements. School differences also suggest that little has changed since 25 years ago when attention was first drawn to this by a number of groundbreaking studies on school effectiveness (Rutter *et al.*, 1979). Interestingly, the extensive school effectiveness literature that followed Rutter's seminal study has largely focused upon government preoccupations with academic achievement rather than upon what is perhaps more illuminative from the standpoint of inclusive schooling, namely the social and affective dimensions of children's experiences of schooling.

The statistics suggest that very little has changed, not only over the last six or seven years, but over the last 25 years since the Warnock Report (DES, 1978) first advocated the abolition of categories of special educational need and movement toward a more inclusive system based upon a continuum of needs which were themselves significantly related to the quality of education being received. The much acclaimed technical ability to address the factors producing educational disadvantage by intervening with those individuals at an early age has it seems come to very little. More importantly, special education continues to fulfil its traditional function *vis-à-vis* the mainstream sector of containing troublesome individuals and depoliticising educational failure through the technologies of measurement and exclusion.

Is the education system more inclusive?

The policy contradictions of New Labour's approach to inclusion are striking and have been widely commented upon (Tomlinson, 2001; Armstrong, 2003a). Under the banner of inclusion, educational equality is being reconceptualised in terms of conformity to quite narrowly defined performance criteria, a definition that is designed to select, place value upon, and advance the opportunities of certain individuals. Yet such a utilitarian system of performativity inevitably promotes exclusion for those who do not meet the standard. In these circumstances, special educational needs continues to be a legitimating label for the failure of the system to address itself to the aspirations, dignity and human worth of so many young people. As Benjamin has argued that:

> For students who are not going to succeed in dominant terms, the standards agenda is instrumental in constructing barriers to their participation. Herein lies one of the most fundamental contradictions at the heart of New Labour's educational policy.
>
> (Quoted by Barton, 2003, p. 16)

Narrowly conceived performance criteria are central to the rhetoric of inclusion advanced by New Labour's education policy. Inclusion is a normative concept. Its colonisation, under the banner of academic opportunity and high standards for all, serves to normalise the values of individual responsibility for individual achievement. The policy of inclusion is aimed not at promoting equity whilst recognising and supporting the richness of social diversity, but at establishing narrow cultural parameters of normality to which all must have the opportunity to conform. The role of education as a mechanism of assimilation, ironically, but inevitably, constructs the role of inclusion as a disciplinary force, regulating the lives of those disabled by their lack of utilitarian value to the interests of an individualised society.

The narrative of inclusion that features so strongly in the social policy agenda of New Labour can be understood as a product of what Andrew Gamble (2000) has described as the attempt of governments in late modern societies to dominate what's left of the state in the face of the uncertainties of a highly marketised civil society, leading to fewer opportunities for citizen rights to be articulated and organised for within a public sphere. The freedom of citizens within the public sphere is squeezed between the market and the state. In education, the marketisation of services within a preferential system of private choices is balanced by a highly regulated system of state-organised prescriptive demands around standards and measures of performance, which leave little room for alternative educational values and goals to be formulated, debated and pursued.

This world, in which the public sphere is increasingly ordered and regulated by the state and the market, is a world from which certainty has disappeared and individuals lack the ability to control the flow of events. This tension between regulation and uncertainty has led to a situation described by Zygmunt Bauman (1990, pp. 182–183) where 'only the vigilant management of human affairs seems to stand between order and chaos'.

During the New Labour period, policy targeted on social prevention measures has increased significantly. In particular, policy has focused on children, parents, communities and schools that are seen as potentially problematic. Those not conforming to certain norms and values have become the subject of intensive state interventions aimed at correcting the social deficits that place children at 'risk'. What we see in this new policy is a widening of what constitutes legitimate sites of state intervention, based upon beliefs about the moral importance of early intervention and prevention and the technical possibilities that science creates for the policy maker and implementer.

State intervention in the governance of children, families, schools and communities who are deemed to be potentially problematic is legitimated on the basis of moral beliefs in pathologies of risk for which technical solutions of risk management can be specified under the ideological formulation of an inclusive society. The process of educational assessment is transformed from a formative and educative process into a risk management system. On the one hand, failure is conceptualised entirely in moral terms as the consequence of individual, family, community and/or school inadequacies. On the other hand, a technical solution to these moral deficiencies is proposed, which involves early identification of at-risk populations on the basis of risk factors 'known' to correlate with the likelihood of failure or anti-social behaviour in the future. Thus, the idea of inclusive education is used to justify the growth of surveillance and management of troublesome populations based on the assumption that special educational needs are an outcome of dysfunctional individuals and communities and that these individuals can be identified through an assessment process determined by experts (Rose & Miller, 1992). Nikolas Rose (1999, p. 134) has described this process as one in which 'The soul of the young person has become the object of government through expertise'.

Such regulation, however, has not been confined to the troublesome. Just as important is the establishment of criteria for what is 'normal'; and it is the values prescribing normality that in turn are used to define the parameters of an inclusive school, community and society and which encourage self-regulation. A process of governmentality is embedded in the moralisation of political values in terms of assumptions about the nature of 'inclusion' supported by technical judgements that masquerade as expertise. It is a masquerade because the 'science' which defines inclusion is decontextualised from the contested beliefs and values which give meaning and relevance to particular representations of normality and social order. Thus, the linking of the science of 'risk assessment' to 'inclusion' supports an anti-welfare rhetoric (Culpitt, 1999) that legitimises the redistribution of social resources into a privatised world of individual responsibility and risk management, replacing 'need' and equity as the core principles of educational and social policy (Kemshall, 2002).

Conclusion

New Labour has from the beginning of its first term pursued a vigorous agenda around the issues of social and educational inclusion. It is an agenda that has taken from the disability movement what were transformatory values drawn from a critique of the cultural politics of disability and reconstructed these in terms of the regulatory and normalising functions of the neoconservative state. At one level the inclusive policies of New Labour go no further than to redress the traditional deficit-driven discourse of special educational needs in the fashionable but illusionary language of inclusion. More perniciously, the discourse of children at risk within whose parameters the policy of inclusive education has been constrained represents a new assault on the public sphere of democratic practice. The contribution of New Labour's inclusive educational policy has been to forward a process of assimilation based upon an uncritical view of 'normality', itself structured by the values of performativity that legitimate state regulation and control. The risks to the self that are generated in the institutionally structured risk environments of the risk society are individualised (Kelly, 2001) and marshalled in support of policies of inclusion as mechanisms for managing the excluded. Thus, the meaning of inclusion has been colonised by political and moral values that articulate, sometimes imprecisely and ambiguously, the fears and desires of an increasingly authoritarian state.

References

Alexander, R. (2003, September 19) 'For Blair 1997 is year zero,' *Times Educational Supplement* (Friday Magazine, p. 11).

Armstrong, D. (2003a) *Experiences of special education: re-evaluating policy and practice through life stories* (London, RoutledgeFalmer).

Armstrong, D. (2003b) 'Partnership with pupils: problems and possibilities,' *Association for Child Psychologists and Psychiatrists Occasional Papers*, 20, 39–45.

Armstrong, D. (2004) 'A risky business? Research, policy, governmentality and youth offending,' *Youth Justice*, 4(2).

Barton, L. (2003) Professorial Lecture. Inclusive education and teacher education: a basis for hope or a discourse of delusion (London, Institute of Education).

Barton, L. & Oliver, M. (eds) (1997) *Disability studies: past, present and future* (Leeds, Disability Press).

Bauman, Z. (1990) *Thinking sociologically* (Oxford, Blackwell).

Bessant, J., Hil, R. & Watts, R. (2003) *'Discovering' risk: social research and policy making* (New York, Peter Lang).

Blyth, E. & Milner, J. (eds) (1996) *Exclusion from school* (London, Routledge).

Booth, T. (2000) Inclusion and exclusion policy in England: who controls the agenda? In: F. Armstrong, D. Armstrong & L. Barton (eds) *Inclusive education: policy, contexts and comparative perspectives* (London, David Fulton).

Copeland, I. (1999) The making of the backward pupil in education in England: 1870–1914 (London, Woburn Press).

Culpitt, I. (1999) *Social policy and risk* (London, Sage).

Department for Education (DfE) (1994) *Code of practice on the identification and assessment of special educational needs.* (London, DfE).

Department for Education and Employment (DfEE) (1997a) *Excellence in education* (London, DfEE).

Department for Education and Employment (DfEE) (1997b) *Excellence for all children: meeting special educational needs* (London, DfEE).

Department for Education and Employment (DfEE) (1998) *Meeting special educational needs: a programme for action* (London, DfEE).

Department for Education and Skills (DfES) (2001a) *Special educational needs: code of practice* (London, DfES).

Department for Education and Skills (DfES) (2001b) *Inclusive schooling: children with special educational needs* (Statutory Guidance) (London, DfES).

Department for Education and Skills (DfES) (2003a) *Statistics of education: special educational needs in England: January 2003* (London, DfES).

Department for Education and Skills (DfES) (2003b) *Every child matters* (London, The Stationery Office).

Department for Education and Skills (DfES) (2004) *Removing barriers to achievement: the Government's strategy for SEN* (London, DfES Publications).

Department of Education and Science (DES) (1978) *Special educational needs: report of the committee of enquiry into the education of handicapped children and young people* (The Warnock Report) (London, HMSO).

Department of Health (DoH)/The Home Office (2003) *The Victoria Climbie Inquiry.* Report of an inquiry by Lord Laming (London, The Stationery Office).

Dyson, A. (2001) 'Special needs education as the way to equity: an alternative approach?' *Support for Learning*, 16(3), 99–104.

Ford, J., Mongon, D. & Whelan, M. (1982) *Special education and social control: invisible disasters* (London, Routledge & Kegan Paul).

Fulcher, G. (1989) *Disabling policies: a comparative approach to educational policy and disability* (Lewes, Falmer Press).

Galloway, D. & Goodwin, C. (1987) *The education of disturbing children: pupils with learning and adjustment difficulties* (London, Longman).

Gamble, A. (2000) *Politics and fate: themes for the twenty first century* (Cambridge, Polity Press).

Gillborn, D. & Youdell, D. (2000) *Rationing education: policy, practice, reform and equity* (Buckingham, Open University Press).

HMSO (2001) *Special educational needs and disability act* (London; HMSO).

Hurt, J. (1988) *Outside the mainstream: a history of special education* (London, Routledge).

Kelly, P. (2001) 'Youth at risk: processes of individualisation and responsibilisation in the risk society,' *Discourse: Studies in the Cultural Politics of Education*, 22(1), 23–33.

Kemshall, H. (2002) *Risk, social policy and welfare* (Buckingham, Open University Press).

Lupton, D. (ed.) (1999) *Risk and sociocultural theory: new directions and perspectives* (Cambridge, Cambridge University Press).

Mason, M. & Rieser, R. (1990) *Disability equality in the classroom—a human rights issue* (London, Disability Equality in Education).

Murray, P. (2004) *Living with the spark: recognising ordinariness in the lives of disabled children and their families*. Ph.D thesis, University of Sheffield.

Murray, P. & Penman, J. (eds) (1996) *Let our children be: a collection of stories* (Sheffield, Parents With Attitude).

Murray, P. & Penman, J. (eds) (2000) *Telling our own stories: reflections on family life in a disabling world* (Sheffield, Parents With Attitude).

Oliver, M. (1996) *Understanding disability: from theory to practice* (London, Macmillan).

Oliver, M. & Barnes, C. (1998) *Disabled people and social policy: from exclusion to inclusion* (London, Longman).

Pritchard, D. G. (1963) *Education and the handicapped 1760–1960* (London, Routledge & Kegan Paul).

Rose, N. (1999) *Governing the soul: the shaping of the private self*, 2nd edition (London, Free Association Books).

Rose, N. & Miller, P. (1992) 'Political power beyond the state: problematics of government,' *British Journal of Sociology*, 43(2), 173–205.

Rutter, M., Maughn, B., Mortimore, P., Ouston, J. & Smith, A. (1979) *Fifteen thousand hours: secondary schools and their effects on pupils* (London, Open Books).

Sigmon, S. B. (1987) *Radical analysis of special education: focus on historical development and learning disabilities* (London, The Falmer Press).

Slee, R. (2001a) ' "Inclusion in Practice:" does practice make perfect?' *Educational Review*, 53(2), 113–123.

Slee, R. (2001b) 'Social justice and the changing directions in educational research: the case of inclusive education,' *International Journal of Inclusive Education*, 5(2/3), 167–177.

Susser, M. (1998) 'Does risk factor epidemiology put epidemiology at risk? Peering into the future,' *Journal of Epidemiology and Community Health*, Accessed online at: http://proquest.umi.com/pqdlink? (21 May 2002).

Thomas, G. & Loxley, A. (2001) *Deconstructing special education and constructing inclusion* (Buckingham, Open University Press).

Tomlinson, S. (1981) *Educational subnormality: a study in decision-making* (London, Routledge & Kegan Paul).

Tomlinson, S. (1982) *A sociology of special education* (London, Routledge & Kegan Paul).

Tomlinson, S. (2001) *Education in a post-welfare society* (Buckingham, Open University Press).

Index

14–19: extending opportunities, raising standards 425
14–19 education: *Aiming Higher* 339, 343, 349, 351; assessment of policy 420–8; Conservative legacy 339–43; future strategy 349–52; Labour policy aims 417–20; *Learning to Compete* 338; rationale 416–17; stages of development 343–9; *see also* further education; higher education
2001 Code of Practice 438–41
2001 Special Educational Needs and Disability Act 434, 441–3

ability: definition 397
ability difference: research method 202–4
ability grouping 44
academic selection *see* selection
accountability 91, 94, 97, 98, 372, 425
action plans 334
action research 244, 249, 251–3
Adelstein, David 18
adjudicators 392–3, 408
admissions 328–9, 370, 391–5
admissions criteria study 395–409
admissions policies 392–5
adult education 100
Adult Learning Inspectorate (ALI) 424
Adult Training Centres 230
Advanced Extension Award 421–2
advisers 249–51
age-segregated phenomena 87
Aiming Higher 339, 343, 349, 351
A levels 341–2, 347, 348, 421–2
Alexander, Robin 435
Alexander, Sir William 96
ALI (Adult Learning Inspectorate) 424
American magnet schools 285, 291, 365, 366

Annan, Noel 264
apprenticeships 136
aptitude: definition 397
APU (Assessment of Performance Unit) 99–100
Archer, M. S. 226
Arnot, Madeleine 272
arts subjects 429–30
AS levels 347, 422
assessment: and league tables 332; and National Curriculum 324–6; of special needs 438–9
Assessment of Performance Unit (APU) 99–100
assisted places scheme 283–4
Atkinson, R. C. 44
attainment 26, 340
auditions 393, 394
Australian Curriculum Development Centre 241–2
authoritarianism 51–2
authority 68–74

baccalaureate concept 348–9
Baker, Kenneth 269, 270, 317, 319, 322, 325–6, 361, 365, 366
Banbury Special Needs Project 243–4
banding 399–401
Bantock, G. 51
Barry, Brian 21, 31
Bauman, Zygmunt 448
Beaumont Review 341
behavioural units 228
benefit systems 145–6
Benn, C. 289
Berlin, Isaiah 12, 99
Better Schools 322
Beyond Contract 73
biometrical genetic analysis 41
Black Papers 84, 316, 365

Black student teachers 274–5
Blair, Tony 336, 435
Blatch, Emily, Baroness Blatch of Hinchingbrooke 368–9
Blau, P. 33
Blunkett, David 293, 435–6
Bodmer, W. F. 36
Booth, A. 225
Booth, T. 437
Boudon, R. 40
Bowes, Samuel 36–7
Boyle, Sir Edward 22
Boyson, Rhodes 84, 316
British Baccalaureate, A 345, 348
BTEC (Business and Technical Education Council) 423
BTEC National Diploma 345, 347
Bulletin 16/83 179–81, 184–8
Bullock, Alan 1, 388
Bullock Report 99, 174
bureaucracy 74–81
bureaucratic organisations 79–80
Burnage Report 276–8
Burt, Sir Cyril 36, 225
Business and Technical Education Council (BTEC) 423

CAI (computer-assisted instruction games) 44–5
Callaghan, James 3, 4, 68, 69, 71, 82, 93, 256, 316
Capey Review 341
Carlisle, Mark 316
Carterton School 243
Casey, Terry 97
Cashmore, Ellis 267
Catholic schools 381–2, 386
Cavalli, L. L. 36
CBI (Confederation of British Industry) 134
central control 314–15
central initiatives 240–1
centralisation 95, 100
central–local government relations 92–3, 100–2
centre-periphery model 241–5
'century of the child' 86–7
Certificate of Pre-Vocational Education (CPVE) 344
CGLI (City and Guilds of London Institute) 423
charismatic authority 69, 71, 79
Cheetham, Paul 70
Chesterton, G. K. 81, 86

Chief Education Officers 92
Child Benefit 145–6
child-centredness 271
child labour 24
child-minding 87
child protection 443
children: in public care 404, 408; with special needs 43–4, 225, 333; *see also* special education
Children First 274, 275
Chitty, C. 289
choice: assumptions 296–7; and competition 327–31; and inequity 298–302; personal costs of 302–7; of school 151–2, 153–4, 159, 161; sponsored grant-maintained schools 362–4
choice$_m$ 297, 306
choice$_s$ 297, 298–302
Christian pressure groups 367–9
Christian Schools Campaign 368–9
Christian socialism 82–3
Chubb, J. 287
Churchill, Winston 71
Church of England 379–81
Circular 10/65 163–4
citizenship 137–8, 267, 420
City Academies 426, 428
City and Guilds of London Institute (CGLI) 423
City Technology Colleges 260–1, 269, 285–7, 331, 359, 360–2, 365–7, 369–70, 372, 426
civil servants 74–5, 92
class: concept of 30; difference 87, 255; and educational movement 30–1; and university access 27–8
classical humanism 51–2, 55, 63
CLEA (Council of Local Education Authorities) 102
Cleveland LEA 248–9
closures: of schools 153–5
Code of Practice (2001) 438–41
Code of Practice on School Admissions 392–3, 407–8
Code of Practice on the Identification and Assessment of Special Educational Needs (1994) 438, 439
Coleman, James 26, 34, 275
Communist countries 43
community schools 88
competition 159–60, 304–5, 306, 327–31

comprehensive schools 163, 228–9
compulsory education 26, 32, 42–3
computer-assisted instruction games
   (CAI) 44–5
Comte, Auguste 77
Confederation of British Industry (CBI)
   134
ConneXions 418, 420
Conservatism 267–9, 274
Conservatives 336, 339–43, 359–60
Constitution of Liberty, The 39
Consultative Council on Local
   Government Finance 102
consumer choice *see* parental choice
cooperatives 78, 79
core curriculum: Callaghan's speech 82;
   demand for 256; educational
   priorities 57–9; and ideology 50–4;
   'knowledge-based approach' 54–5;
   national tests 59–60; needs-based
   approach 55–7; social needs 56–7,
   64–6; White on Harris 62–7
Core (Key) Skills 347
corporatism 73
cost-effectiveness 259
Council of Local Education Authorities
   (CLEA) 102
Counter Course 16–17
Cox, Brian 84, 270–1, 327
Cox, Caroline 164, 366–7, 368–9; *see
   also Standards in English Schools*
CPVE (Certificate of Pre-Vocational
   Education) 344
'cream skimming' 392
Crick Report 420
Crosland, Anthony 3, 93, 163
Crossman, R. H. S. 78–9, 81
cultural analysis 57
cultural capital 88, 300
cultural transmission 268–9
culture 269–70
curriculum: core *see* core curriculum;
   post-16 142–3; special education 229
Curriculum 2000 421, 422
curriculum development 241–2
curriculum policy 322–7
curriculum theory 56
Czechoslovakia 43

DDR (East Germany) 43
Deakin, Ruth 367, 369
Dearing, Sir Ron 319, 325, 327
Dearing Report (1994) 292
Dearing Report (1996) 341, 347–8, 421

decision-making: balance of power
   90–1; central–local relations
   92–3
declining rolls 150–1, 156–7, 161
De Maistre, J. 77
democracy 71–4, 78
demographic curves 132
Dennis, Norman 79
denominational schools *see* faith-based
   schools
Department of Education and Science
   (DES) 97–8, 100, 149
Department of Employment (DEE)
   133–4, 149
DES (Department of Education and
   Science) 97–8, 100, 149
determinism: in social change 29–31
devolved management 359–60
disability: social construction 441–2
Disability Discrimination Act (1995)
   441
disability legislation 441, 442–3
Disabled People's Movement 441
Disappearing Data 181–2
discrimination 441
disengagement 423, 424
diversity 296–7, 303–4, 362–4
Dobson, Frank 183
Dobzhansky, T. 39
drama teaching 429–30
dual curriculum 51
Duncan, O. D. 33
Dunn, Bob 365–6
Durkheim, Emile 77
Dworkin, G. 296, 302
Dyson, A. 444

East Germany (DDR) 43
economic inequality 34
economic relevance 419–20
*Education, Opportunity, and Social
   Inequality* 40
Education Act (1944) 90, 151
Education Act (1976) 95
Education Act (1980) 151
Education Act (1981) 227, 238, 257,
   259, 438
Education Act (1991) 319
Education Act (1993) 360, 362, 368
Education Action Zones 418, 423
educational attainment 26
*Education and Training for the 21st
   Century* 341
education goals 257–8

Education Reform Act (1988) 237,
239–40, 267, 314, 318, 321–2, 332,
359–60
education reforms: support for 274
Education (Schools) Act (1992) 334
educational embourgeoisement: liberal
theory of 22–9
educational equality 447
educational expenditure 93, 94
educational maintenance allowances
(EMAs) 135, 145–6, 418
educational needs 257–9
educational priorities 57–9
educational psychologists 239, 253
educational theory 54–9, 63–4
educational vouchers 365
effectiveness 218–21, 446
'effective schools' movement 275–6
egalitarianism 12, 15–19, 20, 43, 44
egalitarian policies 46, 47
Elmore, R. F. 299
EMAs (educational maintenance
allowances) 135, 145–6, 418
embourgeoisement theory 22–9
employment skills 83–4
enterprise 420
entrance procedures 370
environmental influence 40, 46–7
equality: concept of 11–19, 262–4;
educational 447; of endowment
39–48; of entitlement 263; of esteem
427; objections to 255; obstacles to
31–7; of opportunity 12–15, 22,
26–7, 41–2, 83, 275; of outcome 42;
racial 267, 272, 275; sociological
debate 20–37; of treatment 43–6
Equal Opportunity in Education 22
equal rights: teacher and pupil 15–19
ESN pupils 43–4
esteem: parity of 427
ethos 119–20
European vocational education 136,
139
evangelical Christian schools 385
Every Child Matters 443
examination results 284, 333
*Examination Results in Selective and
Non-selective Schools* 175–7, 184–8,
194–206, 208, 209–10, 213–14,
215–16, 217
examinations 142–3, 163
examinations-based studies:
*Examination Results in Selective and
Non-selective Schools* 175–7, 184–8,

208, 209–10, 213–14, 215–16, 217;
future research direction 188–91;
*Reconstructions of Secondary
Education* 177–9, 184–8, 208–9,
211–13, 216–17, 218–19; *Standards
in English Schools* 164–73, 181–8,
208, 210–11, 214–15, 217–18, 219;
*Statistical Bulletin 16/83—School
Standards and Spending: Statistical
Analysis* 179–81, 184–8
examination system 421–2
Excellence for all Children 417, 434,
435, 437
Excellence in Cities 423
Excellence in Education 435
Excellence in Schools 364, 418
expectations 340
expenditure 93, 94
Eysenck, Hans 35

failing schools 300–2, 306, 315–16,
335
failure: perception of 315–18
faith-based schools 362–4, 376–89
family background 88–9, 111–14
FAS (Funding Agency for Schools) 353,
364
Federation of British Industries (FBI) 24
fee-paying schools 260
Fifteen Thousand Hours: adjustment
equations 117–18; administrative
differences 114–15; behaviour
outcome 118–19; caveats 107–8;
data collection 108–10; dependence
123–4; examination success 111;
family background 111–12, 113–14,
122; intake differences 107, 110–11;
intellectual mix 122–3;
neighbourhood differences 116–17,
122; parental occupation 116;
parental subscription rates 115–16;
physical differences 114–15; primary
schools 114; process items 117–18;
pupils' influence 122–4; school ethos
119–20; statistical analysis 105–6;
successful schools 106–7; verbal
reasoning 111, 112; voluntary-aided
schools 115–16
financial support systems 135, 145–8
Fisher Act (1918) 24
Floud, Jean 93
'forms of thought' 54–5, 63
'fortune' 35
foundation schools 331

Fox, Alan 73
framework approach 348–9
fraternity 29
Fulcher, Gillian 445
Fuller, B. 299
funding 342–3, 362, 376, 378–9, 424, 425
Funding Agency for Schools (FAS) 363, 364
funding formula 332
further education 425–6; *see also* 14–19 education; higher education
Future of Socialism, The 93

Gamble, Andrew 447
GCE A level *see* A levels
gender stereotyping 439
General Certificate of Education 317
General Certificate of Secondary Education 317
genetic determination 39–48
genetic distributions 35–7
genetic diversity 39–40
Genetic Diversity and Human Equality 39
Genetics and Education 35
Germany–England study 190–1
Gewirtz, S. 291, 298, 299, 302
Gintis, Herbert 36–7
GNVQs 341, 347–8, 421
goals, educational 57, 257–8
Goldthorpe, J. 28, 29
Good Education for All 274, 275
Goodman, Geoffrey 70
Gould, Sir Ronald 96
governing bodies 98–9, 329–30
government staff 74–5
grammar schools 283–4, 291, 370–1
grant-maintained schools 287–8, 330–1, 359, 360, 362–4, 426
Gray, J. 177, 181–2, 219; *see also Reconstructions of Secondary Education*
Gray, Robbie 17
Great Debate 4, 68, 93, 97, 100, 255–7, 257
Green Papers: *14–19: extending opportunities, raising standards* 425; *Every Child Matters* 443; *Excellence for all Children* 417, 434, 435, 437; *The Learning Age* 417
Griffiths, Brian 366, 367

Halls, W. D. 2

Halsey, A. H. 2, 276
Hamilton, James 256
Hargreaves, D. 292, 296, 300, 301
Hayek, F. A. 39, 48
Hayes, Christopher 137, 138
Heath, Anthony 2
Heath, Edward 3
hereditability 40–1
heredity 40–1, 46–7
Her Majesty's inspectors 86, 333
higher education 144–5, 318–20; *see also* 14–19 education; further education
Higher Education Funding Council 319
Higher Still 348
Hill, Christopher 270
Hillgate Group 366–7
Hirst, Paul 54
Hobbes, Thomas 20, 69
Hodgson, A. 421
Hoggart, Richard 86
Holland 42–3
home background *see* family background
Howarth, Janet 2
humanities subjects 429–30
human needs approach: to core curriculum 55–7
Hungary 43
Hutchinson, Dougal 213–14

ideologies 50–4, 63–4
Illich, Ivan 22
inclusion 340, 417–18, 433, 434–5, 436, 440–1, 445–9
Increased Flexibility Programme 423
independent schools 260, 269, 283–4, 333
Individual Learning Accounts 417
industrial democracy 73
industrial training 136, 137, 138–40
Inequality of Man, The 44
inequity: and choice 298–302
information provision 332–3
Ingram, D. 393
inspection 333–6
inspectorial roles: of LEAs 249–51
institutional provision 425–7
intake differences 107, 110–11
integration 238–9, 248–9
intelligence 40–1
inter-generational occupational mobility 27, 34
international affairs 72–3

international comparisons 316–17
intervention strategies 443–5, 446, 448
interviews 286, 291, 370, 393, 394, 404–5
IQ 36–7, 40, 47

Jencks, Christopher 33–5, 36, 275
Jencks pessimism 33–5
Jensen, Arthur 35–7, 43
Jewish schooling 382–3
Jinks, J. L. 41
John Loughborough School 372
Johnson, Paul 73, 75
Jones, D. 181–2
Jones, Jack 75
Jones, Neville J. 243, 244, 253
Joseph, Sir Keith 79, 142, 269, 270, 316, 317, 318–19, 320, 322
Judge, Harry 2
justice: and equality 11
juvenile labour 24

Kamin, L. J. 39–40
Keep, Ewart 425
Kelvin, Lord 46
Kennedy, Kerry J. 241–2
Kennedy Commission 343
Kepler, J. 46
'knowledge-based approach': to core curriculum 54–5

labour, skilled 24
Labour Government policies: 14–19 aims 417–20; 14–19 assessment 417–20; disability 441, 442–3; education 435; inclusion 433, 434–5, 443–5, 445–9; special education 435–8
labour market 229–31
Labour movement 78–9
Labour Party 274–6, 293, 330, 331, 336
Layfield Committee Report 95, 96
leadership 247
league tables 301, 332, 333
Learning Age, The 417
Learning and Skills Council (LSC) 425
Learning for the Future Initial Report 349
Learning to Compete 338
Learning to Succeed: a new framework for post-16 learning 418, 425
Learning to Succeed: a radical look at education today 345

LEAs (Local Education Authorities): and 1981 Education Act 248–51; and central government 92–6; closures 155–6; curriculum control 322–3; LMS 329–30; logistics 152–5; politicisation of 101–2; reductions 156–9; special educational needs 237–41, 243–53
Leith, G. V. M. 41
Lenin, V. 77–8
Lewis Committee 131
liberal theory 22–9
Liberal Theory of Justice, The 21
life-long education 144–5
Life-Long Learning 343
literacy 51, 52, 53, 58, 59, 99, 418–19
litigation 332
'Little Englandism' 266–7
LMS (local management of schools) 287–8, 329–30
Local Education Authorities (LEAs) *see* LEAs (Local Education Authorities)
Local Government Finance 95
local management of schools (LMS) 287–8, 329–30
Lockwood, D. 28
Loreto School 371
Loxley, A. 433
LSC (Learning and Skills Council) 425
luck hypothesis 34–5

MacDonald, I. 276–8
MacGregor, John 270, 273
Maclure, Stuart 93
Macmillan, Harold 93
McMurty, J. 308, 309
McPherson, A. F. 177; *see also Reconstructions of Secondary Education*
Maden, Margaret 250, 251
magnet schools 285, 291, 365, 366
Major, John 331
management: local 329–30
Manpower Services Commission (MSC) 130–1, 133–4, 136, 137
Mansell, Jack 137
Mao Tse Tung 69, 71
Marjoribanks, Kevin 2
market forces 365
marketisation 342–3
market philosophy 259–62, 333
Marks, J. 164; *see also Standards in English Schools*
Marshall, Alfred 23–9

Marshallian theory 23–9
Marxism 43
Mathematics Counts 418–19
mathematics study 190–1
Mather, K. 41
Meade, James 35
medical needs: admissions criteria
   402–3
Meeting special educational needs
   437–8
Mercer, Kobena 267
meritocratic principles 43
Merrit, John 56
Michel, Robert 81
Milwaukee Choice Program 299–300
mobility: social 27–8
Modern Apprenticeship Scheme 341,
   347, 424
Moe, T. 287
monitoring 83, 86, 99–100
Morris, Max 97
Morris, William 81
Mortimore, Peter 276
Moser Report (1999) 418
mothers: financial support 88
MSC (Manpower Services Commission)
   130–1, 133–4, 136, 137
MSC's New Training Initiative 130–1,
   133–4, 137–40
multicultural education 271–2, 277–8
Multicultural Education 274
Murder in the Playground 276–8
Muslim education 383–4, 386

National Association for the Teaching
   of English (NATE) 327
National Child Development Study 26,
   40
National Children's Bureau studies:
   *Examination Results in Selective and
   Non-selective Schools* 175–7, 184–8,
   194–206, 208, 209–10, 213–14,
   215–16, 217; *Progress in Secondary
   Schools* 173–5
National Curriculum 262, 269–74,
   322–7
national objectives 93–4
national qualifications framework
   341–2, 346–8, 421
national tests 59–60, 83; *see also* testing
needs-based approach: to core
   curriculum 55–7
NEETs (Not in Education, Employment
   or Training) 418, 423

networking 251, 252
Newcastle LEA 249
New Labour Government policies *see*
   Labour Government policies
New Right ideologues 267–9, 276, 314,
   321, 333, 372
Newsom Report 22
New Training Initiative 130–1, 133–4,
   344
'New Vocationalism' 344–5
Niebuhr, Reinhold 86
No Child is Ineducable 257
Northern Ireland 386
Nuffield College social mobility survey
   27–8
Nuffield Review 423
numeracy 51, 52, 59–60, 418–19
NVQs 341, 346–7, 421

Oak Hill School 369
objections: admissions decisions 393–4
occupational change 84
occupational hierarchy 31–3
occupational mobility 27, 34
occupational status 33–5
OFSTED (Office for Standards in
   Education) 334–6
open enrolment 328–9
openness: in social change 29–31
opinion polls 274
Opportunities and Excellence 420
opportunity: equality of 12–15, 83
Origins and Destinations 112, 113
Orwell, George 86
Our Age 264–5
oversubscription criteria 393–5
Oxford Review of Education 1–3
Oxfordshire LEA 243–4
Oxford Social Mobility Survey 27–8

parental choice 150, 151–2, 153–4,
   159, 161, 260, 273, 297, 328–9
parental interviews 286, 291, 370,
   393
parental involvement 85–6, 88, 98–9,
   151
parent power 98–9, 327–8
Parents English Education Rights
   (PEER) 277
parish schools 380
parity of esteem 427
partial selection 289–91, 394, 397–8
participation: in education policy
   making 96–7; in further education

339–41, 417–18, 419–20, 422–3;
parental 98–9
Patten, John 282, 325, 327
pay and conditions dispute 317
PEER (Parents English Education
Rights) 277
personal development 137–8
Peston, Maurice 99
Peters, R. S. 18
Phillips, David 2
Planned Admission Levels 156
Plowden, Lady Bridget 276
Plowden Committee 30
Poland 43
policy and practice model 245–53
policy-making 90–1, 96
Political Argument 21
political pressure: core curriculum 50
politicisation 92, 101–2, 326–7
Politics of Vision 77
Pomian-Srzednicki, M. 164; *see also
Standards in English Schools*
positive discrimination 88–9
post-16 education 140–7
post-school education 100
poverty 444
Powell, Enoch 266, 268
power: balance of 90–1; distribution of
93–6
practice and policy model 245–53
Prais, Sig 316
Prentice, Reg 70, 71
pressure groups 367
priorities, educational 57–9
Private Learning Providers 424
private schools 283–4
privatisation 372–3
process skills 138–9
product skills 138–9
professional authority 80–1
Progress in Secondary Schools 173–5
progressivism 52–3, 63, 321
pupils: with special needs 43–4, 225,
333; *see also* special education

QAA (Quality Assurance Agency) 418
QCA (Qualifications and Curriculum
Authority) 346
Qualifications for 16–19 Year Olds
341, 347–8
qualifications framework 341–2
qualifications reform 421–2
Quality Assurance Agency (QAA) 418
'quasi-markets' 359–60, 391

Quicke, John 268

Race, Intelligence and Education 35
race-IQ 35–7
racial equality 267, 274–6
racial stereotyping 439
Raffe, D. 177; *see also Reconstructions
of Secondary Education*
rational–legal authority 69, 71
Rawls, John 21
reconstructionism 53–4, 63
*Reconstructions of Secondary
Education* 177–9, 184–8, 194–206,
208–9, 211–13, 216–17, 218–19
recurrent education 32–3
redistribution of wealth 25–6
references: admissions procedures 406
reflective practitioners 246–7
reforms 351; support for 274, 316
refugees 394, 395
Rehn, Gosta 32
religious schools 362–4, 370–2, 401–2
remedial departments 228
Removing barriers to achievement 434,
443–5
Report of the Layfield Committee 95, 96
research projects: *Examination Results
in Selective and Non-selective Schools*
175–7, 184–8, 194–206, 208,
209–10, 213–14, 215–16, 217; future
direction of 188–91;
Germany–England 190–1; National
Children's Bureau studies 173–7,
194–206; *Progress in Secondary
Schools* 173–5; *Reconstructions of
Secondary Education* 177–9,
194–206, 208–9, 211–13, 216–17,
218–19; *Standards in English Schools*
164–73, 181–8, 194–206, 208,
210–11, 214–15, 217–18, 219;
*Statistical Bulletin 16/83—School
Standards and Spending: Statistical
Analysis* 179–81, 184–8; *see also
Fifteen Thousand Hours*
retention rates 422–3
Revised Code of Practice (2001) 434
Reynolds, D. 228
Richard, Ivor 132
risk factors 443–4, 448
Roberts, Iolo 139
Roman Catholic schools 370–1, 381–2
Rose, Nikolas 448
Ruskin College speech 4, 68, 82–4, 93,
256, 316

Russia *see* USSR
Rutter, M. 105, 276, 446; research
    project *see Fifteen Thousand Hours*

safety-net 260–1
St Ambrose School 371
St Anselm's College 371
St Edward's School 371
St Joseph's School 371
Samuel, Raphael 270
Schon, Donald A. 246
school closures 153–5
'school effects' argument 275–6
school ethos 119–20
school governors 98–9, 329–30
school-leaving patterns 140–1
schools adjudicators 392–3, 408
Schools Council 97
Schools Standards and Framework Act
    (1998) 364, 392
school type: classification for research
    196–8
science and technology education 261
Scientology schools 385
SCIs (Senior Chief Inspectors) 335–6
Scotland 290, 385–6
Scruton, Roger 268
Secretary of States for Education 82,
    91, 92, 320, 336; Anthony Crosland
    163; John MacGregor 270, 273; John
    Patten 282, 325, 327; Kenneth Baker
    see Baker, Kenneth; Margaret
    Thatcher 3, 326; Norman Tebbit
    266; Sir Keith Joseph *see* Joseph, Sir
    Keith
sectarian violence 388
Section 11 (Local Government Act
    1966) 272, 275
Segal, Stan 257
selection 151–2, 207, 218, 282–3,
    286–7, 289–91, 369–72
self-government 287–8, 329–30
SENCOs (Special Educational Needs
    Coordinators) 241, 439
Senior Chief Inspectors (SCIs) 335–6
SEN Strategy 434
September 11th 2001 (terrorist attack)
    388
Sexton, Stuart 290, 366, 367, 368
Shaw, B. 228
Silman, Robert 17
Silver, Harold 22
'sink' schools 301–2, 306
sixth-form colleges 426

sixth-form studies 143–4
Skilbeck, Malcolm 51, 57
skilled labour 24, 428
'skills revolution' 419, 426
Slee, R. 434, 442
Smith, David 276
Smith Report (2004) 418–19, 422
Smyth, W. John 247
social change: determinism 29–31;
    openness 29–31
social class: differences 299;
    measurement of 201–2
social education 137–8
social engineering 84, 255
social factors 46–7
social inclusion 417–18
socialism: and bureaucracy 75, 78–9;
    and education 93; as fellowship 29
social justice 402–4
social mobility 27–8, 40
social needs: admissions criteria 402–3;
    and core curriculum 56–7
social prevention measure 448
socio-economic conditions:
    improvements in 25–6
Somerset LEA 238–9
special education: and DES 257;
    discourses 433–4; expansion of
    223–32; Labour Government policies
    435–8; and LEAs 237–41, 243–53;
    Somerset experience 238–9
Special Education Advisers 249–51
Special Educational Needs and
    Disability Act (2001) 434, 441–3
Special Educational Needs
    Coordinators (SENCOs) 241, 439
specialisation 282–3, 288–93, 331
specialist schools 398, 426
special needs: admissions criteria
    403–4; awareness of 259; ideology of
    231–2; and league tables 333; as a
    term 257
special schools 238
speeches: Baker 269; Callaghan 4, 68,
    82–4, 93, 256, 316; Joseph 269
sponsored grant-maintained schools
    360, 362–4, 367–9, 370–2, 373
sponsorship 360, 362, 366, 373
Spours, K. 421
Squibb, P. 225
standards 418–19
Standards in English Schools 164–73,
    181–4, 184–8, 194–206, 208,
    210–11, 214–15, 217–18, 219

Standards Task Force 418
StARs (Strategic Area Reviews) 425
state intervention 306–9, 448
statementing process 238, 436, 438,
    445–6
statements of special educational need
    404, 408
statistical analysis 105–6
*Statistical Bulletin 16/83—School
    Standards and Spending: Statistical
    Analysis* 179–81, 184–8
Steedman, J. 173; *see also Examination
    Results in Selective and Non-selective
    Schools; Progress in Secondary
    Schools*
Steel, David 69
Stephens, Jo 250
Strategic Area Reviews (StARs) 425
Strategy for SEN 443–5
stratification hierarchy 28–9
stratified random selection 286
streaming 44
student grants 144, 147
student loans 147
student unrest 316
studies: admissions procedures
    395–409; Germany–England 190–1;
    National Children's Bureau studies
    173–7, 184–8, 194–206; *Progress in
    Secondary Schools* 173–5, 184–8;
    *Reconstructions of Secondary
    Education* 177–9, 184–8, 194–206,
    208–9, 211–13, 216–17, 218–19;
    Standards in English Schools 164–73,
    181–8, 194–206, 208, 210–11,
    214–15, 217–18, 219; *Statistical
    Bulletin 16/83—School Standards
    and Spending: Statistical Analysis*
    179–81, 184–8
study credits 32–3
Success for All 425
successful schools 106–7
Sullivan, M. 228
Supplementary Benefit 145–6
support services 252
Surrey LEA 239
Susser, M. 445
Sutherland, Stuart 335
Swann, W. 225
Swann Report 274

Tanzania 53
target setting 425, 436–7
Tawney, R. H. 21, 24

Taylor, Barry 140, 238–9, 250
Taylor, Cyril 366
Taylor, Denise 252–3
Taylor Committee of Inquiry 98
teacher and pupil rights 15–19
teacher control 96–7
teachers' associations 96
teacher training 315, 320–1
Teacher Training Agency (TTA) 320
Tebbit, Norman 266
Tebbit White Paper 130–1, 133–4, 137,
    140, 142, 145
Technical and Vocational Educational
    Initiative (TVEI) 344–5
technical schools 136
Technology Schools Initiative 289
technology skills 261
terrorist attack 388
Tertiary Colleges 426
testing 324–6, 332
tests, national 59–60, 83
Thatcher, Margaret 3, 326
Thatcherism 259, 267, 314–15
Theory of Justice, A 21
Thomas, G. 433
Thompson, E. P. 268
Thompson, J. 231
Tolley, George 139
Tomlinson, Sally 276
Tomlinson Working Group 420, 422
top-down methods 321–2
Trade Union Congress (TUC) 73, 75,
    134
trade unions 73, 78, 79
traditional authority 69, 71, 79
traineeship scheme 130–4, 137–40,
    147, 148
training allowance 135
traveller families 394, 395
Tredgold, A. F. 226
triple-track system 341–2
Trown, E. S. 41
TTA (Teacher Training Agency) 320
TUC (Trade Union Congress) 73, 75,
    134
Tullock, Gordon 74
TVEI (Technical and Vocational
    Educational Initiative) 344–5

UGC (University Grants Committee)
    318
unemployment 129–31
unification 348–9
United Sates of America 386–7

universities 145, 319–20
university graduates: origins 27–8
University Grants Committee (UGC) 318
Upton Hall Convent School 371, 373
USSR 43
utility 261–2

value choice 32
vocational education 83–4, 136, 142–3, 416–17, 428
voluntarism 78–9
voucher schemes 301, 365, 368

Wales 364
Walford, Geoffrey 2, 297, 303
Waller, J. H. 47
Warnock Committee 225, 228–9, 257, 438, 446
wealth: redistribution of 25–6
Weaver, Sir Toby 90
Weber, Max 76–7, 79, 81
welfare state 255, 262–3
West, A. 393
West, E. G. 307
White, John 54–5
White, P. 395
White Papers: (1981) 130–1, 133–4, 137, 140, 142, 145; (1985) 322;
(1991) 341, 347; (1992) 282, 287, 291; (1996) 286, 287, 291–2; (1997) 338, 364, 418, 425, 435; (1999) 418; (2003) 420
Whitty, G. 365
Williams, Shirley 135, 316
William Tyndale primary school 256
Wilson, Harold 3
Wilson, John 2
Winch, C. 308
Wolin, Sheldon 77
Wollheim, Richard 12
women: and children's learning 86–7; financial support 88
Woodhead, Chris 335 ·
work based learning 424
working-class children 30–1
work relations 73
work skills 83–4
Wragg, E. 182

YOP (Youth Opportunities Programme) 131, 134, 147, 148
Young Person's Benefit 145–6
youth labour market 229–31
Youth Training Scheme 229–31, 340, 344
youth unemployment 130–2, 340, 344